本书编委会

主　编：俞　钢

副主编：杨龙波　刘兰英　顾绍泉　孙　励

图1：2015 年 9 月，2300 余名研究生新同学进入上海师范大学开始了研究生学习生涯，学校为他们举行了隆重的开学典礼暨科学道德和学风建设宣讲教育。

图 2:2015 年 10 月,学校承办了由上海市学位办主办的上海市"都市文化与法治文明"研究生学术论坛,来自全国 17 所高校的 200 余名研究生与专家学者们相互交流思想,畅谈学术观点。同时,学校还对获得 2014 年度上海市优秀学位论文的导师和研究生进行了表彰。

图 3：2015 年，学校研究生院进一步推动研究生实习基地建设，取得丰硕成果。其中所建 5 个高端教育实践基地获得了全国教育硕士专业学位教学成果二等奖；上海市实验学校高端实践基地获得了全国教育硕士专业学位研究生联合培养示范基地和上海市专业学位研究生实践示范基地；上海师大附中高端实践基地和徐汇区人民法院实践基地获得了上海市专业学位研究生实践示范基地。

图 4:2015 年,学校研究生院(部)组织选拔了 40 名研究生分赴台湾师范大学和美国南加州大学进行研习交流,有效提升了研究生在全球化背景下的从教能力,受到《上海教育》、《青年报》等多家媒体的关注。

图 5：2015 年，学校研究生工作部组织研究生开展了"感受都市文化"、迎新歌会、辩论赛、拔河比赛、篮球赛等一系列丰富多彩的活动，提升了研究生综合素养，引领了校园文化。

图 6:2015 年,学校研究生工作部积极开展研究生就业指导和服务工作,邀请世界 500 强企业 HR 为研究生开设职业生涯讲座 9 场;举办招聘会 2 场;组织研究生参加高层次人才洽谈会 3 场;举办教师资格考试专题讲座和考博经验交流会 3 场。2015 年,我校的研究生就业率达到 94.88%。

图 7:2015 年 6 月,学校分别为博士、硕士毕业生举行了隆重的毕业典礼暨学位授予仪式,1813 名硕士毕业生和 74 名博士毕业生喜获学位,挥别母校。

图 8：2015 年，学校研究生工作部创立了研究生会微信公众号，推出了《你不知道的师大》、《研之梦想》等反映研究生学习生活的短片，获得一致好评，受到《上海教育》、《中国研究生》、上海电视台、东方卫视等多家媒体的关注，社会影响力提升。

序 言

一

年复一年,蓦然回首,又已过 2015 年的春夏秋冬。平凡充实的耕耘,似乎循规蹈矩,清清淡淡,无声无息,却在四季的流变中蕴藏着韧劲和创意,使日子过得忙碌飞快,有滋有味,充满希望。我们相信,努力做好每一件平凡的事儿,就会收获不平凡的成果,犹如静心培护的校园树木,在叶绿叶黄间又粗壮了一圈,还伸出了许多新枝丫,耐看而有活力。

其实,越是平凡的事越难做,尤其是将平凡的事做出些许新意则更难。好在我们这个团队既富有经验又充满智慧,早已形成了稳中求进、进中求质、质中求精的共识,全然适应了团结、紧张、严肃、活泼的节奏,加上得到各级领导、导师和研究生的大力支持,才使年初设定的工作目标得以圆满完成,快乐的笑容替代了艰辛的劳苦。

2015 年上海师大研究生教育发展的进步,集中体现在研究生的学术成果再创新高。据不完全统计,本年度我校博士和硕士研究生公开发表学术论文共 642 篇,比上一年度增加 44 篇;研究生获全国挑战杯、宝钢奖、数学建模竞赛、青少年科技创新奖、英语竞赛等各类奖项共 105 项,计 207 人次,分别比上一年度增加 27 项和 64 人次。这些研究生学术新成果的取得,凝聚着师生们的智慧和心血,为提升学校的综合实力注入了新能量。

正是因为我校研究生追求学术创新的孜孜努力,才使得每年编集的《学思林》郁郁葱葱,生机盎然。本次汇编的《学思林》第五集,共选录2015年度我校博士和硕士研究生独立或合作发表的高质量学术论文35篇,其中博士研究生发表的学术论文10篇,硕士研究生发表的学术论文25篇;文科研究生发表于A类期刊的学术论文6篇,B类期刊的学术论文11篇;理工科研究生发表于SCI一区的学术论文18篇;研究生以第一作者署名的28篇,第二作者署名的7篇,展示了我校研究生最高的学术成果,也将激励莘莘学子不断前行,勇攀学术创新的高峰。

二

过去的一年,是"十二五"发展的收官之年,进步伴着感动,历历在目,特别令人难忘。

学位点的建设,是研究生教育发展的重要平台。我们在持续建设6个一级学科博士点和29个一级学科硕士点的基础上,着重对13个专业硕士学位点加强了内涵建设,包括制订培养方案、课程资源建设、实践基地建设、指导教师团队建设等,有效促进了这些专业硕士学位点的可持续发展,并顺利完成应用心理硕士、应用统计硕士、翻译硕士、法律硕士、体育硕士、汉语国际教育硕士、艺术硕士和公共管理硕士等8个专业硕士学位点的国家级专项评估,取得了令人满意的成绩,其中的一些还获得了优秀。

我们全面推进了被列入上海市教育综合改革重点项目之一的上海市创新中小学见习教师规范化培训与教育硕士专业学位培养相结合改革模式探索与实践的建设,完成了新培养方案和课程质量标准的制订,构建了校、院两级课程教学体系,深化教育理论与学科实践的互融互通,并在2014年专项招录16名研究生的基础上,2015年又招录了86名研究生,社会影响进一步扩大。

同时,我们还有力推动了学校相关学科与中科院在沪四个研究所联合培养研究生的计划,首次选派研究生25名进入联合培养中心学习,迈出了新一轮创新人才培养的坚实步伐。

三

2015年,我们大胆探索与市属重点师范大学发展相适应的研究生招生规模和方式的新途径,进一步完善学术学位研究生与专业学位研究生的结构体系,合理控制在职攻读博士研究生的招生数量,取得了重大的突破,研究生生源质量总体得到了改善。

这一年值得载入校史,我们通过艰难的努力,共招录各类研究生2601名,较上一年度大幅增加近500名,招生规模实现了一次历史性的飞跃。

招录全日制学术硕士研究生1240名,其中来自985高校49名,来自211高校135名,生源质量有所提升。招录全日制专业硕士研究生962名,占全日制硕士研究生总数的43.7%,较上一年度增加8个百分点,结构更趋于合理。

招录全日制博士研究生128名,其中定向生68名,非定向生60名,定向生比例下降11%。

招录非全日制硕士研究生230名,留学生和港澳台学生41名。

大量研究生新生的加盟,使我校研究生在校生人数逼近七千人,研究生日益成为学校创新发展的生力军。

四

随着研究生规模的不断扩大,研究生培养质量体系的建设任务就显得十分繁重,这是比拼眼光和耐力的活儿。好在我们思路清晰,勤于耕耘,足够耐心,终于收获了不平凡的果实。

这一年,我们新设了一级学科课程体系改革项目12个、专业学位案例教学改革项目13个、精品课程建设项目19个和高端教育实践基地建设项目8个,并巩固了海外研习项目2个,着力于提高学术学位研究生学术创新能力和专业学位研究生实践应用能力,取得了明显的进步。特别是在研究生的"两翼"培养,即高端教育实践基地建设和海外研习项目实施方面,呈现出了可喜的特色,受到社会的广泛关注。

在加大力度建设 18 个上海市教委专业硕士研究生社会实践基地的基础上,我们重点深化 5 个高端教育实践基地的建设,继续选派 100 名研究生进入基地参加"浸润式"、高质量的研习,聘请基地专家担任研习导师,凸显了专业硕士研究生培养强化双导师制和产学研结合等特色,有效提升了专业硕士研究生的专业应用能力,并由此获得全国教育硕士专业学位教学成果二等奖 1 项;"教育部教育硕士专业学位联合培养示范基地"1 项,成为全国首批 18 个示范性基地之一;"上海市专业学位示范实践基地"3 项,初步形成了部、市、校、院四级实习基地建设体系。

实施研究生海外研习交流计划,拓宽研究生的国际视野,这是一流专业人才培养的有效途径。本年度,我们进一步加强了与美国南加州大学和台湾师范大学的合作交流,继续组团选派 16 名研究生赴美国南加州大学和 24 名研究生赴台湾师范大学进行为期 2—3 个月的研习交流。持续的选派,研习的实在,收获的丰硕,深受研究生的欢迎和海外研习交流学校的认肯,由此也吸引了沪上多家媒体的眼球,并作了大篇幅的报道。

五

研究生学位论文的质量,是衡量研究生培养水平的重要观测点。因此,完善研究生学位论文质量监控制度,提升研究生学位论文质量,就自然成了研究生教育常抓不懈的核心工作。

近年来,我校连续设立上海市研究生优秀成果(论文)培育项目共 230 项,研究生取得全国百篇优博论文提名奖 3 篇,上海市优秀学位论文 72 篇,具有显著的成效。本年度,我们继续设立研究生优秀成果(论文)培育项目 60 项,旨在进一步激励研究生潜心完成高质量的学位论文;研究生获得上海市优秀博、硕士学位论文 15 篇,含优博学位论文 5 篇和优硕学位论文 10 篇,其中所获上海市优秀博士学位论文的数量,位居市属高校之首。

2015 年,我们通过完善研究生学位论文全员重复率检测、学位论文全员盲审、学位论文预答辩和答辩等一系列质量保障制度,强化了导师负有对研究生进行学科前沿引导、科学方法指导和学术规范教导的责任,取得明显成效。在学位论文全员重复率检测方面,首次将学位论文重复率检测标准整体控制在 20％以下。在学位论文全员盲审方面,推出导师签名后提交学位论文等措施。在学位论文预答辩方面,规定了时间要求和质量标准。通过多管齐下的质量监控,使我校研究生学位论文质量呈现出市双盲评审优秀率大幅度提高、双盲评审异议率优于上海高校平均水平等新特征。

本年度我校共授予博士学位 77 名,科学硕士学位 1218 名,专业硕士学位 671 名。在双盲评审中,获得双优的博士学位论文共 9 篇,优秀率为 10.98％;获得优秀的硕士学位论文共 293 篇,优秀率为 15.06％。在抽中的市盲审学位论文 149 篇中,有 5 篇博士学位论文、19 篇硕士学位论文获得优秀,优秀率为 16.78％,创历年之最。

同时,这一年我校被教育部学位办抽检的 2014 年度博士学位论文共 4 篇,都获得通过;被上海市学位办抽检的 2014 年度硕士学位论文共 86 篇,其中学术学位论文计 66 篇,专业硕士论文计 20 篇,除了被认定为"存在问题"的 1 篇学位论文外,其他学位论文皆获得通过,名列市属高校前茅。

六

2015 年我校研究生的校园文化活动精彩纷呈,青春活力和创新火花光芒四射,品牌和辐射效应进一步凸现,真正成为了校园文化的引领者。

我们围绕"三纵三横"的理念,通过开展"感受都市文化"系列活动,组织所有研究生新生分批赴凸现上海都市文化特色的地标性建筑、文化场馆等地进行观摩,使研究生新生感受上海城市的文化底蕴,增进对上海社会文化的了解;通过打造品牌项目——上海市研究生学术论坛"都市文化与法治文明"主题论坛,以及开展"师道杯"学术演讲大赛、"学思节"、学术沙龙、主持人大赛等活动,尽显我校研究生的风采,社会影响不断扩大;通过举办各类研究生就业招聘会、宣讲会、高洽会等,加强职业指导与服务,有效提升了研究生的就业率和签约率,2015 年我校研究生的就业率为 94.88%,比上一年度提高了 1.62 个百分点;签约率为 83.54%,比上一年度提高了1.7 个百分点,实现了年度工作目标。

这一年,还有两件事值得一提:其一是我校研究生创新创业能力培育取得了新进展,共获"上海市研究生创新创业能力培养"专项资助项目 9 个,含孵化类项目 5 个,创业培养类项目 4 个,非常不易。其二是研究生建设微博、微信平台凸显特色,不仅制作精美,趣味高雅,还配合推送了"五一劳动节专辑——你不知道的师大"、"研之梦想"、缤纷毕业季专辑、"学霸的世界"等一系列活动,吸引研究生数万人次关注,线上线下相结合的新形式,适应了年轻学子的阅读习惯,使研究生在自我教育中提升了综合素质。

七

2015 年我们无惧繁重任务的挑战和考验,更好地担当了研究生管理服务的责任。确实,我们碰到了快速发展带来的许多困难,有过迷茫和劳苦,但大家从未有过松懈的念头,通过一人负责、全院(部)配合的有效管理机制,消化了大量阶段性工作的沉重压力,体现了团队的荣誉,应该为有这样一支勤奋和谐、敬业实干的管理队伍而感到骄傲!

细数我们主办的各类大型活动,就有毕业典礼 3 场、开学典礼 2场、入学考试 3 场、就业招聘会 1 场,以及各类文化学术活动几十场,其中投入的时间和精力无法计量,更何况一些活动还需要策划设计和精心组织。让人记忆犹新的是每年一度硕士研究生入学考试的考场和考务工作,我们顶着星星出动,又在灯火通明中收工,干活累到无语,盒饭吃到想吐。然而,我们头脑清醒,竭尽全力,严格把控,高质量完成了任务,并代表上海考区接受了主流媒体的采访,这实在是一次艰苦的洗礼。

我校研究生管理水平的提升,还得益于这个团队多年来养成的踏实作风。本年度,我们加快落实大学章程规范下的各项管理制度,重新修订了《上海师范大学研究生教育工作条例》和《上海师范大学研究生手册》,研制了《上海师范大学硕—博连读攻读博士学位研究生试行办法》、《上海师范大学研究生学业奖学金管理暂行办法》、《上海师范大学研究生科技创新成果奖励管理办法》等若干文件,进一步细化了研究生管理制度,初步建立了集生源奖学金、学业奖学金、国家奖学金、国家助学金、科研成果奖励、"三助一辅"(助教、助研、助管,辅导员)计划等于一体的研究生奖助体系,优化了长效保障的机制。同时,我们还完成了《2014—2015年上海师大学位与研究生教育年度质量报告》,并在上海高校中率先提交,受到上级领导和同行的好评;完成了《上海师大研究生就业白皮书》,以大量具体数据全面反映了我校2015届研究生就业的状况,为推进我校研究生就业工作提供了依据。

此外,我们继续组织开展了新导师培训活动,邀请资深导师传授指导研究生的经验,宣讲我校研究生管理条例,强化导师是第一责任人的意识,有效促进了新导师指导能力的自我完善。

做好常规平凡的管理工作,看似容易不起眼,却最考验管理者的耐心和定力,我们真诚合作,汇聚创意,互相补台,使每一个流程都走得格外顺畅和完美,也赢得了师生们的尊重。

八

过去的一年,又是"十三五"发展的规划之年,催人思考和奋进。我们顶着日常管理工作的巨大压力,积极参与了学校深化综合改革方案、"十三五"发展规划等的研制工作,完成了《上海师大深化研究生教育综合改革方案》和《上海师大研究生教育十三五发展规划》的编制,基本勾画了新五年我校研究生教育发展的蓝图。

至 2020 年,努力使我校一级学科博士点达到 10 个左右,一级学科硕士点将达到 35 个左右(含博士点所属),拥有"教育博士"专业学位点 1 个,专业硕士学位点 15 个左右,进一步优化我校学位点授权体系。

以提升培养质量和服务需求为导向,依托上海市高峰学科和高原学科建设项目,与一批国家和市级重点、一流、特色学科建设同步前行,重点打造中国语言文学、教育学、数学、世界史、中国史、哲学等一级学科博士点的特色和品牌;全力建设发展与教育心理学、环境科学、马克思主义中国化研究等 3 个二级学科博士点并使之建成一级学科博士点,并带动物理学、法学、政治学、经济学、外国语言文学、美术学等硕士点的整体发展。

争取使研究生总规模达到 9000 名左右,其中博士研究生达到 600 人左右;学术学位研究生与专业学位研究生的结构比例调整为 1:1,甚至使专业学位研究生的人数略超学术学位研究生的人数。同时,健全招生选拔、培养模式和社会评价等研究生教育质量保障体系,提高研究生学术创新能力和创业实践能力。

重点培育研究生优秀学位论文 400 项,设立研究生精品课程建设 60 门,研究生一级学科课程体系建设项目 30 个,专业学位案例教学和案例库建设项目 50 个,高端社会实践实习基地建设 35 个(含教育部示范基地 5 个,上海市示范基地 10 个,校级高端基地 20 个),上海市级示范基地导师工作站 3 个。将研究生学位论文重复率检测标准控制在 20% 以下,使参加上海市学位论文(含专业学位)双盲评审异议率控制在 2%～4%;争取每年研究生获上海市优秀学位论文数在 15 篇左右,在国内外顶级学术刊物上发表论文和在各类专业技能大赛中获奖的数量逐年提升,就业率达 95% 左右。

建立海外研习基地 5 个,每年选派研究生 100 名左右。大力支持各学院拓展研究生海外交流新渠道,通过境外研习、交流访问、联合培养、学术会议等多种途径,使参加海外交流的研究生人数逐年提升,努力实现每届研究生 20% 具有海外交流经历的目标。接收外国留学生人数达到 200 名左右,其中学习期限超过 6 个月的长期生比例占 60％左右。

立足于高原,遥望远处的高峰,任重而道远,实在不容歇脚,让我们打起精神赶紧出发!

九

我们精心推出的上海师范大学研究生《学思林》,已经连续出版了四集,这是第五集,放在一起已是蔚为大观,不仅见证了我校研究生学术创新的能力,还可透过五篇序文和若干照片一窥我校研究生教育进步的轨迹。

2015 年版《学思林》的问世,副部长杨龙波,副院长顾绍泉和刘兰英,以及辅导员孙励、陆祺等做了大量编集和校核工作,值此深表谢忱。衷心感谢为指导研究生高质量学术论文付出辛劳的导师们;感谢一直以来对我校研究生教育工作给予大力支持的市学位办领导,以及校、院领导和相关职能部门;感谢长期为我校研究生教育发展默默尽力的同仁们。

抬头望去,树枝上绿芽初露,春天的气息正在悄然回归,新的一年,新的五年,只要我们勤于护树种木,"学思林"一定会更加生机勃勃!

研究生院常务副院长、研工部部长　俞　钢

2016 年 2 月 18 日于行政楼 507 室

目　录

托勒密埃及油类专营制度考 ………………… 陈　恒　李　月 （ 1 ）

中国省域金融顺周期效应异质性的影响因素研究
　　——基于技术进步与产业调整的空间经济分析视角
　　………………… 王周伟　伏开宝　汪传江　胡德红 （ 19 ）

中国创业投资地域集聚现象及其影响因素研究
　　………………………………… 张玉华　李　超 （ 47 ）

国际文凭课程引入的本土改造对策
　　——以上海市为例 ……………………… 刘茂祥 （ 64 ）

论语文教学理论的"内卷化"困境及其破解路径 ……… 石耀华 （ 74 ）

1927～1937 年吴县湖匪活动及时空分布研究 ……… 胡勇军 （ 89 ）

上海公共租界纳税人会议代表性研究 ……………… 李东鹏 （113）

为学生毕业后生活做更好的准备
　　——英国"2014 国家课程"述评 ………… 李国栋　夏惠贤 （131）

宋元与明清时期嘉兴城中的"坊" ……………… 来亚文 （143）

上海离全球城市有多远？
　　——基于城市网络联系能级的比较分析
　　………………………………… 刘江会　贾高清 （167）

特大型城市多层级城市中心的特征及其发展规律
　　——基于上海从业人口空间分布结构变化的分析
　　………………………………… 朱　敏　汪传江 （184）

上海共有产权保障住房运作模式及效果分析
　　………………………………… 崔光灿　姜　巧 （199）

碳减排视角下上海低碳城市发展路径研究
　　………………… 卓德保　吴玉海　潘植强 （214）

基于旅游数字足迹的目的地关注度与共现效应研究
——以上海历史街区为例 ·················· 梁保尔 潘植强 (229)

A Short-term load forecasting model of natural gas based on optimized genetic algorithm and improved BP neural network
·································· Feng Yu, Xiaozhong Xu (254)

Microwave-assisted synthesis of Ag-doped MOFs-like organotitanium polymer with high activity in visible-light driven photocatalytic NO oxidization
······ Wei Zhu, Peijue Liu, Shuning Xiao, Wenchao Wang,
Dieqing Zhang, Hexing Li (293)

Biochemical composite synthesized by stepwise crosslinking: An efficient platform for one-pot biomass conversion
······ Wei Wei , Cong Wang , Yu Zhao , Shichao Peng ,
Haoyang Zhang , Yipeng Bian , Hexing Li , Xinggui
Zhou , Hui Li (312)

An imidazolium-based organopalladium-functionalized organic-inorganic hybrid silica promotes one-pot tandem Suzuki cross coupling-reduction of haloacetophenones and arylboronic acids
·················· Dacheng Zhang, Tanyu Cheng, Guohua Liu (334)

Ru-Catalyzed Asymmetric Transfer Hydrogenation of α-Trifluoromethylimines
········· Meng Wu, Tanyu Cheng, Min Ji, and Guohua Liu (353)

C_{60}-Decorated CdS/TiO_2 Mesoporous Architectures with Enhanced Photostability and Photocatalytic Activity for H_2 Evolution
······ Zichao Lian, Pengpeng Xu, Wenchao Wang, Dieqing
Zhang, Shuning Xiao, Xin Li, and Guisheng Li (371)

A flexible spiral-type supercapacitor based on $ZnCo_2O_4$ nanorod electrodes
············ Hao Wu, Zheng Lou, Hong Yang and Guozhen
Shen (395)

Graphene oxide-$BaGdF_5$ nanocomposites for multi-modal imaging and photothermal therapy

·········· Hao Zhang, Huixia Wu, Jun Wang, Yan Yang,
Dongmei Wu, Yingjian Zhang, Yang Zhang, Zhiguo Zhou,
Shiping Yang, (414)
A highly selective magnetic sensor for Cd^{2+} in living cells with
(Zn, Mn)-doped iron oxide nanoparticles
······ Yang Zhang, Jinchao Shen, Hong Yang, Yan Yang,
Zhiguo Zhou, Shiping Yang (451)
Rapid and label-free Raman detection of azodicarbonamide with
asthma risk
·········· Menghua Li, Xiaoyu Guo, Hui Wang, Ying Wen,
Haifeng Yang (469)
Gd (Ⅲ) complex conjugated ultra-small iron oxide as an
enhanced T_1-weighted MR imaging contrast agent
······ Li Wang, Hongwei Zhang, Zhiguo Zhou, Bin Kong,
Lu An, Jie Wei, Hong Yang, Jiangmin Zhao
and Shiping Yang (492)
Pt/single-stranded DNA/graphene nanocomposite with improved
catalytic activity and CO tolerance
······ Mengzhu Li, Yuxia Pan, Xiaoyu Guo, Yinhua Liang,
Yiping Wu, Ying Wen and Haifeng Yang * (512)
Construction of Dandelion-like Clusters by PtPd Nanoseeds for
Elevating Ethanol Eletrocatalytic Oxidation
······ Yuxia Pan, Xiaoyu Guo, Mengzhu Li, Yinhua Liang,
Yiping Wu, Ying Wen, Haifeng Yang (531)
Highly Sensitive Naphthalimide-Based Fluorescence Polarization
Probe for Detecting Cancer Cells
······ Ti Jia, Congying Fu, Chusen Huang, Haotian Yang,
and Nengqin Jia (546)
Sensitive detection of tumor cells by a new cytosensor with 3D-
MWCNTs array based on vicinal-dithiol-containing proteins
(VDPs)
·········· Yanan Xu, Hui Wu, Chusen Huang, Caiqin Hao,
Beina Wu, Chongchong Miao, Shen Chen, Nengqin Jia (571)

Functionalized Au nanoparticles for label-free Raman determ-
ination of ppb level benzopyrene in edible oil
········· Shuyue Fu, Xiaoyu Guo, Hui Wang, Tianxi Yang,
Ying Wen, Haifeng Yang （587）
A glucose-responsive pH-switchable bioelectrocatalytic sensor
based on phenylboronic acid-diol specificity
············ Peiyi Gao, Zhihua Wang, Lele Yang, Tengfei Ma,
Ling Yang, Qianqiong Guo, Shasheng Huang （604）
DYT1 directly regulates the expression of *TDF1* for tapetum
development and pollen wall formation in Arabidopsis
········· Jing-Nan Gu, Jun Zhu, Yu Yu, Xiao-Dong Teng,
Yue Lou, Xiao-Feng Xu, Jia-Li Liu and Zhong-Nan Yang （630）
Withholding Response to Self-Face Is Faster Than to Other-Face
························ Min Zhu, Yinying Hu, Xiaochen Tang,
Junlong Luo, Xiangping Gao （654）
Influence of Entrepreneurial Experience, Alertness, and Prior
Knowledge on Opport-unity Recognition
····························· Yu Li, Pei Wang, and Ya-Jun Liang （670）
Online Emotion Regulation Questionnaire for Adolescents:
Development and Prelimi-nary Validation
····················· Dengfeng Xie Jiamei Lu Zhangming Xie （683）

托勒密埃及油类专营制度考[*]

陈恒 李月[**]

在托勒密王朝早期,埃及统治者在埃及对一系列产品的生产、收购、调拨、销售等环节进行严格管控,并通过敕令使之制度化。对于这种或与之类似的古代经济现象,西方学者借用近代才产生的"monopoly"一词加以概述。该词源于古希腊语"μονοπωλεῖν"(由古希腊语单词前缀"μονο-"[英译为"one"]和"πωλεῖν"[英译为"to sell"]组合而成),直译为"单独销售",而在古代经济语境下,我们通常将之译为"专营"或"专营制度"。托勒密埃及专营范围甚广,从农作物种植、家畜饲养到手工业生产,几乎无所不包,加之托勒密埃及庞大行政管理体系对专营行业事无巨细的管理,专营制度已融入到当地生活的方方面面。从这一层面上说,研究托勒密埃及专营制度对于深入了解托勒密埃及经济生活有重要意义。[①]

鉴于托勒密埃及专营制度在托勒密埃及经济中的重要作用,许多研究托勒密埃及经济的西方学者都对这一经济制度有所涉及。例如,罗斯托夫采夫(M. I. Rostovtzeff)介绍了托勒密埃及诸如谷物、纺织品、盐、纸草、啤酒、蜂蜜、鱼、油、木材等一系列产品的专营

---

  *　本文为"上海高校一流学科(B类)世界史"规划项目,受教育部"新世纪优秀人才支持计划"资助。

  **　作者简介:陈恒,上海师范大学都市文化研究中心研究员;李月,上海师范大学人文与传播学院世界史博士生。

  ①　对该制度的学术史梳理请参阅陈恒、李月:《托勒密埃及专营制度的多因素透视》,《世界历史》2013 年第 3 期。

情况;①弗雷泽(P. M. Fraser)提到了香料专营问题;②宾根(Jean Bingen)论述了托勒密埃及油产品的专营问题;③沙伊德尔(Walter Scheidel)等人主编的《剑桥希腊罗马经济史》探讨了专营产品的销售问题。④ 近年来,国内学者对托勒密埃及专营制度也有所关注。郭子林在《从托勒密埃及国王的经济管理透视专制王权》中谈到了国王对油、纺织等行业的专营问题。⑤但迄今为止,国内学者对托勒密埃及专营制度尚未有过专门研究。托勒密埃及专营制度的特色之一就是专营范围几乎囊括了所有行业,但由于史料局限,要想重构托勒密王朝对所有行业的专营情况是不现实的。本文选取史料相对较多、⑥

---

① M. I. Rostovtzeff, *A Large Estate in Egypt in the Third Century B. C.*, Madison: University of Wisconsin Press, 1922, pp. 77, 91 – 92; M. I. Rostovtzeff, *The Social and Economic History of the Hellenistic World*, vol. 1, Oxford: Oxford University Press, 1986, pp. 279, 287, 296 – 297, 301, 307 – 311. 虽然罗斯托夫采夫的这些研究成果已略显过时,著述所用史学方法屡遭批判,已被摒弃,但他基于大量考古成果进行的许多论述对今人来说仍有一定学术价值,值得借鉴。关于罗斯托夫采夫在托勒密时期经济史研究领域的成果的评价可参阅 J. G. Manning, "The Relationship of Evidence to Models in the Ptolemaic Economy, 332BC – 30BC", in J. G. Manning and Ian Morris, eds., *The Ancient Economy: Evidence and Model*, Redwood City, CA: Stanford University Press, 2005, p. 172。

② P. M. Fraser, *Ptolemaic Alexandria*, vol. 1, Oxford: Oxford University Press, 1972, pp. 141, 175.

③ Jean Bingen, *Hellenistic Egypt: Monarchy, Society, Economy, Culture*, Berkeley: University of California Press, 2007, pp. 173 – 181.

④ Walter Scheidel, Ian Morris and R. P. Saller, eds., *The Cambridge Economic History of the Greco-Roman World*, Cambridge: Cambridge University Press, 2007, p. 445.

⑤ 郭子林:《从托勒密埃及国王的经济管理透视专制王权》,《史学月刊》2009 年第 7 期。

⑥ 许多纸草文献都专门提到托勒密埃及油专营问题(主要是王室颁布的敕令),例如,《托勒密二世油专营敕令》(*The Oil Monopoly of Ptolemy II Philadelphus*)专门记载了托勒密埃及的油专营情况。亨特(A. S. Hunt)和埃德加(C. C. Edgar)编译的《纸草选集》(*Select Papyri*)和奥斯丁(M. M. Austin)编译的《从亚历山大到罗马征服的希腊化世界》(*The Hellenistic World from Alexander to the Roman Conquest: A Selection of Ancient Sources in Translation*)都收录了这篇文献,相比之下,后者的评注更新,也更细致。本文主要参考的是奥斯丁的版本,见 A. S. Hunt and C. C. Edgar, eds., *Select Papyri*, vol. 2, The Loeb Classical Library, Cambridge, MA: Harvard University Press, 1963, pp. 11 – 35; M. M. Austin, *The Hellenistic World from Alexander to the Roman Conquest: A Selection of Ancient Sources in Translation*, Cambridge: Cambridge University Press, 2006, pp. 524 – 531. 此外《托勒密二世收益敕令》(*Revenue Laws of Ptolemy Philadelphus*)对油专营问题也有大量规定,见 *Revenue Laws of Ptolemy Philadelphus*, Cols. 38 – 72. 该文献最早出版于1896 年,见 B. P. (转下页)

在专营制度中较为重要、[1]专营程序也较深[2]的油类行业为例,以最大限度还原托勒密埃及油类专营制度的内容和原因,并评估其实施效果。

一、油类专营制度的基本内容

政府对油类行业的专营管制从油料作物种植开始。这些油料作物主要有芝麻、巴豆、药西瓜、红花、亚麻子等,[3]其中芝麻和巴豆(生产蓖麻油的植物)主要出自王田和由官僚经营管理的赠田。[4]

(接上页)Grenfell, ed., *Revenue Laws of Ptolemy Philadelphus*, Oxford: The Clarendon Press, 1896. 最新版本见 B. P. Grenfell, ed., *Revenue Laws of Ptolemy Philadelphus*, New York: Ulan Press, 2011. 曼宁(J. G. Manning)认为,关于油类专营的内容是《托勒密二世收益敕令》保存最好、最重要的一部分,详细评论见 J. G. Manning, *Land and Power in Ptolemaic Egypt: The Structure of Land Tenure, 332 - 30B. C. E*, Cambridge: Cambridge University Press, 2003, pp. 141 - 146。

①　对油类专营问题的规定占到《托勒密二世收益敕令》近 1/2 的篇幅,这说明托勒密王朝统治者对油类行业的重视,见 *Revenue Laws of Ptolemy Philadelphus*, Cols. 38 - 72. 曼宁将油类行业列为专营制度中的三个关键行业之一(另外两个行业是盐和纺织品),见 J. G. Manning, "The Relationship of Evidence to Models in the Ptolemaic Economy, 332BC - 30BC," p. 177. 而科斯特(Helmut Köester)则认为油类行业是托勒密埃及专营制度中最重要的行业,见 Helmut Köester, *History, Culture and Religion of the Hellenistic Age*, New York: Walter de Gruyter &. Co. , 1987, p. 48。

②　托勒密埃及政府对油料作物种植到油产品销售的整个产业链都有详细的规定和严格的监管,相比之下,政府对啤酒、亚麻、羊毛等行业的专营管理就没有那么严格,见 M. I. Rostovtzeff, *The Social and Economic History of the Hellenistic World*, vol. 1, pp. 307 - 308。宾根曾将托勒密埃及政府对油和酒这两个行业的专营管理进行对比,并指出政府对油类行业的专营管理更复杂也更严格,见 Jean Bingen, *Hellenistic Egypt: Monarchy, Society, Economy, Culture*, p. 173。

③　M. M. Austin, *The Hellenistic World from Alexander to the Roman Conquest*, p. 525.

④　Jean Bingen, *Hellenistic Egypt: Monarchy, Society, Economy, Culture*, 2007, p. 171. 罗斯托夫采夫将托勒密埃及土地所有制形式分为王田和授田两类,其中授田又可分为赠田、私田、庙田,见 M. I. Rostovtzeff, *The Social and Economic History of the Hellenistic World*, vol. 1, pp. 274 - 298. 这种划分方式是当前学界较为认同的划分方式。不过也有学者对这种划分方式提出过质疑,如曼宁就认为上埃及地区(埃及南部地区)的庙田和私田实际不受国王控制,不应被纳入授田范围,见 J. G. Manning, *The Last Pharaohs: Egypt under the Ptolemies, 305 - 30BC*, Princeton: Princeton University Press, 2010, p. 124. 笔者倾向于接受罗斯托夫采夫的划分方式,在笔者看来,上埃及地区庙田虽不受控制,但名义上仍属国王所有,因为托勒密王朝国王沿袭法老君权,既是一国之主,也是埃及宗教的最高祭司。至于私田,则是前朝历史遗存,一方面数量极少,似可忽略不计,另一方面,当托勒密 (转下页)

同其他农作物一样,油料作物的种植区域和规模依照《种植计划表》进行,[①]种子由政府供应,[②]并由奥伊口诺摩斯(Oikonomos)[③]监督播种情况,未播撒的种子也由奥伊口诺摩斯负责回收。[④] 而根据《托勒密二世油专营敕令》的规定,如果应耕土地未被耕种,诺姆长、[⑤]区长、奥伊口诺摩斯和审计官应向国王缴纳 2 塔兰特[⑥]的罚款,并按一定比例支付承包商[⑦]损失的利润。[⑧]播种之后,奥伊口诺摩斯须巡视

(接上页)王朝王权鼎盛,能够强化对上埃及地区的控制时,国王也随时可将那里的土地没收。

① 罗斯托夫采夫认为,《种植计划表》由中央政府制定,通过自上而下、各级摊派的方式执行,见 M. I. Rostovtzeff, *The Social and Economic History of the Hellenistic World*, vol. 1, pp. 302 - 303。而最新的研究成果表明,《种植计划表》是基于地方书吏对农作物的考察,再由各诺姆(nome)讨论后上报亚历山大里亚备案,奥斯丁收录了一份关于《种植计划表》的政府报告,显示了这种上报的过程,见 M. M. Austin, *The Hellenistic World from Alexander to the Roman Conquest*, pp. 554 - 555。而且,这种《种植计划表》并非用于给各个村庄强制摊派生产任务,而是用于预测来年的收益,关于《种植计划表》的讨论可参阅 J. G. Manning, "The Relationship of Evidence to Models in the Ptolemaic Economy, 332BC - 30BC," p. 178; Jean Bingen, *Hellenistic Egypt: Monarchy, Society, Economy, Culture*, p. 178。

② 对于享有税收减免或一些作为赠田的土地来说,情况有所不同,当地耕种者需在收获时自留种子,见 M. M. Austin, *The Hellenistic World from Alexander to the Roman Conquest*, p. 526。

③ 根据"Oikonomos"音译而来,其职能相当于地方财政官,这里沿用了刘文鹏先生的译法,见刘文鹏:《古代埃及史》,北京:商务印书馆,2000 年,第 591 页。

④ M. M. Austin, *The Hellenistic World from Alexander to the Roman Conquest*, p. 559.

⑤ 诺姆,相当于一个省的行政区划。诺姆长即其最高行政长官。

⑥ 托勒密王朝沿用了古希腊的货币单位。一般而言,托勒密埃及货币单位具有下面的对应关系:1 塔兰特(Talent)=1500 斯塔特(Statae)=6000 德拉克马(Drachma)=36000 奥波尔(Obols)。这里需要说明的是,托勒密埃及流通的货币主要是以德拉克马为基本单位的银币和以奥波尔为基本单位的铜币,自托勒密二世货币改革之后,由于政府大量发行铜币,铜币大幅贬值,银币与铜币间的兑换比率也常有波动,相应地,物价也会有所变动,因此,文中所引《托勒密二世油专营敕令》中的数据仅能反映敕令颁布时(公元前 259 年,托勒密二世统治的第 27 年)的情况,关于托勒密埃及的货币流通和银、铜币兑换可参阅 Sitta von Reden, *Money in Ptolemaic Egypt: From the Macedonian Conquest to the End of the Third Century BC*, Cambridge: Cambridge University Press, 2007, pp. 63 - 67,70,111。

⑦ 在托勒密王朝承包某一行业收益的人。关于承包商在托勒密埃及专营制度中的作用,可参阅 B. P. Muhs, *Tax Receipts, Taxpayers, and Taxes in Early Ptolemaic Thebes*, Chicago: Chicago University Press, 2004, p. 73; M. M. Austin, *The Hellenistic World from Alexander to the Roman Conquest*, p. 531。

⑧ M. M. Austin, *The Hellenistic World from Alexander to the Roman Conquest*, pp. 525 - 526.

农作物生长情况,解决可能存在的问题。① 收获之时,耕种者须通知诺姆长和区长,在无诺姆长和区长情况下通知奥伊口诺摩斯,再由这些官员通知承包商亲自到耕地现场估价,并根据估价结果订立契约(一式两份),耕种者要以书面形式立誓确认已种农作物的土地数量及评估产量,而后在契约上签字。诺姆长、区长、奥伊口诺摩斯或他们的代理人也要对评估结果负责,并在契约上签字,如有差错,他们也须向承包商支付规定的罚款,并向耕种者索取补偿。②

收获之后,除用于纳税的部分外,③其余产品须按规定价格交由政府指定的代理人收购,根据《托勒密二世油专营敕令》的规定,具体收购价格为:对于筛选干净可直接用于加工的油料作物,以1阿塔巴(Artaba)为标准量,④芝麻8德拉克马,巴豆4德拉克马,红花1德拉克马2奥波尔,药西瓜4奥波尔,亚麻子3奥波尔;对于未筛选干净不可直接用于加工的油料作物,以100阿塔巴为标准量,芝麻增加7阿塔巴,巴豆增加7阿塔巴,红花增加8阿塔巴;对于享有税收减免或一些作为赠田的土地来说,以1阿塔巴为标准量,芝麻6德拉克马,巴豆3德拉克马2奥波尔,红花1德拉克马。⑤收购工作完成后,代理人应向村长递交一份附有收购清单并加盖封印的收据,否则村长不得放行,如在未拿到收据的情况下放行,村长要承担1000德拉克马的罚款,还要赔偿因此造成的契约损失。⑥

收购上来的油料作物会被运往王室仓库,然后由奥伊口诺摩斯

---

① M. M. Austin, *The Hellenistic World from Alexander to the Roman Conquest*, pp. 558-559.

② M. M. Austin, *The Hellenistic World from Alexander to the Roman Conquest*, p. 526.

③ 税率为产出的1/4,见 *Revenue Laws of Ptolemy Philadelphus*, Cols. 39-40. 8,42. 3-43. 19.

④ 阿塔巴(Artaba)和考易斯(Choenices)均为托勒密埃及容量单位。1阿塔巴=40考易斯;1阿塔巴约等于40升,也就是说1考易斯约等于1升。

⑤ M. M. Austin, *The Hellenistic World from Alexander to the Roman Conquest*, pp. 525-526.需要指出的是,这些价格并不是完全不变的,政府会根据情况进行更改和变动。

⑥ M. M. Austin, *The Hellenistic World from Alexander to the Roman Conquest*, p. 525.

统一调拨给辖区的榨油作坊。① 榨油作坊大多归政府所有,神庙也拥有一些,私人不得拥有。② 新建立的榨油作坊要持有奥伊口诺摩斯的签章许可。③ 作坊内的研钵和压榨机等榨油工具由政府提供,④奥伊口诺摩斯监管,生产时供应,不生产时封存,如果监管不利,出现非生产期间生产工具未封存的情况,奥伊口诺摩斯将面临1塔兰特的罚款。⑤ 奥伊口诺摩斯还需负责给每个榨油作坊供应适量的油料作物原材料,数量以确保不超过作坊现存压榨机的实际用量为准。如果奥伊口诺摩斯因未供应油料作物原材料而造成契约损失,他会受到财政大臣的审判,如被判有罪,他将被处以2塔兰特的罚款,并双倍补偿契约损失。⑥

榨油工人由政府分配,⑦安置在各诺姆的榨油工人不得随意迁往其他诺姆,否则承包商、奥伊口诺摩斯,以及其他地方官员都有权力将其逮捕。⑧任何人不得收留来自其他诺姆的榨油工人,否则每收留一个榨油工人处以3000德拉克马罚款。⑨ 榨油工人每天必须完成不少于1阿塔巴芝麻、4阿塔巴巴豆、1阿塔巴红花的榨油量,并按照一定标准获得工资。⑩ 榨油工人工资及其剩余产品利润

————————

① M. M. Austin, *The Hellenistic World from Alexander to the Roman Conquest*, pp. 526,560.

② *Revenue Laws of Ptolemy Philadelphus*, Cols. 44 – 47.9.

③ M. M. Austin, *The Hellenistic World from Alexander to the Roman Conquest*, p. 526.

④ *Revenue Laws of Ptolemy Philadelphus*, Cols. 49.1 – 50.5.

⑤ M. M. Austin, *The Hellenistic World from Alexander to the Roman Conques*, p. 527.

⑥ M. M. Austin, *The Hellenistic World from Alexander to the Roman Conquest*, pp,526 – 527,560.

⑦ *Revenue Laws of Ptolemy Philadelphus*, Cols. 49.1 – 50.5. 托勒密埃及时期的榨油工人往往世代都从事这一行业,并被束缚在所在的诺姆内,供政府调配。

⑧ *Revenue Laws of Ptolemy Philadelphus*, Cols. 44.8 – 18; M. M. Austin, *The Hellenistic World from Alexander to the Roman Conquest*, p. 526.

⑨ M. M. Austin, *The Hellenistic World from Alexander to the Roman Conquest*, p. 527.

⑩ M. M. Austin, *The Hellenistic World from Alexander to the Roman Conquest*, p. 527. 关于榨油工人的工资标准,《托勒密二世油专营敕令》也有明确规定,具体按所榨油料作物的种类和数量支付工资,只是由于文献的这一部分残损不全,我们不得而知。

份额①由奥伊口诺摩斯及其代理人支付,如因未支付工资或利润份额导致作坊停工,奥伊口诺摩斯要向国王支付 3000 德拉克马罚款,并双倍补偿契约损失。榨油工人榨油期间,奥伊口诺摩斯和承包商需要时常到所在诺姆的各榨油作坊中巡察监督,既保障榨油工作顺利进行,②也防止榨油工人将生产工具带走,一经发现,他们要负责将生产工具追回,并对相应的榨油工人处以 5 塔兰特的罚款。③

榨油作坊生产出来的油由奥伊口诺摩斯和承包商及其代理人安排运输和销售。他们须提前十天将下个月用油送到辖区内各城镇的竞标机构,④并在这十天内公示当地零售商所出的最高竞标价格,之后与中标的零售商签订承销合同,并要求他们按照政府规定价格出售。无论零售商同意处理多少数量的油产品,奥伊口诺摩斯都必须在一个月开始之前将足量的油送到各个村子,并量出五天的销售量分给零售商,而承包商须在当天收到货款,并上交王室银行,当天收不到货款的也应在五天之内收讫。⑤ 零售商主要在各市、镇、村的中心区域进行销售,⑥价格以政府规定为准,具体为:每米特拉芝麻油或红花油 48 德拉克马铜币,每米特拉蓖麻油、药西瓜油或灯油 30 德拉克马铜币。零售商销售时所用的量具须经过奥伊口诺摩斯和审计官检验。⑦

私制、私售油产品是明令禁止的。如果有人被发现从零售商以外的其他人那里购买任何油类产品,那么此人必须向承包商支付

---

① 当市场销售了足够的油类产品,足以抵消所有生产成本,剩下的待销售产品就被称为"剩余产品",关于剩余产品的销售利润分配,见 M. M. Austin, *The Hellenistic World from Alexander to the Roman Conquest*, p. 527。

② M. M. Austin, *The Hellenistic World from Alexander to the Roman Conquest*, p. 527.

③ M. M. Austin, *The Hellenistic World from Alexander to the Roman Conquest*, p. 528.

④ 关于竞标机构在油产品专营中的作用详见 *Revenue Laws of Ptolemy Philadelphus*, Cols. 59 - 60。

⑤ M. M. Austin, *The Hellenistic World from Alexander to the Roman Conquest*, p. 528.

⑥ *Revenue Laws of Ptolemy Philadelphus*, Cols. 40. 9 - 20.

⑦ M. M. Austin, *The Hellenistic World from Alexander to the Roman Conquest*, p. 525.

3000 德拉克马的罚款,并被没收一切油类产品,罚款由奥伊口诺摩斯或其代理人监督执行,如其无法支付罚款就会被逮捕入狱。[1] 猪油须在承包商监督下用光,不得以任何借口出售给他人,违者处每块猪油 50 德拉克马的罚款。[2] 神庙榨的油也不得私制、私售。它们的榨油作坊须在承包商、奥伊口诺摩斯及其代理人的监督下用两个月的时间生产出一年所需,且只能生产芝麻油,所产油的数量须登记造册,上呈国王和财政大臣,所产之油只能自用,不得外售,违者处每米特拉 100 德拉克马的罚款。[3] 如果承包商或其下属声称有人制售私油,他可以要求奥伊口诺摩斯或其代理人到场搜查,[4]如果奥伊口诺摩斯或其代理人不去,他们会被处以相当于私油价值两倍的罚款,如果搜查未发现私油,被搜查者有权要求承包商在神庙发誓,承认搜查结果,如果承包者当天或第二天并未发誓,那么他应向被搜查者支付相当于先前声称私油价值的两倍罚款。[5]

　　外来油类产品在托勒密埃及的流通也受到严格限制。《托勒密二世油专营敕令》和《托勒密二世收益敕令》都专门提到亚历山大里亚、佩鲁修姆(Pelusium)与诺姆间的油类产品运输问题。[6] 按照规定,外来油类产品不得带入内地,违者处每米特拉 100 德拉克马的罚款。[7] 如出于自用目的需将外来油类产品带入内地的,应按 1 米

　　① M. M. Austin, *The Hellenistic World from Alexander to the Roman Conquest*, p. 528.

　　② M. M. Austin, *The Hellenistic World from Alexander to the Roman Conquest*, p. 529.

　　③ M. M. Austin, *The Hellenistic World from Alexander to the Roman Conquest*, p. 529.

　　④ 公元前 114 年的一封请愿书反映了承包商要求奥伊口诺摩斯的代理人查禁私油的过程,见 A. S. Hunt and C. C. Edgar, eds., *Select Papyri*, vol. 2, pp. 253－254。

　　⑤ M. M. Austin, *The Hellenistic World from Alexander to the Roman Conquest*, p. 530.

　　⑥ *Revenue Laws of Ptolemy Philadelphus*, Cols. 52. 7－53. 3, 54. 6－19; M. M. Austin, *The Hellenistic World from Alexander to the Roman Conquest*, pp. 529－530. 这两个地方是托勒密埃及主要的海陆贸易中转站,国外和来自叙利亚、巴勒斯坦地区的油产品在缴纳 50％关税之后进口到这两个地区,并在那里的严格监管下消费,除非两地借道互运,否则这些油产品不得作为商品进入内地,见 A. S. Hunt and C. C. Edgar, eds., *Select Papyri*, vol. 2, p. 29, n. a。

　　⑦ M. M. Austin, *The Hellenistic World from Alexander to the Roman Conquest*, p. 529.

特拉 12 德拉克马的标准征税,税款上缴至目的地所在诺姆的王室银行,并要有证明人随往,违者处 1 米特拉 100 德拉克马的罚款,所携油类产品也一并没收。① 此外,承包商还应指派代理人在亚历山大里亚和佩鲁修姆核查外来油类产品,他们须清查仓库,并核查分派出去的油类产品,以加强对源头的监管。②

二、实行油类专营制度的原因

正如我们所看到的,托勒密王朝在埃及对专营产品的生产与销售进行了严密监控,并对相关各方的权利与义务进行了细致规定,由此建立了一种较为严密、完整的专营制度。这种专营制度在埃及的建立是托勒密王朝主观需要和埃及客观条件共同作用的结果。

在希腊化早期,托勒密王朝面临各种巨额开支。除土地开发、③神庙捐助、④文化投入、⑤王室耗费⑥等一系列开支外,主要开支来自外交、军事方面。在爱琴海和小亚细亚地区,托勒密王朝早期统治者一直试图通过扶植亲托勒密王朝的希腊城邦来遏制马其顿王朝,⑦并致力于建立一支庞大的海军用于保卫塞浦路斯、埃及,以及

---

① M. M. Austin, *The Hellenistic World from Alexander to the Roman Conquest*, p. 530.

② M. M. Austin, *The Hellenistic World from Alexander to the Roman Conquest*, p. 530.

③ 例如对法尤姆(Fayûm)的农业开发,可参阅郭子林:《古埃及托勒密王朝对法尤姆地区的农业开发》,《世界历史》2011 年第 5 期。

④ 关于托勒密王朝早期统治者对埃及神庙的捐助可参阅 J. A. S. Evans, "A Social and Economic History of an Egyptian Temple in the Greco-Roman Period," *Yale Classical Studies*, vol. 17(1961), p. 267. 转引自郭子林:《古埃及托勒密王朝对法尤姆地区的农业开发》,《世界历史》2011 年第 5 期;Justin Pollard and Howard Reid, *The Rise and Fall of Alexandria: Birthplace of the Modern World*, New York: Penguin Books, 2006,pp. 82 – 83。

⑤ 文化投入最明显体现在亚历山大里亚的博物馆和图书馆上,可参阅 P. M. Fraser, *Ptolemaic Alexandria*, pp. 312 – 335; Andrew Erskine, "Culture and Power in Ptolemaic Egypt: The Museum and Library of Alexandria," *Greece & Rome*, 2nd Ser., vol. 42, no. 1(Apr. 1995), pp. 38 – 48。

⑥ C. G. Starr, *Past and Future in Ancient History*, Lanham, MD: University Press of America, 1987,p. 31。

⑦ 如对米利都的扶持,见 S. M. Burstein, *The Hellenistic Age from the Battle of Ipsos to the Death of Kleopatra VII*, Cambridge: Cambridge University Press, 1985,pp. 117 - 118。

罗德岛和海上贸易线①不受马其顿海军的威胁,也用于对希腊城邦的军事保护或威慑,确保其对岛国同盟的领导地位。② 科艾勒-叙利亚(Coele-Syria)地区③对托勒密王朝来说也至关重要,这块领土是托勒密王朝防范塞琉古王朝进攻埃及的重要军事缓冲带;位于黎巴嫩的森林是托勒密王朝打造海军舰队的基础;④巴勒斯坦地区是中东商队汇集之地,也是埃及陆上贸易的重要延伸;⑤这里也是托勒密王朝招募雇佣兵的重要兵源地。但这块土地对塞琉古王朝来说同样重要,塞琉古王朝统治者也从未放弃对这块土地的所有权,一直伺机夺回这块本属于它的土地。⑥ 因此,托勒密王朝统治者在这里建有许多军事要塞和据点,⑦并常年驻扎大量军队。此外,为对抗塞琉古王朝的战象,⑧托勒密二世还专门组织人力到红海沿岸今埃塞

① 关于罗德岛对托勒密王朝的重要作用见 Polybius, *The Histories*, V. 88. 4 - 90. 3。

② 公元前 306 年,托勒密王朝的舰队在萨拉米斯(Salamis)与狄米特里乌斯(Demetrius)的舰队对抗时全军覆没,托勒密王朝也失去了岛国同盟的领导地位,见 Diodorus, *Library of History*, 20. 47 - 53; M. I. Rostovtzeff, *The Social and Economic History of the Hellenistic World*, vol. 1, p. 14; R. M. Errington, *A History of the Hellenistic World*, *323 - 30 BC*, Malden, MA: Blackwell Publishing, 2008, p. 43. 后来,托勒密二世重建了托勒密王朝的舰队,但这支舰队在克雷莫尼迪恩战争(Chremonidean War)中又遭到重创,见 M. I. Rostovtzeff, *The Social and Economic History of the Hellenistic World*, vol. 1, p. 37; Günther Hölbl, *A History of the Ptolemaic Empire*, trans, Tina Saavedra, London and New York: Routledge Ltd. , 2001,pp. 40 - 43。

③ 在史料中,这一地区通常被简称为"叙利亚",但巴勒斯坦和腓尼基都被包括在内,见 Martin Hengel, *Judaism and Hellenism: Studies in Their Encounter in Palestine during the Early Hellenistic Period*, vol. 1, Philadelphia: Fortress Press, 1974,p. 7。

④ 埃及树木不能满足埃及本土的需求,而且埃及出产的木材大多不宜用于造船,见 W. W. Tarn, *Hellenistic Civilization*, London: Edward Arnold &. Co. , 1952, p. 195; M. I. Rostovtzeff, *The Social and Economic History of the Hellenistic World*, vol. 1, p. 299。

⑤ 关于巴勒斯坦地区对托勒密王朝的商业价值见 Martin Hengel, *Judaism and Hellenism: Studies in Their Encounter in Palestine during the Early Hellenistic Period*, vol. 1, p. 39。

⑥ 关于两国争夺科艾勒-叙利亚地区的起因见 F. W. Walbank, *Hellenistic World*, Cambridge, MA: Harvard University Press, 1993,p. 101。

⑦ 古罗马研究专家琼斯(A. H. M. Jones, 1904 - 1970)通过将巴勒斯坦地区的城镇名称与埃及城镇名称比对的方法证实,巴勒斯坦的许多据点都是由托勒密王朝统治者建造的,见 A. H. M. Jones, *Cities of the Eastern Roman Provinces*, Oxford: Oxford University Press, 1937,p. 242。

⑧ 据斯特拉波记载,塞琉古一世于公元前 303 年从印度旃陀罗笈多处获得了 500 头战象,见 Strabo, *Geography*, XV. 2. 9。

俄比亚地区捕猎非洲象。① 军队的维持也需要巨额资金。在希腊化早期,托勒密王朝的军队主要由雇佣兵构成。② 要维持这样一支军队,统治者需要为他们提供军备,③并向他们支付工资。④ 此外,统治者还需要通过大量赏赐来维持军队的忠诚。⑤

所有这些开支决定了托勒密王朝在公元前 3 世纪的经济政策目标是尽可能多地谋取收益,⑥而托勒密王朝早期统治者设计和建立经济制度也主要基于这一动机。⑦ 在田赋、税赋都已很重的情况

---

① 据老普林尼(Gaius Plinius Secundus,公元 23/24—79)记载,托勒密王朝统治者还可能专门遣使到印度重金聘请驯象师(见 Pliny, the Elder, *Nature History*, VI. 58),不过这一说法有待考证。实际上,托勒密王朝用非洲象对抗印度象的策略效果并不好,据波里比阿所说,托勒密的大多数战象拒绝进行战斗,它们害怕印度象庞大的身躯和力量,当它们接近印度象的时期就会掉转尾巴,逃离战场,见 Polybius, *The Histories*, V. 84. 5。

② 在希腊化时代,使用雇佣兵作战是十分常见的事,他们在各个希腊化军队中都形成了可观的数目,可参阅 G. T. Griffith, *The Mercenaries of the Hellenistic World*, Cambridge: Cambridge University Press, 1933, pp. 108 - 117; F. W. Walbank, *Hellenistic World*, p. 67。这种情况直到公元前 217 年拉斐亚战役才得以改变,在这场战役中,托勒密王朝由于兵力短缺征召了两万埃及人入伍,见 Polybius, *The Histories*, V. 65. 9; F. W. Walbank et al. , eds. , *Cambridge Ancient History*, vol. 7, part 1, Cambridge: Cambridge University Press, 2006, p. 436。

③ 关于托勒密王朝为雇佣兵提供装备的情况可参阅 Nick Sekunda, *Seleucid and Ptolemaic Reformed Armies 168 - 145 BC*, vol. 2, Stockport: Montvert Publication, 1995, pp. 21 - 22。生产装备所用的铁是托勒密王朝非常紧缺的,需从国外进口,见 F. W. Walbank, *Hellenistic World*, p. 103。

④ 托勒密王朝早期统治者通过支付工资来维持雇佣兵军队,后来财政紧张无力维持时,改用土地来代替工资,可参阅 R. S. Bagnall, "The Origins of the Ptolemaic Cleruchs," *Bulletin of the American Society of Papyrologists*, vol. 21, 1984, pp. 7 - 20。高报酬、赠土地、免赋税等政策培养出了职业军人阶层,见 Martin Hengel, *Judaism and Hellenism: Studies in Their Encounter in Palestine during the Early Hellenistic Period*, vol. 1, p. 14。

⑤ 这是自亚历山大以来通行的做法,而且十分必要,在继承者战争中,军队倒戈是常有的事,可参阅 M. I. Rostovtzeff, *The Social and Economic History of the Hellenistic World*, vol. 1, pp. 9, 20, 22。塔恩更直白地形容希腊化时期的战争是迫使敌军的雇佣兵投降,然后再将其召募过来,见 W. W. Tarn, *Hellenistic Civilization*, pp. 60 - 61。

⑥ 尽可能多地获取收益一直是托勒密王朝的经济目标之一,可参阅 J. G. Manning, "The Ptolemaic Economy, Institutions, Economic Integration, and the Limits of Centralized Political Power," *Princeton/Stanford Working Papers in Classics*, Apr. 2005, p. 9; Andrew Monson, *From the Ptolemies to the Romans: Political and Economic Change in Egypt*, Cambridge: Cambridge University Press, 2012, p. 23。

⑦ F. W. Walbank, *Hellenistic World*, p. 103。

下,①托勒密王朝统治者急于引入专营制度来解决财政紧张问题,②但并不是托勒密王朝的所有领地都适合实行专营制度。③塞浦路斯孤悬海外,统治不易;④科艾勒-叙利亚战火不断,且民情复杂,无法有效控制;昔兰尼加则保持着相当程度的独立,⑤至于色雷斯、爱奥尼亚、卡里亚、西里西亚、吕西亚等地,托勒密王朝的统治力量十分薄弱,统治时间也十分短暂。⑥相比之下,埃及在各方面具有得天独厚的条件,成了培植专营制度的沃壤。

第一,埃及固有的地理条件为专营制度的实行创造了有利条件。埃及南靠埃塞俄比亚高原,北临地中海,东西两侧被沙漠包围,是一个较为封闭的区域,其对外联系主要依靠经西奈半岛通往巴勒斯坦地区的陆上交通和经亚历山大里亚港通往地中海的海上航线,这意味着,仅控制西奈半岛和亚历山大里亚就能控制埃及的货物进出口流通。⑦埃及境内只有一条尼罗河,埃及人也大多依河而居,因此,希罗多德把埃及称为"尼罗河的赠礼"。从第一瀑布到三角洲地区,尼罗河河谷把所有拐弯处都算在内才 490 英里,且宽度十分有

---

① 托勒密王朝的田赋很重,王田的绝大部分产出都要上缴,可参阅 M. M. Manning, *Land and Power in Ptolemaic Egypt*, Cambridge: Cambridge University Press, 2003, pp. 103 - 124. 托勒密王朝的税赋也很重,可参阅 M. I. Rostovtzeff, *The Social and Economic History of the Hellenistic World*, vol. 1, pp. 290, 295 - 296, 305, 308 - 310; W. W. Tarn, *Hellenistic Civilization*, p. 199.

② 专营制度在托勒密王朝建立之前就已存在,古希腊一些城邦在财政紧张的情况下就会对某些产品施行专营,见苗力田主编:《亚里士多德全集》第 9 卷,北京:中国人民大学出版社,2009 年,第 297—319 页。

③ 关于托勒密王朝除埃及以外的其他领地的情况可参阅 R. S. Bagnall, *The Administration of the Ptolemaic Possessions Outside Egypt*, Leiden: E. J. Brill, 1976.

④ 托勒密王朝对塞浦路斯的控制需要依赖海军,但在希腊化早期,托勒密王朝海军几经重创,萨拉米斯海战兵败后,托勒密王朝也一度失去了对塞浦路斯的控制,见 R. M. Errington, *A History of the Hellenistic World*, 323 - 30 *BC*, p. 44.

⑤ 关于希腊化早期昔兰尼加的情况可参阅 R. S. Bagnall, *The Administration of the Ptolemaic Possessions Outside Egypt*, pp. 25 - 37; Günther Hölbl, *A History of the Ptolemaic Empire*, pp. 45 - 46.

⑥ 关于托勒密王朝对其各个领地的统治时间可参阅 Katja Mueller, *Settlements of the Ptolemies: City Foundations and New Settlement in the Hellenistic World*, Dudley, MA: Peeters, 2006, p. 45.

⑦ 《托勒密二世油专营敕令》也仅对亚历山大里亚和佩鲁修姆两地的外来油类产品向内地运输作了规定,见 M. M. Austin, *The Hellenistic World from Alexander to the Roman Conquest*, pp. 529 - 530.

限,最宽处距两岸沙漠也不超过9.2英里。① 如此狭小、集中的生产生活区域也有利于政府对经济活动的监管。而且,该区域又被碎化成42个诺姆,②各诺姆独立组织生产,这又进一步降低了政府监管的难度。由于依河而居,埃及交通运输以水运为主,各诺姆货物一般都通过骡子运到尼罗河的港口再装上驳船,运往他处,③这也有利于政府对埃及境内货物运输的监管。④

　　第二,埃及传统的行政管理体系为专营制度的实行奠定了重要基础。从法老时期第一王朝开始,埃及便确立了中央集权统治,并在之后漫长的岁月里逐渐形成庞大的行政管理体系。⑤ 及至托勒密王朝统治时期,王朝统治者出于政治目的延续了法老旧制,并几乎完全照搬了法老时期埃及行政管理体系。⑥ 由于中央对地方的绝对控制,中央的计划或决策在地方能够得到有效执行和监督,加之官僚数量众多,职责明确,这就在客观上强化了政府对经济事务的干预能力,促进了政府对产品生产、销售等经济活动事无巨细的管理。

---

　　① 数据见亚历山大·莫瑞、G. 戴维:《从部落到帝国:原始社会和古代东方的社会组织》,郭子林译,郑州:大象出版社,2010年,第104页。

　　② 托勒密二世由于对法尤姆地区的开发又在法尤姆建立了新的诺姆,使托勒密埃及的诺姆数增至43个,见 D. J. Thompson, "Economic Reforms in the Mid-Reign of Ptolemy Philadelphus," in Paul McKechnie and Philippe Guillaume, eds. , *Ptolemy II Philadelphus and His World*, Leidon: E. J. Brill, 2008, p. 30。

　　③ 关于托勒密埃及的货物运输可参阅 Strabo, XVII, 1. 7; D. J. Thompson, "Nile Grain Transport under the Ptolemies," in Peter Garnsey, Keith Hopkins and C. R. Whittaker, eds. , *Trade in the Ancient Economy*, Berkeley and Los Angeles: University of California Press, 1983, p. 65。

　　④ 《托勒密二世油专营敕令》对油类产品专营过程中的生产和销售作了细致规定,关于产品运输大多涉及外来油类产品向内地各诺姆运输的限制,对于内地各诺姆间的产品运输问题涉及极少,这或许也能说明托勒密埃及境内货物运输环节易于监管,见 M. M. Austin, *The Hellenistic World from Alexander to the Roman Conquest*, pp. 524 – 531。

　　⑤ 关于法老时期埃及行政管理体系可参阅 A. B. Lloyd, ed. , *A Companion to Ancient Egypt*, vol. 1, Malden, MA: Wiley-Blackwell, 2010, pp. 218 – 236。

　　⑥ 需要说明的是,奥伊口诺摩斯是托勒密王朝统治者在埃及旧有行政管理体系之外新设的职位,其职能与古希腊的市场监理类似,只是又根据统治需要增加了许多新内容,奥伊口诺摩斯在托勒密埃及行政管理体系中的职能相当于地方财政官、地方经济监察官,这也进一步强化了旧有行政管理体系在经济监管中的作用。有一份纸草文献专门详述了奥伊口诺摩斯在托勒密埃及经济体系中的职责,见 M. M. Austin, *The Hellenistic World from Alexander to the Roman Conquest*, pp. 558 – 562。

第三,埃及自身的社会环境对专营制度的实行起到了推动作用。首先,专营制度对埃及来说并非完全陌生。在托勒密王朝实行专营制度之前,埃及就已存在一些类似专营的经济现象,有些产品(例如油)只有神庙才进行生产,周边村民则通过与神庙物物交换来获得这些产品。① 其次,埃及社会人口流动性存在限制,农民往往世代被束缚在固定的土地上,未经官员允许不得擅离;②工匠也世代从事着同样的职业,不得随意在诺姆间迁徙,③这有利于政府对人员的控制和监管。再次,埃及地区以埃及人为主,民族成份较为单一,且埃及人口集中,主要聚居在各村庄中,受村长和书吏约束,便于组织和管理。

三、油类专营制度的实施与社会控制

鉴于托勒密王朝迫切的统治需要和埃及有利的生态、经济、政治条件,托勒密王朝早期统治者在埃及建立了独具埃及特色的专营制度。而且,托勒密王朝早期统治者通过改革币制、④提高关税⑤等

---

① W. W. Tarn, *Hellenistic Civilization*, p. 187; M. I. Rostovtzeff, *The Social and Economic History of the Hellenistic World*, vol. 1, p. 301.

② W. W. Tarn, *Hellenistic Civilization*, p. 187.

③ M. I. Rostovtzeff, *The Social and Economic History of the Hellenistic World*, vol. 1, p. 304;杜丹:《古代世界经济生活》,志扬译,北京:商务印书馆,1963年,第128页。

④ 法老时期的埃及并不存在货币的概念,当时的埃及人通过金、银、铜等金属作为一般等价物进行物物交换,金、银、铜等金属用重量计,单位是德本(deben),各金属之间也有固定的兑换比例,见 J. J. Janssen, *Commodity Prices from the Ramessid Period*, Leiden: E. J. Brill, 1975, p. 101. 波斯王统治时期,孟菲斯地区的统治者可能出于支付希腊雇佣兵工资的目的仿造了少量的希腊银币,见 Sitta von Reden, *Money in Ptolemaic Egypt: From the Macedonian Conquest to the End of the Third Century BC*, p. 32. 亚历山大征服埃及后,阿提卡币制金、银币开始在埃及流通,但流通范围有限。及至托勒密王朝统治时期,王朝统治者建立了与阿提卡币制不同、类似腓尼基制的独特币制,外来货币进入埃及均须入炉重铸成当地货币,这就使埃及货币体系与希腊化世界其他地区货币体系隔绝开来。关于托勒密埃及封闭的货币体系可参阅 Sitta von Reden, *Money in Ptolemaic Egypt: From the Macedonian Conquest to the End of the Third Century BC*, pp. 43 - 48.

⑤ 为保障专营收益,托勒密王朝对进入埃及的外来产品征收的税额是很高的,对某些产品(例如橄榄油)的征税比率甚至高达50%,对埃及以外托勒密王朝领地的产品也不例外,可参阅 M. I. Rostovtzeff, *The Social and Economic History of the Hellenistic World*, vol. 1, p. 305.

措施构建了相对封闭的经济环境,通过引入包税制①保障收益稳定,
这又进一步促进了专营制度在埃及的有效实施。在这种制度保障
下,托勒密王朝几乎把埃及所有行业都纳入了专营体系,以图最大
限度地谋取收益,用塔恩(W. W. Tarn)的话说,"埃及变成了制造金
钱的机器"。②但实际上,托勒密王朝对许多行业的专营管理远达不
到敕令或制度所要求的程度。最明显的是啤酒业,私酿者甚众,但
政府无力监管;③而对亚麻纺织业的监管,政府更是有心无力;④甚
至对监管最为严密的油类行业,政府也做不到绝对专营。⑤ 如此,正
如霍普金斯所言,"政府想要规范和控制所有行业,但实际上,他们
什么也没控制住"。⑥

托勒密王朝统治者在埃及实行专营制度受到多种因素制约,最
明显的是来自埃及本土祭司集团的束缚。长久以来,埃及本土祭司
集团都是作为埃及重要政治、经济力量存在的,及至托勒密王朝统
治时期,王朝统治者在埃及继任法老、确立王权并保持统治的稳定
性仍有赖于埃及本土祭司集团的认可和支持,⑦这种政治上的考虑
促使托勒密王朝统治者在经济上对埃及本土祭司集团有所照顾和

---

① 关于托勒密埃及包税制可参阅 Sitta von Reden, *Money in Ptolemaic Egypt：From
the Macedonian Conquest to the End of the Third Century BC*, p. 95. 关于托勒密埃及包税制的
由来,可参阅 J. G. Manning, *The Last Pharaohs：Egypt under the Ptolemies, 305 - 30BC*,
p. 152.引入包税制被视为托勒密二世经济改革的重要内容,汤普森认为,这一举措在保障收
益上是十分成功的,见 D. J. Thompson, "Economic Reforms in the Mid-Reign of Ptolemy
Philadelphus," p. 38.

② W. W. Tarn, *Hellenistic Civilization*, p. 179.

③ M. I. Rostovtzeff, *The Social and Economic History of the Hellenistic World*, vol. 1,
p. 308.

④ 托勒密埃及亚麻制品中质量最为上乘的当属"拜索斯"(Bysus),这种产品一直由神
庙进行生产,而托勒密王朝统治者对此未加干涉,只是要求将一定数量的"拜索斯"上贡,见
M. I. Rostovtzeff, *The Social and Economic History of the Hellenistic World*, vol. 1, p. 302。

⑤ 如前文所述,神庙也有榨油作坊,虽受限制,但独立于油专营体系之外,也能进行生
产,见 M. M. Austin, *The Hellenistic World from Alexander to the Roman Conquest*, p. 529。

⑥ N. S. Hopkins, *Agrarian Transformation in Egypt*, Boulder：Westview Press, 1987,
p. 98.

⑦ 保持政治统治稳定性对托勒密王朝统治者来说同样重要,曼宁认为,获取收益、保
持政治稳定、建立军田是托勒密王朝统治的主要目标,见 J. G. Manning, "The Ptolemaic
Economy, Institutions, Economic Integration, and the Limits of Centralized Political Power,"
p. 9.

扶持,①而正如我们之前在《托勒密二世油专营敕令》中所看到的,其在实行专营制度涉及埃及本土祭司集团经济利益时也有所妥协。而且,专营制度在底比斯地区很难有效实行。这一地区是埃及本土祭司集团的传统势力范围,到托勒密王朝统治时期,埃及本土祭司集团仍对这一地区的政治、经济事务保持着很大影响力,②这种局面即便在托勒迈伊斯(Ptolemais)建立之后也未有改变。③ 在底比斯地区,土地所有制实质上仍保持着传统埃及特征,大量农民或家庭经营着属于庙产的小份土地。④ 虽然到公元前3世纪末,包税制、王室银行等机构已在底比斯地区出现,⑤但大量反映托勒密王朝早期底比斯地区经济情况的纸草文献显示,专营制度在这一地区并未得到有效推行,⑥主要经济活动仍然与神庙息息相关。⑦

　　托勒密王朝在乡村统治力量的薄弱也制约了托勒密埃及专营制度的有效实行。作为外来统治者,托勒密王朝在埃及的统治主要依赖希腊-马其顿人群体,⑧但这一群体人数相对较少,⑨且主要生活在城市和法尤姆等希腊人聚居地,以至于托勒密王朝缺乏人力对

　　① 例如兴建寺庙、捐助物资等,见 Justin Pollard and Howard Reid, *The Rise and Fall of Alexandria*, pp. 82 - 83;又如在税收方面的妥协,见 Andrew Monson, *From the Ptolemies to the Romans: Political and Economic Change in Egypt*, p. 7。
　　② 底比斯的阿蒙(Amun)神庙甚至建立过神权政权,与托勒密王权统治分庭抗礼,见 Andrew Monson, *From the Ptolemies to the Romans: Political and Economic Change in Egypt*, p. 17。
　　③ 托勒密王朝早期统治者在埃及南部(上埃及)建立托勒迈伊斯,以加强对埃及南部地区的统治,但实际上,托勒密王朝对托勒迈伊斯本身的统治很有限,托勒迈伊斯在形式上拥有一定的自治权,可参阅 W. W. Tarn, *Hellenistic Civilization*, p. 179。
　　④ J. G. Manning, *Land and Power in Ptolemaic Egypt: The Structure of Land Tenure, 332 -30B. C. E*, p. 65.
　　⑤ J. G. Manning, "The Ptolemaic Economy, Institutions, Economic Integration, and the Limits of Centralized Political Power," p. 7.
　　⑥ 关于托勒密埃及底比斯地区的专营情况见 B. P. Muhs, *Tax Receipts, Taxpayers, and Taxes in Early Ptolemaic Thebes*, pp. 73 - 83。
　　⑦ 关于托勒密埃及底比斯地区的神庙经济见 B. P. Muhs, *Tax Receipts, Taxpayers, and Taxes in Early Ptolemaic Thebes*, pp. 87 - 99。
　　⑧ 这种情况在其他希腊化国家同样如此,可参阅 F. W. Walbank, *Hellenistic World*, p. 66。
　　⑨ 虽然在希腊化早期有大量马其顿人、希腊人到埃及定居,但他们在人数上只占到了托勒密埃及人口总数的10%,见 Walter Scheidel, Ian Morris and R. P. Saller, eds., *Cambridge Economic History of the Greco-Roman World*, p. 441。

除法尤姆之外的乡村进行有效管理,因此,托勒密王朝对广大乡村地区的控制在很大程度上依赖当地村长、书吏等埃及地方精英的协助。[①] 这些埃及地方精英是托勒密埃及行政管理体系中的基层管理者,也是包括专营制度在内的中央政策的践行者,但语言障碍、文化差异都影响中央政策在乡村的切实有效实行。而且,在托勒密王朝统治时期,许多乡村的土地契约仍是在当地见证人或神庙公证人在场的情况下做出的,[②]当地的水力灌溉系统也不在政府的管控之中,[③]在这种情况下,如果当地农业生产等经济活动得不到政府有效监管,专营产品生产也得不到保障。

军田制的推行对专营制度也有一定影响。为保障兵源,同时维持军队忠诚度,托勒密王朝统治者在埃及实行军事殖民,在特定区域按军衔高低分配给军人 7—100 阿鲁拉(aroura)[④]不等的土地,以田养兵。[⑤] 这些土地名义上仍归国王所有,在军人死后由国王收回,[⑥]但世袭的情况也很多,[⑦]许多土地逐渐成为军人的私产。对于这些土地,托勒密王朝除了征税之外并没有其他限制,军人自己或雇佣当地埃及人开垦和耕种土地,自行组织生产,所得收益在扣除税收之后用作军饷。也就是说,这部分土地未被纳入专营体系之中,在很大程度上不受政府监管。

综上所述,限于各种因素的制约,托勒密埃及专营制度在实行的程度和范围上都存在局限。托勒密王朝统治者既不能保证对土

---

① 关于托勒密王朝对乡村地区的管理可参阅 Samuel Alan, "The Internal Organization of the Nomarch's Bureau in the Third Century B. C. E.," in *Essays in Honor of C. B. Welles*, American Studies in Papyrology, vol. 1, New Haven: American Society of Papyrologists, 1966。

② Andrew Monson, *From the Ptolemies to the Romans: Political and Economic Change in Egypt*, p. 8.

③ 在此之前,埃及历史上从未有过中央政府官员对灌溉系统进行管控,见 J. G. Manning, "The Ptolemaic Economy, Institutions, Economic Integration, and the Limits of Centralized Political Power," p. 4.

④ 1 阿鲁拉约等于 2/3 美制英亩,或 2756 平方米。

⑤ A. S. Hunt and C. C. Edgar, eds. , *Select Papyri*, vol. 2, pp. 71,237.

⑥ 一份纸草文献明确说明国王在骑兵死后收回他们的份地,见 M. M. Austin, *The Hellenistic World from Alexander to the Roman Conquest*, p. 426。

⑦ N. S. Lewis, *Greeks in Ptolemaic Egypt*, Oxford: Oxford University Press, 1986, p. 142.

地等生产资料的绝对控制,也不能如专营制度所设计的那样对生产经营活动进行严密监管,无法保障专营制度在埃及所有地区切实有效实行。

(原载于《历史研究》2014 年第 6 期)

中国省域金融顺周期效应异质性的影响因素研究[*]

——基于技术进步与产业调整的空间经济分析视角

王周伟　伏开宝　汪传江　胡德红[**]

一、引　言

　　金融顺周期效应是指金融与实体经济之间存在着正向反馈机制。在内生地放大金融体系的不稳定性的同时,该效应也会加剧经济波动。因此金融顺周期效应是经济调控与金融审慎监管都必须始终关注的核心问题。目前,大量文献研究已经表明,中国金融体系具有显著的顺周期效应,也呈现出不同的行业周期与时变特征。但这些相关研究主要集中于国家层面上,较少从省域经济层面上探讨金融顺周期效应。而中国省域经济的规模发展、技术进步、产业发展与结构调整、金融发展以及空间经济特征因素存在着很大差异,这些因素的差异都会使省域货币金融体系与经济体系运行呈现异质性,金融与实体经济的顺周期效应也会具有省域异质性。围绕

　　＊　基金项目:本文为国家社科基金重大项目"推进经济结构战略性调整的重点、难点与路径研究"(13&ZD016)、教育部人文社科研究项目《中国宏观审慎货币政策的调控机制研究》(11YJA790107)与上海市教委重点课题《综合风险网络传染的系统性风险评估与分析框架研究》(12ZS125)的阶段性成果;获国家自然科学基金面上项目《限额与交易机制下多特性质量设计与优化研究》(71371126)、《通货膨胀惯性、金融市场摩擦与结构性冲击——债务危机下 DSGE 模型的扩展与应用研究》(12YJC790020)资助。

　　＊＊　作者简介:王周伟(1969—　　),男,山西闻喜人,博士后,副教授,上海师范大学金融工程研究中心副院长,研究方向:区域金融管理、金融计量分析。

金融顺周期效应的省域异质性及其影响因素展开具体研究,对于合理确定定向精准调控与审慎监管政策组合力度,提升结构化货币政策效率,提高省域金融体系对于创新驱动、转型发展及城镇化建设的支持力度都有着非常重要的指导意义。特别是在经济运行总体平稳、结构调整与转型升级需要稳步推进的"新常态"下,新型城镇化建设与区域经济协调发展亟需差别化结构调控。因此,从理论分析与实证检验两个方面,本文将探讨中国金融顺周期效应是否具有省域异质性? 该异质性的影响因素有哪些? 它们是如何发挥作用的?

本文的主要贡献在于,利用扩展的 C-D 生产函数,构建空间经济分析框架,推算了中国省域金融顺周期效应的异质比率的计算式,从理论上分析了其显著存在性、区域异质性,从创新驱动与产业结构调整视角分析了该效应的影响因素;在分别利用地理距离、技术距离与产业距离准则度量空间相关性的同时,设计了地理-技术-产业组合距离准则,构建了有效的组合空间权重矩阵,利用空间探索性分析与地区固定效应的空间面板杜宾模型及其解释变量效应分解分析方法,实证研究了中国省域金融顺周期效应的异质性影响因素及其作用路径。

二、文 献 综 述

从维护金融稳定角度研究顺周期效应,兴起于 2008 年金融危机发生后。大多数现有文献是在全国层面上对其成因与作用原理进行理论分析,对其存在性、程度及特征进行实证研究。其中成因分析多数是从资本监管、银行经营行为与公允会计准则三个方面进行的。

新颁布的资本充足监管准则允许银行使用内部评级法,而使用内部评级法计算监管资本的三个风险参数是顺周期的。与使用固定风险权重的标准法相比较,这提高了监管资本的风险敏感性,也提高了监管资本的顺周期效应(Tanaka,2002 等);沿着资本监管与银行经营行为视角,Gai 等(2006)认为在市场不完美情况下,抵押资产的流动性放大了金融周期[1];李文泓、罗猛(2010)运用最小二乘法与广义矩分析法,证实我国商业银行的资本充足率具有一定的顺周期效应[2],因此要增加逆周期资本缓冲(Jacques,2010)[3];高国华、潘英丽(2010)依据银行资本跨期持有成本最小化的局部均衡调整模型,设计了商业银行的资本顺周期效应检验模型。他们发现监管资本的亲周期性使资本充足率变动具有顺周期效应,其顺周期调整也具有不对称性[4]。比较综合的是,方芳、刘鹏(2010)从金融市场、金融监管与经济波动三个方面定性地分析了金融顺周期效应的内在成因及其作用机理,利用 M2 与贷款对经济增长的相关性描述分析与 VAR 模型检验,证实中国金融体系存在着信贷顺周期效应[5];通过回顾相关文献,张金城、李成(2011)认为金融体系存在双重顺周期,其成因不尽相同。盈利能力与外部融资成本的顺周期性以及借贷双方的信息不对称造成了银行信贷的顺周期效应;最低监管资本要求、信贷萎缩效应及内部评级法使银行资本充足率也具有顺周期效应[6];Albertazzi 等(2013)通过观察雷曼公司破产前后的意大利银行信贷发放情况,认为银行对外信贷具有顺周期性[7];对于美国商业银行与储蓄银行,Laux 等(2014)认为盯市规则并不是亲周期的主要驱动因素,而是经营杠杆与资本比率的目标管理引发亲周期性[8];Olszak 等(2014)利用欧盟的跨国家跨银行数据与两步系统 GMM 法,研究了贷款损失准备金与商业周期之间的作用,以及银行管理与运营特征、国家特征对其差异性的影响。结果显示,规模较大与稳健经营的商业银行贷款损失准备金的顺周期效应较强;较好的市场约束无法抵消其敏感性,但收入平滑、资本管理与信用风险管理可以减弱亲周期效应[9]。

从公允价值会计准则视角,Sole 等(2009)认为公允价值会计准则是导致顺周期效应的原因之一[10];黄静茹、黄世忠(2013)模拟计算了在两种商业情景下两种计量模式对银行资产负债表科目波动性的影响,其结果与 Laux 等(2009)相似[11],即应用公允价值计量模式会产生增强经济自身波动的波动,不一定具有顺周期效应[12];而梅波(2014)用扩展后的 Feltham 和 Ohlson(1995)模型实证研究结果表明,价值相关性较强的公允价值计量具有顺周期性[13]。

为更好地把握顺周期效应,学者们已经开始探讨其运行特征了。程棵、刁思聪、杨晓光(2012)依据金融加速器理论提出信贷顺周期效应的不对称性命题,用带有马尔科夫转换机制的回归模型和状态空间模型,证明了信贷投放具有一定的顺周期效应,并且具有金融加速器效应[14];俞晓龙(2013)利用银行资本优化模型,建立了银行资本充足率的面板数据实证模型。其研究结果表明,中国不同类型的商业银行资本具有不同的周期性特征,国有商业银行与农村商业银行的资本充足率没有周期性,而城市商业银行资本充足率具有逆周期特征,只有全国性股份制银行具有顺周期效应[15];金雯雯、杜亚斌(2013)运用 TVP-VAR 模型研究发现,在控制货币政策效应后,信贷顺周期效应具有时变性,部分时段上是逆周期变化的,而且短期信贷顺周期效应小于中长期顺周期效应[16]。

从研究方法方面讲,现有文献主要选用的都是非空间的统计与计量方法,这对于概括研究国家金融顺周期效应是适用的。但是,探索分析一国经济体系内部各区域的经济效应时,需要考虑区域经济的异质性与溢出效应,这就需要依据新经济地理理论与空间经济理论框架,用适宜的空间探索分析方法与空间经济计量分析方法构建模型,研究省域金融顺周期效应的异质性及其影响因素。

三、理 论 分 析

金融与实体经济具有顺周期效应,需要实施逆周期监管。由于省域经济的金融、科技与经济特征不尽相同,中国金融顺周期效应在省域上应当是异质的。本文将利用省域生产函数,从经济增长来源分解视角,说明金融顺周期效应存在着省域异质性,并从技术、产业、金融与空间经济特征方面,分析影响因素及其作用路径。

(一) 中国金融顺周期效应的省域异质性研究

传统的 C-D 生产函数产出仅考虑劳动投入和资本投入两个要素,这不完全符合现代经济发展的现实情况。许多学者在研究经济增长对传统的 C-D 生产函数进行了扩展,Devarajan、Swaroop 和 Zou(1996)将公共支出分成两类分别纳入生产函数[17];King & Levine(1993)认为在不发达国家中信贷主要被用来为国内企业的投资活动进行融资,是单一的最为重要的投资资金来源,信贷被认为是推动经济增长的一项重要金融要素,对经济增长至关重要[18]。在对经济增长和全要素生产率研究中,我国学者也对生产函数进行了相应的类似扩展,史永东等(2003)、郭庆旺等(2005)、张钢等(2006)、张军等(2005)都建立了新的扩展模型,研究分析了财政支出与信贷金融因素对于经济增长、全要素生产率的影响[19—21]。

相邻地区经济总量规模较大时,往往对本地区产品的需求能力较大。市场潜能(Market Potential)可以很好地度量这种具有空间正溢出效应的有效需求,它对本省域经济增长具有正向拉动作用,其对省域人均GDP的增长拉动弹性超过了固定资产投资的投入产出弹性(潘文卿,2012;赵增耀、夏斌,2012)[22—23]。

根据上述相关研究结论,本文把资本要素分为私人资本与公共资本,其中私人资本由私人信贷支持的私人投资形成,公共资本由主要源自财政收入的地方政府公共投资形成,把地方政府公共投资作为投入要素;另外,市场潜能增大可以提高各要素的投入产出,把市场潜能作为省域经济发展的需求拉动因素用乘法方式直接引入,得到扩展的省域C-D生产函数:

$$Y_t = A_t K_t^\alpha L_t^\beta G_t^\gamma MP_t^\varphi \tag{1}$$

其中,Y为总产出;A为技术水平;K表示物质资本存量;用L表示劳动力投入;G表示地方政府公共投资;α,β,γ为相应要素的投入产出弹性系数;φ是市场潜能对产出的拉动弹性。为符合实际经济运行特征,假设该生产函数具有一次齐次性与二阶连续可微两个性质。另外,技术进步可以提高要素生产率,且具有偏向性(雷钦礼,2013;陆雪琴、章上峰,2013)[24—25],省域内产业集聚具有规模经济与范围经济效应,于是参数α,β,γ,φ是随着技术进步及其效率与偏向以及产业集聚与结构的变化而变化的。

对式(1)两边取对数得到:

$$\ln Y_t = \ln A_t + \alpha \ln K_t + \beta \ln L_t + \gamma \ln G_t + \varphi \ln MP_t \tag{2}$$

对式(2)两端对时间t求导得到经济增长率分解等式:

$$\frac{\dot{Y}_t}{Y_t} = \frac{\dot{A}_t}{A_t} + \alpha \frac{\dot{K}_t}{K_t} + \beta \frac{\dot{L}_t}{L_t} + \gamma \frac{\dot{G}_t}{G_t} + \varphi \frac{\dot{MP}_t}{MP_t} \tag{3}$$

设 D 表示信贷余额,假定每期中新增信贷在当期全部用于固定资产投资,并在当期全部形成生产资本,资本折旧损耗很小,可以不考虑,则有:

$$\dot{K}_t = K_t - K_{t-1} = I_t = D_t - D_{t-1} = \dot{D}_t \tag{4}$$

$$K_t = \sum \dot{D}_t = D_t \tag{5}$$

把式(4)、(5)代入式(3)可得:

$$\frac{\dot{Y}_t}{Y_t} = \frac{\dot{A}_t}{A_t} + \alpha\frac{\dot{D}_t}{D_t} + \beta\frac{\dot{L}_t}{L_t} + \gamma\frac{\dot{G}_t}{G_t} + \varphi\frac{\dot{MP}_t}{MP_t} \tag{6}$$

式(6)表示省域经济增长率由技术增长率、信贷增长率、劳动力增长率、地方政府公共投资增长率、市场潜能增长率及各要素投入产出弹性共同决定。用小写字母表示变量的增长率,则有:

$$y_t = a_t + \alpha \cdot d_t + \beta \cdot l_t + \gamma \cdot g_t + \varphi \cdot mp_t \tag{7}$$

在规模经济与范围经济及学习效应等作用下,式7中参数一般都为正,信贷变化与经济是同方向变化的,这表明尽管省级政府不具有完全的货币金融调控权力,但在省域经济体系中也存在着金融顺周期效应,即省域金融体系与实体经济之间存在动态的正向反馈作用机制。在该机制作用下,省域信贷增长会推动省域经济增长,反过来,省域经济增长会带来省域信贷增长的进一步增加。由于信息不对称、市场不完美、羊群效应与有限理性,省域经济波动使省域外部融资风险溢价逆向升降,金融加速器效应使省域金融体系经营杠杆率同方向变化;在收入与估值效应作用下担保抵押品价值会随着经济波动同方向变化,资产负债表效应会使省域借款人的信用质量发生同方向变化;在金融机构风险承担因素与竞争效应作用下,在追逐利润动机驱动下,省域金融机构的信贷扩张意愿与行为具有顺周期效应;在财富效应与托宾 Q 效应作用下[26],金融资产质量、公允价值核算的绩效与外部融资成本也受到经济周期的正向作用,使得省域风险资本监管也具有顺周期效应。通过上述作用微观经济行为路径,在省域层面上省域金融体系形成了顺周期效应。

在经济增长来源分解等式(7)中,不同省域经济的资源禀赋及各参数值的大小及其显著差异程度,就决定着中国省域金融体系顺周期效应是否存在、是否具有异质性、异质性的大小及其显著差异程度。在规模经济阶段,如果省域信贷增长率的投入产出弹性值显著且为正值,一般不等于0,则说明中国金融顺周期效应具有省域异质性,即省域金融顺周期效应是显著存在的。新经济地理学与空间经济学理论与实证研究都表明,省域金融、技术与经济禀赋特征及其运行机制都存在明显差异,在这些具有空间异质性的因素作用下,省域金融顺周期效应就是异质的。于是提出本文第一个命题与原假设 H1:中国省域金融体系存在顺周期性效应,而且该效应具有省域异质性。

(二) 中国省域金融顺周期效应异质性的影响因素分析

为进一步分析省域金融顺周期效应异质性的影响因素,下面构建省域金融顺周期效应差异指标进行具体分析。在三大类十多个指标中,用信贷余额增长率与 GDP 增长率之间的比值判断金融经济繁荣与危机的效果最好[27](巴塞尔委员会,2012)。本文用省域经济增长率与省域信贷增长率之比反映省域金融顺周期效应,即经济增长与信贷增长的协调性。该比值大于 0 则表明二者是顺周期协同增长或下降。

式(7)两边除以 d,可得反映省域金融顺周期效应大小的省域经济增长率与信贷增长率之比:

$$\frac{y}{d} = \frac{a}{d} + \alpha + \beta \cdot \frac{l}{d} + \gamma \cdot \frac{g}{d} + \varphi \frac{mp}{d} \tag{8}$$

这表明省域金融顺周期效应大小取决于技术进步与产业经济方面的特征因素,即各经济增长动力要素的投入增长率与信贷增长率之比,包括技术水平增长率(即技术进步)与信贷投入增长率之比、劳动力投入与信贷投入增长率之比以及公共投资投入与信贷投入增长率之比;也取决于空间经济特征,即市场潜能增长率与信贷增长率之比及其拉动弹性;也取决于三个要素的效率,即省域投入产出弹性,包括信贷资本投入产出弹性、劳动力投入产出弹性与公共投资投入产出弹性。

两个不同省域的金融顺周期效应差异可以用省域金融顺周期效应之比来度量,即这两个省域的经济增长率与省域信贷增长率之比的比值(本文定义为异质比率)来度量。对于省域 i、j,则有金融顺周期效应的异质比率为:

$$\frac{y_i/d_i}{y_j/d_j} = \frac{a_i/d_i + \alpha_i + \beta_i \cdot l_i/d_i + \gamma_i \cdot g_i/d_i + \varphi_i \cdot ma_i/d_i}{a_j/d_j + \alpha_j + \beta_j \cdot l_j/d_j + \gamma_j \cdot g_j/d_j + \varphi_j \cdot ma_j/d_j} \quad (9)$$
$$= f(X_1^i, X_1^j; X_2^i, X_2^j; X_3^i, X_3^j; X_4^i, X_4^j)$$

综合式(8)与(9),我们可以知道,省域金融顺周期效应异质性的主要影响因素可以归纳为四个方面:

第一类为省域经济投入的规模经济因素。式(9)中,$X_1^i = (a_i, d_i, l_i, g_i)$,$X_1^j = (a_j, d_j, l_j, g_j)$ 分别是两个省域的技术水平、信贷、劳动力与公共投资等要素投入增长率向量,反映技术进步与要素投入增长率。技术进步是技术水平的增长率。它可以使用全要素生产率(TFP)间接度量[28]。利用 DEA 分析的非参数估计 Malmquist 指数度量,可以把全要素生产率(TFP)分解为技术效率(EC)与纯技术进步(TC);而按照来源,技术效率(EC)又可以分解为纯技术效率(PEC)与规模效率(SEC)[29]。

这些指标反映的是省域金融、科技与实体经济系统向生产领域投入的生产要素增长情况。微观经济主体与地方政府是总体理性的,在规模经济与范围经济阶段中才会加大要素投入,推动本地经济增长,要素投入增长率不同会带来省域金融顺周期效应的差异。这些因素属于影响省域金融顺周期效应异质性的规模经济因素。

第二类为省域要素效率因素。式(9)中,$X_2^i = (\alpha_i, \beta_i, \gamma_i)$,$X_2^j = (\alpha_j, \beta_j, \gamma_j)$ 分别是两个省域的信贷、劳动力与公共投资等要素投入产出效率向量,反映技术效率与要素投入产出弹性,各要素投入产出弹性之差反映了技术进步偏向[30]。按照偏向性,纯技术进步(TC)可以分解为希克斯中性技术进步(MTC)与偏向性技术进步(BTC),后者又可以分为产出偏向型技术进步(OBTC)与要素偏向型技术进步(IBTC)(汪克亮等,2014)[31]。由于每个决策单元仅有一个产出变量,所以 $OBTC = 1$。则全要素生产率可以得到如下分解式:

$$TFP = EC \times TC$$
$$= (PEC \times SEC) \times (MTC \times BTC) \quad (10)$$
$$= (PEC \times SEC) \times (MTC \times OBTC \times IBTC)$$
$$= (PEC \times SEC) \times (MTC \times IBTC)$$

在规模经济与范围经济作用下,这些指标都是正值,在正弹性作用下会把上述规模经济因素的影响作用以杠杆倍数方式放大,这些因素属于放大推动省域金融顺周期效应异质性的要素效率因素。

第三类为本地产业经济特征因素。式(9)中,$X_3^i = (a_i/d_i, l_i/d_i, g_i/d_i)$,$X_3^j = (a_j/d_j, l_j/d_j, g_j/d_j)$ 是同一省域的技术、不同要素投入与市场潜能的增长率之间的比例向量,反映各省域实体经济产业的结构、专业化与多元化特征。省域信贷只有投放到省域产业经济实体中,经过产业运营,才能带来经济增长。所以,这些指标是基础性的,属于影响省域金融顺周期效应异质性的本地产业经济特征因素。

第四类为空间经济特征因素,主要包括市场潜能与产业集聚相关指标。式(9)中,$X_4^i = (ma_i, \varphi_i, ma_i/d_i; a_i/a_j, l_i/l_j, g_i/g_j, ma_i/ma_j)$,$X_4^j = (ma_j, \varphi_j, ma_j/d_j; a_j/a_i, l_j/l_i, g_j/g_i, ma_j/ma_i)$ 是市场潜能以及不同省域之间的技术及不同要素投入增长率与市场潜能增长率之比的向量,后者反映了不同省域经济资源分布的产业集聚情况。市场潜能反映了规模报酬递增、考虑贸易成本的空间总市场需求,是空间经济相互作用下本地实体经济体系对应的总有效需求,有需求支持的经济生产才是可持续的。通过规模效应、知识溢出效应和学习效应,产业集聚可以产生正的行业内集聚(专业化)外部经济和跨行业集聚(多元化)外部经济。这些指标属于拉动省域金融顺周期效应异质性的空间经济特征因素。

在上述省域金融、规模经济、技术、产业与空间经济特征的综合作用下,这种双重顺周期效应就呈现出省域异质性。如图1所示。

由此可以提出本文的第二个命题与原假设 H2:中国省域金融顺周期效应异质性的影响因素主要来自本省域经济的金融发展、技术进步、规模经济、本地产业调整与空间经济四个方面的特征,它们的作用包括直接作用与空间溢出。

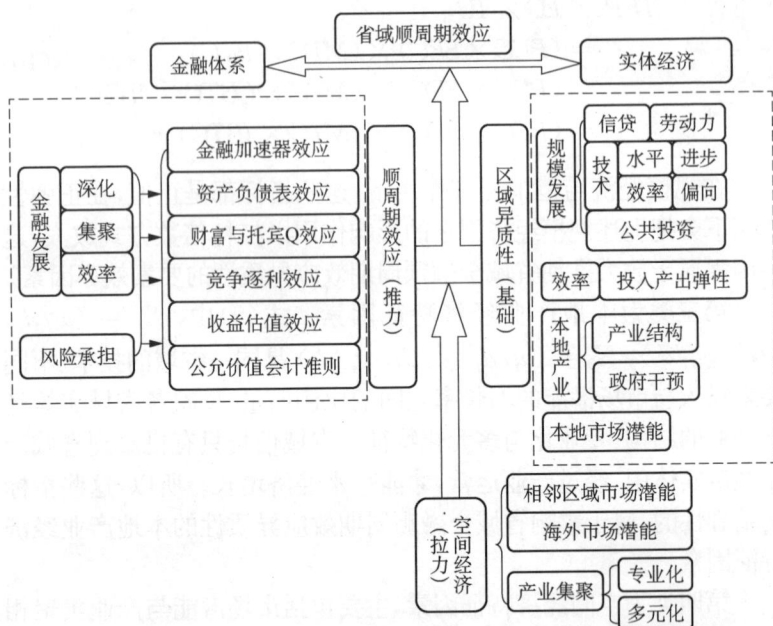

图 1 中国省域金融顺周期效应异质性的影响因素及其作用路径

四、数据来源、变量选择与模型设计

(一) 样本选择与数据来源

从 1998 年 1 月 1 日起,我国取消了对国有商业银行信贷规模的限额控制。因此,我们选用了中国 31 个省、直辖市、自治区在 1998 年—2012 年期间相关指标的年度数据,共有 15 年 31 个省市的面板空间数据。数据来自于《中国工业经济统计年鉴》、《万德数据库》、《中国统计年鉴》、《60 年中国统计资料汇编》、《中国科技统计年鉴》、《中国金融统计年鉴》、《地理信息系统》《中国区域金融运行报告》。

(二) 变量选择

根据理论分析结论,我们分别选择了被解释变量、解释变量与控制变量指标。

1. 被解释变量的指标选用

信贷余额增长率与GDP增长率之间的比值将经济和金融联系起来了,该指标对其长期趋势值的偏离度(GAP)能够反映金融体系中金融顺周期性,又能够综合考虑金融深化引起的经济波动和金融扩张之间的趋势,因此我们选用省域GAP值作为省域金融顺周期效应的代理变量。

2. 解释变量的指标选用

(1) 技术进步类指标。利用基于DEA的非参数估计Malmquist指数及其分解方法,计算全要素生产率(TFP)、技术效率、纯技术进步、纯技术效率与规模效率;技术进步偏向利用技术进步偏向指数反映。根据希克斯的定义,在不考虑要素替代性情况下,技术进步偏向指数(即资本边际产出增长率与劳动边际产出增长率之差)可以近似度量技术进步偏向,计算式为:

$$B = \frac{\partial F_K/\partial t}{F_K} - \frac{\partial F_L/\partial t}{F_L} \qquad (11)'$$

如果B大于0,则属于资本偏向型技术进步;如果B小于0,则属于劳动偏向型技术进步;如果等于0,则属于希克斯中性技术进步。

(2) 产业调整类指标。我们构建产业专业化、产业多元化、产业升级三个指标。产业专业化指数由各省三次产业分别占全国三大产业的比重乘以各产业从业人员占全国各行业总从业人员来表示,该指标反映在全国水平上各行业在省市水平上的加总;产业多元化程度用赫芬达尔指数反映,计算公式为:$HF_j = \sum_{i=1}^{n}(p_{ij}/p_j)^2$,式中$p_{ij}$表示$j$区域$i$行业的总产值;$p_j$是$j$区域总产值;赫芬达尔指数可以反映各行业在省市水平上的加总,能够度量省内产业结构情况,其值越小表示区域产业结构越多元化;产业升级程度用第三产业增加值与第二产业增加值之和占省域GDP的比重来反映。

(3) 金融发展类指标。我们选择金融效率、金融集聚、金融深化三个指标来反映省域金融发展现状。其中,金融效率是指金融体系动员与跨期配置社会资金的效率,用各地银行部门的贷款余额与存款余额之比表示;金融集聚是金融机构与金融要素资源在某些特定区域汇聚的经济现象,本文用各省金融从业人员占总从业人员之比与当年全国各省上述比重平均值的比表示;金融深化程度是指金融体系的发展通过金融市场的资源配置作用对经济发展的推动作用,本文用各省当年贷款与 GDP 之比表示。

（4）市场潜能。某省域的市场潜能等于本地市场潜能、邻近省域市场潜能与海外市场潜能之和,它反映了本区域的市场潜力及其受相关区域经济溢出效应的大小。在考虑距离加权情况下,某省域的市场潜能计算式为:

$$MA_{it} = \frac{GDP_{it}}{d_i^{\delta}} + \sum_{j \in china} \frac{GDP_{jt}}{d_{ij}^{\delta}} + \frac{X_{it}}{d_{fi}^{\delta}} \tag{12}$$

式中,MA_{it} 是第 i 省市在 t 时刻的市场潜能;GDP_{it}、GDP_{jt} 是 t 时刻第 i、j 省市的 GDP;省市内部径向距离 $d_i = \left(\frac{2}{3}\sqrt{area_i/\pi}\right)$;$d_{ij}$ 为第 i、j 省市地理中心之间的距离;距离加权权重取值为 $\delta = 1.5$（李宏兵、蔡宏波、王永进,2014）[32];X_{it} 是第 i 省市在 t 时刻的出口金额,d_{fi}^{δ} 是本地到前五大出口国首都的平均距离。

（5）政府干预。作为一种外生因素,地方政府公共投资对于地方经济发展有着重要的推动作用和挤出效应,对于地方信贷的投放量也有一定的影响,用省域政府财政支出占其财政收入的比重可以表示省域政府干预程度。

3. 控制变量的指标选用

人均 GDP 能够反映一个地方经济发展的绝对水平,为了消除量纲偏大的影响,我们对人均 GDP 取对数;因此,我们选择人均GDP 的对数作为控制变量。

(三) 模型设定与空间效应检验

本文前面的理论分析结论表明,空间经济特征因素是省域金融顺周期效应异质性的主要拉力性影响因素,该作用决定了空间经济溢出效应的大小与空间经济的相关性。前者用解释变量中的市场潜能反映,后者则由空间经济计量分析模型与空间权重矩阵来刻画。因此,依据式(9)与图1描述的逻辑框架,本文构建了空间经济计量分析模型。面板数据分析常用的空间经济计量分析模型主要有空间滞后模型(Spatial Autoregressive Model, SAR)、空间误差模型(spatial error model, SEM)与空间面板杜宾模型(Spatial Durbin model, SDM)。三个空间计量模型描述的空间相关来源不同,SAR模型描述了不同省域因变量之间的空间相关性及其效应,SEM模型描述了不同省域的误差项之间的空间相关性及其效应,但两者都没有考虑自变量之间的空间相关性以及对因变量的作用,SDM模型则同时包括因变量之间和自变量之间的空间相关性。按照理论分析与变量选择结论,本文实证研究中面板数据的 SAR 模型、SEM模型与 SDM 模型的表达式分别为:

$$y_{it} = \alpha + \rho \sum_{j=1}^{31} w_{ij} y_{jt} + \sum_{k=1}^{13} x_{itk} \beta_k + \sum_{m=1}^{2} a_m z_{itm} \\ + \tau_i + \theta_t + \varepsilon_{it} \tag{13}$$

$$y_{it} = \alpha + \rho \sum_{j=1}^{31} w_{ij} y_{jt} + \sum_{k=1}^{13} x_{itk} \beta_k + \sum_{m=1}^{2} a_m z_{itm} \\ + \rho \sum_{j=1}^{31} w_{ij} \varepsilon_{it} + \tau_i + \theta_t + v_{it} \tag{14}$$

$$y_{it} = \alpha + \rho \sum_{j=1}^{31} w_{ij} y_{jt} + \sum_{k=1}^{13} x_{itk} \beta_k + \sum_{k=1}^{13} \sum_{j=1}^{31} w_{ij} x_{jtk} \gamma_k \\ + \sum_{m=1}^{2} a_m z_{itm} + \tau_i + \theta_t + \varepsilon_{it} \tag{15}$$

其中,y_{it} 是被解释变量;x_{itk} 是解释变量;z_{itm} 是控制变量;w_{ij} 是空间权重矩阵的元素;τ_i 是省域固定效应项;θ_t 是时间固定效应项;ε_{it}、v_{it} 为均值为 0、方差为 σ^2 的随机误差向量;α 是常数;β、a 分别是解释变量的参数、控制变量的参数;ρ、γ 是空间滞后参数,可以通过 ρ、γ 是否显著为 0 来判断是否应该建立空间计量模型或是普通面板数据模型。当 $\gamma=0$ 且 $\rho \neq 0$ 时,SDM 模型可以缩减为空间滞后模型(SAR)模型;当 $\gamma + \rho\beta = 0$ 时,SDM 模型缩减为空间误差模型(SEM),因此 SDM 模型更具有一般性。

为进一步合理确定模型形式,本文也根据空间效应检验结果进行判断。首先利用 Moran's I 检验结果判断被解释变量之间与解释变量之间是否存在空间相关性;再用 LM-lag 检验与稳健 LM-lag 检验判断被解释变量之间是不是存在空间滞后相关,用 LM-Error 检验与稳健 LM-Error 检验判断是不是存在空间误差相关。如果只有被解释变量之间存在空间滞后相关,则建立 SAR 模型;如果只存在空间误差相关,则建立 SEM 模型;如果被解释变量之间与解释变量之间都存在空间相关性而且是空间滞后相关,则建立 SDM 模型。

(四) 解释变量作用效应的分解分析

SDM 模型中包含了被解释变量的空间相关项和解释变量的空间相关项,也包含了解释变量的非空间相关项,解释变量空间相关项矩阵 WX 和非空间相关项的系数都没有反映解释变量的全部作用效应。为综合分析解释变量的作用路径,可以通过微偏分的方法把解释变量对被解释变量的综合影响按照来源分为直接效应和间接效应。其中,直接效应为某个省域自变量的变化导致自身因变量的改变,即在第 t 年第 k 个解释变量在第 i 个省域的一个单位变化对第 i 个省域的被解释变量 y_{it} 的平均影响。它可以分为两种影响路径,一种是各自变量对本省域因变量的直接影响,另一种是该自变量影响相邻省域因变量后产生的反馈效应,该反馈效应可以通过计算自变量的直接效应和自变量系数的差值得到。间接效应就是解释变量的空间溢出效应,即在第 i 个省域周围的每个省域中第 k 个解释变量同时发生一个单位变化,通过溢出效应对第 i 个省域的被解释变量 y_{it} 的平均影响。它也可以分为两种影响路径,一是邻近省域自变量对于本省区因变量的影响,另外一种是邻近省域自变量变化使得其自身省地因变量的变化,进而对省域因变量产生的影响。在不考虑诱发效应时,第 k 个解释变量的总效应等于直接效应与间接效应之和。

为得到两个效应的计算式,先把 SDM 模型式(15)移项整理为一般形式[33]:

$$Y = (I-\rho W)^{-1}\boldsymbol{n}_n + (I-\rho W)^{-1}(X\beta + WX\gamma) \quad (16)$$
$$+ AZ + (I-\rho W)^{-1}\varepsilon$$

再求被解释变量向量关于第 k 个解释变量的偏微分方程可得[34]：

$$\left(\frac{\partial Y}{\partial X_{1k}} \quad \frac{\partial Y}{\partial X_{2k}} \quad \cdots \quad \frac{\partial Y}{\partial X_{nk}}\right) = \begin{pmatrix} \dfrac{\partial Y_1}{\partial X_{1k}} & \dfrac{\partial Y_1}{\partial X_{2k}} & \cdots & \dfrac{\partial Y_1}{\partial X_{nk}} \\ \dfrac{\partial Y_2}{\partial X_{1k}} & \dfrac{\partial Y_2}{\partial X_{2k}} & \cdots & \dfrac{\partial Y_2}{\partial X_{nk}} \\ \vdots & \vdots & \ddots & \vdots \\ \dfrac{\partial Y_n}{\partial X_{1k}} & \dfrac{\partial Y_n}{\partial X_{2k}} & \cdots & \dfrac{\partial Y_n}{\partial X_{nk}} \end{pmatrix}$$

$$= (I-\rho W)^{-1}\begin{pmatrix} \beta_k & w_{12}\gamma_k & \cdots & w_{1n}\gamma_k \\ w_{21}\gamma_k & \beta_k & \cdots & w_{2n}\gamma_k \\ \vdots & \vdots & \ddots & \vdots \\ w_{n1}\gamma_k & w_{n2}\gamma_k & \cdots & \beta_k \end{pmatrix} \quad (17)$$

在式(17)中，第 k 个解释变量的直接效应就是等式右端矩阵中主对角线上的元素的平均值；第 k 个解释变量的间接效应就是等式右端矩阵中主对角线元素之外的所有元素值的平均值 $\frac{1}{n^2}\sum_{i=1}^{n}\sum_{j=1}^{n}w_{ij}\gamma_k$。

(五) 空间权重矩阵的构建

空间权重矩阵反映不同省域经济之间的相互关联程度，其元素取值包括邻接标准与距离标准。在区域经济研究中邻接标准不符合实际，所以本文选用距离标准的空间权重矩阵。地理学第一定理告诉我们，任何事物之间都存在联系，而距离较近的事物之间比距离较远的事物之间的联系更为加紧密。而根据上述理论分析可知，技术进步与产业结构是金融顺周期效应的主要作用因素，所以，本文选用地理距离、技术距离、产业距离的倒数分别作为单一距离准则的空间权重矩阵的元素。

地理距离用各省、直辖市的地理中心之间的直线距离表示。以地理距离的倒数作为权重元素构建地理距离空间权重矩阵 W_D，各省域中心的经纬度坐标取自国家基础地理信息系统。即第 i 行第 j 列元素取值为：

$$w_{ij} = \begin{cases} 1/d_{ij} & i \neq j \\ 0 & i = j \end{cases} \tag{18}$$

其中，d 为两地区地理中心之间的直线距离。

技术距离等于两个省域的高技术产业产值占工业总产值比重之差的绝对值。以技术距离的倒数作为权重元素构建得到技术距离空间权重矩阵 W_T；产业距离为两个省域的产业机构的错位程度（即相似指数的倒数），其计算式为：

$$ID_{ij} = \sqrt{\sum_{k=1}^{m} I_{ik}^2 \sum_{k=1}^{m} I_{jk}^2} \Big/ \sum_{k=1}^{m}(I_{ik}I_{jk}) \tag{19}$$

式中，I_{ik} 是第 i 省市第 k 个工业产业的总产值。以产业距离的倒数作为权重元素构建得到产业距离空间权重矩阵 W_I。其中计算技术距离、产业距离所用到高新技术产值、工业总产值、工业中所含各产业产值均为样本期各自均值。

地理距离、技术距离与产业距离不仅分别对空间相关性产生影响，而且它们两个或者三个整合起来共同对省域金融顺周期效应发挥着作用，所以本文也利用三个相关因素的组合距离构建了组合空间权重矩阵。把地理距离空间权重矩阵与技术距离空间权重矩阵相乘得到地理-技术组合距离空间权重矩阵：

$$W_{DT} = W_D * W_T \tag{20}$$

把地理距离空间权重矩阵与产业距离空间权重矩阵相乘得到地理-产业组合距离空间权重矩阵：

$$W_{DI} = W_D * W_I \tag{21}$$

把地理距离空间权重矩阵、技术距离空间权重矩阵与产业距离空间权重矩阵相乘得到地理-技术-产业组合距离空间权重矩阵：

$$W_{DI} = W_D * W_T * W_I \tag{22}$$

五、实证结果及其分析

(一) 中国省域金融顺周期效应异质性的统计分析

省域 GAP 值可以作为省域金融顺周期效应的代理变量。省域 GAP 值的离散与不均等程度就反映了省域金融顺周期效应的异质性程度。我们利用方差、标准差反映绝对离散程度,用离散系数反映相对离散程度,用基尼系数反映省域 GAP 值的不均等程度。计算结果如表 1 所示。

表 1　不同年份的省域金融顺周期效应异质性分析

指标	1998	1999	2000	2001	2002	2003	2004	2005	2006	2007	2008	2009	2010	2011	2012
均值	0.027	0.050	0.004	0.005	0.046	0.101	0.038	−0.045	−0.056	−0.095	−0.141	0.042	0.042	0.012	0.052
方差	0.069	0.099	0.078	0.057	0.072	0.074	0.048	0.035	0.040	0.045	0.047	0.048	0.045	0.036	0.064
标准差	0.005	0.010	0.007	0.003	0.005	0.005	0.002	0.001	0.002	0.002	0.002	0.002	0.002	0.001	0.004
离散系数	2.561	1.990	18.913	11.043	1.575	0.732	1.270	−0.781	−0.708	−0.476	−0.333	1.142	1.072	2.979	1.234
基尼系数	0.641	0.635	0.778	0.753	0.564	0.346	0.546	0.408	0.381	0.258	0.183	0.483	0.393	0.729	0.564

从表 1 中的方差与标准差值可以看出,在不同年份,省域金融顺周期效应都有绝对波动;从离散系数看,在不同年份,省域金融顺周期效应都有较大幅度的相对波动,最小为 0.333 倍的均值,最大为 18.913 倍的均值;从基尼系数看,有 10 年的基尼系数值大于 0.4,有 2 年的基尼系数值接近于 0.4,说明不均等的差距较大,其中 4 年大于 0.6,已属于差距特别悬殊,需要考虑省域金融顺周期效应的异质性问题,另有 3 年的基尼系数值皆小于 0.4,其中 2007、2008 年是处于国际金融危机期间。

为观察空间相关性与集聚性,我们用 ArcGIS 软件画出 GAP 的空间分布图,计算了每年每个变量之间 Moran'I 指数。限于篇幅,这里仅就 2012 年各省域 GAP 值与 Moran'I 指数值进行分析。

从图 2 可以看出,省域 GAP 值分布具有明显地区差异。东北和西北地区 GAP 值大,西南、华中、东部沿海除江苏地区比较小,集

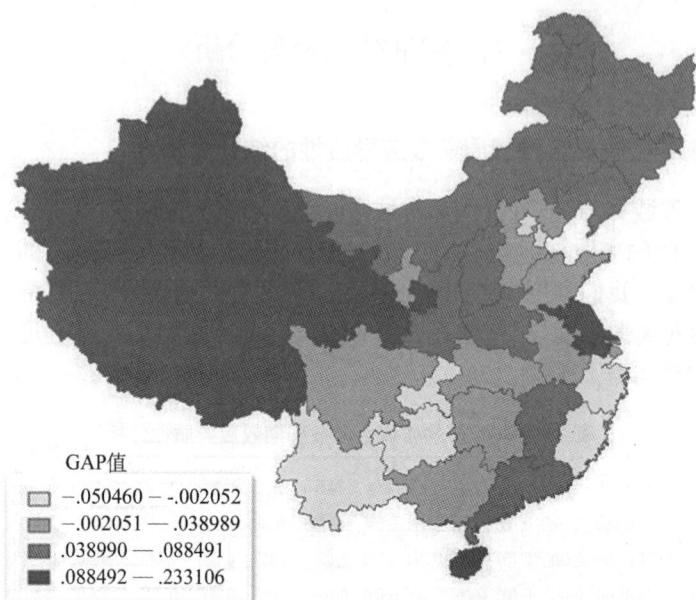

GAP值
- □ −.050460 − -.002052
- ▨ −.002051 − .038989
- ▩ .038990 − .088491
- ■ .088492 − .233106

图 2　2012 年中国省域 GAP 值的四分位分布图

聚现象也比较突出,而 2012 年被解释变量之间的 Moran'I 指数值为 0.410,且在 1% 显著性水平上显著,表明 31 省域 GAP 值具有显著的空间相关性。因此,本文提出的第一个命题是成立的。

(二) 数据平稳性与协整关系检验

为了验证面板数据的平稳性和消除伪回归,我们对各个变量做了单位根检验及协整检验。LLC、IPS、ADF、PP 四种检验结果均表明,原始变量中市场潜能、专一化指标、产业多元化指数、人均 GDP 四个变量不平稳,对不平稳的变量进行一阶差分后再进行检验,所有的变量均在 1% 显著性水平水平下显著,表明变量一阶差分平稳。

由于变量存在一阶单整,于是需要检验模型中变量是否存在协整关系。KAO 检验得到的 ADF 值为 −6.148,在 1% 显著性水平上显著,因此,模型中被解释变量与各解释变量之间存在着协整关系。

(三) 前期检验与模型选择

为了判定模型的具体形式,通过似然比检验和 Wald 检验,我们进一步判断空间面板杜宾模型(SDM)是否可以简化为空间滞后模型(SAR)和空间误差模型(SEM)。检验结果表明,在不同的空间权重矩阵下,Wald_spatial_lag 值和 LR_spatial_lag 值分别在 5% 水平上显著,因此拒绝了 γ 为 0 的原假设,同时 Wald_spatial_error 值和 LR_spatial_error 值分别在 5% 水平上显著,也拒绝了 $\gamma + \beta$ 为零的原假设,这说明选用空间面板杜宾模型更为适合。

面板数据存在着固定效应和随机效应问题,我们进行了Hausman 检验,结果建议选用固定效应模型。对于地区固定效应模型、时间固定效应模型与时空固定效应模型,我们也分别进行了参数估计与模型检验,结果表明在不同的空间权重矩阵下,采取省域固定效应的空间面板杜宾模型的拟合优度、F 检验效果最好,对数最大似然值也都最大,因此我们最后选用省域固定效应的空间面板杜宾模型作为本文最终选用的模型。

(四) 中国省域金融顺周期效应异质性的影响因素及其效应分解结果与分析

不同空间权重矩阵模型估计的结果见表 3 与表 4。表 3 是不同空间相关准则下的空间面板杜宾模型参数估计结果,表 4 为影响因素的直接效应和间接效应估计情况。

表3 不同空间相关准则下的空间面板杜宾模型参数估计结果

指标	单一距离准则		组合距离准则			
	地理	技术	产业	地理 * 技术	地理 * 产业	地理 * 技术 * 产业
市场潜能	−0.002 ***	−0.001 **	−0.001 **	−2.59E−4 **	−0.001 **	−1.62E−4 **
技术效率	7.603 ***	10.168 ***	9.032 ***	9.379 ***	9.343 ***	8.518 ***
纯技术进步	0.9667	0.694	2.930 *	2.757	2.368	2.752

指标	单一距离准则		组合距离准则			
	地理	技术	产业	地理＊技术	地理＊产业	地理＊技术＊产业
纯技术效率	−6.717***	−9.567***	−6.193***	−6.709***	−7.111***	−5.850***
规模效率	−6.831***	−9.581***	−6.214***	−6.756***	−7.139***	−5.887***
TFP	−0.852	−0.617	−2.845	−2.676	−2.252	−2.671
技术偏向	−0.024	−0.022	−0.015	−0.018	−0.008	−0.019
产业专业化	−0.712***	−0.688***	−0.687***	−0.869***	−0.838***	−0.731***
产业多元化	0.424***	0.265*	0.237	0.336	0.376**	0.452***
产业升级	0.002	−1E−04	0.001	9.05E−05	0.001	1.08 E−4
金融深化	0.385***	0.407***	0.369***	0.372***	0.342***	0.371***
金融效率	2.77E−07	−2.67E−07	2.30E−06	2.75E−07	−1.66E−07	7.18E−07
金融集聚	−0.069***	−0.053***	−0.059***	−0.081***	−0.044***	−0.081***
政府干预	0.005	0.002	1E−04	.0012	0.003	0.002
人均GDP	−.045	−0.006	−0.020	−0.044	−0.049	−0.041
rho	0.353***	0.379***	0.256***	−1.541***	−10.242***	−20.624***
R^2	0.764	0.741	0.769	0.788	0.759	0.775
对数似然比	820.208	806.378	827.846	859.462	860.045	880.149

注：*表示在10％水平下显著，**表示在5％水平下显著，***表示在1％水平下显著(下同)。

从表3可以看出，不同空间相关准则下，空间滞后回归系数rho均在1％显著水平下显著，表明我国各个省份的顺周期效应存在空间相关性，对其他省份存在溢出效应，模型的拟合效果比较好。从不同空间权重矩阵模型估计得到的参数值和显著性来看，虽然系数大小有差异，但除技术进步变量的显著性和产业升级的正负号有区别外，其他变量系数的正负号与显著性都没有差异。

从不同模型的拟合效果来看，采用地理-技术-产业组合距离构建的空间权重矩阵的模型拟合效果优于采用其他距离准则构建的空间权重矩阵模型的拟合效果，因此下面我们以采用地理-技术-产业组合距离为空间权重矩阵的空间面板杜宾模型估计结果进行影响因素作用效应分解分析。

根据表4可以得知，本文第二个命题及原假设是成立的，具体

分析如下:

表4　地理-技术-产业组合距离准则下影响因素的效应估计

指标	直接效应	间接效应	总效应
市场潜能	−2.36E−4	−2.16E−4***	−0.002***
技术效率	8.311***	−13.018***	−4.707**
纯技术进步	2.882	−0.781	2.102**
纯技术效率	−5.508**	12.412***	6.9032***
规模效率	−5.529**	12.304***	6.775***
TFP	−2.805	0.560	−2.245***
技术偏向	−0.0205	−0.021	−0.041***
产业专业化	−0.717***	0.630*	−0.087
产业多元化	0.472***	0.980***	1.452***
产业升级	1.023E−4	0.005**	0.005**
金融深化	0.393***	0.660***	1.053***
金融效率	9.87E−7	1.26E−5***	1.35E−5***
金融集聚	−0.101***	−6.23E−01***	−0.723***
政府干预	0.002	−0.003	−9.69E−4
人均GDP	−4.01E−2*	0.025	−0.015
R^2	0.775		
对数似然比	880.149		
rho	−20.624***		

注:* 表示在10%水平下显著,** 表示在5%水平下显著,*** 表示在1%水平下显著

1. 技术进步方面的因素:技术进步因素对于 GAP 的影响是十分复杂的,它可以促进劳动生产率的提高与经济发展,但同时又加大了资金需求。在模型回归结果的直接效应中,TFP、纯技术进步是不显著,技术效率系数有正向影响且显著,间接效应中纯技术进步与技术效率的系数与直接效应中相反,表明了纯技术进步、技术效率具有溢出效应,能够促进其他省域的纯技术进步而带动经济发展;纯技术效率与规模效率的系数显著为负,表明本省域有效利用生产技术、提高投入要素在使用上的效率,提高规模效率都能够促进产出进而减小 GAP 值,纯技术效率与规模效率高的区域会吸引其他区域人才的流入和集聚,因此会产生显著的反向间接效应。较

高的人力资本水平在吸收先进技术、驾驭先进设备的能力方面比较强,能够为提高纯技术效率奠定基础,可以通过提高教育投资来提高人力资本水平和优化要素投入比例提高规模效率来促进产出同时降低信贷/GDP对其长期趋势的偏离程度,同时在重视对各省域人才培养的同时,也应逐渐完善人才流动机制,引导并激励人才流向落后地区。

2. 技术进步偏向因素:文中我们根据式(15)计算所得的技术进步偏向表明我国各省的技术进步大多数属于劳动偏向型技术进步,因为长期以来我国劳动力相对充裕,因此在经济发展中劳动密集型产业所占比重较大,进而在生产中选择多使用劳动而少使用资本的技术,因此技术进步偏向对于GAP影响的直接效应系数为负值,直接效应和间接效应的系数都不显著,表明技术进步偏向对于GAP影响不显著。随着我国刘易斯拐点的到来,应该大力发展知识密集型产业。

3. 产业调整方面的因素:产业专业化反映的是全国水平上各行业在省市水平上的加总,因此专业化程度越高,外部经济越容易产生,从而也就越有利于产业创新以及劳动生产率的提高,因而直接效应中对GAP影响为负,各省份的产业之间存在竞争性,本地产业专业化程度高,周边地区则低,因此间接效应系数相反。产业多元化指数反映的是地区内部产业结构的多元化,越小表明产业越多元化,而地区内部产业的多元化通过适度竞争有正向的外部性,促进本地经济的发展,因此随产业多元化指数增大GAP增大,其间接效应也为负,表明综合距离近的区域在内部发展模式与产业发展上有相互模仿效应。产业升级伴随着工业与服务业的发展,工业越发达服务业越多需求的资金也越多,同时产业升级又可以促进经济发展与资源利用效率提高,直接效应中产业升级系数为正且不显著,说明样本期间产业升级还不是影响GAP的主要因素,产业升级的间接效应为正与直接效应相同,并且是显著的,表明产业升级存在溢出效应,能够带动和促进其他地区产业的升级。

4. 金融发展方面的因素:金融深化与金融效率越高,越有利于金融体系对于实体经济发展的支持,能够促进有效信贷量的增加,推动经济发展,在正反馈机制作用下,进一步加大了信贷的投放量,两个变量系数为正表明金融深化与金融效率越高 GAP 越大,同时金融深化的间接效应为正而且显著,表明金融深化程度越高,其扩散效应能够带动更多其他省域的金融发展,金融效率的直接效应和间接效应系数比较小表明目前金融效率对 GAP 影响不大,因此在金融发展、金融效率提高的同时,需要提高信贷资金的配置与利用效率。金融集聚程度越高,表明本地金融产业越发达,在经济增长中金融因素的作用不可忽视。本地金融业发达能够促进本地经济的发展,直接效应中系数显著为负,金融集聚反映了金融发展的不平衡,本地金融发展程度高,则其他地区金融发展程度低,不利于金融业对实体经济发展的支持,因此间接效应为负。

5. 空间经济方面的因素:市场潜能的直接效应为负并且显著,表明市场潜能大的地区 GAP 值小,市场潜能通过外部性对于生产效率具有正向影响,因此市场潜能对于经济发展具有正向的作用,市场潜能越大,地区经济规模与发展水平越高,GAP 值越小;市场潜能的间接效应为负且显著,说明综合距离近的省地域市场潜能之间相互产生正向影响,能够相互促进经济发展,相应地使得 GAP 值变小,因此可以通过基础设施建设发展发达的海陆空交通网络和信息通讯网络以缩小距离因素的影响,同时各省也应该积极拓展对外贸易,增大市场潜能,促进经济的发展,也有助于降低信贷/GDP 对其长期趋势值的偏离程度。

六、结论与建议

利用扩展的生产函数,本文构建了金融经济分析框架,推导出省域金融顺周期效应的度量指标及其异质比率的计算式,论证了该效应的存在性与异质性,并从规模经济、技术进步、产业调整与空间经济特征方面,系统分析了异质性的影响因素及其作用路径。随后用标准差、离散系数与基尼系数三个离散分布指标,结合四分位数空间分布图,描述分析了省域金融顺周期效应的空间异质性与集聚相关性;在计量分析部分,基于技术、产业、地理视角的单一距离及其组合距离准则分别构建了空间权重矩阵,利用省域固定效应的空间面板杜宾模型,实证检验了省域异质性影响因素的显著作用程度与路径。研究结果表明,中国省域金融经济体系存在着差异显著的顺周期效应;组合距离准则的空间面板杜宾模型效果最好;从三个单一距离准则及其组合距离准则度量的空间相关看,市场潜能、纯技术效率、规模效率、技术进步偏向、产业专业化、金融集聚的总效应与直接影响都是显著为负向作用的,省域金融顺周期效应之间也是负空间自相关的;而技术效率、产业多元化与金融深化的总效应与直接影响都是显著为正向作用的;总效应与直接影响是一致的,说明这些影响因素的直接作用是主导性的。但是在不同的距离准则下影响因素的间接溢出效应表现差异较大,这也说明了影响因素及其作用机制的省域异质性;从组合距离准则看,市场潜能与金融集聚的间接溢出效应是显著为负向溢出效应,而产业专业化、金融深化、金融效率的间接溢出效应是显著为正向溢出效应。

根据上述结论,我们抑制省域顺周期效应,需要做出以下安排:

1. 分省域差别化地设置前瞻性动态调整机制。不同时期或不同省域的经济发展动力与结构特征是不同的,使得中国金融顺周期效应在不同时期的不同省域是具有显著异质性。所以,应当完善省域经济信息共享机制和金融综合统计体系,持续监测与挖掘省域金融经济周期运行规律,依据各省域的金融顺周期效应大小及其影响因素变化,在时间维度上抑制系统性风险的逆周期资本计提应当在计提区间与计提比例等方面分省域差别化地设置前瞻性动态调整机制,抑制金融过度扩张。比如,对于要素市场比较发达、资源配置效率较高的省域,可以设定起点较低、组距较宽的资本计提区间与较低的计提比例,而对政府干预的领域较多力度较大、要素市场欠发达、资源利用效率低下的省域,可以实施起点略高、组距较窄的资本计提区间与较高的计提比例。另外,目前的分省域逆周期资本监管,还要特别关注中国新常态经济特征的省域异质性。由于经济增长潜力下降,资源紧缺环境压力大,较少依赖要素投入推动发展的服务业发展迅速等因素的综合作用,新常态下中国经济总体上进入增长速度的结构性换档期,从8%—10%的高增长速度转为基本维持在7%—8%的中高等经济增长速度,但在省域层面上,省域金融经济周期运行机理的本质性变化、波动形态与结构及其在各省域的表现会有明显不同,逆周期资本监管要因地制宜才能适度有效控制时序上的系统性风险积累。

2. 构建综合挂钩指数,量化设定资本计提区间临界值。省域系统性金融风险来源是多方面的,各类金融风险之间又是相互传染的,省域金融与经济之间顺周期效应的作用路径是多元化的,而且省域金融顺周期效应异质性的显著影响因素主要有技术效率、纯技术效率、规模效率、产业专业化、产业多元化、金融发展规模与金融集聚程度等方面。因此,《巴塞尔协议 III》提出的以信贷/GDP 与其长期趋势的偏离度 GAP 计提为基础的逆周期资本监管框架虽然抓住主要表现指标,但是在可靠性方面还需要补充完善,例如加入顺周期效应的动力因素、异质性影响因素、路径因素及其他综合性风险观测因素,构建综合挂钩指数;在前瞻性方面,利用当期结束后的经济指标计算的指标确定计提比例与时机存在时滞性,需要纳入影响因素等先行指标,再结合极端增长情况下的宏观压力测试结果综合确定。在计提区间的划分临界值确定方面,应当用带有区制变换的量化技术如门限回归技术与平滑转换技术,识别风险状态变迁,分阶段构建相应的上行积累与下行释放机制,合理平衡有效消除顺周期性与平滑经济增长。当前中国经济步入了新常态,也表现出了"优结构、新动力、多挑战"特征。其中,优结构表现在产业结构优化升级,需求结构转为消费为主,城乡一体化趋势不断强化;收入结构转为居民收入为主;新动力表现在消费对经济增长的贡献会持续提升,近期"投资+消费+创新"拉动经济增长将成为常态,市场在资源配置中将起决定性基础作用;多挑战表现为原来高速增长下的隐性风险因素开始凸现,如房地产市场风险、地方债风险等因素。这些都需要我们时变地动态量化设置计提机制各要素,必须分省域因地因时制宜地合理设计挂钩指数与动态资本计提方式。

3. 逆周期资本监管要把省域计提与总体管控紧密融合起来。省域经济是溢出关联与收敛稳定的。从创新驱动与产业调整视角的空间经济计量分析结论看,省域市场潜能是显著影响省域金融顺周期效应异质性的,省域金融顺周期效应不仅总体上存在空间相关性,而且这些省域经济特征方面的影响因素对此异质性影响既有直接效应,也有间接的空间溢出效应与引致诱导效应。因此,在利用逆周期资本监管与资本留存缓冲控制金融过度投放时,要把省域计提与总体管控分别做好,也要在宏观与微观层面上紧密融合起来。在宏观管控层面上,要向价格型调控工具为主、与审慎监控工具及结构化定向精准调控相结合的方式转型,创新推出如补充抵押贷款等新型省域结构化流动性管理的货币政策工具,丰富和优化政策工具组合,构建货币金融审慎新调控框架模式[35];也同时前瞻性地发挥差别化准备金动态调整机制与资本留存缓释等逆周期风险缓释调节作用,发挥信贷政策支持再贷款的促进优化信贷投向方向作用。在微观层面上,用改善与加强资本监管促进金融机构风险管理的功能再造与业务结构优化,利用 RAROC、EVA、资本预算等先进资本管理技术,从业务管理、资本计提、公允价值准则、准备金要求等方面,对银行、证券与保险分类全方位地系统构建逆周期监管体系,强化激励约束机制,提高资源配置效率,推动金融资源合理利用。

参考文献

[1] Gai, Prasanna and Kondor, Peter and Vause, Nicholas. Procyclicality, collateral values and financial stability [R]. Bank of England, Working Paper No. 304. 2006.

[2] 李文泓,罗猛.关于我国商业银行资本充足率顺周期性的实证研究[J].金融研究,2010(2):147—157.

[3] Jacques, Kevin T., Procyclicality, Bank Lending, and the Macroeconomic Implications of a Revised Basel Accord [J]. Financial Review, 2010, 45 (4):915-930.

[4] 高国华,潘英丽.我国商业银行资本充足率顺周期效应研究[J].经济与管理研究,2010(12):82—89.

[5] 方芳,刘鹏.中国金融顺周期效应的经济学分析[J].国际贸易问题,2010(8):120—128.

[6] 张金城,李成.银行信贷、资本监管双重顺周期性与逆周期金融监管[J].金融论坛,2011(2):15—22.

[7] Albertazzi, Ugo and Bottero, Margherita. The procyclicality of foreign bank lending: evidence from the global financial crisis [R]. Bank of Italy, Working Paper No. 926. 2013.

[8] Laux, Christian and Rauter, Thomas. Procyclicality of US bank leverage [R]. Vienna University of Economics and Business Administration, Working Paper. 2014.

[9] Olszak, Malgorzata Anna and Pipien, Mateusz and Kowalska, Iwona and Roszkowska, Sylwia. What drives heterogeneity of procyclicality of loan loss provisions in the EU? [R]. University of Warsaw Faculty of Management, Working Paper No. 3. 2014.

[10] Sole, Juan A. and Novoa, Alicia and Scarlata, Jodi. Procyclicality and fair value accounting [R]. IMF Working Papers, Vol. , pp. 1 - 40, 2009.

[11] Laux, Christian and Leuz, Christian. Did fair-value accounting contribute to the financial crisis? [J]. Journal of Economic Perspectives, Forthcoming.

[12] 黄静茹、黄世忠. 资产负债表视角下的公允价值会计顺周期效应研究[J]. 会计研究, 2013(4):3—11,95.

[13] 梅波. 顺周期效应下公允价值计量的价值相关性研究——兼论多重计量属性[J]. 山西财经大学学报, 2014,36(4):106—114.

[14] 程棵,刁思聪,杨晓光. 中国信贷投放对经济增长影响的实证研究[J]. 经济理论与经济管理, 2012(1):44—58.

[15] 俞晓龙. 资本充足率顺周期效应的实证研究[J]. 金融论坛, 2013(11):44—49.

[16] 金雯雯,杜亚斌. 我国信贷是持续顺周期的吗——基于期限结构视角的时变参数研究[J]. 当代经济科学, 2013,35(5):12—19,124.

[17] Shantayanan Devarajan, Vinaya Swaroop and Heng-Fu Zou. The Composition of public expenditures and economic growth [J]. Journal of Public Economics, 1996,6(7):221 - 240.

[18] King R, Levine R. Finance, entrepreneurship and growth [J]. Journal of Monetary Economics, 1993(32):513 - 542.

[19] 郭庆旺,贾俊雪. 积极财政政策的全要素生产率增长效应[J]. 中国人民大学学报, 2005(4):53—62.

[20] 张钢,段澈. 我国地方财政支出结构与地方经济增长关系的实证研究[J]. 浙江大学学报, 2006(10):88—94.

[21] 张军,金煜. 中国的金融深化和生产率关系的再检测:1987—2001[J]. 经济研究, 2005(11):34—45.

[22] 潘文卿. 中国的区域关联与经济增长的空间溢出效应[J]. 经济研究, 2012(2):54—65.

[23] 赵增耀,夏斌. 市场潜能、地理溢出与工业集聚——基于非线性空间门槛效应的经验分析[J]. 中国工业经济, 2012(11):71—83.

[24] 雷钦礼. 偏向性技术进步的测算与分析[J]. 统计研究,2013,30(4):83—91.

[25] 陆雪琴,章上峰. 技术进步偏向定义及其测度[J]. 数量经济技术经济研究,2013(8):20—34.

[26] 昌忠泽. 金融顺周期性与逆周期金融宏观调控研究述评[J]. 湖北大学学报(哲学社会科学版).2014,41(3):57—64.

[27] 巴塞尔委员会. 各监管当局实施逆周期资本缓冲指引[R]. 2012-12-16.

[28] 郑君君,韩笑,潘子怡. 基于 Malmquist 指数的房地产开发企业全要素生产率变动及收敛性研究[J]. 中国软科学,2013(3):141—151.

[29] 李苍舒. 我国金融业效率的测度及其对应分析[J]. 统计研究,2014,31(1):91—97.

[30] 陆雪琴,章上峰. 技术进步偏向定义及其测度[J]. 数量经济技术经济研究,2013(8):20—34.

[31] 汪克亮,杨力,杨宝臣,程云鹤. 考虑技术进步偏向性的全要素生产率分解及其演变——来自 1992~2009 年中国省际面板数据的经验依据[J]. 软科学,2014,28(3):12—15,25.

[32] 李宏兵,蔡宏波,王永进. 市场潜能加剧了性别工资不平等吗?[J]. 数量经济技术经济研究,2014(1):22—41.

[33] 马子量,郭志仪,马丁丑. 西部地区城市化动力机制研究[J]. 中国人口·资源与环境,2014,24(6):9—15.

[34] 朱玉杰,倪骁然. 金融规模如何影响产业升级:促进还是抑制?——基于空间面板 dubin 模型(SDM)的研究:直接影响与空间溢出. 中国软科学,2014(4):180—192.

[35] 茆训诚,王周伟,吕思聪. 宏观审慎调控框架下系统性风险管理体系的构建研究[J]. 金融管理研究,2013(2):42—54.

（原载于《中国软科学》2014 年第 11 期）

中国创业投资地域集聚现象及其影响因素研究*

张玉华 李 超**

我国依靠创新驱动、建设创新型国家的战略实施,离不开创业投资的助力和催化。基于资本自由流动的新古典经济学假设,创业投资在一定空间内也应该是自由流动的。然而作为一种独特的金融资本,创业投资呈现出地域集聚现象[1]。也正是这种地域集聚,为集聚地社会创造了惊人的财富和价值,未来甚至还会影响和改变世界经济格局。人们已逐步意识到硅谷等地创业投资的集聚不应简单地被看作是一种经济机制,而应注意其"生态环境",也就是其为创业投资及高新技术发展提供的"土壤和气候"。因此,创业投资地域集聚及其影响因素目前已是各国政府、投资机构、创业者关注的重要话题,也引起了国内外学者的广泛关注。

一、创业投资独特的地域集聚现象

自 1970 年 Tribus 最早指出创业投资空间非均衡发展的现象以来,众多学者(Chen 等(2010)[2]、Cumming(2013)[3]、Kolympiris (2011)[4]、Mason 等(2013)[5]、Avnimelech 等(2010)[6])对美国、英

  * **基金项目**:国家社科基金单列项目"学习型组织知识共享机制和效率熵评估指标研究"(BKA110089)。

  ** **作者简介**:张玉华(1968—),男,湖北荆州人,上海师范大学商学院教授,博士,研究方向:投资经济学、管理学。

国、加拿大、法国、德国等发达国家创业投资地域集聚现象进行了研究,阐述了创业投资地域集聚发展的趋势。另有学者(Subhash(2007)[7]、Cumming 和 Dan(2010)[8]、Sahut 等(2011)[9])研究发现创业投资存在"空间临近效应",创业投资机构普遍选择在一定地域集聚。

目前对创业投资地域集聚现象的研究大都限于描述性分析,缺乏对其集聚程度进行准确衡量的指标,相关研究大都使用创业投资的绝对量来衡量其地域集聚程度(Guilhon 和 Montchaud(2006)[10]、胡海峰(2008)[11])。但是我国各地区的经济规模差距较大,金融资源分配不均,如果用创业投资的绝对量指标来衡量各地区的创业投资集聚水平是不精确的。本文借鉴产业经济学中衡量产业集聚度的指标"区位熵"的形式,构建了衡量创业投资集聚程度的指标。

关于创业投资地域集聚影响因素的研究主要集中在三个方面:区域环境、信息不对称以及供求关系。

首先,创业投资地域集聚的一个重要原因是不同地域创业投资环境的差异。Chahine 等(2012)研究了"硅谷"创业投资发展的优势因素,其先进的科技创新能力、丰富的金融资源促使"硅谷"成为全球创业投资中心[12]。Hirukawa 等(2011)认为创业投资地域集聚会受到区域地理环境的影响,但更重要的是区域人文、科教及产业发展对创业投资的影响[13]。我国学者崔毅等(2011)使用因子分析法,研究了我国创业投资地域集聚现象明显的五个省市,从经济、产业、科技、金融等方面构造了环境指标体系,得出了不同环境对创业投资的影响[14]。佘金凤等(2007)从区域创新资源优势对创业资本的吸纳效应、创业投资的"空间邻近效应"等方面分析了区域创业投资不平衡的原因[15]。张海燕等(2012)从投资环境、投资成效、物理距离和经济一体化四个方面分析了影响创业投资地域集聚的原因[16]。

其次,也有研究(Fritsch 和 Schilder(2012)[17])从信息不对称的角度分析了创业投资地域集聚的影响因素:创业投资机构与创业企业之间存在信息不对称,创业投资机构从本质上讲是风险规避者,为了降低不确定性,会将投资集中在信息透明度高的区域。Tian(2012)认为区域集聚投资可以获得投资过程中需要的信息,有利于创业投资机构监管被投资企业,及时做出反应以节省投资成本[18]。

我国学者也做出了类似的分析,胡海峰(2008)利用投资项目与金额数量两个指标分析了创业投资的地域集聚现象,认为区域集聚可以有效分享信息,降低信息不对称性和不确定性带来的不利因素,从而降低交易成本[11]。

最后,还有学者从供求关系方面分析创业投资地域集聚的影响因素,Shachmurove 等(2007)的研究表明,区域资源供需之间的矛盾会导致投资集聚分布:创业投资会投资于金融创新资源集聚、创业氛围浓厚、评估及咨询等中介机构云集的区域[19]。张晓辉等(2012)实证分析了中国创业投资的区域分布特征以及影响因素,金融市场资源、人力资本丰富的地区对创业投资具有较强的吸引力[20]。

上述研究很少涉及定量分析,回归方法的选择也局限于传统的截面数据、时间序列和面板数据模型。相关研究在分析的时候假设各个地区均为彼此独立的个体,忽略了地区创业投资的空间相互关系对其空间分布的影响。基于以下原因,创业投资地域集聚极有可能存在空间相关性:首先,创业投资作为一种特殊的金融资本,其投资行为具有一定的辐射作用[21]。例如创业投资发达的北京对于附近省域创业投资的流向及规模具有影响;其次,我国东、中、西区域经济发展不平衡,区域之间形成了一定的"俱乐部"[22—23]。因此,忽视创业投资集聚的空间相关性,得到的结论显然是不精确的,各种因素的影响方向和程度更是无法衡量。

综上所述,具有明显空间相关性的创业投资地域集聚现象及其影响因素仅用传统的计量模型分析是不够的。本文应用空间计量分析方法,实证分析创业投资集聚的空间相关性,在此基础上利用空间面板数据模型研究创业投资地域集聚及其影响因素。

二、中国创业投资地域集聚程度及其空间相关性

(一) 创业投资地域集聚程度的测算

衡量创业投资地域集聚程度的指标如下:

$$LQ_{it} = \frac{(I_i / I_n)}{(S_i / S_n)} \quad (1)$$

式(1)中,LQ_{it} 为地区 i 在 t 年的创业投资集聚指数,用于衡量

该地区创业投资的集聚程度,大于 1 表示集聚程度高于全国平均,小于 1 表示低于全国平均;I_i/I_n 为 i 地区的创业投资额占当年全国创业投资额的比重,S_i/S_n 为 i 地区金融机构年末存款余额占全国金融机构年末存款余额的比重。

(二) 数据来源及描述

本文研究包括 2005—2012 年中国 29 个省级行政区,由于数据缺失,西藏、海南、港、澳、台除外。创业投资数据来源于各年《中国风险投资年鉴》以及《中国创业投资年度统计报告》,相关数据的描述性统计分析见表 5。

创业投资地域集聚的现象出现极端化。以 2012 年为例,北京的创业投资总额占全国总额的 20% 以上,上海和广东也都超过了 10%,而最少的省份如贵州的观测值为 0[①]。总体说来,东部地区的份额都较高,而中西部地区的份额普遍较低。

(三) 创业投资地域集聚的空间相关性分析

空间自相关有两种指标:全局指标与局部指标。前者主要是用于测算整个区域的空间自相关程度;后者主要是用于测算某个区域与邻近区域的空间相关性。本文采用最为常用的 Moran's I 指数对空间相关性进行测度。传统空间权重矩阵为地理邻接矩阵,但是结合创业投资的实际情况,不同地域之间的相互影响不一定仅取决于地理上的邻近性。随着现代交通、通讯的发展,区域之间的相互影响已经跨越了地理上的障碍,而创业投资的发展与当地的经济发展水平等因素息息相关。因此我们构造了基于经济发展水平的权重矩阵,元素为 $\omega_{ij} = 1/\mid PGDP_i - PGDP_j \mid$,式中分母为区域 i 和 j 之间人均 GDP 差距的绝对值[②]。

计算我国 2005—2012 年 29 个省域的创业投资集聚指数,利用 Moran's I 指数测算我国 29 个省域创业投资地域集聚的空间相关性,得出的 Moran's I 如表 1 所示。

---

① 贵州的观测值为 0 并不意味着该区域的实际投资额为 0,只是说明相关调查抽样缺少有效样本,但是观测值为 0 并非离群值,对实证研究的结果不会产生影响。
② 关于空间权重矩阵的设置及使用文献较多,在此不再赘述。

表 1   Moran's I 指数

年份	2005	2006	2007	2008	2009	2010	2011	2012
Moran's I	0.1404*	0.1261*	0.1430*	0.1710**	0.1640**	0.2034**	0.2126**	0.2304**

注:*** 表示显著水平为 1%,** 表示显著水平为 5%,* 表示显著水平为 10%。

　　结果表明我国省域创业投资地域集聚存在很显著的空间依赖特征,高(低)投资额地区和高(低)投资额地区相邻,随着时间的推移这种效应有逐步增强趋势。Moran's I 从整体上反映了我国省域创业投资地域集聚的空间自相关性,局域 Moran 散点图则具体反映其地域集聚情况,2012 年的局域 Moran 散点图如图 1 所示。

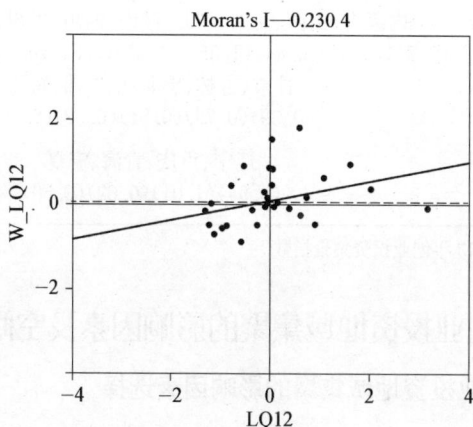

图 1   2012 年创业投资集聚的局域 Moran 散点图

　　由局域 Moran 指数散点图可见大部分省域都属于高-高和低-低两种类型①,这两种类型所占的比例约为 80%,其中高-高地区大约占了 20%,低-低地区约占 60%。高高聚集的省份大多为东部地区,如表 2 中第一象限的省份,各省的创业投资集聚指数均较高,低低聚集的省份多为中西部地区,如表 2 中第三象限的省份,各省的创业投资集聚指数均较低。可以看出我国省域创业投资集聚程度

──────────
　　① "高-高"集聚地区为高创业投资省份的集聚地区,即位于散点图中右上角第一象限的地区;"低-低"集聚地区为低创业投资省份的集聚地区,即图中左下角的第三象限地区;其余地区不存在属性一致的情况。

存在明显的区域差距,中西部地区明显落后于东部地区,呈现出"两极分化"的趋势。

表2　2012年创业投资集聚的局域 Moran 散点图对应的地区及相应创业投资集聚指数

象限	地区与集聚程度
第一象限 H—H	北京、天津、上海、江苏、浙江、福建、山东、广东 (2.75)(1.1)(2.64)(1.78)(1.89)(1.26)(1.34)(2.37)
第二象限 H—L	河北、江西、安徽 (1.21)(0.83)(0.56)
第三象限 L—L	内蒙古、山西、河南、湖北、湖南、四川、贵州、云南、陕西 (0.75)(0.87)(0.44)(1.35)(1.01)(0.81)(0.51)(0.93)(0.77) 甘肃、吉林、黑龙江、广西、新疆 (0.39)(0.79)(0.81)(0.62)(0.45)
第四象限 L—H	辽宁、重庆、青海、宁夏 (0.94)(1.01)(0.32)(0.50)

注:括号内值为2012年创业投资集聚指数。

三、中国创业投资地域集聚的影响因素及空间计量分析

(一)中国创业投资地域集聚的影响因素选择

创业投资地域集聚现象主要集中在欧美发达国家创业投资市场。中国的创业投资是在经济转型中发展起来的,因而在区域分布上更具特殊性,与欧美国家差别较大[24]。我们在分析欧美国家创业投资地域集聚现象及结合中国创业投资特殊性的基础上,将影响创业投资集聚的因素总结如下表所示:

表3　创业投资地域集聚的影响因素

因素分类	具体方面
区域环境	政府政策、创新资源、科技创新水平等
供求关系	交通和通讯基础设施建设水平、金融等服务业水平等

　　结合数据的可得性,本文选取下列解释变量作为影响创业投资地域集聚的影响因素,因变量为前文创业投资的地域集聚指数:

　　(1) 政府政策。中国经济具有转轨特征,尽管社会主义市场经济体制已经建立和不断完善,但是政府在经济的运行过程中仍旧发挥着重要作用。本文使用政府科技支出占财政支出的比重反映政府对高新技术的重视程度。

　　(2) 服务业水平。创业投资中介服务机构是联系投资机构和创业企业的桥梁和纽带,投资的各个环节都需要中介机构的广泛参与[25]。本文使用第三产业产值占 GDP 的比重反映区域中介机构等服务业的水平。

　　(3) 创新资源。创业投资一般投向成长潜力大、技术水平高的项目,而高新技术产业恰好满足这些要求,这就决定了创业投资追随高新技术成为现实。本文使用专利申请授权量反映区域创新资源的丰富程度。

　　(4) 人力资本水平。和物质资本及自然资源相比,人力资本是"软生产要素"。创业投资机构对投资项目的评价很大程度上是对创业者素质的评价。本文使用每十万人口高等学校平均在校生数反映区域人力资本水平。

　　(5) 区域市场容量。创业投资主要投向高科技产业,但是其"逐利性"决定了某些项目只要是具有高成长潜力,即便是传统产业,创业投资也会进行投资。而这些传统产业项目往往具有一定的地域性,如零售业,对于这些项目就要考虑区域市场规模。本文使用人均消费支出量反映区域市场容量的大小。

　　(6) 区域交通。创业投资的运行机制决定了投资机构在向创业企业提供资金之后,还需要向企业投入管理和各种市场资源,并对创业企业进行积极的干预,通过监督与控制创业企业来降低投资风险。基于创业投资的投资特征与降低成本的需要,创业投资机构会将自己的投资活动限制在一定范围之内,即投资活动具有"空间邻近效应"。本文使用机场旅客吞吐量反映区域交通的发达程度。

　　为降低模型的异方差及减少数据变幅,对数据进行对数化处理。因变量、自变量的数据定义如表4所示。

表4　模型变量说明

变量	变量名称	变量定义
因变量	LQ	创业投资集聚指数
自变量	Gov	政府科技支出占财政支出的比重
	Ser	第三产业产值占 GDP 的比重
	LOGtech	专利申请授权量的对数
	LOGedu	每十万人口高等学校平均在校生数的对数
	LOGcons	人均消费支出的对数
	LOGtrans	机场旅客吞吐量的对数

　　本文机场旅客吞吐量根据民航总局公布的《全国机场统计公报》分省加总所得,其余数据来源于《中国统计年鉴》、《中国金融统计年鉴》等。数据的描述性统计分析如表5所示,下面结合具体数据对其进行补充说明:机场旅客吞吐量及专利申请授权量差距较大,显示我国省域之间交通发展程度及区域创新能力存在较大差异。数据显示 2012 年广东省的机场旅客吞吐量为青海省的 41 倍,交通运输差距与创业投资的区域集聚程度差异相似。

表5　变量的统计描述

	LQ	LOGtech	Gov	Ser	LOGedu	LOGcons	LOGtrans
均值	0.6094	3.8046	0.0188	0.4011	1.8082	3.9287	4.1080
中位数	0.3530	3.7691	0.0127	0.3882	1.8662	3.9117	3.1112
最大值	2.9202	8.4312	0.0720	0.7645	2.1846	4.5669	8.2666
最小值	0.0010	1.8976	0.0038	0.2830	0.9542	3.5126	0.1578
标准差	3.9017	1.6452	0.8260	0.8193	0.2622	0.2219	2.2312
观测数	232	232	232	232	232	232	232

(二) 空间计量模型的构建

本文构建的创业投资地域集聚影响因素模型如下,其中式(2)为空间面板滞后模型,式(3)为空间误差滞后模型:

$$LQ_{it} = \rho \sum_{j=1}^{N} \omega_{ij} LQ_{it} + \beta_1 \, LOGtech_{it} + \beta_2 \, Gov_{it} + \beta_3 \, Ser_{it} + \\ \beta_4 \, LOGedu_{it} + \beta_5 \, LOGcons_{it} + \varepsilon_{it} \tag{2}$$

$$LQ_{it} = \beta_1 \, LOGtech_{it} + \beta_2 \, Gov_{it} + \beta_3 \, Ser_{it} + \beta_4 \, LOGedu_{it} + \\ \beta_5 \, LOGcons_{it} + \varphi_{it} \tag{3}$$

$$\varphi_{it} = \rho \sum_{j=1}^{N} \omega_{ij} \varphi_{it} + \varepsilon_{it}$$

式中 ε_{it} 为随机扰动项,φ_{it} 代表空间自相关误差项,ρ 代表空间自相关系数。面板数据模型的估计需要考虑固定效应和随机效应,根据 Baltagi(2005)的研究,固定效应更加符合实际需要,因为个体效应不一定是服从某一分布的随机变量[26]。空间面板数据模型中存在空间效应与时间效应问题,因此在实际分析中就有三种模型:时间效应、空间效应、时空效应,需要根据模型的估计结果进行选择。由于本文只是分析"固定效应",因此综合来说需要估计的模型为以下几种:空间固定效应、时间固定效应、时空固定效应模型。

(三) 中国创业投资地域集聚影响因素的空间计量分析

空间面板模型的判定和选择一般采用 Anselin(1988)[27] 提出的拉格朗日检验法。相关检验结果如表 6 所示:

表 6　LM 及 robust LM 检验结果

	LM-lag	LM-lag-robust	LM-error	LMerror-robust
统计量的值	161.8818	153.0136	9.0235	0.1553
对应 P 值	0.0000	0.0000	0.0027	0.6935

从表 6 可得:由于 LM-lag 和 LM-lag-robust 的检验值较 LM-

error 和 LMerror-robust 值显著,所以选取空间面板滞后模型较为合适①。

本文估计了两个模型:一是全国整体模型,包含涉及到的 29 个省份,以便从全国视角分析创业投资集聚的影响因素;二是区域模型,对中国东、中、西三个地区分别进行模型估计,以便比较不同区域创业投资集聚影响因素的差异②。

表 7 全国 29 省份模型估计结果

解释变量	传统固定效应模型	空间面板滞后模型			空间面板误差模型		
		空间固定	时间固定	时空固定	空间固定	时间固定	时空固定
LOGtech	0.384**	0.600***	2.124**	0.503***	0.461***	1.258***	0.532***
Gov	0.238**	0.439***	0.211*	0.354**	0.549***	0.205*	0.441**
Ser	0.254**	0.336**	0.246***	0.451*	0.375**	0.239**	0.350*
LOGedu	0.035**	0.041***	0.023**	0.087***	0.077**	0.057***	0.058**
LOGcons	0.008*	0.009**	−0.031	0.007	−0.006**	−0.001*	0.005
LOGtrans	0.082**	0.078	0.463**	0.089**	0.014*	0.378**	0.061**
ρ	—	0.715**	0.307**	0.575*	0.601**	0.232	0.412*
调整后的 R^2	0.787	0.891	0.862	0.875	0.883	0.854	0.873
log-likelihood	—	250.431	−24.478	197.213	230.285	−21.322	212.987

注:* 表示 10%水平下显著,** 表示 5%水平下显著,*** 表示 1%水平下显著,下同。

模型一:全国整体模型分析

分析表中模型估计结果,可以得出结论:

1. 比较传统的固定效应模型与考虑空间因素的模型,就调整后的 R^2 来说,在考虑了空间效应之后该值明显优于没有考虑空间效应的模型,说明纳入空间因素的模型能够更好的解释影响创业投资集聚的因素。

---

① 本文将空间面板误差模型的估计结果同样表示出来,以便对创业投资集聚的空间模式进行比较。

② 本文所有回归结果均为使用 Lesage 和 Elhorst 等人编写的空间计量模型的 Matlab 软件包实现,可通过网址:http://www.spatila-econometrics.com/下载。

2. 空间自回归系数 ρ 的估计值均较为显著,除了时间固定效应空间面板误差模型中不显著外,其余几个模型中 ρ 通过了 10% 的显著性水平检验,进一步验证了中国各省创业投资集聚存在空间相关性。

3. 进一步比较六个纳入空间因素的面板数据模型,在综合衡量调整后的 R^2 以及对数似然估计值 log-likelihood 之后,空间固定效应模型的估计效果是最好的,即面板数据中出现的非观测效应主要是个体间的固定效应。本文给出如下解释:首先,由于数据限制,本文研究所选取的面板数据的年份个数小于截面个数,这就出现了"短面板"的现象,进而产生了不同截面的个体效应要强于时间效应[28];其次,从前文分析中我们可以看出,中国不同地域之间的创业投资水平差异十分巨大,这就造成了个体之间的差异效应大于时间上的变化带来的差异效应,这也在一定程度上解释了中国创业投资地域集聚不平衡的现象。

4. 根据表中各解释变量的系数及显著性水平,各省域专利申请授权量和每十万人口高等学校平均在校生数两个解释变量几乎在所有模型中都通过了 1% 的显著性检验,且符号为正,说明省域创新资源优势以及人力资本优势会对创业投资产生吸纳效应;此外,第三产业产值占 GDP 的比重、政府科技支出占财政支出的比重两个解释变量也通过了至少 10% 的显著性水平检验,且符号为正,说明发达的金融中介服务能够对省域创业投资集聚水平产生显著的正向影响,良好的政府政策环境对于创业投资集聚也具有促进作用。除此之外,机场旅客吞吐量这一指标除了在空间滞后模型的固定效应中不显著外,其他模型中都在 10% 的水平下显著为正,说明机场旅客吞吐量对中国省域创业投资集聚具有正向的影响。

5. 各省份人均消费支出这一指标的显著性水平较低,其符号在不同的模型中是不相同的,而且系数的绝对值也比较小,可以认为该指标对创业投资集聚的影响方向和程度是不确定的。我们给出如下解释:中国创业投资地域选择在市场取向上不明确,这与现阶段中国创业投资流向的行业领域有关,以 2013 年为例,当年全年创业投资中互联网行业占比 29%,电信及增值和 IT 行业也分别占比 18％和 15％,结合前面创业投资对创新资源的依赖这一因素,可以认为当前中国的创业投资倾向于高科技产业与传统产业,而这两大产业对市场不敏感,市场取向明显的现代服务业没有得到创业投资的青睐,与此同时,中国国内创业投资市场发展不成熟,可投资创业项目不足,也可能导致部分创业资本流向传统产业。

模型二 东、中、西区域模型

为了比较分析中国不同地区省域创业投资集聚的影响因素,本文分东、中、西三个地区对样本进行了估计[1]。限于篇幅,我们仅列出东部地区的回归结果,中部地区与东西部的区别在于估计的空间效应不显著。

分析比较三个地区的估计结果,可以得到以下结论:

1. 和整体模型一致,纳入空间因素的模型相对于传统模型来说能够更好地解释影响创业投资地域集聚的因素。即便是将全国分为东、中、西三个地区之后,在六个空间模型中,空间固定效应模型的估计效果仍旧优于时间固定效应模型,这与前面我们分析的整体模型中固定效应优于时间效应略有不同,很明显此处的三个地区模型不符合"短面板"的情况。我们给出如下解释:中国不同地区内部省份之间的创业投资水平差异十分巨大,造成了个体之间的差异效应大于时间上的变化带来的差异效应,这和全国各省创业投资的差异是一致的。

2. 分析比较各个解释变量的估计结果,我们可以得到三个地区之间影响创业投资地域集聚的因素的一些相同点和不同点。就相同点来说,各省域专利申请授权量、每十万人口高等学校平均在校生数、政府科技支出占财政支出的比重,这三个解释变量几乎在所有模型中都是显著的,且符号均为正,说明省域创新资源优势以及人力资本优势会对创业投资产生重要影响,政府政策支持有利于创业投资在我国各个地区的发展。下面就各解释变量在东、中、西三个地区表现出来的不同点进行说明。

---

① 东部地区包括:北京、河北、辽宁、上海、江苏、浙江、天津、福建、山东、广东;中部地区包括:山西、安徽、河南、湖南、湖北、吉林、黑龙江、江西;西部地区包括:内蒙古、青海、陕西、新疆、云南、甘肃、贵州、四川、宁夏、重庆、广西。

表8　东部10省份模型估计结果

解释变量	传统固定效应模型	空间面板滞后模型			空间面板误差模型		
		空间固定	时间固定	时空固定	空间固定	时间固定	时空固定
LOGtech	1.125**	0.671***	1.240*	0.622**	1.410**	1.328*	0.841**
Gov	0.285**	0.271***	0.491*	0.552**	0.132***	0.532*	0.217**
Ser	0.214**	0.361**	0.436***	0.541*	0.735**	0.327**	0.501*
LOGedu	0.235**	0.343**	0.031**	0.234***	0.201*	0.152*	0.422**
LOGcons	-0.024*	0.015**	−0.042	0.027	0.016**	−0.055*	0.025
LOGtrans	0.043**	0.067	0.631**	0.058*	0.064*	0.467*	0.072**
ρ	—	0.091*	0.005*	0.075*	0.201*	0.002	0.041
调整后的 R^2	0.701	0.848	0.802	0.835	0.843	0.814	0.823
log-likelihood	—	121.041	54.478	111.033	132.985	51.302	115.087

（1）第三产业产值占 GDP 的比重与机场旅客吞吐量两个解释变量显示出了一些相同的模式：在东部地区，两个指标均通过了至少10％的显著性水平检验，且系数符号均为正值；但是在中、西部地区，两个解释变量变得不再显著，在西部地区甚至出现了负值。这说明金融中介机构以及交通运输条件两个因素对东部地区创业投资的集聚具有重要作用，而在中西部却出现了一定程度的抑制作用。本文解释如下：我国东部沿海地区交通等基础设施完善，区位优势明显，市场经济体制较为完善，能够为创业投资提供必要的成长环境，降低交易成本；而我国中西部地区由于地理上以及政策上的原因，虽然国家实施了"西部大开发"和"中部崛起"等政策措施，但是在金融发展水平以及交通等基础设施建设方面仍旧处于较为落后状态。这就造成了创业投资的区域选择青睐于我国东部地区，而对中西部地区的关注较小。

（2）整体模型中人均消费支出系数不显著且符号为负，我们可以看到，该变量在中、西部地区模型中仍旧不显著，但是在东部地区却通过了显著性检验，且符号显著为正。结合我国东、中、西三个地区经济发展的实际情况，我们可以认为，随着我国东部沿海地区的产业结构升级,广大东部地区在大力发展高新技术产业的同时,也在大力发展市场导向明显的现代服务业,而且现代服务业在经济发展当中的比重呈现越来越高的态势;与此同时,2010年出台的《关于中西部地区承接产业转移的指导意见》引导和支持中西部地区发挥自身优势,加快承接产业转移。这使得中西部地区的产业结构以及创业投资结构发生了变化,其中的传统产业很明显对市场不敏感,这就导致了中西部地区市场容量对创业投资的影响不大。

四、中国创业投资集聚示范区设立的战略安排

本文构造了衡量创业投资集聚程度的指标,探索了应用空间计量经济学的方法,研究我国省域创业投资地域集聚及其影响因素的新思路,解决了传统研究忽视定量分析及空间相关性的问题,为创业投资地域集聚的研究提供了新的思路和方法。本文实证结果表明:我国省域创业投资集聚存在显著的空间相关性;创业投资东部区域"高高"集聚与西部地区"低低"集聚的两极分化现象较为明显,呈现出创业投资地域集聚的"马太效应";不同因素在不同区域显示出了不同的影响方向和程度。

鉴于我国较多省市都提出要大力打造创业投资集聚区的现状,本文建议尽快在东部地区尤其是上海自贸区设立国家级创业投资集聚示范区,从国家层面合理规划创业投资集聚的全国布局。

1. 尽快在东部创业投资发达地区设立国家级创业投资集聚示范区

将创业投资集聚区的打造上升为国家战略,统一规划、统一布局,建议利用政府创业投资引导基金及各项政策形成杠杆[①],尽快在东部创业投资发达地区(如长三角、珠三角及环渤海等地区)特别是上海自贸区设立国家级创业投资集聚示范区,充分发挥其创业投资

---

① 据财政部统计,截至2012年全国共有188家创业风险投资机构获得各类政府引导基金支持,政府创业风险投资引导基金累计出资260.08亿元,引导带动的创业风险投资管理资金规模达1407亿元,平均放大6倍。

的引领带动作用,撬动全球创业投资向中国集聚,力争打造和形成全球又一个新的创业投资中心。

(1) 本文实证研究得出了创业投资地域集聚现象之间存在空间相关性的结论。因此,我们不能将区域创业投资集聚的发展与其他区域相孤立,应该在促进本区域创业投资集聚发展的同时考虑到对其他地区的外部性,要加强区域协调,探讨和设计区域互利共赢的模式,发掘区域之间正向的空间溢出效应,从而有利于整体创业投资产业的发展。我们应该注重创业投资集聚程度较高的东部地区对于中西部地区的整体辐射带动作用,通过东部地区经验的推广,为东部地区创业投资的转移和中西部地区创业投资集聚区的打造创造机遇。

(2) 创业投资的地域集聚是我国创业投资以及经济发展所必经的过程,但是东西部地区创业投资集聚发展"两极化"趋势的出现,将不利于我国东西部区域发挥各自的资源禀赋优势,对全面实施创新驱动发展的战略也会产生不利影响,更有可能会造成区域之间科技创新乃至经济发展新的差距。缩短创业投资的发展差距,需要有统一的制度安排特别是需要国家相关部门统筹协调。

(3) 由于我国创业投资集聚空间相关性的存在,在创业投资规模一定的情况下,各省市为争取创业投资,在区域政策设计、投资环境优化及基础设施建设上难免会出现恶性竞争,这在我国创业投资集聚水平普遍落后的西部地区尤为明显。因此我们要打破区域之间的行政壁垒,加强各省的宏观协调,促进中国创业投资市场的统一。

(4) 国家级创业投资集聚示范区的打造与我国"上海自贸区"建设的战略重合点较多。两者均需要我们不断探索对外开放的新路径和新模式,形成投资合作与竞争的开放性区域,在扩大服务业开放、税收更加优惠等政策方面需要改进,两者紧密的关系可以形成协同发展的态势。

(5) 市场经济就是信用经济,我国中西部地区社会信用体系的建设滞后于经济发展,企业信用缺失、政策朝令夕改、政府随意、行政等行为已明显成为制约创业资本投资中西部的障碍。为促进创业投资的发展，必须从根本上营造一个诚信的投资环境。国家级创业投资集聚示范区的设立可以为西部地区树立"样板"，中西部地区可以借鉴集聚示范区的制度安排，优化信誉环境，为创业投资集聚提供健康的氛围。

综上所述，我国目前将创业投资集聚区的打造上升为国家战略，在东部特别是在上海自贸区设立国家级创业投资集聚区的时机已经成熟，应尽快实施。国家级创业投资试验区的设置也将是继"上海自贸区"等改革试验区建设之后，继续深化改革，培育中国面向全球的竞争新优势，打造中国经济新"升级版"的重要举措。

2. 国家级创业投资集聚示范区的打造思路

(1) 初步形成国家级创业投资集聚示范区，打开创业投资集聚发展新局面

统筹创业投资集聚区域协调发展，形成全国创业投资发展的合力，发展初期可以通过设立并合理使用政府创业投资引导基金，引导国内外创业投资资本、机构及高端人才聚集，将政府引导基金定位为创业投资的"母基金"，强调其引导性及其杠杆效应，可以不直接投资和运作，而是通过与优选的创业投资机构或者合作伙伴共同投资，以保本微利经营，用风险分摊的方式，最大限度地调度创业投资向创业投资集聚区集聚，在此基础上初步形成创业投资集聚示范区。

(2) 探索中国创业投资集聚发展的新模式，形成可复制、可推广的经验

对于国家级创业投资集聚示范区的打造，我们可以依托"上海自贸区"建设的经验，同时也要结合创业投资集聚发展的特殊性，尤其在高科技、人才、服务业、现代物流及资本流通方面要加强改革开放力度，结合中国国情形成一些可复制、可推广的经验。

(3) 开展国家级创业投资集聚示范区的推广试点

一方面，通过上述创业投资集聚示范区的打造，将创业投资集聚示范区的打造经验进行推广试点，充分发挥试点的"引路"意义，节省各地创业投资集聚区打造的时间及投入，推进创业投资集聚的全国发展。

　　另一方面,在试点推广过程中,针对我国中西部地区信用环境的缺失,要借鉴集聚示范区的经验,把基础社会信用体系建设作为西部地区创业投资集聚发展的重要内容,进一步推进西部地区的政务诚信、商务诚信和社会诚信建设。

（原载于《中国软科学》2014 年 12 期）

国际文凭课程引入的本土改造对策 *

——以上海市为例

刘茂祥 **

国际文凭课程（International Baccalaureate Diploma Program）为国际文凭组织（International Baccalaureate Organization）创设的面向16—19岁学生学习的高中课程项目，值得我国高中课程改革关注。其作为一种被广泛认可的国际课程，因其课程结构的完整性与竞争力、课程内容的现代性与生命力、课程体系的融合性与适应性等方面的优势，我国许多省市的学校将其引入并加以实践。笔者认为，对国际文凭课程的引入需要加强本土规范，既要维护我国教育主权，又要从中找到为"我"所用的元素，并且结合我国、地区实情进行改造、创新，从而进一步推进我国高中的课程改革。本文主要从省市层面和学校层面探讨国际文凭课程的本土改造对策。

一、省市层面上的本土改造对策

(一) 强化我国教育主权地位的维护与学生核心价值观的树立

在《上海市中长期教育改革与发展规划纲要（2010—2020年）》

* 本文系上海市哲学社会科学规划·教育学课题、上海市教育科学研究重点项目"优质高中国际课程的实践研究"（A1011）终期成果之一。

** 作者简介：刘茂祥，1975年生，男，湖南邵阳人，上海师范大学教育学院2014级博士生、上海中学教育科研高级教师，上海市基础教育国际课程比较研究所办公室主任，主要从事基础教育改革研究。

中，上海市专门提出了"试点高中国际课程"的要求，力求借鉴国际课程经验，深化高中课程改革。作为落实这一要求的重要行动，上海市教委颁布了《上海市教育委员会关于开展普通高中国际课程试点工作的通知》（沪教委基〔2013〕37 号）这一文件。[1]在这一文件中明确了一条这样的原则：开展中外融合课程试点的学校，课程方案、课程计划及其教材需审查，其中我国国家课程中的语文、思想政治、历史和地理四门课程应为必修课程。也就是说，无论哪一所学校引入涉外课程，都必须经过行政部门的审批，如果课程内容与教材中涉及有意识形态冲突的地方，或者内容中有不符合我国发展实际的情形，可以强制要求不得引入实践，或进行调整（如采取补充教材等方式），才可引入实践。这也是引入国际文凭课程等国际课程的必要前提。与此同时，如果一所学校要获得开展中外融合国际课程的试点，其试点课程方案与实施计划中必须保证我国语文、思想政治、历史和地理四门课程的开设，这是必备条件。也就是说，即使该校被审核有权开设国际文凭课程，哪怕已获得了国际文凭组织的授权，也要求学习国际文凭课程的学生必学语文、思想政治、历史、地理，进行必要的公民教育。而且尤其强调在对学生的教育过程中，必须加强社会主义核心价值观教育，开展形式多样、效果明显的思想品德教育，这是审查学校是否能够试行国际文凭课程的必要前提。这样从政策上保证国际文凭课程的引入与实践必须强调我国教育主权的维护，加强对公民教育与社会主义核心价值观的引领。

（二）委托第三方机构进行课程试行的专业评估

对普通高中试行的国际文凭课程的认证与评估，上海市采取了委托第三方教育机构——上海市基础教育国际课程比较研究所（以下简称"研究所"）进行专业评估。研究所组织熟悉国际课程的专家进入申请试点的学校进行专业评估。专业评估共分成几个环节进行：首先，由六名左右的评估专家审读申请试点国际文凭课程的学校自评报告，要求被评估学校准备该校拟试点开设该课程的第一年教学计划与内容、教材清单、师资准备、对可能涉及与我国意识形态、主权观点相悖或有异议内容自查工作或处理方案、聘请外国专家单位资格认可证书等材料。然后,由研究所派出评估小组进行现场评估。现场评估安排一天左右的时间,主要内容有听取学校汇报,专家分四个小组分别与学校管理人员、课程负责人员、教学与人力资源负责人员、后勤与学生服务负责人员进行交流或实地材料、场所考查与听课、座谈等。现场评估要点主要有试点经费来源、课程架构、师资准备、运行模式、资质具备、资源匹配、学生服务等方面。最后,由各评估小组组长汇总各小组形成分管审查领域的评估意见,完成被审查学校的评估报告。评估报告分办学理念和培养目标、课程、管理、教职员工、学生服务、资源、学生生活、最终评审意见等八大部分。专业评估报告不给予学校是否通过试行评估的明确结论,主要提供考察的事实材料、存在的问题等意见,供行政决策。行政决策权归属"上海市普通高中试点开设国际课程项目领导小组"。

(三) 建立一系列评估流程与标准加以有效指引

在对国际文凭课程等国际课程审查中,作为专业评估的机构——研究所建立了一系列的评估流程与标准加以有效引领。在材料审查流程上,采取先预先审查材料,再进行现场评估的方式;在专家现场审查上,先进行专家培训,再进入实地考察;在学校审查流程上,先进行试点或示范评估,再进行面上的全面铺开;在现场评估流程上,采取先听取学校汇报,然后进行访谈、座谈、听课、资源察看等方式进行;在审核流程上,先进行专业评估,然后再进行行政决策。在评估标准上,研究所先后制定了《上海市基础教育国际课程试点学校认证评估指标体系》《上海市普通高中试行国际课程评估考察要点参考(公办学校、民办学校分开单列)》《上海市普通高中试行国际课程评估听课要点》等一系列标准。在评估标准的制定过程中,尤其注重对课程结构与教材内容的审查,以保持对我国教育主权的维护以及对课程内容、教材中涉及与我国意识形态、教育观点等相冲突或有异议的内容的及时处理(视内容情况要求采取摒除相应内容、补充教学处理、禁止引入某一类教材等方式进行处理)。例如,某学校在国际文凭课程实施中选用的 11 年级原版进口的生物英文教材中,有诸如"中国 17% 的水稻为杂交水稻,这些杂交水稻在口感上要比种间育种的水稻差"等内容的主观评论,则需要提供相应补充教材,让学生对我国的杂交水稻有一个正确认识。[2]

(四) 注重发挥学校引入国际文凭课程的主体作用

无论是上海市普通高中试行国际课程的文件引领,还是研究所的专业引领,都强调普通高中在引入国际文凭课程中发挥自身的项目主体地位,这主要包括在试行国际文凭课程中,学校自身是否为独立实施主体,还是与中介结构合作推进;学校与中介机构的产权关系是否理顺,中介或合作方在该项目运行中是辅助作用还是主体作用;对合作方的资质是否合法等都需要进行考察。在评估引领中,作为实施国际文凭课程的主体——学校要能够逐步发挥主体作用(可以有中介一定的辅助过渡,但主体作用在学校方,这一点必须明确),主要考核点有:实施该课程的管理方是学校自身还是外方或中介方;承担国际文凭课程教学任务的主体是本土教师还是外籍教师;是否有意识地引进与培养胜任该课程的本土教师,形成良好的培养计划与长效机制;在国际文凭课程的实施过程中是否有意识地将其中的有价值元素迁移、改造或运用到其他学生的学习上等。当前我国许多学校尽管引入了国际文凭课程,获得了国际文凭组织的授权,但实质运作方不是学校,而是中介机构。这些中介机构的介入,更多的是考虑某种经济利益诉求(如从学习该课程的学生收费中提取大量所谓的购买服务费用),而不是考虑如何从中汲取有价值的元素来推进我国学校课程的改革,这种方向需要得到扭转。

(五) 培育学校领导者与教师团队的探究精神

对国际文凭课程的引入实践与认证评估,省市层面的引领应尤其注重学校管理者与教师团队的探究精神。引入国际文凭课程这一高端国际课程,遇到的问题会很多,包括怎样有效通过国际文凭组织长达两年的授权审批;其科目内容相当于大学预科课程,对教师的专业要求与英语要求都很高,如何吸引一批优秀的教师从事国际文凭课程的教学;该课程教学要求与国内课程要求有很大的区别,包括对学生的探究性实验设计指导、学习方法论指导;对于其六个学科群的高选择性要求,课程编排与管理怎样应对;国际文凭课程对实验学科的探究性教学与实验设备的要求增强,学校如何创设相应的教育资源环境;如何处理国际文凭课程与我国课程的共生(两种课程取长补短)关系;如何根据国情、校情进行适合我国学生的改造、运用,进而推进学校课程体系的现代性变革等,需要校长的课程领导力与教师的课程驾驭能力持续提升,需要培育学校领导者与教师团队的探究精神。必须指出的是,任何不顾及教师感受的国际文凭课程引入实践与探究,实际上是忽视了那些能够真正贯彻改革的人。积累学校管理者、教师在该课程探索与本土化改革探索方面的经验,对于国际文凭课程的引入与改造的长期性是有价值的。[3][12]

当前我国课程改革正处在如何为我国教育从大走向强提供支撑的十字路口,省市层面对国际文凭课程的规范化本土引入对策,在一定程度上是指向国家课程改革要求上的改革应对。在这个十字路口上,无论是国家还是省市层面,都意识到对国际教育先进元素引入与改造的必要性,因为我们的"强"不是面向国内、同类群体,而是面向国际、一流群体。只有使我们的改革视野站在国际的视野上,立足我国本土的发展需求,在保留我国特色的同时,进行创造性的整合、运用,才能使我国正在推进的新课程改革与标准修改朝着有利于培养具有国际视野、竞争力的人才方向发展。

二、学校层面上的本土改造实践对策

(一) 把握在实践中学习的发展方向与要素

引入国际文凭课程,首先要学习,而且应当在实践中学习。在实践中学习,应当明确校本应用的目的与方向,分析其在学校实践中需要把握的要素,这也是校本改造的前提与基础。在实践中学习国际文凭课程,要把握学习与实践运用的方向。当前高中引入该课程的学习与实践,主要有四种:其一,既关注为国内的境外人士子女提供与国际接轨的教育,又注重从中把握有价值的元素推进我国学生的教育;其二,主要是为我国境外人士提供与国际接轨的教育;其三,是为我国的学生今后出国留学服务;其四,并非为学生今后出国留学做准备,而是看中了其中育人的先进性而引入,旨在推进我国学生国际视野的拓展与具有国际竞争力的能力提升。[4]对于我国大多数高中来说,主要是趋向于前三种,对第四种方向的认识与改造还没有充分显现。对于我国的高中来说,引入国际文凭课程的学习与实践方向应当是借鉴其中有价值的元素来推进我国基础教育的课程改革,尤其是学校课程的建设与完善,为我国学生国际视野拓展与素养提升提供养分。

对国际文凭课程的学习与思考,需要把握有哪些共同的、核心的、反映国际教育发展趋势的、值得为基础教育阶段学校加以充分关注的要素。对于国际文凭课程,值得在校本改造中加以重视与运用的要素有以下五个。(1)课程的选择性与促进学生的个性化知识构成。国际文凭课程只规定了"三高(高水平)三低(标准水平)"的选学原则,没有严格意义的选修课程与必修课程的界限,促进了学生差异性发展。(2)课程的现代性与学生现代素养的提升,如 IBDP课程教材,注重将最新科技及时融入教育内容,其注重课程结构的现代性设置。(3)课程的探究性与学生创新思维、人格的养成,如国际文凭课程实验学科注重学生的探究性实验,实验内容教学占到总课时的 35%左右。(4)关注数字化内容整合与学生学习方式变革。(5)关注高校等社会资源的运用与学生潜能认识、开发。[5]对这些要素的把握,有利于高中在推进国际文凭课程的学习与实践改造中,提升学校课程体系化与现代化建设水平。

(二) 审问所处体系的性质与改造空间

对国际文凭课程的校本改造,不仅要认真审问其所处体系的结构与性质,而且要思考引入后的校本改造空间。任何一种国际课程都有自身所在课程体系以及隐含着该国育人的价值形态与育人观念,有其特定的属性。当然,该国际课程如果不是国别课程,而是具有跨国性质的课程,则更加需要把握其整体的教育理念与性质。为此,"当我们在借鉴国外课程改革的经验教训时,当我们在把自己的课程方案与国外的课程方案进行分析比较时,应该清晰地意识到各国社会制度上的不同,并揭示出各种方案背后所隐含的基本假设和价值取向,这不仅有助于明确课程改革方案的性质,而且有利于课程的设计和实践朝着既定的目标展开[6]。"只有在正确审视国际文凭课程所处性质的基础上,才能更好地挖掘与拓展该国际课程的校本改造空间。

审问国际文凭课程所处体系的性质,要思考整体与局部的关系。譬如,该课程体系包含高中项目、初中项目、小学项目、职业生涯项目,各个项目具有相对独立性,学校可以只开设高中项目,也可以只开设初中或小学项目、职业生涯项目,每个项目均有阶段性的培育要求,开设的语言要求也不同。在审问国际文凭课程所处体系性质的基础上,寻求校本改造的空间,需要考虑以下几个环节。一是课程体系差异性之间的兼容问题。该国际课程有自身的课程体系,而我国中小学也有自己的课程体系,如何在两者之间达成有效的兼容是国际课程校本改造中亟待解决的难题。二是课程价值取向的求同问题。国际文凭课程的课程体系所追求的价值取向是不一样的,我国中小学对国际课程的校本改造,要关注求同问题,尤其是实验学科与科技方面的价值追求中相同的元素,如关注学生探究、创新等,然而从中借鉴有利于学校课程进一步提升的元素。三是课程内容改革的取舍问题。对国际文凭课程的校本改造,一个十分关键的内容是如何完整地将其引入运用到我国学生的教育中,还是摘取其中的部分内容为我所用,这涉及内容的取舍,主要原则是取其精华而非完整的引入。

(三) 慎思有价值内容迁移的生长土壤

对国际文凭课程有价值内容的迁移,首先要发现哪些是值得迁移而且在我国具有生长的土壤。对于哪些有价值内容值得迁移的认识,不能凭空想,需要在做的过程中了解、研究,发现真正能为"我"所用且有学校实践基础与运用空间的东西。显然,国际文凭课程的数学、实验科学不涉及意识形态的东西,因而主要以这些学科为例来探索。从数学而言,其分数学学习、数学标准水平、数学高水平、加深数学四个水平供选学,强调对原创性数学思想的揭示、数学知识发展过程的揭示以及与社会生活、经济问题的联系,这启示我们中小学在推进数学课程的选择性以及数学与发展、创新、生活的联系上加强迁移运用。从实验科学来讲,其物理、化学、生物实验学科的实验内容要占到课程内容的 35％左右,且大多关注探究性实验;在教育内容的安排上注重教学内容基础性与现代性的平衡,教材定期更新且多元化;十分凸显选择性,如物理学科,不仅有标准水平与高水平之分,而且在每个水平层次内都有必修与选修的内容。实验科学的校本改造内容很大,因为我们现有的这方面课程与国际文凭课程的实验学科内容不同的地方超过了 60％,且主要是现代科技内容。深入到具体学科领域的实践来认识其中值得迁移的元素,也能更深入地思考其中哪些元素迁移到我国学生教学需要怎样的条件,包括师资的英语水平、课程选择内容的多少设置以及配备怎样的实验设备、采取怎样评价措施等因素。

寻求国际文凭有价值内容迁移的生长土壤,需要注重运用以下几个方略。第一,将国际文凭课程中有价值的思想融入学校课程体系改革中,如选择性的观念与学校课程体系建设联系,推进必修课程的分层、科目选择与发展课程的自由选学。第二,将国际文凭课程中学科现代内容以必修或选修模块的方式进入到课程教学,如在数学、物理、化学等进行部分内容的学科双语教学,这些双语教学内容就可从中选择现代内容加以运用。第三,以单独的课程形态运用到发展型课程中。如国际文凭课程物理学科高水平可选择的六个内容,如天体物理、通信技术、电磁波、相对论、生物物理、粒子物理,就可以直接成为学校发展课程中的六个科目。第四,采用双语双课本同步学习。如采用上海教材与国际文凭课程原版引进教材同时授课。对有价值内容迁移的校本生长土壤,一方面是把握学校原有的条件、实情来选择迁移的内容,另一方面是积极培育能够有利于先进内容迁移的土壤。只有将原有条件、基础的考量与可能培育的生长土壤紧密结合,才能推进有价值内容迁移的成功以及成功迁移后的持续成长。

(四) 明辨在学校重建与发展的特色选择

对国际文凭课程的校本改造,是基于实践取向的,目的是为了促进学校课程的特色建构与学校个性、特色的持续生长,最终促进学生具有国际视野、国际合作与竞争实力的素养提升。基于实践取向的国际课程校本改造,需要遵守这样的原则:"强调实践的探究不否认理论的思考和指导,但它却是反对对'外来的'理论过分的、无根据的依赖。实践的课程探究模式反对过分依赖外来的理论,强调的是课程理论的重建与发展。"[6]对于国际文凭课程的校本改造,需要强调学校的重建与发展,促进学校具有自身个性的特色彰显。每一所学校,完全可以根据自身的实践,选择符合自身发展需要的国际文凭课程科目进行改造与运用,如有的学校专门针对拓展性论文课程进行运用,有的针对创造·实践·服务课程进行创新,还有的针对艺术课程进行了整合,进一步推进自身的特色选择与创建。

国际文凭课程在学校重建与发展的特色选择上,需充分把握自身的实情与特点。在上海乃至全国其他地方的许多学校,都根据自身的实际、特色的选择引入了国际文凭课程进行校本改造,而且这种校本改造正从原来更多的是留学准备逐步扩展到对我国学生国际视野、国际理解能力提升的素养培育上,这是一种可喜的现象,也符合国家对高中涉外课程引入的方向。据悉,教育部正在制定有关高中引入涉外课程进行实践的规范政策,对民办学校引入加强认证、规划布局与引领;对公办学校则主要是两个倾向,一是不能高收费与独立编班,二是不鼓励整体引入而强调单科融合或在拓展课程中开设,从学校特色与个性发展出发选择适合自身的国际课程中有价值的科目,以保证公办学校改革的公平性与普惠性。国际文凭课程在学校重建与发展的特色选择好了以后,还需要根据学校的发展战略与方向努力创建,努力推进管理、师资、评价上的变革。在管理上,要树立与国际通用的管理法则,按照国际课程实施的基本规则加以落实;在师资培养上,需要进一步深化其实施的教师英语运用能力,提升他们基于实践的国际课程研究与校本改造、深化、形成自身教学个性的能力;在评价上,要做到与国际课程匹配的评价方式,包括对该国际课程校本改造后的实施评价、学生学习评价。

总而言之,在国际文凭课程的省市层面和学校层面的本土改造中,"对于我们准备学习和借鉴的国外课程研究成果,我们不能照抄照搬,也不能简单地进行所谓地'中国化改造',而应该把握其内核、实质,以中国自己的课程实践为基点和框架,从实质性的层次将国外的课程研究成果吸纳、融合到中国的课程实践框架中来"。[7]最后需要指出的是,本文借助国际文凭课程这一具有影响的国际课程发展与本土管理的分析,旨在通过对这一课程的认识与管理,让更多的学者与学校关注像国际文凭课程这样的涉外课程引入应当关注的问题。随着上海等地的本土化管理与改造对策的实施以及学校自发的本土化管理对策探索,正推进自下而上的国家导引政策的酝酿,在近年也将马上出台,将成为全国的规范化引领方向性文件。在国家、省市、学校三级本土化规范推动下,将进一步指导国际文凭课程等涉外课程的本土规范化管理,使我国的教育在拓展国际视野的同时,进一步维护我国教育的主权,关注我国学生的核心价值观教育与作为我国公民应有素养的提升,培育一批能够胜任国际教育、并推进我国课程改革的一线骨干师资力量,进一步推进了我国课程改革的现代化进程。通过对国际文凭课程等国际课程引入的本土化改造与规范管理,将有利于有影响的涉外课程引入实践在推进我国课程的改革走向深入上发挥积极、主动的价值。

参考文献

［1］上海市教育委员会.上海市教育委员会关于开展普通高中国际课程试点工作的通知(沪教委基〔2013〕37 号)[EB/OL].[2013 - 5 - 9].http://www.shmec.gov.cn/html/xxgk/201305/402162013002.php.

［2］上海市基础教育国际课程比较研究所.上海市普通高中试行国际课程评估专家培训手册[G].2013 - 10 - 18.

［3］Doherty C, Shield P. Teachers' Work in Curricular Markets: Conditions of Design and Relations between the International Baccalaureate Diploma and the Local Curriculum [J]. *Curriculum Inquiry*. 2012,42(3):414 - 441.

［4］唐盛昌.我国高中引入国际课程应关注的几个问题[J].教育发展研究,2010(22):12.

［5］唐盛昌,李英.高中国际课程的实践与研究[M].上海:上海教育出版社,2011:342.

［6］施良方.课程理论:课程的基础、原理与问题[M].北京:教育科学出版社,1996.

［7］丁念金.课程论[M].福州:福建教育出版社,2007:586.

（原载于《课程・教材・教法》2015 年第 4 期）

论语文教学理论的"内卷化"困境及其破解路径*

石耀华**

"内卷化"又叫"过密化",在社会学、人类学领域,它常被用来描述这样一类社会现象:当一种社会体系、社会制度达到了某种形态以后,既没有办法稳定下来,也没有办法使自己转变到新的形态,取而代之的是不断地在内部变得更加复杂,[1]具体表现为"有增长无发展、制度变迁的路径依赖、习俗与习惯的精致固化"等不同形态。[2]从美国人类学家戈登威泽的"文化模式内卷化"到格尔茨的"农业内卷化"以及英国汉学家黄宗智"中国农业发展的内卷化",再到美国学者杜赞奇"国家政权内卷化",该理论的视域不断延展,逐渐发展为一种颇具解释力的理论分析范式,已广泛应用于政治学、经济学、历史学、文化哲学等学科领域。用"内卷化"理论研究教育,始于蓝希瑜、杜慧对赣南畲族传统教育蜕变的分析,[3]深化于陈坚对农村教育变革过程中遭遇困境的深度解析。[4]当今语文教学理论一定程度上也陷入了"内卷化"的困境。这种"内卷化"是指,在复杂多变的社会现实与快速推进的语文教改面前,语文教学理论的建构难以获得新的突破,转而在系统内部不断精细化、复杂化,但其整体效益却并未得到质的飞跃,止步于低水平的重复与循环。审思并破解这种困境,对于语文教学理论本身的优化与语文课堂实践的转

* 教育部人文社会科学研究青年项目"资本与地位:农村教师专业身份认同的实证考察——以 A 省 16 地市为例"(14YJC880060);安徽省 2014 年度教学研究项目"卓越教师"研课技能微课程设计研究(2014jyxm228);地方高师院校教师教育精品化战略的理论与实践(2014jyxm752)

** 作者简介:石耀华,安徽安庆人,上海师范大学教育学院博士生,阜阳师范学院文学院教师,主要从事语文课程与教学研究、教师教育研究。

型,都具有十分重要的意义。

一、语文教学理论"内卷化"的表现形态

(一) 有规模上的增长,鲜内涵式发展

这里的"增长",是指语文教学理论"量"的积累;而"发展",则是指"质"的飞跃。从"量"的方面来看,进入 21 世纪以来,语文教学理论的建构取得了突飞猛进的增长。在数据库"中国知网"以"语文"为主题词检索相关文献,1977 年 35 篇,1978 年 104 篇;进入 21 世纪,伴随基础教育课程改革的深入推进,研究成果百花齐放,势不可当,2009 年激增到 10060 篇,2013 年为 14732 篇,这还不包括其他与"语文"有关的相关成果。就"研究项目"来说,以中部教育不甚发达的某省为例,2013 年公示的教育科学规划立项共 442 项,其中跟语文有关的 59 项,所占比例超过 13%,2014 年 367 项,与语文相关的 63 项,占 17%强,该省西北部教育欠发达地区某地级市 2014 年教育科学规划立项 56 项,其中与语文有关的 12 项,超过总数五分之一。以代表语文教育理论的较高水平、具备较高学术含量的"硕博论文"来说,在"中国知网博硕士论文库"检索,与"语文"主题有关的,截至 2015 年 1 月 20 日,共计 13777 篇,其中 2013 年就有 1854篇。

单就数量指标而言,语文教学理论的体量似乎已相当可观。然而,深度分析这些成果,不论是对于语文教学理论本身还是对于语文课堂教学,其价值何在,却是个未知数。就理论本身而言,很多研究甚至没有区分"语文活动"与"语文学习"。"语文是生活""语文的外延与生活的外延相等"等认识本身没有问题,因为语文是母语。但是当一门学科的外延无限延展,大到不可捉摸的时候,这门学科的价值如何体现,答案就不得而知了,"语文"的外延同生活的外延相等并不意味着"语文学科"的外延同生活的外延相等,不能把生活中处处发生的"语文活动"等同于"语文教学"或"语文学习",此其一。

其二,"大语文""真语文""绿色语文"等理念的提出,也的确给人新的启发,但是在"语文"前面无限施加定语,本就暴露我们对于

语文的模糊认知。换句话说,我们讨论的对象是"语文",却少有论题对于"这个对象到底是什么"作出建设性的解释。在对语文课堂实践的指导层面,至少到目前,鲜有研究真正揭示语文教学的基本原理,进而削减了理论的实践品格。以阅读教学为例,我们甚至很少思考"阅读"与"阅读教学"的区别,很少区分不同文体的"阅读"与"阅读教学"。研究到底指向人类的"阅读活动"还是语文教师的"阅读教学",到底指向哪种文体的"阅读"与"阅读教学"这个前提性的问题都不甚明了,其对于语文教学实践的作用就可想而知了。"语文学习功在平时""语文学习要依靠大量的课外阅读"等论断本是成立的,但是从语文教育研究者和语文教师的嘴里说出来,潜台词就是"如何进行有效的语文学习,我是没办法的"。语文学习"得法于课内,发展于课外",我们往往也只关注"课外"的发展,对于课内之"法"则缺乏深入的研究,而这却是关乎语文教学的根本性问题。

　　总之,貌似繁荣的语文教学理论背后,真正立足"语文"、扎根"课堂"开展研究,并对理论建设有所突破、对实践产生实质影响的委实不多,理论与实践似乎是在两条轨道上各自运行,这在某种程度上背离了理论研究的价值旨归,使得语文教学理论陷入"内卷化"困境,难以获得"内涵式"发展。

(二) 多异见纷呈,少知识建构

　　这里的"异见纷呈"多指由主体的经验甚至主观臆想生产出来的意见与观点。有一定证据支持的、比较系统的经验总结或者主观臆想,我们可以称之为"观点",没有证据支持的、零散的、即时生成的经验或者臆想,只能称为"意见"。

　　在语文研究领域,正如学者指出的那样,长期以来一直存在"三多三少"现象:意气用事的多,充分说理的少;自以为是的多,逻辑论证的少;消极批判的多,有效建构的少。[5] 所谓的理论建构要么脱离鲜活的语文教学实践,满足于社会学、教育学一般理论的评介;要么仅仅停留在经验的描述,将感性混同于理性,将感受等同于知识。例如,语文科的"正名"问题,"正名"是揭示概念内涵的重要思路。严格地说,"语文"这一概念的出现是新中国成立以后的事。关于

"语文"的具体所指,一直以来,许多人按照"节缩词还原"的方式将其简单解释为"语言文字""语言文章""语言文学""语言文化"或者"语言文字文章文学文化综合",并借鉴文章学知识、语言学知识、文学知识从各自视野衍生出相应一套语文教学理论。[6] 实际上,这种思路很难谈得上准确揭示语文的本质内涵,恰恰相反,正是这种"正名"实践搅动的迷雾,干扰了我们对语文价值的判断,直接影响课程与教学的实施。再如,语文课程的"性质"问题,一直存在"工具说""人文说""工具人文统一说"等多种理解。长期以来,我们或多或少都是在界定语文课程性质的基础上定位语文课程的功能,再据此建构自己心目中理想状态的语文,并以此为标杆建构语文教学理论,考量语文教学实践。然而,这种关于语文课程性质的解读,多采用"我主张""我认为"的言说方式,各执一词,众说纷纭。深度解析这些"我主张""我认为",会发现其思考路径多指向"课程取向",实际上是个价值判断问题,很难回答事实层面的课程性质问题。[7] 循此思路所定位的语文课程功能也就未必是语文课程的真实功能,所建构的语文教学理论对于理论本身与教学实践的价值自然也就不得而知了。再有,语文课程的"三维目标",不管是官方文本对于"标准"的解读,还是教学中的实际情况,三维目标都是个有机体,它们统整于教学实施过程,这几乎是个常识。但是至少到目前,在很多关于语文课程与教学目标的研究以及语文教师的教学设计中,还是以简单化的思维解读三维目标,粗暴地将其割裂为"知识与能力、过程与方法、情感态度价值观"三个维度进行处理,架空了内在于三维目标水乳交融的教学价值。

所谓"知识",在现代知识型看来,它应基于实证而来,"既能得到观察和实验证实又能得到严格的逻辑证明",它应该"同认识对象的本质相一致或符合",具有客观性、普遍性和可靠性。诚如孔德所言,那些"研究比较简单的自然现象的知识",比如天文学、物理学、生物学等,在较早时代就进入实证的科学轨道,而"社会学、政治学、伦理学等研究社会和人这种比较复杂现象的知识",则是最后到达科学阶段。[8] 在社会转型、科学昌明的今天,我们有理由相信,在教育、教学领域,只有基于科学知识型的知识才具备成其为知识的合法资格。然而,在语文教学研究中,却鲜有真正基于科学知识型的知识建构。首先，从"关于语文的知识"层面来说，诚如前述，在"语文""语文课程性质""语文课程目标"等基本问题的讨论中，多采取"我主张""我认为"的思考路径，多停留在"观点""意见"层面。尽管观点与意见也有助于揭示研究对象的内涵，但这种研究思路很难谈得上"科学知识的建构"。其次，从"作为语文的知识"、即学生在语文课堂中实际学习的语文知识来看，长期以来，语文教学中的语文知识一直存在"滞后于相关学科的研究，一些明显过时或明显错误的语文知识占据语文课堂""带有'原创'意味的语文知识缺乏严格的学术检验"等不良倾向。例如，描写本是一种常见的表达方式，但是"有限的几种人物描写方法从初中一直讲到高中"，并且"一遇到记叙文、小说，就一定要分清哪里是肖像描写、哪里是神态描写或者动作描写"。[9]再有，很多语文教师在阅读、写作教学中机械理解"文体"，片面强调"主题""思想"，偏爱华美、铺陈的语言表达等现象，在今天的语文教学中仍然十分普遍。

语文教学理论的建构要基于科学、合理的知识，学生语文能力的形成也要依托适宜的语文知识。当前语文教学理论的建构却多停留在意见、观点或经验总结的层面，缺乏科学知识体系的支撑，使得所建构的理论失去应有的理论品格，陷入"内卷化"泥淖难以前行。

（三）重抽象理论建构，轻真实教学实践

对于语文教学研究而言，如果说存在理论建构的话，则又会陷入另一种困境：注重抽象理论，为了理论而理论。

首先，简单移植其他学科理论用于语文教学研究。例如，接受美学理论被引介到阅读教学领域，一度引起"阅读领域哥白尼式的革命"。固然，基于各自知识修养、文化背景与人生经验，不同读者面对同一部作品会产生不同的解读，再顺应课程标准强调"尊重学生个人见解""鼓励学生批判质疑"，提倡"多角度、有创意的阅读"等理念，语文阅读教学也提倡多元解读。然而生硬移植过来的理论却将阅读教学多元解读实践导向另一个极端：不入文本曲解，不知人而妄论，不论世而谬说，不察己而乱议。[10]令人忧虑的是，面对这些不良取向的多元解读实践，很多语文老师还表

示理解,并冠以"发散思维"的帽子予以鼓励。这种未经"语文化"改造地简单移植其他学科理论阐释语文问题的倾向,实际上不利于语文教学理论的建构,只能是让语文成为验证其他学科理论合理与否的试验场。

其次,抽象理解某些概念,对语文教学问题进行简单化处理,并据此建构理论。例如《义务教育语文课程标准(2011年版)》在"课程性质"部分指出:"语文课程是一门学习语言文字运用的综合性、实践性课程"。按照汉语习惯,这句话中的关键概念"语言文字运用"可简称为"语用",于是便有"语用教育观"的提出,并逐渐被人们所接受。[11]然而,稍作分析会发现,作为"语言文字运用"简称的"语用"与语用学中的"语用"虽然都指向语言功能,但二者内涵与外延却有较大区别,此"语用"非彼"语用",用"语用学"的理论指导"语用教育观"的建构,可能还有很长的路要走。再如,"教材无非是个例子"这个著名论断本身也没有问题,揭示出了文选型教材的某些特质,据此也可以得出语文教学"教语文"而不是"教课文"的结论。但是,深入分析却会发现,由这个论断可以衍生出两个问题:第一,所有教材都是例子吗? 对于一些构成学生人文世界、构筑学生精神大厦的文化经典,仅作"例子"处理,是否合适? 第二,就算教材都是例子,那么利用这些例子教给学生的到底是什么? 毋庸讳言,不管是"语用论"还是"例子论",我们在依托这些概念建构相关理论的过程中,实际上缺乏对相关概念的深入理解,而是采取一种简单化的处理方式,这样势必削弱理论的阐释力,删减理论的生命力。

再次,一些貌似源于语文教学实践的理论建构,对于语文课堂实践的意义也不大。我国语文教育研究者和语文教师从教学实践中生发出来的一些"理论"或者叫"准理论",除了固化教师的思维、束缚教师的教学外,实在难以看出其对于语文课堂生态的改善有何价值。例如阅读教学中,小说教学"人物、情节、环境"的认知框架,散文教学"形散神不散""借景抒情""托物言志"的言说方式,诗歌教学"体裁""韵律""意象"的分析套路,除了帮助教师以一种简单化的方式进行相应文体的教学,并且有利于"考试"外,对于学生不同文类阅读能力的培养与综合素养的提升,似乎没有多大帮助。再如写作教学,记叙文、说明文、议论文的"教学分类"本就不甚明确;记叙、描写、说明、议论、抒情五种基本表达方式的具体所指也比较含混,彼此夹杂,很难看出这样的理论对写作教学实践与学生写作能力的提高具有多大价值。换句话说,教师基于这些理论产生的"写什么""怎么写"等基本问题的认识就出了问题,从而导致我国的语文教学中"几乎没有写作教学"。[12]

总体看来,当前很多语文教学理论的建构,要么忽视真实的语文教学实践,移植、套用相关理论解释语文教学,为了理论而理论;要么简单理解语文教学实践,曲解甚至忽视语文教学的实践逻辑,建构不适宜、不合理的语文教学理论。如此一来,势必导致理论在实践面前的"乱语",即理论过分自信,显得傲慢、自大,然而具体言说所指却非实践的真实状况,只能是自说自话;或者"失语",即理论无法解释实践的真实问题,更难谈得上"解决",从而显得自信不足,将无法解释、无法解决问题的责任推给某些"不可控"因素,主动让出本该属于自己的阵地。

二、语文教学理论"内卷化"的归因分析

(一) 语文科的先天不足

学科发育过程中的先天不足,是导致语文教学理论"内卷化"的根本原因。这种先天不足有这样几个方面的表现:

首先,就学科发展轨迹而言,语文科有着漫长的过去,却只有短暂的历史。在漫长的古代社会,语文科是与文学、经学、史学等其他学科杂糅在一起综合发展的。清末民初,伴随社会、政治的需要,方始走上独立发展的轨道。但是这种发展进程却是漫长的、曲折的,从开始阶段的"读经讲经""中国文学"等"多名期",到后来的"国语""国文"并称,以致新中国成立以后的"语文",这一名称的演变轨迹本身就颇能说明问题。

其次,不同于物理学、化学、数学等自然科学,语文科的学科归属也比较模糊,涉及语言学、文学、语用学等多个学科。因为语文的研究对象非常复杂,跨越语言学、文学、语用学甚至教育学、心理学等多个领域,同时因为它是母语,跟我们每个人都息息相关,正是因

为我们对它太熟悉了,反而不能清晰地认识它。语言学也好,文学也好,语用学也罢,似乎都是语文科的归属学科,又似乎不全是。正基于此,有人提出建构"语文学"作为语文科的母学科,但语文学到底是门什么样的学科,该如何建构,到目前为止也还是个未知数。这种模糊的状态导致很多关于语文教学的研究实际上是从哪种视角入手、是在哪个层面进行等问题的认识,都不甚明了,影响到语文教学理论的建构。

最后,就研究方法而言,长期以来,语文教学研究一直没能发展自己的专属方法,自上而下的理论建构多直接移植社会学、教育学等相关方法,用这些学科的思维诠释语文教学;自下而上的理论创新虽顾及了语文教学实践与语文教师的经验,但又容易滑入"我主张""我认为"的观点、意见,而欠缺理论品格。即便有些立足教学实践的理论创生或基于教师经验的总结与提炼颇有价值,但在应试理性的僭越与商业大潮的裹挟下,也多难以实现应有的生命张力,难以持续发展。正是这些学科发展中的先天不足,最终导致语文教学理论陷入"内卷化"困境,多止步于低水平的循环或重复。

(二)语文教学研究的价值指向不明

所谓语文教学研究的价值指向,是指语文教学研究"为了什么"的问题。毋庸讳言,当前语文教学研究的价值指向是含混的,这也直接影响到理论的建构。深入分析会发现,语文教学研究含混的价值指向又可细分为两个方面。

首先,就研究主体而言,专业研究人员的存在是一门学科走向成熟的标志之一,也是该学科顺利成长的重要保障。但是,语文教学研究的主体却比较复杂,既有高师院校语文教学论方向的专业研究人员,又有各地市教育研究院、教研室的教研员,更有队伍庞大的基于实践反思语文教学的一线语文教师,甚或其他社会阶层基于"感受""见解"而来的"语文教学门外谈"。这种复杂的主体构成,表面上促成了语文教学研究的繁荣局面,实际上却大大降低了语文教学研究的专业含量,直接影响到研究工作的价值指向。

其次,为了什么而研究,即研究目的的问题。承前所述,由于语文科的先天不足,研究对象关涉多门学科领域,"研究什么"的问题本就不甚明了。同时,多元主体构成导致研究人员从各自不同的角度切入语文教学研究,采取不同的研究取向而不自知。再加上应试思维模式与市场经济造就的浮躁心态,导致研究人员多采用一种简单化的固化思维处理语文教学问题,研究工作可能指向"语文",可能指向"教学",还有可能指向其他某种外在于语文的功利性东西,使得原本含混的研究指向更加迷离,由此建构的理论体系肤浅、苍白,也就不足为奇了。

(三) 芜杂的话语体系湮没了对话平台

语言是存在的家。在语言学看来,语言是一套符号系统,言语是对符号的运用,运用的结果、即言语作品,就是话语。在哲学、社会学领域,话语已经成为一种研究对象,话语分析则成为一种重要的研究方法。在理想状态上,研究共同体所使用的话语体系应具有一定的统整性,对基本概念与命题的内涵应能达成基本共识,并以此为平台展开对话,唯其如此,才能保证研究工作的顺利开展与理论体系的逻辑自洽。然而,在语文科的研究中,话语体系却显得芜杂、散乱。

首先,从话语存在的角度来看。第一,宏观地说,当前语文教学研究的话语表达起码存在三套体系:一是传统的,如"文与道";二是西方的,如"科学与人文";三是中国现当代的,即传统与西方结合的产物,如"知识与能力",还有诸多基于经验而来的"我主张""我认为"的观点与意见。第二,微观来看,当前语文教学研究话语体系具体又包含"认知过程"和"文本内容"两个维度,所谓"认知过程"即着重描述学习者认知加工层面的话语表达,如"理解""感悟""分析""概括""鉴赏""运用",等等。所谓"文本内容"即重在表述语文学习内容的话语体系,如"主题思想""人物形象""文章技法""表现手法""情感取向"等等。深入分析会发现,"认知"维度的话语表达实际上涵括"感性""理性""移情""运用"等多种不同层面,"内容"维度的话语体系则又来自文学、文章学、语言学、语用学等不同领域。这些来自不同领域、从不同视点立论的话语类型共生于语文教学理论框架之内,造成对话平台的丧失,严重制约了理论功能的发挥与价值的实现。

其次,从话语运用的角度来说。当前语文教学研究话语实践中,甚至缺乏对于一些基本概念的统一认知,或者说清晰的认知。例如,语文课程"文与道""科学与人文"的性质表述,其具体所指到底是什么? 语文课程"知识与能力""过程与方法""情感态度价值观"的目标表述,其真实内涵又是什么? 语文教师教学实践中的高频词汇"理解""感受""体会""鉴赏"等概念,到底指什么? 彼此之间有着怎样的关系? 客观地说,我们对这些话语的认识还是比较模糊的,不同人从不同角度、在不同语境中使用这些概念,其具体所指却是千差万别的。正是由于缺乏对于常见概念真实内涵的清晰认知,导致研究者在研究实践中不分语境、不加鉴别地使用这些概念。例如,"快速默读课文","默读"是"快速"进行的吗? 哪些课文适合"默读"? 哪些课文适合"快速"读? 再如读完课文,要求学生说说"理解和感受","理解"和"感受"是同一个层面的东西吗? 将二者对举合适吗? 等等。

正是由于语文教学研究中芜杂、散乱的话语体系造成的对话平台的丧失,导致所建构的理论难以妥帖、确切、系统地反映语文课程与教学的真实状况,制约了语文教学理论的良性发展,滞于"内卷化"困境的同时,也影响了语文教学实践的开展。

三、语文教学理论"去内卷化"的路径探析

在基础教育课程与教学改革快速推进、课堂实践面临重大转型的背景下,语文教学理论要真正体现内在价值,必须找寻合理路径跳脱"内卷化"的困境。我们认为,寻求新的突破,可从以下方面入手。

(一) 立足"语文"开展基础性研究

作为一门独立的学科,总会存在一些基础性的核心论题需要解决,其他研究都是在这些基础论题构成的基架上展开。基础论题的研究程度直接影响到由此派生出的其他研究工作的开展。

对于语文科的一些基础论题,如上文的分析,目前的研究还十分不够,正是这种原发性欠缺,导致了语文教学理论的芜杂与"内卷化"。我们认为,在语文教学研究中,必须对这些基础性论题进行深

入研究,"正视听"的同时夯实语文教学理论的基架。例如,宏观梳理语文科的发展脉络,李海林认为现代语文教育历经"经义教育""语言专门化""语用"三种取向的发展路径。肇始于五四新文化运动的白话文教学反"经义教育",但不反"总体性教育",为"经义教育"留下了后门;叶圣陶等人既反"经义教育",又反"总体性教育",实现了语文教育的"语言专门化"。并指出,从"经义教育"到"语言专门化"是现代语文教育面临的第一个岔路口,当今正面临第二个岔路口,即从"语言专门化"到"语言功能化"。[13]再如,针对语文科研究对象模糊、研究领域混乱的问题,王荣生区分了这样七个层面的研究:语文活动层面,语文学习层面,语文课程与教学论层面,语文课程具体形态层面,语文教材具体形态层面,语文教学具体形态层面,语文教育评价层面。[7]又如,关于语文课程性质的争论,于源溟主张对于这个问题进行分解,思考"谁的性质""什么性质的性质""为什么要研究性质"等问题,在语文学科性质"工具论""人文论""言语论"等传统观点之外,另立"消解论":语文学科性质问题本质上是一个被虚构出来的学术假问题,争论这个问题,是没有意义的,也没有必要。[14]还有"目标"问题,王荣生区分了"课程目标"与"教学目标",认为课程目标是宏观的,指向国家课程,教学目标是微观的,指向具体课堂与学生。在语文科中,课程目标有三类:内容目标,直接指明学生需要学习的内容;能力目标,表明学生在某方面的学习需要达到的水平;活动目标,指明需要开展什么样的活动实现语文学习。而在这三类目标中,又以能力目标为主,这直接制约了语文课程内容的合理生成与教学过程的有效开展。[15]因为围绕某一目标,不同主体可以创生不同的课程与教学内容,形成不同的课程理解,使得语文课程内容缺乏内在一致性,也使得建基于此的语文教学理论缺乏科学含量。

这些围绕语文科核心论题的基础研究,既有助于研究者明了自己的研究工作是基于哪种视角、在哪个层面进行,是采取哪种取向、指向何种目的开展,促进语文教学研究走向有序化,又能为语文教学实践指明方向,产生引领作用。不管对于理论本身,还是教学实践,类似基础性研究都具有实质性价值,能为语文教学理论建设指明方向。

(二) 立足语文课堂实践生发理论

理论价值的体现要源于实践、立足实践,并最终归于实践。语文教学理论要走出"内卷化"怪圈,必须扎根语文课堂,实现其与教学实践的有效对接。扎根理论是一种社会学领域的质性研究方法。陈向明教授指出,它的主旨是"从经验资料的基础上建立理论",研究者在研究开始之前一般没有理论假设,直接从实际观察入手,从原始资料中归纳出经验概括,然后上升为理论,这是"一种从下往上建立实质理论的方法,即在系统搜集资料的基础上寻找反映社会现象的核心概念,然后通过这些概念之间的联系建立相关的社会理论"。[16]扎根理论明确强调"社会学需求建构理论"目标,弥补了过去质性研究"只偏重经验的传授与技巧的训练"等局限,转而"提供了一套明确有系统的策略,以帮助研究者思考、分析、整理资料,挖掘并建立理论"。[17]

以扎根理论指导语文科的研究,引导语文教学理论源于课堂、立于课堂、归于课堂,会给语文教学理论带来新的启发与新的气象。例如,崔允漷基于理论假设与实证调查,将初中语文课型分解为讲授Ⅰ型、讲授Ⅱ型、互动型和指导型,并用数据说明经过10多年的课程改革,当前初中语文课堂是以讲授Ⅱ型、互动型为主(从时间维度看占81.1%,从行为维度看占85.1%),讲授Ⅰ型与指导型所占比例不到20%。[18]再如"课例研究",在传统教研活动的基础上,王荣生开发了"课例作为研究成果的表达形式""课例作为研究对象""课例作为研究问题的载体""课例作为研修内容或研修方式"等若干类型,主张区分"课例研讨""课例研习"等不同取向的研究实践。[19]这些研究都是基于语文课堂实践,结合观察资料与数据分析,对鲜活、真实的课堂经验进行的理论提升,在具备理论应有品格的同时,能够与教学实践进行较好对接,为语文教学理论的建构指明了方向。

(三) 重构语文教学研究的话语体系

针对当前语文教研缺乏统整对话平台,话语体系参差不齐、模糊难辨等痼疾,我们认为,语文教学理论走出"内卷化"困境的一个重要思路就是对语文科的流行话语进行深度解析,明了相关概念、命题的具体所指，重构话语体系。换句话说，就是搞清楚"谁在说""从哪个层面如此言说""说的究竟是什么"等问题。这种话语分析关注的焦点不在"话语是否为真，以及那些是否被证明为真的话语规则"，而是话语本身，"在不考虑话语本身是否为真的前提下，讨论话语形成的过程，以及各种话语之间的关系、规律"，追问"只是它们而不是别种话语——在某时某地的出现究竟意味着什么"等问题。[20]

　　例如，《义务教育语文课程标准(2011年版)》指出："在通读课文的基础上，理清思路，理解、分析主要内容，体味和推敲重要词语在语言环境中的意义和作用"。[21]作为官方文本，如此表述本来没有问题。但是对于这段表述中的关键概念，研究者和教师在使用时，却不得不思考："通读课文"是如何读？"理解"和"分析"又是什么样的关系？靠"理解和分析"能把握"主要内容"吗？或者说哪些"主要内容"靠"理解和分析"可以把握、哪些不可以？"推敲"和"体会"又是什么？"推敲"什么？"体会什么"？课标还指出："阅读简单的议论文，区分观点与材料(道理、事实、数据、图表等)，发现观点与材料之间的联系，并通过自己的思考，作出判断"，[21]"简单的议论文"是种什么样的议论文？观点与材料之间的"联系"指什么？如何"判断"？"判断"什么？等问题都需深入探讨。再比如，语文教学设计中的"教学目标"，我们知道，教学目标是具体的，针对"这一篇课文""这一班学生"而言，课程目标则是宏观的，针对国家课程而言。很多教学设计中的"教学目标"实际上是"课程目标"，这就架空了"这一篇课文"对于"这一班学生"的教学价值。因此，从某种意义上说，在语文教学设计中，"教学点"比"教学目标"更容易将语文教师的关注重心导向具体课文与具体学生，而不至于同"课程目标"混同。对于这些概念话语，在语文教学研究中，不仅要深度分析它们的真实内涵，而且要力争达成共识，为语文教学研究"共同体"提供统一的对话平台。

　　总体看来，从"语文教学大纲"到"语文课程标准"，从"一纲一本"到"一纲多本"，从貌似繁荣的理论建树到丰富生动的语文课堂，通过对语文教学研究成果所作的深度分析，我们发现，其背后潜隐着的是颇为无奈的"内卷化"实况。不可否认，学术探究是个耕织不辍、螺旋晋升的过程。我们从"内卷化"的视野对语文教学理论进行反思与重构,也只是对语文教学理论大厦的构筑所做的一点尝试而已。

参考文献

[1] 陈坚. 延续的痛苦——身体社会学视域中的农村教育研究[M]. 长春:东北师范大学出版社,2012:43.

[2] 张天雪,黄丹. 农村教育"内卷化"的两种形态及破解路径[J]. 教育发展研究,2014(11):30—35.

[3] 蓝希瑜,杜慧. 赣南畲族传统教育颓变的原因分析[J]. 赣南师范学院学报,2006(4):60—62.

[4] 陈坚. 内卷化:农村教育研究的新视角[J]. 教育发展研究,2008(17):31—34.

[5] 倪文锦. 语文科课程论基础·序[M]. 上海:上海教育出版社,2003:1.

[6] 李海林. 言语教学论[M]. 上海教育出版社,2002:4.

[7] 王荣生. 语文科课程论基础[M]. 上海:上海教育出版社,2003.

[8] 石中英. 知识转型与教育改革[M]. 北京:教育科学出版社,2005:63—65.

[9] 顾德希. 建立实际应用语言的知识系统——张志公先生对语文教学科学化的一个重要设想[J]. 课程·教材·教法,1992(12):19—23.

[10] 甘其勋. 个性化阅读要教学相长[J]. 中学语文教学,2007(11):7—10.

[11] 李宇明. 语文生活与语文教育[J]. 语文建设,2014(2):4—7.

[12] 王荣生. 我国的语文课为什么几乎没有写作教学?[J]. 语文教学通讯,2007(12):4—8.

[13] 李海林. 现代语文教育的定位问题[J]. 课程·教材·教法,2015(5):61—68.

[14] 于源溟. 预成性语文课程基点批判[D]. 湖南师范大学博士学位论文,2004:106.

[15] 王荣生. 语文课程目标:转化与具体化——基于《义务教育语文课程标准(2011年版)》的语文教学建议[J]. 中小学管理,2012(4):13—16.

[16] 陈向明. 扎根理论的思路和方法[J]. 教育研究与实验,1999(4):58—63.

[17] 王锡苓. 质性研究如何建构理论[J]. 兰州大学学报:社会科学版,2004(5):76—80.

[18] 崔允漷,雷浩. 新课程改变了中小学的课型了吗?基于证据的初中课堂教学形态分析[C]. 第十六届两岸三地课程会议论文.

[19] 王荣生,高晶. "课例研究":本土经验及多种形态[J]. 教育发展研究,2012(10):44—49.

［20］于龙.现代语文课程话语考论［D］.上海师范大学博士学位论文,2008:12.

［21］中华人民共和国教育部.义务教育语文课程标准(2011年版)［S］.北京:北京师范大学出版社,2012:15.

（原载于《课程·教材·教法》2015年第10期）

1927～1937年吴县湖匪活动及时空分布研究*

胡勇军**

历史社会地理作为历史人文地理的一个重要的研究分支,引起了学术界的广泛关注。① 学者对历史社会地理的概念内涵、基本内容等方面进行了详细阐述。王振忠认为人群的地理分布,人群的形成、发展及与社会文化环境的关系,人群的特征和心理差别等等,都是历史社会地理研究的重要内容。② 吴宏岐进一步认为历史社会地理学的研究内容应为历史时期的社区研究、不同区域人群兴衰的地理背景、不同区域人群的空间结构及其时空演变规律、不同区域人群的社会行为和历史时期社会问题的空间研究。③ 由此可见,人群的空间分布是历史社会地理研究的重要内容之一。土匪作为历史时期一种特殊的社会人群,其活动空间除了受社会环境的影响之

* **基金项目:**本文获上海地方高校大文科研究生学术新人培育计划(B—6002—13—003073)资助。

** **作者简介:**胡勇军(1986—),男,江苏泰兴人,上海师范大学人文与传播学院博士研究生,主要研究方向为历史人文地理。

① 葛剑雄提出历史人文地理包括狭义的历史人文地理和广义的历史社会地理。蓝勇进一步认为广义的历史社会地理包括历史政治地理、历史经济地理、历史军事地理等方面;狭义的历史人文地理包括历史文教地理、历史宗教地理、历史风俗地理等方面。参见蓝勇:《中国历史地理学》,(北京)高等教育出版社,2002年,第6页。

② 王振忠:《社会史研究与历史社会地理》,《复旦学报》(社会科学版),1997年第1期;《历史社会地理研究刍议》,《中国历史地理论丛》,2005年第4辑。

③ 吴宏岐、王洪瑞:《历史社会地理学的若干理论问题》,《陕西师范大学学报》(哲学社会科学版)2004年第3期。

外,还受到自然地理环境的影响,尤其是太湖地区的盗匪,湖泊往往是他们藏匿之所,错综复杂的河道为他们提供便利的作案条件。

关于江南地区的盗匪现象,最早引起学者注意的是太平天国战争时期的枪匪。20 世纪 50 年代,徐力和曹国祉曾分别撰文予以探讨,此后引起了中日学者的注意。他们对太湖地区枪匪的发生、发展、变化及其与清政府和太平天国间的关系进行了详细的论述。[①]另外,刘平对清末民初太湖土匪的成因、帮派以及活动特点和社会危害等几个方面进行了研究;同友分析了抗战前后太湖土匪的分化和演变的原因。[②] 然而受资料和研究方法的局限,学界大都从社会史的角度对土匪进行研究。本文则借用历史地理学的方法[③],以吴县为研究个案,先对 1927—1937 年《申报》关于吴县地区盗匪报道进行数量统计,利用 Access 软件建立数据库,再对匪患发生的地点进行定位,在此基础上分析湖匪的活动特点以及匪患的时空分布与地方防护和自然地理环境之间的内在关系。

一　资料来源及研究思路

本文的数据资料主要来源于《申报》,同时还参考了苏州地方报纸《苏州明报》和《吴县日报》的报道。南京国民政府成立之后,《申报》在吴县各区设有通讯记者,对当地的匪患进行了详细报道。《苏州明报》和《吴县日报》这类地方报纸也对匪患进行了报道,但因报

---

① 徐力:《太平天国革命时期的枪船》,《中学历史教学》,1957 年第 4 期;曹国祉:《关于"太平天国革命时期的枪船"问题》,《中学历史教学》1957 年第 6 期;《太平天国时期江浙太湖地区"枪船"的性质问题》,《史学月刊》1960 年第 2 期;王卫平:《太平天国时期太湖地区枪匪研究》,《江苏社会科学》2003 年第 1 期;[日]针谷美和子:《太平天国革命期、江浙太湖地域の枪船集团》,《中国史における社会と民众》,汲古书院,1983 年 1 月;《太平天国占领地域の枪船集团——太湖周边地域を中心にして》,《历史学研究》1983 年第 11 号;《太平天国镇压后の枪船集团》,《一桥论丛》,第 89 卷第 1 号。

② 刘平:《清末民初的太湖匪民》,《近代史研究》,1992 年第 1 期;同友:《略论抗战前后太湖土匪的分化和演变》,《江苏教育学院学报》(社会科学版)1995 年第 3 期。

③ 类似的研究有郝红暖对乾隆前期直隶留养局空间分布及其原因的探讨,见郝红暖:《乾隆前期直隶留养局的空间分布特点及原因分析》,《中国历史地理论丛》2010 年第 2 辑。

道时断时续,且大部分信息与《申报》雷同,①为了不影响数据统计的系统性,本文匪患数据主要来自《申报》。当然,由于种种因素,报纸报道的数量可能与实际情况存在一定的偏差,但并不妨碍我们对当时吴县地区匪患的整体认识。

笔者通过对《申报》的检索,共统计出 591 条匪患数据。检索的字段主要以吴县区名和市镇的名称为主,如"木渎"、"光福"、"望亭"、"善人桥"等。因《申报》在对匪患报道的时候,往往会详细记录发生的地点,如"县属木渎金山浜蔡姓家"、"县属西跨塘乡马庄地方"、"胥门外东跨塘附近"等,这一方面便于笔者对匪患的检索,另一方面也便于空间定位。为了防止数据遗漏,另外还检索了"湖匪"、"土匪"、"太湖"、"阳澄湖"、"吴淞江"、"安徽帮"、"浦东帮"、"河南帮"等相关字段。匪患数据的类型主要有三种:一、湖匪已经实施抢劫;二、湖匪并未抢劫,但行踪被发现;三、警匪相遇,并发生交火,其中以第一种为主。在对资料详细阅读后,利用 Access 软件建立数据库,设立了 13 个字段名称(见图 1),基本上囊括了资料中所包含的信息。

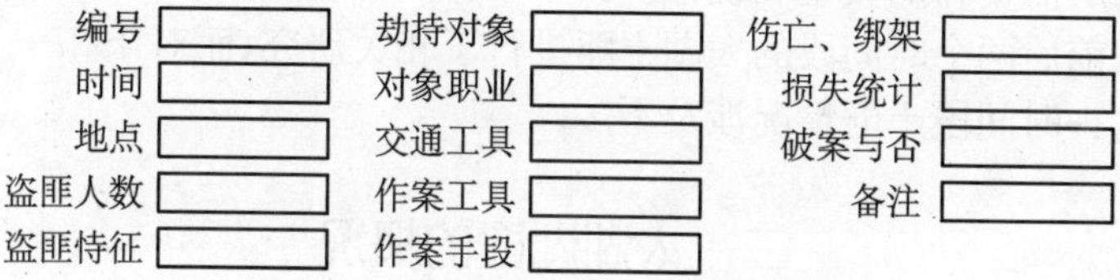

编号		劫持对象		伤亡、绑架	
时间		对象职业		损失统计	
地点		交通工具		破案与否	
盗匪人数		作案工具		备注	
盗匪特征		作案手段			

图 1　1927—1937 年吴县地区匪患数据库

本文研究的空间范围是苏州吴县,1927—1937 年,吴县政区经历了四次变化。南京政府建立之前,吴县原有 7 市 21 乡。1929 年 8 月因市县划界,吴县重新划定地方行政区为 19 个区。1930 年江苏省政府决定撤销苏州市,将苏州市并入吴县,苏州市 7 个市政区划为 3 个城厢区,吴县原有的 19 个区名称不变。1931 年 10 月经省民政厅核准,划善人桥、北山湾等 13 个乡镇为善人桥实验区,列为吴

---

　　① 如《苏州明报》在 1930—1933 年间主要以报道全国性的时政要事为主,很少报道苏州本地新闻。其他年份的匪患报道也多与《申报》相似,有抄袭《申报》之嫌,《吴县日报》也存在这样的情况,因此只作参考之用。

县第二十区。1934 年江苏省政府通过《江苏省各县整理自治区域办法》,以面积、户口、经济状况等为划分标准,重新调整分区和划分乡镇,吴县 20 个乡区并为 12 个区,城厢 3 个区并为一个区。[①] 为了方便起见,本文以 1929 年的行政区划进行空间定位。原因在于,1929 年吴县社会调查处对各区的政治、经济、文化教育、风俗民情、地方治安等方面进行了详细调查,其中对各区的警力配置以及地方保卫力量进行了详细的统计,这就便于探讨匪患的空间分布与地方防护之间的关系。另外,还绘制了各区的详细地图,也便于空间的定位。

本文研究的具体时段为 1927—1937 年,原因有二。其一,这一阶段是《申报》发展的鼎盛时期。从新闻报道的数量来看,相比以前明显增多,尤其是关于江浙两省的新闻报道更是如此;从新闻报道的内容来看,这一时候国内环境相对和平,新闻报道也多关注社会民生等方面。1937 年抗日战争爆发,战争导致交通和通信受阻,《申报》报道的文章大为减少,且多关注国内外时政要事。总的来说,这一阶段《申报》新闻报道较为丰富集中,且具有一定的系统性,便于本文所需资料的收集和统计。其二,刘平和同友分别对清末民初和抗战前后两个时间段的太湖土匪进行了相关研究,而对 1927—1937 年这一时间段土匪情况涉及不多。

二 太湖湖匪的概况

1. 湖匪的定义

民国时期,土匪十分泛滥,据保守估计,到 1930 年中国约有土匪人数 4000 万左右。[②] 当时人们对"土匪"一词泛滥使用,只要是不符合自己意愿的人或行为,都可以"匪"相称。关于土匪的定义,《辞海》中解释说"匪"又叫"强盗,为非作歹的人。""土匪"指以聚众抢劫为生,残害人民,或者窝藏盗匪,坐地分赃的分子。[③] 相较《辞海》而

---

① 苏州市地方志编纂委员会编:《苏州市志(一)》,(南京)江苏人民出版社,1995 年,第 115—117 页。

② 朱新繁:《中国农村经济关系及其特质》,(上海)上海新生命书局,1930 年,第 298 页。

③ 《辞海》,(北京)商务印书馆,1988 年,第 439、1353 页。

言,研究土匪的学者则更强调它的社会属性,英国社会学家埃瑞克·霍布斯鲍姆(Eric Hobsbawm)将土匪活动纳入政治权力史中进行研究,他认为"匪徒指那些拒绝服从的,并踞于权力可控制范围之外的人","他们以自己的方式行使权力,反抗现有的政权"①。贝思飞(Phil Billingsley)继承了霍氏的观念,他注重强调了土匪的"越出法律进行活动"的特点,同时他认为农民的土匪活动也可以简单概括为"数十或数百人结伙的武装抢劫行为"。②蔡少卿认为土匪就是超越法律范围进行活动,而又无明确政治目的,并以抢劫、勒赎为生的人。③

关于太湖地区土匪的称呼,徐力和曹国祉将此种土匪命名为"枪船"。"枪船"约在道光末年兴起,它本身是一种武器战船的名称,同时又是太湖沿岸地区一种赌徒和武装土匪的组织。日本学者针谷美和子将其称为"枪船集团"。王卫平将此股土匪定义为"枪匪",指道光以后活跃于太湖地区以"枪船"为作案工具的水上土匪武装组织。刘平将清末民初太湖地区的土匪称为"太湖匪民",这一称呼强调土匪主要来自失去土地或职业的贫困农民和裁撤的兵卒。同友则将此称呼为"太湖土匪"。

本文结合当时的新闻报道及实际情况,将太湖地区的土匪称为"湖匪"。关于湖匪的称呼,明代就有,据《吴门表隐》记载:"嘉靖二十六年,诛湖匪叶永春等,始至北寺后教场。"④1905 年《申报》报道"浙西帮匪蠢蠢欲动,滋扰商务"。浙江巡抚在回复商部询问的时候,将其称为"湖匪"⑤,这是报纸关于湖匪称谓的最早记载。民国时期,各类报刊及政府公报中关于湖匪的报道比比皆是。曾任江南剿匪司令的钱大钧将江南的盗匪分两种,"在西部的是刀匪,溧阳、溧水、句容、高淳、金坛、镇江各县都有,他们的窟宅大概在茅山附近;在东部的是湖匪,湖匪不仅在太湖,太湖以外澱(淀)山湖、阳城(澄)

① 〔英〕埃瑞克·霍布斯鲍姆:《匪徒》,李立玮、谷小静译,(北京)中国友谊出版社,2001年,第15页。
② 〔英〕贝思飞:《民国时期的土匪》,徐有威等译,(上海)上海人民出版社,2010年,第14页。
③ 蔡少卿:《民国时期的土匪》,(北京)中国人民大学出版社,1993年,第3页。
④ 顾震涛:《吴门表隐》卷1,(南京)江苏古籍出版社,1999年,第3页。
⑤ 《询问湖州匪患来往各电杭州》,《申报》,1905年11月13日,第3版。

湖等以及黄浦江、娄江水道纷歧之处,他们随时出没,为患地方"①。不管是前人所提的"枪船"、"枪匪"、"太湖匪民"、"太湖土匪",还是本文所说的"湖匪",都是指在太湖地区从事武装抢劫、勒赎或杀人的土匪,他们使用的交通工具往往是船,错综复杂的水道系统为他们提供了作案和躲避的条件。

2. 太湖湖匪帮派

太湖面积三万六千顷,横跨江浙两省,地形复杂,湖面岛屿众多,正所谓"支流细河,处处皆盗贼可出可入之地,来去甚易,捕获最难"。② 加上苏州沿太湖区域是江南最富裕地区之一,这更容易滋生湖匪的生长。宋元以来,太湖地区时有盗匪出没。明末长洲人卢径将盗匪问题视为苏州、嘉兴、湖州等府的"三大害"之一,盗匪往往藏匿在嘉兴、湖州两地之间的湖荡中,"每聚至千人,劫掠于吴,而逃庇于浙",故称此害为"吴盗浙窝"。③ 明清鼎革之际,地方社会混乱,盗匪出没无常。顺治二年(1645),"群盗蜂起,太湖沈泮、柏相甫流毒十余年始息"。④ 清代,大量客民迁入浙西杭、嘉、湖三府,其中温州、台州、河南与湖北人主要迁入浙西的北部和西部地区。⑤ 太平天国战争之后,由于政府实行"招垦、招佃"政策,客民迁入人数达到一个高峰。据行龙研究,在江、浙两省交界的各县,到19世纪80年代末,外来客民已超过土著,达数十万人。⑥ 随着外来棚民的大量涌入,潜伏于地方治安中的深层危机很快浮出了水面,长兴山中的棚民垦山,导致浮土随流沉淀于吴江,"遂有游民垦湖,数万佣工,播种而集,割获而散,散无所归,黠者聚而肆劫,且垦湖必先筑园,筑园尤须多人,良莠庞杂,匪类遂起于此时"⑦。这一时期,土匪势力"小且

---

① 钱大钧:《弭平江南匪患的几个办法》,《江苏旬刊》1929年第12/13期,第57页。

② 金友里撰:《太湖备考》卷4《兵防·湖防论说》,(南京)江苏古籍出版社,1998年,第171页。

③ 卢径才:《上史大司马东南权议四策》,见冯梦龙编撰《甲申纪事》卷11,(上海)上海古籍出版社,1993年。

④ 王逋肱:《蚓庵琐语》,见同治《长兴县志》卷31上,清同治修光绪增补本。

⑤ 葛剑雄、曹树基、吴松弟:《简明中国移民史》,(福建)福建人民出版社,1993年,第466页。

⑥ 行龙:《论太平天国革命前后江南地区的人口变动及其影响》,《中国经济史研究》1991年第2期。

⑦ 《太湖剿匪方略》,《湖州月刊》1930年第3卷第7期,第50页。

股单志小",加上清朝设有太湖协镇、太湖水师等专门管理剿匪的机构,湖匪势力并不猖獗。

　　清末民初,伴随着社会剧烈动荡,太湖地区的盗匪蜂拥而起,并形成了不同帮派。据刘平研究,主要有巢湖帮、湖南帮、河南帮、江北帮、浦东帮、湖北帮、湖广帮、山东帮、温台帮、水火帮等,其中又以巢湖帮势力最大,为害之烈。[①] 这一时期"匪股虽多而无结合,虽有枪弹,不足抗官军"。[②] 1924 年江浙战争之后,大量溃兵散勇加入湖匪,不仅使湖匪在枪械弹药方面得到补充,甚至还有专门的组织和训练,太湖匪患变得越来越严重。南京国民政府成立初期,太湖湖匪依旧猖獗,并形成了分别以张兆华(原名张佩尧)、田侉子(原名田仲德)、吴大金、太保阿书(原名徐天雄)为首的江北帮、河南帮、安徽帮和浦东帮四大匪帮团体。这四帮主要横行于江、浙、沪三地,尤其在太湖周边地区异常猖獗,四帮之中以江北帮实力最为雄厚,但在地位和优势方面却不及河南帮。这是因为河南流民很多在太湖种地,他们聚则为匪,散则为民,另外还有大刀会为基础。据不完全统计,四帮匪徒人数不下四五千人,枪械半数,并且各在上海设立秘密机构,在行劫时,各帮之间也多有联合。

　　1928 年 4 月 25 日,江苏和安徽边境的刀匪劫掠溧阳县城,并放走监狱和看守所中的 93 名囚犯和犯罪嫌疑人(28 人已判决,65 人未判决)。1932 年 4 月 3 日,太仓遭到日军飞机轰炸,监狱和看守所中的 179 名囚犯和犯罪嫌疑犯乘机全部逃脱(133 人已判决,46 人未判决)。事发后,两个县政府都公布了逃犯的名单,其中涉及的罪名有窃盗、土匪、强盗、贩卖鸦片、吸食鸦片、伤人致死、妨害公务、拐诱、妨害自由等。本文选取其中关于"土匪"和"强盗"两项罪名进行统计,从籍贯上看,太仓地区的盗匪主要以江北籍人为主,而溧阳地区的盗匪则是河南籍人和江北籍人并存。另外,根据《江苏高等法院公报》公布的 1928 年 7 月至 1929 年 11 月枪决的 149 名盗匪的统

---

　　① 刘平:《清末民初的太湖匪民》,《近代史研究》,1992 年第 1 期。
　　② 《太湖剿匪方略》,《湖州月刊》1930 年第 3 卷第 7 期,第 50 页。

计,其中江北籍 71 人,江南籍 20 人,外省籍 58 人。① 由此可见,南京国民政府时期,太湖周边及西部地区的盗匪主要以江北帮和河南帮为主。

表1　1928、1932 年溧阳和太仓监狱、看守所逃犯的籍贯统计　单位:人

	太仓		溧阳	
	合计	县市分别	合计	县市分别
本地	10	太仓	10	溧阳
江北	25	盐城 7、阜宁 5、海州 4、沭阳 1、涟水 3、赣榆 1、宝应 1、南通 3	15	阜宁 1、海州 6、淮安 1、江北 1、江都 1、泗阳 1、泰州 1、兴化 1、徐州 1、盐城 1
江南	11	嘉定 2、武进 1、吴县 1、常熟 3、崇明 1、金山 1、松江 1、南京 1	1	句容 1
外省	8	河南 2、湖北 2、山东 2、浙江 1、安徽 1	31	安徽 1、河南 25、湖北 1、山东 2、安徽 1、直隶 1

资料来源:《通缉溧阳被刀匪纵出要犯》,《江苏省政府公报》,1928 年第 37 期,第 40—47 页;《通缉太仓监所已未决逃犯》,《江苏省政府公报》,1932 年第 1026 期,第 5—13 页。

　　从年龄结构上来看,太仓脱逃的囚犯(嫌疑人)中,10—20 岁 1 人,21—30 岁 25 人,31—40 岁 16 人,41—50 岁 9 人,51—60 岁 3 人。1928 年 7 月至 1929 年 11 月枪决的盗匪中,10—20 岁 2 人,21—30 岁 69 人,31—40 岁 61 人,41—50 岁 11 人,51—60 岁 4 人,61—70 岁 2 人。由此可见,从事抢劫活动的盗匪主要以 20—40 岁的青壮年为主。

　　3. 湖匪作案的特点

　　从匪患数据的统计来看,湖匪作案的时间往往选择在晚上八点

----

　　① 《民国十七年七月分依惩治盗匪暂行条例案件执行人犯一览表》,《江苏高等法院公报》1928 年第 1 期,第 181—182 页;《民国十七年九月分至十一月分依惩治盗匪暂行条例案件执行人犯一览表》,《江苏高等法院公报》1929 年第 1 期,第 183—185 页;《民国十七年十二月份依惩治盗匪暂行条例案件执行人犯一览表》,《江苏高等法院公报》1929 年第 10 期,第 152—155 页;《民国十八年一月份至七月份依惩治盗匪暂行条例案件执行人犯一览表》,《江苏高等法院公报》1929 年第 12 期,第 163—170 页;《民国十八年八月份至十一月份依惩治盗匪暂行条例案件执行人犯一览表》,《江苏高等法院公报》1930 年第 3 期,第 118—124 页。

到凌晨五点的这段时间里,这时人们都已经熟睡,警惕性降低,难以被发现。抢劫的对象包括农民、商铺、船只、业户、基础干部、公安局、商团、保卫团及其他,其中主要以农民为主。根据统计,抢劫农民占据明确记载湖匪抢劫对象数据(247件)中的57%(报道中有些明确没有记录抢劫对象的职业,根据其他一些材料的佐证,很多为农民),这主要是因为乡村中保卫力量比较薄弱,而又不乏家道小康之户。湖匪抢劫之后,往往鸣枪而去,遭到抵抗的非常少,而且破案率很低。这种情况也跟抢劫的地点非常吻合,根据对抢劫地点的统计,其中544件发生在乡村,47件发生在市镇之中。

表2　湖匪抢劫对象统计　单位:件

对象	农民	商铺	船只	业户	基础干部	公安局	商团	保卫团	其他
数量	141	48	16	13	11	8	2	2	6

注:基层干部主要包括甲长、保长、村长、乡长、图董;业户包括船户、渔户、机户、窑户等。其他包括:商人3件、公司职员1件、外科医生1件、寺庙1件。

相对乡村来说,市镇的防护力量较强,一些市镇上驻有水上公安队、警察队、公安分局、保卫团、商团等防护机构,小股的湖匪一般不敢抢劫。尽管如此,一些市镇还是经常遭到大股湖匪的洗劫,人数都在50人以上,甚至达到200—300人,武器装备也比较精良。与乡村不同,抢劫市镇的时间往往选择商铺营业的白天。湖匪抵镇后首先是剪断长途电话线,防止镇上公安分局与县公安取得联系,请求增援。然后包围公安分局、保卫团、商团,一方面打击抵抗力量,便于洗劫商铺,另一方面抢走枪械,增加自身的武装力量。最后就是抢劫镇上商铺,掳走人质,勒索钱财①。由于市镇集聚了众多商铺,因此损失要比农村严重很多,有时候甚至高达数十万元。1928年12月19日,湖匪五十余人洗劫斜塘镇28家商铺,损失甚巨。1929年4月20日,斜塘镇上的警察队、公安分局、商团、建设局以及

---

① 从伤亡和绑架的情况来看,在有记录的260件数据中,其中165件都涉及绑架,绑架往往成为湖匪勒索金钱的重要手段。

数十家商铺再次遭劫,损失数万元。① 1929 年元旦,湖匪五十余人先将驻扎在光福镇上的水上公安分队包围,击毙门岗卫士,抢走快抢 12 支、子弹 2 箱,随后上街搜劫商铺 35 家,全镇损失数万元。② 1930 年 12 月 11 日,湖匪五六十人携带机关枪 2 架,抢劫浒墅关通安桥镇。登岸后湖匪先将长途电话线剪断,然后包围保卫团,抢走七九步枪 4 支、林明敦步枪 10 支,同时抢走商团毛瑟枪十余支,镇上商铺全遭搜劫,损失数千元。③

盗匪有职业性与非职业性两种类型。太湖湖匪的构成极为复杂,有农民、商贩、盐贩、流民、叛军以及无业游民等等,如河南帮大都在湖边垦荒种田为名,安徽帮与浦东帮聚而为匪,散则贩卖私盐,随集随散。④ 据统计,在 591 件匪患中,具体记载作案人数的案件有 402 件,其中人数在 1—10 人有 105 件(1—3 人为 15 件,4—6 人为 36 件,7—9 人为 54 件);10 人以上的有 297 件,占到整个案件的 70％以上。湖匪抢劫不同于乡村中盗贼小偷小摸活动,单人作案的比率很小,1—3 人仅有 15 件,4—6 人为 36 件,大都集中在 10 人以上,甚至有百人以上的规模,具有一定的组织性和职业性。另外,在

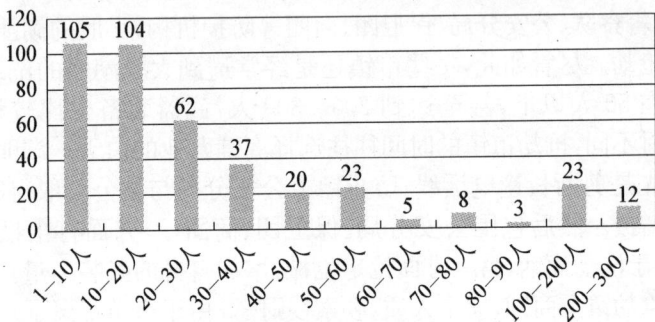

图 2   吴县地区湖匪作案人数统计(1927—1937)   单位:件

---

① 《斜塘乡被劫二十八家》,《申报》,1928 年 12 月 21 日,第 9 版;《苏属车坊斜塘两巨劫案》,《申报》,1929 年 4 月 21 日,第 11 版。

② 《元旦日帮匪洗劫光福镇》,《申报》,1929 年 1 月 4 日,第 12 版。

③ 《湖匪洗劫通安桥镇详情》,《申报》,1930 年 12 月 12 日,第 9 版。

④ 《江浙防剿太湖土匪计划书》,《兴华》1928 年第 25 卷第 48 期,第 44 页。

177 件记载具体作案工具的案件中,明确记录持有枪械者 141 件①,占 80%,其他有短刀、铁尺、铁棒等工具,这也说明了吴县地区湖匪以职业性盗匪为主。

三　匪患的时间分布

1. 年份分布

关于南京国民政府时期土匪活动的概况,学界指出呈现出衰落的态势,然而未有定量的统计,缺乏具体的论证。② 本文通过对 591 件案件分析,以图直观地呈现出这一阶段湖匪衰落的总体态势。由图 3 可知,1927—1937 年吴县地区的匪患分布总体呈现波浪形的特征。南京政府建立初期的 1927—1931 年是湖匪最为猖獗的时候,1932 年匪患程度明显下降,其后出现两次反弹,但始终没有初期那样严重。这一发展轨迹并非是偶尔的,北洋军阀时期,地方治安混乱,导致江南地区盗匪横生。南京国民政府建立初期,地方残留大

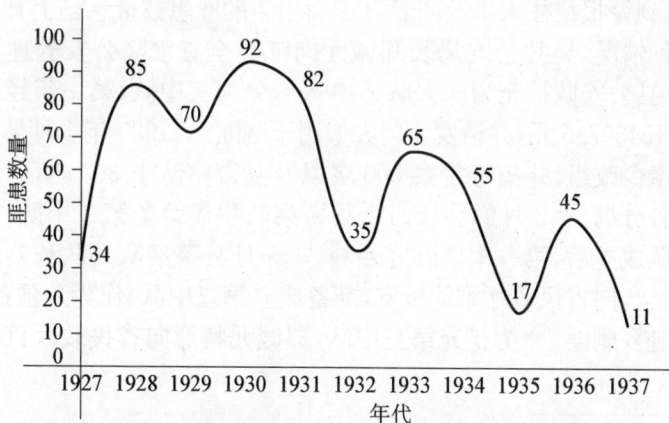

图3　吴县地区太湖匪患年份分布(1927 年—1937)③单位:件

---

① 枪械中主要有盒子炮、快枪、手枪、马枪,甚至还有机关枪之类的枪械。

② 邵雍:《中国近代绿林史》,(福州)福建人民出版社,2004 年。

③ 由于受《申报》报道的影响,1927 年的数据可能出现偏差;另外受抗日战争的影响,1937 年《申报》的报道重点开始转向国内外时政要事,关于湖匪报道相较以前数量减少,可能跟当时的实际情况存在一定的偏差。

量乱军,湖匪依旧猖獗。为了维护地方治安,1928—1931 年吴县公安局不断扩充警力,增强乡村防护体系,同时南京国民政府先后在苏州设立江南剿匪司令部和太湖剿匪总指挥部,对湖匪进行围剿,匪患程度有所减轻。

南京国民政府建立之初就深感土匪是一个严重的社会问题,并开始加大剿匪力度。1927 年裁撤水上警察厅,设立江苏省水陆公安管理处,统一管理全省水陆公安。① 江苏原来的五个水警区由公安管理处直接管辖,并参照水警原定编制,设水上公安队,分为一所七区。苏州为第二区,下辖吴县十一队、昆山十二队、常熟十三队、吴江十四队、平望十五队。②

1928 年内政部公布了《各级公安局编制大纲》,规定在县一级设置警察局,各省省会、特别市设公安局。公安局在管辖范围内依自治区划分为若干区,每区设公安分局一所。公安分局在管辖区内分设警察分驻所,按照居民每千人以上二千人以下划为一巡逻区,设置警察巡逻。③ 当时吴县公安局仅有三百余名警员,分配于 27 市乡,遇到警报往往来不及调遣,④因而当年的匪患数量急剧上升。鉴于此种情况,吴县公安局长郑诚元向江苏全省水陆公安管理处呈请,将县公安队扩充为一大队(540 人),分为三中队,第一年经费预算为 154507.5 元,并请发 4 门大炮用于剿匪。⑤ 1929 年 1 月吴县公安局奉令改组,并招考警察 500 名以及县警察队士 300 名,录取后派往各分局。⑥ 2 月彭县长命令县警察队积极筹备第二中队,待第二中队成立后,第一中队驻守乡村。⑦ 9 月县警察队大队长刘英请求彭县长向省民政厅添购枪支,准备成立第三中队,作为总预备队,专门赴乡剿匪。⑧ 为扩充第三中队,郑诚元特意向省民政厅订购步

① 《裁撤苏州水上警察厅》,《江苏省政府公报》1927 年第 15 期,第 33 页。
② 《苏省水陆公安管理处条例》,《申报》,1927 年 11 月 25 日,第 9 版。
③ 王云五:《中华民国现行法规大全》,(上海)商务印书馆,1935 年,第 372 页。
④ 吴县县政府编辑处:《吴县县政公报》,1929 年第 3 期,第 4 页。
⑤ 《各乡防盗计划》,《申报》,1928 年 6 月 24 日,第 10 版。
⑥ 《公安局扩充招考警士》,《申报》,1929 年 1 月 10 日,第 10 版。
⑦ 《县警察之大扩充》,《苏州明报》,1929 年 2 月 14 日,第 3 版。
⑧ 《县警队再须扩充》,《苏州明报》,1929 年 7 月 9 日,第 3 版。

枪 100 支,手提机关枪 13 架,子弹 5 万发。①

　　基层警力缺乏是南京国民政府时期警政体系中薄弱的一环。郝遇林认为:"中国现有之警察,仅都市警察略具规模,对于乡村警察甚少注意及之"。② 1929 年 4 月 27 日,彭县长以"各乡湖匪猖獗,警力单薄"为由,电呈省民政厅请求补充乡警 260 人,与吴县原有第一、二两中队一起改编为十队,其中七队分驻各乡,三队组成水上游巡队,"常川游弋各乡,一遇匪警,则立即集合防剿"。③ 9 月为了防止南通海盗流窜入境,郑诚元将县城中警队分驻各乡要冲之处,第一中队第一分队驻防渡村,第二分队驻防车坊,第三分队留守队部。第二中队第一分队驻防泖泾,第二分队驻防三山,第三分队暂留队部。④ 同时为了弥补乡村警力的不足,县公安局拟招募便衣警察三千人,由各区区长保荐,"专任密报盗匪行动"。⑤ 在短短的一年中,吴县公安局扩充成三个中队,并增加了乡村警力,保卫力量增强。1936 年内政部警官高等学校校长李士珍曾对江苏省警力做了一个推算,江苏省人口为 3646 万余人,依每千人设警察一名之理想标准计算,则须有警察 34600 余名,但该省原有员警总数,仅有 19900 余名,缺额 16400 余名,缺额 47%。⑥ 1929 年吴县全境共有 629695 人,警员 496 人,⑦依每千人设警察一名的理想标准计算,缺额约 21%,如果加上水上公安,已经超过理想标准。

　　除了扩充警察之外,1928 年南京政府以"苏省大江南北匪势猖獗,民难安枕",任命原淞沪警备司令、第三师长钱大钧为江南剿匪司令,司令部驻扎苏州。⑧ 整个江南地区被划分为三个驻防区域,并制定分期防剿办法,第一期为准备期,第二期为实行期。⑨ 1929 年 1

① 《郑诚元领导枪械》,《苏州明报》,1929 年 9 月 18 日,第 3 版。
② 郝遇林:《模范乡村警察制度》,(北京)独立出版社,1948 年,第 39 页。
③ 《扩充乡警之请示》,《申报》,1929 年 4 月 28 日,第 11 版。
④ 《县警队分驻各乡》,《苏州明报》,1929 年 9 月 11 日,第 3 版。
⑤ 《县公安局拟招募便衣警察三千名》,《苏州明报》,1929 年 10 月 20 日,第 2 版。
⑥ 中国第二历史档案馆:《李士珍拟改进中国警政建议计划三种》,《民国档案》,2004 年第 1 期。
⑦ 乔增祥编:《吴县》,吴县县政府社会调查处 1930 年编印,南京图书馆藏。
⑧ 《国府会议纪要》,《申报》,1928 年 9 月 8 日,第 4 版。
⑨ 《江浙防剿太湖土匪计划书》,《兴华》1928 年第 25 卷第 48 期,第 44 页。

月江南剿匪司令部奉令结束，未完成的剿匪、清乡等事务移归省政府办理。[①] 1930 年 2 月海陆空军总司令部以"太湖流域为江浙两省繁富之区，迭被湖匪滋扰"，为了肃清土匪，任命第五师十三旅旅长胡祖玉为太湖剿匪总指挥，另调四十五师及第六师各团协助剿匪。剿匪司令部在吴兴、无锡两县各驻一旅部，此外对滨湖的宜兴、吴江、吴县派精兵分道进攻。[②]

军、警密切配合，多次对安徽帮、海州帮、浦东帮、河南帮进行围剿，并抓捕匪首吴大金、张兆华、田仲德、太保阿书等人。部分匪众溃散后转移到其他地方，如巢湖帮钟世慕部回安徽郎溪；海州帮毛子龙部携械窜往外海，毛本人则匿上海；[③]安徽帮一部窜入安徽广德一带。[④] 尽管如此，零碎的小股湖匪依然存在，如浦东帮太保阿书余孽王八妹横行于苏浙交界之处，犯案累累；[⑤]海州帮仲兆奎聚众 160 人，船 18 艘，枪械俱全。[⑥] 据 1932 年《吴县县政公报》披露，吴县公安局自 1930 年以来剿匪 17 次，破获盗案 61 件，枪决匪首 14 人，捕获各类盗犯 142 人，救回肉票 23 人，夺获步枪 34 支，手枪 6 支。[⑦]由于剿匪力度不够以及湖匪活动的流动性特点，吴县的匪患始终难以完全消除。

2. 季节性变化

盗匪活动与季节有一定的关联性，贝思飞在研究民国土匪时指出，在华北，农活一般集中在 8 月底到 10 月底的秋季，还有就是 2 月底到 3 月间的早春季节以及 5 月到 6 月底的夏季，"在这段时间内，由于农活繁忙，所以土匪现象极少发生"，而其他季节，特别是 11 月到次年的 2 月间，由于无事可做，所以土匪活动就特别强烈，而 6 月底到 8 月中旬的这段时间，由于农活相对较少，田野间又有大量的高粱等高

---

① 《江南剿匪司令部奉令撤消》，《申报》，1929 年 1 月 26 日，第 11 版。

② 《太湖剿匪计划已确定》，《申报》，1930 年 2 月 13 日，第 10 版。

③ 《匪众散帮消息》，《申报》，1930 年 2 月 17 日，第 9 版。

④ 《四帮湖匪消灭其三》，《申报》，1930 年 4 月 24 日，第 15 版。

⑤ 《女匪王八妹》，《吴县日报》，1933 年 7 月 1 日，第 3 版。

⑥ 《王武升出险详志》，《申报》，1930 年 8 月 7 日，第 8 版。

⑦ 吴县县政府编辑处：《吴县县政公报》，1932 年第 2 期。

秆作物可以做掩护,所以此时也是一个土匪活动的高峰期。① 美国学者安乐博(Robert J. Antony)在研究 19 世纪广东盗匪时也指出,盗匪在农作淡季的农历 11 月和 12 月时最为猖獗,在农忙的夏季(农历 5 月至 7 月)则大为减少。② 王加华认为,在民国时期的江南,盗匪活动的发生频率也与此地的农事周期紧密相关,即农闲时期多,农忙时期少。③ 以上三位学者都是从农事周期的角度探讨盗匪活动与季节的关联性,下文将用图直观地表现吴县地区匪患发生的月份情况,并说明湖匪活动除了与农事有关外,还受到其他因素的影响。

根据图 4 可知,吴县地区的匪患主要集中在 2—3 月和 9—10 月两个时间段,4—8 月匪患逐渐减少,11 月到次年的 1 月匪患也相对减轻,这跟贝思飞对华化土匪研究的结果完全相反,与安乐博对华南盗匪的研究也存在差异性。江南地区,春末和夏末往往是青黄不接的季节,匪患数量有明显的下降。9 月农忙新谷登场之际,这时湖匪开始蠢蠢欲动。正如当时《苏州明报》所说:"太湖中帮匪,因

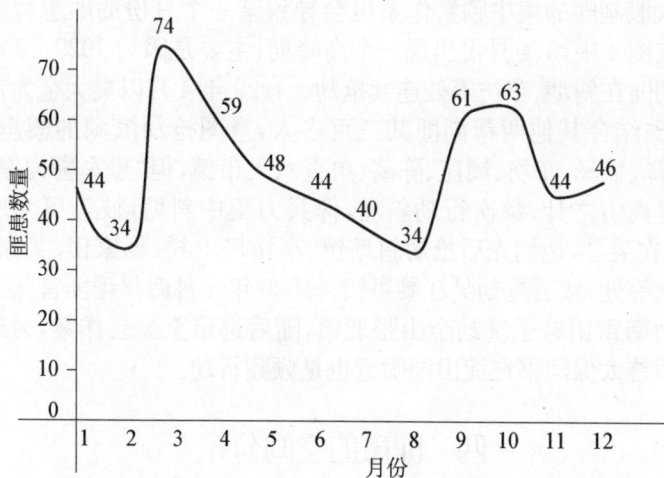

图 4　吴县地区太湖匪患月份分布(1927—1937)　单位:件

---

① ［英］贝思飞:《民国时期的土匪》,徐有威、李俊杰等译,(上海)上海人民出版社,1992 年,第 26—27 页。

② ［美］安乐博:《盗匪的社会经济根源:十九世纪早期广东省之研究》,载叶显恩主编《清代区域社会经济研究》,(北京)中华书局,1992 年,第 539 页。

③ 王加华:《近代江南地区的农事节律与乡村生活周期》,复旦大学 2005 年博士论文。

秋风已起,又将结帮纠股,在四乡滋扰。"①

除了受季节和农事影响之外,其他因素也影响着盗匪的活动。盗匪有职业性与非职业性两种类型,非职业性盗匪与农事节奏的关系更为密切,而职业性盗匪与季节性关系就不那么明显。根据上文的分析,吴县地区的湖匪具有一定的组织性和职业性,因此他们抢掠活动并非集中于农闲的季节,而是四季都有分布。

每年的 11 月到次年的 2 月份,农事最为清闲,应该是一年之中盗匪活动最为剧烈的时期,但在上图中表现得并不明显,这是因为湖匪的活动还受到地方冬防的影响。为了防范湖匪骚扰,每年 10 月至次年 2 月,吴县县政府都会组织冬防,水上公安队、公安局、水巡组、保卫团和商团等各种防卫力量都会积极参与。因而这段时期地方防护较其他时间更为严备,盗匪有所顾忌,活动频率因此有所降低。而在冬防前、后的 9 月和 3 月,地方防护相对松懈,湖匪有机可乘,匪患相对严重。

大股湖匪的集中频繁作案也会导致某一个月份的匪患程度加重。在图 4 中,3、4 月份出现一个高峰期,主要是因为 1929、1930 年大股湖匪在斜塘、车坊等处连续抢劫。1929 年 4 月以吴大金为首的安徽帮,结合其他两帮湖匪共三百多人,意图抢劫滨湖的黎里、同里、震泽、盛泽、车坊、周庄、陈墓、甪直八大市镇,但"恐军警力厚,故用调虎离山之计,数次行劫斜塘,俾兵力集中斜塘,彼等可为所欲为。② 在吴县,他们先后抢劫斜塘镇、车坊塔上村、杨家田、吴家湾、长家浜等处,然后抢劫吴江黎里镇。1930 年 4 月海州帮匪首张兆华勾结河南帮田侉子洗劫金山张堰镇,随后逃窜至吴县作案,另外浦东帮匪首太保阿书在淀山湖附近也是频频行劫。③

四 匪患的空间分布

1. 与自然环境的关系

太湖湖匪使用的交通工具往往是船,据统计,明确记载乘船的

---

① 《秋风起矣! 严防湖匪与共党》,《苏州明报》,1929 年 10 月 21 日,第 3 版。
② 《周庄获匪之供词》,《申报》,1929 年 4 月 29 日,第 9 版。
③ 《阳澄湖匪已击退》,《申报》,1930 年 4 月 9 日,第 11 版。

数据有 185 件(1—10 艘 149 件,10—20 艘 15 件,20—30 艘 4 件,30—40 艘 4 件,40—50 艘 1 件,50—60 艘 1 件,80—90 艘 1 件,数量不详者 10 件)。吴县地处太湖之滨,境内湖泊众多,河道纵横,港汊密布,错综复杂的水道系统为他们提供了作案和躲避的条件。1928 年江南剿匪司令部对太湖及周边水利环境进行调查,"太湖与内地河道息息相通,通苏州内地各河者,有茅岐口、庙桥港、胥口、光福等处……而西山、东山突峙湖中,港湾曲折,通湖之东西,他如吴县所属之金鸡湖、独墅湖、吴淞江、黄天荡、尹山湖、白蚬湖、九里湖,吴昆交界之洋(阳)澄湖……均可以通至太湖,是以匪船可以出没其间,随地可以逃窜。"①根据图 5 可知,匪患主要分布在横泾、斜塘、周庄、东山、湘城等几个区,这主要跟吴县的地理自然环境有极大的关联。

表 3　吴县各区匪患数量统计表(1927—1937)　单位:件

各区	数量	各区	数量	各区	数量	各区	数量
浒墅	30	陆墓	36	周庄	59	蠡墅	24
木渎	31	湘城	42	黄埭	19	东山	38
光福	28	北桥	8	斜塘	68	香山	9
望亭	15	唯亭	26	郭巷	26	西山	18
横泾	82	甪直	22	五潨泾	10	总计	591

横泾全区滨临太湖,港汊纷岐,尤其是与吴江县之间的水域多为滩涂之地,农民多在此围田种茭,因而芦苇、荡草丛生,一望无垠,"每当青纱帐起,辄为盗匪匿迹之渊薮"②。为了消除隐患,横泾和东山乡董曾多次呈请县政府下令铲除,但因地方豪强"罔顾民害,仗势横行",以致"无妥善办法可收实效"。另外,吴县和吴江两县,"犬牙相错,办法不能一致"。③ 因此,横泾与吴江之间的水域经常受到湖匪骚扰,海州帮首毛子龙部就曾盘踞在沿太湖的茅圻港一带。另外,横泾南部"自东山交界摆渡口起,讫渡村、黄垆湖桥一带,客民草

①　《江浙防剿太湖土匪计划书》,《兴华》1928 年第 25 卷第 48 期,第 44 页。
②　《太湖股匪》,《青复月刊》第 4 卷第 1 期,第 13 页。
③　《滨湖各区长会拟铲除太湖荡草办法》,《苏州明报》,1934 年 11 月 1 日,第 6 版。

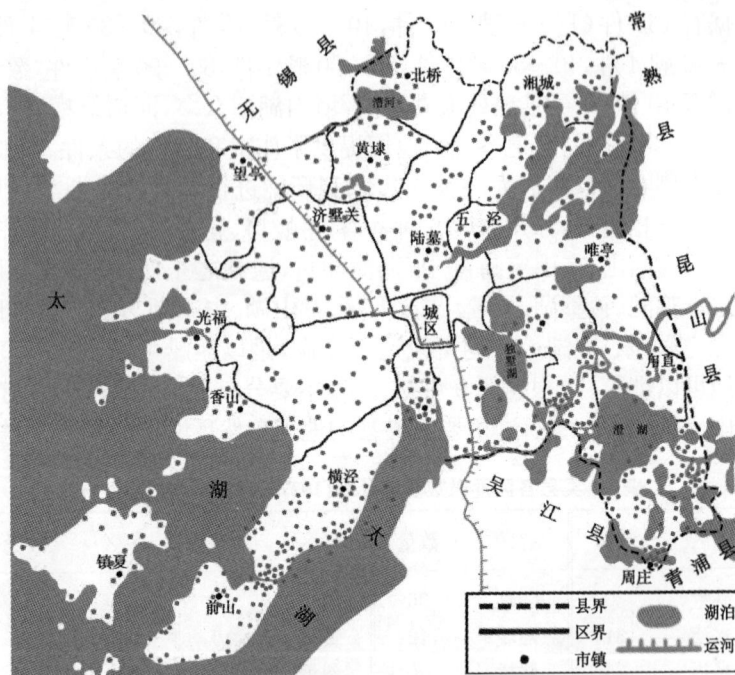

图 5　吴县地区太湖匪患点状分布图(1927—1937)

说明:1.底图来源乔曾祥编:《吴县》,吴县县政府社会调查处 1930 年,南京图书馆藏。原书中所载地图为每一个区的,此图是笔者将吴县 19 个区合拼而成。2.图中每一个点代表一件匪患。

棚林立,千百成群",①这些客民或入湖为匪,或为匪之向导,因而成为横泾匪患另一频发带。

斜塘区匪患主要集中在斜塘镇周围以及吴淞江流域。斜塘镇位于金鸡湖、独墅湖、黄天荡三湖交界之处,这一地区往往是湖匪时常出没地带,匪患相对较为严重。东南部为吴淞江流经之处,而吴淞江是太湖湖匪往来于苏沪之间的必经之路,青浦、金山地区的土匪经常经此水道来苏抢劫。此外,吴淞江南部与吴江、周庄交界之处湖泊众多,便于湖匪的流窜。因此斜塘南部吴淞江流经之地盗匪横生,尤其是濒临吴淞江的车坊镇,成为吴县匪患较为严重的市镇

———————————

① 《吴县俞武功条陈治匪四则》,《江苏省政府公报》1928 年第 37 期,第 33 页。

之一。

　　周庄区位于吴县、吴江、青浦三县交界之处,地处澄湖、长白荡、太史田荡、淀山湖、白蚬江之间,有岛中之镇之称。淀山湖是浦东帮湖匪经常出没的地区,沿淀山湖可以直接进入周庄,这也是湖匪往来苏沪之间的主要河道之一。另外,湖匪也可以通过吴淞江支流可以进入澄湖,抢劫区内的陈墓镇,这是湖匪往来沪苏的另一通道。

　　湘城区因濒临阳澄湖,而成为匪患较为严重之区。海州帮曾在阳澄湖中的阳澄村设立总机构(老巢),湖匪在此处精密布置,每一港隘险要处驻守匪船五六艘,有小网船、农船、快船,以备万一之需。在食物供给方面,专门预备两艘快船用来运输粮食,鱼肉、菜疏、烟酒、油火等物品都到附近的肖泾镇购买,因而"食料不虞缺乏"。[1] 周边的湘城、陆墓、泖泾、五㵎泾、太平桥等镇时常受到此股湖匪的骚扰。此外,海州帮还在阳澄湖东北部、与昆山巴城区相连的杨三太庙设立办事处,此处三面环湖,背后港汊纷岐,草木丛林,地势颇为险恶,便于藏匿。他们聚集匪船三十余艘,匪众二百余人,每隔二三日登岸操练一次。

　　太湖之中孤山众多,"青苍矗立者,为山七十有二,马迹、东西两洞庭,其最大者也。以西北之小山十有四,为马迹之从;以中央之小山四十有一,为西洞庭之从;以东南之小山十有七,为东洞庭之从"[2]。这些孤山往往容易成为湖匪流窜和藏匿之处,东、西两山为众山最大者,地处太湖之中,四面环湖,时常受到湖匪的骚扰。三山"在东山之西,三峰连接",清代此处"居民五百余家,多服贾"。[3] 民国时期,成为太湖湖匪聚集的老巢,为了抵御湖匪的骚扰劫掠,当地贤达和乡绅出面,组织成立三山保卫团。1937 年 4 月,叶圣陶曾与友人登岛游玩,后来他在《记游洞庭西山》一文写道:"据说山上很有些家底殷实的人家,他们备有枪械自卫,子弹埋在岸边的芦苇丛

　　① 《大帮湖匪啸聚澄湖畔》,《申报》,1930 年 2 月 28 日,第 10 版。
　　② 金友里撰:《太湖备考》卷 4《兵防·湖防论说》,(南京)江苏古籍出版社,1998 年,第172 页。
　　③ 金友里撰:《太湖备考》卷 5《湖中山》,(南京)江苏古籍出版社,1998 年,第 197 页。

中,临时取用,只有他们自己有数。"①独山"在县治西南十八里,锡山山脉西来,至是中断……盗艘劫掠,必从此走太湖,避追捕"②。西山北部数里的横山也时有湖匪出没,1928 年 2 月,盘踞在安吉西北龙山的匪首金老三将吴兴练市镇富户邱宏成和重兆镇富商陈云轩及家属五人,绑架至横山,索价勒索。③ 4 月,吴兴北门外万盛米行店主孙祥清儿子回西山完婚,在太湖中被湖匪掳走,家属随即赴横山用二千元将其赎回。④

2. 与地方防护的关系

除了与自然地理环境有关之外,匪患的分布还跟各区防护力量有一定关联。吴县地方防护力量主要包括水上公安队、县警察以及商团、保卫团等地方基础组织。由表 4 可知,吴县各区大都设有公安分局,在基层乡村设有守望所,但因地理位置的关系,各地区的警员配置存在较大的差异。如濒临太湖的商业重镇横泾、木渎、东山和光福警员相对较多,且驻扎了水上公安队,而西北地区的湘城、黄埭以及商业欠发达的郭巷、香山等镇警员相对较少。另外,一些商业较发达的市镇,通过自身的筹备和建设,商团和保卫团力量相对较强,如望亭、横泾、甪直、蠡墅。

表 4　1929 年吴县各区警力与地方保卫人数统计　单位:人

区名	警察力量				地方保卫力量			总计
	水上公安	县公安	缉私队	合计	商团	保卫团	合计	
蠡墅	0	23	0	23	12	33	45	68
木渎	178	43	0	221	0	31	31	252
光福	112	25	0	137	0	30	30	167
望亭	7	17	0	24	92	81	173	197
横泾	100	100	0	200	49	51	100	300

① 叶圣陶:《记游洞庭西山》,《越风》,1936 年第 13 期。

② 金友里撰:《太湖备考》卷 4《兵防·湖防论说》,(南京)江苏古籍出版社,1998 年,第 171 页。

③《重兆陈姓发生绑架案》,《申报》,1928 年 2 月 27 日,第 10 版;《邱宏成函家取赎》,《申报》,1928 年 3 月 17 日,第 10 版。

④《肉票脱险志》,《申报》,1928 年 5 月 4 日,第 10 版。

续　表

区名	警察力量				地方保卫力量			总计
	水上公安	县公安	缉私队	合计	商团	保卫团	合计	
陆墓	0	43	0	43	40	26	66	109
湘城	0	0	0	0	0	15	15	15
北桥	0	8	0	8	0	16	16	24
唯亭	0	14	0	14	32	49	81	95
甪直	0	33	47	80	110	11	121	201
周庄	0	22	0	22	0	24	24	46
黄埭	0	0	0	0	0	18	18	18
斜塘	0	27	0	27	37	13	50	77
郭巷	51	0	0	51	0	46	46	97
五潨泾	0	50	0	50	0	34	34	84
蠡墅	0	24	0	24	69	50	119	143
东山	202	35	0	237	0	106	106	343
香山	0	8	0	8	0	0	0	8
西山	62	24	0	86	0	0	0	86
总计	712	496	47	1255	441	634	1075	2330

资料来源:乔增祥编:《吴县》,第八编《公安》,吴县县政府社会调查处,1930 年,南京图书馆藏。

注:驻光福西华镇寺桥水上省公安队七队三分队警员人数未详,根据同驻光福镇七队一分队警员 62 名,可以估算出七队三分队警员人数在 50 名左右。驻横泾水上省公安游击队、水上省公安队七队二分队、吴县警察二中队三分队、吴县警察三中队三分队人数未详,均遵照规程,根据其他分队情况,估算总人数在 200 名左右。蠡墅保卫团团丁人数未详,根据每月饷银 180 元,估算出团丁 50 人左右。

　　濒临太湖地区尽管通过驻扎水上公安队,增加警员的配置以及加强商团和保卫团的建设多种等方式来增强地方防护力量,但是从图 5 中可以看出,匪患相对其他地区依然较为严重,这主要是因为地理位置过于突出。东山和西山孤悬太湖之中、横泾三面濒湖,难免时常受到湖匪的骚扰。木渎和蠡墅临湖,都为要冲之所,这些地区往往是湖匪上岸行劫或者逃亡流窜的必经之途。清人金友里曾指出吴县境内出入太湖的六处重要关隘,"曰胥口,曰石湖,曰五龙

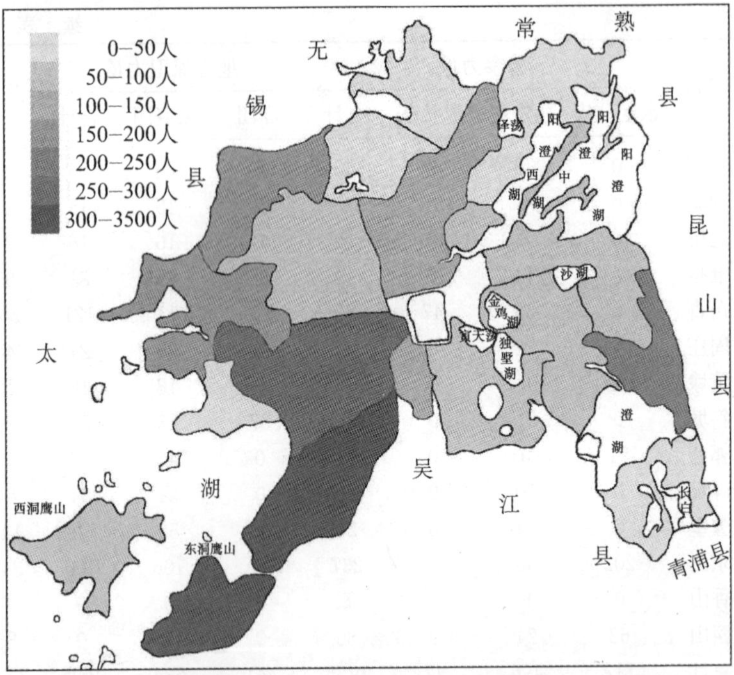

图6 1929年吴县地区保卫力量分布图

桥,曰洞庭东山,曰洞庭西山,其一则内地只枫桥也",①以上六处地
方正好分别位于木渎、蠡墅、东山、西山四区。另外,这些地区平常
出现警队的换防和抽调,导致防护力量分散,使湖匪有乘可趁。如
1928年横泾由水警七队二分队驻防,原有船8艘,后抽调1艘至木
渎,每艘又经区部抽调巡士1人编练游击队,于是防务骤然单薄,盗
匪因而生心。②

　　从图6中可以看到,县域交界和经济欠发达地区,由于地方政
府重视程度和自身经济实力的不足,防护建设较为落后,如黄埭、斜
塘、北桥、湘城、周庄、香山等区。尤其是斜塘、周庄、湘城地处县域
交界之处,境内湖泊众多,但警员的配置却相对较少。冯贤亮在研

---

　　① 金友里撰:《太湖备考》卷4《兵防·湖防论说》,(南京)江苏古籍出版社,1998年,第
167页。
　　② 《吴县俞武功条陈治匪四则》,《江苏省政府公报》1928年第37期,第33页。

究明末清初江南的地方防护时候时所指出，"在行政地理区划交错地带或自然边界区，正是一个控制薄弱地带；为盗匪多发之地。"[①]地方保卫力量的薄弱给湖匪有机可乘，如在1929年吴县行政区域调整中，尹山和郭巷两区合并成新的郭巷区。全区辖境相较之前增加一倍，共计三镇五十乡，而公安机构仅有两个守望所，"殊不足以保地方公安"，尤其是高垫（店）村"为东南各乡往来要道，匪船时有出没"。[②] 1930年太湖剿匪总指挥胡祖玉率军抵达苏州后，根据当时的设防需要，将军队驻扎在太湖和内湖两处。太湖方面有西山、东前山、东后山、泽山、渡村、胥口、光福、涵庄、和桥、横芦、金墅；内湖方面有青浦庙、雪垆庙、盘龙浦、油泾、车坊、斜塘、尹山、高店。[③] 这一方面加强了环太湖地区的防护力量，另一方面弥补了内湖地区警力不足的缺陷，对此后围剿湖匪起到了极为重要的作用。

五 结 语

南京国民政府建立之初，吴县地区匪患严重，这主要是因为北洋政府时期盗匪丛生，地方防护力量较弱。1928—1931年，地方政府通过增强警察力量、派驻军队、组建保卫团和商团以及恢复传统的保甲制度等一系列措施，加强了乡村治安及防控体系建设。尤其是通过军、警的配合，沉重打击了安徽帮、海州帮、浦东帮、河南帮的势力，匪患程度明显减轻，乡村治安有所改善。但是这些战绩，主要是在军队的配合下完成的，兵来匪去，兵去匪来，因而难以从根本上消除。由于受自然地理环境与地方防护等因素的影响，匪患主要分布在西南太湖、东南吴淞江流域以及西北阳澄湖地区，而西北地区相对较少。太湖是湖匪活动的大本营，四通八达的河流有利于湖匪的流窜，吴淞江是湖匪流窜于苏州与上海之间的主要通道。另外，经济欠发达地区以及县与县的交界处，往往防护力量较弱，给湖匪可趁之机。

---

① 冯贤亮：《明末清初江南的地方防护》，《云南社会科学》2001年第3期。
② 《尹郭区请厚警力》，《苏州明报》，1929年10月13日，第2版。
③ 《规定剿防湖匪地点》，《申报》，1930年2月7日，第11版。

土匪现象是近代历史上一个非常复杂的问题,其内部的组成人群、活动特点、社会危害以及与会党、军队之间的关系异常复杂。限于篇幅,本文主要探讨匪患的时空分布与自然地理环境和地方防护之间的内在关系。在研究的过程中,主要借用历史地理的研究方法和思路,是历史地理与社会史研究结合的一种尝试。目前历史社会地理方兴未艾,研究理论和实践严重不足,而历史地理与社会史研究的结合,一方面社会史可以借鉴历史地理学的研究方法,汲取新的养分,深化自身的研究;另一方面历史地理学也可以拓宽研究领域,推动历史社会地理的发展。本文研究的吴县,濒临太湖,经济发达,匪患程度相对较为严重。然而湖匪活动具有很大的流动性,单凭一个县的研究还不足以说明当时整个太湖地区的盗匪情况。太湖周边其他地区以及不濒临太湖地区的盗匪活动又是如何,只有将每个县域的情况弄清楚,才能对此有更加全面清晰的了解。

(原载于《中国历史地理论丛》2014 年第 4 期)

上海公共租界纳税人会议代表性研究

李东鹏[*]

从 1870 年第一次会议召开到 1941 年退出历史舞台,上海公共租界纳税人会议(后文简称"纳税人会议")[①]存续 70 余年,并逐步发展成为完善的制度。纳税人会议历来备受研究者重视,有的研究以"三权分立"的政权组织原则定位纳税人会议、工部局和会审公廨在上海公共租界的地位,认为纳税人会议"相当于资本主义国家政权体系中的议会"。[②] 也有的研究认为纳税人会议是"半殖民地袖珍王国中的小议会",[③]并着重凸显纳税人会议的立法职能。但是也有学者却并不认为纳税人会议等同于议会,如徐公肃称纳税人会议为"类似议会者之存在,与立法权之行使",[④]并从财产资格限制的角度得出纳税人会议"富豪政治"的特点;阮笃成认为纳税人会议在上海公共租界的立法、司法和行政三个领域发挥职能。此外,亦有学者认为纳税人会议为公共租界的议政机构或议事机构。概括言之,纳税人会议"议会"与"类似议会"问题的判定并未解决,而关于纳税人会议的职能研究则主要侧重于其立法职能,尚未深入到从纳税人与所代表人群的角度探究纳税人会议的职能与权

---

  * **作者简介**:李东鹏,上海师范大学人文与传播学院博士研究生

  ① 纳税人会议前身为租地人会议。按照 1845 年《上海租地章程》规定,英国领事巴富尔召集在沪租界租赁土地的英国商人于 1846 年 12 月 22 日在理查饭店召开第一次租地人会议,初步形成了在沪外侨的公共集会议事的制度。1869 年召开的租地人会议年会上改为纳税人会议。

  ② 张仲礼主编《近代上海城市研究》,上海人民出版社 1990 年版,第 608 页。

  ③ 袁燮铭:《晚清上海公共租界政权运作机制述论》,《史林》1999 年第 3 期。

  ④ 蒯世勋:《上海公共租界史稿》,《上海公共租界史稿》,上海人民出版社 1980 年版,第 102 页。

力地位。

　　纳税人会议汇聚各国侨民的利益诉求,这种共同利益凝聚成一种公共权力,代表了上海公共租界的权力秩序,工部局作为行政机构,只是权力秩序的践行者。正如亨廷顿所言:一个社会所达到的政治共同体水平反映着其政治制度和构成这种政治制度的社会势力之间的关系。①各方利益的和谐维系着上海公共租界社会的发展,纳税人会议职能的履行使得公共租界各个团体成为一种共同体,这种共同体保证了租界的稳定有序。但上海公共租界历经百年,纳税人的代表性发生了一些改变,这种改变亦引起了权力秩序的分散和转移,成为后期纳税人会议裂变的重要原因。

一　纳税人会议的职能

　　纳税人会议制度是移植近代西方国家(特别是英国)政治制度的产物。纳税人会议不仅掌控工部局董事的选举、租界规章的制定、征税等权力,更从政治、经济、法律等宏观方面指导工部局的工作,正如费唐法官所言,"工部局财政建议之必须经由纳税人年会核准,工部局立法建议之必须经由纳税人特别大会核准,厥为公共租界生命之重要原素"。②作为公共租界的最高权力机关,纳税人会议权力的行使以其多种职能的发挥为基础。维系上海公共租界纳税人会议权力的法理来源于《土地章程》。1869年《上海洋泾浜北首租界章程》第九款中有明确规定:"需用银两,或应行借支,或另行措办,有约各国领事官(或其中已有大半位数)于西历每年之正、二月初旬择定日期(必于两礼拜之前宣示于众),按照后开章程,选举办事公局之董事;各国领事官又于正、二月内宣示,限二十一天,齐集众人,会同筹议举办上开各项事宜之经费银两;并准此会内齐集之人(执业租主有阘者离境给据代办之人亦在此内)将抽收捐款及发

————————

　　① 塞缪尔·P.亨廷顿:《变化社会中的政治秩序》,上海世纪出版集团2008年版,第7页。
　　② 费唐:《费唐法官研究上海公共租界情形报告书》第2卷,工部局华文处译述,1931年,第312页。

给执照等事,议定施行;亦准将地基价值、房屋租金自行估算,以凭收捐。"①依托租界根本大法赋予的权力,纳税人会议从单纯的议事机构延展出三大职能:

1. 依托人事权和议事权的行政职能

纳税人会议直接选举工部局董事和地产委员会委员。早期工部局董事在纳税人年会上选举产生,1866年后举行专门的工部局董事选举会议。② 1900年成立地产委员会后,纳税人会议掌管地产委员会委员的人事权。此外,工部局若要签订聘期3年以上的职员合同,必须经纳税人会议批准,否则工部局不得聘用。③ 如果工部局各机构雇员管理中遇到工部局董事会不能决定的人事安排,须由纳税人会议决定其去留。此外,1869年《上海洋泾浜北首租界章程》第24款规定"除特会公同议准之员缺薪费外,其余人额缺不得逾3年",④即工部局及下属各委员所雇佣的工作人员所签订的合同一般不能超过3年。只有经纳税人会议批准,工部局才可以签订3年以上的雇用合同,如1883年为了改组巡捕房,纳税人特别会"授权董事会同聘用的警官和巡捕等人员签订为期5年的聘约"。⑤

租界的决策体系分为三级:最高决策机构为公共租界纳税人年会和特别会;其次由纳税人大会选举产生工部局董事,工部局董事通过定期召开董事会议对总办提交的日常事务提出处理意见,审议工部局下属委员会的工作报告;工部局总办负责执行工部局董事会提出的具体意见、计划和其他日常事务,各委员会遇特殊情况也要向总办汇报。假若工部局在执行纳税人市政计划时不达标,或工部局存在拖沓、敷衍行为,而纳税人会议认为在工部局能力范围内必须完成,便会改"建议"为"命令"工部局限期完成。例如租界的粪便处置问题一直困扰在沪西侨,1898年3月1日纳税人年会

① 王铁崖编《中外旧约章汇编》第1册,三联书店1957年版,第294页。
② 上海市档案馆编《工部局董事会会议录》第2册,上海古籍出版社2001年版,第550页。
③ 王铁崖编《中外旧约章汇编》第1册,第298页。
④ 王铁崖编《中外旧约章汇编》第1册,第298页。
⑤ 上海市档案馆编《工部局董事会会议录》第8册,第534页。

上第 9 号决议便命令工部局"限期 3 个月内将租界内所有大便清除"。①

2. 依托征税、工部局预决算和债券审批权的经济职能

租界的捐税主要有地税、房捐、码头捐和执照捐等,均按照纳税人会议商定的税率标准征收。纳税人会议为集体会议,所形成的决议具有契约性质,在公共租界外侨中具有事实上的"法律"效用,对于抗税、漏税的洋行和外侨,纳税人会议可命令工部局强制征收。② 事实上,直到 1879 年,工部局已成立并开展征税工作 25 年之后,仍有人对其征税的权力表示质疑。当年 5 月,一名叫恒德森的纳税人写信给工部局,表示"他认为工部局从法律上来说是没有权力征收此税的,但他准备缴纳向他征收的数额,但这只是作为对租界境内维持治安和安装路灯的一种志愿捐献"。③ 只有由纳税人会议作出征税决议,才能保障征税工作顺利开展。1872 年 2 月 26 日工部局董事会上,工部局的法律顾问伦尼就指出:"在拟定《土地章程》第 9 款时已含有这样一种意图:将一切征税权利授予纳税人会议,藉以防止任何不合理的征税行为。"④

《土地章程》赋予纳税人会议审批工部局的预决算的权力。每年年初举行的年会先审批工部局前一年的决算执行情况,再就工部局制定的预算报告中如税率标准、经费开支等具体事项逐项讨论,各位纳税人提交修正案,通过的修正案附于预算报告之后,形成最终的未来年度工部局市政工作纲要。会上若有纳税人对工部局的预算报告不满,可以提出意见交与大会表决,纳税人会议不同意的预算事项,将不被执行。例如 1884 年 2 月 28 日举行的纳税人年会上,参会者就工部局的经费开支问题展开大讨论,最后通过修正案:"预算报告 219 页的 111.95 两和用于菜场选址的 1222.96 两开支不

---

① Annual Meeting and Special Meeting(1898),U1-1-821,上海市档案馆藏。
② 早期工部局强制征收捐税主要依靠各国驻沪领事对本国侨民施加影响及采取法律途径。1865 年 11 月 15 日工部局起诉韦尔斯地产遗嘱的执行人欠税,领事法庭做出有利于工部局的判决,事实上肯定了工部局征税的权力。
③ 上海市档案馆编《工部局董事会会议录》第 7 册,第 674 页。
④ 上海市档案馆编《工部局董事会会议录》第 5 册,第 536 页。

予通过。"①

近代上海公共租界进行了大规模的市政建设,必然有庞大的资金需求,公共租界收入稳定,发行债券一般较容易,而债券的发行决定权则掌握在纳税人会议手中。发行债券支持市政建设则有两方面的积极作用:第一,专项经费,专款专用。1872 年 10 月 15 日纳税人会议在上海共济会堂(Masonic Hall)召开,并通过决议:"工部局发行上海市政债券,每券 100 两,总额为上海纹银 4 万两,或工部局视情况酌予减少的款额。自发行日起 5 年至 20 年内按票面还本,年息 8 厘,每半年付息一次。"②第二,弥补短期财政资金不足。例如,为修建老闸区新捕房,1888 年 2 月份举行的纳税人会议批准了30000 两的开支。但 6 月份工部局工务委员会的报告预计的花销达到41000 两,而工部局的绝大多数董事都不同意缩小新捕房的规模和减少内部设施,而按照 1884 年纳税人年会上威尔金森(H. S. Wilkinson)的讲话:"当纳税人会议为某一特殊目的表决通过一笔特定数额的款项后,如要使用超过这数额的款项时,则应获得纳税人会议的特别批准。"③由 30 名纳税人签名要求召开的特别会议于1888 年 7 月 16 日下午举行,研究承建新老闸捕房的投标书,并批准董事会发行债券以筹集按照平面图修建捕房所必需的资金,其数字估计约为 15000 两白银。④

3. 依托立法权的议会职能

纳税人会议的议会职能体现在历次的《土地章程》的修订当中。《土地章程》的修订必须首先经纳税人会议批准后,才提交领事或公使,而领事或公使的反馈意见也必须再经纳税人会议通过之后方正式施行。例如,1869 年《上海洋泾浜北首租界章程》通过后,上海外侨、工部局、各国驻沪领事和驻华公使及清政府皆对其不满。工部局于 1873 年 5 月 12 日纳税人年会上提出修订《土地章程》以改变和延伸市政府的体系,纳税人会议第 23 号决议"要求领事团与即将履任的新工部局董事会充分考虑修改《土地章程》的计划,并成立由不

---

① Meeting of Ratepayers(1884),U1-1-802,上海市档案馆藏。
② 上海市档案馆编《工部局董事会会议录》第 5 册,第 583 页。
③ Meeting of Ratepayers(1884),U1-1-802,上海市档案馆藏。
④ Special Meeting of Rate-Payers(1888),U1-1-807 上海市档案馆藏。

少于 7 名纳税人的委员会协助领事团处理此事"。① 为促进《土地章程》修订,1874 年 6 月 8 日纳税人特别会议决定对修改章程委员会进行改组,会议第二号决议:"成立不少于 9 名纳税人组成的修改章程委员会,并提供不超过 2000 两的专项经费,由纳税人特别会议专门审核修改章程委员会所提草案",柏登(Purdon)对此提出动议,要求"会议投票选举 9 名纳税人为修改章程委员会委员"。② 1875 年 5 月 8 日纳税人年会通过了一款《土地章程》修正案,第 14 号决议:在 1869 年《土地章程》第 19 款中"在选举工部局董事纳税人会上有选举权"后加入"出席会议的纳税人代投票权只有在被代理人不在上海公共租界或因病不能出席会议的情形下行使"。③ 纳税人年会通过的修正案很快提交给驻沪领事并递交各国驻北京公使,在同年 6 月驻沪领事团便批准此修正案。④ 到年底,各国北京公使也相继批准。之后,《土地章程》又经历了多次修订,才有了 1898 年的《增订上海洋泾浜北首租界章程》。

　　上海公共租界有来自世界各国的侨民,加之"华洋杂居",这种异常复杂的社会结构使得租界当局的任何治理举措必须取得"全体同意",必须均衡各方的势力,又要彰显西方文明的优越性,而这一切因为纳税人会议制度而成为可能。同时,纳税人会议制度是租界权力体系的重要部分,纳税人会议的职能的履行使得纳税人代表了上海公共租界的权力秩序。进入 20 世纪后,时势的改变使得纳税人会议的适应性问题凸显出来,而隐藏在制度背后的则是由纳税人所组成的权力秩序。纳税人的改变使得上海公共租界纳税人会议的代表性发生改变,权力秩序亦随之转移。正如当时的西人报纸评论道:"如果我们回头看上海公共租界的根本大法,会发现纳税人个体被赋予的权力几乎不受任何限制,这是所有问题产生的根源。"⑤

---

① Rate-Payers' Meeting(1873),U1-16-4813,上海市档案馆藏。

② "Special Meeting of Ratepayers(1874)," *Ratepayers' Meeting*(1870—1884),版本不详,上海徐家汇藏书楼藏。

③ Meeting of Ratepayers(1875),U1-1-788,上海市档案馆藏。

④ 上海市档案馆编《工部局董事会会议录》第 6 册,第 684 页。

⑤ "The Building of 'Greater Shanghai'," *The China Weekly Review*, Dec. 4th, 1926,p. 1.

二　纳税人的代表性分析

纳税人会议代表通常都在租界中具有一定社会地位。民国时期的部分学者将纳税人会议称为"富豪政治"，[①]批评纳税人会议财产资格限制过高。代议制机构治理下的群体必然是所有成员享有同等权利，但事实上"使议会真正得以生长的传统土壤往往会产生一个贵族统治或者财阀统治的社会"，[②]英国议会便是如此。烙着英国传统印记的纳税人会议之所以成为商人或富豪治理的社会，其间关系可谓一脉相承。

《土地章程》和《纳税人会议议事规章》规定了纳税人会议的投票制度和合格纳税人财产资格限制标准，1863 年 11 月 30 日召开的租地人大会通过决议，规定租界内凡拥有地产价格 1000 两或不满 1000 两的租地人，均享受一份投票权；土地估值每增加 1000 两便增加一份投票权；部分地产估值在 500 两以上的租地人也可以获得一份投票权。[③] 下表是租地人会议时期出席会议的租地人人数与票数统计：

表 1　租地人会议时期租地人数统计

年份	会议类型	出席人数	代表票数
1863 年 11 月 30 日	年会	46	不详
1864 年 8 月 18 日	特别会	31	112
1865 年 4 月 15 日、25 日	年会	60	165
1865 年 6 月 30 日、7 月 1 日	特别会	21	158
1866 年 4 月 18 日	年会	33	118
1867 年 2 月 25 日	年会	40	113
1867 年 9 月 10 日	特别会	32	99
1868 年 1 月 10 日	特别会	45	135

---

① 徐公肃、丘瑾璋：《上海公共租界制度》，《上海公共租界史稿》，第 85 页。
② 马克斯·韦伯：《经济与社会》第 1 卷，阎克文译，上海世纪出版集团 2010 年版，第 414 页。
③ General Meeting of Land Renters(1863)，U1 - 1 - 877，上海市档案馆藏。

（续　表）

年份	会议类型	出席人数	代表票数
1868 年 3 月 11 日	年会	不详	216
1868 年 5 月 4 日	特别会	不详	90*
1868 年 5 月 11 日	特别会	不详	157
1869 年 5 月 27、28 日	年会	不详	240

资料来源：1863—1866 年数据来自 1863—1865 年工部局年报中附租地人会议记录，U1-1-877-879，上海市档案馆藏；1867—1869 年数据来自上海公共租界工部局西人纳税人会议报告(1866—1869)，U1-1-1049，上海市档案馆藏；1868 年 3 月 11 日数据来自 1868 年工部局年报，U1-1-881，上海市档案馆藏。

说明：* 1868 年 5 月 4 日特别会未达到 1/3 的出席票数，会上讨论了有关事项，在 5 月 11 日重新举办租地人特别会议。

　　这一时期租地人会议的出席人数大体呈 V 型变化，中间下降的原因很大程度是因为 1864 年太平天国运动失败后，大批避难于租界的难民返乡，造成了一次房地产业的萧条。此外，这一时期发生的棉花投机的破灭和第一次金融风潮也严重影响外商来沪贸易。19 世纪 60 年代后期经济运行企稳，人数开始回升。

　　1869 年《土地章程》第 19 款规定："此等发阄议事之人，必所执产业地价计五百两以上，每年所付房地捐项，照公局估算计十两以上（各执照费不在此内），或系赁住房屋，照公局估每年估算计在五百两以上，而付捐者。"①按章程规定可以归纳为三方面的要求：一是拥有地产价值 500 两以上的地产主；二是每年付房捐地税 10 两以上的纳税人；三是没有房地产业，但如果其所租赁房屋的租金在 500 两以上，这部分缴纳房捐的纳税人也可以参加纳税人会议。以上三类纳税人即本文所称参会纳税人或合格纳税人。自 1870 年正式进入纳税人会议时期，出席会议的纳税人包括在租界租赁土地的地产主、房产主和缴纳房租达到标准的纳税人，成为参会纳税人的渠道变多。下图中我们可以看到从 1870 年到 1939 年近 70 年中，出席纳税人会议的人数的变动趋势：

---

　　①　王铁崖编《中外旧约章汇编》第 1 册，第 297 页。

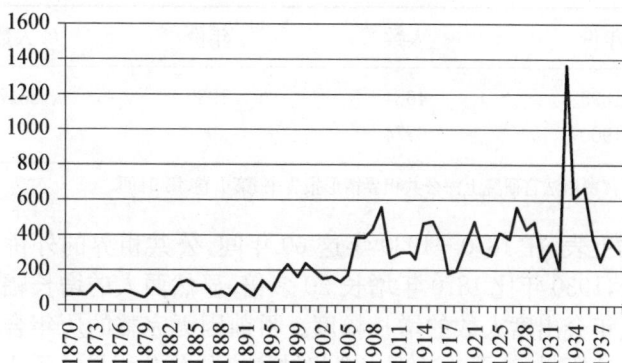

图1　历年纳税人会议出席人数

資料来源:《上海公共租界西人纳税人年会材料(1870—1939)》,U1-1-784-822,上海市档案馆藏。

说明:1894、1897、1919 和 1922 年因档案材料破损,不予阅览,故无法统计其数据;1940、1941 年纳税人年会报告中无出席人数统计。

　　上图显示历年纳税人年会出席人数波动很大,但明显呈上升趋势。具体到各个时段,在 20 世纪以前,人数大都在 200 以内。进入 20 世纪,人数则呈现区间波动,波动区间为 200—600 人,峰值出现在 1933 年,达到 1349 人。一个基本常识是:人数越多,决策成本越高。假如每一个参与者都享有独立的发言权,则决策者人数同决策成本成正比。考察参加纳税人年会的人数变化趋势,最大的原因应归于公共租界外侨人数的增长,下表是 1870 年至 1930 年公共租界的外侨人数统计:

表2　1870—1930 年公共租界外侨人数

年份	人数	年份	人数
1870	1666	1905	11497
1876	1673	1910	13536
1880	2197	1915	18519
1885	3673	1920	23307
1890	3821	1925	29947

(续 表)

年份	人数	年份	人数
1895	4684	1930	36471
1900	6774		

资料来源:《费唐法官研究上海公共租界情形报告书》第1卷,第94页。

据上表,在1870—1930年这60年间,公共租界的外侨人数快速增长,1930年比1870年增长20多倍,显然西人的增长幅度大于纳税人年会出席人数的增长幅度。目前因无完整的历年合格纳税人数统计资料,暂无法整理出合格纳税人与公共租界外侨人数二者的相关性。上表呈现的外侨人数呈持续上升趋势,而参加纳税人年会的人数在进入20世纪以后宽幅波动,有增有减。因此,我们可以得出整体性结论,即纳税人年会参会人数与公共租界外侨人数,二者为上升趋势,19世纪以前基本为正相关,20世纪以后,纳税人年会人数增长变缓,而公共租界外侨人数继续快速增长。另纳税人年会西侨比例详见下表:

表3 纳税人年会人数和外侨比例

年份	公共租界外侨人数	纳税人年会人数	纳税人年会人数占外侨比例(%)
1870	1666	59	3.54
1880	2197	80	3.64
1890	3821	118	3.09
1900	6774	236	3.48
1910	13536	273	2.01
1920	23307	328	1.41
1930	36471	252	0.69

资料来源:据图1、表2中有关数据制作。

由上表可见,在沪外侨能参加纳税人年会的人数比例非常之低,原因可能是两方面:一是达到条件的合格纳税人数较少;二是外侨参加会议的积极性不高。按照1869《上海洋泾浜北首租界章程》第19款所规定合格纳税人的条件,据资料记载公共租界合格纳税

人数 1920 年为 1676 人,代表 2083 票,[①]占公共租界外侨人数的
7.19%;1925 年为 2420 人,代表 2743 票,[②]占公共租界外侨人数的
8.08%。进行合理的预估,合格纳税人数占外侨人口的比重不会超
过 10%,所以资产限制条件过高,造成与会人数较少。因纳税人特
别会出席人数需要达到法定票数的 1/3 才可以召开,所以纳税人特
别会议参会情况与西人参会的积极性相关。据纳税人会议记录记
载,从 1870 年到 1939 年,共召开了 29 次纳税人特别会议,其中有 2
次因为未到达法定票数而流产,有 7 次是与年会一起召开,专门召
开的纳税人特别会议一共有 20 次。在 1920 年以前,纳税人特别会
议召开次数较多,而从 1920 年到 1939 年一共计划召开 6 次纳税人
特别会议,其中有 2 次因票数不足而未成。一般来说,凡涉及租界
重大问题而召开的纳税人特别会,合格纳税人的积极性较高,直到
20 世纪二三十年代才逐渐降低。可以得出结论,资产条件限制过
高是影响纳税人年会人数的主要原因。

　　解析纳税人年会的人群构成,必须回到《土地章程》。正常条件
下,纳税人以其地产或纳税的资格获得一票,租赁房地产的洋行也
可派一人参加纳税人会议,因此正常条件下一人至多可拥有两票。
因为《土地章程》规定可以委托他人代理投票,导致纳税人会议经常
出现一人身拥数票甚至几十票的投票权。可以说,拥有 2 票以上投
票权的纳税人必然是公共租界中资产雄厚的"显贵",因此笔者对历
年纳税人年会中拥有 2 票以上的出席人数作了统计:

表 4　1870—1939 年纳税人年会拥有 2 票以上投票权的人数及其代理票数

年份	人数	占出席人数比例(%)	票数	占总票数比例(%)	年份	人数	占出席人数比例(%)	票数	占总票数比例(%)
1870	27	45.76	164	81.59	1905	40	24.10	279	63.99
1871	17	28.30	156	74.64	1906	49	13.03	301	43.81

---

　　① Report of the Annual and Special Meeting of Ratepayers(1920),U1-1-852,上海市档
案馆藏。

　　② Report of the Annual Meeting of Ratepayers(1925),U1-1-857,上海市档案馆藏。

年份	人数	占出席人数比例（%）	票数	占总票数比例（%）	年份	人数	占出席人数比例（%）	票数	占总票数比例（%）
1872	22	33.33	151	72.95	1907	48	12.60	332	45.73
1873	23	22.12	248	71.06	1908	53	12.16	344	42.80
1874	29	38.66	263	79.22	1909	60	10.70	378	38.65
1875	20	25.97	159	67.09	1910	44	16.12	303	52.79
1876	24	33.80	149	70.95	1911	37	12.71	281	47.79
1877	20	27.03	138	66.03	1912	47	15.46	332	50.92
1878	18	33.69	122	72.60	1913	46	17.90	321	54.50
1879	20	48.78	135	83.80	1914	57	12.26	353	40.95
1880	19	23.75	142	65.14	1915	46	9.73	321	38.25
1881	16	23.88	131	66.84	1916	52	14.29	330	46.09
1882	13	20.00	121	64.70	1917	38	20.43	277	61.97
1883	24	20.87	160	57.55	1918	36	17.82	235	54.39
1884	24	18.32	175	55.91	1920	36	10.97	200	37.45
1885	28	25.00	198	65.35	1921	42	8.90	241	32.97
1886	20	17.86	157	58.15	1923	26	8.60	151	32.54
1887	22	31.88	175	73.53	1924	27	9.60	161	35.77
1888	20	25.97	164	68.90	1925	37	9.27	222	35.69
1889	15	25.42	141	71.94	1926	36	9.54	213	35.20
1890	30	25.42	215	66.56	1927	42	7.68	224	28.35
1891	22	30.99	167	71.67	1928	39	8.90	224	33.68
1892	12	21.82	128	70.33	1929	29	6.19	186	27.56
1893	22	16.18	154	52.74	1930	24	9.52	160	38.65
1895	18	22.22	150	64.94	1931	28	8.02	152	29.86
1896	31	18.10	209	53.09	1932	22	10.62	138	39.42
1898	31	13.96	209	47.72	1933	63	4.67	325	18.54
1899	34	20.36	227	57.90	1934	22	3.62	139	17.79
1900	43	18.22	266	52.16	1935	31	4.63	208	23.19
1901	38	19.89	259	57.17	1936	22	5.89	122	23.74
1902	36	24.32	253	63.25	1937	12	4.78	66	19.76
1903	38	24.52	283	66.20	1938	17	4.57	95	19.55
1904	20	14.71	176	54.32	1939	13	4.38	77	19.54

资料来源：据上海公共租界西人纳税人年会材料(1870—1939)整理，U1-1-784-U1-1-822，上海市档案馆藏。说明：1894年、1897年、1919年和1922年档案材料因破损，无法阅览，故无法统计其数据；1940年、1941年纳税人年会报告中无出席人数统计。

　　由上表可得,每年纳税人年会2票以上投票权的纳税人占出席
人总数变化大致稳定在15%—40%的区间,平均数为每年31人,其
所拥有的投票权数量的变化与人数变化趋势相同,波动区间为
100—300票,平均数为206票。平均每人约有7票的投票权。下图
反映的是拥有2票以上投票权的纳税人占出席会议纳税人数比例
和拥有2票以上投票权的纳税人所代表票数占总票数的比例的变
动趋势:

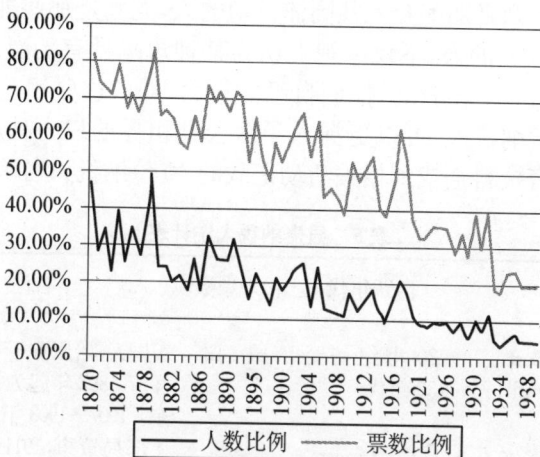

**图 2　1870—1939 年纳税人年会 2 票以上纳税人占总人
数比例、代表票数占总票数比例**

说明:据表 4 相关数据制作。

　　图 2 显示,人数比例和票数比例都明显呈下降趋势,原因之一
是投票权越来越分散;二是参加会议的纳税人越来越多。在纳税人
会议早期,如 1870 年,27 位纳税人所拥有的票数占总票数的
81.59%,可以说他们完全控制了纳税人会议。按照纳税人会议的
规定,票数过半即可通过决议,图 2 显示在 20 世纪前 10 年,约占会
议 20%—30% 纳税人占有 50% 以上的票数,在此时段这一群体事
实上掌控纳税人会议,而通过纳税人会议也就间接控制着公共租界
权力秩序。1910 年以后,纳税人会议的投票权明显分散,观察历年
纳税人年会报告,可见代表 1 票的纳税人数量明显增多,稀释了 2

票以上纳税人的投票权。20世纪30年代,这一群体的人数所占比例已不足10%,所代表的票数比例仅剩20%左右。

在拥有2票以上投票权的纳税人群体中,有一部分拥有10票以上投票权纳税人,可称为"显贵"纳税人。纳税人会议实行代投票制,2票以上纳税人所代表的票具有随机性和临时性,但"显贵"纳税人所代表的票不仅数量多,而且稳定,他们无疑是租界中最富有或最有权势的群体。马克斯·韦伯认为:在一个团体里,真正具有决定性的因素乃是那些介入共同体行动的人,尤其是那些拥有相当重要的社会权力的人,不仅主观上认为某种规范具有妥当性,并且实际依此而行——换言之,他们自己的行为,即以这些规范为准则。[1]观察"显贵"纳税人,可以更深入了解公共租界的权力秩序,下表为笔者据现有资料查找到相关活动记载的10位纳税人名单:

表5 显贵纳税人统计表

名字	活跃年代	代理票数	备注
伯基尔(Albert William Burkill)	20世纪初至30年代	10—13	英国人,始服务于克劳姆祥茂洋行,1897年起为祥茂洋行股东。1907—1908年为公共租界工部局董事,1911—1912年间为工部局副总董,又担任工部局电气委员会主席数年,在有关电气处的事务上颇为活跃
恺自威(William Johnston Keswick)	20世纪30年代	11—13	英国人,1928年任怡和洋行机器部经理,1936年进入工部局董事会,1939年任副总董,1940年以怡和洋行经理身份当选公共租界董事会总董
莱斯特(Hugh William Lester)	20世纪初至20年代	12—15	英国人,服务于天祥洋行,后为该洋行上海分行经理,1922～1923年为工部局董事

---

① 马克斯·韦伯:《社会学的基本概念——经济行动与社会团体》康乐、简惠美译,广西师范大学出版社2011年版,第313页。

（续　表）

名字	活跃年代	代理票数	备注
葛司会（J. J. Keswick）	19 世纪 80 年代	12—15	1880、1881 年任工部局董事，1884、1885 年任总董
高易（G. J. W. Cowie）	19 世纪 70 年代	12—20	律师，1877 年当选为工部局董事
莫西（D. M. Moses）	19 世纪末 20 世纪初	11—17	1896 年当选工部局董事
杜达尔（Chas. Dowdall）	19 世纪 80 年代至 20 世纪初	20—25	1883、1884 年当选董事，1898 年当选为副总董
沃德（W. C. Ward）	19 世纪 20 年代至 90 年代	20—25	1882 年当选为工部局总董
梅博阁（A. Myburgh）	19 世纪 70 年代至 80 年代	25—30	1881 年被选为法租界副总董，1882 年当选为工部局董事，1883 年当选为工部局总董
伊布格（C. L. H. Iburg）	19 世纪末至 20 世纪初	25—30	1905 年当选为工部局董事

资料来源：活跃年代与票数统计，据《上海公共租界西人纳税人年会材料(1870—1939)》，U1-1-784～U1-1-822，上海市档案馆藏。

说明：人名翻译与人物简介，据《近代上海大事记》(汤志钧编，上海辞书出版社 1989 年版)、《近代来华外国人名辞典》(中国社会科学院近代史所翻译室编，中国社会科学出版社 1981 年版)、《上海租界志》(史梅定主编，上海社会科学院出版社 2001 年版)相关内容整理。

上述 10 位纳税人是众多"显贵"纳税人中的一小部分，活跃在租界存续期的各个年代，代理票数也不尽相同。所选取样本虽不能反映这一群体的整体面貌，但根据现有资料可见，在纳税人会上拥有 10 票以上投票权纳税人，大都曾在工部局任董事。工部局作为租界的行政机构，工部局董事会是工部局的最高权力机构，主持公共租界的日常管理事务，工部局的董事可谓是位高权重，名声显赫，又大多拥有实业，人脉广泛，大量未出席纳税人会议的纳税人往往将投票权委托给他们，而在纳税人会议上，显贵纳税人则以其拥有的大量投票权，为自己争取权益。

余　论

　　以往的研究者认为上海公共租界"纳税人资格限制过严,造成富豪政治之事实",[①]这是事实,而更主要的原因应归于工部局董事的身份、地位,也即因其控制资源多,他们可称为"身份群体",[②]这一群体以其自身的"超凡魅力",实际上成为众多因故不能参加纳税人会议的缺席人所选举出来的"代表",以此来影响租界的西侨社会。以纳税人会议为权力机构,以工部局为施政机构,通过纳税人会议所掌控的行政职能、经济职能、议会职能等,塑造着近代上海公共租界,正如布罗代尔所说,"特权阶级在全部政治制度的中心",[③]纳税人会议制度塑造了这一社会阶层,而显贵纳税人又维持并推动纳税人会议制度发展、变革。但租界洋商富豪,一方面担任着工部局的董事,一方面又以其掌控的资源占有纳税人会议上的绝大多数投票,造成了自己管理自己、自己审查自己的局面,这是以往研究不曾注意到的。

　　此外,以往研究中纳税人会议"议会"定位须重新判定。纳税人会议不具备一个条件,即其会议参加者不是在西方的"代议制"下由选举产生的议员。"代议制"是西方议会政治的核心或灵魂,为议会制度的根本特征。显然,通过设定财产资格标准而直接产生的合格纳税人不是由选举产生的租界西人的代表,故在纳税人会议虽移植西方政治制度,但却不是民主宪政的复制,纳税人会议应称为"宪政主义原则"指导下的集体决议机构。20 世纪 20 年代《密勒氏评论报》对此评论道:"上海的外国人数量大约是 40000 人,但由于投票权是基于财产资格的,只有相对较少的一些外国人对外人区域的管理有发言权……管理租界的工部局不是代议制团体,在某种意义上

---

　　① 徐公肃、丘瑾璋:《上海公共租界制度》,《上海公共租界史稿》,第 109 页。

　　② 身份可能要依赖于一种清晰的或者模糊的阶级地位,"身份群体"则意味着一个大型群体内部的众多成员成功地得到了一种特有的社会评价。参见马克斯·韦伯:《经济与社会》第 1 卷,第 425 页。

　　③ 费尔南·布罗代尔:《15 至 18 世纪的物质文明、经济和资本主义》第 3 卷,施康强、顾良译,三联书店 1993 年版,第 211 页。

他们甚至不是住在当地外国人的代表。"①

费唐法官在其报告书中总结租界现有治制的两大优点：一是自治，即公共租界的管理以租界投票人的意志为转移，通过纳税人会议和工部局来实现自治；二是法治，即工部局的统治权限定在组织法内，工部局无法独断行政权。此外，他还认为，工部局的自治非常公开化，因为每年都要在纳税人会议上审议其工作报告、审批预决算。②其分析不无道理，近代上海公共租界纳税人会议已尽可能从公开化、民主化方面进行程序设计，已经形成马克斯·韦伯所认为的"规约式秩序"。③纳税人会议通过推动制定和修改《土地章程》《纳税人会议议事规章》和其他规约章程，规范自身运行程序，制定工部局行动规则，发挥各种职能。④但任何制度设计都需要面对不断更新变化中的社会。在西方现代知识体系的不断影响下，城市发展与社会更新同步进行，极大地改变了近代上海公共租界的社会结构和城市图景。在此背景下，公共租界的参会纳税人数量和构成皆发生变化，纳税人会议的代表性亦随之发生嬗变。由参会纳税人为代表的公共权力是上海公共租界的权力秩序，纳税人会议参会纳税人的代表性事实上是公共租界的权力秩序的体现。但进入20世纪后，伴随着纳税人会议参会纳税人代表性的分散和一般参会纳税人的增多，以纳税人会议为代表的公共租界旧权力秩序已发生分散和稀释。虽然公共租界的显贵纳税人群体依然存在，依然发挥着能量，但正如20世纪20年代纳税人特别会屡次未达到法定人数而流产的事实所彰显，公共租界秩序的变化不以显贵纳税人的意志为转移。

纳税人会议制度能维系近一百年，这正说明纳税人会议有其存在的价值，而纳税人会议只有随着现实情况的变化而调整，才能很好地运行。虽然在19世纪后半期华人已成为贡献公共租界税收的

---

① "The Building of 'Great Shanghai,'" *The China Weekly Review*, Dec. 4, 1926, p. 2.

② 《费唐法官研究上海公共租界情形报告书》第 2 卷，工部局华文处译述 1931 年版，第 136—137 页。

③ 马克斯·韦伯：《社会学的基本概念——经济行动与社会团体》，第 92 页。

④ 李东鹏：《上海公共租界纳税人会议制度研究——从〈土地章程〉、〈议事规章〉看纳税人会议》，《江西师范大学学报（哲学社会科学版）》2015 年第 4 期。

主力军,但华人力量的真正崛起则出现在 20 世纪,以纳税华人会的成立和华人董事进入工部局董事会为标志,上海公共租界的权力秩序已部分转移至华人手中,清醒的外国人都已正视此问题。

(原载于《史林》2015 年第 05 期)

为学生毕业后生活做更好的准备[*]

——英国"2014 国家课程"述评

李国栋　夏惠贤^{**}

英国自 1988 年推行国家课程以来，其义务教育课程标准曾经历过数次修订。2013 年 4 月，英国教育部新颁布了《变革资格与课程：为学生毕业后生活做更好的准备》(Reforming qualifications and the curriculum to better prepare pupils for life after school)的政策，一方面指出要提高普通中等教育证书考试和大学入学考试的要求，另一方面决定从 2014 年 9 月开始实施最新修订的"2014 国家课程"(National Curriculum 2014)。① 以这一政策精神为核心取向，英国拉开了新一轮义务教育课程改革的帷幕。

一、英国"2014 国家课程"的出台历程

在最近几轮 PISA 测试中，英国学生的成绩排名不断下滑，引发

---

* 本文系教育部哲学社会科学研究 2013 年度重大课题攻关项目"大中小德育课程一体化建设研究"的阶段性成果。

** **作者简介**：李国栋(1976—　)，男，上海师范大学国际与比较教育研究院博士研究生，盐城师范学院副教授；夏惠贤(1964—　)，男，上海师范大学教育学院院长，教授、博士生导师。

① UK Department for Education. Reforming Qualifications and the Eurriculum to Better Prepare Pupils for Life after School［EB/OL］. https://www. gov. uk/government/policies/reforming-qualifications-and-the-curriculum-to-better-prepare-pupils-for-life-after-school. 2013 - 04 - 22.

了英国民众对义务教育质量的普遍担忧。伴随有关机构的深入调查,人们逐渐将批评的重心聚焦于国家课程之上,认为现行国家课程未能为学生发展提供足够的准备。在目标设计上,关于成就目标的水平描述(level descriptions)过于繁冗,它既给教师、家长的理解带来很大困难,又难以为学生提供明确的指导,而且潜含着"允许部分学生达不到基本水准"的假设;在内容安排上,部分知识技能要求比其他国家明显更低,且未充分体现"宽广且均衡"(broad and balanced)的基本理念;在课程评价上,现有的全国性评价标准过于强调统一,抑制了教师的专业自主性,并导致了教师"为考试而教"的倾向,学生的学习动机因此而受到很大影响。①

为积极回应这些批评,英国教育大臣戈夫(Michael Gove)于2011年1月宣布启动国家课程修订,并提出了以下目标:(1)为学校构建"基准式"(benchmark)的国家课程,为学生提供自信、成功学习的知识标准,兼顾天才儿童和残障儿童的特殊需求;(2)追寻儿童"应学什么、如何学习"的最佳集体智慧,确保国家课程能与国际上最优秀、最成功的课程媲美;(3)在课程组织和实施上赋予教师更多的专业自由;(4)设立严格的学业水平要求,使之与全球最高水准相符合;(5)让家长了解其子女在学校中应该学习什么,并提供有效的支持。② 这一系列目标明确阐释了新一轮国家课程改革的愿景,并为之提供了相应的视角与路径。

随后,教育部将国家课程修订分解成三项工作同时展开进行。一是通过教育部官网、大众媒体和合作刊物等媒介平台,广泛征询校长、教师、学生、家长、研究人员、企业雇主和慈善机构对现行国家课程的意见。二是委托国家教育研究基金会(National Foundation for Educational Research, NFER)开展课程标准的国际比较研究,向PISA表现优秀的国家和地区借鉴经验。三是组建国家课程修订专

---

① UK Department for Education. National Curriculum Review: Initial Findings〔EB/OL〕. https://www. gov. uk/gov-ernment/speeches/national-curriculum-review-initial-findings, 2014 - 12 - 19.

② UK Department for Education. Review of the National Curriculum in England: Summary Report of the Call for Evidence〔EB/OL〕. http://www. education. gov. uk/publications/standard/publicationDetail/Page1/DFE-00136-2011. 2014 - 03 - 20.

家组(Expert Panel for the National Curriculum Review, EPNCR),从专业视角审视国家课程的问题与不足,并提出新的课程设计思路和建议。

截至 2012 年 2 月,三项工作的代表分别向教育部提交了《英格兰国家课程修订:意见征询总结报告》(Review of the National Curriculum in England: Summary report of the call for evidence)、《英格兰国家课程修订:我们从高绩效国家和地区的英语、数学和科学课程中学到了什么?》(Review of the National Curriculum in England: What Can We Learn from the English, Mathematics and Science Curricula of High-performing Jurisdictions?)和《国家课程框架:专家组报告》(The Framework for the National Curriculum: A Report by the Expert Panel)。基于这三份报告,再经过几番"上交议会研讨、下向民众垂询"的轮回,新的国家课程标准——《英格兰国家课程:四阶段完整框架》(National Curriculum in England: Complete Framework for Key Stages 1 to 4,以下简称为《完整框架》)终于在2013 年 9 月正式出炉,并从 2014 年 9 月开始全面实施。

二、英国"2014 国家课程"的变革内容

《完整框架》共由"导言"、"学校课程"、"国家课程"、"包容性要求"、"算术与数学"、"语言与识字"、"学习科目与成就目标"等七个部分组成。从《完整框架》的文本内容可以看出:与先前的国家课程相比,新修订的 2014 国家课程主要在以下方面进行了变革。[①]

(一)明确国家课程与学校课程的关系

受自由主义教育传统的影响,英国国家课程从其推行开始便存在着争议,甚至遭受过部分地区和学校的抵制。其中,国家课程与学校课程之间关系的不明朗,是长久以来令人感到困惑的问题。例

---

① UK Department for Education. National Curriculum in England: Complete Framework for Key Stages 1 to 4 [EB/OL]. https://www.gov.uk/government/publications/national-curriculum-in-england-framework-for-key-stages-1-to-4. 2013 - 09 - 11.

如,教师在开发学校课程时,通常会处于一种两难境地:是在国家课程框架内做自己份内的事情?还是为了适应学校的特定需求而对国家课程进行改编、突破和超越?① 应对此类困惑,《完整框架》对两者关系作出了明确的阐释。

一方面,两者之间存在着"指导与被指导"的关系。国家课程对学校课程具有基础性的指导作用,学校课程在构建原则、科目设置和学习内容上须遵从国家课程的基本要求。另一方面,两者又有"包含与被包含"的关系。学校课程是学校为学生提供的全部经验,国家课程则是学校课程的有机组成部分。

(二) 完善国家课程的目标层次体系

课程目标是建构课程的首要因素,完整的课程目标应包括宏观、中观和微观三个层次的目标。② 从《完整框架》的相关表述可以看出,新修订的国家课程目标层次体系是严格遵循这一原则来加以完善的。

在宏观层次上,《完整框架》分别向学生和教师提出了国家课程的总目标(Aim for the National Curriculum)。对学生而言,国家课程旨在为他们成为有教养的公民提供最基本的知识、最有效的思维和最得体的语言,并使他们学会体验、欣赏人类的创造性活动与成就。对教师而言,国家课程旨在为他们提供核心内容框架,使他们能在更宽广的学校课程中建构起丰富多彩的课堂,有力地促进学生知识、理解力与技能的发展。

在中观层次上,《完整框架》为每一学科设置了相应的学习目的(Purpose of Study)和课程目标(Curriculum Aim)。以英语学科为例,《完整框架》指出:英语学习目的是理解英语在学校和生活中的重要地位,运用口语和书面语清晰流畅地表达思想和情感,并通过阅读和欣赏文学作品促进学生文化、情感、智力、社会和精神的全面发展。英语课程目标是为学生掌握英语口语和书面语提供高质量标准,使他们通过大量趣味性阅读建构起对英语的热爱;确保学生

---

① 徐玉珍:校本课程与国家课程开发关系评析[J],教育科学研究,2002(5),16—18。
② 刘启迪:课程目标:构成、研制与实现[J],课程·教材·教法,2004(8),24—29。

在理解的基础上轻松、流利地阅读，养成为陶冶性情和获取信息而广泛阅读的习惯；获得阅读、写作、对话所需的词汇和语法知识，学会欣赏本民族丰富多样的文化遗产；学会清晰、准确和连贯地写作，并使作文风格适应不同背景、目的和对象的需求；在讨论过程中清楚阐释自己的观点，掌握对话、倾听、演讲和辩论的语言艺术。

在微观层次上，《完整框架》删除了之前饱受非议的成就目标"水平描述"，转而以"法定性要求"（Statutory Requirements）和"非法定性要目与指南"（Non-statutory Notes and Guideline）来规范学生的成就要求。"法定性要求"规定了各阶段学生须达到的学业水准；"非法定性要目与指南"则阐明了学生学习各科知识时应知晓的事项和建议。至此，2014 国家课程的目标体系以更加丰富、多元的方式呈现出来，为教师理解和把握国家课程要义提供了有益帮助。

（三）调整国家课程的学科组织结构

为使国家课程能在刚性规定与柔性要求的互动平衡中保持充分的张力，《完整框架》在学科组织结构上也作出了进一步的调整。

在刚性规定上，《完整框架》延续了以往国家课程的科目设置，强调国家课程的必修科目即以义务教育四阶段为架构而组织起来的 12 门科目。其中，英语、数学、科学等 3 门为核心科目；艺术与设计、公民、计算机、设计与技术、外语、地理、历史、音乐、体育等 9 门为基础科目。

在柔性要求上，《完整框架》提出了两条新的建议。一是国家课程只提供每一阶段必修科目的知识、技能与方法，其具体组织由学校和教师自行决定。二是在第四阶段增设了四大授权领域（entitlement areas），即艺术（含艺术与设计、音乐、舞蹈、戏剧和媒体艺术）、设计与技术、人文（含地理和历史）和现代外语。这四大授权领域虽然不是必修科目，但学校必须至少开设其中一门。倘若学生想选修其中任何一门，学校须为之提供相应机会，而且还要为达到合格要求的学生颁发相应证书。这一学科组织结构上的调整，使新修订的 2014 国家课程显得比过去更具"刚柔并济"的特点。

(四) 强调国家课程实施的适应取向

为体现国家课程对所有学生的全纳性,《完整框架》还特别强调国家课程实施的适应取向,并向课程实施主体——教师提出了两条包容性要求(Inclusions)。

第一条为"设置合适的挑战"。教师应在国家课程实施中对所有学生赋予适切的高期望,为高于一般期望标准的学生提供拓展任务,为持有远大抱负的学生提供额外方法指导,以及为弱势群体家庭的学生提供有针对性的教学方案。

第二条是"积极回应学生需求,克服个体和群体的潜在障碍"。教师应在国家课程实施中为不同种族、性别和信仰的学生提供平等机会,积极回应不同个体的需求:对残障学生实施特殊教育模式,采用特殊方法帮助他们克服潜在的认知障碍;对母语非英语的学生,要根据其年龄特征、侨居时间和先前经验开展灵活的英语教学,扫除他们在国家课程学习中的语言障碍。从两条包容性要求的具体表述中可以看出:2014 国家课程既考虑到了学生认知基础、年龄特征和性别特点等本体性差异,又考虑到了学生家庭经济、宗教信仰和语言文化等背景性差异,体现了它在课程实施上所赋予的动态适应性。

三、英国"2014 国家课程"的理念评析

课程新政的出台及其标准的变化,通常是由教育理念的创新和突破所驱动。从英国 2014 国家课程的出台历程与变革内容中,我们可提炼出三条蕴含其中的理念,即从"外部借鉴"到"内部平衡",再到"自我超越"。

(一) 外部借鉴:突破西方中心的传统阈限,勇于向东方国家和地区借鉴

长久以来,在西方中心论的传统影响下,英国教育的借鉴对象大多限于英国以外的西方发达国家。然而,自 2000 年 PISA 问世后,伴随东方诸国和地区的相继加入,以及这些国家和地区的学生

在 PISA 中的卓越表现,使英国教育界掀起了一股重新认识东方教育智慧的热潮。一方面,他们需要以这种非西方的"他者"作为反省自身的参照;另一方面,他们期望通过研究东方教育来获得有益于发展自我、融入全球的经验。

早在国家课程修订的开端之际,教育大臣戈夫便在向议会提交的《国家课程修订:初步的发现》(National Curriculum Review:Initial Findings)报告中多次提及亚洲国家的高质量教育水准,并反复强调以新加坡为参照来检视自身不足,如:新加坡要求学生在四年级时就应明确自己的学习规划和事项安排,而英国到六年级时才有这一要求;新加坡六年级科学课就涉及到了"动植物细胞以及细胞分裂对生命生长的基础性作用"这一知识,而英国在中学时才涉及。[①] 与此同时,在教育部发布的另一份报告《国家课程修订:国际学科广度报告》(National Curriculum Review:Report on Subject Breadth of International Jurisdictions)中,新加坡、韩国和日本等东方国家也赫然进入了其中 11 个比较对象国之列。[②] 中国上海两度在 PISA 中夺魁后,英国更是加快了向中国学习的步伐,并采取了一系列的"先取经后拜师"举措。先是由教育部副部长特鲁斯(Liz Truss)率团在 2014 年 2 月访华,学习中国数学教育的经验,考察上海学生 PISA 表现优秀的原因;3 月与中方签署了《中英人文交流对话机制:英沪数学教师交流项目》(England-Shanghai Mathematics Teacher Exchange Project in China-UK People to People Dialogue Mechanism);9 月选派了 72 名英国教师赴上海学习;11 月和次年 3 月还先后邀请了两批上海数学教师赴英开设示范课。种种迹象表明,传统以西方为中心的借鉴阈限在本次课程改革中实现了较大的突破。这种勇于向东方学习的精神,反映了英国在融入全球过程中对教育卓越的更高追求。

---

① UK Department for Education. National Curriculum Review:Initial Findings [EB/OL]. https://www.gov.uk/gov-ernment/speeches/national-curriculum-review-initial-findings. 2014 - 12 - 19.

② National Foundation for Educational Research. National Curriculum Review:Report on Subject Breadth of International Jurisdictions [EB/OL]. https://www.gov.uk/government/uploads/system/uploads/attachment_data/file/197636/DFE-RR178a.pdf. 2014 - 02 - 20.

(二) 内部平衡：化解政府、市场与学校的博弈，促进三者的协同合作

任何时代的课程都不是纯粹的知识产品集合。历次课程变革的背后，往往聚藏着政府意志的渗透、市场力量的驱动和学校治理的诉求。尽管国家统一课程的出现已在一定程度上反映了英国对地方分权、学校自治的反思以及向中央集权的靠拢，但在其实施过程中还是表现出了较为明显的"英式妥协"（British compromise）特征。[①] 当然，这种妥协绝非简单意义上的相互调和，更非无原则的彼此退让，而是凭借政府、市场与学校对国家课程的共同关注来化解彼此之间的博弈纷争，促成三者的协同合作。

政府作为本次国家课程改革的主导力量，从广泛征询民众意见、委托开展比较研究到组建修订专家组，均体现了以其"有形之手"振兴教育的决心。在强调国家控制的同时，市场这一"无形之手"的作用也被赋予了空前的关注。这从其改革政策开篇第一句话便可看出："尽管近几年学生识字与算术的优秀率有所提高，但雇主对此仍不够满意，大约有 42％ 的雇主需要为刚加入的毕业生组织额外培训。"[②] 此外，学校治理的诉求也在本次国家课程修订中得到了积极的回应。学校治理既有别于一般意义上的学校管理，又超越了传统的学校自治，它更强调在民主化、信息化的新型背景之下，学校、政府、社会对学校事务的共同参与和决策。这从《完整框架》的以下表述便可见一斑，如"所有学校都必须将每学年各科课程内容及其相关信息公布于网络上，以供公众共同检视和商讨"。[③] 由上可

---

① Nicola Sheldon. Politicians and History: The National Curriculum, National Identity and the Revival of the National Narrative [J]. The Journal of Historical Association, 2012,(4): 256 - 271.

② UK Department for Education. Reforming Qualifications and the Eurriculum to Better Prepare Pupils for Life after School [EB/OL]. https://www. gov. uk/government/policies/reforming-qualifications-and-the-curriculum-to-better-prepare-pupils-for -life-after-school. 2013 - 04 - 22.

③ UK Department for Education. National Curriculum in England: Complete Framework for Key Stages 1 to 4 [EB/OL]. https://www. gov. uk/government/publications/national-curriculum-in-england-framework-for-key-stages-1-to-4. 2013 - 09 - 11.

知,在统筹政府、市场与学校的利益需求上,英国本次国家课程改革付出了诸多的努力,并在一定程度上促成了三者关系从博弈到协同的转变。

(三) 自我超越:以高要求赋予学生高期望,以评价改革引领教师自主发展

在外部借鉴取得了有益经验,内部平衡收获了一定成就之后,改革面临的另一个重大挑战便是,如何将这些经验与成就融入新的国家课程之中,藉此促进学生与教师的发展,以期实现真正意义上的自我超越。

在应对这一挑战的过程中,2014 国家课程一方面提高了英语、数学、科学等核心课程的学习要求,其意图在于赋予学生更高的期望,确保他们在掌握核心概念与知识的基础上,为以后的学习作出更充分的准备。譬如,英语课程频繁使用了"精通"、"准确"、"得体"等高要求措辞来规范学生的语言、知识、技能的学习;数学课程比以往更强调学生对乘法口诀和加减乘除四则运算的"娴熟"掌握;科学课程则提出了"以科学的方式工作"(Working Scientifically)这一富有"价值引领"意味的新概念来表达对该课程的更高追求。① 另一方面,2014 国家课程还在评价上作出了反思性改进,其目的就在于为教师"松绑",使他们拥有更多的自主权来促进教学和发展。譬如,教育部决定从 2015 年开始采用相对性评价替代传统的绝对性评价,其用意就是为了释放教师因分数排名而带来的压力,扭转"为考试而教"的不良倾向。此外,还为有志于参与评价工具研发的教师设立了专项资助,鼓励他们在评价创新的过程中实现自主性发展。② 可见,无论是为促进学生学习而赋予的"高期望",还是为促进教师发展而倡导的"自主性",均体现了 2014 国家课程自觉应对时代挑

---

① UK Department for Education. National Curriculum in England: Complete Framework for Key Stages 1 to 4 [EB/OL]. https://www.gov.uk/government/publications/national-curriculum-in-england-framework-for-key-stages-1-to-4. 2013 - 09 - 11.

② UK Department for Education. National Curriculum and Assessment from September 2014: Information for Schools [EB/OL]. https://www.gov.uk/government/publications/national-curriculum-and-assessment-information-for-schools. 2014 - 08 - 21.

战、超越传统障碍的理念诉求。

四、启 示

总体而言,2014 国家课程的颁布实施,是英国应对激烈的国际教育竞争而作出的一项战略性抉择。它强调以 1988 年《教育改革法》为基石,延续了当初确立的"宽广且均衡"的课程设计思路;结合新时代的问题与挑战,制定了以"为学生毕业后生活做更好的准备"为核心取向的改革框架;基于外部借鉴、内部平衡和自我超越等理念指导,通过政府自上而下的努力推进,使国家课程的目标体系、内容结构、实施取向与评价制度得到了全方位的改进。联系我国义务教育课程改革实际,我们可从中获得如下启示。

(一) 强化课程改革的顶层设计

当前我国义务教育课程改革正处于全面深化阶段,改革牵涉的利益越来越复杂,面临的压力也越来越大。在此关键时期,仅靠传统"摸着石头过河"的经验型探索,可能会让改革陷入更深的迷惘。唯有通过强调理性、关注统筹的"顶层设计",方能使处于"深水区"的课程改革找准定位和方向。借鉴英国 2014 国家课程的相关经验,我们可考虑从以下两条路径来强化顶层设计:一是在国家"全面推进依法治国"战略的指引下,尽快制订出相应的改革方案,为义务教育课程改革提供坚实的立法保障,使之始终在有法可依、理性有序的轨道上行驶;二是凭借《教育部关于全面深化课程改革,落实立德树人根本任务的意见》这一纲领性文件颁发的契机,以"立德树人"为核心取向来统筹修订课程标准,研制新的课程方案,使课程改革在全面深化的过程中朝着明确、稳定的方向迈进。[①]

① 教育部.关于全面深化课程改革,落实立德树人根本任务的意见[EB/OL]。http://www.moe.gov.cn/publicfiles/business/htmlfiles/moe/s7054/201404/ 167226. html, 2014-12-08。

(二) 注重课程决策的多元协商

　　课程决策是综合考虑政治、经济、文化等多方面因素及其影响，对各类预选课程方案进行价值判断和选择的过程。民主、科学的课程决策，需要各界人士的广泛参与和多元协商。英国 2014 国家课程改革虽然是在政府的主导下进行的，但在决策时它非常注重吸纳各界人士的广泛参与，促进学校、市场等不同利益主体的合作，并通过多种渠道保证决策信息的透明度，使其决策机制呈现出"多元协商、共同决策"的特征。借鉴其有效经验，可从三方面来改进我国的课程决策机制。第一，扩大课程决策的参与面。在课程标准的修订过程中，应积极调动教师、学生、家长以及社会人士参与课程决策的积极性，认真听取各界不同的声音，鼓励他们为课程标准的完善献计献策。第二，提升课程决策的开放度。在新课程方案的研制过程中，应将有关信息及时公布于网络、报刊等媒体之上，供公众共同检视和商讨，从而在最大程度上保证课程方案的可接纳性。第三，设立相应的决策协调机构，将其基本职能定位于征询民众意见和提呈政策建议，以使官方与民间在课程决策上有一个更加畅通的沟通渠道。

(三) 提升本土课程的文化自觉

　　文化自觉意指生活在一定文化中的人对其文化有"自知之明"，明白其来历和形成过程，理解其价值意义、所受其他文化的影响及其未来发展的方向。① 在教育全球化浪潮中，当我们在努力追寻西方国家的课程改革步伐时，西方其实也在以我们的课程文化反观其自身发展。这一趋势在英国 2014 国家课程的建构历程中即有着充分的印证。它既强调以东方课程标准为参照来反省自身，又采取了切实的举措向东方学习和借鉴。作为发达国家的英国尚能以如此的心态审视其课程文化的发展，作为发展中国家的我们更应从文化自觉的视角提升本土课程的文化品性。首先，要关注本土课程文化传统的继承性，特别是对那些久经积淀的优秀课程文化传统要有充

---

　　①　靳玉乐，罗生全：课程理论的文化自觉[J]．教育研究，2008，(6)，41—46。

足的自信并加以弘扬。如 PISA 上海项目负责人张民选教授在《英国教师眼中的中国数学教育秘密》一文中谈及的课程规划的"政治优势",课程实施的"小步前进"与"多变式"教学,以及教研组、备课组制度中蕴含的"集体分享"文化等。[①] 其次,要强调本土课程文化的自我反省意识,对制约本土课程发展的不合理因素以及与国外课程文化相对照还存在的制度缺陷要有批判性的认识。最后,还须保持本土课程文化的开放心态,让本国课程改革在关注自身发展的同时,主动、自觉地融入世界课程改革的队伍。

(原载于《比较教育研究》2015 年第 9 期)

---

① 张民选:英国教师眼中的中国数学教育秘密[N],中国教育报,2014 - 12 - 16(1)。

宋元与明清时期嘉兴城中的"坊"*

来亚文**

引　言

　　"坊"的演变是城市史研究中的一个重点课题,其变化也是学界所谓"唐宋变革"的一个主要表现,近年来则更加关注唐宋以来地方城市中"坊"的问题,研究成果也层现迭出。察其方法,多为横向分析同一时期不同区域的城市,以求探寻其共性。这种做法固然可以说明很多问题,然而只能从文献上片面地予以解读,难以深入探究,故而稍感未能鞭辟入里。有鉴于此,本文选择地处太湖南走廊运河沿岸的嘉兴城为研究对象,试在南宋至明清的长时段内对嘉兴城中的"坊"进行纵向的分析观察,并运用文献考证、实地调查及大比例尺平面图复原的方法展示嘉兴城在这一时段内"坊"的发展变化。

_____

　　* 　**基金项目:**国家自然科学基金资助项目(批准号:41271154)。
　　** 　**作者简介:**来亚文(1990—　　),男,河南息县人,上海师范大学人文与传播学院硕士研究生。主要研究方向为历史城市地理。

一 研究方法与图文资料简述

1. 嘉兴城市历史形态学复原方法

对于宋代以来城市内部肌理的研究,城市历史形态学的空间复原方法是极为有效的。即运用城市早期的大比例尺实测地图,结合丰富的历史文献资料,复原出古代某时间断面上的空间平面图,以直观展现出零碎且抽象的文字记载所不能说明的问题,这种方法可以完全适用于嘉兴府城的坊巷研究。

嘉兴于五代后晋时升县为州,拓建了周围 12 里的罗城,宋庆元间升为府,成为南宋三辅之地,元至元间毁城,明初重筑 9 里 13 步罗城,仅于城西南角一隅收缩了三里①,此后一直沿用至民国初期。从宏观上看,其城市历史形态变化甚微,且城内河网密布,也使城市内部结构更具稳定性。通过元代以来的方志文献及地图资料来看,城内屈指可数的河道兴废均有所稽考,街巷之名自明代至民国也大多变化甚微,这使运用城市历史形态学手段研究城中的坊巷成为了可能。

2. 嘉兴坊巷研究的图文资料概况

本文选取民国六年(1917)11 月印行的《嘉兴城市全图》②为工作底本,可供参考的实测旧图还有 1940 年代的《嘉兴城区图》,这两幅图对于民国时期城内街巷的绘制及巷名的标记均为旧方志地图所无,结合 1997 年《嘉兴市志》对旧街道改造的记载可以比较完整、准确地标出嘉兴城内旧巷的名称。

在历代方志附图中,光绪《嘉兴府志》卷一《图说》中所附《嘉兴府城图》详细标出了城内每座桥梁的名称,这些桥梁大多见载于元、明各方志中,这便为在平面图上定位复原明、清乃至宋、元时期的地

---

① 光绪《嘉兴府志》卷四《城池》按语,按西南隅收缩三里之事不见明代各方志载,经笔者实地踏察及图上测量,这一说法可能不属实,但不影响城市坊巷的考证。

② 钟士希测绘,嘉兴永明电灯公司民国六年(1917 年)11 月印行,比例尺 1：5000,上海图书馆藏。此图系笔者所知最早的大比例尺嘉兴城市实测地图,从图上可见当时城垣及城内河道保留均较为完整,在很大程度上反映了拆城之前传统嘉兴城市面貌。

理事物提供了绝好的参照物。自今可见嘉兴城最早的方志图——弘治《嘉兴府志》附图始,各种方志所附城郭图亦反映出不同时间断面上地物的大致变化,可为城市历史形态的平面图复原提供直观且有力的支撑。

现存的历代方志是研究嘉兴城市历史形态的主要文献资料。其中最早者是刊行于元至元二十五年(1288 年)的《至元嘉禾志》(后文简称《至元志》),该志编纂成书距南宋灭亡(1279 年)不过 10 年,可以反映出南宋后期嘉兴城的详细状况,其对南宋城中坊巷的记录也多为明清方志誊录,且该志收录了不少宋代文章和碑碣,关键之处也常引用宋代旧志①原文,是研究南宋嘉兴府城的主要文献。明代可参考的最早方志是刊行于弘治五年(1492)的《嘉兴府志》(后文简称《弘治志》),该志全部收录了《至元志》中记载的 70 个坊,并以衙署为参照,记录了每个坊的大致位置,结合正德七年(1512)刊行的《嘉兴府志补》,可以为南宋坊巷的定位及复原提供十分珍贵的资料。

对明、清两代的坊区最先有文字表现的是刊行于嘉靖二十八年(1549)的《嘉兴府图记》,但也并没有明确的"坊巷"篇记载,而是在当时新建的社学名称中体现了出来。真正完整且比较全面地记载城内坊巷的是万历二十四年(1596)纂修的《秀水县志》,由于明宣德四年(1429)析嘉兴县西北地区置秀水县,府城附郭之地皆属秀水县辖,故除历代《嘉兴府志》之外,县志中以现存的万历二十四年、康熙二十四年(1685)的《秀水县志》和民国十四年(1925)的《重修秀水县志》为主,历代《嘉兴县志》②为辅。对于城中坊巷的记载,清代各府

---

① 据笔者详查《至元嘉禾志》原文摘引及参考张国淦《中国古方志考》,《至元嘉禾志》纂修时至少可见宋代的嘉兴旧志五种,分别为:宋《(秀州)旧经》、宋《(嘉禾)志》(赵某修)、宋《嘉禾志》二十六卷(淳熙间张元成修)、宋《嘉禾志》十六卷(嘉定间岳珂修)、宋《(嘉兴)图经》。张国淦:《中国古方志考》,(北京)中华书局,1962 年,第 337—341 页。

② 与本文相关的文献,现存主要有崇祯《嘉兴县志》(1637 年刊行)、康熙《嘉兴县志》(1685 年刊行)、嘉庆《嘉兴县志》(1802 年刊行)、光绪《嘉兴县志》(1908 年刊行)、民国《嘉兴新志》(1928 年修)五种,其中以崇祯《嘉兴县志》及民国《嘉兴新志》的价值最高。

志①几乎全都一味传抄万历《秀水县志》，因此参考价值很低。虽然如此，各方志中对重要地物的位置记载会提及其所在的坊，同样也是考证坊区的关键线索。

此外，民国十七年（1928）纂修的《嘉兴新志》，以不同于以往的体例对嘉兴各个方面作出了精确的量化记录，详细记载了当年新设村里的边界，有部分里与明清时的坊重合，也为研究提供了十分珍贵的史料。1997年的《嘉兴市志》对于建国之后的城市街道改造也有十分细致的记录，其中收录了大量旧巷名，亦极利于补充明、清时期嘉兴城复原图的街巷信息，以便于通过街巷来考证宋元以降的坊。

宋代以来的"坊"由于其本义出现引申，故各种"坊"常为方志混为一谈。本文所研究嘉兴的明、清之"坊"即"在城之里"②；对宋、元之"坊"则以考证其实指，略窥其城市管理制度为主。为上溯探索宋、明间坊巷状况，笔者以清光绪《嘉兴府志》的成书时间（1878年）为时间断限，参考上述各旧图及方志记载，复原出清代晚期的嘉兴府城街巷详图如图1。

二　明、清两代嘉兴府城内的坊区

1. 城内坊区位置的信息整合

明、清两代嘉兴府附郭嘉兴县辖九坊，皆在府城东门外；秀水县辖十五坊，其中府城内有十坊，这是本文主要考察的区域。附郭两县所辖的24个坊区均比较稳定，甚至民国改设村里后民间仍延用旧称③。对城内十坊的位置记载较为系统的为万历《秀水县志》和民国《重修秀水县志》，汇总其信息如表1、表2。

---

① 清代府志有康熙《嘉兴府志》（1682年刊行）、康熙《嘉兴府志》（1721年刊行）、嘉庆《嘉兴府志》（1801年刊行）、道光《嘉兴府志》（1840年刊行）、光绪《嘉兴府志》（1878刊行）。

② 《明史·食货志》："以一百十户为里……在城曰坊，近城曰厢，乡都曰里。"嘉靖《太平县志》卷5《执掌》："坊长即里长之附郭者，供办官府急需，其他与里长同。"

③ 民国《嘉兴新志》第1章《县城·坊区》："城区自前清以来，分为二十四坊，今民间犹沿用未废。"《中国方志丛书》，（台北）成文出版社，1970年，第54页。

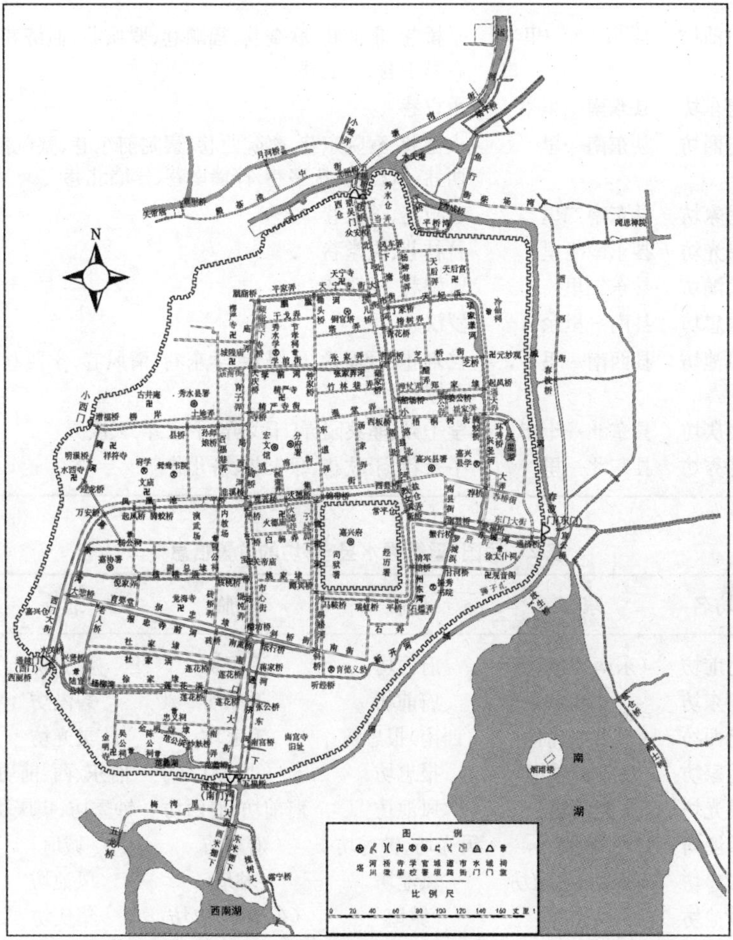

图1 光绪嘉兴府城复原图

表1　万历《秀水县志》坊巷信息

坊名	方位	坊内巷名
府前坊	县①东南一里半	平桥巷、集仙巷、联奎巷、福顺巷、罗城巷、通济巷、石狮子巷、元恺巷
府东坊	县东南一里半	承宣巷
府西坊	县东南一里	火德巷、察院东巷、察院西巷、察院前东巷、察院前西巷、纸行巷、抚字巷、梓墙南巷、梓墙北巷
毛家坊	县东南二里	三板巷、羊血巷
灵光坊	县东南半里	竹林巷、混堂巷
碧漪坊	县东二里	贤娟巷、杨柳巷
报忠坊	县南一里余	罗汉弄
凤池坊	县西南一里	仁寿巷、百福巷、凤凰弄、学东巷、清风巷、学西巷、西城巷
集庆坊	县东北一十步	学子弄、韭菜园弄、干戈弄、平家弄、天庆弄
钟秀坊	县东北一里	平家巷、干歌巷、绿衣巷、塔儿巷

表2　民国《重修秀水县志》坊的位置信息

坊名	东临	西临	南临	北临
府前坊	(东南)府东坊	府西坊	毛家坊	灵光坊
府东坊	城垣	府前坊	毛家坊	碧漪坊
府西坊	(东南)府前坊	(西南)报忠坊	毛家坊	灵光坊
毛家坊	(东南)城垣	报忠坊	(城垣)	府东、西、前坊
灵光坊	碧漪坊	凤池坊	府前坊、府西坊	钟秀坊、集庆坊
碧漪坊	城垣	灵光坊、钟秀坊	府东坊	城垣
报忠坊	府西坊、毛家坊	凤池坊	城垣	凤池坊
凤池坊	灵光坊	城垣	(东南)报忠坊	集庆坊
集庆坊	钟秀坊	城垣	灵光坊	城垣
钟秀坊	碧漪坊	集庆坊	灵光坊	城垣

　　仅从上述二志的记载并不能准确划定城内坊区的准确范围,因

---

① 该"县"即秀水县衙。

此采用新体例编修的民国《嘉兴新志》对于新设村里的记载则提供了更为有效的依据,见表3。

表3　民国《嘉兴新志》载城内新设村里表

里名	固有名称	东界	南界	西界	北界
众安里	碧漪坊	项家漾河	禅杖桥河	北城河	城垣
流虹里	碧漪坊	荐桥河	东城河	西延桥河	禅杖桥河
天星里	碧漪坊	东城基	东城河	荐桥河	秀州校北弄
钟秀里	钟秀坊	北城河	张家弄河	秀学中段	城基
东灵里	灵光坊	西延桥河	集街	局桥河	秀宫河
南灵里	灵光坊	西延桥	集街河	韭溪	道弄上岸
集凤里	南区	市心弄口	报忠埭砖桥街	大西门	楞严寺后
通越里	南区	斜桥河	报忠埭河	大悲桥河	报忠埭上岸后
报忠里	南区	东城河	范蠡湖	西城河	报忠埭河
州东里	南区	东城基狮子汇	南宫	东城河集弄	东城河集弄

由上表可知,1928年新设村里时,众安、流虹、天星三里即旧碧漪坊地,钟秀里即旧钟秀坊,东灵、南灵二里即旧灵光坊,其余集凤、通越、报忠、州东四里,固有名称均为"南区","南区"见载于民国《重修秀水县志》:"城中南区,即南半城,辖府前、府东、府西、报忠、毛家五坊"①,为民国初期新设劝学所时划分的学区,那么上述四里应与旧坊不相重合,故皆统称"南区"。

2. 城内坊区考证与复原

仅从上文的资料来看,并不能准确复原出城内的全部坊区,且民国前期的状况是否与明、清两代相同也尚需考证,因此以万历《秀水县志》中对每个坊内的街巷为线索,结合明、清各坊志中零散的地物位置记载,可以更加真实可信地复原出明、清府城内各坊区的范围,笔者分别予以考证如下:

(1)碧漪坊

民国《嘉兴新志》记该坊被分为众安、流虹、天星三里,各里界详

---

① 民国《重修秀水县志》之《学校》,《浙江图书馆藏稀见方志丛刊》(24—29),(北京)国家图书馆出版社,第463页。

见表3,其坊界也可由此划定出来,即西到北城河、县西河,北、东到城垣,南到东城河,那么这一民国时期的坊区是否与明、清两代相同?

从表1来看,明万历间的碧漪坊内含贤娟、杨柳二巷,这两个巷名一直沿用至三百余年后的建国初期,民国六年及1940年代的城市图中均有表现,1997年的《嘉兴市志》中亦详细记录了这两巷的长宽数据。杨柳巷在北门内;贤娟巷即盐仓巷,在嘉兴县治前(见图1、图2),这便证明了民国《嘉兴新志》对改行村里制时里区对旧坊区继承性的记载是可信的。

在具体地物上,崇祯《嘉兴新志》卷二《公署》载:"道纪司附府,寓玄妙观,在城碧漪坊猪儿桥东";"先师庙在碧漪坊嘉兴县儒学西";《沅湘耆旧集》载:"世传协律仙去嘉兴府治东北碧漪坊建祠祀之,里人祷梦多验。祠三面距水,今为土填焉"①(均见图2)。亦证明明、清时期该坊区一直比较稳定。

(2)钟秀坊、集庆坊

钟秀坊在民国十七年被改设为钟秀里,边界十分明确,万历《秀水县志》载该坊内含平家、干歌、绿衣、塔儿四巷,其中除绿衣巷不明外,其余皆可明确定位。平家巷即1940年代《嘉兴城区图》中的平家弄,干歌巷即干戈弄②,这两条巷弄同时包含于钟秀、集庆二坊,民国《嘉兴新志》载钟秀里之西界在秀学中段,亦即这两条巷的中间,说明两坊的界限在平家、干戈二巷中段,清代各方志在"今巷"条中均记载两个平家、干戈弄,说明了其对万历《秀水县志》不加详察的传抄。

在地理事物的零散记载中,"秀水县忠义祠在集庆坊,节孝祠在钟秀坊"③,前者难以定位,节孝祠则位于秀水县学东,嘉庆、光绪二府志附图中均标明。又"预备济众仓,在城钟秀坊"④;"预备仓,旧名

① 《沅湘耆旧集》卷3《冷协律谦》,清道光二十三年(1843)新化邓氏南村草堂刻本。按冷协律谦祠即冷仙祠。
② 《嘉兴市志》第6篇《市城》,(北京)中国书籍出版社,1997年,第367、383页。
③ 雍正《浙江通志》卷219,清文渊阁四库全书本。
④ 康熙《嘉兴府志》卷4《仓廒》,清康熙二十一年刻本,上海图书馆藏。

济众仓,在钟秀坊天宁寺东"①,则钟秀坊区的范围确与民国无二。

又"城隍庙在城集庆坊"、"楞严寺在城北隅集庆坊"②(见图2),且集庆坊内含"天庆弄",因宋元时天庆观得名,民国旧图中标有"育子弄",该弄"北宋、元时有天庆观"③,故民国育子弄亦在集庆坊内,天庆弄南的百福弄属凤池坊,故连接两巷的秀水县前街应为两坊界线。

(3)灵光坊、凤池坊

由表3可知,灵光坊民国时改设为东灵、南灵二里,整合其边界,其确切范围便十分明确。从表1中看,灵光坊内含竹林(亦名竹篱)、混堂二巷,均可见于民国旧图;又坊内有漱芳亭,"在县西灵光坊旧陆宣公书院后,明正德间知府徐盈建,今为兵巡道署。"④;明代"按察分司,治东北灵光坊"⑤;"宏文馆在府治西北灵光坊"⑥,则明、清灵光坊界与民国时相同。

集庆坊与凤池坊实与表3中的"集凤里"辖区大致相同,这在其名称上即有所体现。从坊内诸巷来看。"百福"之名,甚至今日尚存;"学东"、"学西"二巷则应与位于该坊的嘉兴府学相关;又"杨将军井在县西北凤池坊……今为古井庵";"水西禅寺在城北隅凤池坊爽溪之西";"祥符禅寺在城北隅凤池坊"⑦;"凤池坊娄机故宅,今郡学之前"⑧(见图2);且位于府学南的杨公祠即属报忠坊地⑨,那么凤池坊与报忠坊分界线便应为凤凰池(见图1),从表3可知,集凤里西

① 雍正《浙江通志》卷79。
② 崇祯《嘉兴县志》卷6《祠庙》及卷8《寺观下》,《日本藏中国罕见地方志丛刊》,(北京)书目文献出版社,1991年。
③ 《嘉兴市志》第6篇《市城》,1997年,第367页。
④ 崇祯《嘉兴县志》卷5《古迹》。
⑤ 康熙《嘉兴府志》卷5《公署》,康熙六十年刻本,上海图书馆藏。
⑥ 光绪《嘉兴府志》卷7《公署二》,《中国方志丛书》,(台北)成文出版社,1970年。
⑦ 崇祯《嘉兴县志》卷5《古迹》、卷8《寺观下》。
⑧ 光绪《嘉兴府志》卷15《古迹》。
⑨ 嘉靖《嘉兴府图记》卷4载:"杨公祠在府学南",《中国方志丛书》,(台北)成文出版社,1983年。嘉庆《嘉兴府志》载"杨公祠在府治西北报忠坊",嘉庆六年刻本,上海图书馆藏。万历《秀水县志》、康熙《嘉兴府志》、嘉庆《嘉兴府志》、光绪《嘉兴府志》等附图均标。

界为大西门,这亦与凤池坊一致,明洪武初期建预备仓,"在通越门内五十步……其地为凤池坊"①,该仓亦见于光绪《嘉兴府志》图,足证此处为凤池坊向西南延伸出的区域。

(4) 报忠坊、府西坊

明、清两代的报忠坊与民国时期新设的报忠里并不相同,后者仅为前者的南隅一区,报忠坊北部包括民国时的集凤、通越里一部。

前文所述位于报忠坊北部的杨公祠,本为旧招提寺,古名罗汉院,表1中报忠坊内的罗汉巷或即与此有关;位于图中报忠墭的报忠寺亦在报忠坊②,清雍正时更名觉海寺,至今尚存;另有花园仓也属报忠坊③,据万历《秀水县志》卷十载:"焦家园在通越门内东北百步,宋殿丞焦虎臣之园,即今花园仓也。"又同书卷一《山川》载:"又循(陆宣公)书院之左分流而东,经焦家园为莲花浜。"那么明代花园仓的位置便可大致判定(见图2)。且与花园仓相去不远的陆宣公祠亦"在城西报忠坊"④,位于范蠡湖东的炒麫庵亦属报忠坊地⑤。

从表2可知,报忠坊东临府西、毛家二坊,又据表1,府西坊内有察院东巷、察院西巷等四个因察院命名的巷,察院始建于明嘉靖五年(1526),"治西北百步广平桥南为察院行台"⑥,那么察院东、西两巷及察院前东巷、前西巷位置均可基本确定。同样在府西坊的还有火德巷(因火德庙命名,巷名民国尚存)、梓墙北巷、梓墙南巷(梓墙即子墙,两巷即各方志所称的"子墙脚下")、抚字巷(因府治前向西的"抚字"牌坊得名⑦)、市曹庙、宝花尼寺(俱在府西坊⑧),由此可以

① 崇祯《嘉兴县志》卷3《仓廪》。

② 崇祯《嘉兴县志》卷8《寺观下》:"报忠寺在城西隅报忠坊。"

③ 雍正《浙江通志》卷79:"花园仓在报忠坊"。

④ 崇祯《嘉兴县志》卷6《祠庙》。

⑤ 崇祯《嘉兴县志》卷7《寺观上》、光绪《嘉兴府志》卷18《寺观一》、《檇李诗选》卷十八《炒麫庵》均载其地在报忠坊。《檇李诗选》,清文渊阁四库全书本。

⑥ 万历《嘉兴府志》卷2《公署》,"察院"在万历《秀水县志》及以后的大多方志附图中均有表现,(台北)成文出版社,1983年。

⑦ 万历《秀水县志》卷2《坊表》:"府前街为首藩名郡,左曰承宣,右曰抚字。"该牌坊在嘉庆《嘉兴府志》附《嘉兴府署图》中以图画形式绘出,(台北)成文出版社,1970年。

⑧ 见崇祯《嘉兴县志》卷7《寺观上》,按宝花尼寺明代时为宝花仓。

比较准确地划定府西坊范围(见图 2)。

(5) 府前坊、府东坊

府前坊之地并非皆在府治之前,从表 1 府前坊内的巷名来看,只有"平桥巷"之名与府治前的"平桥"相关,其余均在府治东及东南。如位于"府治东南六十步"①的隐真道院即在府前坊②,因隐真道院前的"集仙"牌坊命名的"集仙巷"也见于表 1,又嘉兴县治东南的舞蛟石亦在府前坊地③,表 1 中的"元恺巷"因"元恺重光"牌坊得名,该牌坊亦在嘉兴"县治东南街"④,"罗城巷"则与府治东名为"罗城"的断头浜相关。与府前坊相邻的府东坊内所含的"承宣巷"因府前街东侧的"承宣"牌坊得名⑤,府东坊的其余各界则可根据表 2 信息予以划定,两坊范围如图 2。

(6) 毛家坊

毛家坊之名应缘于府城南门内通济河支流的一条断头浜,名曰"毛家浜",万历《秀水县志》卷二《山川》载:"湖之东分流……又东,绕南宫前后,疏为三浜水,皆洳浅,而毛家浜差长。"且《至元志》卷八《桥梁》中有"毛家桥,一名熙宁,在澄海门东北一里",其位置可与同在南门东北一里的纸行桥相参照,又有"三板桥,在澄海门北一里五十步",可与在南门东北一里五十步的斜桥相参照,表 1 中的"三板巷"应与该桥有关。

又崇道宫(即上文"南宫")、修真道院均在毛家坊⑥,崇道宫位于南门内南宫浜之畔,修真道院与之相去不远。另外清同治十三年(1874)于毛家坊新建育德义塾⑦,在光绪《嘉兴府志》所附府城图中标出,位于清代新开河北岸,听经桥附近(参见图 1)。结合表 2 信息,可大致判定毛家坊范围。从图 2 来看,毛家与府东两坊之地应

---

① 《至元嘉禾志》卷 12《宫观》,(台北)成文出版社,1983 年。
② 崇祯《嘉兴县志》卷 7《寺观上》。
③ 崇祯《嘉兴县志》卷 5《古迹》。
④ 万历《秀水县志》卷 2《坊表》。
⑤ 崇祯《嘉兴县志》卷 3《坊表》。
⑥ 崇祯《嘉兴县志》卷 7《寺观上》。
⑦ 光绪《嘉兴府志》卷 8《学校一》:"育德义塾,在府治西南毛家坊,旧为塼庵。"

与民国州东里范围相符。

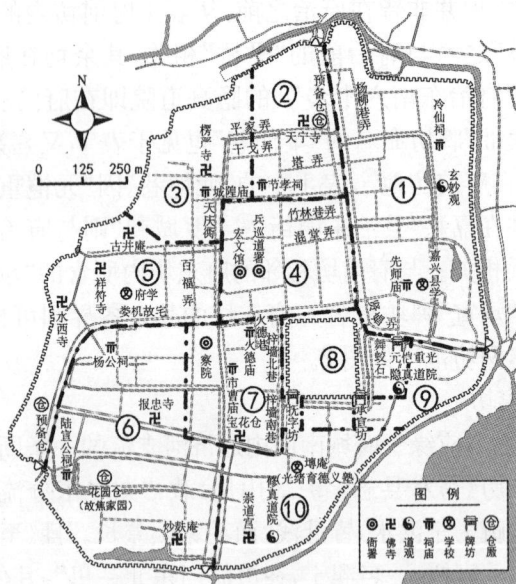

图2 明、清两代嘉兴城内坊区复原①

①碧漪坊②钟秀坊③集庆坊④灵光坊⑤凤池坊
⑥报忠坊⑦府西坊⑧府前坊⑨府东坊⑩毛家坊

三 嘉兴城宋、元时的"坊"与"乡"、"界"

1. 宋元时期嘉兴城内坊名的空间分布

《至元志》中共收录南宋后期的 70 个坊名及其各自的命名缘由,笔者结合弘治《嘉兴府志》及正德《嘉兴府志补》记载,汇总各坊位置信息如表 4。

---

① 城内水系以明代万历时期为断限,清代府治南的新开河、小西门及门内引水河皆无,城西南范公浜可通陆宣公祠南等,详见万历《秀水县志》卷1《山川》。

表4 宋元嘉兴城内"坊"的位置信息

坊名	至元志	弘治志	正德志	坊名	至元志	弘治志	正德志
迎年坊	春波门内		SE180B	四骐坊		SW2L	
正兴坊	朱巷		SE180B	鸣社坊	通社坛		SE40B
登春坊	春波门内		S50B	轻裘坊		SW1L25B	
宜民坊	县治前		N40B	通明坊	醋坊桥	SW1L200B	
流虹坊	兴圣寺西		NE40B	爱稽坊		SW1L80B	
好德坊	盐仓巷	W50B		劝善坊	通咸中坊	SW170B	E200B
通津坊	府东湾			暨容坊	通南营	SW210B	
联魁坊	倪家桥		S80B	天禄坊	石狮子巷	SW200B	
兰锜坊				阅武坊	通教场	SW200B	
碧漪坊	县治西北	NW70B		归鹤坊		SW180B	
集仙坊	隐真道院		S120B	清瑞坊	通澄海门	SW2L	
青绸坊		SW50B		格真坊	通崇道宫	SW2L1B	
环闉坊	府后门东偏			向葵坊	府治前	W120B	
旌烈坊	郡治北	W30B		依莲坊		SW	通节推厅
听履坊	西河上	SW2L		望恩坊	望恩桥西	SW180B	
卿月坊		W1L70B		宝花坊	通宝花寺	S130B	
祥鳝坊	近文学厅	W1L20B		皇华坊		NW100B	
杏坛坊	路学前	W1L20B		广平坊	通广平桥	W1L	
凤池坊		W1L		拥麾坊		NW1L	NE1L
百福坊	通天庆观	W1L		敷闉坊	油车巷	NW300B	
封祝坊	祥符寺	W1L20B		崇梵坊	通兜率寺	NW1L50B	
介宁坊		W1L		钦祐坊	通天宁寺	NW1L50B	
尊耇坊		W1L		遗爱坊	普宁王庙	NW1L	NE1L
率育坊		SW100B	E50B	六一坊	通天庆观	NE300B	
斯才坊		W250B		政桴坊	王鞔鼓巷	NW120B	E100B
咸中坊		W210B	E230B	阜通坊	通税务	W40B	
聚桂坊	市心附近		E200B	金佗坊		NW2L	
丰衍坊	慈济仓	W210B		燕支坊	通燕支桥	NW1L300B	
美俗坊	通瓦子	W180B		澄观坊	通楞严观堂	NW1L300B	
灵光坊	驿巷	W190B		绘麟坊	通金山庙	NW1L300B	
移风坊	通西瓦子	W180B		东陵坊		NW1L70B	

坊名	至元志	弘治志	正德志	坊名	至元志	弘治志	正德志
向道坊	河道人巷	W170B		繡衣坊		NW1L30B	NE1L30B
通阛坊	府后桥西	W170B		瑞龟坊	通精严寺	NW1L	NE1L
织云坊	通蔡织纱巷	W190B		流化坊	通水篆桥	NW100B	
燕春坊	通熙春楼	W200B		兴贤坊	贡院前	NW2L	

（注：《弘治志》以嘉兴县治为参照；《正德志》以秀水县治为参照。E：东；W：西；S：南；N：北；NE：东北；SE：东南；NW：西北；NS：西南；L：里；B：步）

　　据上表信息，结合《至元志》中坊的命名缘由记载，笔者绘制出宋、元嘉兴城中可定位的 69 个坊名的分类分布示意图如图 3：

图 3　嘉兴宋、元各类坊名分布示意图

注：城西南隅处城墙在明初的收缩系示意性表示。

　　从坊名分布图来看，宋、元时期的"坊"多集中分布于子城西北和东南，府城东北及西南区则甚少。从子城北部坊名分布的密集程度来看,宋、元时期的坊明显与明、清时期的坊区不同,其数量甚至超过了后世的巷,这说明宋、元时期嘉兴城内的"坊"应当并不仅仅是城市基层管理区划的名称。

因寺观命名的坊多集中于城西北部,城南及城东则零星散布;名宦宅邸一般占地面积较大,因之命名的坊也多分散在城内四周;而坊名直接源于固有坊巷者均为历史更为久远的坊,此类坊与因旌表教化而命名的坊均可指示出城内居民密集区,从图中看,这两类坊多集中分布在子城北偏西不远的区域,此类可反映出历史层累叠加的街区则是由近及远地研究嘉兴宋、元之"坊"的不二选择。

2. 宋代嘉兴的大市官街

在子城北侧偏西的区域内分布的坊名中,通阛坊因路通大市而名,美俗、移风二坊分别通向东、西瓦子,丰衍坊通宋代的慈济仓,燕春坊通酒库熙春楼,等等。仅从此类坊名的地点指示来看,便不难理解坊名集中于子城西北的缘故了,如万历《秀水县志》所言,"余里生聚久,通衢曲隈,市有坊、街有巷,犹古者井伍遗意。"①城中的大市往往是"坊"聚集的区域,嘉兴子城西北便正是宋代的大市所在。

清嘉庆十五年(1810)嘉兴灵光坊宏文馆东侧东道弄②(今少年路)修街时出土的一块宋代铭文砖,引起了当地文人的关注,时人钱泰吉为之作诗,其序文对该砖作了十分详细的描述:

砖修广各一尺,楷书八字,作二行,字径二寸,曰:"人丰翕集,市井骈阗。"旁二行。左一行云:"大宋政和三年癸巳岁"。字体稍杀而笔法与前八字同。右一行云:"大宋嘉泰元年辛酉正月十六用石重砌"。字寸许,审其笔法,盖重修时加刻也。砖阴文十行,云:"秀州嘉兴县郭五乡居住会首胡公佐、张世隆,精严寺净悟大师有肱,张安言、罗明之、马悦、沈奭、费元实、陈璋、吴拱,遍募众缘,同力重砌大市上官街一道,自韭溪桥东,砌至菩萨桥。圣宋政和三年六月十一日下手兴工甃砌。伏愿保国

① 万历《秀水县志》卷1《坊巷》。
② 东道弄因在杭嘉湖道署东,故名,位置见图1,砖出土位置记载见《桂馨堂集·顺安诗草》卷六《秀水故友葛素如星垣所藏政和砌街砖去岁腊尽归于余》,清道光刻本。

安民,风调雨顺,仍愿舍钱僧俗施主,洎普天之下一切有情,增
延禄算,植福无疆者。书此谨记,泥水都料邵宗仁、弟宗义等崇
信书。"嘉庆庚午里人修宏文馆侧集街,葛君董其役,于土中得
此砖,上有政和钱三百、古镜一、锁二,拓本见贻。①

从砖上铭文及钱泰吉的描述来看,宋代嘉兴大市官街前后修砌
了两次,第一次是在北宋政和三年(1113)六月,后在南宋嘉泰元年
(1201)正月重修,其中韭溪桥和菩萨桥均载于《至元志》,且直至清
代其位置依然如故。由这一铭文记载,结合《至元志》中对南宋地物
的描述可知,嘉兴城内的主要街道格局(至少是子城北部大市官街
及其主要支离街道②)自北宋直至民国,基本未发生大的改变,这便
使我们观察宋代嘉兴大市官街一带的"坊"的形态成为了可能。

一般认为今嘉兴市中山路即宋代以来的大市官街所在,而从宋
代修街砖铭文的出土地点来看,大市官街应以韭溪桥为端,沿集街
而东,至东道弄向北,于张家弄折而向东,至菩萨桥止(参见图1、图
4),这在文献中亦有佐证:作于明代成化五年(1469)《玄真道院建复
旌烈庙碑记》中写道:"计其地,适尽道院东际而巷名'旌烈'者,正直
其取人路……西南距官道,东北肘腋之地皆割没为民居。"③旌烈庙
即杨将军庙,位置便在明、清的混堂弄中,明前期的官道即在该庙西
南,结合宋代修街砖出土处来看这段明前期的碑文,便可以确认东
道弄所在的那条街便是宋代的大市官街主干道。

3. 南宋嘉兴城内"坊"的实指

通过普查南宋后期至明、清两代的方志来看,明、清两代的坊区
在明嘉靖以前完全不见于方志中,其后最先由万历《秀水县志》系统
记录,并在崇祯《嘉兴县志》中高频率出现在地物的地点描述中。而
《至元志》中收录的 70 个南宋的"坊",对其可作补充的记载也仅见
于明代前期的《弘治志》,正德《嘉兴府志补》只收录了十余个,其后

---

① 《甘泉乡人稿》卷21《读旧书室诗》,宋修砖街歌为葛孝廉作并序,清同治十一年刻光
绪十一年增修本。宋砖出土事及文字内容亦见《两浙輶轩续录》卷19、于源《灯窗琐话》卷
125、《养吉斋丛录》卷6、光绪《嘉兴府志》卷86、光绪《嘉兴县志》卷35。

② 宋代该区也极可能存在因明、清两代逐渐侵占而消失的小巷弄。

③ 正德《嘉兴府志补》卷6《碑碣》,明正德七年刻本,上海图书馆藏。

各志均原文照录《至元志》,可见南宋时期的 70 个"坊"至晚在明弘治间仍有遗存,因此用明代前期的文献资料来补充南宋城内"坊"的线索是一种十分有效的办法。

(1) 实即巷弄之"坊"

前文所引的《玄真道院建复旌烈庙碑记》对旌烈庙的地理位置描述中提及了南宋时的"旌烈坊":

> 玄真道院在嘉兴府秀水县南隅韭溪界旌烈坊……计其地迤尽道院东际,而巷名"旌烈"者,正直其取入路。

该碑文作于弘治之前,碑文还述及作者青年时代在该庙读书之事,故其对旌烈坊的描述自然是亲眼所见。从这段文字看,"旌烈坊"位于后世的东道弄(即宋代的大市官道)路东,在后来俗名"混堂弄"的巷口处,标有"旌烈"二字,《至元志》卷二《坊巷》亦载:"旌烈坊在郡治北。名义:巷有郡神杨将军庙,故立此名以旌将军之休烈。"可见所谓"旌烈坊",便是巷口树有"旌烈"坊匾的巷弄。这在《至元志》记载的其他坊巷中也有体现。如"向道坊,在何道人巷口,故以是名。"①此处"何(河)"字应为"向"字之讹;"人"应为"入",即"向道坊,在向道入巷口"。再如织云坊"通蔡织纱巷"、介宁坊"俗曰陈婆儿巷"、率育坊"俗曰杨洗麸巷"、斯才坊"俗曰马坊巷"等等,此类坊或由旧巷更名而来,或在明前期更名为巷,其实质只是一条巷弄的雅称而已。

又如南宋的"灵光坊",同样存在于明弘治时期,《至元志》记载该坊"在驿巷,名义:通灵光寺,故立是名"。"灵光寺"是精严寺的古称,同样"通精严寺"的还有"瑞龟坊",而精严寺前只有一条横巷,且"瑞龟坊"并不在"驿巷",明显两坊不在一处。又弘治时有"灵光巷",嘉靖《嘉兴府图记》卷二载"稍东北入灵光街,为按察分司并司府馆,为布政分司,宋为监仓东厅,元为廉访分司"。明代按察分司便在后来的道前街(街道今同名)路北,故该街也即明代前期的灵光街、灵光巷,同样也是宋、元时期的灵光坊、驿巷。

---

① 其中"何"字《至元志》钞本写为"河"。

百福巷弄是嘉兴城中唯一一条将宋代坊名沿用至建国后的巷子,且如《至元志》所载,百福坊"巷通天庆观",百福巷弄的北段确可通向古天庆观所在的育子弄,也即宋代的"六一坊",而作于宋淳祐五年(1245)的《重建慈恩塔院记》①中载:"余幼肄举子业,周游问学诸郡,则憩天庆坊刘氏邸。""天庆坊"不见《至元志》所载的 70 个坊名,而明万历后有"天庆巷"见于诸志。又如宋代"好德坊,在盐仓巷",盐仓巷中因有苏小小墓,故本名"贤娼",后取其谐音,也常两名并用,"好德"二字即取"欲使人知有好色不如好德之义"。该巷直至建国后尚存,《嘉兴市志》载:"北起中山路中段,南向折东与县南街相交,长 180 米,宽 4 米,沥青路面,旧时名贤娼弄。"②该巷在民国六年旧图中亦有标明。所谓"好德坊",实即立于盐仓巷中,书有"好德"二字的牌坊,而盐仓巷也因此雅称为好德坊。

另外比较特殊的有咸中坊和劝善坊,《至元志》卷二《坊巷》载:

咸中坊,名义:俗曰幢子巷,乃宋刑人于市之所,故立此名,盖取"吕刑咸中有度"之义。

劝善坊,名义:通咸中坊刑人之所。《尚书·多方》云:"殄戮多罪,亦克用劝",孔子传曰:"戮众罪亦能劝善"。因立此名。

由上文来看,咸中坊为立于大市上的一座牌坊,该坊内的刑场在通往劝善坊的巷口,又表 4 可知其距嘉兴、秀水二县治的方位距离,但仅凭此依然无法予以准确定位。对此,作于弘治六年(1493)的《修建市曹庙碑记》③中的记载可予以补充:"市曹庙在嘉兴郡治西,去秀水县治东南二百步,咸中坊市心巷之中区。"宋、元时期的坊在明弘治时皆有遗存,故时人所记自然具有很高的可信度。从文中看,市心巷应是咸中坊的一部分,该巷建国后尚存,且有修街砖可证明其至晚于宋代便已存在(详见后文)。市心巷北通集街,可知咸中坊所在的"市"应为大市官街的集街段,市心巷应为大市官街主干道

① 《至元嘉禾志》卷 18《碑碣三》。
② 《嘉兴市志》第六篇《市城》,1997 年,第 382 页。
③ 正德《嘉兴府志补》卷 6《碑碣》。

的一条主要支离巷,劝善坊应在大市官街路北的西道弄(见图 4),这应即"以坊统巷"或坊内有坊的现象①。

图 4　宋代嘉兴大市附近的"坊"

可在图中准确定位的坊还有巷内有铜官塔的遗爱坊(即塔弄)、位于嘉兴县治西北,路通天星湖的碧漪坊(即梧桐树街)、巷通广平桥的广平坊(即砖桥弄北段)、内有报忠寺的听履坊(即报忠埭一段)②等等,均可坐实南宋后期嘉兴城内的"坊"多为巷之雅称的结论。

(2) 实即牌坊之"坊"

《至元志》中所录南宋嘉兴城内的坊名也出现了坊巷和牌坊不分的状况,如"聚桂坊"为表彰神童而立、"联魁坊"为表彰孝子而立,到了明代则被方志同时收入"坊巷"和"坊表"两目中,且注文并无二致。"归鹤"、"集仙"二坊,则明确可知为隐真道院门前的两座牌坊①。再如通阛坊"在府后桥之西偏,通大市"。那么其位置约在集街与东道弄交汇处,正是大市入口;环阓坊"在府后门之东偏,通回环子城之路"(见图4),实际上也只是一座牌坊。那么由此来看,"在嘉兴县前"的宜民坊、"在路学前"的杏坛坊、"通南营"的暨容坊、"通教场"的阅武坊等等,均应与"归鹤"、"集仙"一样,只是实体建筑的牌坊。那么大市官街附近为坊名集中之处的问题便可得到解答,在官街附近因东、西瓦子命名的"移风"、"美俗"二坊,因熙春楼命名的燕春坊,因慈济仓命名的丰衍坊等等,均可能是设立在大市沿街或街内小巷中各种地物之前的牌坊。

而此类牌坊之所以被收录进"坊巷"条,也不一定全都是混淆了"坊"的概念,如聚桂坊,本为旌表牌坊,而后其所在的巷因此而被称为聚桂坊,宋宝祐四年进士唐天麟即是"县之聚桂坊人"②,集仙坊在明代也有因之命名的巷,这种现象明代也比较普遍,前文提及的"抚字"、"承宣"、"元恺重光"等牌坊均有与之对应的巷名存在。

4. 宋代嘉兴城内的乡和界

学界已有学者发现并提出"以乡统坊"的现象,认为这是"由于这些州县城郊都市化后,其基层行政管理单位却并未能及时从乡里制转变成厢坊制,而是变成了独特的乡坊制"③的缘故。但是从嘉兴的个案来看,这一观点似乎并不适用。

前文所引的大市官街修街砖文中有"秀州嘉兴县郭五乡居住会首胡公佐、张世隆"之文,清代人不解其中"郭五乡"所指,作诗云:"已没灵光井,谁知郭五乡?",并自作注曰:"乡名不载旧志,今见砖刻。"④这是对"郭五乡"的误解,"郭五乡"应即宋代嘉兴县的五个附郭乡,而非一乡之名,且是方志中所详载的。前文所引宋宝祐二年(1254)的《报忠观记》,有"在郡之五福乡听履坊西门"语,说明南宋嘉兴城内有以乡统坊的现象。听履坊即后世的报忠埭一段,五福乡自然便是城内之乡。另外,1967年嘉兴市心弄施工时,出土了两块

① 《至元志》卷17载端平改元(1234年)《隐真道堂记》提及:"院北两坊导其所从人之路,东榜'集仙'、西标'归鹤'。"
② 最早见嘉庆《嘉兴县志》记载。
③ 前揭包伟民:《宋代城市研究》第2章,《管理制度》,第125页。
④ [清]朱休度:《小木子诗三刻》之《俟宁居偶咏》卷下,清嘉庆刻汇印本。

宋代修街砖^①，其一铭文：

> 大宋国秀州嘉兴县嘉禾乡子州西界市心内清信募绿弟子宋□□朱希建，□从□谨募重新甃砌碏□，长伍拾丈，计钱肆拾贯文……岁次丙寅六月初八日，募绿□□朱希建。

文中的嘉兴尚称"秀州"，故在南宋庆元元年(1195)升府之前，则"丙寅"应至晚为绍兴十六年(1146)。"市心"即出土修街砖的市心巷，那么该巷在宋代便属于附郭嘉禾乡管辖，嘉禾乡便也是"郭五乡"之一。

宋代的嘉兴罗城拓修于后晋天福四年(939)，至上述时间最晚的宝祐二年，诸乡被囊括于城中已然经历了三百余年，自然不会有"未能及时从乡里制转变成厢坊制"的问题，且经查后世方志，五福乡至清代犹存，嘉禾乡在明初时析为四隅。那么嘉兴以乡统坊的现象该如何解释？

《至元志》卷三《乡里》中对"嘉兴县郭五乡"有比较详细的记录，这五乡分别为：五福乡(管里4)、嘉禾乡(管里4)、由拳乡(管里4)、劝善乡(管里4)、时清乡(管里1)。崇祯《嘉兴县志》对唐代以来嘉兴所辖的乡里进行了考证和记录，其中除五福乡外，其余四乡均在五代前便已存在。对宋代之后的乡里记载比较详细，其各自所管里数与《至元志》同，且增加了各乡位置的记录，统计如下：

表5　嘉兴县附郭五乡宋、明位置(治、州治即子城衙署，县即嘉兴县治)

乡名	五福乡	嘉禾乡	由拳乡	劝善乡	时清乡
宋代位置	治北	州治	治南	县东	县北
明代位置	县西二里	——	县南一里	县东北二里	县北二里

由此来看，嘉兴城的附郭乡是长期存在的行政单位，且到了明代以后才改为"隅"或渐渐移出城外，以乡统坊的现象并非是偶然，

---

① 铭文拓片现藏于嘉兴市博物馆二楼，第二片有"宝祐三年(1255)，岁次乙卯八月初四日重甃砌"文。

而应是一种常态。

又《至元志》在上述五乡之后载:

> 五乡凡十有二界:天庆上界、天庆下界、盐仓上界、盐仓下界、大悲东界、大悲西界、府东界、府西界、韭溪界、薛向界、南官界、南菓子界。

这又引出一个由陈振提出过的问题,陈振认为"一部分大中城市则开始实行厢统界,界辖坊(巷)的'厢界坊(巷)制'"[①],依据主要为《嘉泰吴兴志》卷二《坊巷·州治》、《乾道临安志》卷二《坊市·界分》及《淳祐临安志》卷七《坊巷》。其中《嘉泰吴兴志》明确记载:"坊名乡地久废,官司乡贯止以界称,今为界十七,分属四厢。"惜陈文论之甚简,包伟民则对其观点提出怀疑,认为宋代湖州的"界"可能只是坊的一种别称,杭州的"界"则应"只是一个点或线,而非一个区域"[②]。从宋代嘉兴城的状况来看,"界"则很可能是专门设立的城市管辖区域,且在嘉兴并非由厢统界,而是由附郭乡,附郭乡在城市的管理中似乎发挥着不可低估的作用,如修筑大市官街的工程便主要由附郭五乡的"居住会首"主持。

前文提及的砖文中有"秀州嘉兴县嘉禾乡子州西界市心内"的表述,由于当时嘉兴尚为秀州,故该"子州西界"应即《至元志》中的"府西界";又前文所引明成化五年的《玄真道院建复旌烈庙碑记》中亦有"玄真道院在嘉兴府秀水县南隅韭溪界旌烈坊"的表述,而这种用"界"作为地点描述的方式此后便不再出现,逐渐为明代的坊区所替代。

仔细分析嘉兴城内 12 个界名中之带方位者,皆可找到与之对应的地名:"天庆"即天庆观;"盐仓"即盐仓巷;"大悲"即大悲河(西门流入之河[③]);府东、府西均以府治为参照;从这些地名上看,无一不在明、清时期的坊界上。其他界名除"薛乡"不明外,其余亦皆可

---

① 陈振:《略论宋代城市行政制度的演变——从厢坊制到隅坊(巷)制、厢界坊(巷)制》,《漆侠先生纪念文集》,(保定)河北大学出版社,2002 年,第 347 页。
② 详见前揭包伟民:《宋代城市研究》第 2 章,北京中华书局,《管理制度》2014 年版,第 155—160 页。
③ 万历《秀水县志》卷 1《山川》:"大悲河,长一百五十丈。水从西运河来,下从韭溪河去。"

考:"韭溪"即韭溪桥或其所跨之河的古称;"南宫"即崇道宫;"南菓
子"即菓子巷之南①。且宋代嘉兴城内有12个界,与明、清时期的10
个坊在数量上也相差不大。又宋代在"子州西界"(即府西界)内的
市心巷,明、清时期也在府西坊内。由此来看,至晚在明嘉靖之后出
现的城内坊区应并非骤然设置,而可能对前代有所继承。笔者根据
其大致方位及前文对明、清坊区的考证,将可与宋元界名对应的明
清坊名列表如下:

表6　宋元界名与明清坊名方位对应
(注:按古代惯称,上南下北。)

宋元界名	明清坊名	宋元界名	明清坊名
盐仓下界	碧漪坊	盐仓上界	府前坊
天庆下界	集庆坊	天庆上界、大悲西界	凤池坊
韭溪界	灵光坊	南宫界	毛家坊
府西界、南菓子界	府西坊	府东界	府东坊
薛乡界	钟秀坊(可能)	大悲东界	报忠坊

四　余　论

　　明、清两代嘉兴府城中的坊区约在明正德至嘉靖间(16世纪
初)设置,崇祯时已被常用于地名描述。坊区为城市管理、赋役征收
的基本单位,设置之初,还曾以坊为单位建立了社学,后均废。又清
康熙《秀水县志》卷二《公廨》中记录了各坊的"铺",即更铺,亦称巡
警铺,明清时期的地方城市中,坊区亦为巡警消防区,如明代宁波府
"每坊旧设巡警铺夫,以防盗备火"②。坊区的设置,更可作为控制城
市的有力手段,如顺治二年(1645)嘉兴民众抗清时,即令"各坊居
民,不许往来,逾界者即亲识,立时禽杀"③,由此可见一斑。

---

①　正德《嘉兴府志补》卷2《坊巷》:"菓子巷在府治西五十步,旧传锦带河傍多栽李柰菓
子,取菓珍李柰之义。"则南菓子可能为梓墙南巷。
②　嘉靖《宁波府志》卷25《传一》之《余文升传》,明嘉靖三十九年刊本。
③　屈起:《嘉兴乙酉兵事记》卷1《郡城之骚乱》,世界书局民国三十六年版,第3页。

　　至晚于明弘治以前,南宋遗留下的古坊(以实体建筑为标志)尚存于嘉兴城中,因此这之前的记载可与《至元志》互为参照。这些古坊虽然在弘治后废弃,但在巷名中仍有部分遗存,由于街巷形态的稳定性,仍可以此观察南宋之"坊"的原形。可以说所谓"坊巷",应即入口有牌坊的街巷,其意与"街坊"相类。明嘉靖之前不见后世的坊区记载,而可见以宋元时的界名用于地点描述中,可以说宋代嘉兴的"界"应为一种类似明、清坊区的行政区划,且沿用至明代前期。在嘉兴,统辖"界"的单位是附郭乡,而非厢,因此嘉兴"以乡统坊"的现象应为乡辖界,界统坊(巷)的表现。宋代的嘉兴城内亦设置了南、北、西三厢[①],但其时嘉兴府城皆为嘉兴县辖地,故城内诸界、坊(可能还包括"里")均属县辖之乡。

(原载于《中国历史地理论丛》2015 年第 3 期)

---

　　① 《至元志》卷1《沿革》:"宋置南、北、西三厢,圣朝至元十三年废,遂置兵马司,至元十四年改为录事司。

上海离全球城市有多远？*

——基于城市网络联系能级的比较分析

刘江会　贾高清**

0　引　言

　　2014年初上海市政府发布了《关于编制上海新一轮城市总体规划的指导意见》，明确提出未来上海发展目标定位是："在2020年基本建成'四个中心'和社会主义现代化国际大都市的基础上，努力建设成为具有全球资源配置能力、较强国际竞争力和影响力的全球城市。"这一城市定位与2001年国务院批准的《上海市城市总体规划(1999—2020)》相比已经发生了变化，即定位从"现代化国际大都市"变为"全球城市"，全球城市要求上海似于纽约、伦敦在全球城市网络格局中成为重要的"全球性节点"城市。上海城市定位这一变化是上海顺应全球政治经济格局变化后的选择，建设"全球城市"是上海在经济转型升级的关键时期，谋求高层次发展的新的奋斗目标。

　　全球城市的形成有两个基本条件：一是全球城市产生于世界经

　　*　**基金项目:** 国家社科基金项目(12BGJ046)；教育部人文社科基金项目(13YJA790067)；上海师范大学第七期重点建设学科"城市经济学"和上海师范大学"原创性与前瞻性预研项目"(DYL201401)

　　**　**作者简介:** 刘江余(1971—　)，男，上海师范大学商学院副教授，硕士研究生导师。研究方向：金融地理。

济增长的重心区域;二是全球城市的形成和发展依赖于城市区域体系的强大支撑。当前,中国已成为世界经济增长新的引擎,上海无疑在这一引擎中发挥重要作用,同时上海又有"长三角"城市群提供的有力腹地支撑。因此,可以说上海已经具备了建成全球城市的基本条件。

但我们也清楚地认识到,与纽约、伦敦等公认的全球城市相比,上海在全球资源配置能力、国际竞争力和影响力方面存在不少差距。搞清楚这种差距有利于上海在建设全球城市的过程中避免走弯路。基于这一认识,本文试图运用"嵌套网络模型"的方法来回答"上海离全球城市有多远?"这一基本问题,同时从城市网络联系能级的角度分析上海与顶级全球城市的差距,并在此基础上有针对性地提出上海建设全球城市的一些政策建议。

1 文 献 回 顾

全球城市研究的开拓者当属英国著名城市规划专家 Peter. Hall,他在《世界城市》一书中详细描述了世界城市[①]的五大基本特征。Hall 之后涌现了大批具有影响力的全球城市理论,比如 Jacobs 的"动态城市理论"、Friedmann 的"世界城市假说"以及 Sassen 的"全球城市三部曲"。这些理论成为 20 世纪 80—90 年代中期全球城市研究的主流理论。但这一时期的全球城市研究有一个共同的局限性就是"有属性无关系",即大量研究成果多是关于单个城市或者是几个城市综合指标的比较,运用的基本测度指标也主要是城市属性数据,如跨国公司总部的集中程度、金融资产控制率等,并认为在这些数据排序中排名靠前的城市即为全球城市。这种只关注城市属性数据而忽略城市之间的联系数据被认为是这一时期全球城市理论广遭诟病的主要原因。

20 世纪末随着信息技术和航空运输业快速发展,使得城市之

---

①　世界城市"的概念最早是由城市和区域规划先驱 P. Geddes 在 1915 年所著《演化中的城市》一书中提出来的,而"全球城市"的概念一般认为是哥伦比亚大学 Saseen 教授在其1991 年出版的《全球城市》(The Global City)一书中提出来的。"世界城市"可以视为是"全球城市"的早期概念。

间的联系越来越紧密。研究者逐渐认识到，城市不能被孤立地研究，应该将其理解为一个由信息、资本、人力等多种"流"所联结起来的庞大的城市网络体系。基于这种认识，Castells 提出了"全球流动空间理论"，认为城市间的网络关系决定了城市的地位，全球城市是"在全球网络中作为一种高级服务生产和消费连接过程的中心"，即一个城市被视为"全球城市"一定是因为其在"全球城市网络"中居于关键性节点地位，Calstells 的这一思想突破了 Sassen 等人"有属性无关系"的全球城市理论研究的缺陷，开创了基于关系连接的全球城市网络研究新框架。但由于数据的匮乏，基于 Castells 理论的城市间网络联系的实证研究成果一开始比较少。拉夫堡大学 Taylor 教授及其领导的"全球化和世界城市"(Globalization and World Cities，简称 GaWC)研究小组则突破了这一困境。Taylor 借鉴 Sassen 研究世界城市时提出先进生产性服务业(Advanced Producer Services，简称 APS)的概念，构建了"嵌套网络模型"，该模型通过统计 APS 企业机构在全球城市体系中的分布情况来获得"城市-公司数量矩阵"，并通过矩阵评分对全球城市联系能级进行排名，从而为城市网络联系的定量化描述提供了方向。GaWC 利用该方法对不同城市网络联系能级的排名获得了广泛的关注，被视为是评估一个城市是否具有"全球性"影响力的重要标准。

GaWC 小组的基于 APS 企业全球分布特征的"嵌套网络模型"的研究方法已获得不少国内学者的关注，并运用该方法取得了很多研究成果。比如倪鹏飞和 Taylor 利用该方法测算了中国 37 个城市在全球网络体系中的联系能级排名情况。赵渺希和刘铮根据中国205 家 APS 企业和 106 个中国城市构成的数量矩阵，测算了中国城市网络体系中不同城市的联系能级。王聪和曹有挥等利用长三角APS 企业分布特征，分析了长三角城市网络中各城市的联系能级。姚永玲和董月等则根据 61 家跨国 APS 企业和 49 个不同国家城市构成的数量矩阵，测算并比较了北京和首尔的城市网络联系能级及其动力因素。

本文试图在上述国内外研究成果的基础上，尝试运用"嵌套网络模型"来研究上海在全球城市网络中的位置。与国内现有相关文献相较,本文所做工作的价值体现在以下三个方面:其一,现有研究上海全球城市建设的文献很多属于战略类研究,即聚焦于研究上海建设全球城市的战略规划、发展路径等问题,本文则利用全球城市关联数据,分析上海在全球城市网络体系中的位置,从而可以为这类战略研究提供客观依据;其二,与那些主要是基于城市属性指标来分析上海的全球竞争力或上海与其他全球城市差距的文献相较,本文则利用全球城市间的联系数据来分析上海的全球影响力问题,因而可以弥补这类文献忽略全球城市之间关联数据的"有属性无关系"的局限性;其三,虽有一些文献在分析全球城市网络中的城市联系能级时涉及到上海,但是关注点不是上海,与这些文献相较,本文的关注点则放在上海,因此对于上海全球城市建设问题而言,本文更具针对性。

2 全球城市网络联系能级的测算方法、样市选择与数据来源

2.1 全球城市网络联系能级的测算方法:嵌套网络模型

全球城市网络理论认为,全球城市是建立在全球经济层面的重要节点,而先进生产性服务业则是全球城市结节成网的基础,APS企业在全球布局办公点和分支机构,从而推动城市间资本、人才和信息流动,这种生产要素在城市间的流动促进了全球城市网络的形成,因此跨国经营的 APS 企业是全球城市网络的真正缔造者。根据这一理论,Taylor 领导的 GaWC 研究小组创造性地利用跨国 APS企业的全球分布特征建立了全球城市间的网络联系分析框架——"嵌套网络模型"。基于该模型对全球城市进行的排名被视为是评估一个城市是否具有"全球性"影响力的重要标准。本文也利用该模型来测算全球城市的网络联系能级,并据此分析上海在全球城市网络中是否居于"关键性节点"位置。

基本步骤如下:首先假设 n 个城市中有 m 个先进生产性服务公司,V_{ij} 表示 j 公司在 i 城市办公机构的服务价值,所以最后会得到 $n \times m$ 的服务型价值矩阵城市网络,其中矩阵的构成元素 V_{ij} 取值如表1所示。

表1 样本跨国公司服务价值判定标准

V_{ij}值	判定标准
0	j 公司在 i 城市没有设立任何机构。
1	j 公司在 i 城市设立一般机构或者办事处。如毕马威在深圳设立办事处经营当地的一般事务。
2	j 公司在 i 城市设立重要机构网点或者地区总部级别的机构。如毕马威在上海设立了中国总部，在北京设立了中国业务发展中心，两个城市都赋予2。
3	j 公司在 i 城市设立公司总部或者具有总部职能的机构。如毕马威行政总部在阿姆斯特丹，业务总部在纽约，两个城市都赋予3。

由服务价值矩阵可以得到两城市通过一个公司的基本连接点：

$$\gamma_{abj} = V_{aj}V_{bj} \tag{1}$$

γ_{abj} 是 a, b 两城市之间通过 j 公司的单位连接，称为单位链接。其中 V_{aj} 即 j 公司在 a 城市的服务价值，V_{bj} 即 j 公司在 b 城市的服务价值。通过两城市之间与某个公司的单位链接，继续求和可以得到两城市与所有公司的链接之和，可以用下面的公式表示：

$$\gamma_{ab} = \sum_{j=1}^{m} \gamma_{abj} \tag{2}$$

网络中的每个城市与剩下的其他城市形成 $n-1$ 个链接，因此可以得到：

$$N_a = \sum_{i=1}^{n-1} \gamma_{ai}, \, a \neq i \tag{3}$$

这被定义为 a 城市与网络中其他城市的链接数量之和，也被称为 a 城市的"网络联系能级"（Na）。我们选取具有"最高网络联系能级"（定义为 N_H）的城市作为参照系，并将其他城市的 N_a 与 N_H 相除，从而可以得到城市 a 的"相对网络联系能级"：

$$P_a = \Delta N_a / \Delta N_H \tag{4}$$

显然相对网络联系能级 P_a 界于 0 到 1 之间，最高网络联系能

级的城市 P_a 值等于1。

2.2 样本选择和数据来源

参照 GaWC 研究小组的方法,我们选取了先进生产性服务业的会计、广告、银行/金融、法律、咨询、物流、信息技术等 7 个行业中最具全球影响力的 50 家公司,这些公司大多为 2014 年财富杂志全球500 强公司,另外,这些公司还要符合以下标准:(1)在全球至少有15 家以上的分支机构;(2)在美洲、欧洲和亚太地区至少有一家分支机构。由于这些样本公司在全球各地基本都有分支机构,考虑到数据处理的工作量,本文只选取了 GaWC 世界城市层级中的 Beta 级以上的部分城市,并补充了最新的财富 500 强在该地区有公司总部的城市,这样就得到了全球 64 个城市。

测算样本城市"网络联系能级"关键是要知道全球性 APS 企业的机构在样本城市的分布数据。这一数据我们只能通过手工逐一查阅这些企业的网站获得。例如,对于摩根斯坦利,首先进入摩根斯坦利公司全球主页,然后点击"global office",我们可以查到摩根斯坦利在本文 64 个样本城市中的 48 个城市中设立了机构。摩根斯坦利总部在纽约,亚太地区总部设在香港,欧洲地区总部设在伦敦,在北京、上海等设有办事处。通过这种方式,我们统计整理得到 50 家样本公司在 64 个样本城市设立了 2180 个机构,其中公司总部和地区总部级共 790 个,分支机构或办事处级1390个。

3 基于"嵌套网络模型"的上海城市网络联系能级的测算结果及其佐证

3.1 基于"嵌套网络模型"上海城市网络联系能级的测算结果

利用上述"嵌套网络模型"我们测算出了 2014 年全球城市的网络联系能级和相对网络联系能级。表 2 中列出全球城市中网络联系能级排名前十的城市。这些城市在全球网络中起着巨大的连通作用,同时在全球金融、经济、文化、政治等各领域都是全球的中心,也起着重大的聚集作用,在世界城市网络中处于关键的枢纽作用。

表2 世界城市网络联系能级排名前十城市(2014)

城市	网络联系能级(N_a)	相对网络联系能级(P_a)	排序
伦敦	6432	1.000	1
纽约	6412	0.997	2
香港	5567	0.866	3
巴黎	5555	0.864	4
新加坡	4989	0.776	5
上海	4851	0.754	6
东京	4796	0.746	7
北京	4498	0.699	8
悉尼	4494	0.699	9
米兰	4450	0.692	10

根据网络联系能级(Pa)得分,并按照 GaWC 世界城市层级的划分方法,我们可以将 64 个样本城市划分为 6 个等级(图 1),相当于 GaWC 世界城市层级中的 Beta 级到 Alpha^{++}级。不难发现,伦敦和纽约具有最高的网络联系能级,处于全球城市的顶层(即 Alpha^{++}层级),主导着全球的生产性服务业,对全球其他城市起着节点控制的作用。上海处于第二层级(即 Alpha$^+$层级)。2000 年以来,上海在全球城市网络联系能级中的排名越来越靠前,2000 年的时候上海在全球排第 31 位,相当于 GaWC 网络城市层级划分的 Alpha$^-$城市,2012 年的时候上海已经跃居到第 6,相当于 GaWC 网络城市层级划分的 Alpha$^+$城市①。

根据"嵌套网络模型"测算了样本城市先进生产性服务业的分行业网络联系能级(N_a)。测算结果表明,上海的法律服务业的 N_a 只相当于伦敦的 46.0%、纽约的 57.9%,咨询业的 N_a 只相当于伦敦的 74.4%、纽约的 85.9%,信息技术服务业的 N_a 只相当于伦敦

---

① 2012 年以前的排名是泰勒(Taylor)领导 GaWC 项目组的排名,2014 年是根据本文样本数据得到的排名。

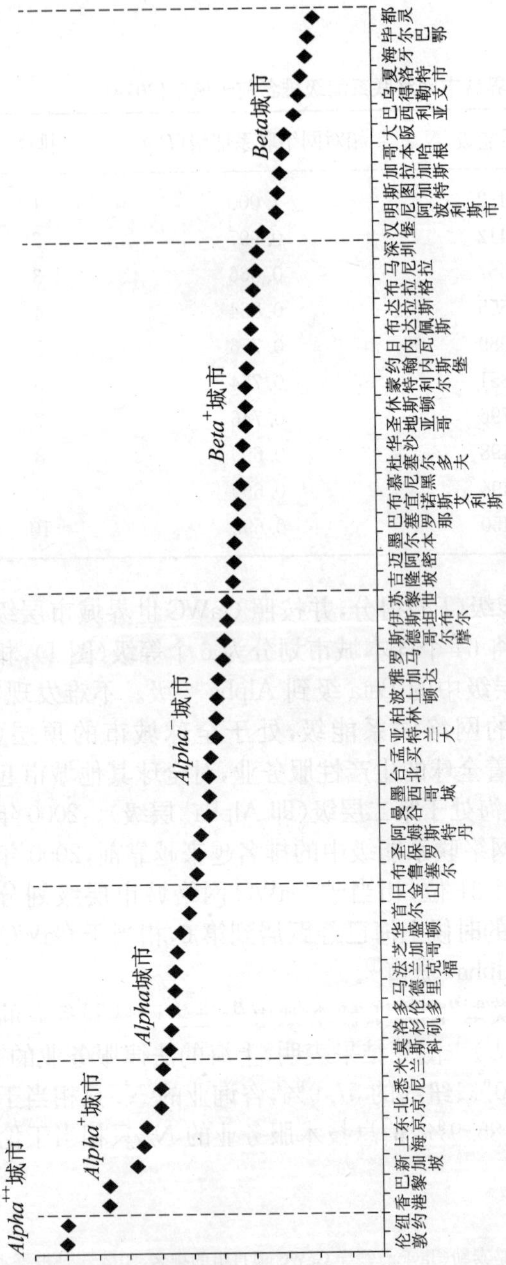

图 1 各个城市在全球网络中相对联系能级层次级划分 (2014)

的 61.0%、纽约的 61.1%。其他先进生产性服务业诸如银行、会计、广告等行业的 N_a 也与伦敦和纽约存在较为明显的差距,图 2 雷达图反映了这一点。

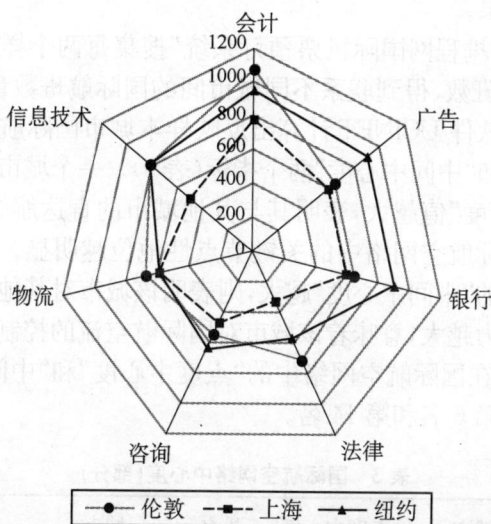

**图 2　上海、伦敦和纽约先进生产性服务业网络联系
能级雷达图**

总体而言,不管是 GaWC 的排名还是根据本文测算结果的排名,上海在全球城市网络的联系能级基本上处于 Alpha$^+$ 层级略靠后的位置,不仅落后于顶级全球城市伦敦和纽约,也略微落后于香港、巴黎和新加坡。

3.2　上海城市网络联系能级的一个佐证:来自"航空联系度"的证据

APS 企业在全球布局办公点推动了生产要素在城市间的流动,导致了全球城市结节成网,全球城市就是这个城市网络中的关键性节点,节点城市支配和控制的要素流量越大,则节点城市在全球网络中的联系能级越大。由于节点城市支配和控制全球城市间要素流量的能力大小与其控制的国际航空流量密切相关,在全球城市网络中居于关键性节点位置的城市其在全球航空网络中也一定居于关键性节点位置,因此 Simith 和 Derudder 等人通过统计国际航空流来测算和比较不同城市在全球城市网络中的重要性。本文也用这一方法来佐证上述基于"嵌套网络模型"的上海城市网络联系能级的测算结果。

通过在"携程网国际机票预订系统"搜集每两个样本城市之间的一周内航班数,得到联系不同城市间的国际航班数量矩阵,并利用矩阵分析软件 UCINET 计算出反映样本城市国际航空联系度的"点中心度"和"中间中心度"两个指标(表 3)。一个城市在航空网络中的"点中心度"值越大,表明其与其他城市的直达航线数量越多,该城市在国际航空网络中的关键节点性地位越明显。一个城市在航空网络中的"中间中心度"越大,则表明该城市对其他城市进行航空中转的能力越大,意味着该城市对国际航空流的控制力越高。表3 显示,上海在国际航空网络中的"点度中心度"和"中间中心度"的排名分别为第 6 名和第 14 名。

表3 国际航空网络中心度(部分)

排名	城市	点度中心度	排名	城市	中间中心度
1	纽约	6118	1	伦敦	196.089
2	伦敦	5454	2	巴黎	157.47
3	芝加哥	3574	3	法兰克福	155.948
4	巴黎	3120	4	阿姆斯特丹	142.039
5	香港	2940	5	纽约	134.667
6	华盛顿	2814	6	北京	94.467
7	上海	2814	7	慕尼黑	94.205
8	法兰克福	2772	8	伊斯坦布尔	86.405
9	洛杉矶	2599	13	东京	51.757
10	多伦多	2590	14	上海	49.88

通过 NetDraw 软件得到了可视化的国际航空网络的"点中心度"和"中间中心度"图(图 3、图 4),图中以节点大小来区分城市中心度的高低,以线条粗细来区分联系强度的强弱。从图中也可以看出上海在全球城市航空网络权力结构体系中所处的位置。

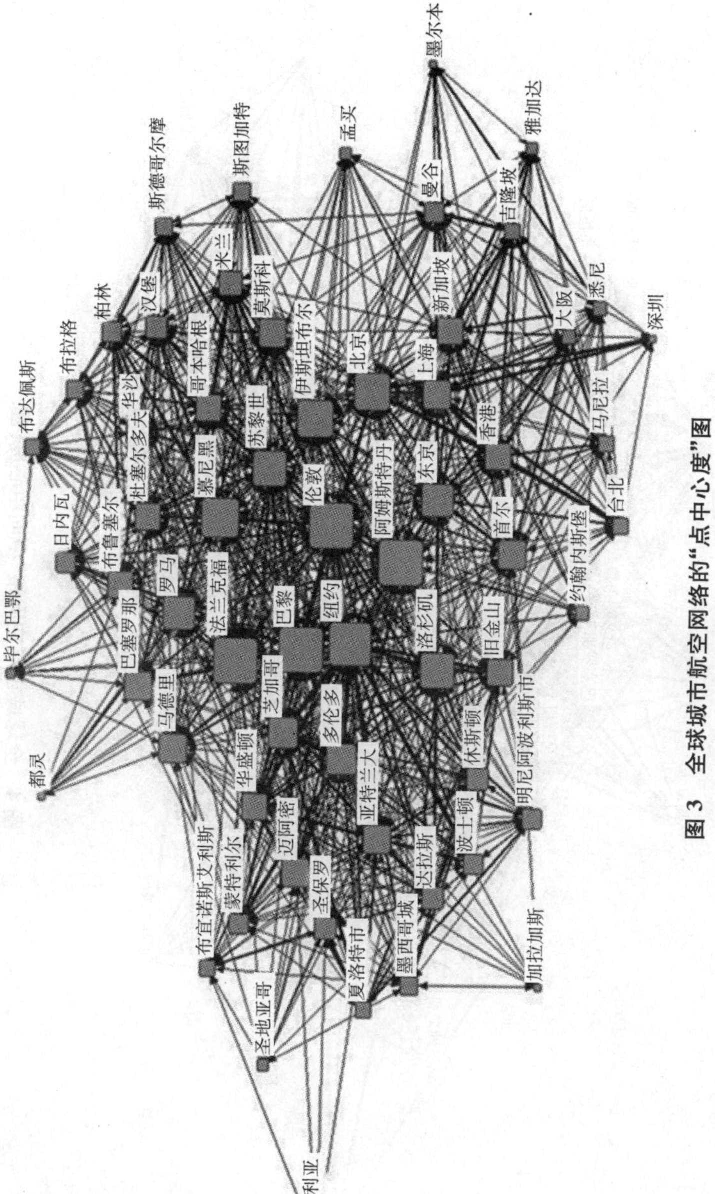

图 3 全球城市航空网络的"点中心度"图

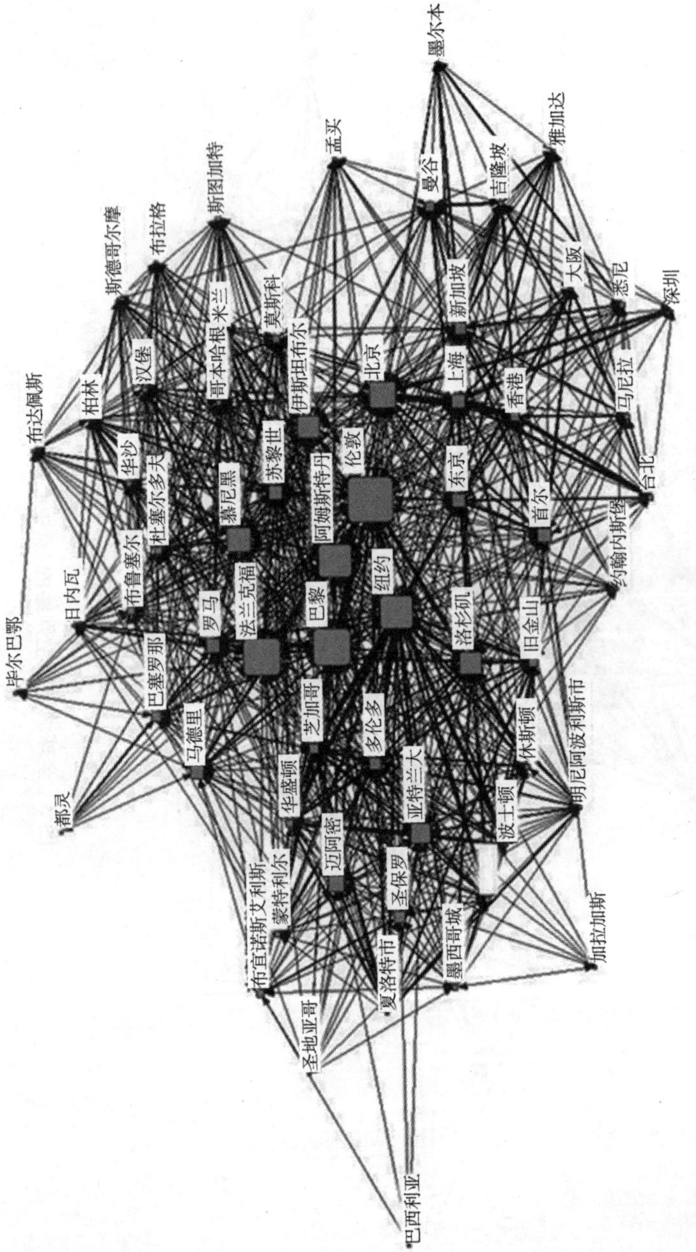

图 4 全球城市航空网络"中间中心度"图

总体而言，上海在航空联系度方面已经处于前列，但依然比伦敦、纽约、香港要低，这与基于"嵌套网络"模型的测算结果基本一致。

4 上海城市网络联系能级与顶级全球城市差距的原因

上海在全球城市网络中的联系能级在不断上升，但是，上述分析显示上海要作为全球经济资源流动与支配的重要空间载体的城市，与顶级全球城市相比还是存在明显的差距，本文认为导致这种差距的主要原因在于以下几个方面。

4.1 上海的跨国公司总部资源还不够

全球城市是通过跨国公司在支配资源，所以一个城市拥有的跨国公司机构的数量越多，它在全球城市网络中的联系能级就越高，在全球经济的影响力也就越大。《财富》世界 500 强排行榜显示，2014 年上海有 8 家 500 强跨国公司总部，而东京有 43 家，纽约有 18 家，伦敦有 17 家。根据上海的总部经济认定标准，截至 2013 年底，累计落户上海的跨国公司地区总部达到 445 家，这一数据与亚太地区的香港和新加坡相较也存在不少差距(图 5)。

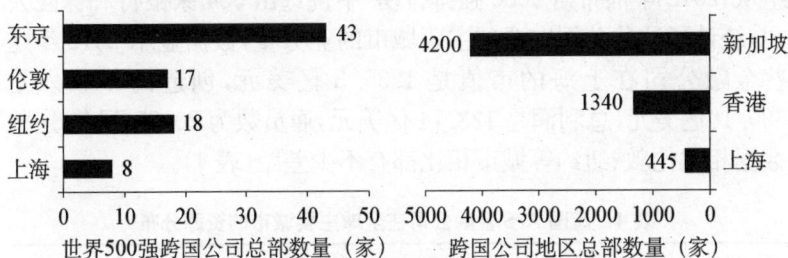

图 5 跨国公司总部和地区总部数量比较①

本文的样本数据也印证了这一点，样本数据中，伦敦拥有 10 家

① 上海的数据参见第一财经：一财网 http://www.yicai.com/news/2014/07/3992903.html。香港和新加坡的数据源于：彭羽、沈玉良. 上海、香港、新加坡吸引跨国公司地区总部的综合环境比较[J]. 国际商务研究，2012，33(4)。

权重为 3 级的跨国公司机构、纽约有 15 家,上海只有 1 家。APS 企业在上海设立的机构的权重基本上 1 级或 2 级。由此可见,相对于高端形态的全球性国际城市而言,上海的跨国公司(尤其是 APS 企业)总部资源聚集度相对较弱,这是导致上海网络联系能级较Alpha^{++}城市要低的重要原因。

4.2 上海的国际高端资源流量相对不足

顶级全球城市具有巨大的国际高端资源流量与交易,是全球资源配置网络中主要节点,因此在全球城市网络中联系能级也最高。以国际高端资源最集中的金融业为例,纽约、伦敦在时间上相互连接形成了全球最大的金融循环网,它们作为金融业的全球服务中心占据了全球经济的策略性位置,理所应当地吸引跨国公司将决策中心和管理管制中心集聚于此。数据显示,上海在金融市场国际化方面与伦敦、纽约还有较大差距,比如 2009 年的时候纽约外资金融银行的金融资产占整个金融资产的 70%左右,而上海的比重才 20%左右[1]。高端国际资源的另一个重要指标是吸纳外籍人才的数量,纽约的海外人口占到 37%,伦敦 24%,东京也超过 3%,而上海只有0.7%[2]。

GaWC 研究小组的研究数据也证实了这一点。GaWC 研究小组从"2012 年福布斯 2000 强排行榜"中挑选出 554 家银行和保险公司,统计了这些公司在全球主要城市的业务量,数据显示 2012 年这些金融公司在上海的市值是 1236.3 亿美元,创造的年收入是690.16亿美元,总利润是 123.74 亿美元,雇员数为 20.37 万人,这些数据相比伦敦、纽约等城市相比都有不少差距(表 4)。

表 4 跨国 APS 金融公司在全球主要城市的资源分布

城市	市值(亿美元)	年收入(亿美元)	利润(亿美元)	雇员数(人)
纽约	8,535.98	6,424.74	887.74	1,076,745

① 数据来源于"瞭望东方周刊",2009 年 6 月 1 日,http://news.sina.com.cn/c/sd/2009-06-01/124317927022_6.shtml。
② 参见第一财经:一财网 http://www.yicai.com/news/2014/07/3992903.html。

续　表

城市	市值(亿美元)	年收入 (亿美元)	利润(亿美元)	雇员数(人)
东京	3,815.47	4,300.25	276.01	558,912
香港	2,305.40	660.84	282.07	298,605
伦敦	4,651.40	4,556.95	382.83	887,979
悉尼	2,479.30	1,578.98	217.58	151,314
巴黎	2,109.30	5,318.21	245.03	685,693
多伦多	2,884.30	2,173.39	224.76	563,185
新加坡	1,017.90	242.84	80.63	72,939
上海	1,236.30	691.	123.74	200,370

数据来源：GaWC, Global Command and Control Centres(2012)

4.3　上海为全球提供服务的能力还不足

按照 Castells 的观点，全球化进程实质上是将先进生产性服务业的生产与消费中心以及它们所连带的地方社会连结到全球网络的过程，因此 Taylor 以及 GaWC 把全球城市定义为"提供全球服务的中心"。从理论上说，一个城市在全球城市网络中的联系能级越高，其为全球提供服务的能级就越大。

相对于顶级全球城市而言，上海先进生产性服务业网络联系能级较低，导致上海先进生产性服务业为全球提供服务能力受到制约，削弱了上海在全球城市网络中的影响力。我国国内体制框架（比如会计准则、金融监管、市场准入）与国际准则之间的矛盾制约了上海先进生产性服务业的快速发展，使得上海不能产生像毕马威（KMPG）、波士顿咨询（BCG）、世达（Skadden，Arps）、高盛（Goldman Sachs）这样业务遍布全球的著名公司。这是导致上海为全球提供服务能力相对不足的重要原因。

4.4　上海作为首位城市的"质量"和"体量"都有待提高

全球城市基本上是一国（或地区）的"首位城市"（Primary City），即一国（或地区）的经济规模和人口规模最大的城市。一般而言，首位城市的"质量"越高和"体量"越大，其在全球城市中的网络体系中的影响力就越大。"人均 GDP 程度高、后工业化经济结构明显,特别是现代服务业发达"是衡量首位城市"质量"的重要标准。"经济总量规模大"则是衡量"首位城市"的"体量"指标。

从反映"首位城市"的"质量"指标而言,相较于纽约、伦敦、东京等"首位城市"而言,上海的人均 GDP、服务业(尤其是现代服务业)的比重都远低于这些城市,从反映"首位城市"的"体量"的指标而言,上海不仅 GDP 总量要远远低于上述城市,并且 GDP 占全国的比重也远低于上述城市,伦敦的 GDP 约占英国 GDP 的 17.0%,纽约的 GDP 占美国 GDP 的 11.5%,东京 GDP 占日本 GDP 的比例更高达 35.2%,而上海的 GDP 只占全国的 3.8%[1],近年来还呈现下降趋势。因此,上海作为"首位城市",不管就"质量"而言,还是就"体量"而言,上海还不够强、不够大[2]。导致上海的经济辐射能力还不够足,从而限制了上海在全球资源配置中的控制力。

5 结 论

本文基于 GaWC 研究小组的"嵌套网络"模型,测算了全球 64 个重要城市的网络联系能级,测算的结果显示,上海在全球城市的网络联系能级和影响力迅速提升,从 2000 年全球排名第 32 位跃升到第 6 位。本文还通过构建国际航班数量矩阵,并运用网络分析软件 UCINET 测算了 64 个样本城市的"国际航空联系度",测算的结果显示,上海在国际航空网络体系中的节点地位与其在基于"嵌套网络模型"的全球城市网络体系中的节点地位相当。研究的结果还显示,不管是基于什么方法,上海与伦敦、纽约等顶级的全球城市相较,还存在相当的差距。

本文认为,上海的跨国公司总部资源不足、国际高端资源流量少、为全球提供服务的能力不强,以及作为"首位城市"的"质量"不高和"体量"不大,是导致上海在全球资源配置网络中的节点控制力

---

① 伦敦、纽约和东京的数据源于维基百科,中国的数据源于中国统计年鉴。
② 陈钊、陆铭的研究显示,即使从人口规模的角度而言,上海作为"首位城市"的"体量"都不算大。参见:陈钊,陆铭.首位城市该有多大?[J].学术研究,2014(5)。

不足的重要原因，也是导致上海与顶级全球城市之间存在较大差距的重要原因。

上海要实现全球城市的规划目标，必须首先成为跨国公司总部资源集聚地、成为国际高端资源及跨国 APS 企业的"指向地"，为此上海迫切需要加快形成与国际接轨的制度环境（包括金融制度、会计准则、贸易规则、市场准入等），只有这样上海才能为跨国总部资源、国际高端人才和资本的流入创造条件，才能吸引更多的跨国 APS 企业的进入，也才有可能产生具有国际影响力和能够在全球布局的上海本土的 APS 企业，从而最终提高上海为全球提供服务的能力并获得国际高端资源的控制力。上海要突破制度壁垒离不开中央政府的政策支持，"上海自由贸易试验区"的落地是上海又一重大发展机遇，上海要充分把握这一历史机遇，尽快形成可复制可推广的经验，促进上海的经济制度环境与国际接轨，这对于上海建设全球城市意义重大。

另外，上海在建设全球城市的过程中要处理好"质"与"量"的关系，一方面要提高现代服务业的比重，形成具有明显后工业化特征的经济结构，从而提升上海作为"首位"城市的"质量"。另一方面，经济结构转型过程中不能忽视量的增长，要充分认识到与顶级全球城市相比，上海作为"首位城市"的"体量"是不够的。近年来，上海经济总量在全国经济总量的比例的下降，制约了上海经济辐射能力的提升，因此上海不仅要大力发展现代服务业，还应加快发展先进制造业。先进制造业的快速发展是上海取得与"首位城市"相匹配"体量"所必需的，也是上海建设全球城市的重要基础。

（原载于《城市发展研究》2014 年第 11 期）

特大型城市多层级城市中心的特征及其发展规律

——基于上海从业人口空间分布结构变化的分析

朱　敏　汪传江*

0　引　言

得益于沉淀性的资源优势,特大型城市的城市中心往往有着极强的要素集聚能力,而商务与居住成本从中心向外逐级下降的经济规律,使得城市在自然成长过程中,往往会形成"单中心"的城市空间结构[1—2]。当城市膨胀到一定程度后,就会带来城市交通拥堵、环境污染严重、商务成本过高等一系列城市病[3—5]。在西方国家,为了应对"单中心"发展带来的城市问题,许多特大型城市通过城市规划,推动"多中心组团"结构模式的发展,将中心城区的人口与产业向城市外沿疏散,从而达到缓解中心城区人口压力的目的[6]。

人口高度集中于中心城区的单中心格局一直是上海城市空间的最突出特征。基于类似的思路,上海市在1999年初编制完成的《上海市城市总体规划(1999年—2020年)》提出了"控制中心城人口与用地规模,有序引导中心城的人口与产业向郊区疏散"的城市多中心建设的规划目标,其特点在于以中心城为主体,形成"多轴、多层、多核"的市域空间布局结构[7—9]。

＊　作者简介:朱敏(1978—　),男,上海人,上海师范大学商学院副教授,硕士研究生导师。研究方向:金融地理。

经过十多年的发展后,上海的城市空间体系是否朝着预期方向发展,城市副中心是否已经发育完成并与规划中的副中心相对应?新城的建设是否已形成一定的人口集聚规模,并成为城市的区域性中心?目前为止,缺乏较为深入的论证分析。

已有研究多是根据多中心模型和单中心模型对城市人口密度分布的拟合效果来确定城市空间结构的类型与转变,吴文钰、马西亚[10]和奉贤宏、魏也华等[11]分别利用以上方法对上海与南京的情况进行了研究。他们的研究存在的主要不足是:①假定城市中心数量与位置已知,这种做法主观性较强;②在对多中心城市的人口密度空间进行拟合时实际上将各级城市中心同等对待,因此无法达到区分各级城市中心的目的。

不同于基于规划或者经验,在已知城市中心的前提下利用各类指标去评价城市中心的研究,本文假设城市中心未知,通过对上海市全境 212 个街道镇(根据 2009 年上海市街道镇的划分标准)1996 年和 2008 年两次经济普查细分数据的量化分析,基于从业人口空间分布结构变化的特征,反向侦测、筛选城市中心,然后再利用从业人口聚集强度、辐射范围、辐射人口数量和辐射形态四个指标度量城市中心的层级,并进一步分析不同层级城市中心的特征和发展规律。

在定量分析的基础上,通过城市多中心发展现状与上海市 1999 年城市总体规划进行对比,分析我国特大型城市多中心规划和实际建设中需要注意的要点。希望通过本文研究的结论抛砖引玉,为我国特大型城市或大型城市的城市规划提供一定的经验借鉴。

1 研究方法以及数据来源

1.1 研究方法

本文的研究思路是先通过从业人口空间分布密度找出若干符合条件的候选中心,然后对候选的区域中心进行聚类分析,通过聚类结果区分各区域中心的类型,在此基础上归纳不同层级城市中心的特点。具体的研究过程主要分为三步。

第一步,通过邻域分析以及栅格重分类的方法,搜索出符合要求的候选中心。经济普查的最小单位是街道(镇)行政区划,把街道

(镇)第二、第三产业的从业总人口除以街道的所辖面积,得到区域内的从业人口密度。利用这一密度作为街道镇的形心处的人口密度,再利用倒数距离插值法获得上海市从业人口密度的栅格图像。

考察从业人口空间密度分布,存在大量的局部密度最大点,筛选符合条件的点的集合至关重要。解决问题的关键在于计算局部密度最大点的辐射范围。如图1,考察某一中心 A 的辐射范围,在市域范围内搜索满足以下两个条件的类似 C 的各点:①C 点的人口密度小于 A 点的人口密度;②C 点到这若干条等高线的最短距离等于 C 点到中心 A 的距离,则由 C 这样的所有点构成的连线就是 A 的辐射边界线,图中阴影部分即为 A 的辐射范围。

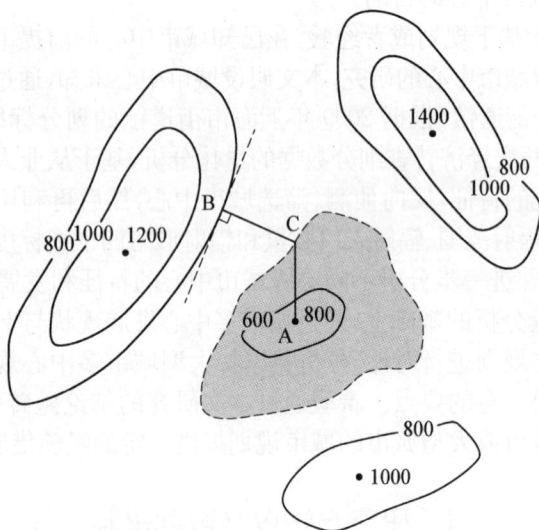

图1　城市中心辐射范围 S 的定义

任意一级的城市中心必然具备一定的"辐射半径",通过设定"辐射半径"的大小,就能够剔除不符合要求的点。本文使用 A 点到其辐射边界各点距离的最小值作为 A 点的"辐射半径"*r*。在具体操作中,"辐射半径"以 0.5 km 为步长向上递增,逐级搜索。筛选搜索结果发现"辐射半径"在 1 km 处,得到的城市中心数量合适而且城市中心的位置与经验相符。因此以 1 km 作为最小"辐射半径"筛选城市中心。

第二步,计算候选中心的四个特征指标。四个分析指标如表1所示,分别选择从业人口聚集强度 D、辐射范围 S、辐射人口数量 N 和辐射形态 P。

第三步,利用两阶段聚类方法,根据四个维度的数据,对候选中心进行自动聚类。如果城市中心的不同类型已经自然形成,那么在多个特征维度上,不同类型之间必然会出现显著的层级差异,通过自动聚类就可以把它们分离出来。这里我们选择 SPSS 中两阶段自动聚类方法。

表1　城市中心特征分析的主要指标

类型	指标	计算方法	说明
强度特征	人口聚集强度(D)	中心位置点从业人口的密度	值越大,中心的集聚强度越大。
广度特征	辐射范围(S)	辐射范围内网格数 n 乘以单位网格面积	值越大,中心的影响范围越大。
体量特征	辐射人口数量(N)	辐射范围内所有网格的人口数加总	值越大,中心的体量越大。
形态特征	辐射形态(P)	中心点到边界最短距离除以最大距离	反映了城市中心在各个方向上辐射能量的对称性,值越小,条带型特征越明显。

1.2　研究数据

研究数据包括上海市所有街道镇 1996 年与 2008 年的从业人口数据、上海市 2009 年街道镇行政区划 GIS 地理信息数据,取自上海市经济普查细分数据。所使用的街道镇的行政区划是以 2009 年的街道镇的行政划分为标准,对于一些街道镇在 1996 年的行政划分与 2009 年不一致的情况,作者根据调整前后面积的变动计算出按照 2009 年行政划分下的新的街道镇的人口数量。

表 2 1996 年与 2008 年上海城市中心聚类结果

年份	聚类数量	最优 AIC	第一类中心	第二类中心	第三类中心
1996 年	2	0.9	外滩街道	其他 22 个城市中心	无
2008 年	3	0.8	外滩街道	南京西路街道、陆家嘴街道、徐家汇街道、虹梅路街道	其他 22 个城市中心

资料来源:根据上海市 1996 年与 2008 年经济普查数据以及上海市 2009 年地理信息基础数据计算

表 3 1996 年上海市各级城市中心及其特征

聚类结果	中心层级	数量	人口聚集强度 D(人/ km²)	辐射形态 P	辐射范围 S(km²)	辐射人口数量 N(人)
第一类	城市主中心	1	285190.00	1.0000	6651.81	9446056.00
第二类	区域性中心	22	16284.57	0.2145	1110.46	851791.10

资料来源:同表 2

表 4 2008 年上海市各级城市中心及其特征

聚类结果	中心层级	数量	人口聚集强度 D(人/km²)	辐射形态 P	辐射范围 S(km²)	辐射人口数量 N(人)
第一类	城市主中心	1	103557.00	1.0000	6651.81	10383650.00
第二类	城市副中心	4	42271.30	0.0250	2930.09	3959321.20
第三类	区域性中心	22	5133.48	0.2632	720.14	594764.60

资料来源:同表 2

2 实证分析

首先利用 ArcGIS 的空间数据和 MATLAB 编写的算法搜索出 1996 年与 2008 年全部候选中心,然后计算每个候选中心的四个指标,并根据这四个指标进行两阶段自动聚类,结果如表 2 至 4 所示。

基于聚类结果,通过雷达图分析不同类型城市中心的特征。首先,比较 2008 年城市主中心与 1996 年城市主中心的特征,如图 2a,可以发现在城市主中心辐射范围不变的情况下,相对于 1996 年,2008 年城市主中心辐射范围内产业人口增加,同时中心位置的产业人口集聚强度下降。这一现象,恰恰说明城市中必然形成新的集聚中心,吸纳新增加的产业人口,同时有效分散了产业人口向城市主中心方向的集聚。

进一步分析 2008 年聚类的类中心特征,如图 2d,可以发现形成了三个城市中心的层级。其中第二个层级相对于第三个层级区域中心,在辐射范围、产业人口集聚强度以及辐射人口数量三个指标上都显著大于区域中心。

如图 2c,可以发现 1996 年只存在两个类型的城市中心。到了 2008 年则出现一个新的类型。那么这一新的城市中心类型与 1996 年低层级的区域中心是否存在差别? 我们把 2008 年、1996 年的区域中心和 2008 年的第二个层级的类中心放在一起比较。如图 2b,可以看到,2008 年、1996 年区域中心的总体形态没有发生大的变化,只是在辐射范围、产业人口集聚强度以及辐射范围内产业人口数量三个指标上有所增强,而第二个类中心的形态显著差别于第三个类别,这说明第二类中心和区域中心存在显著不同,而

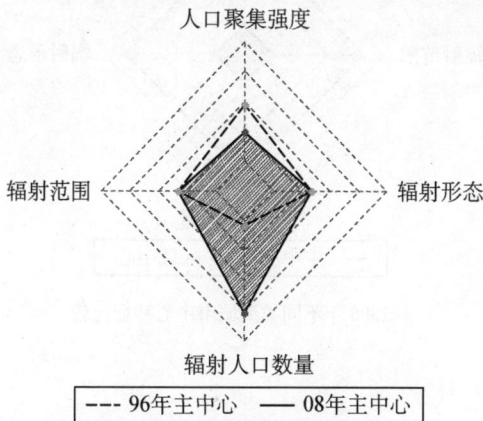

a. 不同时期主中心特征比较

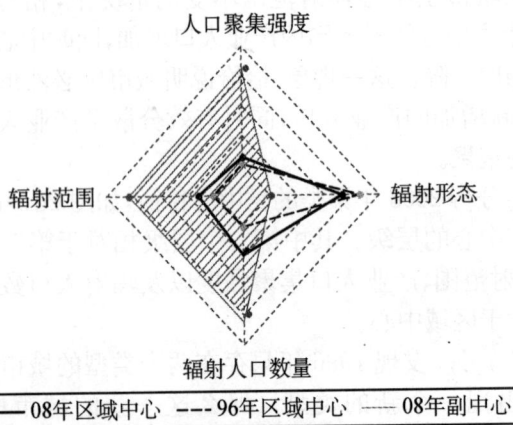

b. 副中心与不同时期区域中心特征比较

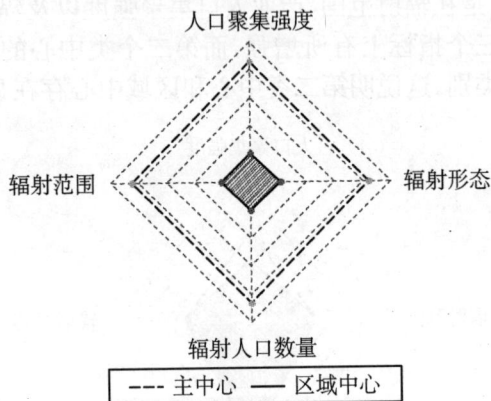

c. 1996 年不同类型城市中心特征比较

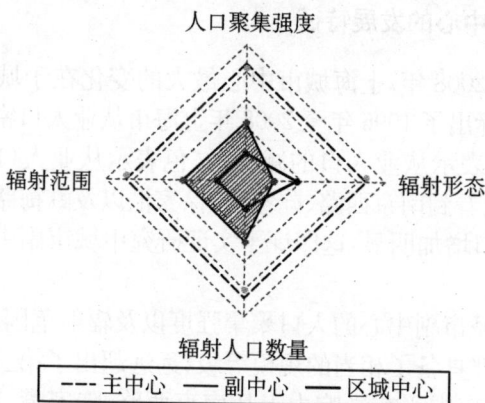

d. 2008年不同类型城市中心特征比较

图2 不同时期聚类中心的特征比较

且层级高于区域中心,这实际就是经过十多年发展,上海城市副中心已初步形成。值得注意的是,目前已经形成的副中心更趋向于狭长的带状分布形态,副中心的辐射影响在方向上存在较大的非均衡性。

3 上海各层级城市中心的发展规律

3.1 城市主中心的发展特征

根据1996年与2008年的分析结果可知,外滩在整个上海城市空间中的中心与主体地位一直没有发生变化。虽然从1996年到2008年外滩这个城市的主中心的人口聚集强度发生了急剧的下降,从1996年的28人/km² 降到2008年的10万人/km²,但是其产业人口的聚集强度仍然远远高于其他城市副中心。特别是随着上海国际金融中心的建设,金融机构总部不断向外滩地区迁移,金融机构集聚已成为外滩地区新的产业结构特色,而外滩作为上海城市的地标由于其独特的城市区位与历史人文条件使得其在整个城市空间体系中的中心地位在相当长的一段时间内都将不会发生改变。

3.2 城市副中心的发展特征

1996 至 2008 年,上海城市中心最大的变化在于城市副中心的出现。图 3 标出了 1996 年至 2008 年上海市从业人口密度的变化趋势,其中蓝色表示从业人口的减少,红色表示从业人口的增加。分析图 3a,可以看到南京西路、陆家嘴、徐家汇以及虹梅路街道这四个地区从业人口增加明显,这印证了实证研究中城市副中心判别的合理性。

从四个城市副中心的人口聚集强度以及辐射范围上来看,四个城市副中心都具备了相当的规模等级,远远超出了第三类的区域性中心,四个城市中心在影响力上从南京西路、陆家嘴、徐家汇、虹梅路街道往下依次递减,这主要与四个城市副中心所处的城市区位、中心发育的先后顺序以及中心的功能定位有关。

从四个城市副中心的地理位置来看,四个城市副中心均位于中心城区。从四个副中心的辐射范围来看,徐家汇中心与虹梅路中心主要的影响范围是南部地区,陆家嘴中心主要的影响地区是浦东新区,而南京西路的影响范围主要是浦西城市的中部地区,虽然四个城市副中心离主中心较近,但是随着四个城市副中心的发育也带动了周边外围地区产业人口的快速聚集,其中徐家汇中心与陆家嘴中心的作用尤为突出,这一点从图 3a 可以直观地反映出来。

从四个城市副中心的空间分布形态上可以看出,四个城市副中心虽然都是围绕在城市主中心周围分布,但是其并非均匀分布在其四周而是与城市主中心一起构成"条带状"结构,这与上海整个城市空间的东北-西南走向的"条带状"形态相一致,这种城市副中心的"条带状"形态表明了城市副中心的空间分布不平衡性以及城市空间发展的不平衡性。

3.3 区域性中心的发展特征

图 3b 标示出了进入候选中心的地理位置变化,其中差号标示 1996 年成为中心而 2008 年未成为中心的地理位置;加号标示 1996 年未成为中心而 2008 年新成为中心的地理位置;圆圈则表示始终

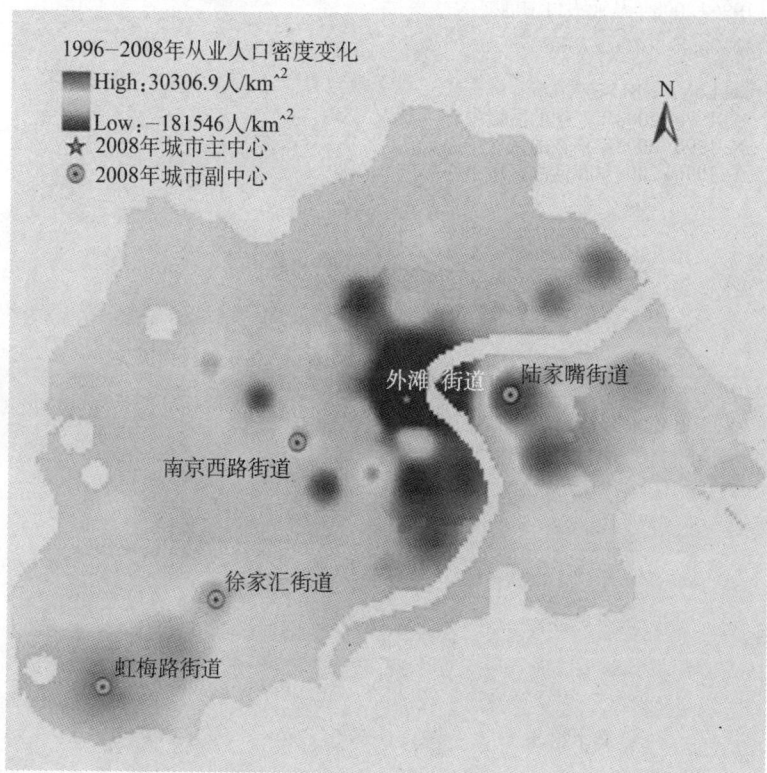

a. 1996—2008 城市副中心变化情况

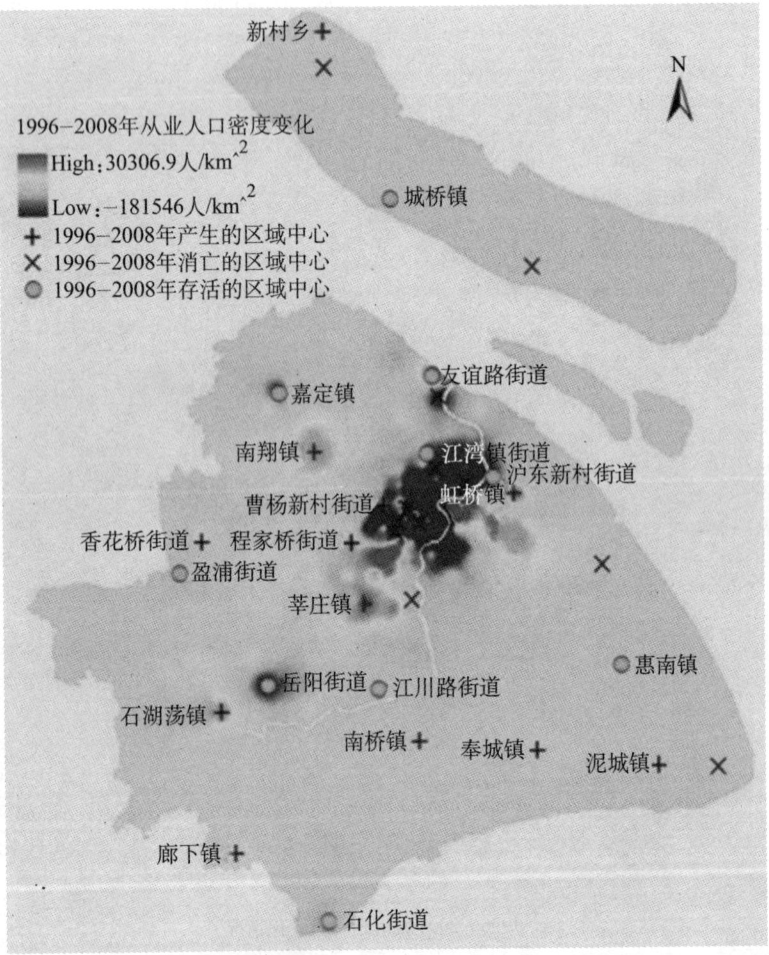

1996-2008年从业人口密度变化

High：30306.9人/km^2

Low：-181546人/km^2

＋ 1996-2008年产生的区域中心

✕ 1996-2008年消亡的区域中心

◎ 1996-2008年存活的区域中心

新村乡

城桥镇

嘉定镇　友谊路街道

南翔镇　江湾镇街道

曹杨新村街道　沪东新村街道

虹桥镇

香花桥街道　程家桥街道

盈浦街道

莘庄镇

岳阳街道　江川路街道　惠南镇

石湖荡镇

南桥镇　奉城镇　泥城镇

廊下镇

石化街道

b. 1996—2008 年城市区域中心变化

图 3　1996—2008 年上海市从业人口空间分布的变动情况

是中心的地理位置。对比 1996 年与 2008 年的区域性中心，虽然中心的数量都是 22 个，但是其空间上的分布出现了重大的变化。中心城区的变化主要体现为原有区域中心消失，被新形成的副中心替代；而对于远郊区随着新城的建设，区域中心数量大幅度上升。

对比 1996 年与 2008 年的区域性中心的演变也可以看出，其中 10 个区域性中心在 1996 年与 2008 年间保持不变，其中大部分或者是当地的区政府所在地或者是当地的制造业基地。由此可见在近郊区与远郊区建设区域性中心的过程中，行政中心与制造业仍然是吸引人口聚集的主要力量。

4　规划视角下上海各层级城市中心的建设成效

4.1　中心城区与城市副中心

按照规划上海将形成以外滩、人民广场、南京路、陆家嘴等周边为市级中心以及以徐家汇、花木、真如和江湾-五角场为副中心的多中心的中心城区空间结构。如果将本文中 2008 年探测出来的南京西路副中心、陆家嘴副中心与外滩主中心一起构成一个更大范围的城市主中心，那么实际形成的城市副中心只有徐家汇-虹梅路城市副中心；由于数据仅到 2008 年，规划中的江湾-五角场中心正在发展，当时的规模等级尚未达到城市副中心应有的特征，只表现为区域性城市中心；而规划中的真如与花木副中心在 1996 年与 2008 年都未进入城市区域性中心的行列。

通过以上分析可知，虽然上海城市多中心建设取得了一定成效，多核结构正在发育并形成，但是真正形成的而且与城市主中心相距一定距离的城市副中心只有徐家汇副中心。徐家汇副中心建设成功主要有三点原因：

① 交通规划合理，拥有广阔的人口腹地。三条地铁线路在此交汇，一号地铁线将莘庄闵行方向的人流聚集过来，九号线将七宝、九亭甚至是松江新城方向的人流聚集过来，而地铁十一号线将上南和三林方向的人流聚集过来，三条地铁线的交汇并延伸向广阔的近郊与远郊地区使得徐家汇商圈具有广阔的人口腹地。

② 徐家汇商圈发展由点及线，最终形成面，这为徐家汇商圈的

商业商务气息的提升打下了良好的基础。徐家汇商圈的发展是由虹桥路、华山路、漕溪北路、肇嘉浜路四个十字路口形成的路口商业街为中心并以这四条道路为轴延伸发展,最终形成现在的徐家汇商圈。

③ 在商圈的发展过程中注重与文化、旅游和休憩的结合,并提供了完善的基础配套公共设施。

相比于徐家汇商圈,其他几个规划中的副中心近十年发展相对比较迟缓,主要是因为在中心区位选择、周边交通设计、商业商务功能的开发以及土地的规划与开发等方面存在或多或少的一些问题。

花木副中心区域的土地主要用于世纪公园与高档居住区建设,商业商务用地体量小而且十分分散,最终形成了以社区型商业占主导地位的不良局面。在副中心规划之初,其商务功能就未受重视,而是将其定位为居住、行政、休闲中心,城市副中心必须具有的商业商务功能的开发未受到应有的重视,这成为其发展迟缓的根本原因。

真如副中心的区位优势和交通条件虽然比较好[12],但区域内项目开发迟缓成为阻碍其发展的根本原因。虽然真如副中心具备一定的发展潜力,却由于已建成的商务区体量太小,无法在短期内快速形成一定规模的商圈。而在建项目由于工程拖拉严重,使得竣工开业遥遥无期,在短期内不会形成具有一定规模的商业集聚。

综上所属,在城市副中心规划与建设的过程中,商务与商业的集聚能力是关键因素。为了形成一定的商业与商务集聚力,城市副中心的选址周边必须具有一定规模的人口腹地,中心位置已经具备一定规模的商业集聚度;在交通规划上,城市快速交通的设计必须具备将人口腹地中的人流集中过来的功能;在土地的开发与利用上必须为商业用地留有足够的空间,这有利于副中心发展的可持续性,同时应该注意土地开发与工程工期的进度安排。

4.2 新城与区域性中心的建设

上海市在 1999 年的上海市总体规划中提出建设 11 座新城和 22 个左右的中心镇。考察图 3b,可以发现 11 座新城在 2008 年形成的区域性中心名单中都能找到,这表明新城建设已经使得其成为当地的区域性中心。从表3和表4中区域性中心的人口聚集强度也可以看出,从1996年到2008年11座新城的人口密度都在上升,这表明新城在一定程度上发挥了阻止人口向中心城区迁入的作用。虽然11座新城都已经成为了局部的区域性中心,但是并不是所有新城都形成一定的人口聚集范围与人口聚集规模。其中,只有松江新城以及嘉定新城依靠工业园区为依托,才形成了一定的人口聚集规模。

新城相对规划发展迟缓的主要原因是新城的定位不明确。其一,没有将新城的建设上升到城市建设的战略核心地位,在市级层面上只是将其作为缓解中心城区人口压力的一种手段,而在区级层面上往往又将其作为推动城镇化的工具,这势必会引起新城的功能定位在整个城市体系的分工中找不到合适的位置;其二,没有将新城的建设纳入到长三角的城市群整体体系之中,这直接导致了新城规划的起点过低,功能定位重叠等问题。另外,由于交通等基础服务设施的配套不到位使得新城对于中心城区居民以及高端劳动力缺少相应的吸引力,使得新城的人口结构仍然以本地居民与外来务工人员为主。

5 结 论

本文利用从业人口聚集强度、辐射范围、辐射人口数量和辐射形态四个指标度量城市中心的层级,并进一步分析其发展特征。研究发现,1996—2008年上海市城市空间结构已由"单中心模式"向"单中心与多中心混合模式"转变,多层级的城市中心体系初具雏形。期间形成了南京西路、陆家嘴、徐家汇与虹梅路四个城市副中心以及二十二个区域性中心,整个城市空间结构已经呈现出由"单核"向"多核"、"双层"向"三层"的空间形态转变。

但在2008年,规划中的四个城市副中心只有徐家汇中心发育完成,其他三个中心则由于商业与商务集聚程度低、土地利用不合理等因素导致其发育缓慢;郊区十一个新城已经发育成为区域性的城市中心,但由于定位不够明确使得其人口与产业的集聚度都相对较低。

因此,作为特大型城市的上海,仍需要进一步加强城市副中心建设,强化上海经济发展的空间平衡;并将新城的建设上升到城市建设的战略核心地位,新城规划的视界提升到把新城纳入长三角城市群体系的长远高度,在整个城市体系的分工中明确新城的功能定位。

参考文献

[1] 张开琳.大城市副中心建设理论与实践[J].城市问题,2005,(2):73—76.

[2] 孙斌栋,石巍,宁越敏.上海市多中心城市结构的实证检验与战略思考[J].城市规划学刊,2010,(1):58—63.

[3] 王旭辉,孙斌栋.特大城市多中心空间结构的经济绩效——基于城市经济模型的理论探讨[J].城市规划学刊,2011,(6):20—27.

[4] 孙斌栋,潘鑫.城市空间结构对交通出行影响研究的进展——单中心与多中心的论争[J].城市问题,2008,(1):19—22.

[5] 孙斌栋,涂婷,石巍,等.特大城市多中心空间结构的交通绩效检验——上海案例研究[J].城市规划学刊,2013,(2):63—69.

[6] 马海涛,罗奎,孙威,等.东京新宿建设城市副中心的经验与启示[J].世界地理研究,2014,(1):103—110.

[7] 王红霞.多中心化空间演变进程中的城镇体系建设——以上海为例的研究[J].上海经济研究,2009,(1):13—22.

[8] 毛佳樑,耿毓修,陈友华,等.上海市城市总体规划回顾与展望——专家座谈会[J].上海城市规划,2011,(4):80—85.

[9] 叶贵勋,金忠民.上海城市总体规划指标体系研究[J].城市规划汇刊,2002,(3):32—36.

[10] 吴文钰,马西亚.多中心城市人口模型及模拟——以上海为例[J].现代城市研究,2006,(12):39—44.

[11] 秦贤宏,魏也华,陈雯,等.南京都市区人口空间扩张与多中心化[J].地理研究,2013,(4):711—719.

[12] 王治,叶霞飞,顾保南,等.上海市真如副中心轨道交通建设规划协调方案[J].城市轨道交通研究,2007,(5):28—31.

(原载于《城市发展研究》2014年第11期)

上海共有产权保障住房运作模式及效果分析*

崔光灿 姜 巧**

0 前 言

共有产权住房作为我国住房供应的一种新模式,近年各地的实践力度不断加大,并形成了不同的发展模式。早期提出共有产权是与经济适用住房相联系,着重解决原经济适用房中存在的漏洞问题,包括覆盖面小,容易被人作为投资手段等[1]。2007年后,随着各地对住房保障力度的加大,一些地区开始在经济适用住房、动迁房等住房供应中试点共有产权,从江苏省姜堰、如皋、淮安等城市共有产权住房试点来看,在产权理论上是可以探讨的,在现行法制下是可行的,在实践中是可操作的[2]。共有产权住房作为一种住房保障制度创新,相对公共租赁住房等保障手段,有助于中低收入家庭的财富积累,在解决住房消费问题的同时解决由住房财富分配不均所引发的问题[3]。保障性住房共有产权模式的建立和运行,对于优化保障性住房的配置效果,加强保障性住房建设的资本化能力,提高住房保障的效率,给予受保障人群改善福利和增加财富的平等机会

基金项目:国家自然科学基金项目(71473166)
** **作者简介**:崔光灿(1970—),男,汉族,河南新乡人,上海师范大学房地产与城市发展研究中心副教授,主要研究方向:城市经济、住房政策。

具有积极效果[4]。从而共有产权住房在住房保障中的地位不断确立,并提出可以共有产权住房模式统领出售型保障房供应体系[5]。后来,一些地区开始将共有产权运用于各类住房,并产生了利用共有产权住房来统领现在的经济适用房、拆迁安置房和限价商品房,明确政府与保障对象之间的责权利,从而建立新住房保障体系,构建合理衔接的住房体系的观点[6]。也有考虑将共有产权方式引入整个住房保障和供应体系,以使共有产权住房进一步推广和可持续发展,将共有产权住房定位为一种政策性住房[7]。

2014 年 4 月,国家确定了北京、上海、深圳、成都、淮安、黄石 6 个城市为共有产权住房试点城市,希望通过各地的实践探索合理的发展模式。上海作为试点城市之一,在完善经济适用住房基础上,形成了共有产权保障住房运作模式,从 2009 年开始试点,供应了近 7 万户家庭,其间相关政策不断完善,基本形成了稳定的共有产权保障住房供应与管理体系。在共有产权住房实践中,其实施效果如何,运作上有哪些难点,未来发展的方向如何? 我们以上海的共有产权保障住房为例进行分析。

1　上海共有产权保障住房产生的背景

上海 1998 年住房制度改革以后,全面停止了实物分房,住房供应以市场化商品住房为主。2000 年以后,与全国多数大中城市一样,房价经历了较快的上涨过程,居民的住房支付能力不足开始显化。上海最早实施廉租住房政策,主要通过租赁方式解决低收入家庭的住房困难。但随着房价进一步上升,许多高于廉租住房收入标准,但又无力通过市场解决住房困难的"夹心层"开始出现,如何通过政府的帮助,使这些家庭在政府与个人共同努力下解决住房困难成为迫切的问题。此前,全国多数地区都在建设经济适用住房,但由于经济适用住房福利性高,寻租空间大,一些地区在经济适用住房政策实施过程中也出现过偏差,使社会对经济适用住房制度产生了质疑,上海考虑到没有很好的收入审核等手段,难以避免经济适用住房中的寻租问题,暂时没有建设经济适用住房。

2007 年 8 月,国务院发布《关于解决城市低收入家庭住房困难的若干意见》,明确提出"把解决城市低收入家庭住房困难作为维护群众利益的重要工作和住房制度改革的重要内容,作为政府公共服务的一项重要职责",各地分别结合自身的特点采用多种住房保障形式,一方面完善原有的廉租住房、经济适用住房制度,另一方面不断探索新的公共租赁住房、限价房、共有产权保障性住房等保障政策。

这一阶段,上海开始考虑在原有经济适用住房制度基础上,充分运用信息化手段,形成规范化的申请审核供应流程,建设经济适用住房,并将共有产权运用于住房保障,定位于新型经济适用住房发展模式,称为共有产权保障住房。使经济适用住房回归到保障本质,充分发挥"政府保障"与"家庭自助"相结合的作用。

将共有产权保障住房作为主要住房保障形式,是基于与上海城市发展的实际需要相适应的考虑,一是上海作为一个大型城市,人多地少的矛盾特别突出,住房供求数量矛盾显著,单纯依靠租赁补贴无法解决所有住房问题;二是通过共有产权住房保障有助于解决上海城市发展所需要的青年人才的住房问题,留住人才,增强城市发展动力;三是符合中低收入家庭的住房需要,上海经济活力较强,就业较为充分,市民的可支配收入总体较高,具有一定的支付能力,但由于当地房价较高,超过市民收入上涨速度,市民单纯自身积累购买住房困难[8];四是有利于提高政府有限财政资金的运行效率,有利于吸引民间资本参与保障房建设[9],更好地利用市场化开发建设机制;五是共有产权保障住房通过明确政府与个人间的产权份额,有利于减少经济适用住房福利性过高产生的寻租空间。

2　上海共有产权保障住房运作的基市模式

2.1　供应对象定位于中等及以下收入住房困难家庭

上海共有产权保障住房供应对象为本市户籍中低收入住房困难家庭,其申请准入条件由收入、财产、住房和户籍等构成,近年准入条件有一个不断放宽的过程,如其中收入标准从 2009 年开始试点时人均月收入 2300 元,到 2014 年已放宽到人均月收入 6000 元。目前的准入条件基本覆盖了大多数的机关和企事业单位的青年职工,这部分人既有一定的购房能力,但购买商品住房的能力不足。通过共有产权保障住房,解决包括"夹心层"住房困难,使城市多数居民"有恒产而有恒心"。

表1 上海共有产权保障住房准入条件

批次	户口年限	人均收入与财产条件	住房困难条件	单身申请年龄
2009年试点批	本市7年本区5年本处3年	人均年收入≤2.76万元人均财产≤7万元	人均≤15 m²	年满30周岁
2011年第一批	本市7年本区5年本处3年	3人以上:年收入≤3.48万元财产≤9万元;2人及以下:上浮10%	人均≤15 m²	年满30周岁
2011年第二批	本市7年本区5年本处3年	3人以上:年收入≤3.96万元财产≤12万元;2人及以下:上浮10%	人均≤15 m²	年满30周岁
2012年批	本市3年本处2年	3人以上:年收入≤6万元财产≤15万元;2人及以下:上浮20%	人均≤15 m²	男年满30周岁,女年满28周岁
2013年批	本市3年本处2年	3人以上:年收入≤6万元财产≤15万元;2人及以下:上浮20%	人均≤15 m²,增加住房面积扣减政策	男年满28周岁,女年满25周岁
2014年批	本市3年本处2年	3人以上:年收入≤7.2万元财产≤18万元;2人及以下:上浮20%	人均≤15 m²,增加住房面积扣减政策	男年满28周岁,女年满25周岁

2.2 严格的准入条件信息化核查机制

在共有产权保障住房的准入过程中,实施严格的审核机制是保障制度规范执行的基础。上海形成了集户籍、婚姻、经济、住房状况四方面为主的申请条件审核系统,并形成了以信息化手段取代纸质的审核信息,借助互联网形成了不同部门间的信息比对机制。其中,户籍申请信息与公安的户籍信息库相比对。婚姻状况申请信息与民政部门的婚姻登记信息相比对。住房状况信息通过全市房地产交易登记系统和公有住房数据库系统进行核查,并建成了上海市住房状况信息中心。经济状况信息核查最难,在市级层面成立了上海居民经济状况核对平台,涵盖社保、税务、公积金、银行、证券、车辆管理等 14 个部门的信息化比对专线,及时准确审核申请家庭的收入、财产状况。

2.3 集中建设与配建两种方式

共有产权保障住房有两种建设方式,一是集中建设,充分利用市场机制,通过项目招投标,确定由具有良好资质和信誉的房地产开发企业进行建设,建好后直接由开发企业按政府定价销售给通过政府审核的保障对象。二是配建,凡新出让土地开发建设的商品住宅项目,按照不低于该项目住宅建设总面积 5% 的比例配建保障房,住房建成后无偿移交政府用于住房保障。所有共有产权保障住房由全市统一建设供应,根据各区的住房保障申请对象数量,分配给各区使用。

2.4 规范的供应程序

共有产权保障住房严格按保障性住房的供应标准,建设面积控制在 40~70 m² 左右。单身或 2 人家庭,可申请购一居室,3 人家庭购二居室,4 人及以上家庭购三居室。

共有产权保障住房每年分批次集中供应,基本一年一批次,集中申请审核,通过审核的家庭都有机会进行选房,选房按区县分项目进行,选房顺序完全按"摇号"的方式实施,并由公证部门全程公证,所有摇号工作通过媒体直播,保证了公平和公正。

针对以往个别地区经济适用住房实践中出现过一些不规范的现象,上海共有产权保障住房在供应环节重点形成规范的制度和操作程序,没有对公务员等特殊人群、特殊对象的特殊政策,在准入标准、审核、供应上完全统一,在统一的受理、公示平台上运行,从制度上保证了供应的公平、公开和公正,当然如何将好制度执行好也是对政府管理能力的一个考验。

2.5　定价及产权份额设定

共有产权保障住房的土地供应方式为划拨出让,定价方式按经济适用住房定价,主要依据共有产权住房建设成本,同时参考周边商品住房价格来确定出售价格,称为销售基准价格。

具体的产权比例按不同地段与商品住房价格的关系确定,计算公式为:购房人产权份额=销售基准价格/(周边房价×90%),这里按周边房价的90%计算主要是考虑周边房价有开发商的利润部分,政府进行了相应的折扣。具体到不同项目,政府与个人的产权比例有3∶7、4∶6等多种情况,这一比例在合同中约定,主要用于以后共有产权住房上市时的收益分成。其中,政府持有的产权份额主要由政府直接或间接的各种投入构成,比如投入的市政、公用等配套资金,减免的土地出让金、行政事业性收费及其他税费等,而购房人的产权份额主要由其购房出资构成。

2.6　产权主体的权利与义务界定

共有产权主体之间关系可有两种基本的形式,一是严格物权法约束下的共有产权,二是经济意义上的共有产权。这也是目前争论较多的问题,如果共有产权住房是物权法约束下的共有产权,则购房家庭和政府作为住房的共有产权人,必须按产权份额来承担后续住房使用过程中的住房维修保养(维修资金)、日常管理(物业费)、房屋安全等责任,而政府如果承担了这个责任后,将可能是难以操作,这将意味着共有产权住房无法持续。而经济意义上的共有产权,仅体现在物权中的财产权或收益权份额上,可不涉及到日常的使用。共有产权住房作为保障性住房,则不宜用物权法约束下的共有产权,政府在住房取得上给予了支持,而在住房使用上,可以由保障家庭负担为主。目前上海的做法是政府作为共有产权人"让渡"了其产权对应的使用权，不对居住人收取租金，但居住人相应要承担所有住房维护保养责任，并承担所有物业管理费。

在共有产权份额确定的方法上，上海是以合同方式约定共有产权住房中政府与购房人的各自份额，由各区县住房保障中心代理行使政府的产权份额。

2.7 后期管理

共有产权保障住房主要是用于解决购房的居住问题，规定共有产权保障住房的房地产权利人、同住人不得将住房擅自转让、出租、出借、赠与或者改变房屋使用性质，不得设定除该住房购房贷款担保以外的抵押权。区（县）住房保障机构可以通过家访等方式，了解房地产权利人、同住人居住和使用该住房的情况。目前开始试点主要由导出区住房保障部门异地管理，通过建立工作站或委托物业企业开展日常巡查。

2.8 上市交易

共有产权保障房可在5年以后上市，上市时购买人取得按产权份额的出售价款，转化为商品住房，但政府有"优先回购"权。政府回购共有产权保障房后，可继续提供给符合条件的家庭作为共有产权保障房或作为其他保障住房。上市的收益分成在购房合同和产权证附注中注明，如购房时共有产权保障住房的价格仅占同类商品住房价格的70%，则该购房人只能拥有70%的产权，将来购房人将房屋出售时，他只能按其70%份额获得出售价款，其余的归政府所有。目前第一批共有产权住房取得产权还未满5年，所以没有上市的实践。

3 共有产权保障住房实施中的几个特征

3.1 明晰了政府与市场的关系

"共有产权"及其收益分配方式，既体现了政府的阶段性住房支持，也符合市场经济规律的基本要求。如果中低收入家庭购买的产权型保障住房不能获得增值回报，将没有购买的积极性。但如果对保障性住房的使用和收益分配没有限制,不能保证其用于最需要的家庭,不能保证公平、公正,还会产生过度的"利益输送",影响社会接受度。

共有产权保障住房由购房人和政府按其"出资额"不同拥有相应的产权,体现了"谁投资谁受益"的市场经济原则。共有产权保障住房低于商品住房价格的部分不是简单"让渡"给购房人,而是政府拥有产权,当共有产权保障住房上市时,政府按其产权份额回收投资并获得相应的收益。在住房的使用阶段,政府将住房的使用权"让渡"给购房人,以支持其解决住房困难。

3.2 衔接了住房保障供应与市场化供应

从国际上多数国家的实践看,如果多数的保障对象没有有效的"上升"通道退出住房保障体系,长期居住在保障性住房中,有可能产生几个后果:一是进入保障性住房中的群体越来越大,社会管理难度加大;二是越来越多的保障性住房(特别是租赁型住房)年久失修,居住质量越来越差;三是由于住房财产的缺失,社会分化日益加重。这都不利于住房保障的可持续和社会的和谐。所以政府在提供住房保障的同时,应考虑使有能力的家庭提高收入,最终离开保障进入市场。

但在大城市的房价上涨速度快于收入增长,房价收入比失衡,居民的收入通过长期的积蓄还远远赶不上住房价格的上涨,甚至,已积累的收入相对增长的房价还在不断缩水,保障对象将很难离开住房保障进入市场。因此,共有产权保障住房既解决保障对象眼前的住房困难,又使保障对象在享受住房保障期间,逐步积累住房支付能力,通过自身的努力,离开住房保障,进入市场改善住房条件。

3.3 平衡了政府帮助与家庭自助的关系

住房保障政策在帮助那些永久失去了生产和劳动能力的人体面地生存下去的基础上,更应注重帮助那些由于在经济、教育、生活和工作技能上存在劣势而暂时处于贫困状态的人们获得居住、工作和学习的机会,使受益者慢慢不再依赖社会福利,逐步成为负责任的和富有成效的社会成员[10]。保障对象通过购房款取得的一部分住房产权,属于"自助"行为;政府将其名下产权的"使用权"部分让渡给保障对象,属于"帮助"行为。由于许多家庭在购买共有产权保障住房时通过银行或公积金贷款支付购房款,这种住房的自助行为体现在整个住房的使用期间。一方面要通过自己的努力来增加收入,归还信贷。另一方面,购房人要取得完全产权,也必须努力工作,增加资金积累。如果共有产权保障住房未来上市或被保障家庭取得了完全产权,政府的帮助也将结束,但如果保障对象长期居住,说明这部分家庭没有能力通过市场改善自己的住房条件,政府仍通过使用权的"让渡"继续帮助。

3.4　均衡了政府的当期与远期土地财政收入

共有产权保障住房的建设中,政府以土地划拨的形式,减少了当期的土地出让金收入,并转化为保障住房的产权份额。将来共有产权保障住房上市时,还可以取得相应收益,是将政府即期的土地财政收入逐步转化为今后中长期收入,在一定程度上也有利于减少城市土地财政中"寅吃卯粮"的现象。同时,相对于建设租赁型保障住房给这些家庭长期居住而言,政府投资和管理的成本较低,而且保障家庭拥有产权住房后顾之忧少,所以是一个"双赢"的制度安排。

4　共有产权保障住房实施效果

上海共有产权保障住房自 2009 年底开展试点供应以来,到 2014 年底,已受理申请家庭共 5 个批次,完成购房签约近 7 万户,多数家庭已经入住。同时,由于在住房保障申请审核、供应过程中,严格按照有关规定操作,有效地避免了各种违规产生的可能,没有发生明显的问题,使共有产权保障住房供应可以规范运行,切实起到了解决居民住房困难的效果。

2014 年 12 月,我们对首个共有产权保障住房居住小区"新凯家园"进行了抽样调查,该小区为 2010 年开始分批入住,调查方式按楼组随机抽样,共调查了 200 户家庭。

4.1　居住现状

共有产权保障住房满足了家庭的基本居住需求,50.8％的住户认为房屋基本满足住房需要,42.5%的住户认为房间面积偏小,还有 10.6%的住户认为房屋内房间太少,10.1%的住户认为房屋空间设计不合理。在调查家庭中,80.2%的家庭居住二户室;18.2%居住一居室;0.5%居住三户室。从共有产权保障住房的居住年限看,该小区于 2010 年交付使用,到 2014 年底,约 65%的家庭实际居住时间在 3 年以上,说明这批保障住房起到了解决居住困难的使用,如图 1 所示。

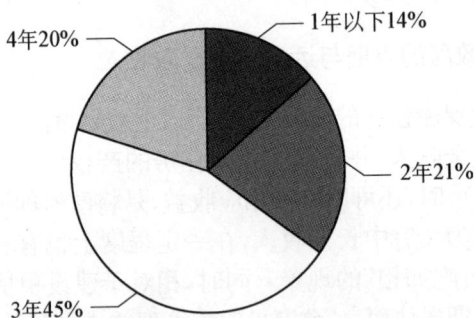

图 1　共有产权保障住房居住年限

4.2　经济自助情况

在购房过程中,70%以上的家庭有贷款或借款,这些家庭都要通过自己的工作收入来还贷款,目前约有 17.6%的住户已还清贷款或借款,如图 2 所示。

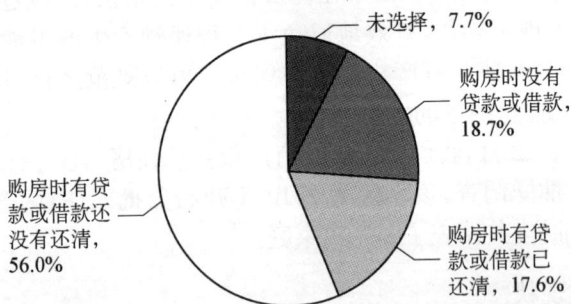

图 2　共有产权保障住房家庭购房借贷款情况

　　从家庭成员的工作情况看,51.2%的家庭成员工作情况没有变化,但有 39.2%的家庭成员工作时间增加了,说明共有产权保障住房在一定程度上起到了工作促进的作用。

　　共有产权保障住房以解决居住为主,只有少数家庭考虑将来上市出售,占 2%,多数家庭考虑长期居住不打算出售,占到 78%。还有部分家庭不确定,或根据将来的家庭情况确定,如图 3 所示。

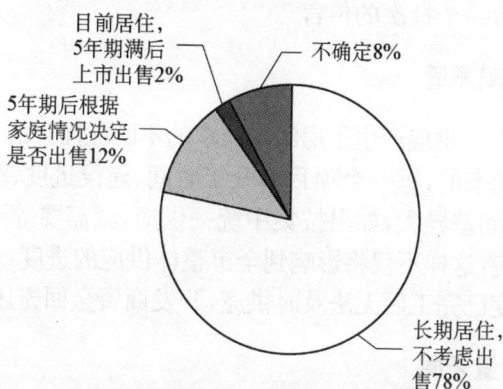

图 3　共有产权保障住房家庭未来住房打算

4.3　后期使用管理情况

　　根据调查,后期使用以自住为主,极少家庭存在转租和空关现象。对于后期使用管理的态度,62.1%的住户认为"经济适用房管理政策禁止转租、转借等行为的规定"完全合理,20.9%的住户认为"不太合理,最好允许转租转借,但产权人应该将租户信息到居委会登记"。对于后期管理的手段,35.7%的住户认为"1 年进行一次摸底调查"最为合适;24.2%的住户认为"根据需要不定期抽查"比较合适。

5　实践中遇到的主要难点和问题

5.1　集中申请受理带来的矛盾

　　上海共有产权保障住房采用的是按批次集中申请受理,即每年规定统一申请受理的时间节点,并按批次进行房源供应的方式。按批次集中申请受理主要是考虑每年政策都在调整。但每批次申请的时间不确定,也产生了一些问题,一是行政受理能力不足,材料审核难度大,短时期内大批量家庭的申请,有的批次达 3 到 4 万户,审批与住房供应时间节点把握难。二是申请家庭预期不明,不知道下一批何时开始申请,不知道还有多少共有产权保障住房供应,社会上常常有最后一个批次的传言。

5.2 供需匹配矛盾

分批次集中供应产生了房源与需求的不匹配性。由于共有产权住房建设是动态的,每一个项目的开工时间、建设进度、竣工时间不一,可预售时间差异大,如果按集中统一供应,就需要等到房源基本落实才能供应,这样不仅将影响到全市整体供应的进度,也可能造成有的项目进度已完工后无法及时供应,开发商资金回笼压力大。

5.3 居住质量矛盾

房源供需矛盾还表现在区域结构上,目前住房困难家庭主要集中在市中心区,而上海中心城区新增土地供应几乎没有空间,共有产权保障住房建设项目主要集中在外环线以外,往往是新建大型居住区,在交通、教育等方面的公共配套不足,从我们对首批家庭的调查看,出行难、就医难、日常购物难是居民反映最强烈的三个焦点,基本公共配套设施不到位方面如图 4 所示。

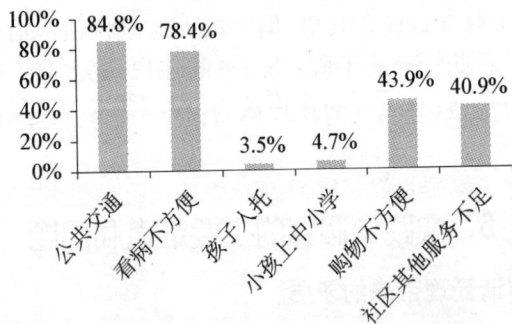

图 4 共有产权保障住房家庭反映的主要困难

5.4 后期管理矛盾

共有产权保障住房保障对象的后期管理有两个难点需要解决，第一是人口导入区与导出区的关系，住房保障对象原来为市中心区人口，户籍及住房保障行政管理仍在原来的市中心区（导出区），而家庭实际居住在外区（导入区），这样就造成了后期社区管理与行政管理职责的不匹配，而且由于住房保障对象有相当一部分是老年、无业人口，为导入区的公共服务配套带来了财政压力。

第二个难点是共有产权保障住房在后期使用中的管理，如何形成一个有效的违规使用发现、查处机制，特别是随着保障住房的数量越来越大，后期管理的工作量也越来越大，目前还没有形成有效的方式。

6 形成常态化供应管理的政策建议

共有产权保障住房在上海实践是基本成功的，但还存在着一些需要解决的问题，要形成可持续的长期住房保障方式，可从以下几个方面入手。

6.1 常态化申请受理，形成持续性预期

一是形成日常申请受理机制。共有产权保障住房申请受理纳入社区事务一门式受理窗口，常年受理。住房保障申请对象可以根据家庭具体的情况，决定申请保障性住房的时间。

二是常年资格审核。住房保障资格审核应改变现有的"批量"审核到单件常态审核，这一制度需要建立在住房保障事务管理的审核系统与住房状况信息管理部门、民政收入核对管理部门建立专线信息网络，形成一套规范的常态化查询机制。

6.2 形成申请家庭轮候机制，实现供需平衡

通过资格审核的家庭，审核结果在一定期限内有效，如3年，称为住房保障轮候家庭。该家庭在3年期间，可随时根据全市公布的房源信息享有进行申请选房资格。共有产权保障住房按项目供应。

共有产权保障住房根据每一个具体项目的建设进度,安排配售时间,具体可一个项目一开盘或多个项目一起开盘。共有产权保障住房轮候对象根据项目情况,决定是否参加申请选房。

轮候机制建立以后,可以根据轮候的家庭数量来确定共有产权保障住房的建设数量和进度,形成共有产权保障住房"人等房"的供需平衡模式。对不同区域、不同项目、不同房型的选房申请情况,可以有效地反映出共有产权保障住房申请家庭的住房需求意愿,根据这一需求意愿的统计分析,政府在共有产权保障住房建设土地供应方面可以有针对性地供地,对于需求比较强的项目,可要求开发企业加快建设进度。对于开发企业而言,这也加快了资金回笼,有利于提高开发企业的积极性,减少住房积压的担心。

6.3 强化居住区管理职能,实现有效后期管理

在处理后期管理问题中,关键是强化保障对象现居住区(导入区)的管理职能,将住房保障行政管理职责也转移到居住区,由居住区建立后期管理的常态化手段,如通过小区居民委员会、物业管理企业等,形成有效动态管理机制,并由全市来统筹管理成本。

共有产权保障住房是共有产权住房的一个重要的形式,在实践中不同城市有不同的做法,如淮安的共有产权住房也是保障住房,但和商品住房衔接,黄石市将共有产权与动迁房、公共租赁住房相结合,都是有益的探索,一般都具有住房保障的功能。通过共有产权住房供应,可以使更多的家庭尽自己所能出资购买或低价租赁住房,这既解决了这些家庭近期的住房困难,也提高了其长期住房支付能力,将是一种可以长期存在的住房供应形式。

参考文献

[1] 贾广葆,马似鹏.共有产权——经济适用房的新模式[J].城市开发,2007(6):36—38.

[2] 吴立群,宗跃光.共有产权住房保障制度及其实践模式研究[J].城市发展研究,2013(2):中彩页7—9.

[3] 陈淑云.共有产权住房——我国住房保障制度的创新[J].华中师范大学学

报(人文社会科学版),2012(1):48—58.

[4] 吕萍,修大鹏,李爽.保障性住房共有产权模式的理论与实践探索[J].城市发展研究,2013(2):中彩页 20—24.

[5] 张娟锋,虞晓芬.以共有产权住房推动我国住房保障体系的发展[J].中国房地产,2015(4):63—65.

[6] 金细簪,虞晓芬.共有产权存在的合理性释义及未来发展思路[J].中国房地产,2014(11):22—26.

[7] 严荣.完善共有产权住房体系建设研究[J].经济纵横,2015(1):24—27.

[8] 王永刚.共有产权住房的制度设计[J].上海房地,2014(9):29—30.

[9] 黎明月,吴憬,胡宝仪.共有产权模式在保障性住房体系中的应用及测算比较[J].建筑经济,2014(9):93—96.

[10] 郑思齐,符育明,任荣荣.住房保障的财政成本承担中央政府还是地方政府?[J].公共行政评论,2009(6):30—46.

(原载于《城市发展研究》2015 年第 7 期)

碳减排视角下上海低碳城市发展路径研究[*]

引　言

　　城市既是人类科技进步与社会文明的智慧结晶,也是环境污染与社会问题的汇集之处[1]。在城市化发展的推动下,人类对资源与能源的使用无论是在规模上还是在速度上都达到了前所未有的高度,碳排量增长所带来诸多问题严重影响着城市可持续发展与居民生活健康[2]。如何协调碳排量与城市发展之间的矛盾已成为城市化发展过程中的焦点问题。

　　在逐渐凸显的能源危机与日益严峻的环境问题双重影响下,倡导"低排放、低污染、低消耗"的"低碳经济"理念逐渐受到国内外学者的重视,建设"低碳城市"的构想也应运而生。"低碳城市"是指城市碳排放速率低于城市发展速率或呈现出负增长状态[3]。换言之,低碳城市是在确保居民生活质量不断提高和城市经济快速发展前提下,实现城市的低碳化和可持续发展[4][5]。

　　近年来,我国在城市化快速发展的同时也付出了沉重的代价,

---

　　* **基金项目**:国家自然科学基金资助项目(71371126);教育部人文社会科学研究规划基金资助项目(10YJA630236);上海师范大学城市经济学重点学科建设资助项目

　　** **作者简介**:卓德保(1965—),男,上海师范大学商学院教授。

城市环境问题逐渐成为制约城市低碳化发展的重要因素。因此,如何在经济快速发展的同时实现城市未来发展向低碳发展模式的转变,成为当今城市化发展研究的重要课题。本文正是基于低碳城市发展理念,分析上海城市发展中存在的问题,在不影响上海经济快速发展的情况下,探索上海低碳化城市发展的模型和路径。

1 文献回顾

"低碳经济"概念最早出现在 2003 年英国政府能源白皮书报告中,是指"以更少的能源消耗与生态环境污染,获取更多的经济产出"。该概念一经提出,便引起国际社会的广泛关注,此后有关"低碳城市"的研究也随之兴起。在国外研究中,Chin 和 Wee 通过深入分析能源消耗、碳减排量与城市规划的关系问题,提出低碳城市发展模式。部分学者认为,城市规划对能源消费、碳排量的控制主要集中于土地综合利用[6]、倡导公共交通[7]等方面的政策引导。随后,国外学者纷纷从城市碳排放影响因素[8]、低碳城市环境治理[9]等方面开展低碳城市建设的相关研究。

伴随着国外低碳研究的影响,国内学者也逐渐将研究目光转向低碳城市,并强调低碳城市研究应关注维持经济快速发展与降低单位产值能耗两方面[10]。从现有文献来看,国内对于低碳城市的研究主要集中于国际视角、政府视角、规划视角三方面。在国际视角方面,黄光宇和陈勇以丹麦太阳风社区为例,指出可再生能源的使用能最大限度减少温室气体的排放[11]。在政府视角方面,国内学者多是从调整产业结构[12]、制定公共交通等角度[13]指出政府在低碳城市建设中应起监督者、促进者以及提供者的作用。在规划视角方面,辛章平与张银太认为,低碳城市发展规划应从城市定位、产业发展、交通规划以及建筑设计四个方面制定[14]。

现有研究主要集中在降低城市碳排量与实现城市可持续发展上,主要结论是:(1)低碳城市建设应遵循"三低"原则(低能耗、低污染、低排放)与"三高"原则(高效能、高产出、高效率);(2)低碳城市建设不仅需要考虑有效降低城市碳排量,同时也应保证经济发展速度以及居民生活质量。但现有研究大多仅从政府低碳政策[12]、企业低碳生产[14]、居民低碳消费[15]单方面考虑减排问题。本文是在分析上海城市发展与碳排放的关系上，从政府、企业以及居民三方面的综合作用探讨上海低碳城市发展路径。

2 上海低碳城市化发展现状及问题

2.1 上海城市化发展与生态环境交互关系的演变

根据上海城市发展演变历程来看，新中国成立以来，上海城市化发展与生态环境交互关系在时间上可分为：协调阶段（1949 年—1957 年）、冲突阶段（1957 年—1978 年）、磨合阶段（1978 年—2009 年）、再协调阶段（2010 年—至今）（表1）。

表 1　上海城市化发展与生态环境交互关系演变

	协调阶段（1949 年—1957 年）	冲突阶段（1957 年—1978 年）	磨合阶段（1978 年—2009 年）	再协调阶段（2010 年—至今）
城市类型	传统城市	现代城市萌芽	现代城市	生态城市
文明类型	农业文明占据主体	工业文明初期	工业文明	生态文明
经济类型	农业经济时代	工业经济时代	类循环经济时代	循环经济时代
产业比重	第一产业占据主体 二、三产业起步	第二，三产业迅猛发展 第一产业比重下降	第三产业快速发展 第二产业比重下降	第三产业继续发展 一、二产业创新发展
生态质量	城市生态环境较好	受工业发展影响开始下降	初期生态迅速恶化 后期恶化速度减缓	生态环境控制

数据来源：根据《上海经济年鉴》、《上海统计年鉴》整理自绘

在再协调阶段中，特别是 2010 年世博会举办后，"与自然共生"生态理念逐步融入城市发展之中，建设生态城市成为上海城市未来发展的主要目标。通过低碳经济与低碳生活模式实现上海城市发

展的低碳城市建设被提上议程,并成为城市发展的趋势。

纵观上海城市化发展的历程,自 2004 年开始城市化率增长速度逐渐放慢,从 2004 年的 81.16% 到 2012 年的 89.76%,年增长率为 0.95%(图 1),与此同时,城市废弃物排放总量却在逐步增加

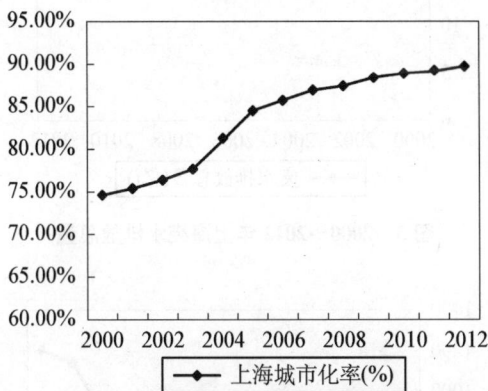

图 1 2000~2012 年上海城市化率

(图 2、3、4)。尤其是工业废气排放量和垃圾产生量远远高于上海城市化增长速率,且有加速趋势,使得环境质量加速下降。这在一定程度上反映因环境污染、碳排放过量等城市化问题所带来的发展瓶颈严重阻碍着上海城市化进程广度与深度的推进。

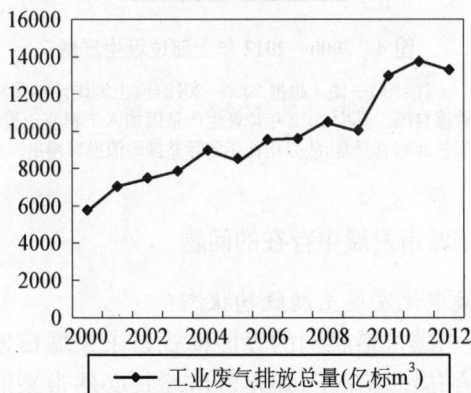

图 2 2000~2012 年上海工业废气排放总量

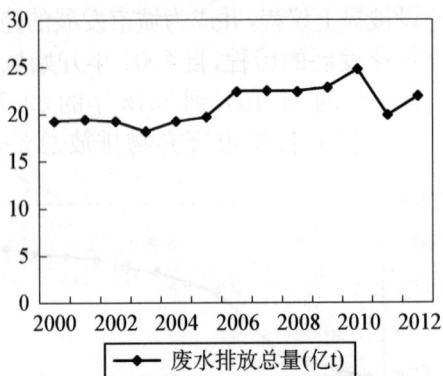

图 3　2000～2012 年上海废水排放总量

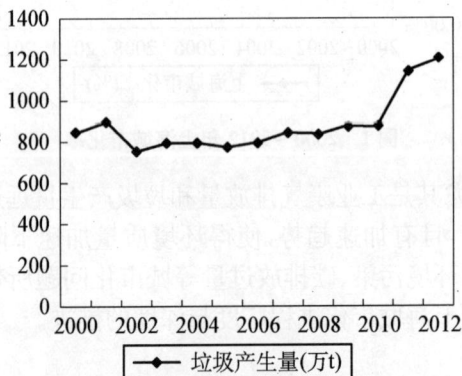

图 4　2000～2012 年上海垃圾生产量

注:图 1—图 4 根据 2000—2012 年《上海统计年鉴》数据自绘。其中 2012 年垃圾生产量因加入工程渣土清运量而略有异常,故采用往年年际差额均值推算得出。

2.2　上海低碳城市发展中存在的问题

2.2.1　城市化发展呈弱脱钩状态

城市发展与碳排量脱钩的发展模式是未来城市发展的理想模式[3](图 5)。在传统经济下,城市经济增长必然带来能源消耗与碳排量的增加(图 5 左半部分);然而在低碳经济下,则是追求在城市经济增长的同时,实现能源消耗与碳排量的减少(图5右半部分)。

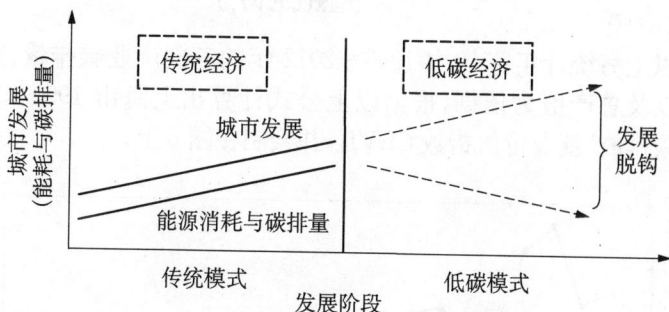

图5 城市发展与碳排量脱钩发展模式

目前,上海已逐渐倡导低碳城市建设并落实相应低碳发展措施。根据 2001～2013 年《上海统计年鉴》[16] 中的数据可以看出:自 2000 年以来,每万元 GDP 能源消耗强度从 2000 年的 1.15 t 标准煤下降至 2012 年的 0.56 t 标准煤,碳排量从 2000 年的 2.82 亿 t 下降至 2012 年的 1.37 亿 t。尽管 GDP 增长速度略高于碳排量增长速度,但由于仍然依赖能源消耗并带来碳排量的增加,这也说明上海城市化发展呈弱脱钩状态。

2.2.2 城市碳排放贡献价值不高

城市社会经济发展和碳排放强度一直为低碳研究所关注,单位碳排量所贡献的价值是低碳城市发展研究的独特视角。城市碳排放的贡献价值反映单位碳排量提供物质创造和提供就业的价值或能力,本文采用碳排放-就业价值指数[15]($CEVI_i$):

$$CEVI_i = \sqrt[n]{\frac{g_i P_i X_1 X_2 \cdots X_n}{C_i S_i}}$$

其中:$CEVI_i$ 表示第 i 个部门碳排放-就业价值指数;g_i 表示 i 部门的人均 GDP;P_i 表示 i 部门就业人数;$X_1 \cdots X_n$ 表示与碳排放产出效益有关的其他因子;C_i 表示 i 部门碳排量;S_i 表示 i 部门相对应的占地面积。

采用正向指标的标准化方法,对 $CEVI_i$ 进行无量纲化处理,得出最终碳排放-就业价值指数 $CEVI_0$:

$$CEVI_0 = \frac{CEVI_i}{\max(CEVI_i)}$$

以上海统计年鉴[16]中 1990—2012 年的三次产业碳排量、就业人数以及总产值为依据,根据以上公式计算出上海市 1990—2012年的碳排放-就业价值指数 $CEVI_0$,并绘制在图 6 上。

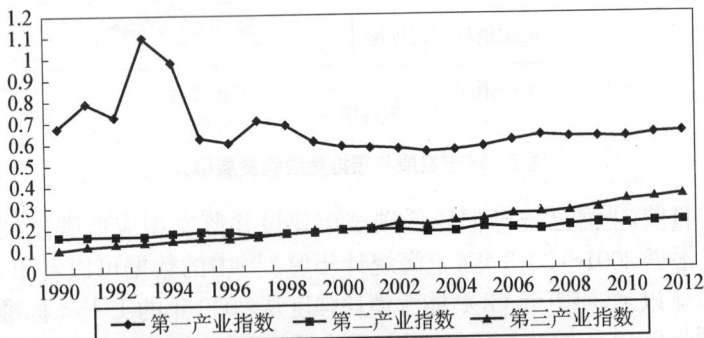

图 6 1990~2012 年碳排放-就业价值指数

数据来源:根据上海统计年鉴数据计算绘制

从图 6 可以看出:

① 从 1990 年至 2012 年,第三产业碳排放-就业价值指数上升幅度略大于第二产业,表明第三产业的碳排放价值提升最为显著,是城市未来低碳化发展的优势产业。

② 第一产业的碳排放-就业价值指数最高,但与内含高附加值的第二、三产业相比而言,第一产业并不符合保障经济发展水平的标准,其 GDP 贡献率要低于第二、三产业。

3 上海城市化发展对碳排放的影响分析

3.1 上海城市化发展对碳排放的影响因素

现有研究和大量实践表明:城市化发展必然带来城市碳排量的增加。分析城市化发展中影响碳排放的因素,度量各因素对城市碳排放影响的大小,对于探索上海低碳城市发展的路径至关重要。具体来说,城市生产总值、居民收入水平以及人口数量增加,会导致城市对煤炭、石油等能源需求量提升,城市碳排放年增长量也随之增加。此外,城市化进程的提升也使城市建设面积不断增加,因城市建筑面积而产生的废弃物及碳排放增长量也随之增长。

因此,综合现有研究并结合上海城市化发展现状,本文以碳排放年增长量为研究对象,构建上海城市化发展对碳排放增长量影响的概念模型(图7),影响碳排放增长量(Y)的因素包括城市人口数量(X_1)、城市生产总值(X_2)、城市居民收入(X_3)、城市建筑面积(X_4)。

3.2 上海市城市发展对碳排放增长量影响的模型构建与实证分析

根据图7的概念模型,建立现象 y 与 x_1、x_2、x_3、x_4 之间的多元线性回归方程。为了避免伪回归现象,采用变量的增量 Y 与 X_1、X_2、X_3、X_4 分别代替变量 y 与 x_1、x_2、x_3、x_4,并建立多元线性回归方程:

$$Y = a_1 X_1 + a_2 X_2 + a_3 X_3 + a_4 X_4 + b$$

其中,a_1、a_2、a_3、a_4 为回归系数,b 为回归常数。

碳排放(y)的计算采用联合国政府间气候变化专门委员会(IPCC)2006 年版碳排放指南计算公式:$y = \sum_{i=1}^{n} B_i \times C_i$,其中 y 为碳排量,B_i 为按标准煤计算而得的能源 i 消耗量,C_i 为能源 i 碳排放系数,i 为能源种类。结合上海市实际情况,上海市能源消耗品种为煤炭、焦炭、燃料油、汽油、煤油、柴油、天然气,故设定 $i = 7$。

将 1995—2012 年《上海统计年鉴》相关数据,通过 SPSS19.0 软件 pearson 相关分析得出自变量与因变量的相关性,具体结果如表 2 所示。

表 2　碳排放增长量与影响碳排放因素之间的相关性

指标		城市人口数量(X_1)	城市生产总值(X_2)	城市居民收入(X_3)	城市建筑面积(X_4)
碳排放增长量(Y)	Pearson 相关性	.894*	.938**	.863*	.845***
	显著性	0.017	0.002	0.013	0.004
	N	18	18	18	18

注:** 表示相关性在 0.01 水平上显著,* 表示相关性在 0.05 水平上显著

表 2 的结果表明：X_2、X_4 与 Y 在 0.01 水平上呈显著相关性，X_1、X_3 与 Y 在 0.05 水平上呈显著相关性。再通过 SPSS19.0 软件对回归模型进行分析，得到表 3 的结果。

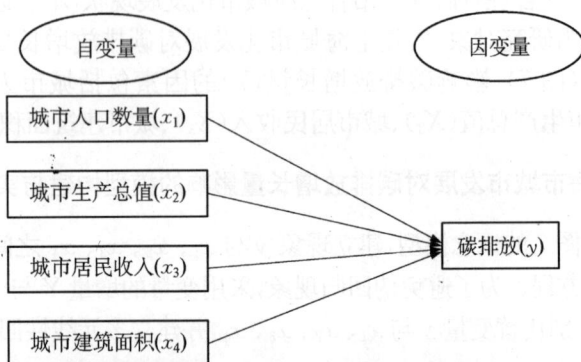

图 7　上海城市化发展对碳排放影响的概念模型

表 3　碳排放增长量与城市发展指标间关系的回归结果

Variable （解释变量）	Unstandardized Coefficient （非标准化系数）		Standardized Coefficient （标准化系数）	t	Sig.
	B	Std. Error （标准误差）	Bate （试用版）		
X_1	.216	.163	.154	3.726*	.0217
X_2	.469	.012	.431	9.659**	.0013
X_3	.161	.069	.137	2.317**	.0029
X_4	.257	.006	.223	5.376*	.0175
b	365.412	336.412	—	2.2175*	.0291

注：** 表示相关性在 0.01 水平上显著，* 表示相关性在 0.05 水平上显著

从表 3 可知，依据 t 检验情况来看，X_2 与 X_3 通过 Sig. ≤ 0.01 下的参数显著性检验，X_1 与 X_4 则通过 Sig. ≤ 0.05 下的参数显著性检验。这表明该概念模型较为合理，变量 X_1、X_2、X_3、X_4 均可以作为解释变量存在于模型中，以解释上海城市化发展对碳排放增长量的影响。

因此,由上述分析可知多元线性回归方程为:

$$Y = 0.216X_1 + 0.469X_2 + 0.161X_3 + 0.257X_4 + 365.412$$

同时,对碳排放增长量影响的模型进行拟合优度及其他检验,得到结果如表4所示。

表4 拟合优度及其他检验结果

R	R^2	调整 R^2	标准估计误差	D-W
.853	.728	0.713	0.036	1.975

从表4可看出,拟合优度检验指标 R、R^2、调整 R^2 均接近于1,这表明多元概念模型拟合度较好,通过模型拟合度检验。同时,由于DW=1.916,查DW检验表得:$d_L = 0.82$,$d_U = 1.87$。所以 $d_U <$ DW $< 4 - d_U$,即 X_1、X_2、X_3、X_4 之间不存在自相关性,通过模型自相关检验。

因此,从显著性检验、拟合度检验、自相关检验可以看出:由解释变量 Y 与 X_1、X_2、X_3、X_4 所构建的概念模型合理有效。这表明随着城市化发展进程不断深入,城市碳排放增长量(Y)随着解释变量要素基数的增加而增加。此外,解释变量城市生产总值(X_2)在模型中所占比重最大,即城市生产总值对城市碳排放增长量影响程度最大,这也在侧面体现出上海城市化发展呈弱脱钩状态——上海城市化率增长依赖于碳排量增加。

4 上海低碳城市发展路径

从上文分析可以看出,上海城市化发展依赖于能源资源消耗,呈现弱脱钩状态。此外,作为解释变量的 X_1、X_2、X_3、X_4 等因素也显著影响着城市碳排放水平。因此,要真正解决低碳城市发展的问题,就必须在政府、企业以及居民3大层面上实施碳减排目标,形成"三轴一核"低碳城市发展模式(图8),才能实现真正意义上的低碳城市发展。

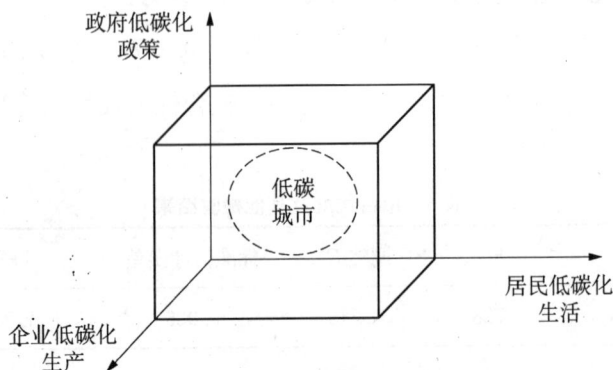

图8 "三轴一核"低碳城市发展模式

作为城市发展的三大参与主体：政府、企业和居民，三者在构建低碳城市发展过程中是一个相互影响、相互促进的有机整体（图9）。

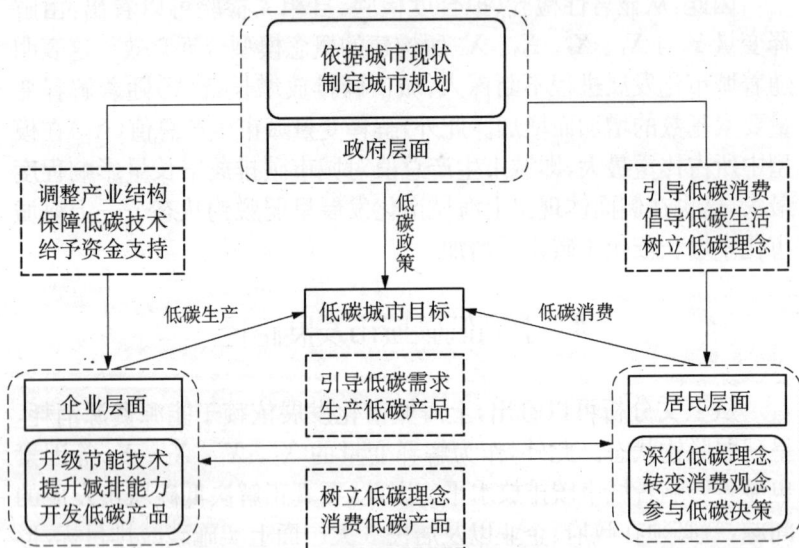

图9 上海低碳城市发展路径

4.1 第一阶段:政府层面

在低碳城市发展过程中,政府低碳政策的制定是其关键所在。政府应通过低碳监管机制、低碳政策引导以及产业结构调整等方面,推动城市向低碳建设的转型升级。

4.1.1 制定低碳发展规划,构建低碳监管机制

从表1的演变阶段可以看出,建设"生态城市"与"低碳城市"已成为上海城市发展的必由之路。上海应以"最大限度上保障经济发展、最大限度上减少碳排量"作为低碳规划的制定标准,从居民低碳住宅建筑、企业低碳生产减排等方面指导低碳城市建设。同时,积极推行节能减排技术,建立健全城市低碳监管机制,促进低碳城市建设的顺利开展。

4.1.2 树立公众低碳理念,引导居民低碳消费

城市化进程的不断推进也使得城市人口数量(X_1)增加,并影响着上海低碳城市发展。因此,政府引导居民树立低碳消费理念,应通过各种媒体推广低碳理念,引导城市居民,将倡导"低碳生活、低碳消费"作为低碳城市发展中不可或缺的部分。

4.1.3 调整产业结构,提供资金技术保障

低碳城市建设需要理念更新,更需要产业结构调整与生产技术支持。从表3中可知,城市生产总值(X_2)的高值回归系数(0.491)体现生产总值对碳排量的影响最大。说明上海必须强化城市发展的脱钩效应。由于城市生产总值源于第一、二、三产业产值,因此解决各产业碳排放低价值贡献问题,就必须进行产业结构的优化调整。

因此,在上海低碳城市建设中,应调整、优化产业结构,大力发展城市低碳化优势产业——第三产业,合理降低第二产业比重。积极发展知识密集型、技术密集型产业,加大现代服务业等低碳行业的比重。对符合"三低"、"三高"的企业应给予低碳技术的扶持保障,对节能减排较为突出的企业给予资金补贴和税收减免等优惠政策。

4.2 第二阶段:企业层面

企业是连接政府与居民的纽带,是低碳城市建设的关键,在城市低碳化发展过程中起着必不可少的作用。

4.2.1 加强低碳技术创新,提升节能减排能力

在政府层面给企业低碳技术支撑的同时,企业也应加强低碳技术的应用与创新[12]。因此,根据图6反映的上海三产碳排放低价值贡献状况,企业在注重低碳技术引进的同时,也要积极向知识密集型、技术密集型转型,实现对碳排量的有效控制。

4.2.2 加快低碳产品生产,强化企业内部管理

随着城市人口数量与城市居民收入对碳排量显著性影响的凸显,引导城市居民低碳消费应是企业未来发展战略。因此,企业应将低碳技术引入到生产过程中,积极生产低碳产品。同时,健全节能减排指标体系、检测体系与考核体系,将节能减排工作纳入企业的考核体系之中。

4.3 第三阶段:居民层面

居民作为城市主体,是低碳城市建设的源动力,其生活方式与消费模式直接决定着低碳城市建设的成功与否。

4.3.1 树立低碳生活理念,养成低碳消费习惯

低碳城市建设,离不开居民的低碳消费。随着城市化水平的不断提升,城市人口数量与居民收入水平的增加对城市碳排量的影响逐渐凸显。城市居民在日常生活和工作中不仅要最大限度降低对能源的消耗,还要树立低碳消费概念,通过对产品的低碳偏好促使企业生产低碳产品。

4.3.2 倡导低碳生活方式,参与城市低碳决策

城市低碳生活不仅要求居民树立低碳理念,同时也倡导低碳居住方式。城市人口数量、居民收入水平与城市建筑面积对城市碳排量增长量的影响显著。因此,应倡导居民在居住选择与设计中崇尚低碳居住方式,减轻居民建筑对城市环境的负荷。同时,城市人口数量、居民收入水平的提升带来城市交通需求的增加。因此,政府应加快发展城市公共交通系统等低碳交通方式建设,以减少城市车

辆尾气碳排量。

5　研 究 结 论

　　低碳城市建设既不同于自由市场的经济模式,也不同于政府高度掌控的环境治理模式。而是一种政府同企业、居民三方共同参与的新型城市化发展模式。本文通过研究表明:将低碳理念融入经济发展和居民生活之中,是我国社会经济持续发展的关键所在。通过对上海低碳城市发展现状的深入分析,得出以下结论:

　　(1) 低碳城市建设是一个多目标问题,涉及政府、企业以及居民三方面,其中政府起着引导作用,居民则是低碳城市建设的源动力,企业作为连接政府与居民的纽带,在建设低碳城市过程中起着必不可少的作用。

　　(2) 低碳城市建设应遵循的"三低"原则与"三高"原则;不仅需要考虑到降低城市排放量问题,同时也要保证经济发展速度以及居民生活质量。

注释

① 碳排放增长量(Y)的计算采用联合国政府间气候变化专门委员会(IPCC)2006年版碳排放指南计算公式: $Y_o = \sum_{i=1}^{n} B_i \times C_i$,其中 Y_o 为碳排量, B_i 为按标准煤计算而得的能源 i 消耗量, C_i 为能源 i 碳排放系数, i 为能源种类。结合上海市实际情况,上海市能源消耗品种为煤炭、焦炭、燃料油、汽油、煤油、柴油、天然气,故设定 $i = 7$ 。因此,碳排放增长量(Y) 则为年际间碳排量 Y_o 之差。

参考文献

[1] 倪深海. 城市生态化与可持续城市发展的生态原则[J]. 山东农业大学学报(自然科学版),2001,(4):525—528.

[2] 李鱼,范英英,孙钊,李都峰. 基于经济增长约束的低碳城市碳排放总量优化模型研究[J]. 安徽农业科学,2012,(2):334—336.

[3] 陈飞,诸大建. 低碳城市研究的内涵、模型与目标策略确定[J]. 城市规划学刊,2009,(4):7—13.

［4］王家庭.基于低碳经济视角的中国城市发展模式研究［J］.江西社会科学，
2010,(3):85—89.

［5］刘中文,高朋钊,张序萍.我国低碳城市发展战略模式研究［J］.科技进步与
对策,2010,(22):67—70.

［6］Masanobu K, Kenji D. Multiagent land-use and transport model for the policy
evaluation of a compact city ［J］. *Environment Planning B: Planning Design*,
2005,(4):485 - 504.

［7］Shim G E, Rhee S M, Ahn K H, Chung S B. The relationship between the
characteristics of transportation energy consnmption and urban form ［J］. *The
Annals of Regional Science*, 2006,(2):351 - 367.

［8］Neil S, Steve P, Ramachandran K. The iterative contribution and relevance of
modelling to UK energy policy ［J］. Energy Policy, 2009,(3):850 - 860.

［9］Castelnuovo E, Galeotti M, Gambarelli G, Vergalli, S. Learning-by-Doing vs.
Learning by Researching in a model of climate change policy analysis ［J］.
Ecological Economies, 2005,(2):261 - 276.

［10］陈飞,诸大建.低碳城市研究的理论方法与上海实证分析［J］.城市发展研
究,2009,(10):71—79.

［11］黄光宇,陈勇.生态城市理论与规划设计方法［M］.北京:科学出版社,2004.

［12］何建坤,张希良.中国"十一五"期间能源强度下降趋势分析——如何实现能
源强度下降20％的目标［J］.中国软科学,2006,(4):33—38.

［13］李增福,郑友环."低碳城市"的实现机制研究.经济地理,2010,(6):
949—954.

［14］辛章平,张银太.低碳经济与低碳城市［J］.城市发展研究,2008,(4):
98—102.

［15］宋婷,沈清基.城市碳排放价值指数研究及规划应用［J］.城市发展研究,
2013,(3):15—20.

（原载于《城市发展研究》2014 年第 11 期）

基于旅游数字足迹的目的地
关注度与共现效应研究*

——以上海历史街区为例

梁保尔　潘植强**

引　言

　　作为人类文明发展里程的显著标志,互联网已成为人类生活不可或缺的重要组成部分。据中国互联网络信息中心(CNNIC)发布的《第33次中国互联网络发展状况统计报告》显示,截至2013年12月,我国网民规模达6.18亿①。网络已逐渐扩展成人们获取信息数据、表达自身观点乃至具有重要现实影响的社交空间[1]。与此同时,互联网凭借其开放、共享、交互的特性使得大量旅游信息得以有效交汇[2],游客在旅游过程中对旅游目的地的真实体验与关注偏好逐渐被网络文本所反映[3];越来越多的游客以文本、图片等表达形

　　*　**基金项目:**本研究受上海市教委科研创新重点项目"世界遗产视野中的上海历史街区旅游功能优化研究"(12ZS195)和2015年中国旅游研究院优奖计划专项基金项目"基于旅游数字足迹的目的地景观关注度及共现效应研究——以上海3A级及以上旅游景区为例"资助。〔The study was supported by a grant from Key Project of Innovation and Scientific Research of Shanghai Municipal Education Commision (to LIANG Baoer) (No. 12ZS195) and China Tourism Academy Projects for Talent Youth in 2015 (to PAN Zhiqiang). 〕

　　**　**作者简介:**梁保尔(1953—　),男,上海人,博士、教授,研究方向为遗产旅游、旅游文化研究,E-mail:lbaoer@shnu. edu. cn;潘植强(1991—　),男,安徽芜湖人,硕士研究生,研究方向为旅游地理、旅游文化与区域旅游规划。

　　①　资料来源:http://www. cnnic. net. cn/hlwfzyj/hlwxzbg/hlwtjbg/201403/t20140305_46240. htm, 2014 - 10 - 18。

式在微博、博客等网络社交空间中发布网络游记,并逐渐形成游客在网络社交空间中的旅游数字足迹。

然而出于不同动机与意图,官方与游客对旅游目的地景观的关注与感知并不一致,官方试图宣传的旅游目的地景观与游客所关注的旅游目的地景观也存在一定差异。因此,正确认识官方与游客两者差距之所在,不仅能使目的地旅游规划与营销推广更加符合游客意愿与需求,同时也能有效增强游客对目的地的满意度及重游意愿[4]。基于此,本研究以上海历史街区为例,利用发布于网络空间的官方宣传文本与网络游记文本进行对比分析,通过统计各历史文化风貌区的关注次数及关注度来识别官方与游客对上海历史街区的关注偏好;并运用社会网络分析法描绘上海历史街区各景观相互间的共现效应,分析官方与游客两者感知共现效应差异之所在,以促进官方营销与宣传更加符合游客意愿与需求。

1 文 献 回 顾

当前,网络媒体影响力的增加不断推动着研究者利用旅游数字足迹,对游客关注度、旅游动机与消费偏好等方面进行研究。旅游数字足迹是指游客在旅游过程中和旅游结束后在微博、博客等网络社交空间上以文本、图片等表达形式所主动发布或共享的旅游游记、旅游攻略以及旅游点评等[5]。因此,旅游数字足迹作为因游客活动所形成的具有地理标签或位置信息的电子痕迹[6],能够反映出游客在旅游目的地的空间移动;故而以此研究游客时空行为,可以快速获得游客在目的地实际地理空间中的移动轨迹与关注热点。

在针对旅游目的地关注的研究中,国外研究者 Reilly、Andsager 等较早将旅游关注研究与网络数据相结合,并通过特征高频词汇深入揭示出游客关注偏好及其对目的地认知形象所在[7—8];此后,部分研究者也通过网络口碑研究旅游目的地对游客信任度[9]与忠诚度[10]的显著影响。受国外研究影响,国内研究者逐渐运用旅游数字足迹研究旅游现象,主要集中在旅游形象感知、旅游网络关注与客流关系、游客旅游行为三个方面。在旅游形象感知研究中,张文等以赴台大陆游客的网络游记为样本,指出大陆赴台游客对台湾旅游地形象的感知以正面评价为主[11]；部分研究者也先后以鼓浪屿、嘉峪关为例，依据特征高频词汇将网络游记文本中游客所感知的目的地形象划分成多个维度[12—13]。与此同时，在旅游网络关注与客流关系研究中，路紫较早指出旅游网站访问人数与景区实际接待游客人数存在较高关联度[14]；此后，李山、龙茂兴等通过百度指数验证旅游网络关注与客流量之间存在显著正向关系[15—16]，张妍妍等人则以代表游客旅游数字足迹的文本和照片分析西安旅游流的时空网络结构[17]。随着研究的不断深入，研究者发现旅游数字足迹蕴含游客旅游动机及其重游意愿。在此情况下，陈钢华等人以泉州为例，根据影响游客重游决策的因素不同，将重游者划分为"大众平衡型""满怀期待型"和"无所谓型"三类[18]；赵振斌等则以太白山背包客为例，通过网络游记的特征高频词汇归纳得出"登顶""穿越""徒步"是其旅游动机[19]。

上述研究成果利用网络游记为样本，在分析旅游形象感知、客流响应机制等多重问题的同时，为解决旅游地营销推广、应急机制等方面提供了重要依据；然而，已有研究多倾向于从游客视角出发，忽视了作为目的地宣传主体的官方才是弥补目的地营销宣传短板之所在。同时，目的地关注度及共现效应的生成是游客对目的地景观主观感知的结果[20]，但以网络游记为样本的现有研究仅仅对游客行为、感知、动机问题进行探讨，故而单纯以迎合网络游记所折射出的游客关注偏好来改进目的地营销宣传，将使得目的地陷入被支配、被接受地位[21—22]。

因而，作为真实反映官方宣传意图与游客实际关注的旅游数字足迹，能在一定程度上反映官方和游客对目的地景观的宣传与关注偏好，这无疑为深入了解游客关注偏好，并以此为基础调整目的地营销策略提供了新途径。因此，如何通过官方宣传文本与网络游记文本得出官方和游客对上海历史街区关注度与共现效应的差异及成因，这将是本研究的研究重点。

2 研 究 设 计

2.1 研究对象

本研究以上海市 2003 年批准划定的"中心城历史文化风貌区"

(以下简称"上海历史街区")①为例,将构成上海历史街区旅游景观的衡-复路②、外滩、南京西路、人民广场、虹桥路、山阴路、新华路、愚园路、提篮桥、老城厢、龙华、江湾这 12 个历史文化风貌区作为研究对象,并由"FMQ01"至"FMQ12"进行逐一编号。目前,历史街区内部拥有新天地、田子坊、景云里等特色里弄以及宋庆龄故居、孙中山故居、巴金故居、周公馆等名人故居,也拥有多伦路、武康路、衡山路等人文街道,极具美学艺术价值和历史人文价值,是上海都市旅游的热点区域。同时,构成上海历史街区的 12 个组成部分分布于徐汇、黄埔、静安、长宁、虹口等地,然而受区域面积、交通区位等多方面因素影响,使得官方与游客关注偏好在这一研究区域中存在差异,这对本研究分析两者差异及成因来说具有重要意义。

2.2 研究样本

为深入研究官方与游客关于上海历史街区旅游关注度与共现效应差异之所在,本研究采用网络搜索引擎对各历史文化风貌区相关官方宣传文本与网络游记文本加以采集,以资进行两者关注度与共现效应比较分析。

2.2.1 官方宣传文本获取方式

对于官方宣传文本的获取,本研究以上海官方旅游部门网上所发布的宣传文本为主。官方宣传文本来源网站主要为"上海市旅游局政务网""乐游上海""上海旅游网"以及上海市各相关区县旅游局政务网。针对这 4 个数据信息来源版块,借助"火车头采集器"软件采集 2009 年 6 月到 2014 年 6 月期间的官方宣传文本共 1243 篇,经人工识别剔除内容重复、转载的文本后,最终得到1027篇有效的官方宣传文本,并逐一编号为"GFTXT0001"……"GFTXT1027"。

2.2.2 网络游记文本获取方式

对于网络游记文本的获取,本研究以游客在旅游活动中或旅游结束后通过社交网络分享的旅游体验及感知评价文本为主,分别选

---

① 为便于研究分析与理解,本文采用《雅典宪章》和《华盛顿宪章》中所提出的"历史街区"这一概念作为上海市中心城 12 个历史文化风貌区的统称。

② 衡-复路历史文化风貌区全称"衡山路-复兴路历史文化风貌区",跨徐汇、静安、黄浦、长宁 4 个行政区。

取"新浪博客""携程""百度旅游"以及"蚂蜂窝"等知名度高且交互性强的网站。针对这 4 个数据信息来源板块,借助"火车头采集器"软件采集 2009 年 6 月到 2014 年 6 月期间的网络游记文本共 3765篇,经人工识别剔除内容重复、转载、图片为主以及与街区无关的文本后,最终获得 933 篇有效的网络游记文本,并逐一编号为"YKTXT0001"……"YKTXT0933"。

2.3 研究方法

本研究对上海历史街区旅游关注度与共现效应的研究,借助计算机构建共现处理平台①,分析官方宣传文本与网络游记文本,统

while(GFTXT′. read())//依次读取每一篇官方宣传文本正文
    match collection mc＝regex. matches(GFTXT′. Get String(0),@FMQ number i);//设定变量 FMQ name i 为当前指定景区
   {GFTXT′ number＝GFTXT′. Get String(1);//获取参与当前统计的官方宣传文本编号
find_FMQ number i＝mc. count;//判断指定风貌区在当前官方宣传文本中是否出现
  if(find_FMQ number i!＝0){find_FMQ number i＝1;}//若在当前官方宣传文本中出现,则 FMQ name i 关注次数不累计
    then match collection me＝regex. matches(GFTXT′. Get String(0),@FMQ number j);//设定变量 FMQ name j 为共现风貌区
      if strfind(GFTXT′,FMQ name{j});//若在当前官方宣传文本中,FMQ name i 与 FMQ name j 共现
        result_temp(FMQ name i, FMQ name j)＝1;//则 FMQ name i 与 FMQ name j 共现次数＝1
        end
      end
    end
  fclose(GFTXT′number_txt);//关闭官方宣传文本
end

注:上图仅显示官方宣传文本统计代码,网络游记文本统计代码构建则需将"GFTXT′"替换为"YKTXT′"。

图 1 上海历史文化风貌区官方宣传文本关注次数和共现频次统计代码

Fig. 1 The Shanghai historical and cultural features of the official promotion district concerned and the co-occurrence frequency statistical code number

---

① 本文所提及的共现处理平台是在 Windows XP 操作系统中使用 Visual Studio 2008开发工具构建而得。

计各历史文化风貌区的"关注次数"与"共现次数"两个指标(图 1)。在本研究中,"关注次数"是指某一历史文化风貌区在网络文本中被提及的次数。对于共现效应研究来说,景区间共现主要是在某一景区样本中出现对另一景区的描述[2,23~24]。因此,本文所提及的"共现次数"则是指两个历史文化风貌区在同一网络文本中被同时提及的次数。据此,依据官方宣传文本与网络游记文本可形成官方关注次数、官方共现次数、游客关注次数、游客共现次数这 4 类统计指标。

但需要指明的是,为避免各历史文化风貌区在某一网络文本中多次重复出现而导致研究结果产生偏移,本研究设定,在单篇网络文本中所指的历史文化风貌区无论被提及多少次,其关注次数或共现次数均为 1。

此外,为进一步分析各历史文化风貌区之间共现效应所在,本研究通过社会网络分析官方和游客对不同历史文化风貌区的共现效应进行量化分析,以直观地对各历史文化风貌区共现效应进行分析,并借以对比官方与游客感知共现差异之所在。

3   研究分析与结果

3.1   上海历史街区关注度及其偏好分析

关注次数的大小反映官方和游客对历史文化风貌区的重视程度——关注次数越多则表示关注度①越强,反之则相反[2]。因此,本研究通过"共现处理平台"获得 12 个历史文化风貌区在官方宣传文本与网络游记文本中的关注次数——官方关注次数与游客关注次数;同时采用官方关注度与游客关注度来显示两者对各历史文化风貌区的重视程度(表 1)。

---

①   历史文化风貌区关注度=该历史文化风貌区关注次数/各历史文化风貌区关注次数之和。

表 1 上海历史街区官方与游客的关注次数及关注度一览表

Tab. 1 Attention times and degree of the official and tourists on Shanghai historical streets

历史文化风貌区编码 Code of historic districts	网络文本 Network text			
	官方宣传文本 Official propaganda texts		网络游记文本 Network tourist texts	
	官方关注次数 Official attention number	官方关注度 Official attention degree	游客关注次数 Tourism attention number	游客关注度 Tourism attention degree
FMQ01（衡－复路历史文化风貌区）	189	0.151	183	0.157
FMQ02（外滩历史文化风貌区）	169	0.135	167	0.143
FMQ03（南京西路历史文化风貌区）	148	0.118	132	0.113
FMQ04（人民广场历史文化风貌区）	129	0.103	106	0.091
FMQ05（虹桥路历史文化风貌区）	126	0.101	57	0.049
FMQ06（山阴路历史文化风貌区）	111	0.089	142	0.122
FMQ07（新华路历史文化风貌区）	104	0.083	73	0.063
FMQ08（愚园路历史文化风貌区）	85	0.068	47	0.040

（续　表）

历史文化风貌区编码 Code of historic districts	网络文本 Network text			
	官方宣传文本 Official propaganda texts		网络游记文本 Network tourist texts	
	官方关注次数 Official attention number	官方关注度 Official attention degree	游客关注次数 Tourism attention number	游客关注度 Tourism attention degree
FMQ09（提篮桥历史文化风貌区）	68	0.054	87	0.075
FMQ10（老城厢历史文化风貌区）	53	0.042	114	0.098
FMQ11（龙华历史文化风貌区）	43	0.034	36	0.031
FMQ12（江湾历史文化风貌区）	27	0.022	21	0.018

据表 1 数据结果显示：官方与游客的关注偏好在 FMQ01、FMQ02、FMQ03、FMQ04、FMQ11 以及 FMQ12 这 6 处历史文化风貌区相一致；在 FMQ05、FMQ06、FMQ07、FMQ08、FMQ09 以及 FMQ10 这 6 个历史文化风貌区相偏离，且在前 3 处呈现较强的官方关注偏好，在后 3 处呈现较强的游客关注偏好。

3.1.1　官方关注偏好与游客关注偏好相一致

从表 1 数据可看出，官方与游客关注偏好一致性呈现"两极"分布。具体来说，资源禀赋高、空间区位好且位于中心城核心区的衡-复路（FMQ01）、外滩（FMQ02）、南京西路（FMQ03）、人民广场（FMQ04）这 4 处历史文化风貌区是官方与游客关注的热点区域，因此关注度呈现"高值"一致性分布。以外滩历史文化风貌区（FMQ02）为例，官方宣传文本认为：

对于外滩而言，万国建筑博览群是腔调，外白渡桥是妖娆……如今的外滩已经簇簇新……已成为全中国乃至全世界最耀眼的地标之一①。

与此同时，网络游记文本中的网友"国学牛仔〈〈"认为：

(外滩)这里百年来都是中国第一大城市上海的象征，这里被称为万国建筑博览群……我好像每次来上海都去外滩……外滩当之无愧作为上海的标志②。

从官方宣传文本与网络游记文本所共有的"外滩/万国建筑博览群"词汇可看出，外滩因具有高资源禀赋的"万国建筑博览群"，使得官方宣传偏好与游客关注偏好极为契合；即官方宣传文本中关于外滩的介绍——"地标"，都能在网络游记文本表达中遴选出——"标志"，这使得外滩历史文化风貌区成为官方（0.135）与游客（0.143）共同的关注偏好。

对于资源禀赋低、空间区位差且位于中心城边缘区的龙华（FMQ11）、江湾（FMQ12）这2处历史文化风貌区而言，两者位于上海内环边缘区域，交通便捷性低于其他风貌区；同时两者区内仅有二种类型的旅游资源，旅游资源丰度要弱于其他风貌区，因此既不是官方宣传重点也不是游客关注重点，成为官方与游客关注的盲点区域，从而关注度呈现"低值"一致性分布。

3.1.2 官方关注偏好与游客关注偏好相偏离

对于官方关注偏好与游客关注偏好相偏离的分析，涉及官方关注偏好显著和游客关注偏好显著两种情况。

第一，加强对建筑生态与人文生态极为脆弱地带的环境保护，是官方关注偏好形成主因所在。当前，因旅游发展而造成的诸多环境问题使得目的地可持续发展遭遇阻碍，故而提升目的地社会权能

---

① 资料来源：http://www. tour. sh. cn/index. php/Home～VisitingCard～mapDetail～id～186,2014-09-27。

② 资料来源：http://lvyou. baidu. com/notes/e5041473fe2902a17f34941？=28942bd001b3184b27efe, 2014-09-27。

以保护人文、科研以及艺术价值极高的自然与人文资源就显得尤为重要[25]。从表1可看出,官方关注度偏好显著性主要体现在虹桥路(FMQ05)、新华路(FMQ07)以及愚园路(FMQ08)这3处美学价值极高的风貌区,三者关注度差值分别为0.052、0.02、0.028,尤以虹桥路历史文化风貌区(FMQ05)最为显著。

通过对描绘虹桥路历史文化风貌区(FMQ05)网络文本的分析可知,官方宣传文本中的"别墅/花园/风景线/建筑很美"等词凸显出旅游解说对街区美学价值的重视,官方意图通过旅游解说系统强化对街区建筑遗存的保护,以达成提升游客保护意识的环境教育目标。然而,游客感知能力的有限性以及旅游活动的异地性,使得游客较难获取有关旅游地重要属性的客观信息[26];在此情况下,官方对教育、环保功能的重视使得街区蕴含的人文价值并未被游客所知晓,故而代表游客感知评价的"不知道来处/不理解/不会再来/没意义"等词汇在网络游记中多次出现。因此,两者关注的偏离影响着游客满意度与重游意愿,导致官方关注的热点(0.101,排名第5)反而成为游客关注的盲点(0.049,排名第9)。

第二,满足触摸历史记忆及感知人文内涵的深度旅游动机,是游客关注偏好形成主因所在。目前,城市化进程的快速推进使得城市内部面临"同质化"与"无地方"的双重困境,这唤起了游客对城市记忆的追寻和人文遗存的凝视。这种游客既不同于"追寻虚假旅游吸引物"的肤浅旅游者[27],也不同于"被欺骗而不自觉"的愚昧型旅游者[28]。在此情形下,积淀着历史记忆与人文资源的山阴路(FMQ06)、老城厢(FMQ10)以及提篮桥(FMQ09)这3处风貌区自然而然就成为游客所关注的热点。从表1可看出,FMQ06、FMQ10与FMQ09这3处人文值较高的风貌区的游客关注偏好较为显著,三者关注度数值依次为0.122、0.098、0.075,其中,尤以老城厢历史文化风貌区(FMQ10)最为显著,游客关注度(0.098,排名第5)远大于官方关注度(0.042,排名第9)。

在对网络游记文本中关于老城厢历史文化风貌区(FMQ10)描绘的分析可知,无论是归结为老城厢历史文化风貌区内部蕴含人文价值的"人文历史/文化/信仰"等词汇,还是反映游客对这一风貌区关注与凝视的"踏着/印迹/体味/市井生活"等词汇,均可体现出游客对蕴含浓厚人文价值的历史文化风貌区关注偏好较为集中。然而,这与官方重视保护美学价值极高的风貌区相异,致使官方关注偏好与游客关注偏好相偏离。

3.2 上海历史街区共现效应分布分析

对上文官方与游客关注偏好的研究,主要是基于单个景观的分析。一般而言,旅游产品或旅游路线的设计由多个景观组成,故而深入分析官方宣传文本与网络游记文本中各历史文化风貌区相互间是否存在共现效应,对上海历史街区旅游营销宣传起着至关重要的作用。本研究采用社会网络分析法,根据所统计的各历史文化风貌区共现次数形成官方与游客共现矩阵,并借助可视化工具 Pajek 将其生成为官方与游客的社会网络关系图(图 2、图 3)。

3.2.1 官方宣传文本共现效应分布

从图 2 可看出,在官方宣传文本共现网络图中,官方并未重点宣传某一历史文化风貌,街区总体共现宣传分布较为均衡。同时,衡-复路(FMQ01)、外滩(FMQ02)、南京西路(FMQ03)、人民广场(FMQ04)等 4 处风貌区之间共现效应较为凸显,构成了官方共现核心区域,并与虹桥路(FMQ05)、山阴路(FMQ06)、新华路(FMQ07)、愚园路(FMQ08)、老城厢(FMQ10)等风貌区形成较为显著的关联效应。此外,这 4 处风貌区也在官方关注度中位列前4,这也说明官方联动宣传意识较强,力图通过热点景区带动效应提升景区热度。

3.2.2 网络游记文本共现效应分布

对于网络游记文本所形成的共现网络图,位于共现核心位置的衡-复路(FMQ01)与外滩(FMQ02)历史文化风貌区相互间共现次数最为显著,且两者与其他历史文化风貌区共现次数较为密集,已成为网络游记文本中两大共现核心景区及游客旅游首选之地(图3)。同时,衡-复路(FMQ02)与外滩(FMQ02)历史文化风貌区所共有且共现次数大于 10 的分别是南京西路(FMQ03)、人民广场(FMQ04)、山阴路(FMQ06)、老城厢(FMQ10),形成着网络游记文本中四大共现次核心景区。将这 6 处风貌区与游客关注度排名前 6 位的风貌区作对比分析,可知两者完全一致,这在一定程度上也能

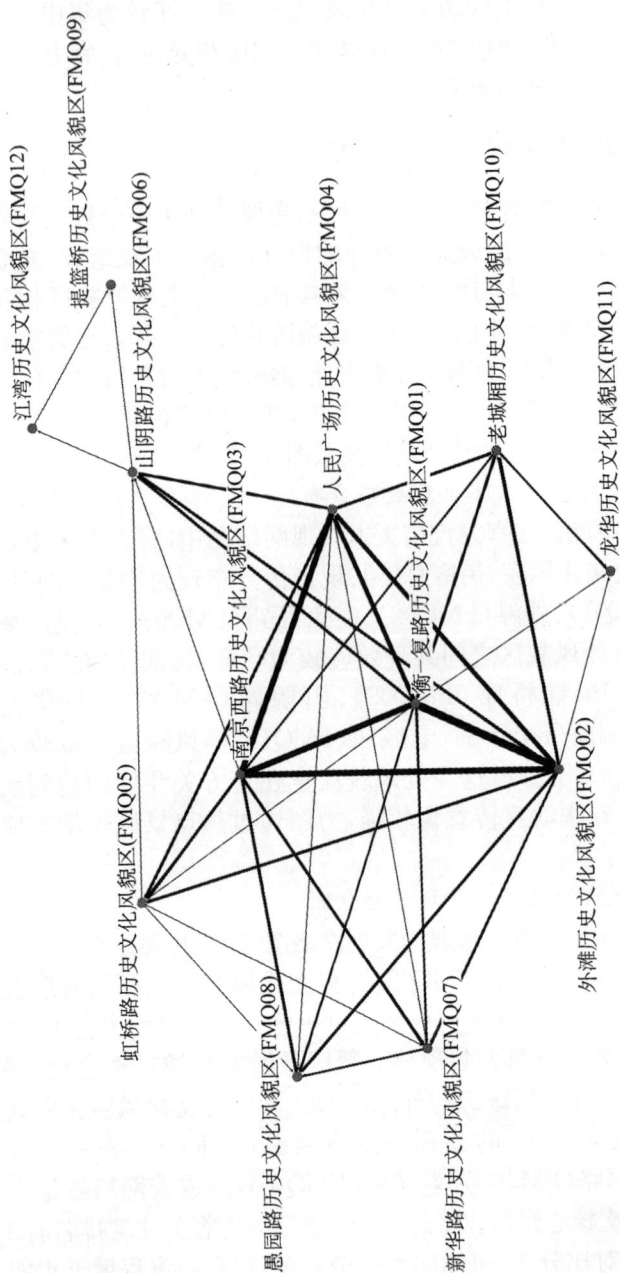

图 2 上海历史街区官方宣传文本共现网络图

Fig. 2 The social network figure based on official promotion of Shanghai historical streets

注:图中线条代表共现强度,线条越粗则共现强度越强,线条越细则共现强度越弱,下列图 3 同此。

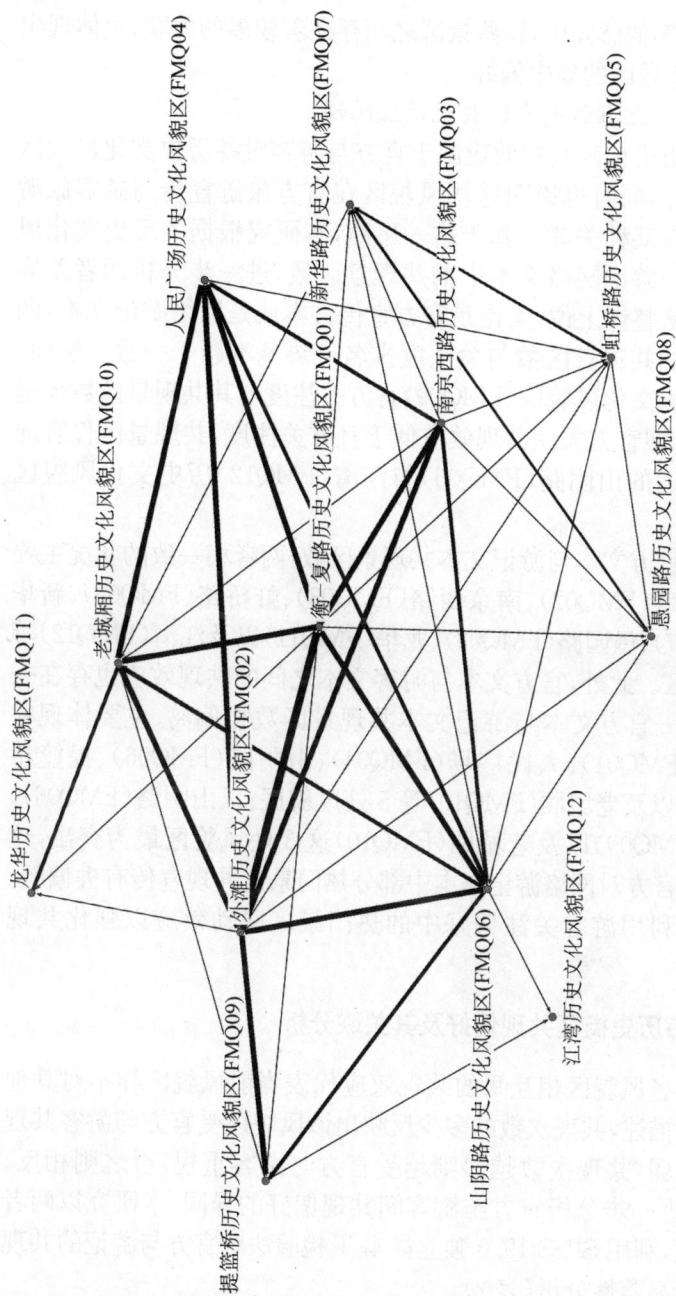

图 3 上海历史街区网络游记文本共现网络图

Fig. 3 The social network figure based on web travel notes of Shanghai historical streets

说明,在游客的感知中,这些景区之间存在着较多的关联,也体现出游客对这些景区的集中偏好。

3.2.3 上海历史街区共现效应比较

上海历史街区共现效应源于官方与游客对各历史文化风貌区的关注偏好,同时也说明这些风貌区在官方旅游宣传与游客旅游感知中具有某种关联。基于这一思路,本研究根据各历史文化风貌区官方与游记网络文本中的共现景区数,进一步分析两者差异之所在。从整体上说,无论是官方宣传文本或是网络游记文本,两者所形成的共现景区数与关注度排名走势基本趋于一致。然而,提篮桥历史文化风貌区(FMQ09)官方关注度与其共现景区数却呈反向分布,即官方关注共现效应低于官方关注度,共现景区仅有地理位置较近的山阴路(FMQ06)与江湾(FMQ12)历史文化风貌区两处。

对比官方文本与游记文本共现景区数,两者相一致的状况主要分布于外滩(FMQ02)、南京西路(FMQ03)、虹桥路(FMQ05)、新华路(FMQ07)、愚园路(FMQ08)、龙华(FMQ11)以及江湾(FMQ12)等7处风貌区。此外,官方文本与游客文本之间的共现效应也存在一定差距——官方文本与游记文本共现景区数相偏离,主要体现在衡-复路(FMQ01)、人民广场(FMQ04)、山阴路(FMQ06)、提篮桥(FMQ09)以及老城厢(FMQ10)等5处风貌区;以山阴路(FMQ06)、提篮桥(FMQ09)以及老城厢(FMQ10)这3处风貌区最为突出,这也反映出官方对网络游记文本中部分热门景区共现宣传有失偏颇,尚未充分利用游客关注偏好中的热门景区联动效应以强化共现宣传。

3.3 上海历史街区共现偏好及其关联分析

由于各风貌区相互间的共现效应代表当前风貌区样本对其他风貌区的描述,共现次数的多少反映出该风貌区受官方与游客共现偏好的强弱,共现次数越多则越受官方与游客重视,否之则相反。因此,为进一步分析官方与游客间共现偏好的异同,本研究以两者共现次数,利用SPSS 19.0独立样本T检验法对官方与游记的共现偏好进行显著性分析(表2)。

表2 上海历史街区官方与游客的共现偏好显著性检验

Tab. 2 The significance test of common preference about the official and tourists in Shanghai historical streets

历史文化风貌区编码 Code of historic districts	官方宣传文本 Official propaganda texts		网络游记文本 Network tourist texts		t统计值 t-Statistic	伴随概率 Prob.	标准误差 Std error	共现偏好 Co-occurrence preferences
	共现次数	共现均值	共现次数	共现均值				
FMQ01(衡-复路历史文化风貌区)	161	13.45	157	13.08	0.107	0.4578	1.9327	共同偏好
FMQ02(外滩历史文化风貌区)	162	13.83	161	13.42	0.068	0.3732	2.2264	共同偏好
FMQ03(南京西路历史文化风貌区)	144	11.97	89	7.42	1.164**	0.0207	4.3719	官方偏好
FMQ04(人民广场历史文化风貌区)	129	10.73	83	6.92	1.059*	0.0409	3.6428	官方偏好
FMQ05(虹桥路历史文化风貌区)	50	4.17	23	1.92	1.358***	0.0032	1.3645	官方偏好
FMQ06(山阴路历史文化风貌区)	55	4.58	98	8.17	−1.187**	0.0117	2.5712	游客偏好
FMQ07(新华路历史文化风貌区)	46	3.83	26	2.17	1.030**	0.0239	1.7743	官方偏好
FMQ08(愚园路历史文化风貌区)	58	4.83	31	2.58	1.129*	0.0329	1.6753	官方偏好

（续 表）

历史文化风貌区编码 Code of historic districts	官方宣传文本 Official propaganda texts		网络游记文本 Network tourist texts		t统计值 t-Statistic	伴随概率 Prob.	标准误差 Std error	共现偏好 Co-occurrence preferences
	共现次数	共现均值	共现次数	共现均值				
FMQ09(提篮桥历史文化风貌区)	2	0.17	40	3.33	-1.855^{***}	0.0047	1.1392	游客偏好
FMQ10(老城厢历史文化风貌区)	52	4.32	105	8.75	-1.127^{***}	0.0013	2.9461	游客偏好
FMQ11(龙华历史文化风貌区)	10	0.83	14	1.17	-0.315	0.2776	0.3174	共同偏好
FMQ12(江湾历史文化风貌区)	2	0.17	7	0.58	-0.394	0.3191	0.6825	共同偏好

注：(1)表中 ***、**、* 分别表示差异显著性在 0.01、0.05、0.1 水平上显著；(2)共同偏好表示为官方与游记共现偏好之间不存在显著性差异，是官方与游记的共同关注偏好。

据表 2 显示,在官方宣传文本和网络游记文本中,官方与游客的共现偏好存在官方偏好、游客偏好以及共同偏好三种情况,可归纳为共现偏好显著性和非显著性两种差异。结合表 2 显示的数据,下文即从这两种差异进行共现偏好分析。

3.3.1 共现偏好显著性差异分析

通过对表 2 中 t 统计值及伴随概率 p 的分析可看出,南京西路(FMQ03)、人民广场(FMQ04)、虹桥路(FMQ05)、山阴路(FMQ06)、新华路(FMQ07)、愚园路(FMQ08)、提篮桥(FMQ09)以及老城厢(FMQ10)这 8 处风貌区则体现为共现偏好显著性差异,这表明官方对这些风貌区存在过度宣传或资源低效利用的现象,对景区宣传的把握有失偏颇,并没有得到同等程度的游客偏好。其中,FMQ03(1.164**)、FMQ04(1.059*)、FMQ05(1.358***)、FMQ07(1.030**)、FMQ08(1.129*)等 5 处为官方共现偏好;FMQ06(−1.187**)、FMQ09(−1.855***)、FMQ10(−1.127***)等 3 处为游客共现偏好。

现有研究表明,在整个旅游目的地范围内,资源禀赋高、旅游吸引力强的旅游产品或产品组合,往往会被官方作为目的地重要的旅游吸引物进行联合宣传,利用其示范效应和带动效应推动目的地旅游业发展[29]。因此,在官方共现偏好中,南京西路(FMQ03)、人民广场(FMQ04)、虹桥路(FMQ05)、新华路(FMQ07)、愚园路(FMQ08)等 5 处风貌区因内部拥有众多风格较为接近且内在关联性较强的优秀历史建筑,如成片集中、风格多样、富有特色的公共建筑、独立式花园住宅建筑、新式里弄建筑等[30],故而成为官方旅游宣传重点,因此在官方宣传中产生共现次数为 3 的五重共现效应集合"FMQ[03:04:05:07:08](3)"①。此外,上述 5 处风貌区亦形成着 3 个四重共现效应"FMQ[03:04:05:07](3)""FMQ[03:04:05:08](3)""FMQ[04:05:07:08](3)"与 6 个三重共现效应,尽管共现次数呈现出低值分布,多介于 3 与 6 之间,但从另一方面来说,官方宣传

---

① 对于历史文化风貌区共现效应集合,[ ]内部编号代表共现样本风貌区,其编号个数代表样本风貌区共现重数,( )内部数值代表样本风貌区共现次数;以"FMQ[03:04:05:07:08](3)"为例,表示 03、04、05、07、08 这 5 处样本风貌区在官方宣传文本中形成共现,共现重数为 5,共现次数为 3。

资源投入较为均衡,相互间共现宣传较为紧密。然而,这5处风貌区因官方"自上而下"的单向营销活动严重影响着营销行为的完整性,导致游客反馈等环节被忽视[31],使得游客实际共现偏好低于官方共现偏好,未得到游客相应的关注,从而存在过度宣传与低效利用问题。

与此同时,表现为游客共现偏好的3处风貌区则反映出历史人文资源对游客关注热点及旅游动机具有显著正向影响[32]。具体来说,随着寻求文化差异、认知人文内涵的后现代旅游消费群体的诞生,作为文化遗产地的历史街区因其独特的文化魅力越来越受到旅游者的青睐[33]。因此,无论是代表现代文学长廊的山阴路历史文化风貌区(FMQ06)、承载上海本土文化的老城厢历史文化风貌区(FMQ10),还是保留犹太文明及其过往的提篮桥历史文化风貌区(FMQ09),三者无一不体现着游客对城市变迁轨迹、居民生活历程等深层人文关注所在,并形成着1个三重共现效应集合"FMQ[06:09:10](9)"以及3个二重共现效应集合"FMQ[06:09](13)""FMQ[06:10](11)""FMQ[10:12](13)"。在此情况下,对积淀城市人文记忆且关注度较高及关注偏好凸显的游客来说,网络游记文本中"多伦路""百年""世事变迁""上海犹太难民""历史/故事""回忆"等词汇,深刻体现出有着寻求文化差异、认知人文内涵动机的游客对山阴路、老城厢以及提篮桥这3处风貌区内部人文价值的关注,形成较为显著的游客共现偏好。同时,无论是三重共现效应集合抑或是二重共现效应集合,游客共现次数数值均要高于官方共现次数,这意味着游客在关注力度上要显著强于官方宣传力度,较少的共现景区数目也间接显现出游客关注偏好的集中。

3.3.2 共现偏好非显著性差异分析

从表2分析可知,共现偏好非显著性差异则体现在衡-复路、外滩、龙华、江湾等4处风貌区,即在官方宣传文本与网络游记文本中所遴选出的共现偏好极为契合,官方对此类景区的宣传与景区本身的受欢迎程度是相匹配,并未出现过度宣传或资源低效利用问题。

具体来说,对于衡-复路和外滩这两处风貌区而言,根据上文两者在官方宣传文本与网络游记文本中相一致的关注度与关注偏好来看,这两处风貌区因资源禀赋高、空间区位好、服务设施完善等因素,已成为官方宣传与游客关注中所共识的标志性历史街区,即在官方宣传文本中有关这两处风貌区的推介都能在网络游记文本的表达中遴选出。因此,衡-复路和外滩这两处风貌区是官方与游客共同共现偏好之所在,不存在共现偏好显著性差异现象。

此外,对于龙华与江湾这两处风貌区而言,两者内部所蕴含的佛教文化及民国文化与其他风貌区人文内涵匹配度与关联度不高,实现共现宣传的契合度较差,因此导致官方共现宣传偏好不强;同时也因地理位置相对较远、旅游资源禀赋较差等多重因素而未被游客所关注。两者所形成的低关注度间接导致在官方与游客共现次数和共现街区数呈较低分布,因此在官方与游客两者间的共现偏好并不显著。

4　研究结论与讨论

4.1　研究结论

本研究借助官方宣传文本和网络游记文本,从关注度与共现效应两方面探寻上海历史街区下辖各历史文化风貌区官方与游客的关注偏好及共现偏好,并分析两者差异之所在。通过对网络文本的比较分析可知,游客游记文本中所表达的关注及共现偏好与官方宣传文本之间存在显著关联。本研究认为,资源禀赋高、空间区位好的风貌区,不仅是游客所追逐的景点,同时也是官方所极力推荐的景点,从而形成较为一致的关注偏好及共现偏好;对于资源禀赋低、空间区位差的风貌区而言,由于官方与游客所形成的低关注度,间接导致官方与游客的共现次数和共现街区数呈较低分布。

此外,历史街区旅游营销策略也存在一定问题,即官方所着重宣传的景点并未被游客所关注,同时游客所肯定的热门景点也未被官方作为宣传重点。具体来说,满足触摸历史记忆及感知人文内涵的深度旅游动机,使得游客对街区内部人文价值关注偏好要明显高于外部美学价值,故而感受人文内涵及历史记忆是游客造访历史街区的核心动机;同时,官方重视对建筑生态与人文生态极为脆弱地带的环境保护,并力图实现对资源禀赋高、旅游吸引强的景点进行联合宣传,故而官方对街区外部建筑风格较为接近、内在关联性较强且美学价值高的风貌区较为关注,是其宣传核心之所在。

4.2 研究启示

本研究通过对官方宣传文本与网络游记文本的对比分析,得出官方宣传与游客关注差异及其成因,更为重要的是,本研究在实践层面对官方旅游营销策略提出以下建议。

4.2.1 强化联动宣传,实现街区协调发展

景区联动协调发展是保证景区营销资源合理、有效利用的关键之所在。因此,应依托具有较高旅游资源禀赋且知名度、美誉度较好的历史文化风貌区,通过跨景区营销方式改变各历史文化风貌区受访率不一致的现状,消除景区过度宣传或资源低效利用问题。在此情况下,官方采取景区联动宣传策略,发挥衡-复路、外滩、山阴路、老城厢以及提篮桥这5处游客关注度较高的热门风貌区优势,采取冷门景区"攀附"策略,加强对龙华与江湾这两处游客关注度较低的冷门风貌区的联合宣传,促进上海历史街区旅游的全面发展。

4.2.2 实施精准宣传,有效瞄准游客偏好

游客在网络游记文本中对上海历史街区内部各历史文化风貌区的关注与评价虽然是主观的,但却表达了游客自身对历史街区的旅游体验与个人感受。因此,官方应在充分了解游客关注偏好并保持原有风貌区关注热度的基础上,适当降低对虹桥路、新华路、愚园路这3处风貌区的宣传力度;同时,根据游客感受人文内涵及历史记忆的核心旅游动机,加强对山阴路、老城厢以及提篮桥这3处风貌区的宣传力度,着力强化对城市变迁轨迹、居民生活历程等深层人文内涵的挖掘,从而提高游客对上海历史街区的满意度及重游意愿。

4.2.3 优化解说系统,强化人文资源解说

旅游解说的形成源于游客感知能力的有限性,使得游客较难获取有关旅游地重要属性的客观信息,致使游客必须依赖解说系统才能顺利完成游览活动。因此,官方未来在利用旅游解说系统传递历史街区建筑美学价值,以达成对游客环保与教育目标的同时,要避免只注重历史街区物质环境而形成"静态消极式""建筑躯壳式"的保护模式;更应注重对以山阴路、老城厢以及提篮桥深层人文价值

的保护与宣传,力图协助游客认知目的地旅游资源的人文、科学及艺术价值所在。只有这样,才能提升游客对虹桥路、新华路、愚园路这3处风貌区的关注,消除因缺乏街区人文内涵信息而造成的负面影响。

4.3 讨论

本研究采用网络文本分析官方与游客关注偏好和共现偏好,并得出相关结论。需要指明的是,本研究从"新浪博客""携程""百度旅游"以及"蚂蜂窝"等知名网站相关版块获取研究样本,并未从词义角度分析样本信息的褒贬含义,这在一定程度上制约了研究样本的全面性。此外,本研究在对景区共现效应的分析中仅限定于2个景区间,而3个及以上景区是否存在共现效应、如何对此进行计算,这也是非常值得深入探讨的话题;由此可见,计算并研究多重景区共现效应以体现共现效应的全面性,应作为下一步研究的方向。

参考文献

[1] Yu Haibo. A probe into the methodology of using network topics as qualitative data source: A case study of tourist motivation [J]. *Tourism Science*, 2011, (1):46 - 53.(于海波. 网络话题作为定性数据来源的研究方法探讨——以旅游动机为例[J].旅游科学,2011,(1):46—53.)

[2] Yao Zhanlei, Xu Xin, Li Limei, et al. An analysis of the co-occurrence phenomenon of scenic areas in online travel note [J]. *Tourism Science*, 2011, (2):39 - 46.(姚占雷,许鑫,李丽梅,等. 网络游记中的景区共现现象分析——以华东地区首批国家5A级旅游景区为例[J].旅游科学,2011,(2):39—46.)

[3] Wang Yuan, Xu Xin, Feng Xuegang, et al. Research on tourists' percieved image of ancient town using web text mining methods: A case study of Zhujiajiao [J]. *Tourism Science*, 2013,(5):86 - 95.(王媛,许鑫,冯学钢,等. 基于文本挖掘的古镇旅游形象感知研究——以朱家角为例[J].旅游科学,2013,(5):86—95.)

[4] Liu Zhixing, Ma Yaofeng, Gao Nan, et al. A research on tourism destination image perception of Mountain resorts: A case study of mountain Wutai scenery area in China [J]. *Journal of Mountain Science*, 2013,(3):370 - 376.(刘智

兴,马耀峰,高楠,等. 山岳型旅游目的地形象感知研究——以五台山风景名
胜区为例[J]. 山地学报,2013,(3):370—376.)

[5] Girardin F, Calabrese F, Fiore F D. Digital footprinting: Uncovering tourists
with user — generated content [J]. *Pervasive Computing IEEE*, 2008,14
(4):36 – 43.

[6] Gartner G, Bennett D A, Morita T. Toward ubiquitous cartography [J].
Cartography and Geographic Information Science, 2007,34(4):247 – 257.

[7] Reilly M D. Free elicitation of descriptive adjectives for tourism image
assessment [J]. *Journal of Travel Research*, 1990,28(4):36 – 43.

[8] Andsager J L, Drzewiecka J A. Desirability of differences in destinations [J].
Annals of Tourism Research, 2002,29(2):401 – 421.

[9] Bickart B, Schindler R M. Internet forums as influential sources of consumer
information [J]. *Internet Market*, 2001,15(3):31 – 40.

[10] Thomas W G, Talai O, Andrew J C. WOM: The impact of customer-to-
customer online know-how exchange on customer value and loyalty [J].
Journal of Business Research, 2006,59(4):449 – 456.

[11] Zhang Wen, Dun Xuefei. Study on image perception of mainland tourists to
Taiwan: Based on content analysis of online travels [J]. *Journal Beijing
International Studies University*, 2010,(11):75 – 83. (张文,顿雪霏. 探讨大
陆游客对台湾旅游目的地形象的感知——基于网上游记的内容分析[J]. 北
京第二外国语学院学报,2010,(11):75—83.)

[12] Fu Yeqin, Wang Xinjian, Zheng Xiangmin. Study on tourism image based on
web text analysis: Case of Gulangyu [J]. *Tourism Forum*, 2012,5(4):59 –
66. (付业勤,王新建,郑向敏. 基于网络文本分析的旅游形象研究——以鼓
浪屿为例[J]. 旅游论坛,2012,5(4):59—66.)

[13] Miao Hong, Ma Jintao, Zhang Huan. A study on tourists perceiving image of
Jiayuguan City based on web text analysis [J]. *Journal of Northwest Normal
University: Natural Science*, 2014,50(2):99 – 104,120. (苗红,马金涛,张
欢. 基于网络文本分析的嘉峪关市游客感知形象研究[J]. 西北师范大学学
报:自然科学版,2014,50(2):99 – 104,120.)

[14] Lu Zi, Zhao Yahong, Wu Shifeng, et al. The time distribution and guide
analysis of visiting behavior of tourism website users [J]. *Acta Geographica
Sinica*, 2007,(6):621 – 630. (路紫,赵亚红,吴士锋,等. 旅游网站访问者行
为的时间分布及导引分析[J]. 地理学报,2007,(6):621—630.)

[15] Li Shan, Qiu Rongxu, Chen Ling. Cyberspace attention of tourist attractions
based on baidu index: Temporal distribution and precursor effect [J].

Geography and Geo-information Science，2008，(6)：102 - 107.（李山，邱荣旭，陈玲.基于百度指数的旅游景区络空间关注度：时间分布及其前兆效应[J].地理与地理信息科学，2008，(6)：102—107.）

[16] Long Maoxing, Sun Gennian, Ma Lijun, et al. An analysis on the variation between the degree of consumer attention of travel network and tourist flow in regional tourism：A case of Sichuan province [J]. *Areal Research And Development*，2011，(3)：93 - 97.（龙茂兴，孙根年，马丽君，等.区域旅游网络关注度与客流量时空动态比较分析——以四川为例[J].地域研究与开发，2011，(3)：93—97.）

[17] Zhang Yanyan, Li Junyi, Yang Min. The tourism flow network structure of Xi'an based on tourism digital footprint [J]. *Human Geography*，2014，(4)：111 - 118.（张妍妍，李君轶，杨敏.基于旅游数字足迹的西安旅游流网络结构研究[J].人文地理，2014，(4)：111—118.）

[18] Chen Ganghua, Huang Yuanshui. Influencing factors on tourists' revisit decision-making：A web-based empirical study [J]. *Tourism Tribune*，2011，23(11)：69 - 74.（陈钢华，黄远水.旅游者重游决策的影响因素实证研究——基于网络调查[J].旅游学刊，2011，23(11)：69—74.）

[19] Zhao Zhenbin, Dang Jiao. The travel behavior of backpackers of Taibai Moutain based on internet text content analysis [J]. *Human Geography*，2011，26(1)：134 - 139.（赵振斌，党娇.基于网络文本内容分析的太白山背包旅游行为研究[J].人文地理，2011，26(1)：134—139.）

[20] Lu Lin, Wang Tianying. A retrospect and prospect of research on tourist gaze in recent years in China [J]. *Journal of Anhui Normal University：Natural Science*，2013，36(5)：497 - 501.（陆林，汪天颖.近年来国内游客凝视理论应用的回顾与展望[J].安徽师范大学学报：自然科学报，2013，36(5)：497—501.）

[21] Bai Z. Ethnic identities under the tourist gaze [J]. *Asian Ethnicity*，2007，8(3)：245 - 259.

[22] Quinn B. Performing tourism：Venetian residents in focus [J]. *Annals of Tourism Research*，2007，34(2)：458 - 476.

[23] Wang Leilei, Zhao Zhenbin, Li Juan. The cognitive hotspots and relevance of inbound tourism in XinJiang [J]. *Human Geography*，2014，29(6)：140 - 145.（王蕾蕾，赵振斌，李娟.新疆入境游客认知热点与关联研究[J].人文地理，2014，29(6)：140—145.）

[24] Wang Ruhui, Zhang Qiong, Zhao Jiming. On the Tourists' preference of ethnic villages based on content analysis：Taking the Tibetan village tourists in Danba

County as an example [J]. *Journal of Sichuan Normal University*: *Social Sciences Edition*, 2013,40(2):51-57.(王汝辉,张琼,赵吉明.基于内容分析法的民族村寨游客偏好研究:以丹巴县甲居藏寨游客为例[J].四川师范大学学报:社会科学版,2013,40(2):51—57.)

[25] Guo Wen, Huang Zhenfang. Study on the development of community power and functions under the background of the development of rural tourism — Based on the investigation of two typical cases in Daizu Garden and Yubeng Community,Yunnan Province [J]. *Tourism Tribune*, 2011,26(12):83-92.(郭文,黄震方.乡村旅游开发背景下社区权能发展研究——基于对云南傣族园和雨崩社区两种典型案例的调查[J].旅游学刊,2011,26(12):83—92.)

[26] Deng Mingyan, Qin Yan. An optimization of tourist interpretation system in heritage scenic areas based on demand analysis: Taking Mt. Emei Scenic Area as an example [J]. *Tourism Tribune*, 2010,25(7):35-40.(邓明艳,覃艳.基于需求分析的遗产景区旅游解说系统优化研究——以峨眉山景区为例[J].旅游学刊,2010,25(7):35—40.)

[27] Boortin D J. *The Image*: *A Guide To Pseudo — Events In America* [M]. New York: Atheneum, 1964.

[28] Maccannell D. Staged authenticity: Arrangements of social space in tourist settings [J]. *American Journal of Sociology*, 1973,(79):589-603.

[29] Yin Shuhua. Research on Government's function of tourism marketing [J]. *Journal of Beijing Technology and Business University*: *Social Science Edition*, 2007,22(4):62-67.(银淑华.试论政府的旅游营销职能[J].北京工商大学学报:社会科学版,2007,22(4):62—67.)

[30] Chen Fei, Ruan Yisan. A comparative study on conservation planing of historic and cultural areas in shanghai and the response of conservation planning [J]. *Urban Planning Forum*, 2008,(2):104-110.(陈飞,阮仪三.上海历史文化风貌区的分类比较与保护规划的应对[J].城市规划学刊,2008,(2):104—110.)

[31] Chi Xiongbiao. On theoretical basis of the governmental tourist promotion acts [J]. *Tourism Tribune*, 2003,18(3):58-61.(池雄标.论政府旅游营销行为的理论依据[J].旅游学刊,2003,18(3):58—61.)

[32] Liang Jiangchuan. Tourism motivations and destination preferences: A study of Guangdong external tourists [J]. *Areal Research and Development*, 2003,32(5):151-156.(梁江川.旅游动机与目的地偏好——以广东外来旅游者为例[J].地域研究与开发,2003,32(5):151—156.)

[33] Wu Chengzhao, Wang Jing. The study on tourism destination image of the

metropolitan space of Shanghai [J]. *Modern Urban Research*, 2012, (2): 82 - 87.(吴承照,王婧.基于游客感知的上海都市空间旅游意象研究[J]. 现代城市研究,2012,(2):82—87.)

(原载于《旅游学刊》2015 年第 7 期)

A Short-term load forecasting model of natural gas based on optimized genetic algorithm and improved BP neural network

Feng Yu, Xiaozhong Xu

College of Information and Electrical Engineering,
Shanghai Normal University

1. Introduction

In the gas supply system, gas load data is of fundamental significance for project planning, engineering design, pipeline operation and optimal scheduling. Load forecasting can provide a basis for gas supply planning, achieving the maintenance plan and distribution dispatching of gas pipe network. Accurate forecasting will improve operational efficiency, save energy and reduce costs. Thus the natural gas consumption forecasting has been widely researched [1 - 3].

Currently, forecasting methods can be roughly grouped into three categories. The first one is statistical method, including time series method, trend extrapolation, etc. The second one is artificial intelligence method, like neural network (NN) [4 - 7], and genetic algorithm (GA) [8,9]. And the third one is combinational method, such as the combination of GA and support vector machine (GA-SVM) [10], the integration of genetic algorithm and neural network (GA-BP) [11 - 14] and so on [15]. Irani and Nasimi [16] presented a hybrid genetic algorithm back propagation for permeability estimation of the reservoir, and the results demonstrated its excellence. Sedki et al. [17] evolved neural network utilizing real coded genetic algorithm for daily rainfall-runoff forecasting and the results showed that the GA-based neural network model gave superior predictions.

Over the years, studies have shown that a combinative model gives better projected results compared to a single model for natural gas prediction. The main direction of research is how to combine and optimize various intelligent algorithms to improve the prediction accuracy. Song [18] introduced an existing GA-BP model, but they did not optimize BP neural network to speed up learning convergence or explain specific algorithm mechanism yet. In contrast to aforementioned paper, this article describes the whole algorithm in detail and puts forward three improvements to obtain higher forecasting precision, including improved additional momentum factor, improved self-adaptive learning rate and improved momentum and self-adaptive learning rate. Also, cat chaotic mapping is introduced to enhance the global search ability of genetic algorithm (CCMGA). Optimized by CCMGA, the neural network will exert maximum performance. The analyses and comparisons of the above several different combinational algorithms show that the CCMGA-BP algorithm improved by improved additional momentum factor gets the optimal prediction solution for short-term gas load forecasting. Besides, we propose a series of data pre-processing technologies and take a full account of more elements affecting natural gas consumption, which make the model approximate the training data very well and ensure more accurate prediction.

The remainder of this paper is organized as follows. The next section describes data pre-processing in detail. Section 3 elaborates the improvements of BP neural network. Section 4 presents the new CCMGA-BP algorithm. Section 5 reports our experiments and relevant discussions. Concluding remarks are drawn in Section 6.

2. Data pre-processing

For gas load forecasting, accurate prediction is based on a large number of true and exact historical load data of the research area. However, "bad data", such as missing data, exception data, etc. are unavoidable because of systematic errors. These data play a serious interference in network training and forecasting process. They will cause the training error beyond the desired range, and then weaken the prediction accuracy, which finally results in a waste of economic and resource. So in order to guarantee the smoothness of the load sequence, the consistency of the order of magnitude and better performance of the network, the pre-processing of the original data is essential.

2. 1. Missing data processing

When confronted with the lack of data on a certain day, we can choose the closest m data to the missing data according to the Euclidean distance or correlation analysis, and then calculate the weighted average:

$$l(d) = w_1 l(d_1) + w_2 l(d_2) + \cdots w_m l(d_m) \qquad (1)$$

where $l(d)$ is the missing data and does not exist, $[l(d_1), l(d_2), \cdots, l(d_m)]$ is the closest data vector to $l(d)$, $[w_1, w_2, \cdots, w_m]$ is the weight vector whose value can be determined by Euclidean distance or correlation coefficient. That is to say, small Euclidean distance or large correlation coefficient leads to a corresponding high weight coefficient.

2. 2. Longitudinal vertical data processing

Because of the effect of random factors (e. g. drastic temperature changes, the occurrence of significant events), the load data will generate abnormal data points sometimes, which will disturb the regularity of the overall data sequence, destroy the similarity of the data curve with the same date type, and then affect the forecasting accuracy. Thus it is very necessary to correct the exception data. However, in the formulation of gas supply planning process, we can make a manual adjustment on predicting outcomes to suit the actual situation. The longitudinal vertical data processing is to ensure the trend of the load curve.

The load curve of one year has obvious seasonal characteristics. In a season, the load data with the same date type are similar to each other. That is to say, the intra-season data have a weekly cycle. So we can assume that $l(h, n)$ is load value, h denotes one day in a week, $h = 1, 2, \cdots, 7$; and n indicates the n-th week of a season, $n = 1, 2, \cdots, N$.

Firstly we can calculate the mean value $E(h)$ and the mean squared error $V(h)$ of the days with the same date type by formulas below:

$$E(h) = \frac{1}{N} \sum_{n=1}^{N} l(h, n) \tag{2}$$

$$V(h) = \sigma_h^2 = \frac{1}{N} \sum_{n=1}^{N} [l(h, n) - E(h)]^2 \tag{3}$$

Then we define the deviation rate as $\rho(h, n)$:

$$\rho(h, n) = \frac{|\, l(h, n) - E(h)\, |}{\sigma_h} \tag{4}$$

The correction process is as below:

$$\begin{cases} \rho(h, n) \geqslant \gamma, \begin{cases} 1 < n < N, \bar{l}(h, n) = \dfrac{l(h, n-1) + l(h, n+1)}{2} \\ n = 1, \bar{l}(h, n) = l(h, n+1) \\ n = N, \bar{l}(h, n) = l(h, n-1) \end{cases} \\ \rho(h, n) < \gamma, \bar{l}(h, n) = l(h, n), \end{cases} \tag{5}$$

where γ is the expected deviation rate. In reference to [19, 20] and numerous trials, we set $\gamma = 1.2$ for Spring and Autumn, $\gamma = 1.5$ for Summer and Winter in this article. The above method is applied to the load data from November 15, 2005 to August 25, 2008 for Shanghai. During the period, 86 data points are corrected.

2.3. *Horizontal level data processing*

The horizontal level data processing is to guarantee the smoothness of a week's load sequence again. The process is as follows:

Suppose a week's load sequence as $l(n) = [l(1), l(2), \cdots, l(7)]$.

Firstly, generate two new load sequences $l^{(1)}(n)$ and $l^{(2)}(n)$ by Eqs. (6) and (7).

$$\begin{cases} l^{(1)}(n) = \dfrac{1}{5}\sum_{i=-2}^{2} l(n+i), & n = 3, 4, 5 \\ l^{(1)}(n) = l(n), & n = 1, 2, 6, 7 \end{cases} \tag{6}$$

$$\begin{cases} l^{(2)}(n) = \dfrac{1}{3}\sum_{i=-1}^{1} l^{(1)}(n+i), & n = 2, 3, 4, 5, 6 \\ l^{(2)}(n) = l^{(1)}(n), & n = 1, 7 \end{cases} \tag{7}$$

Calculate the estimation sequence $\hat{l}(n)$ by Eq. (8).

$$\hat{l}(n) = 0.15 l^{(2)}(n-1) + 0.7 l^{(2)}(n) + 0.15 l^{(2)}(n+1) \tag{8}$$

Then define the deviation rate by Eq. (9).

$$\rho(n) = \frac{|l(n) - \hat{l}(n)|}{\hat{l}(n)} \tag{9}$$

The correction process is as follows:

$$\begin{cases} \rho(n) \geqslant \delta, & l(n) = \hat{l}(n) \\ \rho(n) < \delta, & \textit{cons}\tan t \end{cases} \tag{10}$$

where δ represents the expected deviation rate, we finally adopt $\delta =$

0. 1 after many tests. The above method is applied to the load data from November 15, 2005 to August 25, 2008 for Shanghai. During the period, 158 data points are corrected.

2. 4. The normalization processing

The normalization is a process that cancels the order of magnitude difference between input and output data and avoids causing large prediction error. The results will improve the learning efficiency and the prediction accuracy of network.

The value of Sigmoid function is uniformly distributed in $[0, 1]$. However, we notice that the results are better by using the range of $[0.1, 0.9]$ during the experiment. Therefore, we adopt the latter range. The normalization process is as bellow:

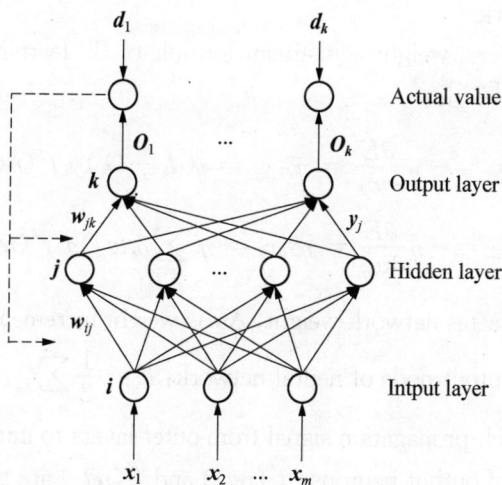

Fig. 1 The three-layer BP neural network structure.

$$y = \frac{x - x_{\min}}{x_{\max} - x_{\min}} \times (0.9 - 0.1) + 0.1 \qquad (11)$$

The anti-normalization method is as follows:

$$x = \frac{y - 0.1}{0.9 - 0.1} \times (x_{\max} - x_{\min}) + x_{\min} \tag{12}$$

where x is the raw data, y is the normalized data, $x_{\max}$ and $x_{\min}$ represent the maximum and minimum values of overall samples.

3. BP neural network prediction model

3.1 *The standard BP algorithm*

BP neural network can theoretically approximate any nonlinear continuous function under the condition of reasonable structure and appropriate weights. It makes use of error gradient descent algorithm to minimize the mean square error between the output value of network and the actual output value. Fig. 1. shows a three-layer BP neural network.

The general weight adjustment formula of BP learning algorithm is as follows [21]:

$$\begin{cases} \Delta w_{jk} = -\eta \dfrac{\partial E}{\partial w_{jk}} = \eta \delta_k y_j = \eta (d_k - O_k) y_j f'(net_k) \\[4mm] \Delta w_{ij} = -\eta \dfrac{\partial E}{\partial w_{ij}} = \eta \delta_j x_i = \eta (\sum_{k=1}^{L} \delta_k w_{jk}) x_i f'(net_j) \end{cases} \tag{13}$$

where w indicates network weight, Δw is weight increment, E is error function of output node of neural network: $E = \frac{1}{2} \sum_{k=1}^{L} (d_k - O_k)^2$, δ_k is error back-propagation signal from outer layers to inner ones, L is the number of output neurons, $f'(net_k)$ and $f'(net_j)$ are the derivative of transfer function of output and hidden layer, the negative sign expresses the gradient descent, the constant $\eta \in (0, 1)$ reflects the learning rate of network.

Although back-propagation algorithm is a significant progress in the study of artificial neural network, the training speed of basic BP algorithm is too slow to meet the actual application while it is

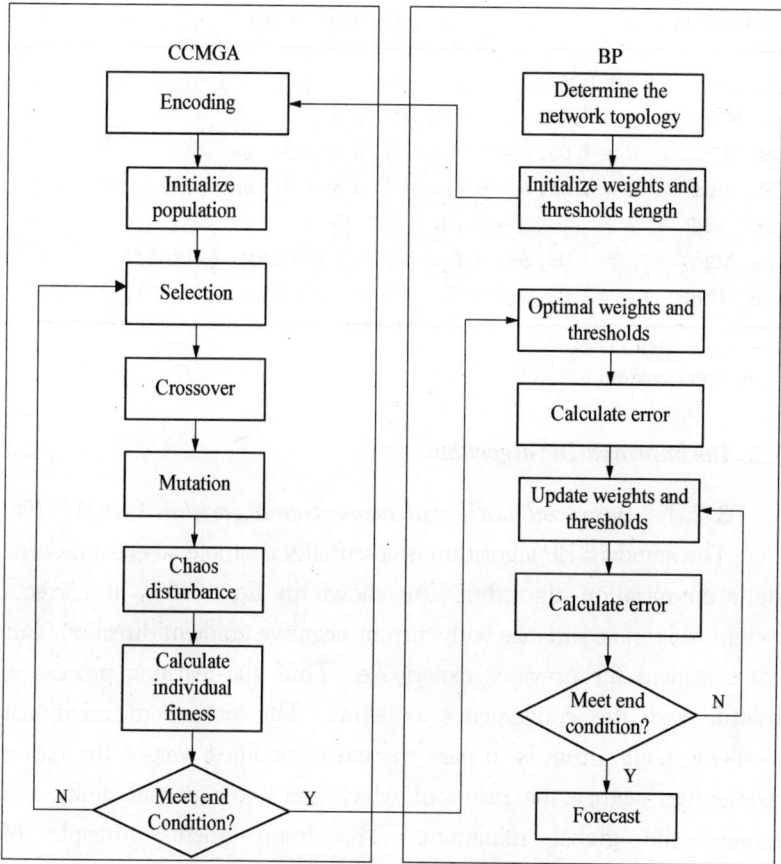

Fig. 2 The flowchart of combinational model.

applied to short-term load forecasting. In addition, the performance surface of multilayer neural network may have many local minima which make it difficult to converge to the global minimum point. Thus it is essential to improve the traditional BP algorithm for load forecasting.

Table 1　The initial parameters of standard and improved BP NN.

Algorithm	The initial values
St[a]_BP	$\eta = 0.05$
St_MBP	$p = 1.04$, $mc = 0.9$, $\eta = 0.05$
St_ABP	$a = 1.05$, $b = 0.7$, $c = 1$, $d = 1.04$, $\eta = 0.01$
St_MABP	$a = 1.05$, $b = 0.7$, $c = 1$, $d = 1.04$, $mc = 0.9$, $\eta = 0.01$
Im[b]_MBP	$p = 1.04$, $\lambda = 0.03$, $\eta = 0.05$
Im_ABP	$a = 1.05$, $b = 0.7$, $c = 0.99$, $d = 1.04$, $\eta = 0.01$
Im_MABP	$a = 1.05$, $b = 0.7$, $c = 0.99$, $d = 1.04$, $\lambda = 0.01$, $\eta = 0.01$

[a]　St_means standard NN.
[b]　Im_means improved NN.

3. 2. *The improved BP algorithm*

3. 2. 1　*Improved additional momentum algorithm* (*Im_MBP*)

The standard BP algorithm is essentially a simple steepest descent static optimization algorithm. As shown in Eq. (13), it corrects weight only in accordance with current negative gradient direction, but not considers the previous experience. Thus the learning process is volatile and the convergence is slow. The nature of additional momentum algorithm is to pass the latest modified weight through a momentum factor, the result of which can avoid partial dinky and achieve the global minimum. The improvement principle of momentum weight adjustment is described as follows:

$$\Delta w(k+1) = (1-mc)\eta\delta_i p_j + mc\Delta w(k) \qquad (14)$$

where k expresses training times, mc is momentum factor, $0 < mc < 1$, p_j is input value from former layer.

Meanwhile, we should note that when model error increases, previous weight matrices and controlling parameters are reserved and adopted for the current iteration and updated values are discarded. The momentum effect needs to be stopped to make the network not fall into larger error surface.

Also, when model error decreases, we can adopt different momentum factor in different training periods to improve the network performance. In the flat portion of the error surface, increasing the momentum factor helps weight vector flee the flat areas of the error surface, which can accelerate convergence. In contrast, in the steep part of the error surface, reducing the momentum factor avoids the instability of the network. In short, the momentum factor can be adaptively regulated according to the gradient of error function about the weight vector.

$$mc = \begin{cases} 0, & E[w(k+1)] \geqslant pE[w(k)] \\ e^{-\lambda - ||\frac{\partial E}{\partial w}||}, & E[w(k+1)] < E[w(k)] \\ mc, & \text{others} \end{cases} \tag{15}$$

where p is the maximum permissible error change rate, we can select appropriate value to meet the actual situation based on the classic value defined in [22]. λ is a random number, $0 < \lambda < 1$.

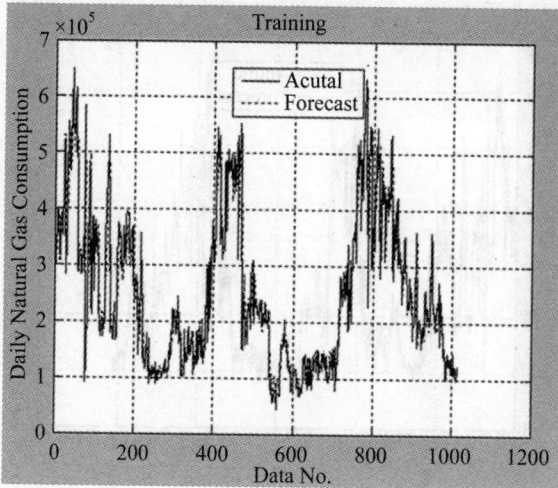

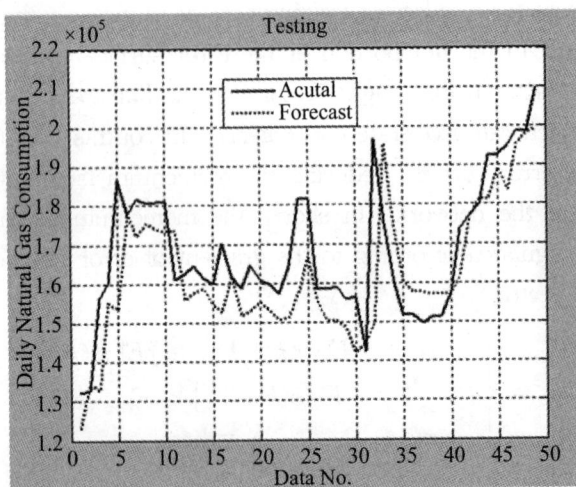

(a) The training and testing results of standard BP NN whose training data are non-processed.

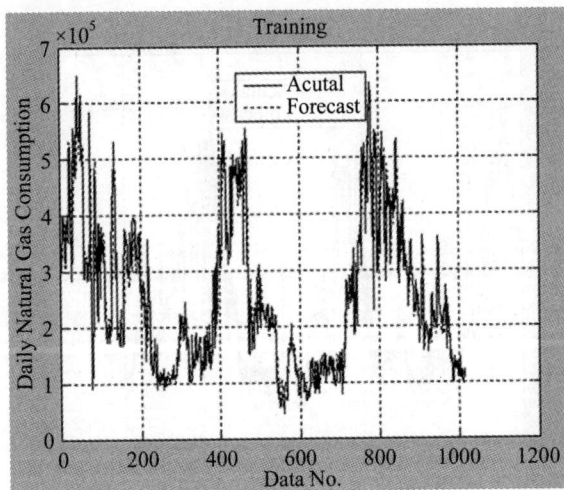

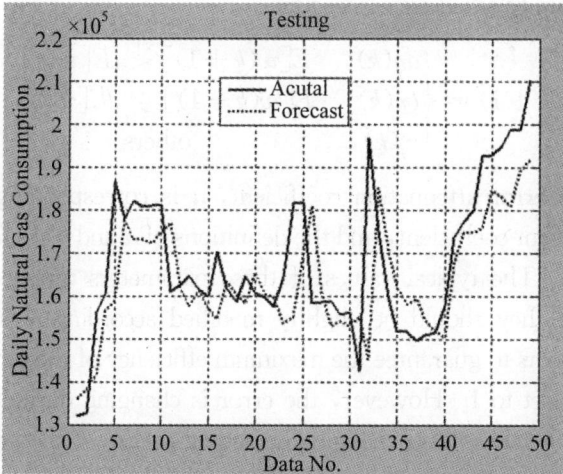

(b) The training and testing results of standard BP NN whose training data are processed.

Fig. 3. Comparison of standard BP NN whose training data are non-processed or processed.

3. 2. 2 *Improved self-adaptive learning rate algorithm (Im_ ABP)*

Another important reason why the standard BP algorithm converges slowly is that the learning rate is constant in training process. However, the learning rate impacts the convergence speed greatly. In fact, smaller learning rate, longer training time and slower convergence; on the contrary, too big learning rate may result in shock and even divergence. Also, the learning rate which is better for the initial training is not necessarily suitable for subsequent training. By making the learning rate adaptive adjustment in iterative process, self-adaptive learning rate algorithm will ensure that the BP neural network is always with maximum acceptable learning rate for training. The criteria is: check whether the weight correction value really reduces the error function during training, and if it does, then add an appropriate amount on selected learning rate; otherwise, reduce the learning rate to avoid excessive tune.

$$\eta(k+1) = \begin{cases} a\eta(k), & E[w(k+1)] < cE[w(k)] \\ b\eta(k), & E[w(k+1)] \geqslant dE[w(k)] \\ \eta(k), & \text{others} \end{cases} \quad (16)$$

where c is error attenuation coefficient, a is corresponding learning rate increment coefficient, and the definitions of d and b are in contrast with them. The typical values of these parameters can be found in [21], but they should be slightly modified according to the actual situation so as to guarantee the maximum efficiency of the network. In [21], c is set to 1. However, the error is changing during training, the learning rate is also changing according to Eq. (16), which will result in the continuous volatility of the network. Here we set c in the interval (0.9, 1) to ensure the relative stability of the network because the subtle change in error does not cause the change of learning rate. We select the initial learning rate as 0.01 in this paper.

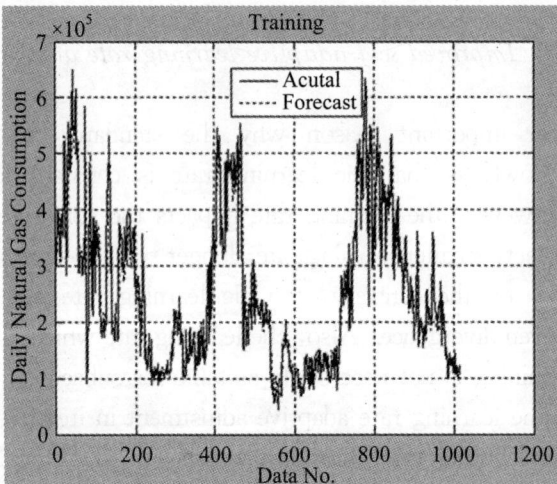

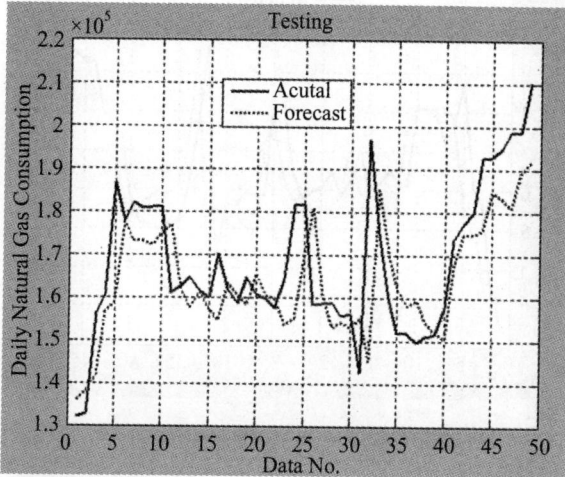

(a) The training and testing results of standard MBP NN.

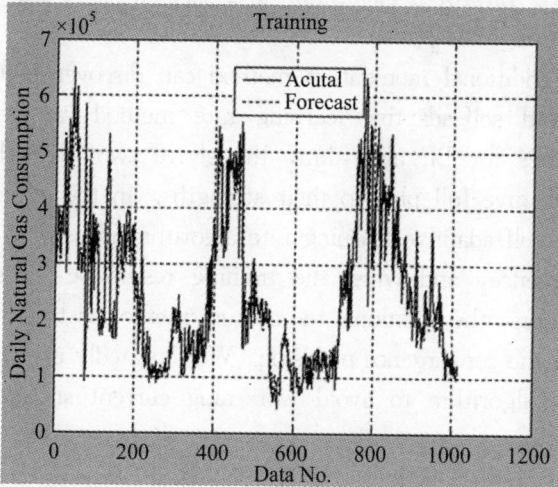

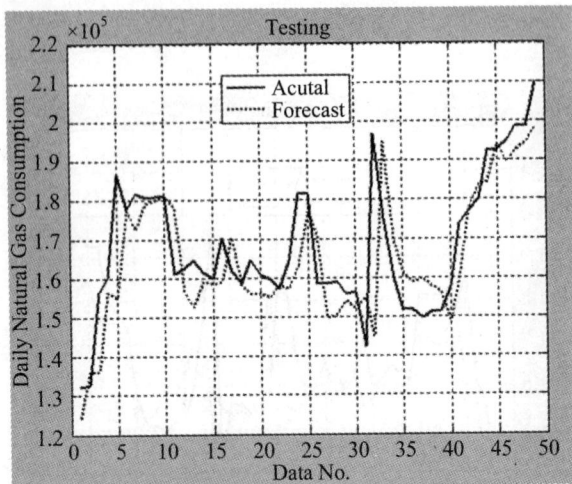

(b) The training and testing results of improved MBP NN.

Fig. 4. Comparison between standard MBP NN and improved MBP NN.

3. 2. 3 *Improved momentum and self-adaptive learning rate algorithm*(*Im_MABP*)

Since additional momentum method can discover better global solutions and self-adaptive learning rate method can reduce the training times for BP algorithm, the above two methods can be combined to give full play to their strengths. In the initial training phase, the self-adaptive learning rate algorithm is used to speed up the convergence, and when the training results are close to the expected value, the additional momentum method is then introduced to improve the convergence precision. We repeatedly use this skill in our tuning algorithm to avoid worsening current situation of the system.

The connection weights and thresholds of BP neural network are randomly initialized to the value in the interval [0,1] before training. This non-optimized initialization often causes BP algorithm uneasy to get optimal result. GA can be used to optimize the initial distribution of weights and thresholds and enable BP neural network approximate the data very well.

4. Genetic algorithm optimizes BP neural network prediction model

GA is an optimization tool that supposedly simulates biological evolution, which simulates the group's collective evolution behavior and each individual indicates an approximate solution of problem search space. Starting from an arbitrary initial population, GA effectively achieves a steady optimized breeding and selection process through individual hereditary and variation, thereby it can evolve population to better area of search space.

This paper combines GA with improved BP neural network to form a new prediction model. The algorithm is formed by three parts [11 - 13]:

(1) Determine BP NN topology. Determine the number of input nodes according to short-term load forecasting influencing factors, decide the number of output neurons based on output parameters, and then define the optimal number of hidden nodes through vast experiments. Finally, we can get the individual length of GA.

(2) Utilize GA to optimize BP neural network weights and thresholds. Generate a population randomly, whose individual represents network weights and thresholds. Then compute fitness value through fitness function (defined in Section 4. 3) and find the best individual by selection, crossover and mutation operations.

(3) Use improved BP neural network to predict. Initialized with the best individual, BP neural network weights and thresholds can be local optimized again during training. The optimized BP NN can obtain an accurate prediction and an excellent efficiency.

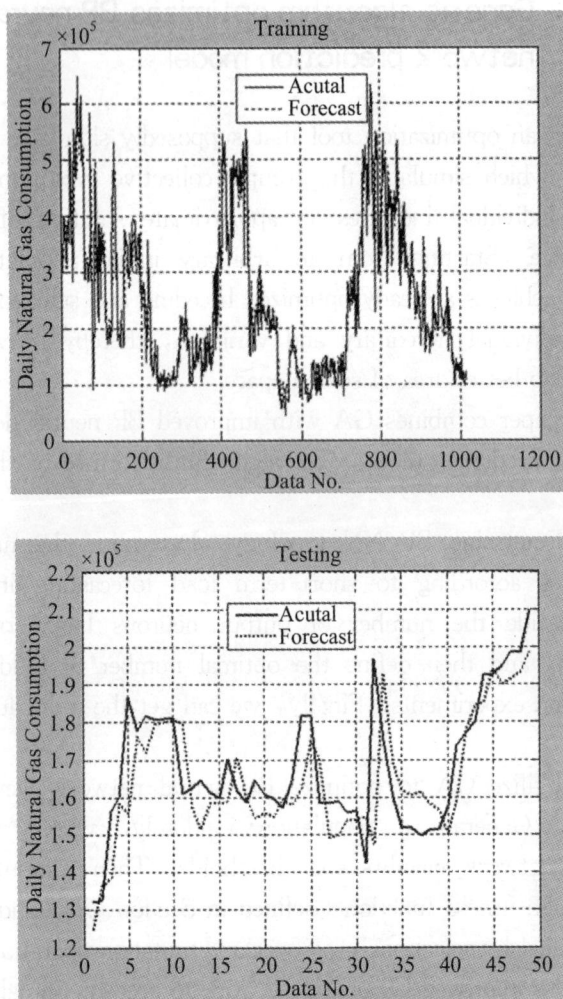

(a) The training and testing results of standard ABP NN.

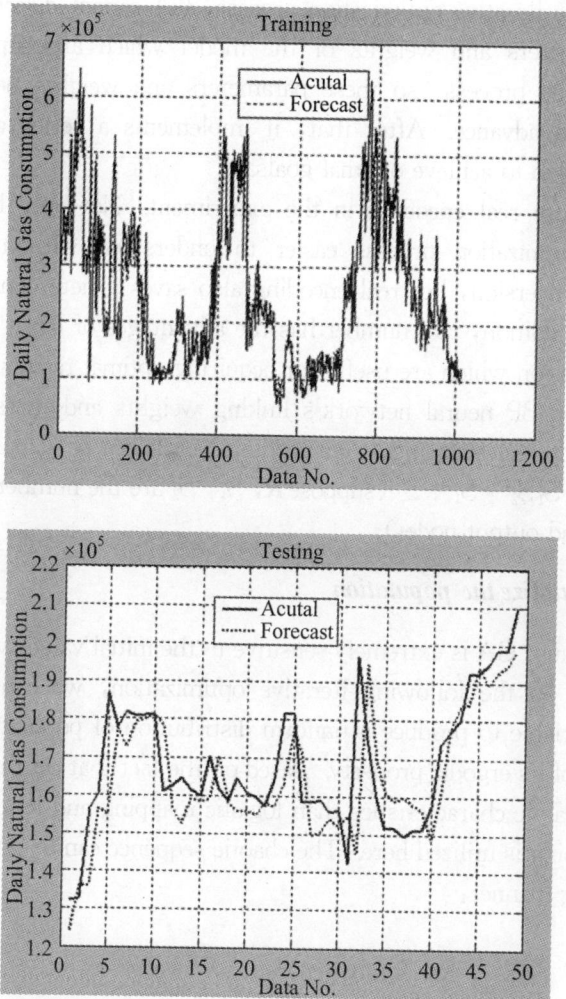

(b) The training and testing results of improved ABP NN.

Fig. 5. Comparison between standard ABP NN and improved ABP NN.

4.1 Determine encoding mode and encoding length

In the iterative optimization process, GA cannot directly act on the parameters and weights of the model which are supposed to describe the process, so these parameters and weights need to be encoded in advance. After that, it implements a series of genetic manipulation to achieve optimal goals.

We use real encoding in the experiment. Not only because it makes optimization process easier to understand without number system conversion, but real encoding also saves genetic manipulation time. In addition, real number has the advantages of large range and high precision which are useful for acquiring optimal results.

When BP neural network's linking weights and thresholds are encoded by real encoding, the encoding length can be calculated by $S = RS_1 + S_1 S_2 + S_1 + S_2$ (suppose R, S_1, S_2 are the number of input, hidden and output nodes).

4.2 Initialize the population

Because GA is extremely sensitive to the initial values which have influence on the following iterative optimization, we can introduce chaos variable to produce a uniform distribution of population by the full use of its ergodic property. Based on the fact that cat mapping has better chaotic characteristics than logistic mapping and tent mapping, cat mapping is utilized here. The chaotic sequence can be generated by following manner:

Step 1. Randomly generate a Sd vector $x_1 = [x_{11}, x_{12}, \cdots, x_{1S}]$, the range for each component is $0 - 1$.

Step 2. Get M chaotic variables by means of cat mapping Eq. (17): $x_1, x_2, \cdots, x_M$.

$$\begin{bmatrix} x_{n+1} \\ y_{n+1} \end{bmatrix} = \begin{bmatrix} 1 & 1 \\ 1 & 2 \end{bmatrix} \cdot \begin{bmatrix} x_n \\ y_n \end{bmatrix} \bmod 1, \; n = 1, 2, \cdots. \quad (17)$$

where $x \bmod 1 = x - [x]$, y is a random number, $0 < y < 1$.

Step 3. Use the following formula to map chaos interval to the range of variables to be optimized:

$$X_i^j = A^j + (B^j - A^j)x_i^j, \quad i = 1, 2, \cdots, M; \quad j = 1, 2, \cdots, S.$$

$$(18)$$

where A^j and B^j are lower and upper limit of optimization variable X^j.

Step 4. Calculate the fitness value, and choose N individuals who have better performance as initial population.

4.3 Fitness function

On the basis of error function E of output node of neural network, the overall goal of genetic operators is to find the minimum value of E, therefore the individual fitness function F is:

$$F = 1/(1 + E)$$

$$(19)$$

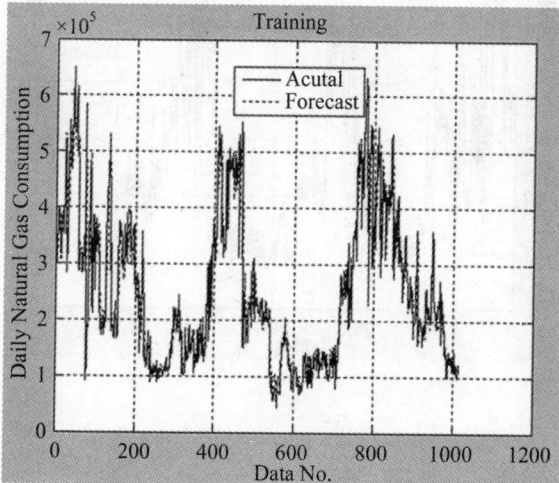

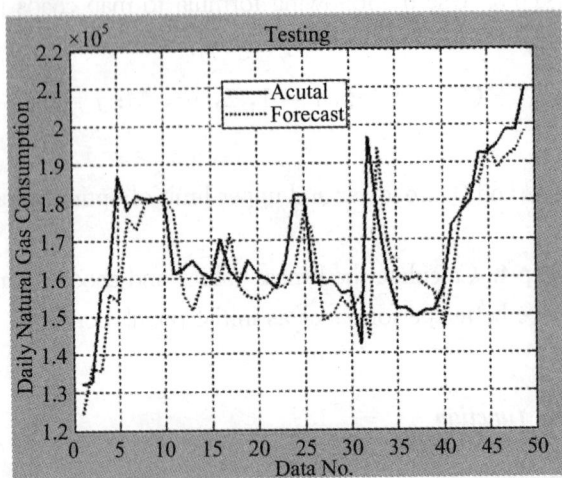

(a) The training and testing results of standard MABP NN.

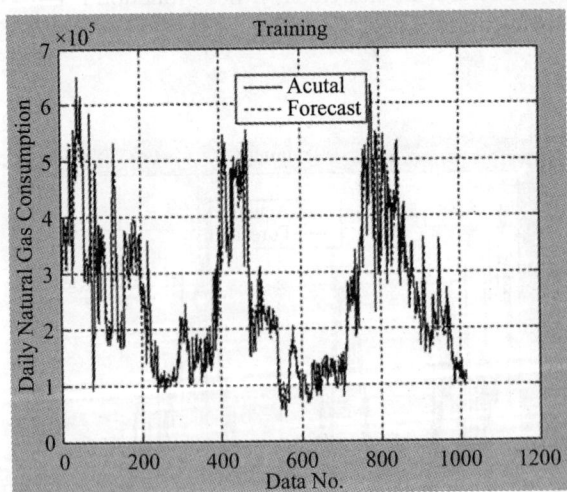

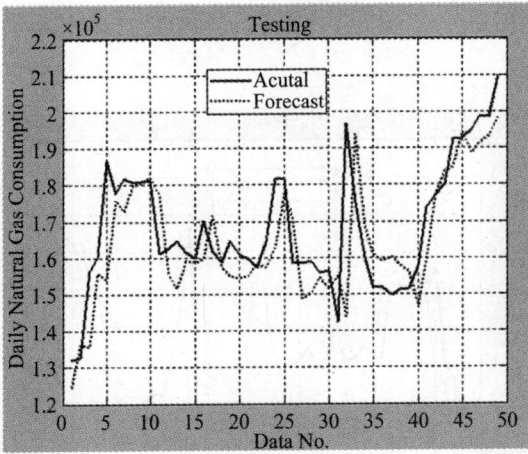

(b) The training and testing results of improved MABP NN.

Fig. 6. Comparison between standard MABP NN and improved MABP NN.

4. 4 Selection

Selection operation is to choose better individual from initial population that can be applied to the subsequent iteration. We use the elite selection method in this article. The method can prevent the best individual from being destroyed by crossover and mutation operators. The specific steps are as follows:

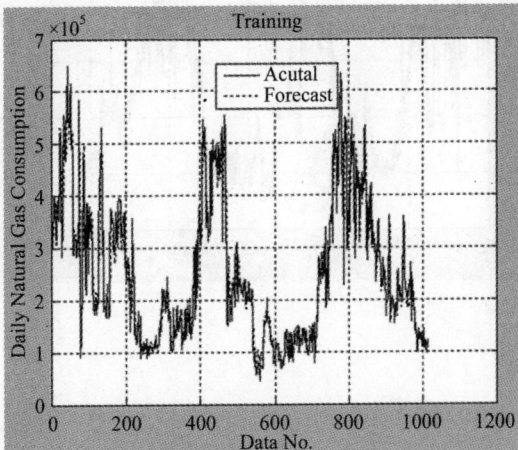

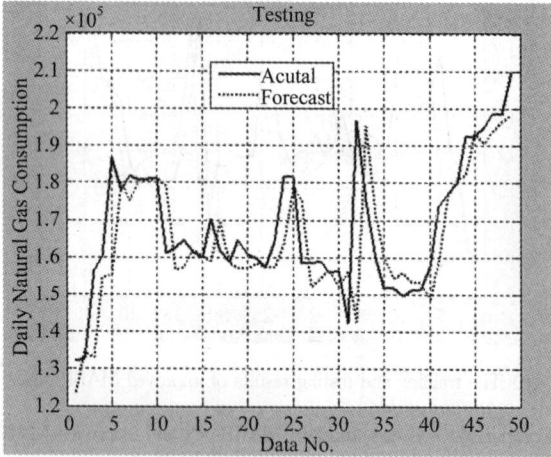

(a) The training and testing results of standard BP NN optimized by CCMGA.

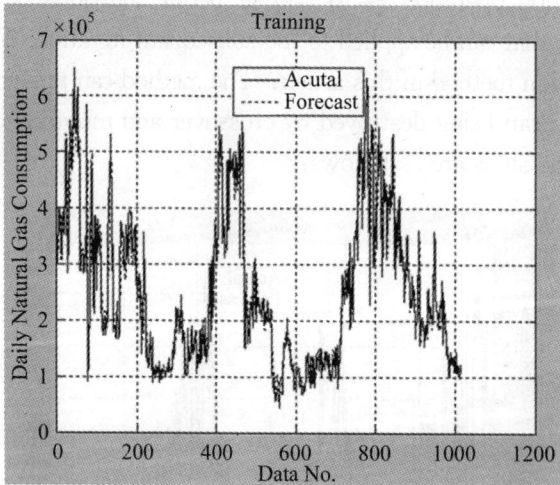

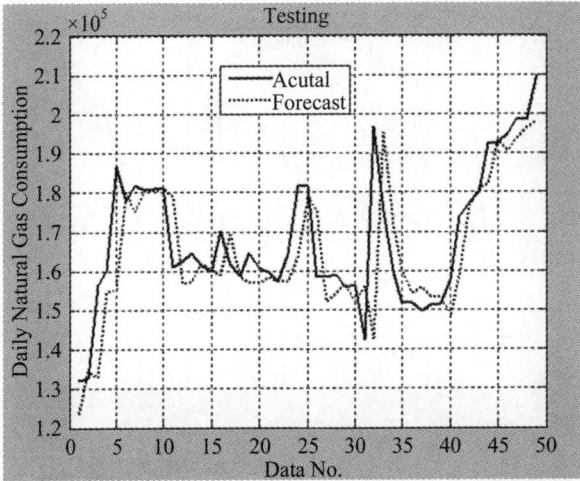

(b) The training and testing results of standard MBP NN optimized by CCMGA.

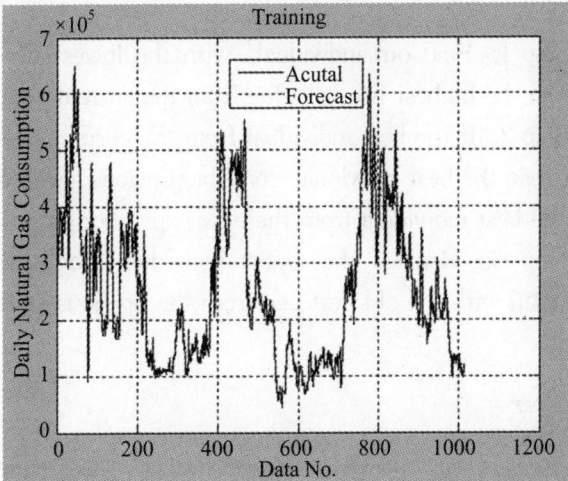

学思林

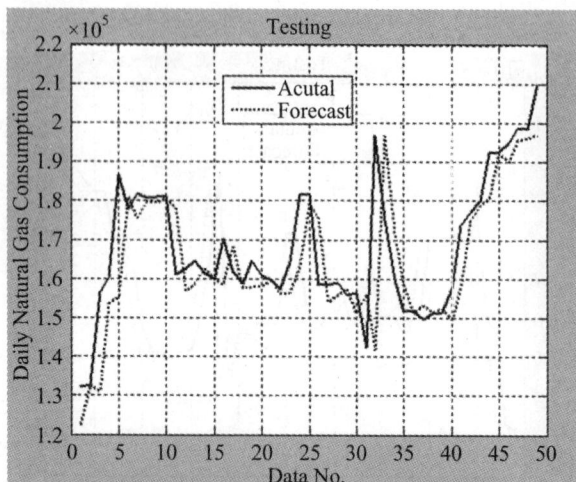

(c) The training and testing results of improved MBP NN optimized by CCMGA.

Fig. 7. Comparison among standard BP NN, MBP NN and improved MBP NN optimized by CCMGA.

Step 1. Find out individuals with the lowest fitness value and with the highest fitness value from the current population;

Step 2. If the best individual from the current population is better than the best individual from the previous generation, then copy the best individual from the new population;

Step 3. Replace the worst individual from the current population with the old best one from the previous generation.

4.5 *Crossover*

Crossover is an operation that exchanges part chromosomes between a pair of parent individuals with a relatively large probability (p_c) and produces two new individuals. This operation can enlarge the diversity of solution and ergodicity of searching space. We adopt 1-point crossover here.

$$\begin{cases} a_i^k(t+1) = a_i^k(t) \times (1-b) + a_j^k(t) \times b \\ a_j^k(t+1) = a_j^k(t) \times (1-b) + a_i^k(t) \times b \end{cases} \quad (20)$$

where a_i^k and a_j^k represent the chromosomes which occur crossover in the k-th bit, t denotes the number of iterations, b is a random number uniformly distributed in $[0, 1]$.

In early iteration, larger crossover probability can bring in new genes to improve the global search ability; but when the population evolve to late, crossover probability should be reduced in order to avoid the loss of excellent genes. So here we use adaptive crossover probability.

$$p_c = \begin{cases} p_{cmax} - \dfrac{(p_{cmax} - p_{cmin})(f_{high} - f_{avg})}{f_{max} - f_{avg}}, & f_{high} \geqslant f_{avg} \\ p_{cmax}, & f_{high} < f_{avg} \end{cases} \quad (21)$$

where f_{max} is the maximum fitness value of an individual, f_{avg} is the average fitness value of the population, f_{high} is the greater fitness value of parent before crossover, $p_{cmax} = 0.9$, $p_{cmin} = 0.6$.

4. 6　Mutation

Mutation is another method to generate new individual by changing one or some gene values of chromosome. The mutation probability should be small as high mutation probability will cause chaotic behavior of the GA.

$$a_i^j(g+1) = \begin{cases} a_i^j(g) + (a_i^j(g) - a_{max}) \times f(g), & r > 0.5 \\ a_i^j(g) + (a_{min} - a_i^j(g)) \times f(g), & r \leqslant 0.5 \end{cases},$$

$$f(g) = r_2 \times \left(1 - \frac{g}{G_{max}}\right)^2 \quad (22)$$

where a_i^j expresses the chromosome which occurs mutation in the j-th bit, a_{max} is upper limit of allele and a_{min} is lower limit, g represents current generation and G_{max} is the max iterations, r and r_2 are random numbers, $0 \leqslant r$, $r_2 \leqslant 1$.

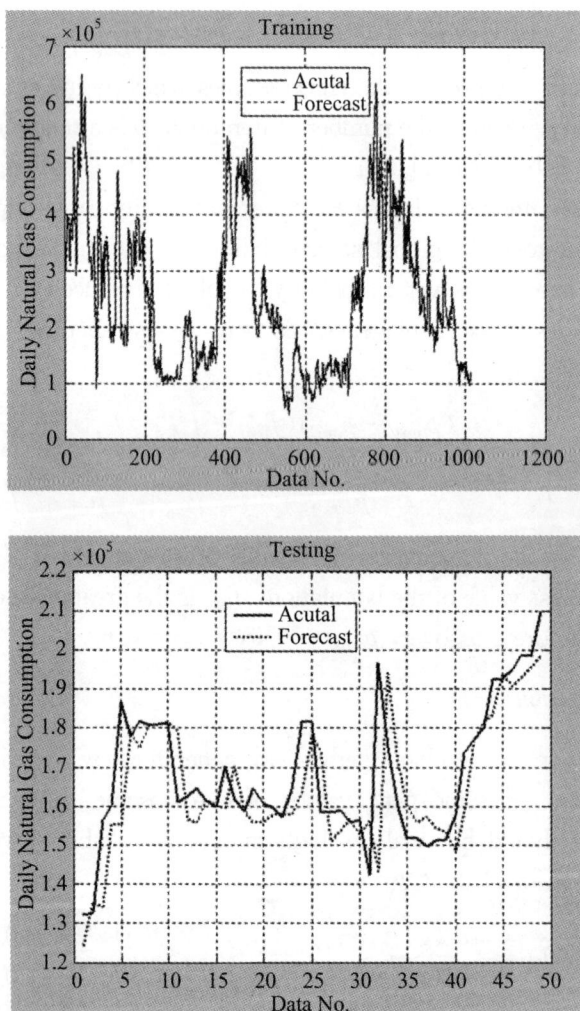

(a) The training and resting results of standard ABP NN optimized by CCMGA.

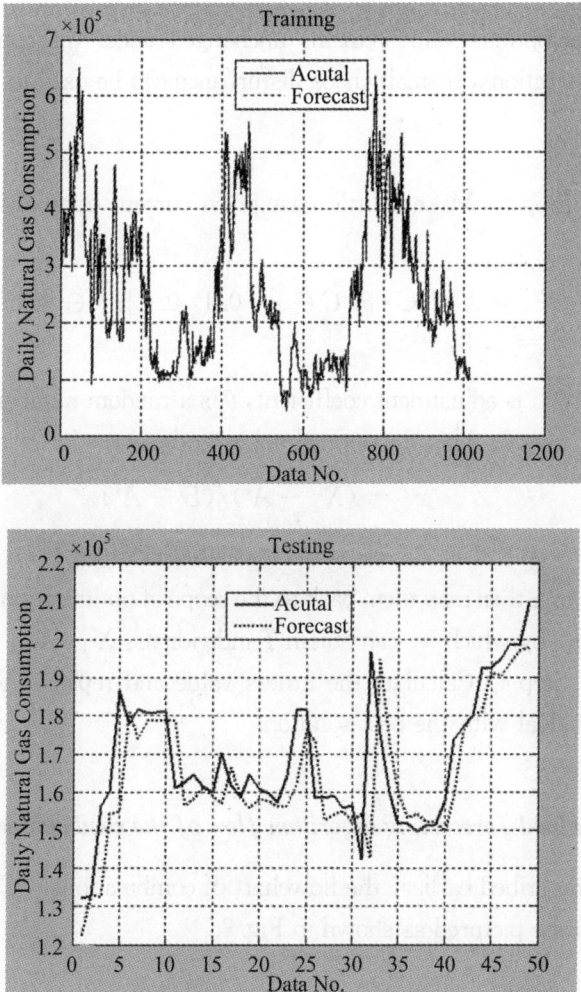

(b) The training and testing results of improved ABP NN optimized by CCMGA.

Fig. 8. Comparison between standard ABP NN and improved ABP NN optimized by CCMGA.

4.7 *Chaos disturbance*

If the optimal value remains unchanged under the condition of multiple iterations, a small chaos disturbance can be used to jump out precocity.

Step 1. Make a little change on current optimal individual X:

$$X^{j\prime} = X^j + C \cdot \theta, \ C \in [-0.1, 0.1]; \ \theta \in (0, 1); \quad (23)$$
$$j = 1, 2, \cdots S.$$

where C is adjustment coefficient, θ is a random number.

Step 2. Map the optimal value to the chaos interval $[0, 1]$:

$$x^{j\prime} = (X^{j\prime} - A^j)/(B^j - A^j) \quad (24)$$

Step 3. Get T chaos variables by means of Eq. (17): x'_1, x'_2, $\cdots$, x'_T; then map them back to the scope of optimization variables again, by which we can obtain T individuals: X'_1, X'_2, $\cdots$, X'_T.

Step 4. Calculate the fitness value and replace the original individual with the best solution.

4.8 *The load forecasting algorithm flow of the combinational model*

As described earlier, the flowchart of combinational CCMGA-BP model can be pictured as shown in Fig. 2.

5. Simulation analysis

We apply the above several different combinational algorithms into short-term gas load forecasting. To evaluate forecasting capacity of the proposed algorithms, some evaluation indexes, such as mean absolute error (MAE), mean absolute percentage error (MAPE), root mean square error (RMSE) and the iteration number under the same training error, are adopted to deal with the forecasting results of BP NN, MBP NN, ABP NN, MABP NN, CCMGA-BP NN, CCMGA-MBP NN, CCMGA-ABP NN and CCMGA-MABP NN.

It is well recognised that temperature and climate have impact on natural gas consumption. In addition, the load forecasting value is also influenced by date type and historical data. So we make the following six factors with large influencing weights as one of the inputs to BP neural network, including maximum, minimum, average tempera-tures, date type, weather conditions of the predict day, and previous day's consumption. The output of network is the predicting outcomes.

In our experiments, the sample data used are recorded from November 15, 2005 to October 13, 2008 for Shanghai. We choose the pretreated data from November 15, 2005 to August 25, 2008 as ' training samples, and the remaining data from August 26, 2008 to October 13, 2008 as testing samples.

The entire algorithm is implemented by MATLAB R2012b. In the process of running different algorithms, we can repeatedly adjust the value of each parameter for training and testing. We adopt 6-8-1 three-layer BP neural network structure. A sigmoid transfer function is chosen for the hidden layer neurons, and a liner transfer function is chosen for the output layer neurons. The initial parameters of GA are given as follows: population size: $N = 70$; individual coding length: $S = 65$; the maximal iterative number: $G_{max} = 200$; mutation probability: $p_m = 0.001$. The initial parameters of standard and improved NN are as shown in Table 1.

For analyzing the performance of proposed data processing method, the non-pretreatment data and pretreatment data are used for load forecasting by means of standard BP NN. The comparison result is shown in Fig. 3. As well, Figs. 4 - 6 respectively show the comparison between standard NN and modified NN for training data

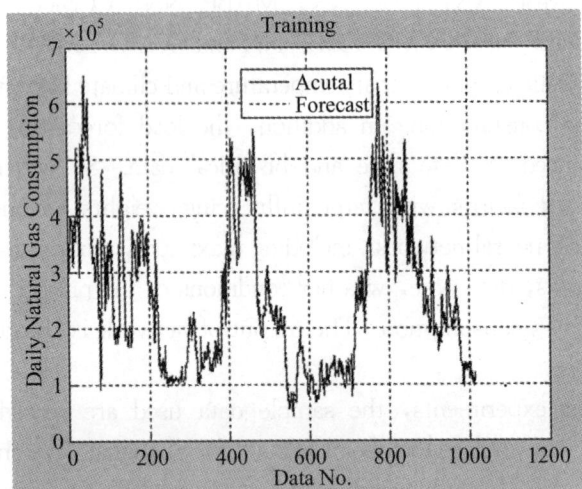

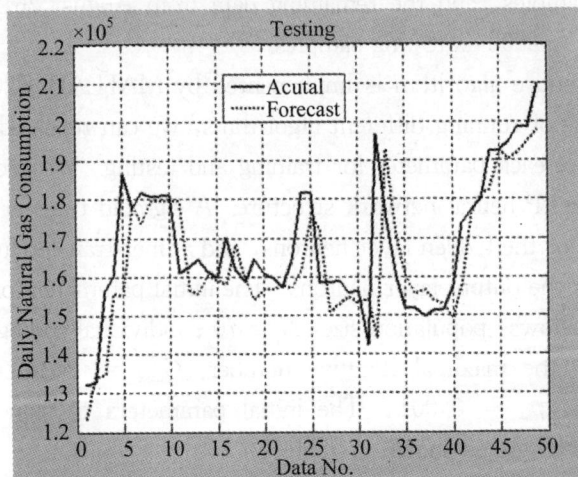

(a) The training and testing results of standard MABP NN optimized by CCMGA.

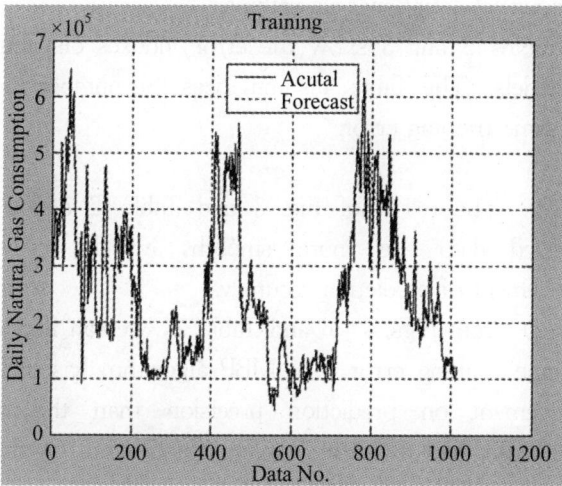

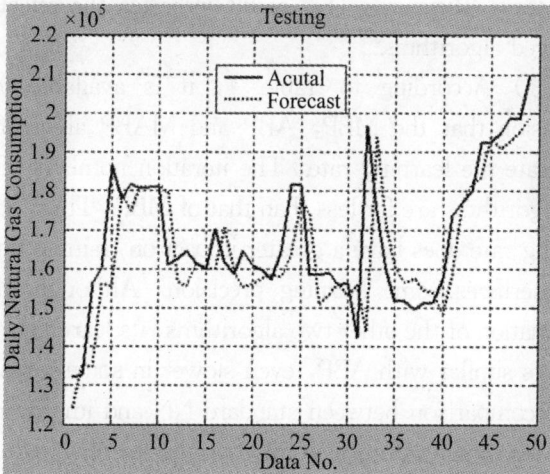

(b) The training and testing results of improved MABP NN optimized by CCMGA.

Fig. 9. Comparison between standard MABP NN and improved MABP NN optimized by CCMGA.

sets and testing data sets. Figs. 7 - 9 respectively show the comparison among various combinational algorithms.

The Tables 2 and 3 show the error indexes distribution from different models. The Table 4 summarizes the number of iterations under the same training error.

(1) The result of Fig. 3 and Table 2 denote that the processed data are more smooth, which result in the improvement of prediction accuracy.

(2) From Figs. 4 - 6 and Table 2, we can find that under the same training error, the MBP algorithm has more obvious improvement on prediction precision than the other two algorithms. And the modifications, carried out on the standard MBP NN, ABP NN and MABP NN, all achieve relatively higher forecasting efficiency. This result indicates the effectiveness of improved algorithms.

(3) According to Table 4, it is available to get the conclusion that the MBP, ABP and MABP algorithms indeed accelerate the learning rate. The iteration numbers of the latter two algorithms are far less than that of MBP. Thus, the adaptive learning rate does have a greater impact on training times, but it also sacrifices some learning precision. Although MABP is a combination of the other two algorithms, its learning convergence speed is similar with ABP, even slower in some cases. In terms of the comparison between standard NN and improved NN, the proposed modifications also improve the learning rate, especially for improved MBP.

(4) The Figs. 7 - 9, Tables 3 and 4 also show the forecasting performance of the improved combinational algorithms. The MAE, MAPE and RMSE of optimized models are better than ones of non-optimized methods. Also, the iteration numbers are

Table 2 Error statistic of standard and improved BP NN for training and testing data sets. Training data sources: November 18, 2005 to August 25, 2008. Testing data sources: August 26, 2008 to October 13, 2008.

	Non_St_BP[a]		St_BP		St_MBP		Im_MBP	
	Training	Testing	Training	Testing	Training	Testing	Training	Testing
MAE	24633	9353.4	24431	9223.0	23512	8549.1	23435	8475.1
MAPE	0.1107	0.0548	0.1095	0.0531	0.1039	0.0505	0.1033	0.0500
RMSE	37951	12669	37878	12859	37264	12233	37186	12308

	St_ABP		Im_ABP		St_MABP		Im_MABP	
	Training	Testing	Training	Testing	Training	Testing	Training	Testing
MAE	23704	8643.6	23587	8606.0	24039	8808.8	23889	8739.2
MAPE	0.1052	0.0510	0.1045	0.0508	0.1072	0.0520	0.1063	0.0515
RMSE	37441	12045	37335	12163	37693	12483	37593	12551

[a] Non_St_BP means standard BP algorithm whose training data are non-processed.

Table 3 Error statistic of standard and improved BP NN optimized by CCMGA for training and testing data sets. Training data sources: November 18, 2005 to August 25, 2008. Testing data sources: August 26, 2008 to October 13, 2008.

	CCMGA-St_BP		CCMGA-St_MBP		CCMGA-Im_MBP	
	Training	Testing	Training	Testing	Training	Testing
MAE	17729	8272.1	17234	7890.0	17131	7857.5
MAPE	0.0763	0.0488	0.0732	0.0463	0.0724	0.0459
RMSE	25965	11963	25486	12368	25323	12582

	CCMGA-St_ABP		CCMGA-Im_ABP		CCMGA-St_MABP		CCMGA-Im_MABP	
	Training	Testing	Training	Testing	Training	Testing	training	testing
MAE	17332	8011.2	17305	7953.2	17454	8169.1	17373	8031.8
MAPE	0.0739	0.0471	0.0737	0.0467	0.0746	0.0478	0.0741	0.0473
RMSE	25593	12273	25564	12278	25717	12250	25639	12199

Table 4 The iteration number of various algorithms under the same training error. Training data sources: November 18, 2005 to August 25, 2008.

The same training error : 0.36						
St_BP	St_MBP	St_ABP	St_MABP	Im_MBP	Im_ABP	Im_MABP
The iteration number 164639	24117	18	8	16542	17	6
CCMGA-St_BP	CCMGA-St_MBP	CCMGA-St_ABP	CCMGA-St_MABP	CCMGA-Im_MBP	CCMGA-Im_ABP	CCMGA-Im_MABP
The iteration number 19506	4233	11	4	1856	10	2

reduced greatly, especially for CCMGA-BP and CCMGA-MBP algorithms. It is obvious that CCMGA can enlarge the ergodicity of searching space.

（5）Under a certain precision requirement, the above analyses show that the CCMGA-Im_MBP model for gas short-term load forecasting has higher prediction accuracy than others, and it also undergoes relatively few iteration numbers.

6. Conclusion

In this paper, we propose a combinational model, which is based on the integration of improved BP neural network and optimized GA, to avoid partial dinky and achieve the global minimum. The simulation results of several different combinational algorithms demonstrate that the CCMGA-Im _ MBP model is ideal for gas short-term load forecasting of Shanghai as it can give us more satisfactory prediction accuracy and relatively few iteration number.

Acknowledgments

The project is supported by the Shanghai Science and Technology Committee (Grant No. 11510502400). The authors appreciate the editor and the anonymous reviewers whose insightful technical comments and useful editorial suggestions improve the quality of this paper.

References

[1] Soldo Božidar. Forecasting natural gas consumption. *Appli Energy* 2012; 92: 26 - 37.

[2] Azadeh Ali, Saberi Morteza, Asadzadeh Seyed Mohammad, Hussain Omar Khadeer, Saberi Zahra. A neuro-fuzzy-multivariate algorithm for accurate gas

consumption estimation in South America with noisy inputs. Int J Electr Power Energy Syst 2013;46:315 - 325.

[3] Yu Yihua, Zheng Xinye, Han Yi. On the demand for natural gas in urban China. *Energy Policy* 2014;70:57 - 63.

[4] Rodger James A. A fuzzy nearest neighbor neural network statistical model for predicting, demand for natural gas and energy cost savings in public buildings. Expert Syst Appl 2014;41:1813 - 1829.

[5] Zhou Hong, Su Gang, Li Guofang. Forecasting daily gas load with OIHF-Elman neural network. Proc Comput Sci 2011;5:754 - 758.

[6] Azadeh A, Asadzadeh SM, Ghanbari A. An adaptive network-based fuzzy inference system for short-term natural gas demand estimation: uncertain and complex environments. Energy Policy 2010;38:1529 - 1536.

[7] Eynard Julien, Grieu Stéphane, Polit Monique. Wavelet-based multi-resolution analysis and artificial neural networks for forecasting temperature and thermal power consumption. Eng Appl Artif Intell 2011;24:501 - 516.

[8] Wang Ju-Jie, Wang Jian-Zhou, Zhang Zhe-George, Guo Shu-Po. Stock index forecasting based on a hybrid model. Omega 2012;40(6):758 - 766.

[9] Thomas Ng S, Skitmore Martin, Wong Keung Fai. Using genetic algorithms and linear regression analysis for private housing demand forecast. Build Environ 2008;43:1171 - 1184.

[10] Hong Wei-Chiang, Dong Yucheng, Zhang Wen Yu, Chen Li-Yueh, Panigrahi BK. Cyclic electric load forecasting by seasonal SVR with chaotic genetic algorithm. Int J Electr Power Energy Syst 2013;44:604 - 614.

[11] Ashena Rahman, Moghadasi Jamshid. Bottom hole pressure estimation using evolved neural networks by real coded ant colony optimization and genetic algorithm. J Petrol Sci Eng 2011;77:375 - 385.

[12] Amin AE. A novel classification model for cotton yarn quality based on trained neural network using genetic algorithm. Knowl-Based Syst 2013;39:124 - 132.

[13] Sanaye Sepehr, Asgari Hesam. Thermal modeling of gas engine driven air to water heat pump systems in heating mode using genetic algorithm and Artificial Neural Network methods. Int J Refrig 2013;36(8):2262 - 2277.

[14] Li Kangji, Su Hongye. Forecasting building energy consumption with hybrid genetic algorithm-hierarchical adaptive network-based fuzzy inference system. Energy Build 2010;42(11):2070 - 2076.

[15] Zhu Suling, Wang Jianzhou, Zhao Weigang, Wang Jujie. A seasonal hybrid procedure for electricity demand forecasting in China. App Energy 2011;88:

3807 - 3815.

[16] Irani Rasoul, Nasimi Reza. Evolving neural network using real coded genetic algorithm for permeability estimation of the reservoir. Expert Syst Appl 2011; 38:9862 - 9866.

[17] Sedki A, Ouazar D, El Mazoudi E. Evolving neural network using real coded genetic algorithm for daily rainfall-runoff forecasting. Expert Syst Appl 2009; 36(1):4523 - 4527.

[18] Song Chao, Song Juan. Parameter optimization for BP neural network with GA on short-term gas load prediction. Ind Contr Comput 2012;25(10):82 - 84. [Chinese].

[19] Ming Liu. The power system load forecasting research based on wavelet and neural network theory [dissertation]. Nanjing: Nanjing University of Science and Technology; 2012 [Chinese].

[20] Chan Lv. Short-term load forecasting based on BP neural network [dissertation]. Hubei: Huazhong University of Science and Technology; 2007 [Chinese].

[21] Kaykin Simon. Neural networks and learning machines. 3rd ed. New Jersey: Pearson Education; 2009.

[22] Jing Guolin, Du Wenting, Guo Yingying. Studies on prediction of separation percent in electrodialysis process via BP neural networks and improved BP algorithms. Desalination 2012;291:78 - 93.

(原载于 applied Energy 2014 年第 134 期)

Microwave-assisted synthesis of Ag-doped MOFs-like organotitanium polymer with high activity in visible-light driven photocatalytic NO oxidization

Wei Zhu, Peijue Liu, Shuning Xiao,
Wenchao Wang, Dieqing Zhang, Hexing Li

Key Laboratory of Resource Chemistry of Ministry of Education, Shanghai Key Laboratory of Rare Earth Functional Materials, College of Life and Environmental Science

1. Introduction

Air pollution becomes crucial problem in damaging the human health and the sustainable development of both society and economy. The sweep-gas from cars, power-plants, chemical industries and plant-burning usually contains nitrogen oxides (NO_x), sulfur oxides (SO_x), carbon monoxide (CO), persistent organic pollutants (POPs) and even mercury (Hg), which were considered as the most important reason for the air pollution, which were considered as the most important reason for the air pollution, which were considered as the most important reason for the air pollution [1 - 3] Thus, removal NO_x is one of common targets in treating air pollution [4]. Recently, photocatalysis has received increasing attention in environmental cleaning [5 - 7] and the photocatalytic NO oxidization represents one of the most promising ways in removing NO_x owing to the simple operation, low cost, high efficiency, and strong durability *etc.* [8,

9]. TiO₂ without or with dopants like non-metals, metals, metal ions, and oxides are frequently employed for photocatalytic NO oxidation under UV lights irradiation [9 - 11], but they usually display much lower activities than thermal catalysts. Under visible-light irradiation, they exhibit extremely low activity in photocatalytic NO oxidation [8], which limits their utilization of solar lights. Recently, metal-organic frameworks (MOFs) become more and more attractive owing to their unique properties and wide applications in sensor, adsorption, catalysis, and energy storage *etc.* [12 - 14]. Their applications in photocatalytic dye degradation, water splitting, and CO_2 reduction have been widely reported, but most of them exhibit very poor activities [12,15 - 18]. No report has been found so far for the photocatalytic NO oxidation on MOFs. Herein, we reported for the first time a new Ag-loaded MOFs-like organotitanium polymer prepared by coordination and polymerization reaction between 2-aminoterephthalic acid and Tetra-*n*-butyl titanate in the presence of Ag NPs under microwave irradiation. The unique coordination bond in MOF-like network absorbed visible lights to generate photoelectrons and holes. The Ag NPs promoted the light harvesting and also facilitated photoelectron transfer to retard their recombination with holes. As a result, the as-prepared Ag@NH₂-MOP(Ti) exhibited excellent photocatalytic activity in both NO oxidization and inactivating bacteria under visible lights irradiation.

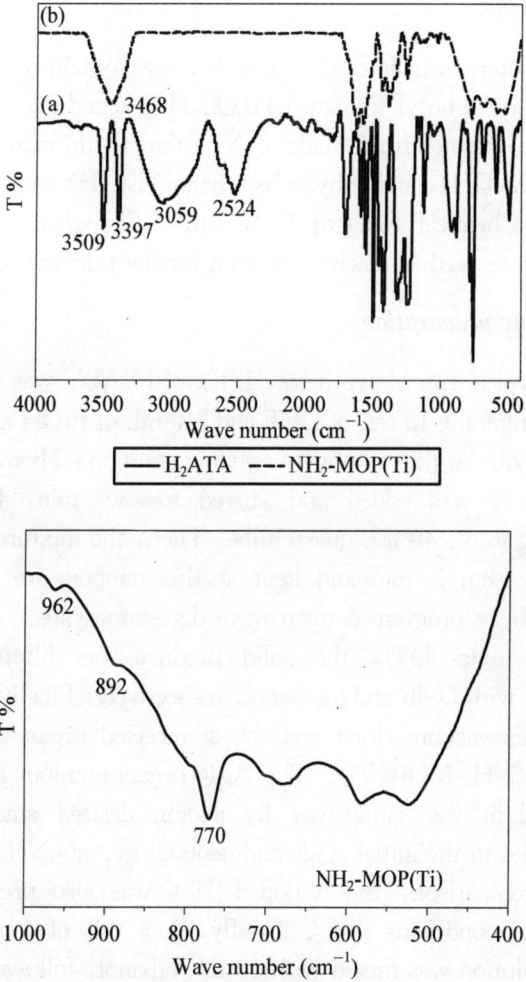

Fig. 1 FTIR spectra of (a) H_2ATA molecule and (b) NH_2-MOP(Ti) polymer. The right is the enlarged FTIR spectrum of NH_2-MOP(Ti).

2. Experimental

2.1 *Materials*

2-aminoterephthalic acid （H$_2$ATA） was obtained from Sigma-Aldrich. Tetra-*n*-butyl titanate （Ti(OC$_4$H$_9$)$_4$） and Ag nanoparticles (NPs) were obtained from Aladdin. *N*,*N*-dimethylformamide (DMF), methanol (MeOH), and anhydrous ethanol (EtOH) were supplied by Sinopharm Chemical Reagent Co., Ltd. （Shanghai, China）. All materials were used as received without further purification.

2.2 *Sample preparation*

In a typical run of synthesis, 1.1 g of H$_2$ATA was added into a solution containing 18 mL of DMF and 2.0 mL of EtOH and stirred at 25℃ for about 20 min to obtain a yellow solution. Then, 1.2 mL of Ti (OC$_4$H$_9$)$_4$ was added and stirred for 30 min, followed by transferring into a 40 mL quartz tube. Then, the mixture was heated to 150℃ within 5 min and kept at this temperature for 15 min controlled by a programed microwave digestion system. After being cooled down to 60℃, the solid product was filtered, washed thoroughly with DMF and methanol, respectively. Finally, the yellow product was vacuum dried and the as-received organotitanium was denoted as NH$_2$-MOP(Ti). The Ag@organotitanium polymer was synthesized in the same way by adding desired amount of Ag nanoparticles in the initial stage and denoted as Ag@NH$_2$-MOP(Ti).

For comparison, the *N*-doped TiO$_2$ was also prepared under supercritical conditions [19]. Briefly, 2.5 mL of 1.0 M HNO$_3$ aqueous solution was mixed with 10 mL ethanol, followed by adding dropwise into a solution comprised of 40 mL ethanol and 10 mL of Ti(OC$_4$H$_9$)$_4$ at 25℃ under vigorous stirring. The formed TiO$_2$ gel was aged for 48 h at 40℃ and then transferred into a 500 mL autoclave containing 200 mL of ethanol and 13 of mL triethylamine (Et$_3$N), followed by treating under supercritical conditions at 280℃

for 2 h. After washed thoroughly with deionized water and ethanol, the obtained product was dried at 80℃, followed by calcining at 350℃ for 8 h to remove the residual organic species.

2.3 Characterization

The morphology was observed *via* field emission scanning electron microscopy (FESEM, HITACHI S-4800) and transmission electronic micrograph (TEM, JEOL JEM-2100). UV-vis diffuse feflectance spectra (DRS) were obtained on a UV-vis spectrpphotometer (DRS, UV-2450). The Brunauer-Emmett-Teller (BET) approach was used to determine the surface area. X-ray photoelectron spectroscopy (XPS) was done on a Perkin Elmer PHI 5000 C ESCA system to analyze electronic states. All the binding energies were calibrated by using the contaminant carbon ($C_{1S} = 284. 6$ eV) as a reference. The Fourier transformation infra-red spectrum (FTIR) experiments were carried out on an AVATAR 370 FT-IR spectrometer. Thermal gravimetric analysis (TGA) was performed with a Perkin Elmer Pyris Diamond TG analyzer under air atmosphere with a heating ramp of 5℃/min. The photoluminescence spectroscopy (PLS) was collected on Varian Cary-Eclipes 500 excited with 280 nm lights. The photocurrent responses in the light on-off process were determined in a homemand three electrode quartz cell containing 0. 5 M Na_2SO_4 aqueous solution under visible lights (> 420 nm) irradiation at an applied potential of 0. 5 V vs. SCE (saturated calomel electrode) with electrochemical workstation (CHI 660D, Chen Hua Instrument Co. , Ltd.)

2.4 Activity test

The photocatalytic NO oxidation was performed at an ambient temperature in a continuous flow setup equipped with an online NO-NO_2-NO_x analyzer (Thermo Scientific, Model 42i) under irradiation with two 150 W tungsten lamps equipped with a UV cut filter to cut off lights with wavelength < 420 nm. The NO conversion was defined as follow:

$$NO \text{ conversion } (\%) = \frac{(C_0 - C)}{/C_0} \times 100\%$$

where C_0 is the initial balanced concentration of NO and C is the concentration of NO at a given time in photocatalytic reaction process.

The photocatalytic disinfection was carried out in a flask containing a photocatalyst and suspension of bacterial cells at 25℃ under stirring and irradiation a 300 W Xenon lamp equipped with a UV cut filter to cut off lights with wavelength < 400 nm. The visible-light intensity was measured by a light meter (LI-COR, USA) and was fixed at 190 mW cm^{-2}. All glass apparatuses used in the experiments were autoclaved at 121℃ for 20 min to ensure sterility. The bacterial cells was incubated in 10% nutrient broth solution at 30℃ for 18 h. The final photocatalyst concentration and cell density were adjusted to 100 mg L^{-1} and about 1×10^7 colony forming units per milliliter (cfu mL^{-1}), respectively. keep the reaction temperature at 25℃ and stir the reaction mixture with a magnetic stirrer throughout the experiment. Before and after the photocatalytic oxidation (PCO) treatment, an aliquot of the reaction solution was sampled at given time and immediately diluted with sterilized saline, followed by spreading onto a nutrient agar. After being incubated at 30℃ for 24 h, the number of colonies formed was counted to determine the antibacterial efficiency.

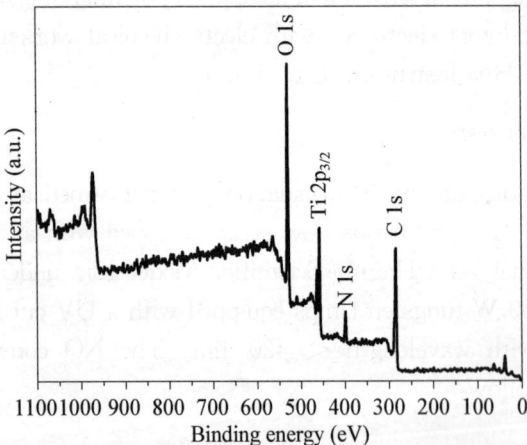

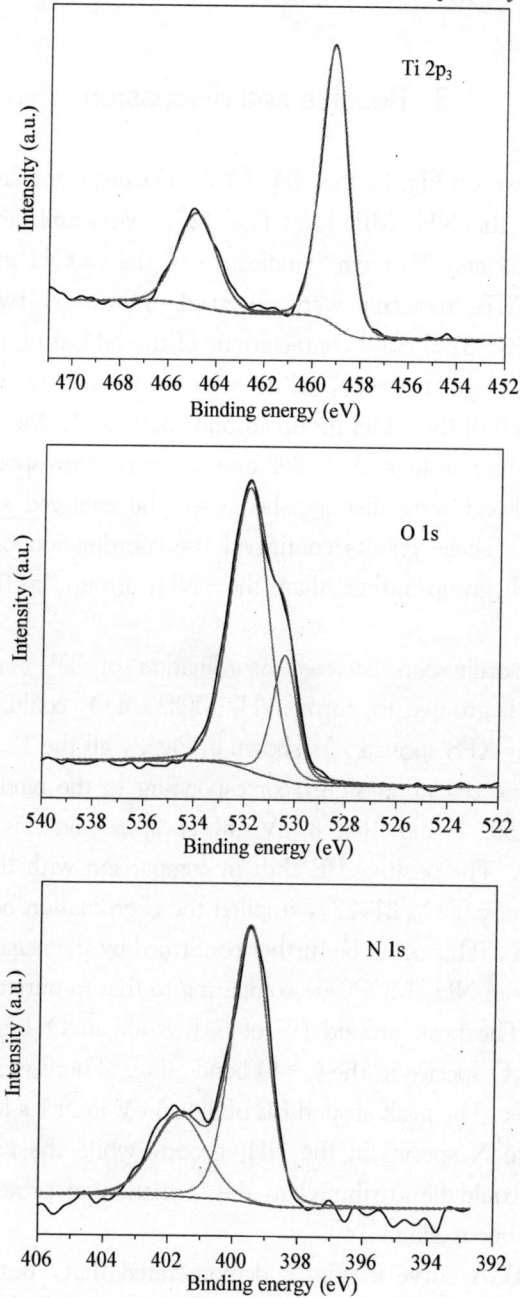

Fig. 2   XPS spectra of NH₂-MOP(Ti) polymer.

3. Results and discussion

As shown on Fig. 1, the NH_2-MOP(Ti) displayed similar FTIR spectrum to the NH_2-MIL-125 (Ti) [12]. No significant vibration bands at 3059 and 2524 cm^{-1} indicative of the COOH group in the original H_2ATA molecule were observed. However, two vibration bands at 3500 - 3150 cm^{-1} characteristic of the-NH_2 group in H_2ATA molecule were still reserved, which were overlapped with the strong vibration band of the—OH group around 3350 cm^{-1}. Meanwhile, the special vibration peaks at 962, 892 and 770 cm^{-1} corresponding to the O—Ti—O bond were distinguished (see the enlarged spectrum on right)[20]. These results confirmed the coordination of Ti^{4+} with the—COOH group rather than the—NH_2 group in the H_2ATA molecule.

The coordination between coordination of Ti^{4+} and H_2ATA *via*—COOH groups to form NH_2-MOP (Ti) could be further confirmed by XPS spectra. As shown in Fig. 2, all the Ti species were present in+4 oxidation state, corresponding to the binding energies (BE) of 459. 1 and 464. 8 eV in Ti $2p_{3/2}$ and Ti $2p_{1/2}$ level, respectively. The positive BE shift in comparison with that observed in pure anatase TiO_2[21,22], implied the coordination between Ti^{4+} and H_2ATA. This could be further confirmed by the negative BE shift of the O 1 s in NH_2-MOP(Ti) comparing to that in pure anatase TiO_2 [21,22]. The peak around BE of 531. 8 eV in O 1 s level could assigned to O species in the C—O bond [23]. There were two kinds of N species. The peak around BE of 399. 5 eV in N 1 s level could be attributed to N species in the NH_2 group, while the peak at about 401. 5 eV could be attributed to the formation of protonated amine group in acidic medium[24].

The TGA curve in Fig. 3 demonstrated that, besides a slight weight loss from 50 to 100℃ due to the desorption of trace solvents, the NH_2-MOP(Ti) displayed a strong weight loss of about 55.6% between 160 and 500℃, corresponding to burning removal of organic ligands to produce TiO_2 (33.3%). The mass ratio between organic ligands and TiO_2 implied that each Ti^{4+} ion coordinated with one H_2ATA in cross-linked network, leading to a porous polymer similar to NH_2-MIL-125 (Ti) [12]. However, the weight of organic ligands was significantly reduced due to the unsaturated Ti^{4+} coordination, which may account for the poor crystallization degree of NH_2-MOP(Ti). As a result, the XRD pattern (Fig. S1a) showed that the NH_2-MOP(Ti) was present only in amorphous state. As show in the Fig. 4, both FESEM and TEM images revealed that the NH_2-MOP(Ti) was comprised of uniform small nanoparticles. The Ag@NH_2-MOP(Ti) remained the morphology and particle size of the original NH_2-MOP (Ti). These Ag particles with average diameter around 60 – 70 nm were dispersed and encapsulated by NH_2-MOP(Ti).

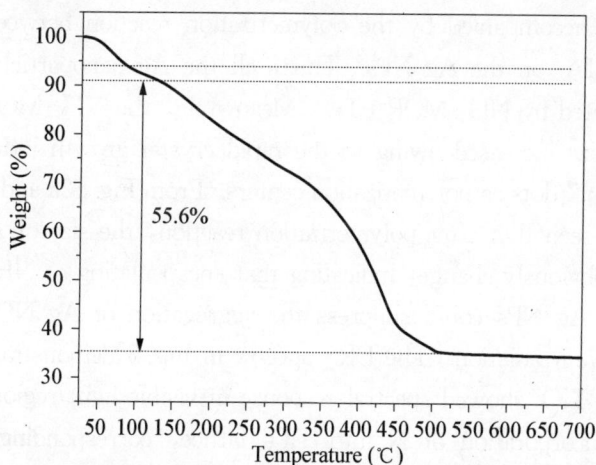

Fig. 3   Thermal analysis of NH_2-MOP (Ti) polymer under air atmosphere.

Table 1 Structural parameters of different samples.

Sample	S_{BET} $(m^2 g^{-1})$	V_p $(cm^2 g^{-1})$	D_P (nm)	D_S (nm)
NH_2-MOP(Ti)	317	0.58	7.3	19
Ag(20 mg)@NH_2-MOP(Ti)	286	0.39	5.9	22
Ag(40 mg)@NH_2-MOP(Ti)	272	0.44	6.5	23
Ag(60 mg)@NH_2-MOP(Ti)	245	0.49	6.3	24
Ag(80 mg)@NH_2-MOP(Ti)	205	0.31	6.1	29

Based on the N_2 adsorption-desorption isotherms (Fig. S1b), they exhibited the typical IV isotherms, indicating the mesoporous structure. In addition, the BET specific surface area (S_{BET}), pore volume (V_P), pore size (D_P) and average particle diameter of different samples (D_S) were calculated. As shown in Table 1, the addition of the Ag nanoparticles caused decrease in S_{BET}, V_P and D_P, while the D_S increased. A possible reason was that microwave irradiation induced local "super hot" dots generated on the Ag surfaces, accompanied by the polymerization reaction between Ti^{4+} and H_2ATA on the Ag NPs. Thus, all the Ag nanoparticles were encapsulated by NH_2-MOP (Ti). Meanwhile, the NH_2-MOP (Ti) particle size increased owing to the rapid crystal growth induced by "super hot" dots as polymerization centers. From Fig. S2a and S2b, it could be seen that after polymerization reaction, the size of Ag NPs did not obviously change, indicating that encapsulating of NH_2-MOP (Ti) on Ag NPs could suppress the aggregation of Ag NPs under microwave irradiation. The DRS spectra in Fig. 5 demonstrated that N-doped TiO_2 showed spectral response in visible-light region owing to the incorporation of N into TiO_2 lattice, corresponding to the formation of intermediate energy levels [5,25]. The NH_2-MOP(Ti) also displayed strong absorbance for visible lights with the absorption edge located at 570 nm. This further confirmed the similar polymer structure to the NH_2-MIL-125 (Ti), in which the COO—Ti^{4+}

coordination bond generated the spectral response in the range from 400 to 570 nm[26]. The Ag@NH$_2$-MOP (Ti) displayed stronger absorbance for visible lights than that of NH$_2$-MOP (Ti). Obviously, the localized surface plasmon resonance (LSPR) effects from Ag NPs could be neglected due to the big size (60 – 70 nm). Meanwhile, the presence of Ag could enhance the dispersion (see the structural parameters in Table 1). Thus, the promoting effects could be mainly attributed to the assembly of NH$_2$-MOP(Ti) polymer onto Ag NPs which promoted light harvesting *via* multiple reflections. The increase of Ag amount could further enhance the visible light absorbance owing to the improved assembly of NH$_2$-MOP(Ti) polymer. Meanwhile, the electrochemical impedance spectroscopy (EIS) responses (Fig. S3) demonstrated the smaller semicircles of the Ag@NH$_2$-MOP(Ti) than that of the NH$_2$-MOP(Ti), indicating that decoration with Ag NPs could significantly reduce the electrochemical impedance since Ag is excellent electric conductor. Meanwhile, the photoluminescence (PL) spectra (Fig. S4) revealed that all the Ag@NH$_2$-MOP(Ti) exhibited much lower peak intensity around 560 nm than the NH$_2$-MOP(Ti), corresponding to the lower photoelectron-hole recombination rate since the rapid transfer of photoelectrons promoted their separation from holes. As a result, the Ag@NH$_2$-MOP (Ti) displayed stronger photocurrent response under visible light irradiation than that of NH$_2$-MOP(Ti) (see Fig. S5) owing to both the enhanced light harvesting ability for generating more photocarriers and the facilitated electron-transfer for diminishing photoelectron-hole recombination rate. With the increase of Ag amount up to 40 mg, the electrochemical impedances decreased gradually owing to the enhanced electron conductivity, leading to enhanced photocurrent due to low photoelectron-hole recombination rate. However, further increase in the Ag amount resulted in an abrupt decrease in photocurrent since too many Ag nanoparticles in the NH$_2$-MOP (Ti) might promote the photoelectron-hole recombination. In addition, the N-TiO$_2$ displayed

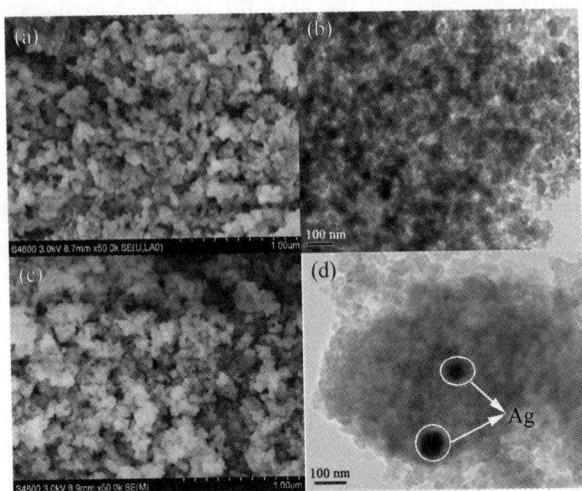

Fig. 4   The FESEM (left) and TEM (right) images of (a and b) NH₂-MOP(Ti) and (c and d) Ag@NH₂-MOP (Ti).

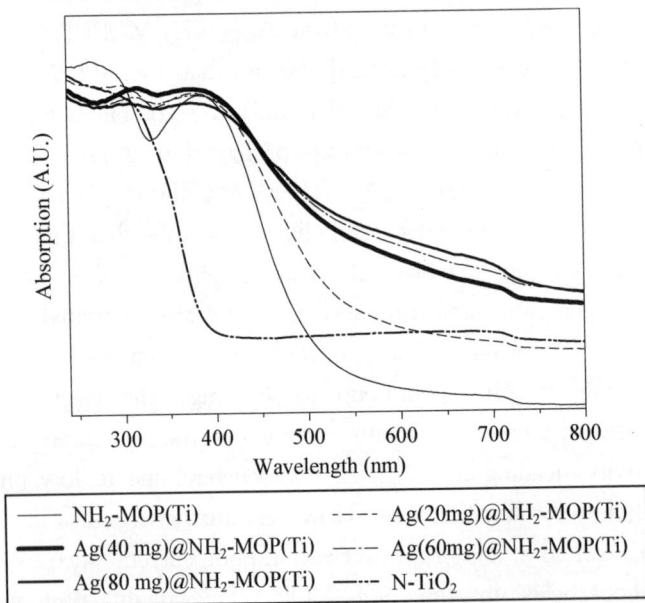

Fig. 5   UV-vis DRS spectra of different photocatalysts.

poor absorbance for visible lights due to very low content of N
($<3.4\%$ N/Ti molar ratio) incorporated into TiO_2 lattice and also
showed high photoelectron-hole recombination rate due to the poor
electric conductivity in the absence of Ag, which is in accordance with
the result of low photocurrent.

As shown in Fig. 6 the NH_2-MOP (Ti) exhibited slightly lower
activity than the typical visible-light photocatalyst (N-TiO_2) in
photocatalytic Nitric oxide (NO) oxidation under visible lights
irradiation. As discussed above, the NH_2-MOP(Ti) showed even
higher visible lights absorbance than the N-TiO_2. Therefore, its low
activity thus could be mainly attributed to the extremely poor
crystallization degree, which was unfavorable for electron transfer
[27], leading to the high photoelectron-hole recombination. The
Ag@NH_2-MOP (Ti) exhibited much higher activity than the NH_2-
MOP(Ti) owing to both the enhanced light harvesting ability and the
reduced photoelectron-hole recombination rate by facilitating photoel-

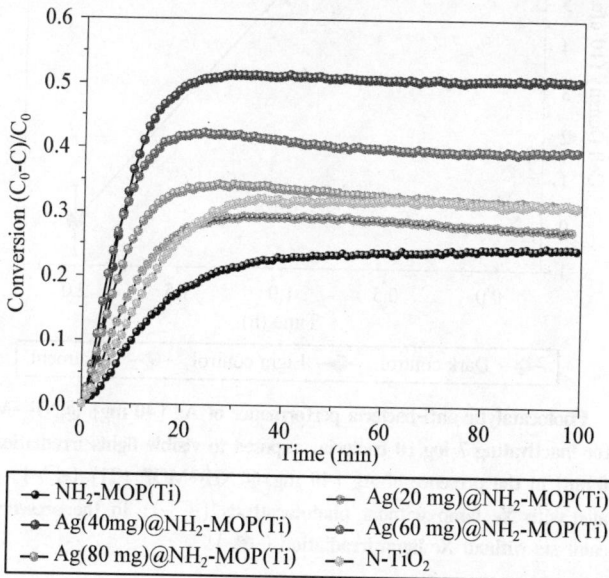

Legend	
NH_2-MOP(Ti)	Ag(20 mg)@NH_2-MOP(Ti)
Ag(40mg)@NH_2-MOP(Ti)	Ag(60 mg)@NH_2-MOP(Ti)
Ag(80 mg)@NH_2-MOP(Ti)	N-TiO_2

**Fig. 6   Reaction profiles of photocatalytic NO oxidation under visible
lights ($\lambda \geqslant 420$ nm) irradiation.**

ectron-transfer. The activity gradually increased with increas-ing Ag content owing to the enhanced promoting effects. However, very high Ag-content was harmful for the photocatalytic activity, possibly due to the gathering of Ag NPs which might promote photoelectron-hole recombination. The Ag (40 mg) @ NH$_2$-MOP (Ti) was thus determined as an optimum photocatalyst, which exhibited the activity almost twice as that of the N-TiO$_2$. Interestingly, as shown in Fig. 7, it also exhibited high activity in killing bacteria under Xenon lamp irradiation with $\lambda \geqslant 400$ nm, while there was no anti-bacterial activity without photocatalyst or light irradiation, indicating the excellent photocatalytic water disinfectants performance working under visible-light irradiation.

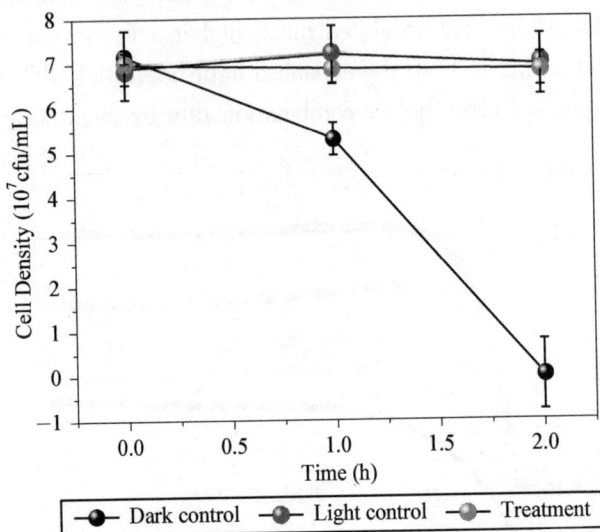

Fig. 7　Photocatalytic anti-bacteria performance of Ag (40 mg) @NH$_2$-MOP (Ti) for inactivating 7 log 10 bacteria, exposed to visible lights irradiation ($\lambda \geqslant 400$ nm) in the presence of Ag (40 mg)@NH$_2$-MOP (Ti) (-○-); only irradiated with Xe lamp without phototacatlysts (-□-); in the presence of photocatalysts without Xe lamp irradiation (-●-).

Fig. 8 schematically illustrated the reaction mechanism for

photoca-talytic NO oxidation over Ag@NH$_2$-MOP (Ti). Similar to the NH$_2$-MIL-125 (Ti) [28], the NH$_2$-MOP (Ti) polymer was formed by cross-linked Ti^{4+}-H$_2$ATA coordination. The visible light irradiation induced the excitation of electrons in the H$_2$ATA-ligand owing to the narrow energy band gap, followed by jumping from the HOMO orbital to the LUMO orbital, resulting in photoelectrons (e_{tr}^-) and holes (h_{tr}^+). Besides the recombination with the h_{tr}^+, other e_{tr}^- would transfer from the H$_2$ATA-ligand to Ti^{4+}, which could directly reduce Ti^{4+} into Ti^{3+} or transfer onto Ag NPs, which may retard their recombination with h_{tr}^+. Both the e_{tr}^- on the Ag NPs or the Ti^{3+} could reduce to O$_2$ to O$_2^{\cdot-}$ [29]. Taking into account of the molecular orbital structure ($(\sigma_{1s})^2$ $(\sigma_{1s}^*)^2$ $(\sigma_{2s})^2$ $(\sigma_{2s}^*)^2$ $(\sigma_{2p})^2$ $(\pi_{2p})^4$ $(\pi_{2p}^*)^1$), a single electron occupied the π antibonding orbital in NO molecule which was unstable and could be easily lost. Thus, the h_{tr}^+ on the HOMO orbital of the H$_2$ATA-ligand could easily capture such a single electron on the

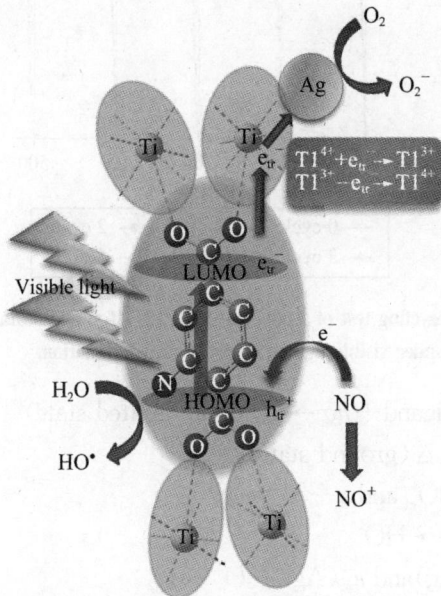

Fig. 8   Schematic illustration of mechanism for visible lights driven photocatalytic NO oxidation over Ag@NH$_2$-MOP (Ti).

π antibonding orbital in NO molecule to form NO^+[30,31]. Other h_{tr}^+ might directly oxidize H_2O to form the $HO^\cdot$ radical or recombine with the e_{tr}^-. The $HO^\cdot$ radicals also served as active sites. According to the online NO-NO_2-NO_x analysis, the $O_2^{\cdot-}$ and the $HO^\cdot$ radicals further oxidized NO^+ into NO_3^-, together with the formation of NO_2^- and as side products (see the following reaction equations)[29]. The important role of the $HO^\cdot$ radicals from H_2O oxidation could be confirmed by the fact that the NO conversion increased by adding trace water moisture (see Fig. S6).

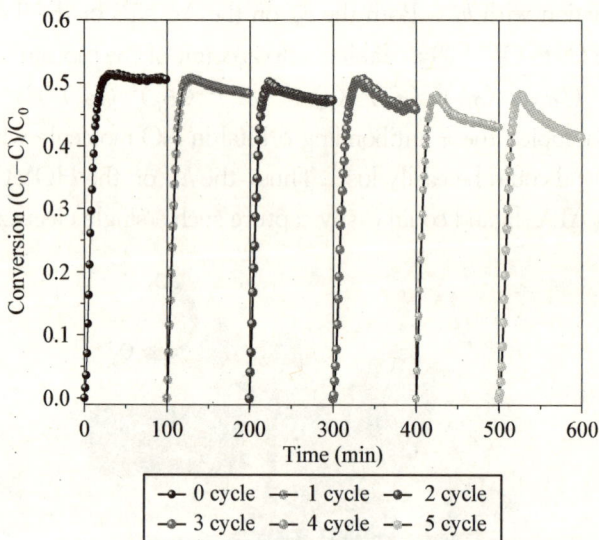

Fig. 9 Recycling test of Ag@NH₂-MOP(Ti) for photocatalytic NO oxidation under visible lights ($\lambda \geqslant$ 420 nm) irradiation.

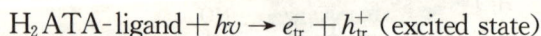

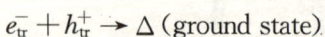

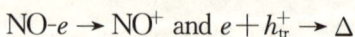

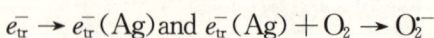

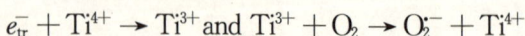

$H_2ATA\text{-ligand} + h\upsilon \rightarrow e_{tr}^- + h_{tr}^+$ (excited state)

$e_{tr}^- + h_{tr}^+ \rightarrow \Delta$ (ground state)

$NO\text{-}e \rightarrow NO^+$ and $e + h_{tr}^+ \rightarrow \Delta$

$h_{tr}^+ + H_2O \rightarrow HO^\cdot$

$e_{tr}^- \rightarrow e_{tr}^-(Ag)$ and $e_{tr}^-(Ag) + O_2 \rightarrow O_2^{\cdot-}$

$e_{tr}^- + Ti^{4+} \rightarrow Ti^{3+}$ and $Ti^{3+} + O_2 \rightarrow O_2^{\cdot-} + Ti^{4+}$

$$NO^+ + O_2^- \rightarrow NO_3^-$$
$$NO^+ + HO^\cdot \rightarrow HNO_2$$
$$HNO_2 + HO^\cdot \rightarrow NO_2 + H_2O$$
$$NO_2 + HO^\cdot \rightarrow HNO_3$$

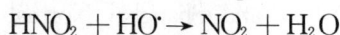

Besides the high activity, the $Ag@NH_2$-MOP(Ti) also showed strong durability and could be used repetitively without significant decrease in activity (see Fig. 9). As shown by the N_2 adsorption-desorption isotherms, FTIR, XRD and TEM results (Fig. S7) of the photocatalyst before and after 5 cycles, no obvious change on the physicochemical properties and morphology of the samples after the cycled reaction was observed. We conclude that the slight decrease in the activity could be mainly attributed to the adsorption of HNO_3 onto the photocatalyst, which was accordance with the previous reports [30,32].

4. Conclusions

This work developed a novel MOFs-like organotitanium polymer *via* Ti^{4+}-H_2ATA coordination in cross-linked network under microwave irradiation. The as-prepared Ag @ NH_2-MOP (Ti) exhibited very high activity and strong durability in visible lights driven photocatalytic NO oxidation and inactivation of bacteria. The NH_2-MOP (Ti) was activated by visible lights to generate photoelectrons and holes, followed by producing $O_2^{\cdot-}$ and $HO^\cdot$ active species. The Ag nanoparticles promoted light harvesting and electron transfer to reduce photoelectron-hole recombination. To further enhance photocatalytic activity and stability, highly crystallized NH_2-MOP(Ti) with well-defined MOFs structure will be designed. Such a work is being under way.

Acknowledgements

This work was supported by NSFC (21477079, 21207090,

21237003, 21261140333）, PCSIRT （IRT1269）, Shanghai Government （14JC1402500, 15QA1403300h）, the Doctoral Program of Higher Education （20123127120009）, and Shanghai Normal University (DXL122 and S30406).

Appendix A. Supplementary data

Supplementary data associated with this article can be found, in the online version, at http：//dx. doi. org/10. 1016/j. apcatb. 2015. 02. 003.

References

［1］ S. Roy, A. Baiker, Chem. Rev. 109(2009)4054－4091.

［2］ X. Huang, M. M. Li, H. R. Friedli, Y. Song, D. Chang, L. Zhu, Environ. Sci. Technol. 45(2011)9442－9448.

［3］ G. Lammel, A. Heil, I. Stemmler, A. Dvorskà, J. Klànovà, Environ. Sci. Technol. 47(2013)11616－11624.

［4］ P. Granger, V. I. Parvulescu, Chem. Rev. 111(2011)3155－3207.

［5］ J. Schneider, M. Matsuoka, M. Takeuchi, J. L. Zhang, Y. Horiuchi, M. Anpo, D. W. Bahnemann, Chem. Rev. 114(2014)9919－9986.

［6］ M. R. Hoffmann, S. T. Martin, W. Choi, D. W. Bahnemann, Chem. Rev. 95(1995)69－96.

［7］ H. Chen, C. E. Nanayakkara, V. H. Grassian, Chem. Rev. 112(2012)5919－5948.

［8］ S. Yin, B. Liu, P. L. Zhang, T. Morikawa, K. -i. Yamanaka, T. Sato, J. Phys. Chem. C 112(2008)12425－12431.

［9］ J. Lasek, Y. -H. Yu, J. C. S. Wu, J. Photochem. Photobiot. C 14(2013)29－52.

［10］ M. Signoretto, E. Ghedini, V. Trevisan, C. L. Bianchi, M. Ongaro, G. Cruciani, Appl. Catal. B 95(2010)130－136.

［11］ J. S. Dalton, P. A. Janes, N. G. Jones, J. A. Nicholson, K. R. Hallam, G. C. Allen, Environ. Pollut. 120(2002)415－422.

［12］ Y. H. Fu, D. R. Sun, Y. J. Chen, R. K. Huang, Z. X. Ding, X. Z. Fu, Z. H. Li, Angew. Chem. Int. Ed. 51(2012)3364－3367.

［13］ J. B. DeCoste, G. W. Peterson, Chem. Rev. 114(2014)5695－5727.

［14］ A. Bétard, R. A. Fischer, Chem. Rev. 112(2011)1055 - 1083.

［15］ C. Wang, Z. G. Xie, K. E. deKrafft, W. B. Lin, J. Am. Chem. Soc. 133 (2011)13445 - 13454.

［16］ M. C. Das, H. Xu, Z. Y. Wang, G. Srinivas, W. Zhou, Y. -F. Yue, V. N. Nesterov, G. D. Qian, B. L. Chen, Chem. Commun. 47(2011)11715 - 11717.

［17］ C. G. Silva, I. Luz, F. X. L Xamena, A. Corma, H. García, Chem. Eur. J. 16(2010)11133 - 11138.

［18］ T. Toyao, M. Saito, Y. Horiuchi, K. Mochizuki, M. Iwata, H. Higashimura, M. Matsuoka, Catal. Sci. Technol. 3(2013)2092 - 2097.

［19］ Y. N. Huo, Z. F. Bian, X. Y. Zhang, Y. Jin, J. Zhu, H. X. Li, J. Phy. Chem. C 112(2008)6546 - 6550.

［20］ J. C. S. Wu, Y. -T. Cheng, J. Catal. 237(2006)393 - 404.

［21］ S. P. Chenakin, G. Melaet, R. Szukiewicz, N. Kruse, J. Catal. 312(2014)1 - 11.

［22］ J. E. Gonçalves, S. C. Castro, A. Y. Ramos, M. C. M. Alves, Y. Gushikem, J. Electron Spectrosc. 114 - 116(2001)307 - 311.

［23］ G. X. Zhang, S. h. Sun, D. Q. Yang, J. -P. Dodelet, E. Sacher, Carbon 46 (2008),196 - 205.

［24］ K. P. Wang, Q. Liu, Carbohydr. Res. 386(2014)48 - 56.

［25］ R. Asahi, T. Morikawa, H. Irie, T. Ohwaki, Chem. Rev. 114(2014)9824 - 9852.

［26］ Y. Horiuchi, T. Toyao, M. Saito, K. Mochizuki, M. Iwata, H. Higashimura, M. Anpo, M. Matsuoka, J. Phys. Chem. C 116(2012)20848 - 20853.

［27］ J. J. Wu, X. Y. Lü, L. L. Zhang, F. Q. Huang, F. F. Xu, Eur. J. Inorg. Chem. 2009(2009)2789 - 2795.

［28］ J. M. Thomas, P. Roy. Soc. A Math. Phys. 468(2012)1884 - 1903.

［29］ T. L. Thompson, J. T. Yates, Chem. Rev. 106(2006)4428 - 4453.

［30］ D. Q. Zhang, M. C. Wen, S. S. Zhang, P. J. Liu, W. Zhu, G. S. Li, H. X. Li, Appl. Catal. B 147(2014)610 - 616.

［31］ K. Hadjiivanov, H. Knozinger, Phys. Chem. Chem. Phys. 2(2000)2803 - 2806.

［32］ Z. B. Wu, Z. Y. Sheng, H. Q. Wang, Y. Liu, Chemosphere 77(2009)264 - 268.

Biochemical composite synthesized by stepwise crosslinking: An efficient platform for one-pot biomass conversion

Wei Wei [a], Cong Wang [a], Yu Zhao [a],
Shichao Peng [a], Haoyang Zhang [a],
Yipeng Bian [a], Hexing Li [a], Xinggui Zhou [b], Hui Li [a]

[a] The Education Ministry Key Lab of Resource Chemistry
and Shanghai Key Laboratory of Rare Earth Functional
Materials, Shanghai Normal University,
[b] State Key Laboratory of Chemical
Engineering, East China University of Science and
Technology

1. Introduction

The production of fuels and chemicals from plentiful and renewable biomass resources has drawn immense attention in recent years [1 - 5]. Sorbitol, a hexitol, is a valuable platform chemical that can be converted by straightforward methods into a variety of useful products [6]. Nowadays, almost all extant sorbitol production processes are usually based on the hydrogenation of glucose catalyzed by metallic catalysts [7 - 13]. In fact, glucose can be facilely obtained from biomass materials, primarily starch [14—16] and even cellulose, [17] through enzymatic hydrolysis bioprocesses. Apparently, a combined, one-pot hydrolysis-hydrogenation of biomass materials to sorbitol displays some advantages in its step-saving and low costs mainly linked to both the separation and the refining procedures [18—20]. Nevertheless, our previous studies revealed the one-pot process contains incompatible parameters. More specifically, enzymes are easily poisoned when contacting with metal catalysts, while metallic active sites would be covered by enzymes and the colloidal substances originated from hydrolysis of biomass materials, leading to a rapid deactivation for the subsequent glucose hydrogenation. Noting that encaging a functional material within another material can form a yolk-shell configuration that provides protecting effect on the individual core [21], very recently, we designed yolk-shell nanoarchitectures consisting of cores made of supported Ru encapsulated within porous silica shells [22, 23]. By combining such materials with amyloglu-cosidase, one-pot hydrolysis-hydrogenation of dextrin has been successfully conducted to produce sorbitol where the porous silica shell separates the incompatible catalysts in different regions. Specifically, the enzymatic hydrolysis of dextrin to glucose occurs outside the yolk-shell nanoarchitectures owing to the blocking effect of the silica shells on the large enzyme molecules. Meanwhile, the permeation-selective porous silica shells offer a convenient path for the produced small glucose molecules crossing into the catalytically active cores for hydrogenation to sorbitol. While promising, the present process still uses free enzyme which decreases the economical attractiveness owing to the difficulty associated with the reusability of enzyme and the protein contamination of the final product. Therefore, immobilization of enzyme directly onto the outer surface of shell is needed to ensure the achievement of a real merging of such yolk-shell nanostructures and enzyme.

With advances in material science, a number of techniques have been developed for enzyme immobilization, such as support binding (physical binding, ionic binding, or covalent binding), entrapment, and crosslinking [24]. To enhance the operational stability and reusability of amyloglucosidases for bioprocessing, they have been immobilized *via* various methods by far. Using polyethyleneimine-coated sepabeads as supports, Torres et al. successfully immobilized glucoamylase *via* ionic adsorption [25]. In comparison with ionic binding, covalent binding of enzyme to insoluble carriers is even stronger. In 2008, Kamal et al. reported the covalently immobilization of glucoamylase on polypropylene-grafted fibers by using carbodiimide as a coupling agent [26]. By using glutaraldehyde [27] or polyglutaraldehyde [28] as coupling agent, amyloglucosidase was attached to silanized magnetic nanoparticles or gelatin. Compared to other coupling agents, glutaraldehyde-based coupling reaction requires mild conditions. In those reports, immobilized amyloglucosidases were found to be more beneficial relative to the corresponding free enzymes. Despite the well-known advantages for enzyme immobilization, the immobilization of amyloglucosidase has not been performed frequently in industrial because the macromolecular enzyme loading is still a tough issue. Crosslinking technique has proved to be a promising approach for carrier-free immobilization of enzyme, which permits multipoint attachment through intermolecular crosslinking between enzyme molecules [29]. Based on this technique, Talekar et al. recently developed a combi-CLEAs strategy to prepare carrier-free co-immobilization of macromolecular enzymes, glucoamylase, and pullulanase [30]. In our research, we sought to address these concerns by *both* covalently attaching of yolk-shell nanostructures onto amyloglucosidase *and* ensuring an insoluble and robust biochemical catalyst.

Herein, we design a recyclable bifunctional biochemical composite. The synthesis of such composite is achieved through a step-wise crosslinking method that involves the covalent attachment of yolk-shell structured chemical catalyst onto amyloglucoamylase with glutaraldehyde and the subsequent coupling of the composite in the presence of modified dextran. The biochemical composite enables the efficient synthesis of sorbitol in one pot from dextrin, cellobiose, and even cellulose. More importantly, the biochemical composite could be used repetitively many times, showing a good potential in industrial applications.

2. Experimental section

2.1 Catalyst preparation

The synthesis of biochemical composite involves the fabrication of yolk-shell structured chemical catalyst (Scheme 1A) and the integrating of the above material and enzyme (Scheme 1B). Firstly, uniform dispersing of Ru-B amorphous alloys within the porous channels of amino-functionalized mesoporous carbon nanospheres (af-mCarbon) was achieved by ultrasound-assisted incipient wetness infiltration of $(NH_4)_2RuCl_6$ onto af-mCarbon, followed by reduction with borohydride (Ru-B/af-mCarbon) [31]. Afterward, the Ru-B/af-mCarbon was coated by co-condensation of tetraethoxysilane (TEOS) and N-(amino-ethyl)-amino-propyl trimethoxy silane (APTES) in the presence of cetyltrimethylammonium bromide (CTAB), generating a core-shell structured Ru-B/af-mCarbon @ CTAB/af-SiO$_2$, where CTAB/af-SiO$_2$ refers to a mesostructured CTAB/silica composite coated on the surface of the Ru-B/af-mCarbon core. Finally, the as-synthesized core-shell structured Ru-B/af-mCarbon@CTAB/af-SiO$_2$ was etched with hot water to achieve a yolk-shell structured configuration (Ru-B/af-mCarbon@ air@ af-mSiO$_2$). The integrating of the yolk-shell structured Ru-B/af-mCarbon@ air@ af-mSiO$_2$ and enzyme was conducted through a stepwise crosslinking method, including covalent attachment of chemical catalyst onto enzyme through a glutaraldehyde-based crosslinking technique (Ru-B/af-mCarbon@ air @ af-mSiO$_2$-A-I) and coupling of the obtained crosslinked composite with modified dextran (Ru-B/af-mCarbon@air @af-mSiO$_2$-A-II). More details about the catalyst preparation can be found in the Supporting Information.

2.2 Catalyst characterization

Fourier transform infrared (FTIR) spectra were obtained using a Thermo Nicolet Magna 550 spectrometer. The bulk composition and Ru loading were analyzed by means of inductively coupled plasma optical emission spectrometry (ICP-OES; Varian VISTA-MPX). Enzyme loading was determined by bicinchoninic acid (BCA) assay. The amorphous structure was investigated by both X-ray diffraction (XRD; Rigaku D/Max-RB with Cu Kα radiation) and selective-area electronic diffraction (SAED; JEOL JEM2100). The material shapes and morphologies were observed by both field emission scanning electron microscopy (FESEM; HITACHI S-4800) and transmission electron microscopy (TEM, JEOL JEM2100). N_2 adsorption-desorption isotherms were obtained at 77 K using a Micromeritics TriStar II apparatus. By N_2 adsorption, the Brunauer-Emmett-Teller (BET) surface area (S_{BET}) was calculated by using the multiple-point

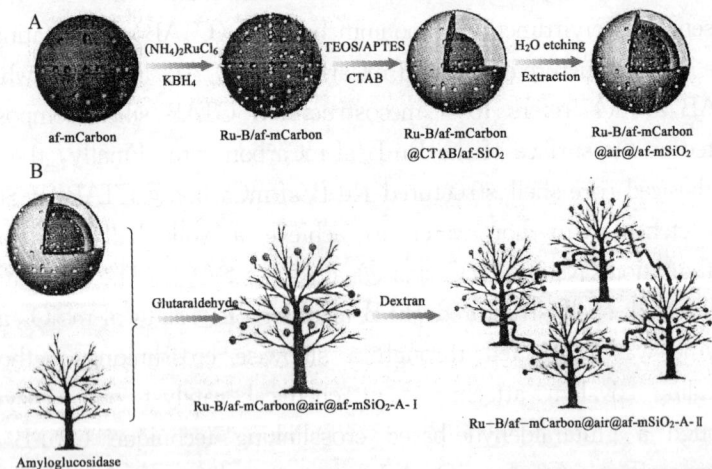

Scheme 1. Illustration of the synthesis process of (A) yolk-shell structured Ru-B/af-mCarbon @ air @ af-mSiO$_2$ and (B) biochemical composite through stepwise cross-linking technique.

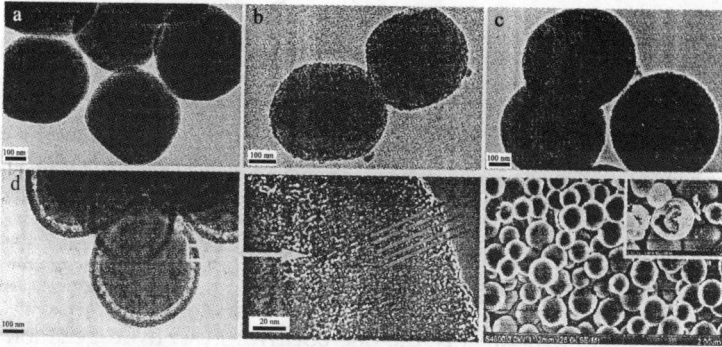

Fig. 1 TEM images of (a) af-mCarbon, (b) Ru-B/af-mCarbon, (c) Ru-B/af-mCarbon@CTAB/af-SiO₂, and (d) Ru-B/af-mCarbon@air@af-mSiO₂. (e) FESEM image of Ru-B/af-mCarbon@air@af-mSiO₂. The inset in (e) is a partially crushed sphere.

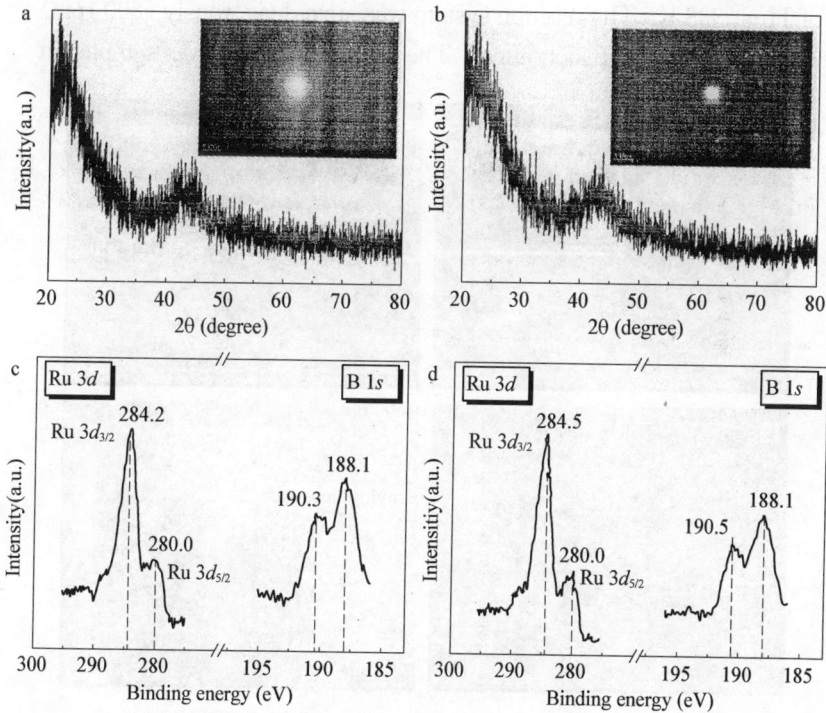

Fig. 2 Wide-angle XRD patterns of (a) Ru-B/af-mCarbon and (b) Ru-B/af-mCarbon @air@af-mSiO₂. XPS spectra of (c) Ru-B/af-mCarbon and (d) Ru-B/af-mCarbon@ air@af-mSiO₂. The insets in (a) and (b) are the SAED images of the Ru-B particles.

BET method in the relative pressure range of $P/P_0 = 0.05—0.2$. The pore volume and pore size distribution curve were obtained by the Barrett-Joyner-Halenda model. The surface electronic states were determined by X-ray photoelectron spectroscopy (XPS; ULVAC-PHI PHI5000 VersaProbe system using AI Kα radiation).

2.3 *Catalytic performances test*

In a typical experiment, the one-pot hydrolysis-hydrogenation of dextrin to sorbitol was carried out in a Parr 4848 autoclave con-taining Ru-B/af-mCarbon@ air@ af-mSiO$_2$-A-II (6.5 mg Ru and 25.9 mg amyloglucosidase), 0.25 g of dextrin, 25 mL of water, and 4.0 MPa of H$_2$ at 333 K. The reaction system was stirred vigorously (800 rpm) to eliminate the diffusion effect. The reaction mixture was sampled at

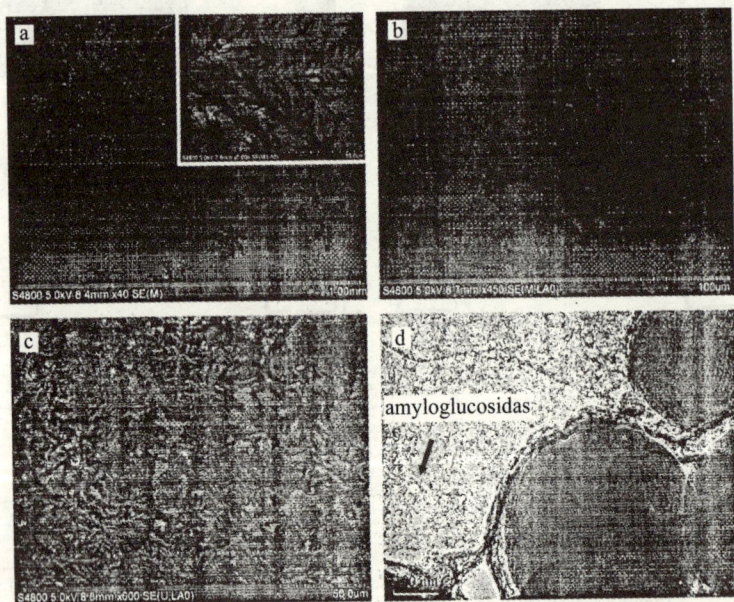

Fig. 3 FESEM images of (a) amyloglucosidase, (b) Ru-B/af-mCarbon@ air@ af-mSiO$_2$-A-I, and (c) Ru-B/af-mCarbon@air@af-mSiO$_2$-A-II. (d) TEM image of Ru-B/af-mCarbon@ air@ af-mSiO$_2$-A-II.

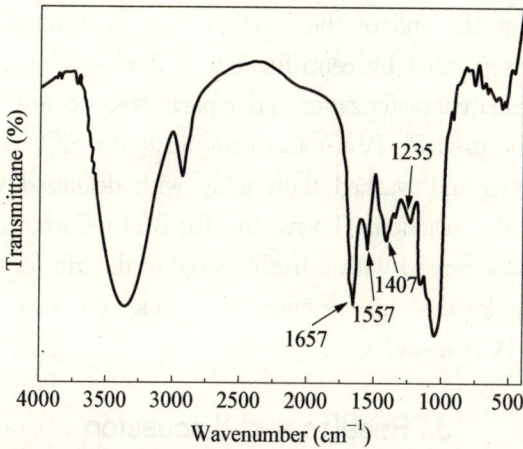

Fig. 4 FTIR spectrum of Ru-B/af-mCarbon @ air @ af-mSiO$_2$-A-II.

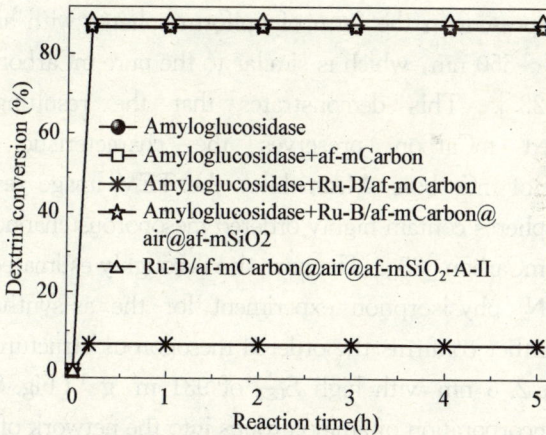

Fig. 5 Dextrin hydrolysis in different catalyst systems. Reaction conditions: dextrin (0.25 g), amyloglucosidase (20 μL), a catalyst (containing 6.5 mg Ru), water (25 mL), T = 333 K, P_{HZ} = 4.0 MPa, stirring rate = 800 rpm.

intervals for product analysis on a liquid-phase chromatograph (Agilent 1200) equipped with a carbohydrate column (Shodex, SC1011) and a refractive index detector at 333 K with water as the movable phase at 0. 6 mL/min. After the mixture cooled to room temperature at the end of the reaction, the biochemical composite catalyst was separated by centrifugation and washed with deionized water for further characterization and applications. To test the catalyst durability, the used Ru-B/af-mCarbon@air@af-mSiO$_2$-A-II catalyst was centrifuged and washed thoroughly with deionized water after each run of the reaction. Then, the Ru-B/af-mCarbon@air@af-mSiO$_2$-A-II was reused with a fresh charge of dextrin for subsequent recycle run under the same reaction conditions. The supernatant was collected for BCA assay.

3. Results and discussion

3.1 *Catalyst characterization*

As shown in TEM image (Fig. 1a), the as-synthesized af-mCarbon is present in the form of uniform spheres with an average diameter of ~550 nm, which is similar to the pure mCarbon reported recently [23]. This demonstrates that the resulting amino-functionalized mCarbon preserves the characteristic spherical morphology of mCarbon. Meanwhile, the TEM image reveals that these nanospheres contain highly ordered mesoporous channels similar to the pure mCarbon [23]. The pore size is roughly estimated to be ~ 2.5 nm. N$_2$ physisorption experiment for the as-synthesized af-mCarbon further confirms the ordered mesoporous structure centered approximate 2.6 nm with high S_{BET} of 931 m^2 g^{-1} (Fig. S1). The successful incorporation of amino groups into the network of mCarbon was demonstrated by FTIR characterization. The FTIR spectra (Fig. S2) reveal that, besides those absorbance bands observed in the pure mCarbon, the acid-treated mCarbon displays additional absorbance bands at 1728 and 1222 cm^{-1}, corresponding to the stretching vibration of C = O bond and the bending vibration of O-H bond from the grafted-COOH groups on mCarbon [32]. Grafting TETA on the acid-treated mCarbon resulted in the remarkable decrease of O-H bending vibration and a blueshift of C = O stretching vibration to 1662 cm^{-1}, indicating the formation of the amide bond [32]. Additionally, other features should be given attention are 3041, 2930, 2849, 1453, and 1112 cm^{-1} due to N-H stretching, C-H asymmetric stretching, C-H symmetric stretching, N-H bending, and C-N stretching, respectively [33]. CO_2 temperature-program med-desorption (CO_2-TPD) was also used to confirm the incorporation of amino group into the surface of mCarbon. In case of the pure mCarbon, no CO_2 uptake was found for the used adsorption conditions (Fig. S3a); while the af-mCarbon shows pronounced CO_2 desorption peaks (Fig. S3b). All of these features indicate that the TETA have been grafted onto mCarbon successfully. Fig. 1b demonstrates that the ordered mesostructure of af-mCarbon can be well maintained after depositing Ru-B nanoparticles (NPs). Meanwhile, it can be observed that the Ru-B NPs are uniformly dispersed into the pore channels. The Ru loading was determined as 2. 2 wt% by ICP analysis. From Fig. 1c, one can see that the Ru-B/af-mCarbon core is completely coated by silica shell with a thickness around 100 nm. To protect the amino functionality attached on the material, hot water (363 K) was used as etching agent for the generating of yolk-shell nanostructures in the present research. Fig. 1d reveals that, after being etched with hot water, the thickness of silica shell decreased about 20 nm, together with the formation of a space around 20 nm between the silica shell and the Ru-B/af-mCarbon core. From the FESEM image (Fig. 1e), the average diameter of the as-prepared Ru-B/af-mCarbon@air@af-mSiO$_2$ was estimated to be ~550 nm, which was in good line with the TEM observation. The attached FESEM image of broken Ru-B/af-mCarbon @ air @ af-mSiO$_2$ further confirms the achievement of yolk-shell structured configuration (inset in Fig. 1e). From the high-magnification TEM image of the yolk-shell structures in Fig. 1d, continuous mesochannels throughout the shell with openings at surface and radially oriented to the sphere surface can be clearly observed for the silica shell. Such a unique pore orientation is due to the perpendicular alignment of surfactant mesophases induced by the equal attractivity to polar and nonpolar species of the interface between the CTAB/silica phase and the water/ethanol solution [34—36]. The perpendicular mesoporosity in the silica shell is anticipated to increase the accessibility of the Ru-B/af-mCarbon core and thus enhancing the efficiency of mass transport. The pore size in the silica shell can be measured to be 2.6 nm by nitrogen physisorption experiment (Fig. S4).

The wide-angle XRD patterns (Fig. 2a and b) reveal that the Ru-B NPs in both the Ru-B/af-mCarbon and the Ru-B/af-mCarbon@ air @ af-mSiO$_2$ are present in the typical amorphous structure, corresponding to a broad peak at$\sim 2\theta = 45°$ [37,38], which is further confirmed by the consecutive diffraction halos in the attached SAED pictures [39]. The XPS spectra (Fig. 2c and d) demonstrate that all the Ru species in both the Ru-B/af-mCarbon and the yolk-shell structured Ru-B/af-mCarbon@air@af-mSiO$_2$ are present in metallic state, corresponding to the binding energy (BE) of 280.0 eV in Ru $3d_{5/2}$, while the B species are present in both the elemental state and the oxidized B, with BE of 188.1 and 190.5 eV in B 1s level. The B 1s BE of the elemental B exceeds that of pure B by 1.0 eV [40], suggesting the formation of Ru-B alloy in which partial electrons transfer from B to Ru. The failure in observing the BE shift of the metallic Ru can be understood by considering its relatively greater atomic weight compared with the B atom. As a result, the XRD, SAED data coupled with that of XPS, confirmed the formation of Ru-B amorphous alloy. Plenty of studies had demonstrated that Ru-B amorphous alloy has enhanced catalytic activity relative to the monometallic Ru in many reactions, including the hydrogenation of glucose to sorbitol [33]. On the one hand, the unique amorphous alloy structure of Ru-B endows them with a stronger synergistic effect between Ru active sites and more highly unsaturated Ru active sites than the monometallic catalyst, which may promote the adsorption of reactants and favor hydrogenation activity [33, 38]. On the other hand, the strong electronic interaction between Ru and B in the Ru-B alloys makes Ru electron enriched. The higher electron density on Ru active sites might facilitate the formation of H^- species, which would be anticipated to increase glucose hydrogenation activity [33,38].

The integrating of the yolk-shell structured Ru-B/af-mCarbon@ air@af-mSiO₂ and amyloglucosidase was conducted through a stepwise crosslinking method. As shown in Fig. 3a, the free amyloglucosidase has tree-like appearance showing pinnatisect. The width of the segments can be determined as 200—300 nm. Glutaraldehyde-based crosslinking technique has proven one of the most facile methods to immobilize an enzyme on functionalized support. Therefore, glutaraldehyde was first used as crosslinker to covalently attach Ru-B/ af-mCarbon@ air@ af-mSiO₂ onto amyloglucoamylase. The resulting Ru-B/af-mCarbon@ air @ af-mSiO₂-A-I preserves the characteristic tree-like shape of the free amyloglucoamylase and Ru-B/af-mCarbon@ air@ af-mSiO₂ particles can be found to hang on the segments of amyloglucosidase, presenting decorated tree-like structure (Fig. 3b). We presume that the crosslinking process to form Ru-B/af-mCarbon@ air@af-mSiO₂-A-I was due to the interaction of glutaraldehyde with both the amino functionalities on the surface of chemical catalyst and the amino group residues in the enzyme. To further enhance the insolubility and robustness of the biochemical composite, additional coupling of Ru-B/af-mCarbon@ air@ af-mSiO₂-A-I was implemented by using the modified dextran as crosslinker. Under SEM, Ru-B/af-m Carbon @ air @ af-mSiO₂-A-II appears as aggregates (Fig. 3c), suggestive of the tying of the decorated tree-like composite with the modified dextran. From the TEM image of Ru-B/af-mCarbon@air@ af-mSiO₂-A-II (Fig. 3d), the yolk-shell structured Ru-B/af-mCarbon @ air @ af-mSiO₂ can be also observed, demonstrating that the stepwise crosslinking was never associated with damage to the structure of chemical catalyst. Because amyloglucoamylase is extremely sensitive to the high-energy electron beam in TEM analysis, only a trail of devastation was left beside the yolk-shell structured Ru-B/af-mCarbon@ air@ af-mSiO$_2$ (marked with arrow). Furthermore, the formation of biochemical composite can be further confirmed by the FTIR spectrum. As shown in Fig. 4, Ru-B/af-mCarbon@ air@ af-mSiO$_2$-A-II displayed additional absorbance bands at 1657, 1557, 1407, and 1235 cm^{-1}, which are ascribed to the functional groups of amino acid in amyloglucoamylase. It should be noted that the C $=$ N vibration peaks (1600—1650 cm^{-1}) as the formation of Schiff's base are covered by the characteristic peaks from amino acid groups.

More importantly, the biochemical composite, denoted as Ru-B/af-mCarbon@air@af-mSiO$_2$-C-II, can be also achieved from the yolk-shell structured Ru-B/af-mCarbon@ air@ af-mSiO$_2$ and cellulase by the same method, demonstrating the generality of this stepwise crosslinking strategy.

3.2 Catalytic performances

The as-prepared biochemical composites were subjected to one-pot production of sorbitol *via* hydrolysis-hydrogenation of biomass materials. We began by exploring the enzymatic efficiency of amyloglucosidase for saccharification of dextrin in different catalyst systems (Fig. 5). Note that blank run performed using amyloglucosidase accompanying with af-mCarbon delivers similar enzymatic efficiency to that of the free amyloglucosidase. Nonetheless, significant inhibiting effects on the dextrin hydrolysis activity can be observed when using amyloglucosidase in the presence of Ru-B/af-mCarbon. This implies that amyloglucosidase is easily poisoned once directly contacting with metallic Ru, in line with the results reported in our recent studies [22,23]. Hardly, any difference in the enzymatic efficiency can be found using amyloglucosidase accompanying with the yolk-shell structured Ru-B /af-mCarbon@ air@ af-mSiO$_2$, apparently

owing to the protective effect of the af-mSiO₂ shell that prevents
amyloglucosidase from crossing over the shell to contact with the Ru-
containing core. Furthermore, almost entire retention of the enzymatic
efficiency for saccharification of dextrin can be observed on Ru-B/af-
mCarbon@ air@ af-mSiO₂-A-II, compared to the free amyloglucosidase. This result indicates that the present stepwise crosslinking
method is promising and the resulting biochemical composite is anticipated to catalyze the one-pot biomass conversion.

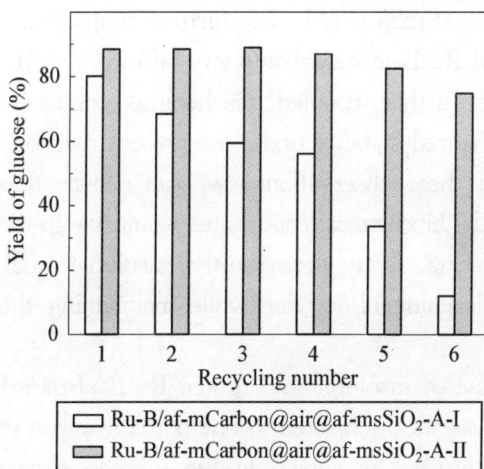

Fig. 6 Recycling test of the biochemical composites for dextrin
hydrolysis. Reaction conditions: dextrin (0. 25 g), biochemical
composite (containing 6. 5 mg Ru and 25. 9 mg amyloglucosidase),
water (25 mL), $T = 333$ K, $P_{H2} = 4.0$ MPa , stirring rate =
800 rpm. Each run was conducted for 5 h in recycling test. Each run
was conducted for 6 h in recycling test.

Industrial application of an enzyme in an immobilized form greatly
relies on its stability and handling convenience [24]. Next, we first
investigated the durability of the biochemical composites during the
hydrolysis of dextrin. Although Ru-B/af-mCarbon@ air@ af-mSiO₂-
A-I retained complete activity of the free enzyme, its stability was
rather undesirable since apparent deactivation occurred during the

recycling test (Fig. 6). During the hydrolysis of dextrin catalyzed by Ru-B/af-mCarbon @ air @ af-mSiO$_2$-A-I, we also determined the leaching amounts of amyloglucosidase by the BCA assay in the supernatants. The analysis results revealed that more than 11% and 75% of the applied enzyme leached out after the first cycle and the six cycle, respectively, suggesting that Ru-B/af-mCarbon @ air @ af-mSiO$_2$-A-I was soluble in water under the present conditions. In an effort to favor the stability of biochemical composite, Ru-B/af-mCarbon @ air @ af-mSiO$_2$-A-I was further coupled with modified dextran to afford Ru-B/af-mCarbon@air@af-mSiO$_2$-A-II. As shown in Fig. 6, the further coupled biochemical composite exhibited substantially enhanced stability under the present reaction conditions. On the basis of these observations, we can deduce that additional crosslinking of the biochemical composites would tie up them together and thus rendering them permanently insoluble and effectively preventing the leaching of enzyme while maintaining the enzymatic efficiency.

The as-prepared insoluble and robust Ru-B/af-mCarbon@ air@ af-mSiO$_2$-A-II was then subjected to one-pot conversion of dextrin to sorbitol (Scheme 2). As shown in Fig. 7, the enzyme catalyzed saccharification of dextrin to release glucose molecules rapidly. The produced glucose would diffuse through the af-mSiO$_2$ shell in Ru-B/af-mCarbon@air@af-mSiO$_2$, followed by the hydrogenation to the final product, sorbitol, over the catalytically active cores. Our observations suggest that the mesoporous silica shell in Ru-B/af-mCarbon@ air@ af-mSiO$_2$ plays a key role in conducting the one-pot dextrin conversion. On the one hand, af-mSiO$_2$ shell blocks the big dextrin molecules and other colloidal substances (100—1000 nm) stemmed from the dextrin hydrolysis out of the yolk-shell nanostructures, efficiently protecting the Ru active sites from being covered. On the other hand, af-mSiO$_2$ shell allows the produced glucose ($\sim$1 nm)

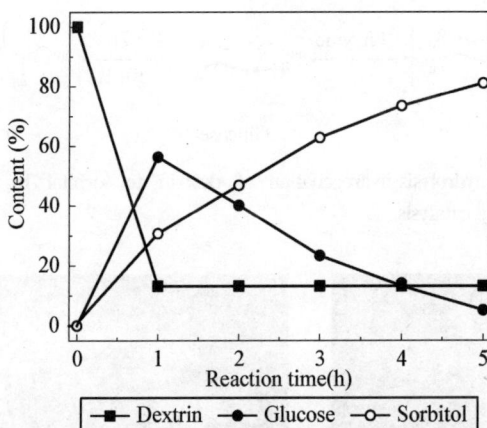

Fig. 7　Reaction profile in one-pot hydrolysis-hydrogenation of dextrin by
Ru-B/af-mCarbon @ air @ af-mSiO₂-A-II.　Reaction conditions: dextrin
(0. 25 g), 0. 9 g of biochemical composite (containing 6. 5 mg Ru and 25. 9
mg amyloglucosidase), water (25 mL), $T = 333$ K, $P_{H2} = 4. 0$ MPa,
stirring rate=800 rpm.

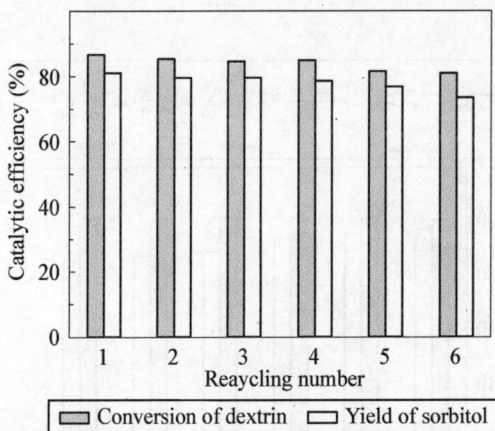

Fig. 8　Recycling test of Ru-B/af-mCarbon@air@af-mSiO₂-A-II for
one-pot hydrol-ysis-hydrogenation of dextrin.　Reaction conditions:
dextrin (0. 25g). 0. 9 g of biochemical composite (containing 6. 5 mg
Ru and 25. 9 mg amyloglucosidase), water (25 mL), $T = 333$ K,
$P_{H2} = 4. 0$ MPa, and stirring rate = 800 rpm.　Each run was
conducted for 5 h in recycling test.

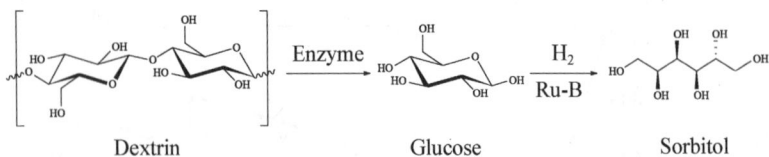

Scheme 2. One-pot hydrolysis-hydrogenation of dextrin to sorbitol by merger of enzymatic and metallic catalysis.

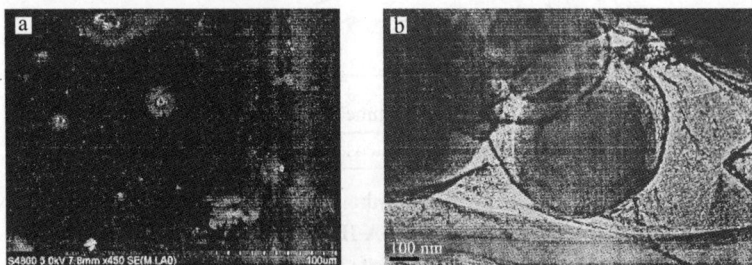

Fig. 9 (a) FESEM and (b) TEM images of the Ru-B/af-mCarbon@air@af-mSiO$_2$-A-II after being reused for 6 times.

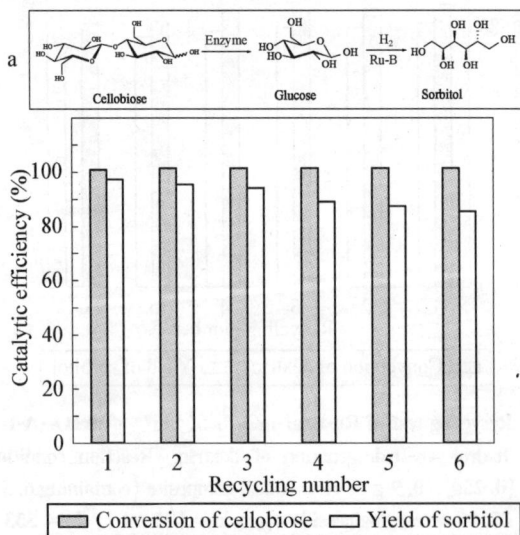

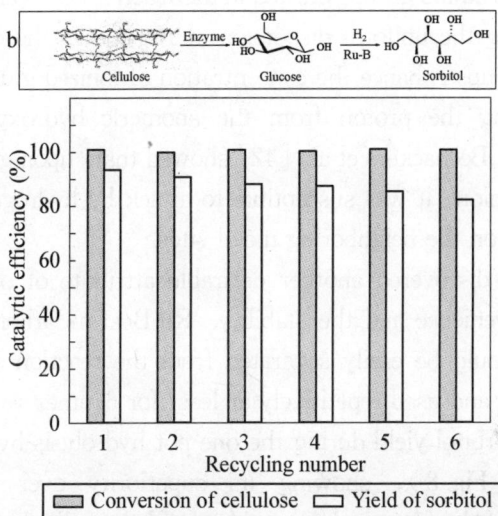

Fig. 10　Recycling test of Ru-B/af-mCarbon@air@af-mSiO$_2$-C-II for one-pot hydrolysis-hydrogenation of (a) cellobiose and (b) cellulose. Reaction conditions: cellobiose or cellulose (0.1 g), 0.68 g of biochemical composite (containing 2.6 mg Ru and 0.33 g cellulase), water (20 mL), $T = 333$ K, $P_{H2} = 4.0$ MPa, and stirring rate=800 rpm. Each run was conducted for 6 h in recycling test.

from dextrin hydrolysis diffuse across the shell and then be hydrogenated to sorbitol over the Ru-B/af-mCarbon core. Notably, the catalytic efficiency of the present biochemical composite exceeds those we reported recently. For example, the present biochemical composite enables the one-pot dextrin conversion to proceed at moderate temperature (333 K vs. 348 K [22] and 343 K [23]). Additionally, only a shorter time (5 h) in the present system is needed to obtain the similar sorbitol yield to the recent results (7 h [22] and 6 h [23]). As demonstrated above, the dextrin hydrolysis efficiency can be retained entirely in Ru-B/af-mCarbon@air@af-mSiO$_2$-A-II, the enhanced catalytic efficiency of the present biochemical composite should be thanks to the superior glucose hydrogenation activity of the Ru-B/af-mCarbon@air@af-mSiO$_2$ to the previous systems. On the one hand, the amino groups grafted in mCarbon serve as anchor points [33], favoring the uniform dispersion of Ru-B. On the other hand, the amino groups enhance the concentration of ionized glucose species *via* abstracting the proton from the anomeric hydroxyl group in glucose [41]. Beenackers et al. [42] showed that, upon generation of the glucose anion, it was susceptible to attack by hydrogen adsorbed dissociatively on the neighboring metal sites.

We also discovered another desirable attribute of our process: handling convenience and the stability. Ru-B/af-mCarbon@air@af-mSiO$_2$-A-II could be easily separated from the reaction solution *via* centrifugation and used repetitively at least for 6 times with only 9% decrease of sorbitol yield during the one-pot hydrolysis-hydrogenation of dextrin (Fig. 8), showing its superiority over the simple combination of the free amyloglucosidase and the yolk-shell structured chemical catalysts [22, 23]. During the recycling test, the dextrin conversion decreased by 7% after being used 6 times. Accordingly, the slight decrease in sorbitol yield after 6 cycles should be attributed to the partial lost in enzymatic efficiency for saccharification of dextrin. The FESEM and TEM images (Fig. 9) showed that both the decorated tree-like structure of the biochemical composite and the yolk-shell structure morphology of the chemical catalyst were still present after 6 cycles. However, the leaching amount of amyloglucosidase was determined as 5% by the BCA assay in the supernatant, demonstrating that leaching of enzyme might be the main factor responsible for the decrease in efficiency.

Finally, further investigations of the generality of the present strategy revealed that one-pot synthesis of sorbitol can be also achieved *via* hydrolysis-hydrogenation of cellobiose and even cellulose by Ru-B/af-mCarbon@air@af-mSiO$_2$-C-II with 6 cycles of successive use (Fig. 10). From the viewpoint of practical applications, transforming the inedible biomass materials into valuable platform chemicals is more economical issue. Therefore, further optimization may eventually make the approach industrially viable for the conversion of non-food biomass into sorbitol as a renewable platform chemical.

4. Conclusions

In summary, our research provides a paradigm for the utility of crosslinking technique for the integrating of chemical catalyst and the macromolecular enzyme into biochemical composite. The recyclable biochemical composite can be used to convert biomass materials into sorbitol in high efficiency. This one-pot process may find important applications for the efficient production of renewable platform chemicals from biomass materials without intermediate purification. Moreover, this strategy can potentially be extended to other biochemical composites with different composition and thus versatile functions.

Acknowledgments

This work is supported by the National Natural Science Foundation of China (21273149), PCSIRT (IRT1269), the Program for New Century Excellent Talents in University (NCET-11-1052), the Shanghai Science & Technology and Education Committee (11JC1408900, 12490502800, 10SG41), and State Key Laboratory of Chemical Engineering (SKL-ChE-14C05).

Appendix A. Supplementary material

Supplementary data associated with this article can be found, in the online version, at http://dx. doi. org/10. 1016/j. jcat. 2015. 04. 021.

References

[1] A. Corma, S. Iborra, A. Velty, Chem. Rev. 107(2007)2411.

[2] R. Rinaldi, F. Schüth, Energy Environ. Sci. 2(2009)610.

[3] D. A. Simonetti, J. A. Dumesic, Catal. Rev. -Sci. Eng. 51(2009)441.

[4] J. C. Serrano-Ruiz, J. A. Dumesic, Energy Environ. Sci. 4(2011)83.

[5] M. Besson, P. Gallezot, C. Pinel, Chem. Rev. 114(2014)1827.

[6] T. Werpy, G. Peterson, Top Value Added Chemicals from Biomass: Results of Screening for Candidates from Sugars and Synthesis Gas, vol. 1, US Department of Energy, Energy Efficiency and Renewable Energy, Battelle, Richland, WA. 〈http://www1. eere. energy. gov/biomass/pdfs/35523. pdf〉.

[7] W. S. Fedor, J. Millar, A. J. Accola, Ind. Eng. Chem. 52(1960)282.

[8] W. M. Kruse, L. W. Wright, Carbohydr. Res. 64(1978)293.

[9] P. Gallezot, P. J. Cerino, B. Blanc, G. Fleche, P. Fuertes, J. Catal. 146 (1994)93.

[10] H. Li, H. X. Li, J. F. Deng, Catal. Today 74(2002)53.

[11] B. Kusserow, S. Schimpf, P. Claus, Adv. Synth. Catal. 345(2003)289.

[12] S. Schimpf, C. Louis, P. Claus, Appl. Catal. , A 356(2009)112.

[13] V. N. Sapunov, M. Y. Grigoryev, E. M. Sulman, M. B. Konyaeva, V. G. Matveeva, J. Phys. Chem. A 117(2013)4073.

[14] D. Yankov, E. Dobreva, V. Beschkov, E. Emanuilova, Enzyme Microb. Technol. 8(1986)665.

[15] R. Hoover, Food Rev. Int. 16(2000)369.

[16] J. Kadokawa, Chem. Rev. 111(2011)4308.

[17] M. Katz, E. E. Reese, Appl. Microbiol. 12(1968)419.

[18] A. Bruggink, R. Schoevaart, T. Kieboom, Org. Process Res. Dev. 7 (2003)622.

[19] C. Simons, U. Hanefeld, I. W. C. E. Arends, T. Maschmeyer, R. A. Scheldon, Top. Catal. 40(2006)35.

[20] M. J. Climent, A. Corma, S. Iborra, Chem. Rev. 111(2011)1072.

[21] N. Ren, Y. H. Yang, J. Shen, Y. H. Zhang, H. L. Xu, Z. Gao, Y. Tang, J. Catal. 251(2007)182.

[22] L. Xu, W. Wei, H. X. Li, H. Li, ACS Catal. 4(2014)251.

[23] W. Wei, Y. Zhao, S. C. Peng, H. Y. Zhang, Y. P. Bian, H. X. Li, H. Li, ACS Appl. Mater. Interfaces 6(2014)20851.

［24］ R. A. Sheldon, Adv. Synth. Catal. 349(2007)1289.

［25］ R. Torres, B. C. C. Pessela, C. Mateo, C. Ortiz, M. Fuentes, J. M. Guisan, R. Fernandez-Lafuente, Biotechnol. Prog. 20(2004)1297.

［26］ H. Kamal, G. M. Sabry, S. Lotfy, N. M. Abdallah, J. Rosiak, E. A. Hegazy, J. Macromol. Sci. 45(2008)65.

［27］ A. Panek, O. Pietrow, J. Synowiecki, Strach 64(2012)1003.

［28］ A. Tanriseven, Z. Ölçer, J. Synowiecki, Biochem. Eng. J. 39(2008)430.

［29］ R. A. Persichetti, N. L. S. Clair, J. P. Griffith, M. A. Navia, A. L. Margolin, J. Am. Chem. Soc. 117(1995)2732.

［30］ S. Talekar, S. Desai, M. Pillai, N. Nagavekar, S. Ambarkar, S. Surnis, M. Ladole, S. Nadar, M. Mulla, RSC Adv. 3(2013)2265.

［31］ Y. Wang, L. Xu, L. Xu, H. X. Li, H. Li, Chin. J. Catal. 34(2013)1027.

［32］ J. Chen, M. A. Hamon, H. Hu, Y. S. Chen, A. M. Rao, P. C. Eklund, R. C. Haddon, Science 282(1998)95.

［33］ S. L. Wang, W. Wei, Y. Zhao, H. X. Li, H. Li, Catal. Today, http://dx. doi. org/10. 1016/j. cattod. 2014. 07. 039.

［34］ B. Tan, S. E. Rankin, J. Phys. Chem. B 108(2004)20122.

［35］ S. B. Yoon, J. Y. Kim, J. H. Kim, Y. J. Park, K. R. Yoon, S. K. Park, J. S. Yu, J. Mater. Chem. 17(2007)1758.

［36］ Y. H. Deng, Y. Cai, Z. K. Sun, J. Liu, C. Liu, J. Wei, W. Li, C. Liu, Y. Wang, D. Y. Zhao, J. Am. Chem. Soc. 132(2010)8466.

［37］ Y. Pei, G. B. Zhou, N. Luan, B. N. Zong, M. H. Qiao, F. Tao, Chem. Soc. Rev. 41(2012)81409.

［38］ H. Li, W. Wei, Y. Zhao, H. X. Li, Catalysis 27(2015)144.

［39］ S. Klein, J. A. Martens, R. Parton, K. Vercruysse, P. A. Jacobs, W. F. Maier, Catal. Lett. 38(1996)209.

［40］ H. Li, H. X. Li, W. L. Dai, W. J. Wang, Z. G. Fang, J. F. Deng, Appl. Surf. Sci. 152(1999)25.

［41］ G. de Wit, J. J. de Vlieger, A. C. K. Dalen, R. Heus, R. Laroy, A. J. Van Hengstum, A. P. G. Kieboom, H. Van Bekkum, Carbohydr. Res. 91 (1981)125.

［42］ J. A. W. M. Beenackers, B. F. M. Kuster, H. S. Van der Baan, Carbohydr. Res. 140(1985)169.

An imidazolium-based organopalladium-functionalized organic-inorganic hybrid silica promotes one-pot tandem Suzuki cross coupling-reduction of haloacetophenones and arylboronic acids

Dacheng Zhang, Tanyu Cheng, Guohua Liu

Key Laboratory of Resource Chemistry of Ministry of Education,
Shanghai Key Laboratory of Rare Earth Functional Materials,
Shanghai Normal University

1. Introduction

Multiple-step organic transformations through an one-pot catalytic process, as an important aspect of green chemistry, have attracted a great deal of interest due to atomic economy and minimum workup [1—5]. However, intrinsic disadvantages of homogeneous organometallic catalysts, such as reuse of expensive organometallic complexes and potential product contamination from leaching of metal, do still hinder their practical applications in industrial process. Thus, development of an immobilized strategy overcomes these barriers is of considerable importance. Silica-based mesoporous materials as supports to immobilize organometallic complexes for catalysis have obtained great achievements [6,7]. In particular, imidazolium-based silica materials as supports have exhibited some salient advantages [8—10]. As a type of environmentally friendly materials, imidazolium-based silica materials possess potential phase transfer function that can promote significantly catalytic efficiency in a biphasic catalysis system [9—10]. Furthermore, functionalized imidazolium-based silica materials can be constructed easily via various assembly strategies, [11—14] particularly some materials containing multi-functionality on their silicate networks can realize potentially a multiple-step organic transformation that is still rare in a heterogeneous catalysis. Accordingly, it is reasonable to expect that the construction of an imidazolium-based silica material with multi-functionality in its silicate network has significant benefits for an one-pot multiple-step organic transformation in a heterogeneous catalysis system.

Suzuki cross-coupling reaction of aryl halides and arylboronic acids to biaryls, and catalytic reduction of carbonyls to alcohols are two type of classic organic reactions, which have been investigated extensively both in theoretically and practically [15—17]. Recently, some successful examples through the combination of above two organic reactions to construct biaryl alcohols from reaction of haloacetophenones and arylboronic acids have been explored [18,19]. In both cases, a triazolyl-diylidene-bridged Pd/Ir-complex enables one-pot tandem Suzuki cross-coupling of aryl halides and arylboronic acids followed by reduction to obtain biaryl alcohols, but the transition-metal contamination for reaction product is still unavoidable problem in its practical application. Therefore, the design of a recyclable imidazolium-based silica-supported organopalladium-functionalized heterogeneous catalyst to realize one-pot tandem Suzuki cross coupling-reduction of haloacetophenones and arylboronic acids to prepare a range of biaryl alcohols is highly desirable.

As an effort to develop highly efficient heterogeneous catalysts, [20 - 25] in this contribution, we utilize the benefits of an imidazolium-based organic-inorganic hybrid silica (IBOIHS) and develop an organopalladium-functionalized heterogeneous catalyst PdPPh$_2$-IBOIHS (3), consisting of uniformly distributive, well-defined confined organopalladium active species within its imidazolium-based silicate network. As expected, the imidazolium functionality and the well-defined confined organopalladium active species within IBOIHS can promote synergistically its catalytic performance. As presented in this study, the heterogeneous catalyst exhibits a high efficiency in the one-pot tandem Suzuki cross coupling-reduction of haloacetophenones and arylboronic acids, providing a range of biaryl alcohols with high yields. Furthermore, the heterogeneous catalyst can be readily recycled and reused repeatedly at least six times without reducing obviously its reactivity.

2. Experimental

Characterization. Pd loading amounts in the catalyst was analyzed using an inductively coupled plasma optical emission spectrometer (ICP, Varian VISTA-MPX). Fourier transform infrared (FT-IR) spectra were collected on a Nicolet Magna 550 spectrometer using KBr method. X-ray powder diffraction (XRD) was carried out on a Rigaku D/Max-RB diffractometer with CuKα radiation. Scanning electron microscopy (SEM) images were obtained using a JEOL JSM-6380LV microscope operating at 20 kV. Transmission electron microscopy (TEM) images were performed on a JEOL JEM 2010 electron microscope at an acceleration voltage of 220 kV. X-ray photoelectron spectroscopy (XPS) measurements were performed on a Perkin-Elmer PHI 5000 C ESCA system. All the binding energies were calibrated by using the contaminant carbon (C_{1s} = 284. 6 eV) as a reference. Nitrogen adsorption isotherms were measured at 77 K with a Quantachrome Nova 4000 analyzer. The samples were measured after being outgassed at 423 K overnight. Pore size distributions were calculated by using the BJH model. The specific surface areas (S_{BET}) of samples were determined from the linear parts of BET plots (p/p_0 = 0. 05 — 1. 00). Solid-state [13] C (100. 5 MHz), [29] Si (79. 4 MHz) and [31] P

(169. 3 MHz) CP/MAS NMR were obtained on a Bruker DRX-400 spectrometer.

Preparation of PdPPh$_2$-IBOIHS (3). A typical procedure was as follows: under argon atmosphere, to a stirred suspension of IBOIHS (1) (1. 0 g) in 20. 0 mL of dry toluene was added a solution of PdCl$_2$ [PPh$_2$(CH$_2$)$_2$ Si(OEt)$_3$]$_2$(2) (0. 19 g, 0. 20 mmol) in 5. 0 mL of dry toluene at room temperature. The resulting mixture was refluxed for 24 h. After cooling to room temperature, the volatiles were removed in vacuum and 50 mL of water was added. Then the residues were filtrated and washed twice with 50 mL of water and 50 mL of CH$_2$Cl$_2$. After Soxhlet extraction in dry CH$_2$Cl$_2$ to remove homogeneous and unreacted start materials, the solid was dried under reduced pressure overnight to afford the catalyst (3) (1. 08 g) as a brown powder. ICP analysis showed that the Pd loading-amount was 8. 48 mg (0. 08 mmol) per gram catalyst. IR (KBr) cm^{-1}: 3430. 5 (s), 3148. 0 (w), 3095. 1 (w), 2934. 5 (w), 1634. 9 (w), 1565. 7 (m), 1448. 9 (w), 1411. 3 (w), 1351. 9 (w), 1245. 5 (w), 1132. 4 (s), 1051. 2 (s), 921. 7 (m), 762. 9 (w), 702. 2 (w), 478. 8 (w); ^{13}C CP/MAS (100. 5 MHz): 9. 4 (SiCH$_2$CH$_2$CH$_2$N), 23. 9 (SiCH$_2$CH$_2$CH$_2$N), 28. 3, 19. 2 (PCH$_2$), 51. 7 (SiCH$_2$CH$_2$CH$_2$N), 123. 0 (CH of imidazolium) 129. 1 (CH-Ph), 135. 8 (CH of imidazolium) ppm; ^{29} Si MAS/NMR (79. 4 MHz): T^1($\delta=-50. 9$ ppm), T^2($\delta=-59. 5$ ppm), T^3($\delta=-69. 0$ ppm); ^{31} P CP/MAS (169. 3 MHz): 10. 4 ppm.

General procedure for one-pot tandem reactions. A typical procedure was as follows. Catalyst 3 (25. 00 mg, 2. 00 μmol of Pd based on ICP analysis), ketones (0. 10 mmol), and arylboronic acid (0. 12 mmol), NaOH (12. 0 mg, 0. 30 mmol) and 4. 0 mL i-PrOH were added sequentially to a 10. 0 mL round-bottom flask. The mixture was then stirred at 82℃ for 12 h. During this period, the reaction was monitored constantly by TLC. After completion of the reaction, the catalyst was separated by centrifugation (10,000 rpm) for the recycling experiment. The aqueous solution was extracted with ethyl ether (3 × 3. 0 mL). The combined ethyl ether extracts were washed with brine twice and then dehydrated with Na_2SO_4. After evaporation of ethyl ether, the residue was purified by silica gel flash column chromatography to afford the desired products.

3. Results and discussion

3. 1 *Synthesis and structural characterization of the heterogeneous catalyst* **3**

The organopalladium-functionalized heterogeneous catalyst, abbreviated as $PdPPh_2$-IBOIHS(3)[$PdPPh_2$: [26, 27]], was prepared as outlined in Scheme 1. Firstly, the imidazolium-based IBOIHS (1) was synthesized *via* the hydrolysis-condensation of 1, 3-bis(3-(triethoxysilyl) propyl)-1 *H*-imidazol-3-ium iodide according to the reported method [28, 29]. The directly postgrafting bis[(diphenylphosphino) ethyltriethoxysilane)] palladium dichloride (2) onto IBOIHS did then afford the rude $PdPPh_2$-functionalized IBOIHS. Finally, the pure catalyst 3 was obtained successfully by thoroughly Soxhlet extraction to clean of rude catalyst, obtaining its pure form as a brown powder (see SI in Figs. S1 – S4).

Incorporation of well-defined site-single $PdPPh_2$-functionality within its IBOIHS silicate network could be proven by solid-state ^{13}C cross-polarization (CP)/magic angle spinning (MAS) NMR spectroscopy. As shown in Fig. 1, catalyst 3 produced strong carbon signals of $SiC\underline{H}_2 \, \underline{C}H_2\underline{C}H_2$ N (at 9. 4, 23. 9 and 51. 7 ppm) and of N$\underline{C}$HCHN$\underline{C}$HN groups (at 123. 0 and 135. 8 ppm), corresponding to the propyl and imidazolium moiety as the IBOIHS main network. Characteristic carbon atoms of -$\underline{C}H_2$ P$\underline{C}_6$ H_5 groups in catalyst 3 could be observed clearly at 28. 3, 129. 1 ppm that were marked in its spectrum, respectively. These peaks were absent in the spectrum of 1, suggesting the successful incorporation 2 in its IBOIHS silicate network. Chemical shifts of 3 were strongly similar to those of its homogeneous counterpart 2 (see SI in Fig. S2), demonstrating that both had the same well-defined single-site active species that could be further confirmed by ^{31}P CP MAS spectra (see SI in Fig. S3) [26]. In addition, its solid-state ^{29}Si MAS NMR spectrum further revealed its

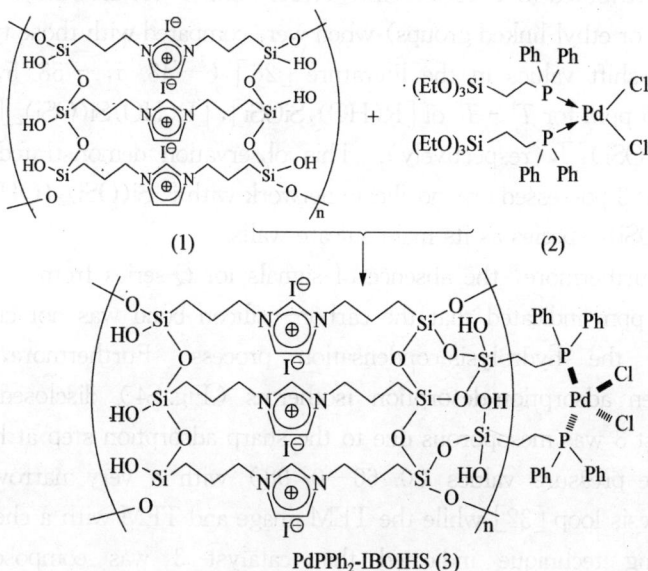

Scheme 1. Preparation of the heterogeneous catalysts.

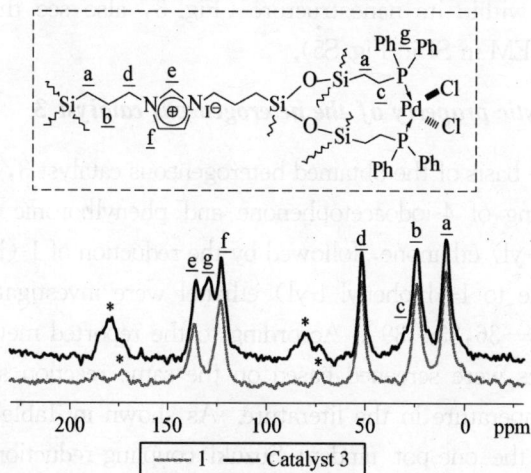

Fig. 1 ^{13}C CP MAS NMR spectra of the IBOIHS (1) and catalyst 3.

organosilicate network as shown in Fig. 2. It was found that catalyst 3 produced one group of exclusive T signals derived from organosilica, suggesting that all Si species were covalently attached to carbon atoms [30,31]. Strong T signals at -59.5 and -69.0 ppm in the spectrum of 3 are attributed to T^2(R-Si(OSi)$_2$(OH)] and T^3(R-Si(OSi)$_3$) (R= propyl or ethyl-linked groups) when were compared with those typical isomer shift values in the literature [26] (-48.5, -58.5, and -67.5 ppm for T^1 - T^3 of [R(HO)$_2$SiOSi], [R(HO)Si(OSi)$_2$], and [RSi(OSi)$_3$], respectively). This observation demonstrated that catalyst 3 possessed organosilicate network with R-Si(OSi)$_2$(OH) and R-Si(OSi)$_3$ species as its main silicate walls.

Furthermore, the absence of signals for Q-series from -90 to -120 ppm indicated that the carbon—silicon bond was not cleaved during the hydrolysis-condensation process. Furthermore, the nitrogen adsorption-desorption isotherms (Fig. S4) disclosed that catalyst 3 was mesoporous due to the sharp adsorption step at higher relative pressure values (0.60—0.98) with a very narrow H1 hysteresis loop [32] while the TEM image and TEM with a chemical mapping technique indicated that catalyst 3 was composed of micrometer particles and the palladium centers were uniformly distributive within its nanostructure (Fig. 3, also see the enlarged SEM and TEM in SI in Fig. S5).

3.2 Catalytic property of the heterogeneous catalyst 3

On the basis of the obtained heterogeneous catalyst 3, the Suzuki cross-coupling of 4-iodoacetophenone and phenylboronic acid to 1-(biphenyl-4-yl) ethanone, followed by the reduction of 1-(biphenyl-4-yl) ethanone to 1-(biphenyl-4-yl) ethanol were investigated at first [18—19,33—36,33—39]. According to the reported method [18], several bases were screened based on the same reaction solvent and reaction temperature in the literature. As shown in Table 1, it was found that the one-pot tandem Suzuki coupling-reduction reactions with weak bases including Cs_2CO_3, K_2CO_3, Na_2CO_3, K_2PO_4 and KF only afforded the side-products of Suzuki cross-coupling. No reductive products could be observed in these cases (entries 1 – 5). Whilst the reactions with the strong basic conditions, the one-pot tandem Suzuki coupling-reduction reactions enabled to transfer 1-(biphenyl-4-yl) ethanone to 1-(biphenyl-4-yl) ethanol from the reaction of 4-iodoacetophenone and phenylboronic acid, but the reactions with *t*-BuOK and KOH as bases afforded a mixture of 1-(biphenyl-4-yl) ethanone and 1-(biphenyl-4-yl) ethanol (entries 6-7). Interestingly, only in the case of NaOH as a base, the reaction could give the clean product of 1-(biphenyl-4-yl) ethanol with 99% yield (entry 8), which only tiny biphenyl produced *via* the self-coupling of phenylboronic acid were observed due to the slightly excess phenylboronic acid. Furthermore, the optimization of substrate-to-catalyst mole ratio disclosed 2.0 mol% of 3 as catalyst is the optimal amount of heterogeneous catalyst (entries 8 – 10). As a result, the one-pot tandem Suzuki coupling-reduction reaction with 2.0 mmol% 3 as a catalyst, NaOH as a base, *i*-PrOH as a hydrogen resource and solvent at 82℃ was determined as an optimal reaction condition.

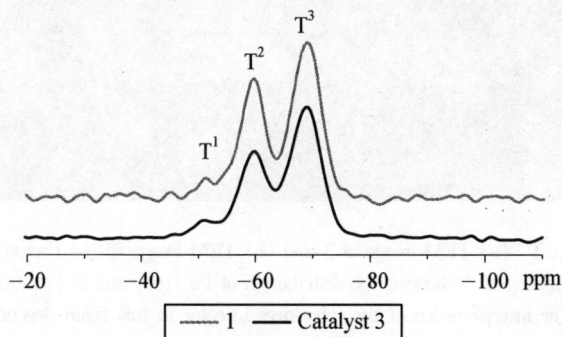

Fig. 2 ^{29}Si CP MAS NMR spectra of the IBOIHS (1) and catalyst 3.

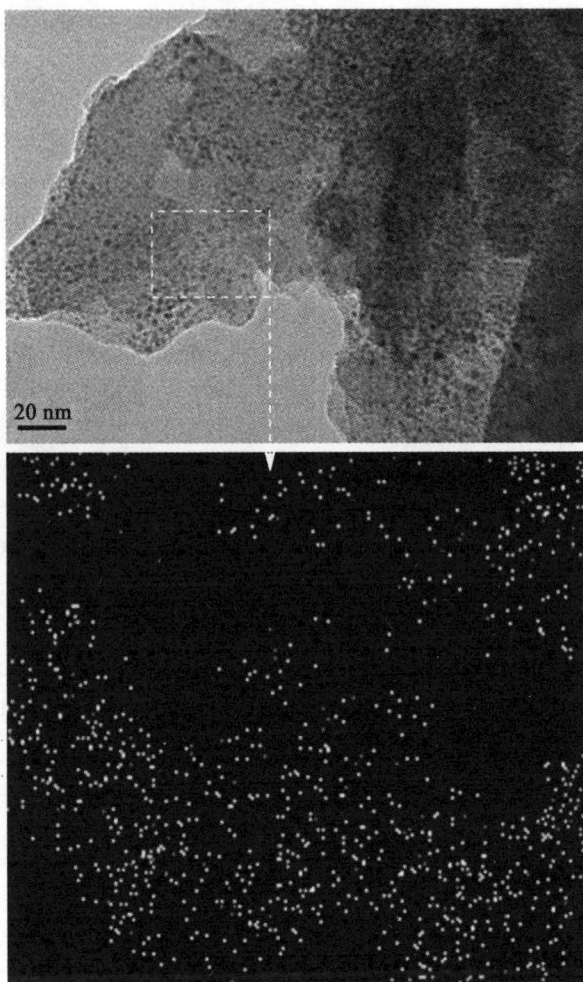

Fig. 3 (a) TEM image of 3 and (b) TEM image with a chemical mapping of 3 showing the distribution of Pd (red) and Si (white). (For interpretation of the references to color in this figure legend, the reader is referred to the web version of this article.)

Based on the clean one-pot tandem Suzuki coupling-reduction reaction in above optimal reaction condition, it provided an opportunity to investigate its reaction time course from the reaction of 4-iodoacetophenone and phenylboronic acid catalyzed by catalyst 3. As shown in Fig. 4, it was found that the Pd-catalyzed Suzuki cross-coupling of 4-iodophenylethanol and phenylboronic acid processes at first, which is fast as seen by the formation of 1-(biphenyl-4-yl) ethanone (B) in a maximum conversion of 77% after 1.0 h of reaction. Subsequently, the reduction of 1-(biphenyl-4-yl) ethanone occurs smoothly with 2-propanol as a hydrogen resource, providing the target product of 1-(biphenyl-4-yl) ethanol (C). This behavior is obviously differed from that observed in our previous report, in which one-pot tandem Suzuki coupling-reduction reaction with the reduction at first, and then followed by Suzuki cross-coupling reaction [25]. Therefore, the different reaction sequence disclosed the inherent role of different reaction conditions in a similar tandem reaction.

Having established that catalyst 3 enabled to catalyze steadily the Suzuki cross-coupling reaction followed by transfer hydro genation reaction of 4-iodoacetophenone and phenylboronic acid to give the clean 1-(biphenyl-4-yl) ethanol, we further inves tigated its general applications in the one-pot tandem Suzuki coupling-reduction reactions with different arylboronic acids. As shown in Table 2, in general, a variety of arylboronic acids were smoothly reacted with 4-iodoacetophenone to afford the clean products in desirable yields (entries 3 - 8). Notably, high cat-alytic performance should be due to the well-defined single-site organopalladium catalytic nature validated by its ^{13}C CP/MAS NMR. Further, evidence supporting this view came from an X-ray photo-electron spectroscopy (XPS) investigation. As shown in Fig. 5, XPS investigation showed that catalysts 3 had the similar Pd $3d^{5/2}$ elec tron binding energy to its homogenous counterpart 2 (337.61 *versus* 337.62 eV). This observation demons-trated that catalyst 3 retained the original coordinated environment of its homogeneous counter-part 2. In addition, it was also found that the one-pot tandem Suzuki coupling-reduction reaction of 4-bromoacetophenone and phenyl boronic acid could afford the products with desirable yield (entry 2). Interestingly, the one-pot tandem Suzuki cross coupling-reduction could also be used toward the synthesis of biaryldiols, in which the reaction of 4-iodoacetophenone and (4-acetylphenyl) boronic acid afforded a 1,1'([1,1'-biphenyl]-4, 4'-diyl) diethanol in 99% yield (entry 9).

Table 1   **Optimization of reaction condition in the tandem Suzuki-coupling/transfer hydrogenation of 4-iodoacetophenone and phenylboronic acid.** [a]

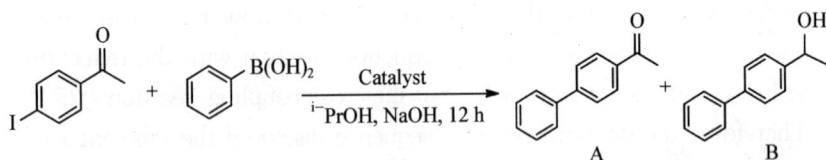

Entry	Base	Yield A (%)[b]	Yield B (%)[b]
1	Cs_2CO_3	99	nd
2	K_2CO_3	97	nd
3	Na_2CO_3	55	nd
4	K_3PO_4	95	nd
5	KF	66	nd
6	t-BuOK	35	65
7	KOH	22	78
8	NaOH	Trace	99
9	NaOH	Trace	95[c]
10	NaOH	Trace	99[d]

[a] Reaction conditions: catalyst 3 (25.00 mg, 2.00 μmol of Pd based on the ICP analysis), base (0.30 mmol), 4-iodoacetophenone (0.10 mmol), phenylboronic acid (0.12 mmol), and 4.0 mL of 2-propanol, reaction temperature (82℃), reaction time 12 h.

[b] Determined by ^{1}H-NMR spectra.

[c] Data were obtained using 1.8 mol% of catalyst 3.

[d] Data were obtained using 2.2 mol% of catalyst 3.

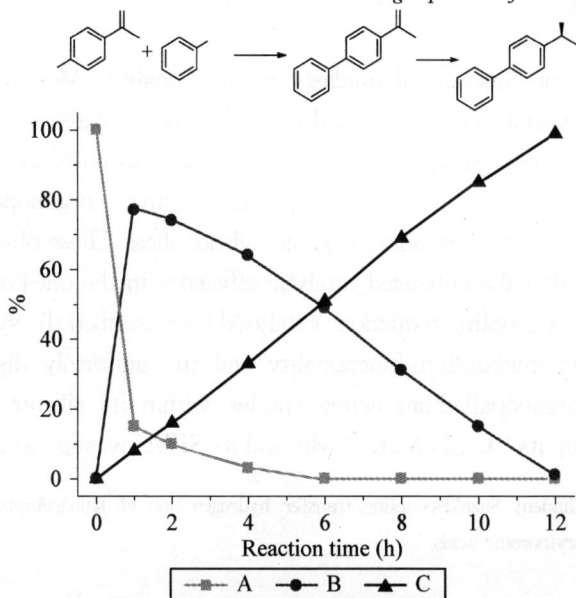

Fig. 4   Time course of the transformation of 4-iodoacetophenone and phenylboronic acid with catalyst 3 (reactions were carried out at 82℃ at substrate-to-catalyst mole ratio of 50 in 4. 0 mL of 2-propanol).

It is noteworthy that this one-pot tandem reaction catalyzed by catalyst 3 presented higher yield than that of its homo geneous counterpart 2 (entry 1 *versus* entry 1 in bracket), suggesting the uniformly distributive palladium species within the imidazolium-based silicate network in catalyst 3 could promote efficiently catalytic performance. To gain better insight into the role of the uniformly distributive palladium species during the catalytic process and the nature of imidazolium-functionality within IBOIHS network, a kinetic profile of the tandem Suzuki cross coupling-reduction of 4-iodoacetophenone and phenylboronic acid catalyzed by 3, by its homogeneous counterpart 2, and by the mixed IBOIHS (1) and 2 were investigated. As shown in Fig. 6, it was found that the initial TOF values of 3, the mixed IBOIHS (1) plus 2, and 2 were 4. 0, 2. 5 and 1. 5 mol/(mol h), respectively. As observed, the reactivity with the mixed IBOIHS (1) and 2 as a catalyst was higher than that obtained with 2, disclosing the function of imidazolium-functionality. Meanwhile, the reactivity with 3 as a catalyst had more than twice increase of reaction rate relative to 2, suggesting both benefits of function of imidazolium-functionality and of uniformly distributive organopalladium-functionality within organic-inorganic hybrid silica. These observations confirmed that the enhanced catalytic efficiency in the one-pot tandem Suzuki cross coupling-reductions catalyzed by 3 ascribed the synergistic role of the imidazolium-functionality and the uniformly distributive confined organopalladium active species within its silicate network validated by its ^{13}C CP/MAS NMR and its SEM investigation.

Table 2   **Tandem Suzuki-coupling/transfer hydrogenation of haloacetophenones and arylboronic acids.** [a]

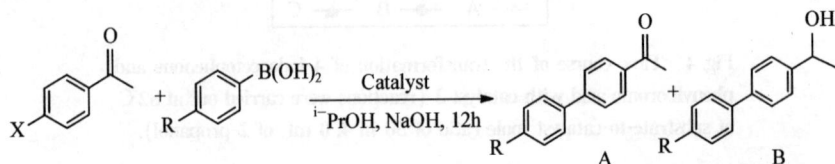

Entry	X	R	Yield A (%)[b]	Yield B (%)[b]
1	I	H	nd (20)[c]	99 (80)[c]
2	Br	H	Trace	94
3	I	4-F	Trace	85
4	I	4-Cl	Trace	90
5	I	4-OCH$_3$	Trace	92
6	I	4-CF$_3$	Trace	98
7	I	4-NO$_2$	nd	99
8	I	4-CN	nd	99
9	I	4-COCH$_3$	nd	99

[a] Reaction conditions: catalyst 3 (25.0 mg, 2.0 mol%, 2.00 μmol of Pd based on the ICP analysis), NaOH (0.30 mmol), 4-haloacetophenone (0.10 mmol), arylboronic acids (0.12 mmol), and 4.0 mL of 2-propanol, reaction temperature (82℃), reaction time 12 h.

[b] Determined by ^{1}H-NMR spectra (see SI in Fig. S8).

[c] Data in the bracket were obtained using its homogenous counterpart 2 as a catalyst.

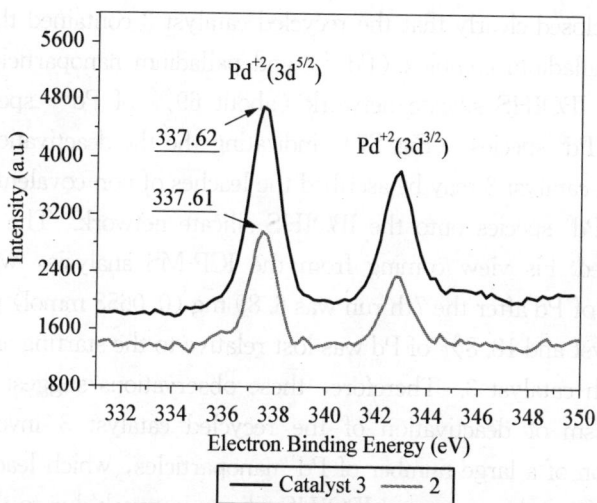

Fig. 5 XPS spectra of catalyst 3 and its homogeneous counterpart 2.

An important feature in design of any heterogeneous catalyst is that that catalyst could be recovered and the recycled catalyst still retains its reactivity after multiple cycles. Remarkably, catalyst 3 was recovered easily and reused repeatedly when one-pot tandem Suzuki cross coupling-reduction of 4-iodoacetophenone and phenylboronic acid was chosen as a model reaction. It was found that, in six consecutive reactions, the recycled catalyst 3 did still afford the desirable product with 95% yield (see SI in Table S1). However, the reactivity of the recycled catalyst 3 dropped sharply in seventh run, where only 76% yield could be obtained. In order to explore the nature of the deactivation of the recycled catalyst 3, the TEM image and XPS spectrum after the 7th run were further investigated (Figs. S6-S7). The TEM image of the recycled catalyst 3 showed that the palladium-functionality was still dispersed and no obvious aggregation onto IBOIHS silicate network could be observed (Fig. S6), suggesting that the deactivation of the recycled catalyst 3 came possibly from the other factors rather than the aggregations of palladium species. The XPS data disclosed clearly that the recycled catalyst 3 contained the mixed organopalladium complex (Pd^{+2}) and palladium nanoparticle (Pd^0) onto its IBOIHS silicate network (about 69% of Pd^{2+} species and 31% of Pd^0 species) (Fig. S7), indicating the the deactivation of the recycled catalyst 3 may be ascribed the leaches of non-covalent absorption of Pd^0 species onto the IBOIHS silicate network. The evidence supported this view coming from the ICP-MS analysis, where the amount of Pd after the 7th run was 6.89 mg (0.0658 mmol) per gram of catalyst and 18.8% of Pd was lost relative to the starting amount of the fresh catalyst 3. Therefore, these observations suggest that the mechanism of deactivation of the recycled catalyst 3 involves the formation of a large number of Pd^0 nanoparticles, which leads to Pd-leaches from the supported IBOIHS silicate network due to their non-covalent physical absorption interactions. Also, in order to explore its recyclability, another attempt through a continuous-flow synthesis was investigated as shown in Fig. 7 [40]. In this case, 4-iodoacetophenone (1.00 mmol) and phenylboronic acid (1.20 mmol) completely dissolved in a diluted aqueous solution of sodium hydroxide in *i*-PrOH (20 mL), while the X-Cube (ThalesNano) instrument was equipped with the packed bed reactor containing the heterogeneous catalyst 3 (500 mg of catalyst was filled this bed reactor, 0.6 mL volume, 70 mm × 4 mm). The reaction parameters/temperature (80 ℃), 0.1 mL/min flow rate were selected on the flow reactor, and processing was started, whereby only a diluted aqueous solution of sodium hydroxide in *i*-PrOH without 4-iodoacetophenone and phenylboronic acid was pumped through the system until the instrument had achieved the desired reaction parameters and stable processing was assured. During the desired reaction parameters and stable processing was observed, the freshly prepared reaction mixture was pumped. After processing through the flow reactor, the product was obtained. The result showed that the product of 1-(biphenyl-4-yl) ethanol in a 91% yield with respect to 4-iodoacetophenone was obtained, which offer a potential application in an industrial interest.

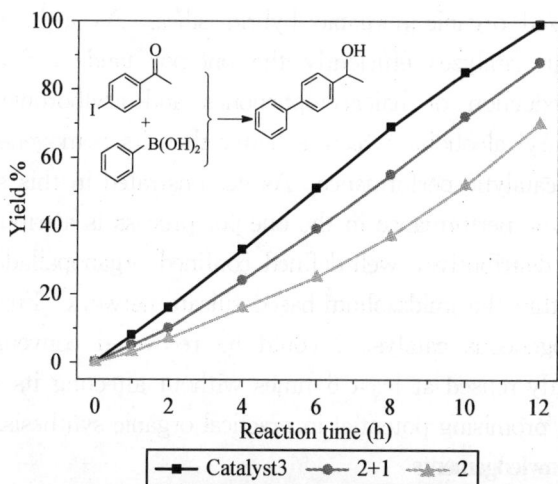

Fig. 6 Comparison of tandem reaction catalyzed by catalyst 3, its homogeneous counterpart 2, and the mixed IBOIHS (1) and 2. Reactions were carried out at 82℃ at substrate-to-catalyst mole ratio of 50 in 4. 0 mL of 2-propanol.

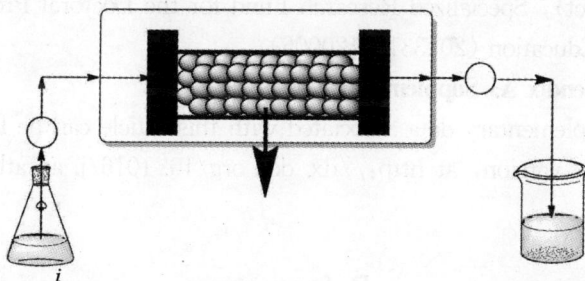

Fig. 7 Schematic of continuous flow process for the tandem Suzuki-coupling/transfer hydrogenation of 4-iodoacetophenone and phenylboronic acid.

4. Conclusions

In conclusion, we take advantage of benefit of imidazolium-functionality to develop an imidazolium-based organopalladium-functionalized organic-inorganic hybrid silica. As a heterogeneous catalyst, it catalyzes efficiently the one-pot tandem Suzuki cross coupling-reduction of haloacetophenones and arylboronic acids to prepare biaryl alcohols, which is better than its homogeneous counterpart in catalytic performance. As demonstrated in this study, the high catalytic performance in the one-pot process is attributed to the uniformly distributive, well-defined confined organopalladium active species within the imidazolium-based silicate network. Furthermore, the heterogeneous catalyst 3 could be recovered conveniently and subsequently reused at least 6 times without affecting its reactivity, showing a promising potential in practical organic synthesis.

Acknowledgements

We are grateful to China National Natural Science Foundation (21402120), the Shanghai Sciences and Technologies Development Fund (13ZR1458700 and 12nm 0500500), the Shanghai Municipal Education Commission (14YZ074, 13CG48, Young Teacher Training Project), Specialized Research Fund for the Doctoral Program of Higher Education (20133127120006).

Appendix A. Supplementary data

Supplementary data associated with this article can be found, in the online version, at http://dx. doi. org/10. 1016/j. apcatb. 2015. 03. 024.

References

[1] L. Tietze, G. Brasche, K. Gericke, Domino Reactions in Organic Synthesis, Wiley-VCH, Weinheim, 2006.

[2] G. Posner, Chem. Rev. 86(1986)831.

[3] C. Grondal, M. Jeanty, D. Enders, Nat. Chem. 2(2010)167.

[4] L. Albrecht, H. Jiang, K. Jørgensen, Angew. Chem. Int. Ed. 50(2011) 8492.

[5] C. Vaxelaire, P. Winter, M. Christmann, Angew. Chem. Int. Ed. 50(2011)

3605.

[6] F. Kleitz, Handbook of Asymmetric Heterogeneous Catalysis, Wiley-VCH, Weinheim, 2008, pp. 178.

[7] H. Zou, S. Wu, J. Shen, Chem. Rev. 108(2008)3893.

[8] J. Dupont, R. de Souza, P. Suarez, Chem. Rev. 102(2002)3667.

[9] B. Karimi, M. Gholinejad, M. Khorasani, Chem. Commun. 48(2012)8961.

[10] B. Karimi, D. Elhamifar, O. Yari, M. Khorasani, H. Vali, J. Clark, A. Hunt, Chem. Eur. J. 18(2012)13520.

[11] P. Borah, X. Ma, K. Nguyen, Y. Zhao, Angew. Chem. Int. Ed. 51(2012) 7756.

[12] M. Waki, N. Mizoshita, T. Tani, S. Inagaki, Angew. Chem. Int. Ed. 50 (2011)11667.

[13] M. Guan, W. Wang, E. Henderson, Ö. Dag, C. Kübel, V. Chakravadhanula, J. Rinck, I. Moudrakovski, J. Thomson, J. McDowell, A. Powell, H. Zhang, G. Ozin, J. Am. Chem. Soc. 134(2012)8439.

[14] M. Mandal, M. Kruk, Chem. Mater. 24(2012)123.

[15] A. Suzuki, Pure Appl. Chem. 57(1985)1749.

[16] N. Miyaura, A. Suzuki, Chem. Rev. 95(1995)2457.

[17] R. Malacea, R. Poli, E. Manoury, Coord. Chem. Rev. 254(2010)729.

[18] A. Zanardi, J. Mata, E. Peris, J. Am. Chem. Soc. 131(2009)14531.

[19] S. Gonell, M. Poyatos, J. Mata, E. Peris, Organometallics 31(2012)5606.

[20] W. Xiao, R. Jin, T. Cheng, D. Xia, H. Yao, F. Gao, B. Deng, G. Liu, Chem. Commun. 48(2012)11898.

[21] D. Xia, T. Cheng, W. Xiao, K. Liu, Z. Wang, G. Liu, H. Li, W. Wang, ChemCatChem 5(2013)1784.

[22] R. Liu, R. Jin, L. Kong, J. Wang, C. Chen, T. Cheng, G. Liu, Chem. Asian J. 8(2013)3108.

[23] G. Liu, J. Wang, T. Huang, X. Liang, Y. Zhang, H. Li, J. Mater. Chem. 20(2010)1970.

[24] D. Zhang, X. Gao, T. Cheng, G. Liu, Sci. Rep. 4(2014)5091.

[25] D. Zhang, J. Xu, Q. Zhao, T. Cheng, G. Liu, ChemCatChem 6 (2014) 2998.

[26] O. Kröcher, O. Köppel, M. Fröba, A. Baiker, J. Catal. 178(1998)284.

[27] N. Linares, A. Sepúlveda, M. Pacheco, J. Berenguer, E. Lalinde, C. Nájera, J. Garcia-Martinez, New J. Chem. 35(2011)225.

[28] V. Polshettiwar, R. Varma, Tetrahedron 64(2008)4637.

[29] B. Karimi, A. Maleki, D. Elhamifar, J. Clark, A. Hunt, Chem. Commun. 46(2010)6947.

[30] S. Inagaki, S. Guan, T. Ohsuna, O. Terasaki, Nature 416(2002)304.

[31] X. Yang, F. Zhu, J. Huang, F. Zhang, H. Li, Chem. Mater. 21(2009) 4925.

[32] F. Fakhfakh, L. Baraket, A. Ghorbel, J. M. Fraile, C. Herrerías, J. Mayoral, J. Mol. Catal. A: Chem. 32(2010)21.

[33] E. Burda, W. Hummel, H. Gröger, Angew. Chem. Int. Ed. 47(2008) 9551.

[34] V. Gauchot, W. Kroutil, A. Schmitzer, Chem. Eur. J. 16(2010)6748.

[35] E. Burda, W. Bauer, W. Hummel, H. Gröger, ChemCatChem 2(2010)67.

[36] A. Prastaro, P. Ceci, E. Chiancone, A. Boffi, R. Cirilli, M. Colone, G. Fabrizi, A. Stringaroe, S. Cacchi, Green Chem. 11(2009)1929.

[37] A. R. Siamaki, A. E. R. S. Khder, V. Abdelsayed, M. S. El-Shall, B. F. Gupton, J. Catal. 279(2011)1.

[38] H. A. Elazab, A. R. Siamaki, S. Moussa, F. Gupton, M. S. El-Shall, Appl. Catal. A. 491(2015)58.

[39] F. Zhang, C. Kang, Y. Wei, H. Li, Adv. Funct. Mater. 21(2011)3189.

[40] I. I. Junior, M. C. Flores, F. K. Sutili, S. G. F. Leite, L. S. de, M. Miranda, I. C. R. Leal, R. O. M. A. de Souza, Org. Process Res. Dev. 16(2012) 1098.

(原载于 Applied Catalysis B Environmental 2015 年第 174 期)

Ru-Catalyzed Asymmetric Transfer Hydrogenation of α-Trifluoromethylimines

Meng Wu, Tanyu Cheng, Min Ji, and Guohua Liu

Key Laboratory of Resource Chemistry of Ministry of Education,
Shanghai Key Laboratory of Rare Earth Functional Materials,
Shanghai Normal University

Enantioselective transformation of strong electron-withdrawing acyclic α-trifluoromethylimines to α-trifluoromethylami-nes through a ruthenium-catalyzed asymmetric transfer hydrogenation has been developed. The method described here is a facile catalytic process with sodium formate as a hydrogen resource and water-dimethylformamide as a cosolvent. The benefit of this enantioselective transformation affords a series of chiral α-trifluoromethylamines with high yields and excellent enantioselectivities (93%—99% ee) under mild reaction conditions.

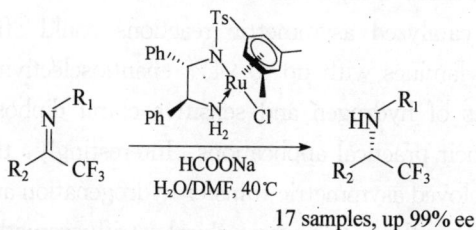

17 samples, up 99% ee

Since the pioneering works reported by Noyori, Ikariya, and co-workers on ruthenium (Ⅱ) (diphosphine) (diamine) di-chloride complexes for asymmetric hydrogenation of ketones and imines,[1] a large number of reviews and researches involving in n-sulfonylated 1,

2-diamines as chiral ligands both in asymmetric hydrogenation and in asymmetric transfer hydrogenation of ketones and imines are well-documented theoretically and practically.[2] Also, various catalytic reaction systems covering 2-propanol, formic acid-triethylamine, formic acid, and sodium formate as hydrogen resources have been explored in asymmetric transfer hydrogenation of ketones and imines.[3] Most prominent examples employ chiral N-sulfony-lated diamine-based η^5-Cp*-M complexes (η^5-Cp* = pentam ethyl cyclopentadiene series) and η^6-arene-M complexes (η^6-arene = aromatic ring series) (M=Ru, Rh, and Ir), which have been applied extensively to various asymmetric transfer hydrogenation of ketones and imine.[4] Although these fruitful achievements have been obtained, their applications in enantioselective transformation of trifluoromethylim-ines remain an unmet challenge.

Optically pure α-trifluoromethylamine, as an important number of biologically active motifs, has been attracting much interest in medical and fluorine chemistry.[5] Recently, besides the methods of diastereoselective reductive aminations and asymmetric addition,[6] the construction of chiral α-trifluoromethylamines through enantioselective reduction of achiral α-trifluoromethylimines had been explored by a few groups.[7] The first two successful examples utilized an asymmetric hydrogenation method reported by the Uneyama and Zhou groups,[7b-d] in which Pd-catalyzed asymmetric reactions could afford chiral α-trifluoromethylamines with up to 94% enantioselectivity. However, high pressures of hydrogen and sensitive chiral diphosphine ligands still limited their practical applications. Interestingly, the latter three examples employed asymmetric transfer hydrogenation and asymmetric hydrosilylation methods to prepare chiral α-trifluoromethyla-mines.[7e-g] As shown in Scheme 1, the Akiyama group[7e] used an asymmetric transfer hydrogenation method through the use of a chiral phosphoric acid as a catalyst and benzothiazoline as a hydrogen resource to provide chiral 4-methoxy-N-(2,2,2-trifluoro-1-phenylethyl)aniline with 96%

ee, while the Benaglia group[7f] utilized an asymmetric hydrosilylation method through the use of a chiral organocatalyst (picolinamide) as a catalyst to obtain 91% *ee* of chiral 4-methoxy-*N*-(2,2,2-trifluoro-1-phenylethyl) aniline. In particular, the Cahard group[7g] took advantage of the η^6-arene-Ru complex (chiral aminoalcohol/ [RuCl$_2$ (*p*-cymene)]$_2$) as a catalyst and 2-propanol as a hydrogen resource to enable enantioselective reduction of achiral 4-methoxy-*N*-(2,2,2-trifluoro-1-phenylethylidene) aniline to chiral 4-methoxy-*N*-(2,2,2-trifluoro-1-phenylethyl) aniline (93% *ee*) through an asymmetric transfer hydro-

(a) Akiyama group (ATH)

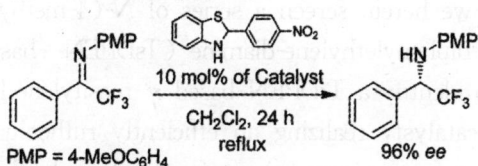
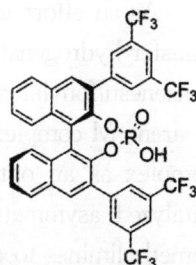

(b) Benaglia group (AHS)

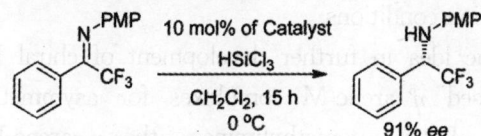
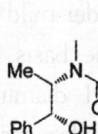

(c) Cahard group (ATH)

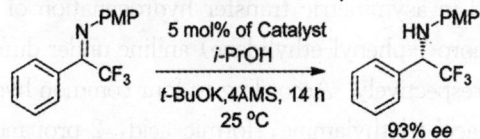
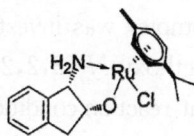

This work (ATH)

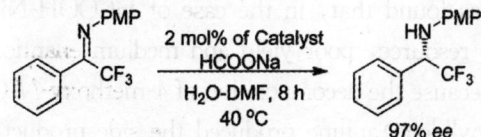
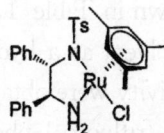

Scheme 1   Asymmetric Transfer Hydrogenation (ATH) and Asymmetric Hydrosilylation (AHS) of 4-Methoxy-*N*-(2,2,2-trifluoro-1-phenylethylidene)aniline

genation method. Although the above three examples had been presented successfully, the first two examples needed 10 mol % of catalyst to reach their enantioselective performances, while *ee* values in Ru-catalyzed asymmetric transfer hydrogenation with 5 mol % of catalyst in the last example needed to be further enhanced. Therefore, by utilizing chiral N-sulfonylated diamine-based catalysts, realization of highly efficient asymmetric transfer hydrogenation of α-trifluoromethylimines with a low catalyst's amount under mild reaction conditions is high desirable.

As an effort to develop highly efficient catalysts for asymmetric transfer hydrogenation,[8] we herein screen a series of N-(4-methyl) benzenesulfonylated 1, 2-diphenylethylene-diamine (TsDPEN)-based η^6-arene-M complexes to identify a TsDPEN-based η^6-mesitylene-Ru complex as an optimal catalyst, realizing an efficiently ruthenium-catalyzed asymmetric transfer hydrogenation of achiral aryltrifluoromethylimines to chiral aryltrifluoromethylamines with 2 mol % of catalyst under mild reaction conditions.

On the basis of the idea in further development of chiral N-sulfonylated diamine-based η^6-arene-M complexes for asymmetric transfer hydrogenation of trifluoromethylimines, the η^6-arene-Ru complex was investigated in asymmetric transfer hydrogenation of 4-methoxy-N-(2,2,2-trifluoro-1-phenyl-ethylidene) aniline under different reaction conditions, respectively. According to four common hydrogen resources, formic acid-triethylamine, formic acid, 2-propanol, and sodium formate, we screened its catalytic performance at first. As shown in Table 1, it was found that, in the case of HCOOH-NEt₃ cosolvent as a hydrogen resource, poor yield and medium enantioselectivity were obtained because the decomposition of 4-methoxy-N-(2, 2,2-trifluoro-1-phenylethylidene) aniline produced the side product of 2,2,2-trifluoro-1-phenylethanol (Table 1, entry 1).[7g] Similarly, the decomposition also existed in the case of HCOOH as a hydrogen resource (Table 1, entry 2). Differing from the above hydrogen resources, the asymmetric reaction with *i*-PrOH as a hydrogen resource had a high enantioselectivity (86% *ee*), but the yield was poor (Table 1, entry 3). To our delight, in the case of HCOONa as a hydrogen resource and water as a solvent that was inspired by the works of the Xiao and Deng groups on asymmetric transfer hydrogenation of quinolines and *N*-sulfonylimines,[9] we found that catalyst A could produce the desirable (s)-4-methoxy-*N*-(2, 2, 2-trifluoro-1-phenylethyl) aniline with 86% yield and 89% *ee* (Table 1, entry 4).

Table 1. Optimization of H Resource and Catalysts for Asymmetric Transfer Hydrogenation[a]

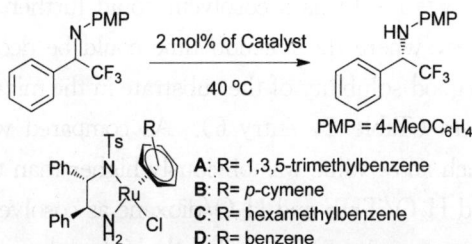

PMP = 4-MeOC₆H₄

A: R= 1,3,5-trimethylbenzene
B: R= *p*-cymene
C: R= hexamethylbenzene
D: R= benzene

entry	cat.	solvent and/or H resource	time (h)	yield (%)	*ee* (%)[b]
1	A	HCOOH-NEt₃	24	49	78
2	A	HCOOH	24	43	68
3	A	*i*-PrOH	24	38	86
4	A	H₂O-HCOONa	24	86	89
5	B	H₂O-HCOONa	24	83	86
6	C	H₂O-HCOONa	24	50	70
7	D	H₂O-HCOONa	24	10	57

[a] Reactions were performed with 4. 0 μmol of catalyst, 0. 20 mmol of 4-methoxy-*N*-(2,2,2-trifluoro-1-phenylethylidene)aniline in 2. 0 mL of solvent at 40℃. [b] Determined by HPLC.

On the basis of this finding, we further investigated the different η⁶-arene-Ru complexes in the asymmetric transfer hydrogenation of 4-methoxy-*N*-(2,2,2-trifluoro-1-phenyl-ethylidene) aniline using HCOONa as a hydrogen resource and water as a solvent. As shown in entries 5 ~ 7 of Table 1, it was found that catalyst A afforded the desirable products slightly higher than that of catalyst B (Table 1, entries 4 ~ 5), and markedly better than those of catalysts C and D (Table 1, entry 4 versus entries 6 ~ 7). Therefore, (S, S)-TsPDEN/ [RuCl$_2$(mesitylene)]$_2$ (A) was identified as an optimal catalyst through the use of HCOONa as a hydrogen resource and water as a solvent.

Due to poor solubility of substrates, optimization of cosolvent using A as a catalyst was further attempted. As shown Table 2, it was found that the enantioselectivity of the asymmetric reaction with H$_2$O/DMF (v/v=1 : 1) as a cosolvent could further enhance from 89% to 97% *ee*, where the reaction time could be decreased to 8 h because of the good-solubility of the substrate in the mixed H$_2$O/DMF cosolvent system (Table 2, entry 6). As compared with the other cosolvents, such an *ee* value was obviously higher than those obtained with the mixed H$_2$O/THF and H$_2$O/dioxane as cosolvents (Table 2, entry 6 versus entries 1 ~ 2), and slightly higher than those obtained with the others (Table 2, entry 6 versus entries 3 ~ 5). Therefore, the mixed H$_2$O/DMF (v/v=1 : 1) was identified as an optimal cosolvent. As a comprehensive result, the asymmetric reaction with 2.0 mmol % of A as a catalyst, HCOONa as a hydrogen resource, and H$_2$O/DMF (v/v=1 : 1) as a cosolvent at 40°C was determined as the optimal reaction condition.

Table 2. Optimization of Cosolvent for Asymmetric Transfer Hydrogenation[a]

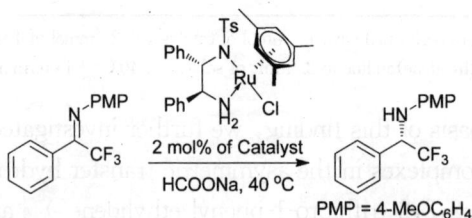

entry	cat.	cosolvent	time (h)	yield (%)	ee (%)[b]
1	A	H_2O/THF(1 : 1)	24	70	54
2	A	H_2O/dioxane(1 : 1)	24	88	nd
3	A	H_2O/i-PrOH(1 : 1)	24	40	96
4	A	H_2O/DMA(1 : 1)	8	91	93
5	A	H_2O/DMSO(1 : 1)	8	92	96
6	A	H_2O/DMF(1 : 1)	8	93	97

[a] Reactions were performed with 4. 0 μmol of catalyst, 0. 20 mmol of 4-methoxy-N-(2,2,2-trifluoro-1-phenylethylidene)aniline, 1. 0 mmol of HCOONa in 2. 0 mL of cosolvent at 40℃. [b] Determined by HPLC.

Having established that catalyst A enabled a highly efficient asymmetric transfer hydrogenation of 4-methoxy-N-(2,2,2-trifluoro-1-phenylethylidene) aniline, we further investigated its general applicability to prepare chiral aryltrifluoromethylamines with a series of aryl-substituted substrates. As shown in Table 3, in general, high yields, no intermediate products, and excellent enantioselectivities were obtained under the optimal reaction conditions for all tested substrates. It is noteworthy that the structures and electronic properties of substituents in the aromatic ring at the R_2 group did not affect significantly their enantioselectivities; that is, various electron-withdrawing and electron-donating substituents in the Ar moiety at the R_2 group were equally efficient (entries 2 – 9). However, the slight effects on yields could be observed, in which electron-withdrawing substituents in the Ar moiety at the R_2 group had slightly higher yields than those of electron-donating substituents (entries 2 – 6 versus entries 7 – 9). In addition, the thienyl-substituted substrate could be also converted to the corresponding chiral products with excellent enantioselectivity (Table 2, entry 10). Moreover, besides the general p-methoxyphenyl (PMP) protection group, other protection groups, such as p-tolyl, Ph, and naphthyl, could also be expanded to the asymmetric transfer hydrogenation, providing the desirable chiral aryltrifluoromethylamines with high enantioselectivities (entries 11 ~ 17).

Table 3. **Substrate Scope for Ru-Catalyzed Asymmetric Transfer Hydrogenation of α-Trifluoromethylimines**[a]

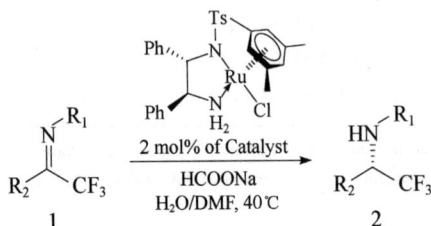

entry	R_1, R_2	2	time (h)	yield (%)	ee (%)[b]
1	PMP, Ph	2a	8	93	97
2	PMP, 4-FC$_6$H$_4$	2b	8	91	97
3	PMP, 4-ClC$_6$H$_4$	2c	8	90	99
4	PMP, 4-BrC$_6$H$_4$	2d	8	88	95
5	PMP, 3-BrC$_6$H$_4$	2e	8	94	95
6	PMP, 4-CF$_3$C$_6$H$_4$	2f	5	93	97
7	PMP, 4-MeC$_6$H$_4$	2g	17	75	96
8	PMP, 4-MeOC$_6$H$_4$	2h	9	87	98
9	PMP, 2-MeOC$_6$H$_4$	2i	8	82	93
10	PMP, 2-thienyl	2j	20	70	97
11	4-MeC$_6$H$_4$, Ph	2k	8	88	95
12	4-MeC$_6$H$_4$, 4-FC$_6$H$_4$	2l	8	93	94
13	4-MeC$_6$H$_4$, 4-BrC$_6$H$_4$	2m	8	89	95
14	Ph, Ph	2n	8	94	96
15	4-ClPh, Ph	2o	8	91	95
16	1-naphthyl, Ph	2p	12	89	96
17	2-naphthyl, Ph	2q	9	90	99

[a] Reactions were performed with 4. 0 μmol of catalyst D, 0. 20 mmol of α-trifluoromethylimines, 1. 0 mmol of HCOONa in 2. 0 mL of water/ DMF (v/v=1/1) at 40℃.
[b] Determined by HPLC.

As mentioned in the part of the Introduction, chiral 2, 2, 2-trifluoro-1-phenylethanamine as an important synthetic motif could be converted to various optically pure biologically active molecules in medical and fluorine chemistry.[5] In this case, in order to obtain optically pure 2, 2, 2-trifluoro-1-phenylethanamine, we attempted to remove the PMP protection group of the hydrogenated product (S)-4-methoxy-*N*-(2,2,2-trifluoro-1-phenylethyl) aniline. Among those reported methods,[6c, 7d, g, 10] it was found that the use of an equivalent of HIO_4 and H_2SO_4 in the cosolvent of $MeCN/H_2O$ (v : v=1 : 1) as a reaction condition could afford the best result,[7g] where the PMP protection group of (S)-4-methoxy-*N*-(2,2,2-trifluoro-1-phenylethyl) aniline could be removed readily to give (S)-2, 2, 2-trifluoro-1-phenylethanamine with the slightly decreased enantiosel-ectivity in 72% isolated yield, as shown in Scheme 2.

Scheme 2. Removal of the PMP Protection Group

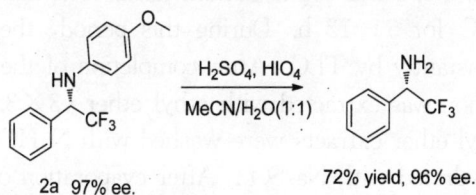

2a 97% ee. 72% yield, 96% ee.

In conclusion, by the further investigation of Noyori's catalysts, we find that $RuCl[(S, S)-TsDPEN)]$ (mesitylene) is an efficient catalyst in the asymmetric transfer hydrogenation of acyclic α-trifluoromethylimines with sodium formate as a hydrogen resource and water-dimethylformamide as a cosolvent, which produces various chiral aryl-substituted α-trifluoromethylamines in high yields and enantioselectivities (93%- 99% ee). Furthermore, the mild reaction conditions make this asymmetric reaction an attractive character for the construction of valuable α-trifluoromethylamines through the transformations of strong electron-withdrawing α-trifluoromethylimines.

■ **EXPERIMENTAL SECTION**

General Methods. All manipulations were carried out under an inert atmosphere using a nitrogen-filled glovebox or Schlenk techniques. Deuterated solvents were purchased commercially and were degassed and stored over activated 4 Å molecular sieves. The α-trifluoromethylimines and (S)-2, 2, 2-trifluoro-1-phenylethanamine were prepared according to the published procedures.[7d-g, 11] All other reagents were obtained from commercial sources and used without further purification. The ^{1}H, ^{19}F, and ^{13}C{1H} NMR spectra were recorded at 400, 376, and 101 MHz, respectively. ^{19}F NMR chemical shifts were determined relative to $CFCl_3$ as the outside standard and low field is positive. Mass spectrometry was performed on a GC/MS spectrometer with the electron impact (EI) ionization technique. HRMS data were recorded on a GC-TOF instrument using the EI technique. The enantiomeric excesses (ee) were determined by an HPLC analysis with a UV-vis detector using a Daicel OD-H or OB-H or AD-H Chiralcel column (Φ 0.46 × 25 cm).

Typical Procedure for Asymmetric Transfer Hydrogenation of α-Trifluoromethylimines. The catalyst (2.49 mg, 4.0 μmol, 2.0 mol %), α-trifluoromethylimines (0.20 mmol), HCOONa (68.0 mg, 1.0 mmol, 5.0 equiv) and 2.0 mL of H_2O/DMF (v/v = 1/1) were added sequentially to a 5.0 mL round-bottom flask. The mixture was then stirred at 40℃ for 5 - 12 h. During this period, the reaction was monitored constantly by TLC. After completion of the reaction, the aqueous solution was extracted with ethyl ether (3 × 3.0 mL). The combined ethyl ether extracts were washed with $NaHCO_3$ and brine, and then dehydrated with Na_2SO_4. After evaporation of ethyl ether, the residue was purified by silica gel flash column chromatography to afford the desired product. The yields were determined by ^{1}H NMR, and the ee values were determined by a HPLC analysis using a UV-vis detector and a Daicel chiralcel column (Φ 0.46 × 25 cm).[7d-g, 10]

2a:.[7d, e] 52.266 mg, 0.186 mmol, 93% yield, 97% ee; ^{1}H NMR (400 MHz, $CDCl_3$): δ 7.49—7.47 (m, 2H), 7.44—7.39 (m, 3H), 6.79—6.75 (m, 2H), 6.66—6.62 (m, 2H), 4.87—4.81(m, 1H), 3.74 (s, 3H); ^{13}C{1H} NMR (101 MHz, $CDCl_3$): δ 153.7, 139.9, 134.7, 129.4, 129.2, 128.3, 125.6 (q, $J_{C-F} = 280$ Hz), 118.3, 116.1, 115.2, 60.7 (q, $J_{C-F} = 30$ Hz), 55.8; GC/MS (m/z): 281; HPLC (OD-H, elute: Hexanes/i-PrOH = 95/5, detector: 254 nm, flow rate: 0.5 mL/min, 25℃), $t_1 = 16.5$ min (major), $t_2 =$

18. 9 min.

2b:[7f] 54. 418 mg, 0. 182 mmol, 91% yield, 97% *ee*; ^{1}H NMR (400 MHz, CDCl$_3$): δ7. 47−7. 43 (m, 2H), 7. 12−7. 07 (m, 2H), 6. 77−6. 74(m, 2H), 6. 60−6. 59 (m, 2H), 4. 85−4. 79(m, 1H), 4. 07 (s, 1H), 3. 74 (s, 3H); ^{13}C{^{1}H} NMR (101 MHz, CDCl$_3$): δ 164. 6, 162. 1, 153. 7, 139. 5, 130. 3, 130. 0, 130. 0, 125. 3 (q, J_{C-F}=279 Hz), 116. 0, 115. 1, 61. 3 (q, J_{C-F}=29 Hz), 55. 8; GC/MS (*m/z*): 299; HPLC (OD-H, elute: Hexanes/*i*-PrOH = 95/5, detector: 254 nm, flow rate: 0. 5 mL/min, 25℃), t_1 = 21. 94 min (major), t_2=26. 1 min.

2c:. [7e, g] 56. 700 mg, 0. 180 mmol, 90% yield, 99% *ee*; ^{1}H NMR (400 MHz, CDCl$_3$): δ 7. 39−7. 33 (m, 4H), 6. 75−6. 71 (m, 2H), 6. 58−6. 54 (m, 2H), 4. 76−4. 86 (m, 1H), 4. 09 (s, 1H), 3. 72 (s, 3H); ^{13}C{^{1}H}NMR (101 MHz, CDCl$_3$): δ 153. 7, 139. 3, 135. 3, 133. 0, 129. 6, 129. 4, 125. 1 (q, J_{C-F} = 280 Hz), 116. 1, 115. 1, 61. 3 (q, J_{C-F}=29 Hz), 55. 9. GC/MS (*m/z*): 315; HPLC (AD-H, elute: Hexanes/*i*-PrOH = 90/10, detector: 254 nm, flow rate: 0. 8 mL/min, 25℃), t_1=12. 0 min(major), t_2=14. 9 min.

2d:. [7e, g] 63. 184 mg, 0. 176 mmol, 88% yield, 95% *ee*; ^{1}H NMR (400 MHz, CDCl$_3$): δ7. 52 (d, J=8. 8 Hz, 2H), 7. 34 (d, J=8. 4 Hz, 2H), 6. 78−6. 73 (m, 2H), 6. 01−6. 56 (m, 2 H), 4. 82−4. 77 (m, 1H), 3. 73 (s, 3H); ^{13}C{^{1}H} NMR (101 MHz, CDCl$_3$): δ 153. 7, 139. 3, 133. 5, 132. 3, 129. 9, 125. 0 (q, J_{C-F}= 281 Hz), 123. 5, 116. 0, 115. 1, 61. 5 (q, J_{C-F}=30 Hz), 55. 9; GC/MS (*m/z*): 359; HPLC (OD-H, elute: Hexanes/*i*-PrOH=95/5, detector: 254 nm, flow rate: 0. 5 mL/min, 25 ℃), t_1 = 23. 4 min (major), t_2=30. 2 min.

2e: 67. 492 mg, 0. 188 mmol, 94% yield, 95% *ee*; ^{1}H NMR (400 MHz, CDCl$_3$): δ 7. 64 (s, 1H), 7. 55−7. 53 (m, 1H), 7. 42 (d, J=8. 0 Hz, 1H), 7. 31−7. 27 (m, 1H), 6. 80−6. 76 (m, 2H), 6. 63 - 6. 59 (m, 2H), 4. 85−4. 79 (m ^{1}H), 3. 75 (s, 3H); ^{13}C{^{1}H} NMR (101 MHz, CDCl$_3$): δ 153. 8, 139. 3, 136. 9, 132. 6, 131. 3, 130. 7, 126. 9, 125. 1 (q, J_{C-F} = 281 Hz), 123. 5, 116. 0, 115. 2, 61. 5 (q, J_{C-F}=30 Hz), 55. 9; ^{19}F NMR (376 MHz, CDCl$_3$): δ-72. 80 (d, J=7. 5 Hz); GC/MS (*m/z*): 359; HR-MS (ESI) [M+H]$^+$

(m/z): calcd for $C_{15}H_{13}BrF_3NO$, 360.0205, found 360.0196. HPLC (OD-H, elute: Hexanes/i-PrOH = 95/5, detector: 254 nm, flow rate: 0.5 mL/min, 25 ℃), t_1=24.5 min (major), t_2=29.9 min.

2f:.[7d, e, g] 64. 914 mg, 0.186 mmol, 93% yield, 97% ee; ^{1}H NMR (400 MHz, CDCl$_3$): δ7.67 (d, J=8.4 Hz, 2H), 7.61 (d, J=8.4 Hz, 2H), 6.77—6.75 (m, 2H), 6.58 (d, J=8.4 Hz, 2H), 4.94 — 4.88 (m, 1H), 3.74 (s, 3H); ^{13}C{^{1}H} NMR (101 MHz, CDCl$_3$): δ 153.9, 139.3, 138.6, 131.7, 131.5, 128.7, 126.1, 125.0 (q, J_{C-F}=280 Hz), 116.1, 115.2, 61.6 (q, J_{C-F}=30 Hz), 55.8; GC/MS (m/z): 349; HPLC (OB-H, elute: Hexanes/i-PrOH=90/10, detector: 254 nm, flow rate: 0.5 mL/min, 25℃), t_1=26.7 min, t_2=33.3 min (major).

2g:.[7d, e] 44. 250 mg, 0.150 mmol, 75% yield, 93% ee; ^{1}H NMR (400 MHz, CDCl$_3$): δ 7.24 (d, J=8.0 Hz, 2H), 7.10 (d, J=8.0 Hz, 2H), 6.66—6.63 (m, 3H), 6.54—6.50 (m, 2H), 4.72—7.66 (m, 1H), 3.62 (s, 3H), 3.39 (s, 1H), 2.26 (s, 3H); ^{13}C{^{1}H} NMR (101 MHz, CDCl$_3$): δ153.5, 139.8, 139.2, 131.5, 129.8, 128.0, 125.4 (q, J_{C-F}=280 Hz), 116.0, 115.1, 61.7 (q, J_{C-F}=29 Hz), 55.9, 21.4; GC/MS (m/z): 295; HPLC (AD-H, elute: Hexanes/i-PrOH = 90/10, detector: 254 nm, flow rate: 0.8 mL/min, 25℃), t_1=10.1 min (major), t_2=14.2 min.

2h:.[7d, e] 54. 114 mg, 0.174 mmol, 87% yield, 98% ee; ^{1}H NMR (400 MHz, CDCl$_3$): δ 7.39 (d, J=8.4 Hz, 2H), 6.96—6.93 (m, 2H), 6.78—6.75 (m, 2H), 6.65—6.62 (m, 2H), 4.82—4.77 (m, 1H), 4.01 (bar, 1H), 3.83 (s, 3H), 3.74 (s, 3H); ^{13}C{^{1}H} NMR (101 MHz, CDCl$_3$): δ160.3, 153.5, 139.9, 129.3, 126.5, 125.5 (q, J_{C-F}=280 Hz), 116.0, 115.1, 114.5, 61.4 (q, J_{C-F}=30 Hz), 55.9, 55.5; GC/MS (m/z): 311; HPLC (AD-H, elute: Hexanes/i-PrOH=90/10, detector: 254 nm, flow rate: 0.8 mL/min, 25℃), t_1=15.4 min (major), t_2=22.8 min.

2i: 51. 004 mg, 0.164 mmol, 82% yield, 93% ee; ^{1}H NMR (400 MHz, CDCl$_3$): δ 7.37 (d, J=7.6 Hz, 1H), 7.33—7.29 (m, 1H), 6.98—6.92 (m, 2H), 6.76—6.71 (m, 2H), 6.64—6.60 (m, 2H), 5.45—5.39 (m, 1H), 4.23 (bar, 1H), 3.88 (s,

3H), 3. 70 (s, 3H); $^{13}C\{^1H\}$ NMR (101 MHz, CDCl$_3$): δ 158. 0, 153. 5, 134. 0, 130. 4, 128. 4, 126. 0 (q, $J_{C-F}=281$ Hz), 123. 1, 121. 3, 116. 0, 115. 8, 115. 2, 111. 5, 56. 0, 55. 8, 55. 0(q, $J_{C-F}=$ 30 Hz); GC/MS (m/z): 311; ^{19}F NMR (376 MHz, CDCl$_3$): $\delta-72.$ 74 (d. J$=7.$ 4 Hz); HR-MS (ESI) [M$+$H]$^+$ (m/z): calcd for C$_{16}$H$_{16}$F$_3$NO$_2$,312. 1206, found 312. 1209. HPLC (AD-H, elute: Hexanes/i-PrOH$=$90/10, detector: 254 nm, flow rate: 0. 8 mL/min, 25℃), $t_1=5.$ 6 min(major), $t_2=11.$ 2 min.

2j : ^{7e}40. 180 mg, 0. 140 mmol, 70% yield, 97% ee; ^1H NMR (400 MHz, CDCl$_3$): δ 7. 34 (dd, J$=1.$ 2 Hz, 1. 2 Hz, 2H), 7. 19 (d, J$=3.$ 2 Hz, 2H), 7. 05 (dd, J$=3.$ 6, 3. 6 Hz, 1H), 6. 83$-$ 6. 79 (m, 1H), 6. 72$-$6. 68 (m, 1H), 5. 16$-$5. 11 (m, 1H), 3. 94 (bar, 1H), 3. 76 (s, 3H); $^{13}C\{^1H\}$ NMR (101 MHz, CDCl$_3$): δ154. 0, 139. 5, 137. 6, 127. 5, 127. 3, 126. 5,125. 0 (q, $J_{C-F}=$ 280 Hz), 116. 4, 115. 2, 58. 3 (q, $J_{C-F}=29$ Hz), 55. 8; GC/MS (m/z): 287; HPLC (AD-H, elute: Hexanes/i-PrOH $=$ 97/3, detector: 254 nm, flow rate: 1. 0 mL/min, 25℃), $t_1=12.$ 0 min (major), $t_2=14.$ 6 min.

2k: ^{7d}46. 640 mg, 0. 176 mmol, 88% yield, 95% ee; ^1H NMR (400 MHz, CDCl$_3$): δ7. 48 (d, J$=6.$ 0 Hz, 2H), 7. 44$-$7. 38 (m, 3H), 6. 99 (d, J$=8.$ 4 Hz, 2H), 6. 58 (d, J$=8.$ 4 Hz, 2H), 4. 93 $-$4. 86 (m, 1H), 4. 23 (d, J$=7.$ 2 Hz, 1H), 2. 24 (s, 3H); ^{13}C $\{^1H\}$ NMR (101 MHz, CDCl$_3$): δ143. 5, 134. 6, 130. 1, 129. 3, 129. 2, 128. 9, 128. 2, 125. 5(q, $J_{C-F}=280$ Hz), 114. 5, 61. 2 (q, $J_{C-F}=30$ Hz), 20. 6; ^{19}F NMR (376 MHz, CDCl$_3$): $\delta-72.$ 90 (d, J$=7.$ 0 Hz); GC/MS (m/z): 265; HPLC (OD-H, elute: Hexanes/ i-PrOH$=$97/3, detector: 254 nm, flow rate: 1. 0 mL/min, 25℃), $t_1=8.$ 5 min (major), $t_2=9.$ 5 min.

2l: 52. 638 mg, 0. 186 mmol, 93% yield, 94% ee; ^1H NMR (400 MHz, CDCl$_3$): δ7. 46 (dd. J$=6.$ 4, 5. 2 Hz, 2H),7. 13$-$7. 07 (m, 2H),7. 00(d, J$=8.$ 4 Hz, 2H),6. 56(d, J$=8.$ 4 Hz, 2H), 4. 93$-$4. 86(m, 1H),4. 22(d, J$=6.$ 8 Hz, 1H),2. 25(s, 3H);^{13}C $\{^1H\}$NMR (101 MHz, CDCl$_3$):δ164. 3, 162. 06, 143. 15, 130. 1, 130. 0, 129. 0, 125. 2(q, $J_{C-F}=280$ Hz), 116. 2, 116. 0, 114. 4,

60. 5 (q, $J_{C-F}=29$ Hz), 20. 6; GC/MS(m/z): 283; HR-MS (ESI) $[M+H]^+$ (m/z): calcd for $C_{15}H_{13}F_4N$, 284. 1057, found 284. 1055. HPLC (OD-H, elute: Hexanes/i-PrOH$=97/3$, detector: 254 nm, flow rate: 1. 0 mL/min, 25℃, $t_1=12$. 9 min (major), $t_2=17$. 6 min.

2m: 61. 232 mg, 0. 178 mmol, 89% yield, 95% *ee*; ^{1}H NMR (400 MHz, CDCl$_3$): δ7. 56－7. 53 (m, 2H), 7. 36 (d, $J=8$. 4 Hz, 2H), 6. 99 (d, $J=8$. 0 Hz, 2H), 6. 54 (d, $J=7$. 6 Hz, 2H), 4. 90－4. 83 (m, 1H), 4. 22 (d, $J=6$. 0 Hz, 1H), 2. 24 (s, 3H). ; ^{13}C{^{1}H} NMR (101 MHz, CDCl$_3$): δ143. 0, 133. 5, 132. 3, 130. 1, 129. 8, 129. 1, 128. 2, 125. 0(q, $J_{C-F}=280$ Hz), 114. 4, 60. 8 (q, $J_{C-F}=30$ Hz), 20. 6; GC/MS (m/z): 343; HR-MS (ESI) $[M+H]^+$ (m/z): calcd for $C_{15}H_{13}BrF_3N$, 344. 0256, found 344. 0254. HPLC (OD-H, elute: Hexanes/i-PrOH$=95/5$, detector: 254 nm, flow rate: 1. 0 mL/min, 25℃), $t_1=14$. 0 min (major), $t_2=19$. 8 min.

2n: ^{7d} 47. 188 mg, 0. 188 mmol, 94% yield, 96% *ee*; ^{1}H NMR (400 MHz, CDCl$_3$): δ 7. 49－7. 38 (m, 2H), 7. 18 (t, $J=7$. 6 Hz, 2H), 6. 80 (t, $J=7$. 6 Hz, 1H), 6. 67 (d, $J=8$. 0 Hz, 2H), 4. 97－4. 91 (m, 1H); ^{13}C{^{1}H} NMR (101 MHz, CDCl$_3$): δ145. 7, 134. 3, 128. 1, 129. 6, 129. 4, 129. 1, 128. 1, 125. 3 (q, $J_{C-F}=280$ Hz), 119. 5, 114. 2, 60. 8 (q, $J_{C-F}=30$ Hz); GC/MS (m/z): 251; HPLC (AD-H, elute: Hexanes/i-PrOH $= 95/5$, detector: 254 nm, flow rate: 1. 0 mL/min, 25℃), $t_1=7$. 7 min (major), $t_2=10$. 0 min.

2o:^{10} 51. 870 mg, 0. 182 mmol, 91% yield, 95% *ee*; ^{1}H NMR (400 MHz, CDCl$_3$): δ 7. 54－7. 47 (m, 5H), 7. 22－7. 18 (m, 2H), 6. 67－6. 63 (m, 2H), 5. 00－4. 93 (m, 1H), 4. 47 (d, $J=5$. 6 Hz, 1H); ^{13}C{^{1}H} NMR (101 MHz, CDCl$_3$): δ 144. 4, 133. 9, 129. 6, 129. 5, 129. 3, 128. 1, 125. 3(q, $J_{C-F}=280$ Hz), 124. 3, 116. 2, 116. 0, 114. 4, 61. 0 (q, $J_{C-F}=30$ Hz), 20. 6; ^{19}F NMR (376 MHz, CDCl$_3$): δ-72. 76 (d, $J=7$. 1 Hz); GC/MS (m/z): 285; HPLC (OD-H, elute: Hexanes/i-PrOH $= 95/5$, detector: 254 nm, flow rate: 0. 5 mL/min, 25℃), $t_1=14$. 8 min(major), $t_2=18$. 3 min.

2p: ^{7g} 53. 578 mg, 0. 178 mmol, 89% yield, 96% *ee*; ^{1}H NMR (400 MHz, CDCl$_3$): δ8. 01 (d, $J=8$. 0 Hz, 1H), 7. 86 (d, $J=$

7. 6 Hz, 1H), 7. 59—7. 52 (m, 4H), 7. 47—7. 43 (m, 3H), 7. 36 (d, J=8. 4 Hz, 1H), 7. 29—7. 25 (m, 1H), 6. 56 (d, J=7. 2 Hz, 1H), 5. 20—5. 07 (m, 2H); $^{13}C\{^1H\}$ NMR (101 MHz, CDCl$_3$): δ 140. 7, 134. 6, 134. 0, 129. 5, 129. 2, 129. 1, 128. 2, 126. 3, 125. 7, 124. 3, 125. 4 (q, J_{C-F}=281 Hz), 120. 0, 119. 9, 107. 4, 60. 8 (q, J_{C-F} = 29 Hz); GC/MS (m/z): 301; HPLC (OD-H, elute: Hexanes/i-PrOH=95/5, detector: 254 nm, flow rate: 0. 5 mL/min, 25℃), t_1=21. 3 min, t_2=30. 6 min(major).

2q:[7g] 54. 180 mg, 0. 180 mmol, 90% yield, 99% *ee*; ^1H NMR (400 MHz, CDCl$_3$): δ7. 71—7. 68(m, 2H), 7. 59—7. 53(m, 3H), 7. 43—7. 36 (m, 4H), 7. 28—7. 24 (m, 1H), 6. 99 (dd, J=2. 4, 2. 4 Hz, 1H), 6. 84 (d, J=1. 2 Hz, 1H), 5. 12—5. 07 (m, 1H); ^{13}C $\{^1H\}$ NMR (101 MHz, CDCl$_3$): δ143. 3, 134. 9, 134. 1, 129. 5, 129. 4, 129. 2, 128. 5, 128. 1, 127. 8, 126. 7, 126. 5, 125. 3 (q, J_{C-F}= 281 Hz), 123. 2, 118. 0, 107. 1, 60. 6 (q, J_{C-F}=29 Hz); GC/MS (m/z): 301; HPLC (AD-H, elute: Hexanes/i-PrOH=95/5, detector: 254 nm, flow rate: 0. 5 mL/min, 25 ℃), t_1 = 19. 0 min (major), t_2=31. 2 min.

(*S*)-2,2,2-*Trifluoro-1-phenylethanamine*:[7g] 25. 20 mg, 0. 144 mmol, 72% yield, 96% *ee*; ^1H NMR (400 MHz, CDCl$_3$) δ 7. 40—7. 33 (m, 5H), 4. 31 (q, J=7. 6 Hz, 1H), 1. 84 (s, 2H); ^{13}C NMR (CDCl$_3$): δ135. 6, 131. 4, 129. 1, 128. 8, 125. 8 (q, J_{C-F}=280 Hz), 58. 1 (q, J_{C-F} = 30 Hz); HPLC (OD-H, elute: Hexanes/i-PrOH=95/5, detector: 254 nm, flow rate: 0. 5 mL/min, 25℃), t_1=20. 5 min (major), t_2=26. 21 min.

■ASSOCIATED CONTENT

Ⓢ Supporting Information

Characterizations and chiral HPLC analysis of the catalytic enantioselective reactions. This material is available free of charge via the Internet at http://pubs. acs. org.

■AUTHOR INFORMATION

Corresponding Author

* Tel: +86 21 64321819. E-mail: ghliu@shnu. edu. cn (G. L.).

Notes

The authors declare no competing financial interest.

■ **ACKNOWLEDGMENTS**

We are grateful to the China National Natural Science Foundation (21402120), the Shanghai Sciences and Technologies Development Fund (13ZR1458700 and 12 nm0500500), the Shanghai Municipal Education Commission (14YZ074, 13CG48, Young Teacher Training Project), and the Specialized Research Fund for the Doctoral Program of Higher Education (20133127120006).

References

[1] (a) Hashiguchi, S.; Fujii, A.; Takehara, J.; Ikariya, T.; Noyori, R. *J. Am. Chem. Soc.* 1995, *117*, 7562. (b) Uematsu, N.; Fujii, A.; Hashiguchi, S.; Ikariya, T.; Noyori, R. *J. Am. Chem. Soc.* 1996, *118*, 4916. (c) Gao, J. X.; Ikariya, T.; Noyori, R. *Organometallics* 1996, *5*, 1087. (d) Fujii, A.; Hashiguchi, S.; Uematsu, N.; Ikariya, T.; Noyori, R. *J. Am. Chem. Soc.* 1996, *118*, 2521. (e) Hashiguchi, S.; Fujii, A.; Haack, K. J.; Matsumura, K.; Ikariya, T.; Noyori, R. *Angew. Chem., Int. Ed. Engl.* 1997, *36*, 288. (f) Noyori, R.; Hashiguchi, S. *Acc. Chem. Res.* 1997, *30*, 97.

[2] (a) Ikariy, T.; John, A. B. *Acc. Chem. Res.* 2007, *40*, 1300. (b) Xie, J. H.; Zhu, S. F.; Zhou, Q. L. *Chem. Rev.* 2011, *111*, 1713. (c) Ikariya, T.; Murata, K.; Noyori, R. *Org. Biomol. Chem.* 2006, *4*, 393. (d) Wang, C.; Villa-Marcos, B.; Xiao, J. L. *Chem. Commun.* 2011, *47*, 9773. (e) Nugent, T. C.; El-Shazly, M. *Adv. Synth. Catal.* 2010, *352*, 753. (f) Wu, X.; Xiao, J. L. *Chem. Commun.* 2007, 2449. (g) Yu, Z. K.; Jin, W. W.; Jiang, Q. B. *Angew. Chem., Int. Ed.* 2012, *51*, 6060. (h) Li, C. Q.; Xiao, J. L. *J. Am. Chem. Soc.* 2008, *130*, 13208. (i) Chen, F.; Ding, Z. Y.; Qin, J.; Wang, T. L.; He, Y. M.; Fan, Q. H. *Org. Lett.* 2011, *13*, 4348. (j) Ding, Z. Y.; Chen, F.; Qin, J.; He, Y. M.; Fan, Q. H. *Angew. Chem., Int. Ed.* 2012, *51*, 5706. (k) Chen, F.; Wang, T. L.; He, Y. M.; Ding, Z. Y.; Li, Z. W.; Fan, Q. H. *Chem.—Eur. J.* 2011, *17*, 1109.

[3] (a) Murata, K.; Ikariya, T.; Noyori, R. *J. Org. Chem.* 1999, *64*, 2186. (b) Barron-Jaime, A.; Narvaez-Garayzar, O. F.; Gonzalez, J.; Ibarra-Galvan, V.; Aguirre, G.; Parra-Hake, M.; Chavez, D.; Somanathan, R. *Chirality* 2011, *23*, 178. (c) Perryman, M. S.; Harris, M. E.; Foster, J. L.; Joshi, A.; Clarkson, G. J.; Fox, D. J. *Chem. Commun.* 2013, *49*, 10022.

(d) Zhang, H. ; Lian, C. ; Zhu, J. ; Deng, J. *Green Chem.* 2007, *9*, 23. (e) Wang, C. ; Li, C. ; Wu, X. ; Pettman, A. ; Xiao, J. *Angew. Chem.*, *Int. Ed.* 2009, *48*, 6524. (f) Han, J. ; Kang, S. ; Lee, H. K. *Chem. Commun.* 2011, *47*, 4004.

[4] (a) Wu, X. ; Liu, J. ; Li, X. ; Zanotti-Gerosa, A. ; Hancock, F. ; Vinci, D. ; Ruan, J. ; Xiao, J. *Angew. Chem.* 2006, *45*, 6718. (b) Zhou, H. ; Li, Z. ; Wang, Z. ; Wang, T. ; Xu, L. ; He, Y. ; Fan, Q. H. ; Pan, J. ; Gu, L. ; Chan, A. S. *Angew. Chem.*, *Int. Ed.* 2008, *47*, 8464. (c) Kwak, S. H. ; Lee, S. A. ; Lee, K. -I. *Tetrahedron*: *Asymmetry* 2010, *21*, 800. (d) Wang, T. ; Zhuo, L. G. ; Li, Z. ; Chen, F. ; Ding, Z. ; He, Y. ; Fan, Q. H. ; Xiang, J. ; Yu, Z. X. ; Chan, A. S. *J. Am. Chem. Soc.* 2011, *133*, 9878. (e) Mashima, K. ; Abe, T. ; Tani, K. *Chem. Lett.* 1998, 1199. (f) Murata, K. ; Ikariya, T. ; Noyori, R. *J. Org. Chem.* 1999, *64*, 2186. (g) Wu, Z. ; Perez, M. ; Scalone, M. ; Ayad, T. ; Ratovelomanana-Vidal, V. *Angew. Chem.*, *Int. Ed.* 2013, *52*, 4925.

[5] (a) Nie, J. ; Guo, H. C. ; Cahard, D. ; Ma, J. A. *Chem. Rev.* 2011, *111*, 455. (b) Lim, J. ; Taoka, B. ; Otte, R. D. ; Spencer, K. ; Marshall, C. G. ; Young, J. R. *J. Med. Chem.* 2011, *54*, 7334. (c) O'Shea, P. D. ; Chen, C. Y. ; Gauvreau, D. ; Hughes, F. ; Gosselin, G. ; Nadeau, C. ; Volante, R. P. *J. Org. Chem.* 2009, *74*, 1605. (d) Zhang, N. ; Ayral-Kaloustian, S. ; Nguyen, T. ; Afragola, J. ; Hernandez, J. ; Lucas, R. ; Gibbons, J. ; Beyer, C. *J. Med. Chem.* 2007, *50*, 319. (e) Imamoto, T. ; Iwadate, N. ; Yoshida, K. *Org. Lett.* 2006, *8*, 2289. (f) Goulioukina, N. S. ; Bondarenko, G. N. ; Lyubimov, S. E. ; Davankov, V. A. ; Gavrilov, K. N. ; Beletskaya, I. P. *Adv. Synth. Catal.* 2008, *350*, 482.

[6] (a) Gosselin, F. ; O'Shea, P. D. ; Roy, S. ; Reamer, R. A. ; Chen, C. -Y. ; Volante, R. P. *Org. Lett.* 2005, *7*, 355. (b) Prakash, G. K. S. ; Mandal, M. ; Olah, G. A. *Angew. Chem.*, *Int. Ed.* 2001, *40*, 589. (c) Kawai, H. ; Kusuda, A. ; Nakamura, S. ; Shiro, M. ; Shibata, N. *Angew. Chem.*, *Int. Ed.* 2009, *48*, 6324. (d) Li, Y. ; Hu, J. *Angew. Chem*,. *Int. Ed.* 2005, *44*, 5882. (e) Li, Y. ; Hu, J. *Angew. Chem.*, *Int. Ed.* 2007, *46*, 2489. (f) Prakash, G. K. S. ; Mandal, M. ; Olah, G. A. *Org. Lett.* 2001, *3*, 2847. (g) Truong, V. L. ; Pfeiffer, J. Y. *Tetrahedron Lett.* 2009, *50*, 1633. (h) Truong, V. L. ; Menard, M. S. ; Dion, I. *Org. Lett.* 2007, *9*, 683. (i) Gosselin, F. ; Roy, A. ; O'Shea, P. D. ; Chen, C. Y. ; Volante, R. P. *Org. Lett.* 2004, *6*, 641. (j) Fries, S. ; Pytkowicz, J. ; Brigaud, T. *Tetrahedron*

Lett. 2005, *46*, 4761. (k) Fustero, S. ; del Pozo, C. ; Catalán, S. ; Alemán,
J. ; Parra, A. ; Marcos, V. ; Ruano, J. L. G. *Org. Lett.* 2009, *11*, 641.

[7] (a) Giacalone, F. ; Gruttadauria, M. ; Agrigento, P. ; Noto, R. *Chem. Soc.*
Rev. 2012, *41*, 2406. (b) Abe, H. ; Amii, H. ; Uneyama, K. *Org. Lett.*
2001, *3*, 313. (c) Suzuki, A. ; Mae, M. ; Amii, H. ; Uneyama, K. *J. Org.*
Chem. 2004, *69*, 5132. (d) Chen, M. W. ; Duan, Y. ; Chen, Q. A. ; Wang,
D. S. ; Yu, C. B. ; Zhou, Y. G. *Org. Lett.* 2010, *12*, 5075. (e) Henseler,
A. ; Kato, M. ; Mori, K. ; Akiyama, T. *Angew. Chem. , Int. Ed.* 2011,
50, 8180. (f) Genoni, A. ; Benaglia, M. ; Massolo, E. ; Rossi, S. *Chem.*
Commun. 2013, *49*, 8365. (g) Dai, X. Y. ; Cahard, D. *Adv. Synth. Catal.*
2014, *356*, 1317. (h) Mikami, K. ; Murase, T. ; Zhai, L. ; Kawauchi, S. ;
Itoh, Y. ; Ito, S. *Tetrahedron Lett.* 2010, *51*, 1371.

[8] (a) Zhang, D. C. ; Cheng, T. Y. ; Zhao, Q. K. ; Xu, J. Y. ; Liu, G. H. *Org.*
Lett. 2014, *16*, 5764. (b) Zhang, D. C. ; Gao, X. S. ; Cheng, T. Y. ; Liu, G.
H. *Sci. Rep.* 2014, *4*, 5091. (c) Gao, X. S. ; Liu, R. ; Zhang, D. C. ; Wu,
M. ; Cheng, T. Y. ; Liu, G. H. *Chem. —Eur. J.* 2014, *20*, 1515. (d) Liu,
R. ; Cheng, T. ; Kong, L. Y. ; Chen, C. ; Liu, G. H. ; Li, H. X. *J. Catal.*
2013, *307*, 55. (e) Zhang, H. S. ; Jin, R. H. ; Yao, H. ; Tang, S. ; Zhuang,
J. L. ; Liu, G. H. ; Li, H. X. *Chem. Commun.* 2012, *48*, 7874. (f) Gao, F. ;
Jin, R. H. ; Zhang, D. C. ; Liang, Q. X. ; Ye, Q. Q. ; Liu, G. H. *Green*
Chem. 2013, *15*, 2208. (g) Xia, D. Q. ; Cheng, T. Y. ; Xiao, W. ; Liu, K.
K. ; Wang, Z. L. ; Liu, G. H. ; Li, H. L. ; Wang, W. *ChemCatChem* 2013,
5, 1784.

[9] (a) Wu, X. ; Li, X. ; Hems, W. ; King, F. ; Xiao, J. L. *Org. Biomol.*
Chem. 2004, *2*, 1818. (b) Wang, L. ; Zhou, Q. ; Qu, C. ; Wang, Q. ; Cun,
L. ; Zhu, J. ; Deng, J. *Tetrahedron* 2013, *69*, 6500.

[10] (a) Johnson, T. ; Lautens, M. *Org. Lett.* 2013, *15*, 4043. (b) Allendörfer,
N. ; Sudau, A. ; Bräse, S. *Adv. Synth. Catal.* 2010, *352*, 2815. (c) Fu,
P. ; Snapper, M. L. ; Hoveyda, A. H. *J. Am. Chem. Soc.* 2008, *130*, 5530.

[11] (a) Enders, D. ; Gottfried, K. ; Raabe, G. *Adv. Synth. Catal.* 2010, *352*,
3147. (b) Abid, M. ; Savolainen, M. ; Landge, S. ; Hu, J. B. ; Prakash, G.
K. S. ; Olah, G. A. ; Török, B. *J. Fluorine Chem.* 2007, *128*, 587. (c) Li,
C. L. ; Chen, M. W. ; Zhang, X. G. *J. Fluorine Chem.* 2010, *131*, 856.

(原载于 Journal of Organic Chemistry 2015 年第 80 期)

C_{60}-Decorated CdS/TiO$_2$ Mesoporous Architectures with Enhanced Photostability and Photocatalytic Activity for H$_2$ Evolution

Zichao Lian, Pengpeng Xu, Wenchao Wang,
Dieqing Zhang, Shuning Xiao, Xin Li,
and Guisheng Li

Key Laboratory of Resource Chemistry of Ministry of Education,
Shanghai Key Laboratory of Rare Earth Functional Materials,
College of Life and Environmental Science, Shanghai Normal
University

1. Introduction

Since Fujishima and Honda had reported that hydrogen evolution could be obtained through photoelectrochemical water-splitting by using TiO$_2$ as electrodes,[1-4] the semiconductor-based photocatalysis induced water-splitting route for hydrogen evolution has been recognized as one of the most effective methods for solving the energy crisis.[5] Also, cadmium sulfide (CdS) with a band gap of around 2.4 eV matches well with the visible part of solar-light spectra and exhibits excellent photocatalytic activity because of its highly effective absorption of solar energy.[6] Thus, it has been applied in different kinds of fields such as optoelectronics,[7] solar cells,[8] chemical sensors,[9] and photocatalysis.[10] However, its photocorrosion effect gas greatly limited its wide application.

In addition, our earlier work proved that ordered mesoporous TiO_2 CdS with quantum dots (QDs) implanted into its framework could be applied in the treatment of both water and air purification under visible-light irradiation. [11] Nevertheless, there still exist some problems in such photocatalytic systems, including the low photocatalytic activity resulting from the low electronic conductivity, low quantum efficiency, and the inherent photocorrosion problem drawback for CdS-based photocatalysts. [12, 13] As is already known, the sulfide ion could easily be oxidized by photogenerated holes, and cadmium ions could be reduced by the photoinduced electrons. Such photocorrosion effects lead to the instability of CdS, seriously prohibiting its practical application. Thus, it is key to seek a new approach to inhibit the photocorrosive effect to the CdS nanoparticles via choosing a surface-modification route involving loading a thin amorphous-carbon layer around CdS, [14] or forming a heterojunction [15] and a Z-scheme [16] to accelerate the photoinduced electron transfer. Thus, carbon nanostructured materials such as activated carbon, multiwalled carbon nanotubes, [17-20] single-walled carbon nanotubes (SWCNTs), [21, 22] fullerenes (C_{60}), [23] and reduced graphene oxide (rGO). [24-27] give us a new space in which to design nanocomposites with excellent photocatalytic performance in recent years. Among these carbon nanostructured materials, C_{60} has gained a lot of attention for its novel properties owing to its special delocalized conjugated structures. [27] The most important role of C_{60} in electron-transfer processes lies in that it could serve as an excellent electron acceptor. This efficiently increases the photogenerated charge separation and decreases the rate of charge recombination, [28] thus enhancing the photocatalytic activity. Therefore, combining photocatalysts with fullerene could provide an excellent route for obtaining rapidly photogenerated charge separation via facilitating electron transfer. [29, 30] Also, C_{60} molecules could be regarded as the antiphotocorrosion agent.[31] Given those advantages, it is highly necessary to implant C_{60} into the mesoporous framework of CdS/TiO$_2$ composites to enhancie the activity and stability.

Herein, we report the fabrication of C_{60}-decorated CdS QDs sensitized mesoporous TiO$_2$ photocatalysts via an evaporation induced

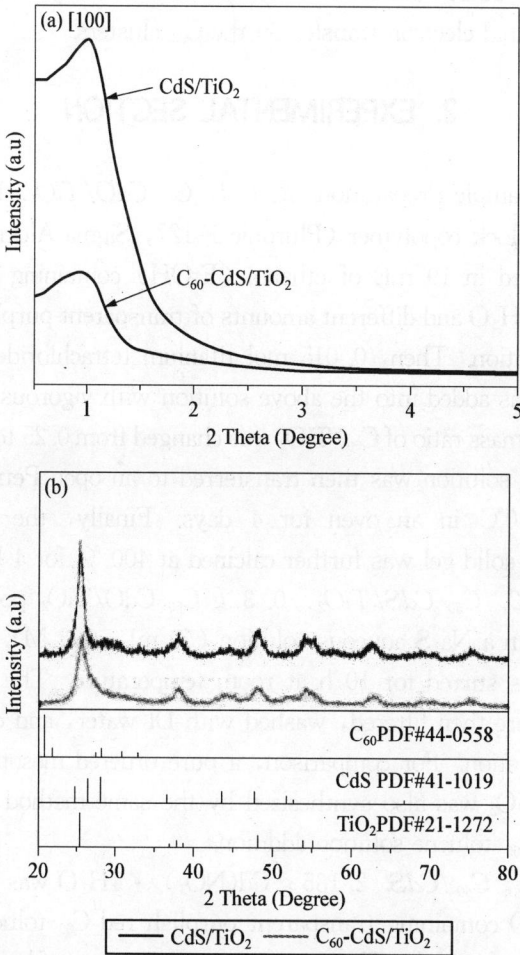

Figure 1　Small-angle X-ray diffraction (SXRD) (a) and wide-angle X-ray diffraction (WXRD) (b) of CdS/TiO$_2$ and C_{60}-CdS/TiO$_2$.

self-assembly (EISA), together with an ion-exchange route.[11] CdS QDs and C_{60} clusters were well embedded into the framework of the well-ordered mesoporous TiO_2 photo-catalyst. The C_{60} cluster protection layers were distributed on the surface of both CdS and TiO_2. Such layers were favorable for enhancing the photocatalytic performance in H_2 evolution with excellent stability, owing to the photogenerated electron transfer on the C_{60} clusters.

2. EXPERIMENTAL SECTION

2. 1. Sample Preparation. 2. 1. 1. C_{60}-CdO/TiO$_2$. Poly-(alkyleneoxide) block copolymer (Pluronic F-127, Sigma-Aldrich, 1. 5 g) was dissolved in 19 mL of ethanol (EtOH) containing 0. 21 g Cd $(NO_3)_2 \cdot 4H_2O$ and different amounts of transparent purplish red C_{60}-toluene solution. Then, 0. 015 mol titanium tetrachloride (Shanghai Aladdin) was added into the above solution with vigorous stirring for 0. 5 h. The mass ratio of C_{60}/TiO_2 was changed from 0. 25 to 1. 5 wt %. The formed solution was then transferred to an open Petri dish, and gelled at 40℃ in an oven for 4 days. Finally, the as-prepared transparent solid gel was further calcined at 400 ℃ for 4 h in air.

2. 1. 2. C_{60}-CdS/TiO$_2$. 0. 3 g C_{60}-CdO/TiO$_2$ powders were introduced in a Na_2S aqueous solution (50 mL, 0. 2 M). The above solution was stirred for 10 h at room temperature. The as-obtained powders were then filtered, washed with DI water, and collected for further utiliation. For comparison, a pure ordered mesoporous TiO_2 and CdS/TiO$_2$ was also synthesized by the same method without Cd source or C_{60}-toluene solution addition.

2. 1. 3. C_{60}/CdS. 2. 135 g Cd(NO$_3$)$_2 \cdot 4H_2O$ was dissolved in 50 mL H_2O containing transparent purplish red C_{60}-toluene solution with stirring for 24 h. The resulting precipitate was filtered, washed with water and ethanol, and dried at 80℃ for 12 h. The as-obtained products were further calcined at 400℃ for 4 h in air to obtain C_{60}/

CdO powders. Then, the as-obtained C_{60}/CdO (0. 3 g) was dispersed in a Na$_2$S aqueous solution (50 mL, 20. 0 g/L) with stirring for 10 h at 80℃. The as-obtained brown products were filtered, washed with water and ethanol three times, and dried at 80℃ for 12 h. The mass ratio of C_{60}/CdS was tuned from 0. 25 to 1. 5 wt %.

 2. 2. Characterization. Both wide and low-angle X-ray diffraction measurements were performed on a Rigacu Dmax-3C X-ray diffractometer using a parallel mode. High-resolution transmission electron microscopy (HRTEM) was measured in a JEOL-2010 at 200 kV. The TEM or HRTEM samples were prepared by grinding and dispersing the photocatalyst powders in ethanol for 20 s under ultrasonic irradiation. Carbon coated copper grids were utilized as holders for loading samples. BET surface area, pore volume, and average pore diameter of photocatalyst were measured by N$_2$ adsorption at-196℃ using TriStar II 3020 system by Micromeritics Instrument Corporation. The binding energies of the elements in the products were investigated by the X-ray photoelectron spectroscopy (XPS) using a PerkinElmer PHI 5000C. The contaminant carbon (C 1s= 284. 6 eV) was chosen as a reference for calibrate the binding energies. The UV-vis diffuse reflectance spectra (200 - 800 nm) were recorded by a MC-2530 UV-vis spectrophotometer system equipped with a Labsphere diffuse reflectance accessory. BaSO$_4$ was used as a reference. Photoluminescence (PLS) emission spectra were recorded on a Varian Cary-Eclipse 500 at room temperature using 280 nm light as the excitation source. Thermogravimetric analyses (TG) were carried out on a DTG-60H thermogravimetric analyzer with a heating speed of 2℃/min under air atmosphere.

 2. 3. Photoelectrochemical Measurements. The photocurrents were recorded on an electrochemical analyzer (CHI 660D Instruments, Chen Hua Instrument Co. , Ltd.) in a standard three-electrode system. Platinum sheet (20 × 20 × 0. 1 mm^3, 99. 99%) was used as the counter electrode, and a saturated calomel electrode

(SCE) was used as the reference electrode. The as-prepared samples electrode was used as the working electrode. In order to drive the photogenerated electron transfer from the working electrode to the platinum electrode, an external bias voltage (0.5 V) was loaded. For preparing the working electrode, the as-obtained photocatalyst powders (20 mg) were ground with polyethylene glycol (PEG, molecular weight 20000, 0.01 g) and ethanol (0.5 mL) to form a slurry. Afterward, the slurry was spin-coated onto an FTO glass electrode $(3 \times 1 \ cm^2)$ for the formation of an active area $(10 \times 10 \ mm^2)$. The as-formed electrodes were further heated at 200℃ for 3 h in a ceramic plate heater. A xenon lamp $(300 \ W, \lambda > 420 \ nm)$ was used as the visible-light source, and the photoelectrochemical cell was positioned 10 cm away from the xenon lamp. Na_2SO_4 aqueous solution (0.5 mol/L) was used as the electrolyte.

2.4. Activity Test. *2.4.1. Photocatalytic H_2 Generation.* Hydrogen production by photocatalytic water-splitting was carried out at room temperature in a three *flat-bottomed* flask reaction cell (100 mL) sealed with aboral rubber plugs. Typically, ordered mesoporous C_{60}-CdS/TiO_2 photocatalyst (50 mg) was suspended in a Na_2S-Na_2SO_3 aqueous solution (80 mL, 0.25 M for Na_2S, 0.25 M for Na_2SO_3). Before light-irradiation, nitrogen flow was introduced into the photocatalyst suspension to remove the dissolved O_2. Four low power UV-LEDs (3 W, 420 nm) (Shenzhen LAMPLIC Science Co. Ltd., China) were utilized as the light source for driving the photocatalytic H_2 evolution. In four different directions, all LEDs were positioned away from the reactor with a distance of ca. 1 cm. Each UV-LED possessed a focused intensity (ca. $6 \ mW \cdot cm^{-2}$) and areas (ca. $1 \ cm^2$) on the reaction flask. For keeping the photocatalysts in suspension status, vigorous magnetic stirring was maintained during the photocatalytic reaction. 0.5 mL of gas was sampled intermittently after 1 h of photocatalytic reaction. The evolved H_2 amount was determined using a gas chromatograph (GC9800 (N),

Shanghai Ke Chuang Chromatograph Instruments Co. Ltd. , China, TCD, nitrogen as carrier gas, and a 5 A molecular sieve column).

The apparent quantum efficiency (QE) was very important to evaluate the photocatalytic performance. And the QE was calculated according to eq 1:[32]

$$QE[\%] = \frac{\text{number of reacted electrons}}{\text{number of incident photons}} \times 100$$

$$= \frac{\text{number of evolved H}_2\text{molecules} \times 2}{\text{number of incident photons}} \times 100 \quad (1)$$

3. RESULTS AND DISCUSSION

For investigating the crystalline phase and mesostructure of the as-formed C_{60}-CdS/TiO$_2$ samples, both wide-angle X-ray diffraction (WXRD) and small-angle X-ray-diffraction (SXRD) were applied in the present work. The small-angle XRD patterns demonstrated that both CdS/TiO$_2$ and C_{60}-CdS/ TiO$_2$ samples exhibited strong peaks indicative of (100) diffraction, suggesting that the samples possessed a highly ordered 2D hexagonal mesoporous structure (p6 mm), as shown in Figure 1a. [33, 34] It revealed that the in situ introducing C_{60} and the transfer from CdO to CdS did not destroy the framework of the ordered mesoporous structure, although a slight decrease of (100) diffraction peak was observed upon coupling C_{60} with CdS/TiO$_2$. Wide-angle XRD of CdS/TiO$_2$ and C_{60}-CdS/TiO$_2$ samples indicated the diffraction peaks at 2θ of 25. 3°, 36. 9°, 38. 2°, 38. 6°, 48. 1°, 53. 5°, 55. 6°, 62. 7°, and 75. 0° of an anatase-TiO$_2$ structure (JCPDF 21-1272) in Figure 1b. Meanwhile, there was an additional diffraction peak at 2θ of 43. 6°, ascribed to the (110) crystal plane of hexagonal CdS crystal phase (JCPDF 41 – 1049). Such low peaks could result from the high dispersity of the as-obtained CdS QDs. Other diffraction peaks related to CdS could be overlapped by the diffraction peaks of anatase TiO$_2$. In addition, the mesoporous C_{60}-CdS/TiO$_2$, with a low C_{60} content (<2 wt%), did not exhibit C_{60} characteristic diffraction peaks. It could be ascribed to the high dispersity of C_{60} in the framework of CdS/TiO$_2$, as shown in Supporting Information (SI) Figure S1. For proving the existence of C_{60} after 400℃ calcination, TG was also utilized to analyze to thermal stability of C_{60} in the presence/absence of CdS/TiO$_2$ framework. As shown in SI Figure S2, the weight loss of C_{60} was observed when the temperature increased to about 400℃ to the case pure C_{60}. In the presence of CdS/TiO$_2$ framework, only 12 wt % loss was observed before 200 ℃ to the case of C_{60}-CdS/TiO$_2$. Such loss was attributed to the removal of water or hydroxyl groups absorbed on the surface of C_{60}-CdS/TiO$_2$. No obvious weight loss could be observed over 400℃. Such excellent thermal stability could be attributed to the protection of TiO$_2$ framework. As known, the thermal conductivity constant of TiO$_2$ was about 3. 8 w/m • k at 400 ℃. Upon being calcined at 400 ℃, most heat will be absorbed by the framework of TiO$_2$, thus C_{60} layers will be maintained. These results indicated that the C_{60} molecules could be obtained in the framework of CdS/TiO$_2$ even after calcination at 400 ℃.

Nitrogen adsorption-desorption isotherms were recorded to evaluate the effect of C_{60} on the porous structure of CdS/TiO$_2$ samples. As shown in Figure 2, all samples exhibited a similar type-IV isotherm, illustrating that these samples possessed mesoporous structure. As shown in Table 1, CdS/TiO$_2$ sample possessed a specific surface area of 191 m^2 • g^{-1}. It clearly indicated that both surface area and pore volume decreased upon increasing the C_{60} content. Such decrease could be ascribed to the occupation of C_{60} clusters in the pore channels of mesoporous structures. These results further suggested that the C_{60} clusters and CdS QDs were embedded in the pore wall of the mesoporous TiO$_2$ networks. From the BET results, one could draw a conclusion that such mesoporous C_{60}-CdS/TiO$_2$ architectures remained opened mesoporous channels and had a large surface area. Such structure is highly required for catalyst design, being beneficial to enhance the molecular transport capacity of reactants and the release of H_2.[35]

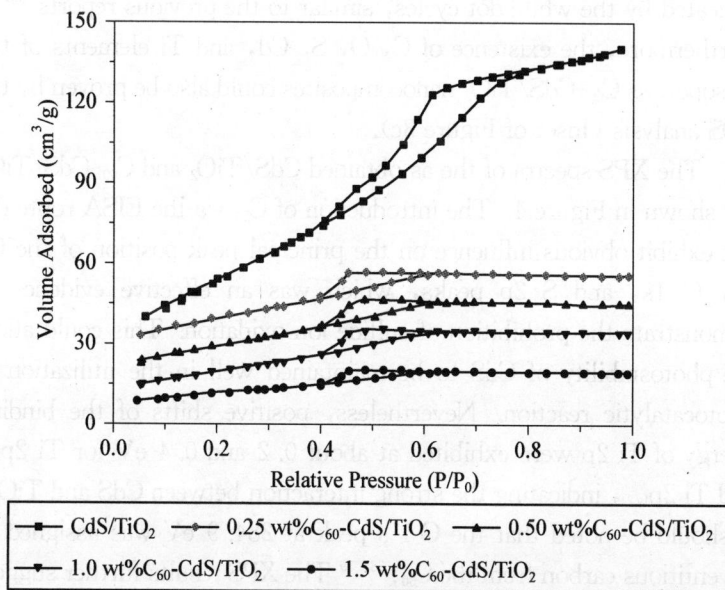

Figure 2. N_2-sorption isotherms of CdS/TiO₂ and C_{60}-CdS/TiO₂ samples.

The transmission electron microscopy (TEM) images were utilized to define the ordered structure and crystal phase of the as-obtained samples. As shown in Figure 3a, a long-range ordered structure was readily observed in the CdS/TiO₂ composites. Upon introducing C_{60}, the long-range ordered structure was still retained except for a slightly twist, as illustrated in Figure 3b. Besides, the nanocrystalline nature of hexagonal CdS and anatase TiO₂ could be well-resolved in the HRTEM image of C_{60}-CdS/TiO₂, as shown in Figure 3c. It was noted that there was no change of lattice structure of TiO₂ (0.352 nm) and CdS (0.316 nm) after embedding C_{60} into the mesoporous framework of TiO₂. It was also found that an amorphous coverture layer was surrounded on the surface of TiO₂ and CdS nanocrystals, and the layer possessed a thickness of 1 – 2 nm, about 2 – 3 times of the diameter of C_{60} molecular (0. 7 nm). Therefore, it could be estimated that C_{60} clusters were attached with TiO_2 and CdS indicated by the white dot cycles, similar to the previous reports.[36, 37] Furthermore, the existence of C, O, S, Cd, and Ti elements of the mesoporous C_{60}-CdS/TiO_2 nanocomposites could also be proven by the EDS analysis (Inset of Figure 3c).

The XPS spectra of the as-obtained CdS/TiO_2 and C_{60}-CdS/TiO_2 are shown in Figure 4. The introduction of C_{60} via the EISA route did not exhibit obvious influence on the principal peak position of the Cd 3d, O 1s, and S 2p peaks, which was an effective evidence to demonstrate the prohibition of sulfide ion oxidation. This could allow the photostability of CdS to be maintained well in the utilization in photocatalytic reaction. Nevertheless, positive shifts of the binding energy of Ti 2p were exhibited at about 0. 2 and 0. 4 eV for Ti $2p_{3/2}$ and Ti $2p_{1/2}$, indicating the strong interaction between CdS and TiO_2. It should be noted that the C 1 s peak at 284. 9 eV was assigned to adventitious carbon from the C_{60}.[38, 39] The XPS results further suggest the formation of heterojunctions between C_{60} and CdS/TiO_2 in the framework of mesoporous TiO_2.

As is known, the light absorption capability (LAC) played an important role in affecting the photocatalytic activity of the photocatalysts. Thus, it is highly necessary to keep or improve the LAC of the as-formed CdS/TiO_2 even after loading the C_{60} clusters. In order to evaluate the LAC of samples, UV-visible diffuse reflectance spectroscopy (DRS) was used. As shown in Figure 5a, the as-obtained samples exhibited the typical absorption, ranging from 400 to 550 nm in the visible-light region. It could be assigned to the embedded CdS QDs in the pore wall of mesoporous TiO_2. Such CdS QDs may change the intrinsic band gap absorption of TiO_2. Furthermore, the introduction of the C_{60} clusters into the mesoporous CdS/TiO_2 framework results in to a high LAC in the visible-light

Table 1. Structural Parameters of All As-Obtained Samples

samples	BET surface area (m^2/g)[a]	pore volume (cm^3/g)[b]	pore size (nm)[c]
CdS/TiO$_2$	191	0.180	3.4
0.25 wt % C$_{60}$-CdS/TiO$_2$	90	0.0604	3.0
0.50 wt % C$_{60}$-CdS/TiO$_2$	83	0.0646	2.9
1.0 wt % C$_{60}$-CdS/TiO$_2$	71	0.0532	2.9
1.5 wt % C$_{60}$-CdS/TiO$_2$	41	0.0304	2.8

[a] BET special surface area calculated from the linear part of the BET plot ($p/p_0 = 0.1 - 0.2$). [b] The total pore volumes were estimated from the adsorbed amount at a relative pressure of $p/p_0 = 0.99$. [c] The pore-size diameters (PSD) were derived from the desorption branches of the isotherms by using the Barrett-Joyner-Halenda (BJH) method.

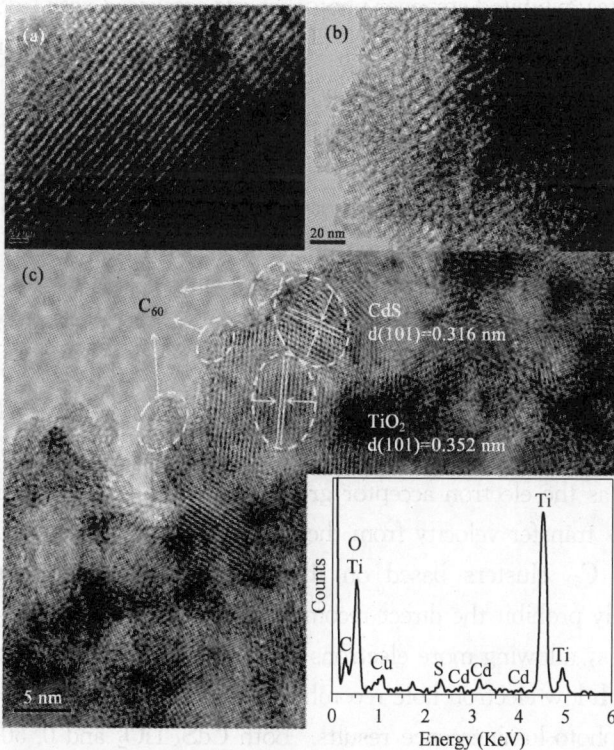

Figure 3 TEM image of CdS/TiO$_2$ (a), 0.50 wt % C$_{60}$-CdS/TiO$_2$ (b), and the HRTEM image and EDS spectrum (inset) of 0.50 wt % C$_{60}$-CdS/ TiO$_2$ (c).

region. Interestingly, the as prepared C_{60}-CdS/TiO$_2$ exhibits the stronger absorption along with the increasing C_{60} content, indicating the increment of surface electric charge and electronic interaction between C_{60} and CdS/TiO$_2$.[20, 40] Such enhanced light adsorption capability owing to the C_{60}-introduction would be highly necessary for making the C_{60}-CdS/TiO$_2$ mesoporous composites an ideal photocatalyst.

For proving the enhancement of the C_{60} clusters on the photoresponse performance of mesoporous C_{60}-CdS/TiO$_2$ composites, transient photocurrent techniques were used to measure and evaluate the performance. As shown in Figure 5b, all of the C_{60}-CdS/TiO$_2$ composites exhibited stronger photocurrents compared with CdS/TiO$_2$ under visible-light ($\lambda > 420$ nm) irradiation at an applied potential of 0. 5 V vs SCE. Among all the C_{60}-modified samples, the 0. 50 wt % C_{60}-CdS/TiO$_2$ sample possessed the highest photocurrent density. Nevertheless, further increasing the loaded amount of C_{60} clusters resulted in the decrease of photocurrent density. This could be attributed to the light shielding effect of excess C_{60} coverage on the surface CdS/TiO$_2$, although the light absorption capability could still be increased upon introducing excess C_{60}, suggested by the UV-vis results (Figure 5a). It should also be noted that photocurrent responses were highly reproducible for numerous on-off cycles and remained stable. As for the 0. 50 wt % C_{60}-CdS/TiO$_2$ sample, C_{60} clusters as the electron acceptor greatly enhanced the photogenerated electrons transfer velocity from the conduction band of both CdS and TiO$_2$ to C_{60} clusters based on the photocurrent results. It could effectively prohibit the direct recombination of photoinduced electrons and holes, allowing more electrons to be captured by protons to from H$_2$. Such low electron-hole recombination rates can also be supported by the photo-luminescence results. Both CdS/TiO$_2$ and 0. 50 wt % C_{60}-CdS/TiO$_2$ displayed peaks at around 560 nm, as shown in Figure 5c. An obvious fluorescence peak decrease can be observed after

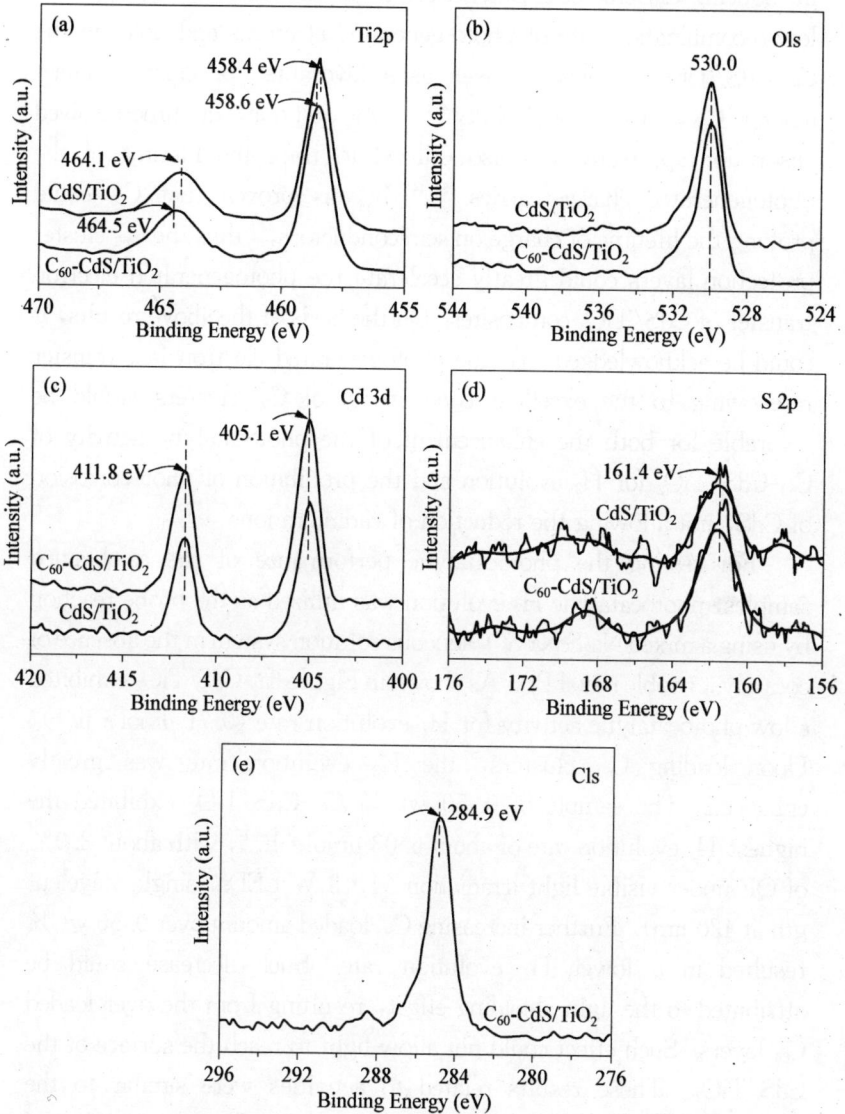

Figure 4 XPS spectra in Ti 2p (a), O 1s (b), Cd 3d (c), S 2p (d) level of CdS/TiO$_2$ and 0.50 wt % C_{60}-CdS/TiO$_2$, respectively, and C 1s level (e) of the C_{60}-CdS/TiO$_2$.

introducing C_{60} clusters. Such decrease of fluorescence indicated the low recombination rate of photo-generated electrons and holes in the C_{60}-CdS/TiO_2 samples, as well as a favorable (or close) contact among C_{60}, TiO_2, and CdS.[41, 42] In addition, a time-resolved absorption spectrum was also utilized to trace the lifetime of the photogenerated charge carries.[43, 44] It was proven that C_{60} could prolong the lifetime of charge on semiconductors,[43] thus the C_{60} cluster protection layers could greatly accelerate the photogenerated electron transfer of CdS/TiO_2 composites. On the basis of the above results, it could be acknowledged that the photogenerated electron fast transfer rate owing to the excellent conductivity of C_{60} clusters would be favorable for both the enhancement of the photocatalytic activity of C_{60}-CdS/TiO_2 for H_2 evolution and the prohibition of photocorrosion of CdS, not allowing the reduction of cadmium ions.

For testing the photocatalytic performance of the as-obtained samples, photocatalytic H_2 evolution was utilized as the probe reaction by using a mixed Na_2S-Na_2SO_3 aqueous solution system in the absence of cocatalyst (noble metal Pt). As shown in Figure 6a, CdS/TiO_2 exhibited a low photocatalytic activity for H_2 evolution rate (0.71 $\mu mol \cdot h^{-1}$). Upon loading C_{60} clusters, the H_2 evolution rate was greatly enhanced. The sample of 0.50 wt % C_{60}-CdS/TiO_2 exhibited the highest H_2 evolution rate of about 6.03 $\mu mol \cdot h^{-1}$, with about 2.0% of QE under visible light irradiation (4×3 W LEDs, single wavelength at 420 nm). Further increasing C_{60} loaded amount over 0.50 wt % resulted in a lower H_2 evolution rate. Such decrease could be attributed to the light shielding effect, resulting from the over loaded C_{60} layers. Such effect could not allow light to reach the surface of the CdS/TiO_2. These results related to activities were similar to the photocurrent results. For further proving the enhancement effect of C_{60}, C_{60}/CdS (with various C_{60} contents) samples were also prepared as comparative candidates. The mass ratio of C_{60}/CdS was tuned from 0 to 1.5%, same to the mass ratio of C_{60}/TiO_2. From SI Figure S3, it could be observed that the optimal ratio of C_{60}/CdS (0.5 wt %) resulted in a hydrogen evolution rate of about 0.11 μmol $\cdot$ h^{-1}, about four times of that of CdS. These results further proved that C_{60} could accelerate the separation of photogenerated electrons for H_2 evolution. As a good photocatalyst for H_2 evolution, the stability played an important role for evaluating its photocatalytic performance. Herein, the sample of 0.50 wt % C_{60}-CdS/TiO_2 was repeated for H_2 evolution from water-splitting via recovering catalysts through centrifugation. As shown in Figure 6b, the H_2 evolution rate of the as-obtained sample could be well maintained even after three times of usage. The remaining reaction solution after reuse was also centrifuged and analyzed with ICP. The results indicated that nearly no cadmium ions were detected. For proving the promotion effect of C_{60} on the stability of CdS/ TiO_2 during the H_2 evolution, the recyclability of pure CdS/ TiO_2 was also investigated. As shown in SI

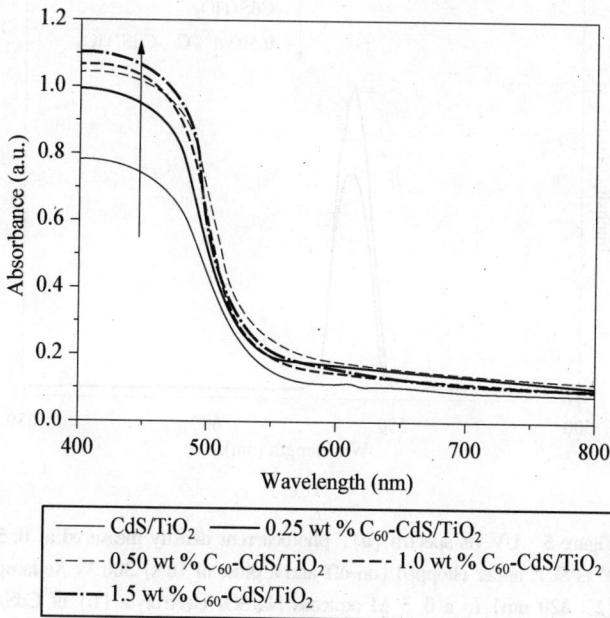

Absorbance (a.u.) vs Wavelength (nm)

— CdS/TiO_2   — 0.25 wt % C_{60}-CdS/TiO_2
---- 0.50 wt % C_{60}-CdS/TiO_2   ---- 1.0 wt % C_{60}-CdS/TiO_2
—·— 1.5 wt % C_{60}-CdS/TiO_2

(a)

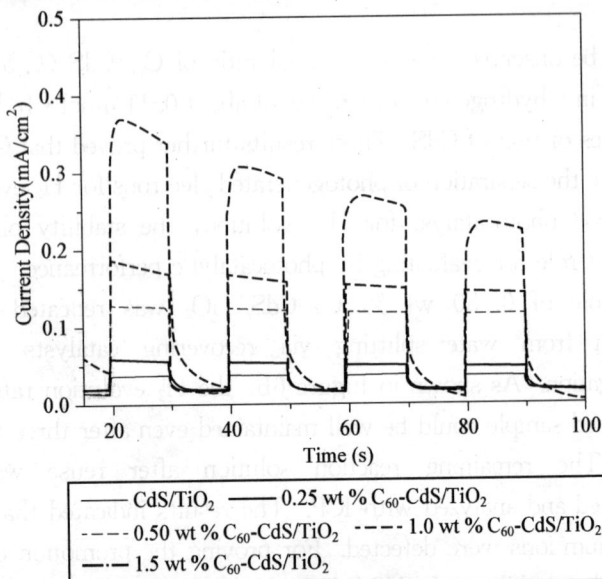

(b)

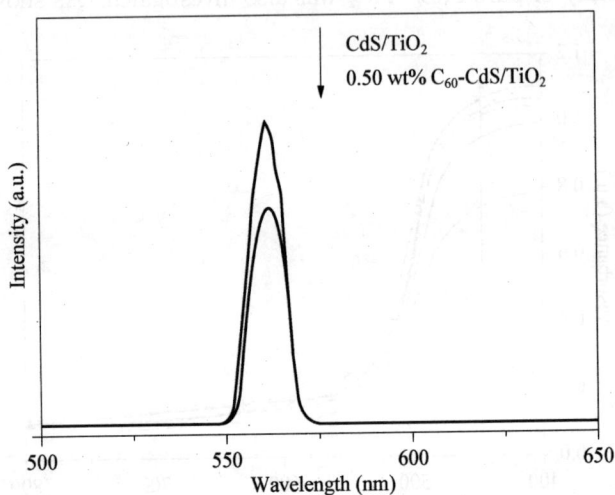

(c)

Figure 5   UV-vis spectra (a), photocurrent density measured at 0.5 V vs SCE under chopped (on-off and a pluse of 10 s) 300 W Xe lamp ($\lambda > 420$ nm) in a 0.5 M aqueous Na_2SO_4 electrolyte (b) of CdS/TiO_2 and C_{60}-CdS/TiO_2 samples, and photoluminescence spectra (c) of CdS/TiO_2 and 0.50 wt% C_{60}-CdS/TiO_2 excited by 280 nm.

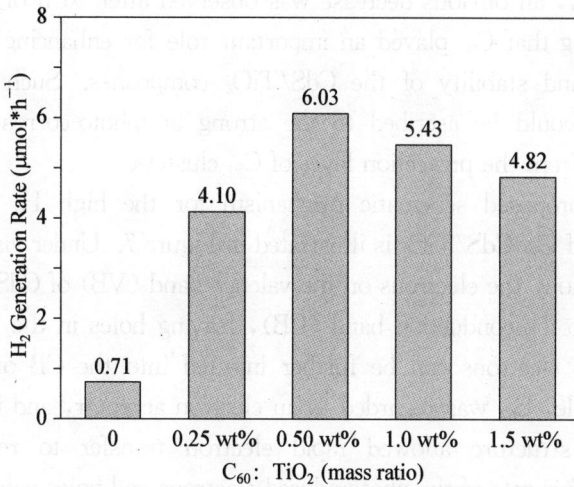

(a)

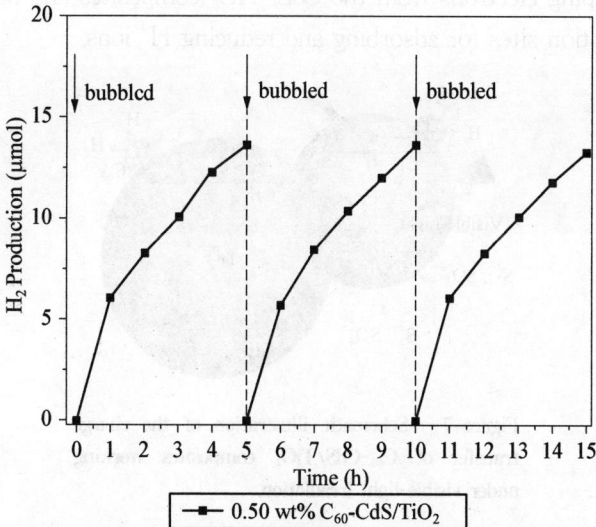

(b)

Figure 6 (a) Photocatalytic activities of the different amount of C_{60} in C_{60}-CdS/TiO_2. (b) Recycling test of the 0. 50 wt % C_{60}-CdS/ TiO_2 for H_2 evolution rate in aqueous solution under visible-light ($\lambda=$ 420 nm) LED light irradiation.

Figure S4, an obvious decrease was observed after 10 h of reaction, suggesting that C_{60} played an important role for enhancing both the activity and stability of the CdS/TiO₂ composites. Such excellent stability could be ascribed to the strong antiphoto-corrosion effect resulted from the protection layer of C_{60} clusters.

A proposed schematic mechanism for the high H_2 evolution activity of C_{60}-CdS/TiO₂ is illustrated in Figure 7. Under visible-light illumination, the electrons on the valence band (VB) of CdS could be excited to the conduction band (CB), leaving holes in the VB. And these CB electrons can be further injected into the CB of TiO₂.[11] Meanwhile, C_{60} was regarded as an electron acceptor, and its special electron structure allowed rapid electron transfer to reduce the combination rate of the photoinduced electrons and holes pairs. Thus, the loaded C_{60} clusters could act as electron transit stations for both fast trapping electrons from the CdS/TiO₂ composites and serving as H_2 evolution sites for adsorbing and reducing H^+ ions.

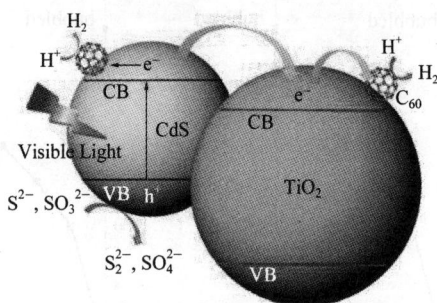

Figure 7   Schematic illustration of the charge transfer of C_{60}-CdS/TiO₂ composites working under visible-light irradiation.

4. CONCLUSIONS

C_{60}-CdS/TiO₂ were prepared using a novel method by preplanting crystal seeds (C_{60} and CdO) into the pore wall of ordered mesoporous TiO_2, accompanied by an ion-exchange route for tuning CdO to CdS. Such C_{60}-CdS/TiO_2 photocatalyst presented excellent photocatalytic activity during the water-splitting for H_2 evolution under visible-light irradiation ($\lambda = 420$ nm) and remarkable photostability owing to the presence of C_{60} cluster protecting layers in the TiO_2 framework. C_{60} layers effectively enhanced the light absorption capability of the prepared catalysts and greatly accelerated the photogenerated electron transfer velocity with the formation of antiphotocorrosion of CdS. Besides, they could also act as the electron transit stations for both fast trapping electrons from the CdS/ TiO_2 composites and serve as H_2 evolution sites for adsorbing and reducing H^+ ions.

■ASSOCIATED CONTENT

⑤ Supporting Information
XRD patterns of different content of C_{60} in C_{60}-CdS/TiO_2, TG analysis, H_2 photocatalytic evolution of C_{60}/CdS samples, and the recyclability of mesoporous CdS/TiO_2 for H_2 photocatalytic evolution. This material is available free of charge via the Internet at http://pubs. acs. org/.

■AUTHOR INFORMATION
Corresponding Authors
* E-mail: dqzhang@shnu. edu. cn (D. Z.).
* E-mail: Liguisheng@shnu. edu. cn (G. L.).
Author Contributions
† Equal contribution.
Notes
The authors declare no competing financial interest.

■ACKNOWLEDGMENTS
This work was supported by the National Natural Science Foundation of China (21207090, 21477079, and 21237003), Shanghai

Government (15QA1403300, 11SG42, 11ZR1426300, 13YZ054, and 14ZR1430900), PCSIRT (IRT1269), Doctoral Program by Higher Education (2012312712009), and by a scheme administrated by Shanghai Normal University (S30406).

References

[1] Schlapbach, L.; Zuttel, A. Review Article Hydrogen-Storage Materials for Mobile Applications. *Nature* 2001, *414*, 353 – 358.

[2] Churchard, A. J.; Banach, E.; Borgschulte, A.; Caputo, R.; Chen, J. C.; Clary, D. C.; Fijalkowski, K. J.; Geerlings, H.; Genova, R. V.; Grochala, W.; Jaron, T.; Juanes-Marcos, J. C.; Kasemo, B.; Kroes, G. -J.; Ljubic, I.; Naujoks, N.; Norskov, J. K.; Olsen, R. A.; Pendolino, F.; Remhof, A.; Romanszki, L.; Tekin, A.; Vegge, T.; Zach, M.; Zuettel, A. A Multifaceted Approach to Hydrogen Storage. *Phys. Chem. Chem. Phys.* 2011, *13*, 16955 – 16972.

[3] Xiang, Q.; Yu, J.; Jaroniec, M. Enhanced Photocatalytic H₂ Production Activity of Graphene-Modified Titania Nanosheets. *Nanoscale* 2011, *3*, 3670 – 3678.

[4] Fujishima, A.; Honda, K. Electrochemical Photolysis of Water at a Semiconductor Electrode. *Nature* 1972, *238*, 37 – 38.

[5] Li, Q.; Guo, B.; Yu, J.; Ran, J.; Zhang, B.; Yan, H.; Gong, J. R. Highly Efficient Visible-Light-Driven Photocatalytic Hydrogen Production of CdS-Cluster-Decorated Graphene Nano-sheets. *J. Am. Chem. Soc.* 2011, *133*, 10878 – 10884.

[6] Yu, J.; Yu, Y.; Zhou, P.; Xiao, W.; Cheng, B. Morphology-dependent photocatalytic H₂-production activity of CdS. *Appl. Catal.*, B 2014, *156 – 157*, 184 – 191.

[7] Li, X.; Jia, Y.; Cao, A. Tailored Single-Walled Carbon Nanotube-CdS Nanoparticle Hybrids for Tunable Optoelectronic Devices. *ACS Nano* 2010, *4*, 506 – 512.

[8] Pan, Z.; Zhang, H.; Cheng, K.; Hou, Y.; Hua, J.; Zhong, X. Highly Efficient Inverted Type-I CdS/CdSe Core/Shell Structure QD-Sensitized Solar Cells. *ACS Nano* 2012, *6*, 3982 – 3991.

[9] Ferancova, A.; Rengaraj, S.; Kim, Y.; Labuda, J.; Sillanpaa, M.

Electrochemical Determination of Guanine and Adenine by CdS Microspheres Modified Electrode and Evaluation of Damage to DNA Purine Bases by UV Radiation. *Biosens. Bioelectron.* 2010, *26*, 314 – 320.

[10] Li, Z. J.; Wang, J. J.; Li, X. B.; Fan, X. B.; Meng, Q. Y.; Feng, K.; Chen, B.; Tung, C. H.; Wu, L. Z. Photocatalysis: An Exceptional Artificial Photocatalyst, NiH-CdSe/CdS Core/Shell Hybrid, Made In Situ from CdSe Quantum Dots and Nickel Salts for Efficient Hydrogen Evolution. *Adv. Mater.* 2014, *25*, 6634 – 6634.

[11] Li, G. S.; Zhang, D. Q.; Yu, J. C. A New Visible-Light Photocatalyst: CdS Quantum Dots Embedded Mesoporous TiO₂. *Environ. Sci. Technol.* 2009, *43*, 7079 – 7085.

[12] Ke, D. N.; Liu, S. L.; Dai, K.; Zhou, J. P.; Zhang, L. N.; Peng, T. Y. CdS/Regenerated Cellulose Nanocomposite Films for Highly Efficient Photocatalytic H₂ Production under Visible Light Irradiation. *J. Phys. Chem.* C 2009, *113*, 16021 – 16026.

[13] Kudo, A.; Miseki, Y. Heterogeneous Photocatalyst Materials for Water Splitting. *Chem. Soc. Rev.* 2009, *38*, 253 – 278.

[14] Hu, Y.; Gao, X.; Yu, L.; Wang, Y.; Ning, J.; Xu, S.; Lou, X. W. Carbon-Coated CdS Petalous Nanostructures with Enhanced Photostability and Photocatalytic Activity. *Angew. Chem.*, *Int. Ed.* 2013, *125*, 5746 – 5749.

[15] Zhang, J.; Qiao, S. Z.; Qi, L.; Yu, J. Fabrication of NiS Modified CdS Nanorod p-n Junction Photocatalysts with Enhanced Visible-Light Photocatalytic H₂-Production Activity. *Phys. Chem. Chem. Phys.* 2013, *15*, 12088 – 12094.

[16] Ding, L.; Zhou, H.; Lou, S.; Ding, J.; Zhang, D.; Zhu, H.; Fan, T. Butterfly Wing Architecture Assisted CdS/Au/TiO₂ Z-Scheme Type Photocatalytic Water Splitting. *Int. J. Hydrogen Energy* 2013, *38*, 8244 – 8253.

[17] Yu, J. G.; Ma, T. T.; Liu, S. W. Enhanced Photocatalytic Activity of Mesoporous TiO₂ Aggregates by Embedding Carbon Nanotubes as Electron-Transfer Channel. *Phys. Chem. Chem. Phys.* 2011, *13*, 3491 – 3501.

[18] Dai, K.; Peng, T.; Ke, D.; Wei, B. Photocatalytic Hydrogen Generation Using a Nanocomposite of Multi-walled Carbon Nanotubes and TiO₂ Nanoparticles under Visible Light Irradiation. *Nanotechnology* 2009, *20*, 125603.

[19] An, G.; Ma, W.; Sun, Z.; Liu, Z.; Han, B.; Miao, S.; Miao, Z.; Ding,

K. Preparation of Titania/Carbon Nanotube Composites Using Supercritical Ethanol and Their Photocatalytic Activity for Phenol Degradation under Visible Light Irradiation. *Carbon* 2007, *45*, 1795 – 1801.

[20] Silva, C. G.; Faria, J. L. Photocatalytic Oxidation of Benzene Derivatives in Aqueous Suspensions: Synergic Effect Induced by the Introduction of Carbon Nanotubes in a TiO_2 Matrix. *Appl. Catal.*, *B* 2010, *101*, 81 – 89.

[21] Zhou, W.; Pan, K.; Qu, Y.; Sun, F.; Tian, C.; Ren, Z.; Tian, G.; Fu, H. Photodegradation of Organic Contamination in Wastewaters by Bonding TiO_2/Single-Walled Carbon Nanotube Composites with Enhanced Photocatalytic Activity. *Chemosphere* 2010, *81*, 555 – 561.

[22] Li, N.; Ma, Y.; Wang, B.; Huang, Y.; Wu, Y.; Yang, X.; Chen, Y. Synthesis of Semiconducting SWNTs by Arc Discharge and Their Enhancement of Water Splitting Performance with TiO_2 Photocatalyst. *Carbon* 2011, *49*, 5132 – 5141.

[23] Yu, J.; Ma, T.; Liu, G.; Cheng, B. Enhanced Photocatalytic Activity of Bimodal Mesoporous Titania Powders by C-60 Modification. *Dalton Trans.* 2011, *40*, 6635 – 6644.

[24] Fan, W.; Lai, Q.; Zhang, Q.; Wang, Y. Nanocomposites of TiO_2 and Reduced Graphene Oxide as Efficient Photocatalysts for Hydrogen Evolution. *J. Phys. Chem. C* 2011, *115*, 10694 – 10701.

[25] Xiang, Q.; Yu, J.; Jaroniec, M. Enhanced Photocatalytic H_2-Production Activity of Graphene-Modified Titania Nanosheets. *Nanoscale* 2011, *3*, 3670 – 3678.

[26] Jiang, G.; Lin, Z.; Chen, C.; Zhu, L.; Chang, Q.; Wang, N.; Wei, W.; Tang, H. TiO_2 Nanoparticles Assembled on Graphene Oxide Nanosheets with High Photocatalytic activity for Removal of Pollutants. *Carbon* 2011, *49*, 2693 – 2701.

[27] Fu, H.; Xu, T.; Zhu, S.; Zhu, Y. Photocorrosion Inhibition and Enhancement of Photocatalytic Activity for ZnO via Hybridization with C_{60}. *Environ. Sci. Technol.* 2008, *42*, 8064 – 8069.

[28] Yu, G.; Gao, J.; Hummelen, J. C.; Wudl, F.; Heeger, A. J. Polymer Photovoltaic Cells: Enhanced Efficiencies via a Network of Internal Donor-Acceptor Heterojunctions. *Science* 1995, *270*, 1789 – 1791.

[29] Li, G.; Jiang, B.; Li, X.; Lian, Z.; Xiao, S.; Zhu, J.; Zhang, D.; Li, H. C_{60}/$Bi_2TiO_4F_2$ Heterojunction Photocatalysts with Enhanced Visible-Light Activity for Environmental Remediation. *ACS Appl. Mater. Interfaces* 2013,

5,7190 - 7197.

[30] Dai, K.; Yao, Y.; Liu, H.; Mohamed, I.; Chen, H.; Huang, Q. Enhancing the Photocatalytic Activity of Lead Molybdate by Modifying with Fullerene. *J. Mol. Catal. A: Chem.* 2013,*374* - 375,111 - 117.

[31] Hassan, N.; Holze, R. A Comparative Electrochemical Study of Electrosorbed 2-and 4-Mercaptopyridines and Their Application as Corrosion Inhibitors at C₆₀ Steel. *J. Chem. Sci.* 2009,*121*,693 - 701.

[32] Yu, J. G.; Qi, L. F.; Jaroniec, M. Hydrogen Production by Photocatalytic Water Splitting over Pt/TiO₂ Nanosheets with Exposed (001) Facets. *J. Phys. Chem.* C 2010,*114*,13118 - 13125.

[33] Li, H. X.; Bian, Z. F.; Zhu, J.; Huo, Y. N.; Li, H.; Lu, Y. F. Mesoporous Au/TiO₂ Nanocomposites with Enhanced Photocatalytic Activity. *J. Am. Chem. Soc.* 2007,*129*,4538 - 4539.

[34] Yang, H. G.; Sun, C. H.; Qiao, S. Z.; Zou, J.; Liu, G.; Smith, S. C.; Cheng, H. M.; Lu, G. Q. Anatase TiO₂ Single Crystals with a Large Percentage of Reactive Facets. *Nature* 2008,*453*,638 - 641.

[35] Yu, J. C.; Li, G. S.; Wang, X. C.; Hu, X. L.; Leung, C. W.; Zhang, Z. D. An Ordered Cubic Im3m Mesoporous Cr-TiO₂ Visible Light Photocatalyst. *Chem. Commun.* 2006,2717 - 2719.

[36] Amer, M. S.; Busbee, J. D. Self-Assembled Hierarchical Structure of Fullerene Building Blocks; Single-Walled Carbon Nanotubes and C₆₀. *J. Phys. Chem.* C 2011,*115*,10483 - 10488.

[37] Kratschmer, W.; Lamb, L. D.; Fostiropoulos, K.; Huffman, D. R. Solid C₆₀: A New Form of Carbon. *Nature* 1990,*347*,354 - 358.

[38] Wang, F.; Zhang, K. Physicochemical and Photocatalytic Activities of Self-Assembling TiO₂ Nanoparticles on Nanocarbons Surface. *Curr. Appl. Phys.* 2012,*12*,346 - 352.

[39] Liu, B.; Zeng, H. C. Carbon Nanotubes Supported Mesoporous Mesocrystals of Anatase TiO₂. *Chem. Mater.* 2008,*20*,2711 - 2718.

[40] Wang, W. D.; Serp, P.; Kalck, P.; Luís Faria, J. Photocatalytic Degradation of Phenol on MWNT and Titania Composite Catalysts Prepared by a Modified Sol-Gel Method. *Appl. Catal.*, B 2005,*56*,305 - 312.

[41] Cheng, B.; Le, Y.; Yu, J. Preparation and Enhanced Photocatalytic Activity of Ag @ TiO₂ Core-Shell Nanocomposite Nanowires. *J. Hazard. Mater.* 2010,*177*,971 - 977.

[42] Yu, J. G.; Xiong, J.; Cheng, B.; Liu, S. Fabrication and Characterization of

Ag-TiO₂ Multiphase Nanocomposite Thin Films with Enhanced Photocatalytic Activity. *Appl. Catal.*, B 2005, 60, 211 – 221.

[43] Stewart, M. H.; Huston, A. L.; Scott, A. M.; Oh, E.; Algar, W. R.; Deschamps, J. R.; Susumu, K.; Jain, V.; Prasuhn, D. E.; Blanco-Canosa, J.; Dawson, P. E.; Medintz, I. L. Competition between Förster Resonance Energy Transfer and Electron Transfer in Stoichiometrically Assembled Semiconductor Quantum Dot-Fullerene Conjugates. *ACS Nano* 2013, 7, 9489 – 9505.

[44] Jing, L.; Cao, Y.; Cui, H.; Durrant, J. R.; Tang, J.; Liu, D.; Fu, H. Acceleration Effects of Phosphate Modification on the Decay Dynamics of Photo-Generated Electrons of TiO₂ and Its Photocatalytic Activity. *Chem. Commun.* 2012, 48, 10775 – 10777.

(原载于 Aca Applied Materials & Interfaces 2015 年第 8 期)

A flexible spiral-type supercapacitor based on $ZnCo_2O_4$ nanorod electrode

Hao Wu,[a, b] Zheng Lou,[b] Hong Yang[a] and Guozhen Shen[b]

[a] The Key Laboratory of Resource Chemistry of Ministry of Education, Shanghai Key Laboratory of Rare Earth Functional Materials, and Shanghai Municipal Education Committee Key Laboratory of Molecular Imaging Probes and Sensors, Shanghai Normal University, Shanghai 200234, China

[b] State Key Laboratory for Superlattices and Microstructures, Institute of Semiconductors, Chinese Academy of Sciences

1. Introduction

The increasing demand for portable and flexible electronics such as roll-up displays, photovoltaic cells, and wearable devices have initiated intensive efforts to explore flexible, light-weight and environmentally friendly energy storage devices.[1-5] As a new class of energy storage devices, flexible supercapacitors (SCs) have attracted much attention as a promising energy source for wearable electronics due to their remarkable advantages such as high power density and relatively large energy density, fast charge/discharge capability, light weight, excellent reliability and flexibility. Despite the significant advances achieved in electrode materials for SCs,[6-11] the practical applications of supercapacitors were still seriously hindered due to the relatively poor performance of the electrode materials, such as low specific capacitance in carbon based materials, poor cycling stability in transition metal oxides, and very high cost of RuO_2 based materials. Therefore, more effort is still desired to further improve the electrochemical performance of electrode materials in order to build better SCs with both high power and energy densities. It has been proven to be an effective strategy to utilise nanostructure engineering, including nanoparticles, hollow nano-architectures and one-dimensional (1D) nanostructures to contribute greatly to the optimization of electrode properties with higher capacity/ capacitance because of the increased active surface areas, short ion transport pathways and so on.[7, 12-16]

$ZnCo_2O_4$ has been considered as an attractive candidate for substitution of the conventional graphite anode in supercapacitors due to its superiorities such as improved reversible capacities, enhanced cycling stability, and good environmental benignity.[17-20] The $ZnCo_2O_4$ with a spinel structure, where the Zn^{2+} occupies the tetrahedral sites and the Co^{3+} occupies the octahedral sites, has been widely investigated as a high-performance material for supercapacitors.[17, 21, 22] In recent years, $ZnCo_2O_4$ as electrode materials for supercapacitors has begun to attract attention for its low cost and excellent electrochemical performance.[23-26] For example, Hope-Weeks's group synthesized the $ZnCo_2O_4$ nanocrystal and tested its supercapacitor properties. However, the tedious preparation process and the low specific capacitance (700 F g^{-1} at 5 mV s^{-1}) made it difficult to meet the demands of practical application.[15] Liu and co-workers recently fabricated a one dimensional $ZnCo_2O_4$ nanorods/nickel foam integrated electrode; although it exhibited good electrochemical performance at low current densities, its specific capacitance (1400 F g^{-1} at 1 A g^{-1}) and cycling stability (only 1000 cycles at 6 A g^{-1} were given) were still unsatisfactory.[21] Gang's group has prepared highly porous $ZnCo_2O_4$ nanotubes, which shows a remarkable cycling ability of 689 F g^{-1} at 10 A g^{-1} after 3000 cycles together with an excellent rate capability of 588 F g^{-1} at 60 A g^{-1} (84% capacity retention).[27] From the above, we can conclude that $ZnCo_2O_4$ could be considered as attractive materials.

Herein, by flexible coaxial fiber assembly of hierarchical $ZnCo_2O_4$ nanorod arrays/Ni wire electrodes, we designed a new class of flexible all-solid-state planar-integrated fiber supercapacitors (FSC), allowing us to obtain good electrochemical capacitance performance, with a high specific capacitance of 10.9 F g^{-1} at a scan rate of 10 mV s^{-1}, an energy density of 76 mWh kg^{-1} and a power density of up to 1.9 W kg^{-1}. To our knowledge, this is the first time that $ZnCo_2O_4$ nanorod arrays have been grown on a Ni wire substrate and directly used as electrode materials for supercapacitors.

2. Experimental

2.1 Synthesis of materials

Hydrochloric acid (HCl), ethanol and acetone were procured from Merck (India) Ltd. Potassium hydroxide (KOH; FW=56.11), urea (CO$(NH_2)_2$; MW=60.06), cobalt nitrate hexa-hydrate (Co $(NO_3)_2$ · $6H_2O$; FW=291.04), ammonium fluoride (NH$_4$F; FW= 37.04) and zinc nitrate hexahydrate-(Zn$(NO_3)_2$ · $6H_2O$; FW=297. 47) were procured from Alfa Aesar A Johnson Matthey company. Polyvinylalcohol (PVA; MW=70000 - 100000) was procured from Himedia Laboratories Pvt. Ltd. Moreover, double distilled water was used for all the experiments.

Synthesis of the $ZnCo_2O_4$ nanorods on a Ni wire. Prior to deposition, commercial Ni wires were cleaned by sonication sequentially in acetone, 1 M HCl solution, deionized water and ethanol for 15 min. After being dried, the Ni wire was transferred into a Teflon-lined stainless autoclave. In a typical synthesis of $ZnCo_2O_4$ nanorods, 1 mmol Zn$(NO_3)_2$ · $6H_2O$, 2 mmol Co$(NO_3)_2$ · $6H_2O$, 6 mmol CO $(NH_2)_2$ and 5 mmol of NH$_4$F were dissolved in 30 mL deionized water by constant stirring, and the mixture was stirred to form a pink solution in the 50 mL Teflon-lined stainless autoclave. Then, the pre-treated Ni wires were put in the above autoclave, heated to 120℃, and kept at that temperature for 6 h. After the autoclave had cooled down to room temperature, the product was collected, washed, vacuum-dried, and then thermally treated at 350℃ for 3 h at a rate of 5 ℃ min^{-1} to obtain $ZnCo_2O_4$ nanorods.

The PVA/KOH polymer electrolyte was prepared as follows: in a typical process, 3 g PVA was dissolved in 25 mL DI water with stirring at 98 ℃ for 1 h. Then, 3 g KOH was dissolved in 5 mL DI water. Finally, the above two solutions were mixed together at 60 ℃ under vigorous stirring until the solution became clear.

2. 2 Characterization

The synthesized products were characterized with an X-ray diffractometer (XRD; X'Pert PRO, PANalytical B. V., the Netherlands) with radiation from a Cu target (Kα, $\lambda=0.15406$ nm). The morphologies of the samples were characterized using electron microscopy (SEM; NANOSEM 650 - 6700F, 15 kV) and transmission electron microscopy (HRTEM; JEOLJEM-2010HT).

2. 3 Electrochemical characterization

CV were examined at the scan rates of 0.01—1000 V s^{-1} and EIS were recorded in the frequency range of 0.01—100 kHz with a 5 mV ac amplitude at a CHI760D electrochemical workstation.

2. 4 Calculation

The specific capacitances can be calculated from the CV curve by using the equation:[28-30]

$$C = Q/V = I/S \tag{1}$$
$$C_V = C/m \tag{2}$$

where C is the capacitance, Q is the charge accumulated in the capacitors, V is the potential in the CV curve, I is the current in the CV curve, and S is the scan rate.[29] The energy density and power density of the device were obtained from the equations:[30]

$$E = C_{sp} \times \Delta V^2 / 7200 \tag{3}$$

$$P = E \times 3600 / \Delta t \tag{4}$$

where E is the energy density (in Wh g^{-1}), P is the power density (in W g^{-1}) and Δt is the total discharge time (in seconds).

3. Results and discussion

The fabrication of the fiber solid-state SC is shown in Fig. 1. First, one commercial Ni wire sample, serving as an anode, was wound around a steel rod and then pulled out, resulting in the formation of a spiral-type electrode (Fig. 1 step 1, 2). $ZnCo_2O_4$ nanorods grown on the Ni wire were synthesized by the hydrothermal method (Fig. 1 step 3), and the spiral-type electrode was then coated with a layer of PVA/KOH gel electrolyte (Fig. 1 step 4). The gel

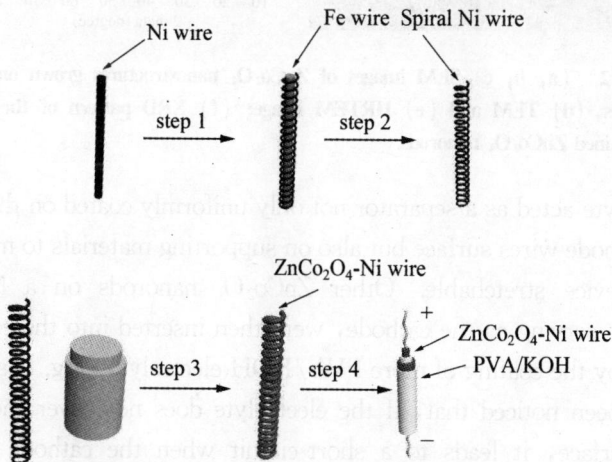

Fig. 1 Schematic illustration for designing of highly flexible coaxial fiber supercapacitors.

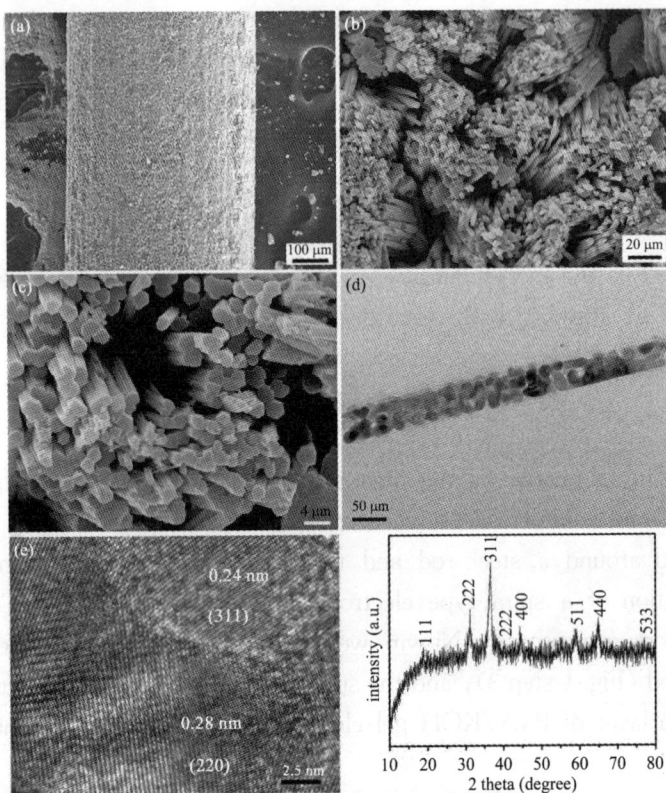

Fig. 2 (a, b, c) SEM images of ZnCo₂O₄ nanostructures grown on Ni wires, (d) TEM and (e) HRTEM image; (f) XRD pattern of the as-obtained ZnCo₂O₄ nanorods.

electrolyte acted as a separator not only uniformly coated on the anode and cathode wires surface but also on supporting materials to make the fiber device stretchable. Other ZnCo₂O₄ nanorods on a Ni wire sample, serving as the cathode, were then inserted into the coil, followed by the coating of more PVA/KOH electrolyte (Fig. 1 step 4). It has been noticed that, if the electrolyte does not cover the whole wire surface, it leads to a short-circuit when the cathode wire is inserted into the anode one. Furthermore, the specifically selected solid-state electrolyte for the fiber SC will overcome the major drawbacks of conventional liquid electrolytes, such as leakage of the electrolyte, difficulty in device integration and environmental stability, which are crucial for the development of useful wearable fiber devices.

The $ZnCo_2O_4$ nanorods were grown on Ni wires *via* a conventional hydrothermal method. Fig. 2a – c shows the scanning electron microscopy (SEM) images of the products with 5 mmol NH_4F. It can be seen that the $ZnCo_2O_4$ nanorods were uniformly grown on a Ni wire, as shown in Fig. 2a. Fig. 2b and c depict the SEM image of the pure $ZnCo_2O_4$ nanorods grown on the Ni wires substrate with a diameter of about 50 nm. The microstructures of the $ZnCo_2O_4$ nanorods were also investigated by using transmission electron microscopy (TEM). Fig. 2d shows a low-magnification TEM

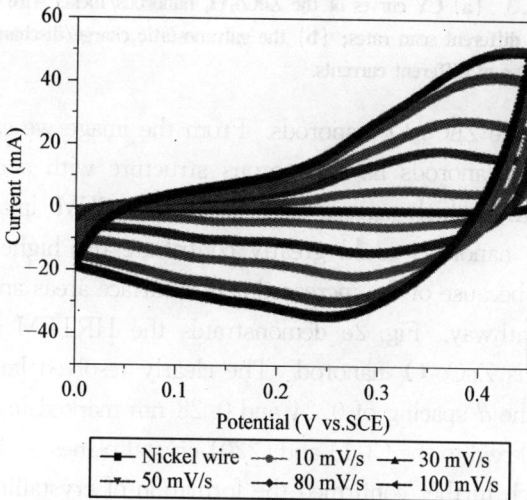

(a)

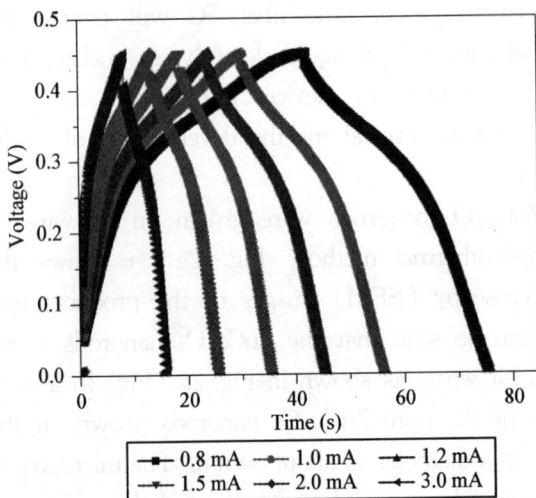

(b)

Fig. 3 (a) CV curves of the $ZnCo_2O_4$ nanorods/nickel wire at the different scan rates; (b) the galvanostatic charge/discharge curves at different currents.

image of single $ZnCo_2O_4$ nanorods. From the image we can see that the $ZnCo_2O_4$ nanorods have a porous structure with a diameter of about 50 nm, which agrees well with the SEM images. One-dimensional nanorods could greatly contribute the higher capacity/capacitance because of the increased active surface areas and short ion transport pathway. Fig. 2e demonstrates the HRTEM image of a single porous $ZnCo_2O_4$ nanorod. The clearly resolved lattice fringes show that the d-spacing of 0.24 and 0.28 nm marked in the pattern could be indexed to the (311) and (220) crystal planes of the $ZnCo_2O_4$ phase, which further confirmed the formation of crystalline $ZnCo_2O_4$ nanorods and agreed well with the result of X-ray diffraction (XRD) data.[31] The phase and composition of the nanorods were investigated by peeling off the nickel wires. As shown in Fig. 2f, the XRD pattern of the precursor is well consistent with previous reports.[32-34] It is obvious that all of the observed peaks' position are in good agreement with the $ZnCo_2O_4$ structure of the standard card of JCPDS card no. 23 - 1390.

The electrochemical properties of the $ZnCo_2O_4$ nanorods on a Ni wire electrode were first measured in a three-electrode cell using a 3 M KOH electrolyte; a platinum electrode and a saturated calomel electrode (SCE) were used as the counter electrode and reference electrode, respectively. Fig. 3a shows the representative cyclic voltammetry (CV) curves recorded at different scan rates ranging from 10 to 100 mV s^{-1}, and one pair of redox peaks can be clearly seen. All of the curves show obvious pseudocapacitance features with a pair of well-defined redox peaks within 0 - 0. 45 V (*vs.* SEC). The pair of peaks is mainly associated with the Faradaic redox reaction related to M-O/M-O-OH, where M refers to Ni or Co. [32, 33] Accompanying the increase in the scan rate, the peak currents were also increased, suggesting that the one-dimensional porous nanorods were beneficial to fast redox reactions, furthermore no redox peaks can be observed in the pure nickel wire at 10 mV s^{-1}. To further evaluate the potential application of the $ZnCo_2O_4$ as electrodes for electrochemical supercapacitors, galvanostatic charge-discharge measurements were carried out between 0 and 0. 45 V (*vs.* SEC) at various currents ranging from 0. 8 to 3. 0 mA, as shown in Fig. 3b. The voltage plateaus during the charge/discharge process were consistent with the CV results and the nonlinear characteristics further verified the pseudocapacitance behavior. The electrochemical reaction of $ZnCo_2O_4$ with the electrolyte can be written as follows:

$$ZnCo_2O_4 + OH^- \rightarrow ZnCo_2O_4/OH + ZnCo_2O_4 - OH$$

Here, $ZnCo_2O_4/OH$ represents the electric double layer formed by the hydroxyl ion, and $ZnCo_2O_4$-OH represents the product formed by the cathode reaction involving the hydroxyl ion. [35]

Fig. 4a shows a galvanostatic charging-discharging test which was conducted in a stable potential window between 0 and 1 V at various current densities ranging from 0.5 to 2 mA. We can observe that the charge/discharge behavior has a good symmetry, indicating that the charge/discharge straight line was provided with excellent

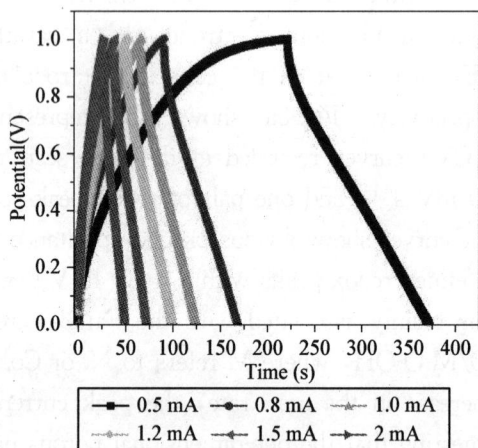

(a)

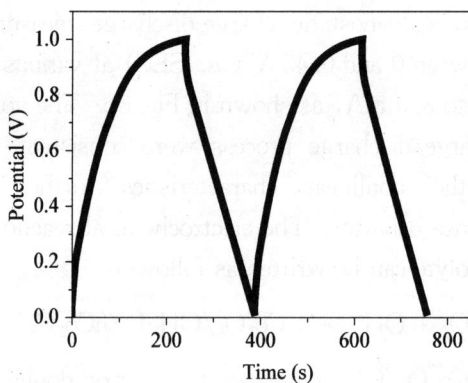

(b)

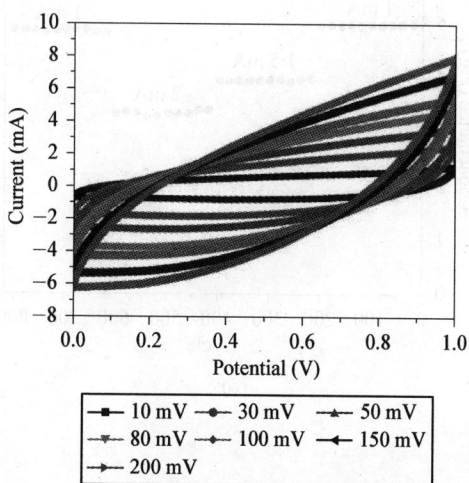

(c)

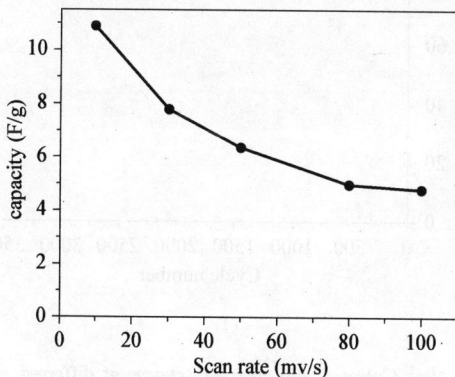

(d)

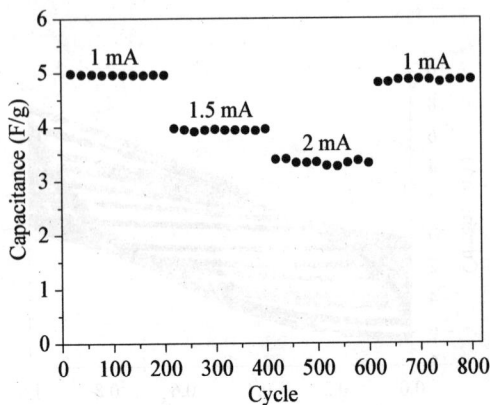

(e)

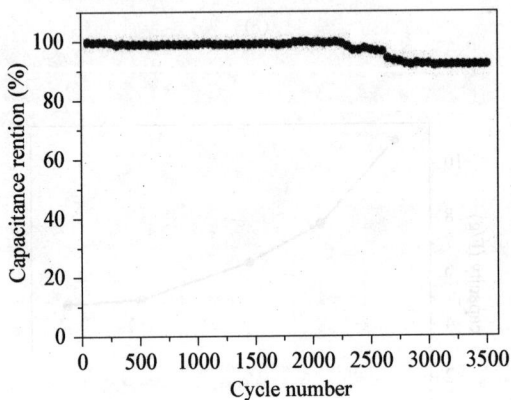

(f)

Fig. 4 (a) Galvanostatic charge-discharge at different currents measured in the voltage window of 0 – 1 V; (b) galvanostatic charge/ discharge curve at a current of 0. 08 mA; (c) cyclic voltammograms from 10 to 200 mV s^{-1}; (d) the plot of the capacitance as a function of potential at various scan rates; (e) cycle performance with the increasing currents; (f) capacitance retention on cycle number at a current of 2 mA.

coulomb efficiency. [36] Fig. 4b illustrates the charge/discharge behavior of the FSC devices at a current of 0. 5 mA. A relatively small voltage drop (0. 15 V) is shown in Fig. 4b, indicating excellent SC performance of the as-designed FSC. From Fig. 4c, we can judge that the FSC devices are operated by scan rates ranging from 10 to 200 mV s^{-1}. From the plot, it can be observed that the curves of the two electrode systems are obviously different from those of the above three-electrode systems (Fig. 3a), which mainly represent the absence of redox peaks. Briefly, supercapacitors can be classified into two categories: the non-Faradaic electrical double-layer capacitor and the Faradaic redox pseudocapacitor. These two mechanisms can work separately or together, depending on the active electrode materials used in the capacitors. For our two-electrode system, it clearly reveals that the feature of electrical double-layer capacitor occupied a more dominant position than that of the typical pseudocapacitor. Besides, no obvious redox peaks are observed in the present work, indicating that the current supercapacitors are charged and discharged at a pseudoconstant rate. [37, 38] Thus, we can draw the conclusion that two-electrode devices are primarily nonfaradaic within their corresponding voltage window. [27] Actually, this common phenomenon is observed in many symmetric supercapacitors reported previously. [26] We calculated the capacity of the flexible device at different scan rates, ranging from 10 to 100 mV s^{-1} and the corresponding result is depicted in Fig. 4d. From the curve, the largest capacitance could be obtained to be about 10. 90 F g^{-1} at a scan rate of 10 mV s^{-1}, and the specific capacitance was calculated to range from 4. 85 F g^{-1} at 100 mV s^{-1} to 10. 90 F g^{-1} at 10 mV s^{-1}, which was higher than that of ZnCo$_2$O$_4$@carbon fibers (0. 4 mF at 100 mV s^{-1} to 0. 85 mF at 30 mV s^{-1})[26] and revealed that one-dimensional ZnCo$_2$O$_4$ nanorods could greatly contribute to the optimization of electrode properties with higher capacity/capacitance. The cycling performance of the FSC at a progressively increased current was carried out as shown in Fig. 4e. After 800 times of continuous cycling at varied current, the current returned to 1 mA and was revealed to be 97. 9% of the initial capacitance at 1 mA. It could then be recovered and maintained for another 200 cycles, which was much higher than previously reported values. [21, 30] Fig. 4f shows cyclic stability, we can find that the capacitance was maintained at 92% of its original value at 2 mA after 3500 charge/discharge cycles, revealing its excellent cycling stability, which can be attributed to the mechanical stability of the active materials and good contact between the electrode and current collector origin of the direct growth of $ZnCo_2O_4$ nanostructures on the Ni wire substrate. Above that, it makes it possible to consider it as an attractive candidate in supercapacitors due to its superior qualities such as improved reversible capacities, and enhanced cycling stability.

Electrochemical impedance spectroscopy (EIS) and rate capability are two important parameters to determine the performances of SCs. Fig. 5a shows the energy density and power density (Ragone chart). The energy density varied from 42 to 76 mWh kg^{-1} with a power density ranging from 0. 50 to 1. 9 W kg^{-1}. Our fabricated FSC also revealed an open circuit voltage of 0. 4 V which can be maintained for 10. 8 h after being fully charged and can also have a low leakage current of 0. 4 mA (Fig. 5b and c), indicating excellent energy storage performance. Fig. 5d and the inset show the Nyquist plots in frequen-

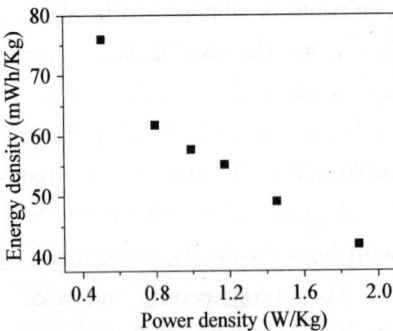

(a)

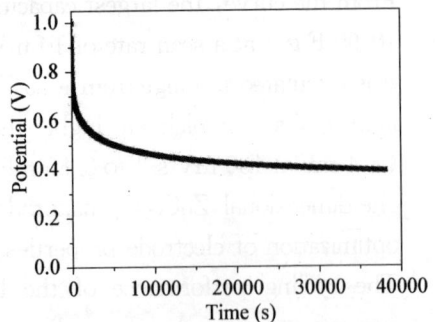

(b)

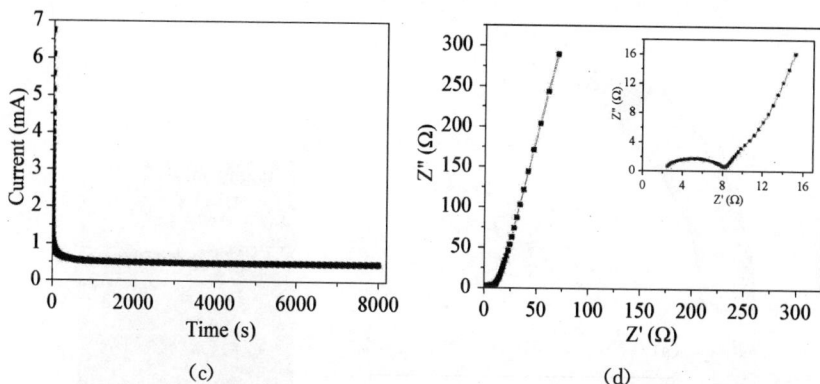

Fig. 5 (a) Volume energy and power density of the fiber solid-state supercapacitor; (b) self-discharge curve and (c) leakage current curve of the device; (d) Nyquist plots showing the imaginary part *versus* the real part of impedance. Inset shows the high-frequency region of the plot.

cies ranging from 100 kHz to 0. 01 Hz with an ac perturbation of 5 mV. In the high frequency region, the intercept of the semicircle with the real axis represents the equivalent series resistance (ESR) including the resistance of the electrolyte solution, the intrinsic resistance of the active material, and the contact resistance of the interface active material/current collector. The x-intercept of the Nyquist plots represents the ESR of two-electrode SC, and the charge transport resistance is 2. 23 Ω,[39] revealing that our electrodes have a very small resistance with good ion response. The reason may be that one-dimensional nanorods could shorten the ion transport pathway and decrease resistance.

The mechanical stability of the FSC under bending states is a key parameter for practical use. Compared with the planar device, the fiber device can be strong enough to bear the generated tensile force, and the performance of fiber supercapacitors is almost the same under different angles, which is very useful in practical applications.[40] Thus the flexibility of our coaxial FSC was further enhanced. A schematic diagram in Fig. 6a shows the FSCs in different bending states. Fig. 6b shows the charge/discharge curves at a current of 1. 5 mA under the

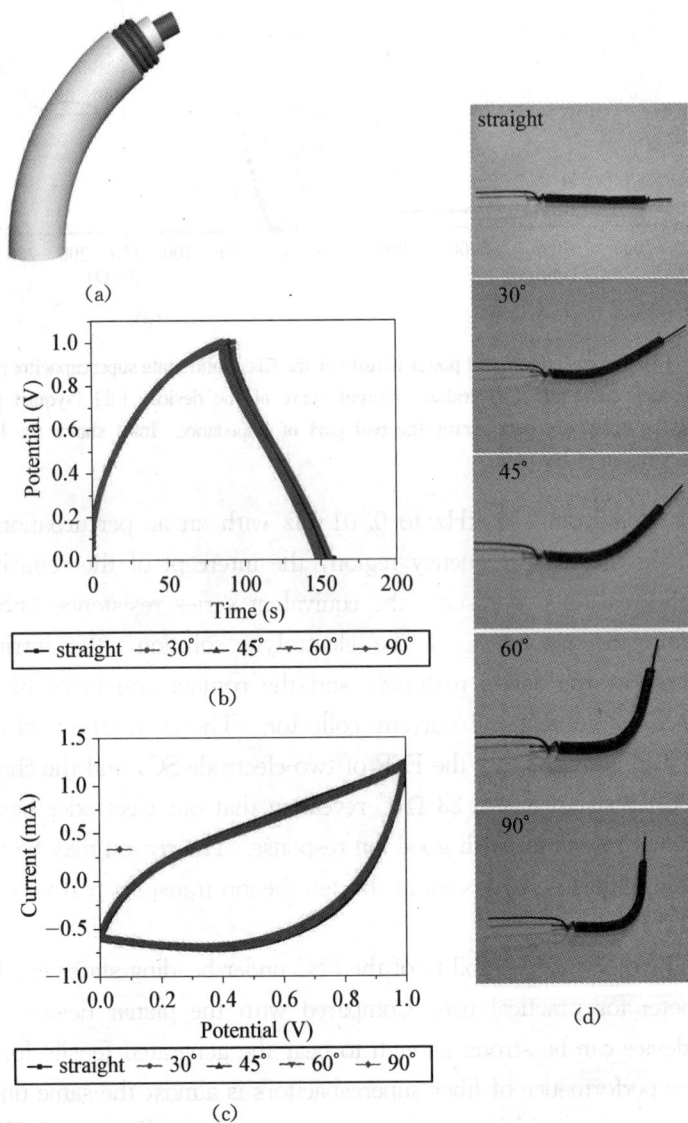

Fig. 6 (a) Fiber SCs in bending states; (b) charge/discharge curves at a current of 1.5 mA in straight and different bending states, respectively; (c) CV curves at 100 mV s⁻¹ in straight and different bending states, respectively; (d) photos of coaxial FSC under the different bending states, straight, 30°, 45°, 60°, 90°.

different angles, which demonstrate that our device can maintain good fiber shape and have excellent flexibility. Fig. 6c demonstrates the CV curves of the FSC deformed from the straight state to the 90° status. Meanwhile the low performance degradation indicates the high stability of the as-fabricated coaxial FSC. Fig. 6d presents the photos of our coaxial FSC under the different bending states (30°, 45°, 60°, 90°), which demonstrated that our device has excellent flexibility. These results make it possible to design patterns for wearable devices applications.

4. Conclusions

We have successfully developed a spiral-type flexible fiber supercapacitor based on $ZnCo_2O_4$ nanorod electrodes as active materials on a Ni wire. The specific capacitances reached 10.9 F g^{-1} at a scan rate of 30 mV s^{-1}, an energy density of 76 mWh kg^{-1} and a power density of up to 1.9 W kg^{-1}. Outstanding cycling ability and excellent flexibility have also been achieved. The enhanced performance is attributed to the one-dimensional $ZnCo_2O_4$ nanorod structure, which increases active surface areas, shortens ion transport pathways and so on. In view of their excellent electrochemical performance and facile and cost-effective synthesis, these $ZnCo_2O_4$ nanostructures might hold great promise as advanced electrode materials for high-performance supercapacitors. Furthermore, by decreasing the diameter of the metal fiber, flexible fiber supercapacitors with smaller diameter and size are expected to be fabricated, which will make it possible to weave the fiber supercapacitor into design patterns for wearable electronic applications.

Acknowledgements

This work was supported by the National Natural Science Foundation (61377033).

References

[1] M. F. El-Kady and R. B. Kaner, *Science*, 2012,335,1326.

[2] G. H. Yu and Y. Cui, *Nano Energy*, 2013,2,213.

[3] X. Lu, Y. Zeng, M. Yu, T. Zhai, C. Liang, S. Xie, M. Balogun and Y. X. Tong, *Adv. Mater.*, 2014,26,3148.

[4] B. Yao, L. Y. Yuan, X. Xiao, J. Zhang, B. Hu and W. Chen, *Nano Energy*, 2013,2,1071.

[5] N. Liu, W. Ma, J. Tao, X. Zhang, J. Su, L. Li, C. Yang, D. Golberg and Y. Bando, *Adv. Mater.*, 2013,25,4925.

[6] P. J. Hall, M. Mirzaeian, S. I. Fletcher and F. B. Sillars, *Energy Environ. Sci.*, 2010,3,1238.

[7] A. S. Aricò, S. A. Antonino, P. Bruce, B. Scrosati, J. M. Tarascon and W. V. Schalkwijk, *Nat. Mater.*, 2005,4,366.

[8] Z. G. Yin and Q. D. Zheng, *Adv. Energy Mater.*, 2012,2,179.

[9] Y. Fang, B. Luo, Y. Y. Jia, X. L. Li, B. Wang, Q. Song and F. Y. Kang, *Adv. Mater.*, 2012,24,6348.

[10] L. Zhang, W. Bin and H. X. W. Lou, *Chem. Commun.*, 2012,48,6912.

[11] T. Zhu, J. S. Chen and X. W. Lou, *J. Mater. Chem.*, 2010,20,7015.

[12] L. L. Wang, J. N. Deng, Z. Lou and T. Zhang, *J. Mater. Chem. A*, 2014, 2,10022.

[13] X. W. Lou, L. A. Archer and Z. C. Yang, *Adv. Mater.*, 2008,20,3987.

[14] L. L. Wang, H. M. Dou, Z. Lou and T. Zhang, *Nanoscale*, 2013,5,2686.

[15] L. L. Hu, B. H. Qu, Q. H. Li and T. H. Wang, *J. Mater. Chem. A*, 2013, 1,5596.

[16] L. L. Wang, T. Fei, Z. Lou and T. Zhang, *ACS Appl. Mater. Interfaces*, 2011,3,4689.

[17] Y. Sharma, N. Sharma, G. Rao and B. Chowdari, *Adv. Funct. Mater.*, 2007,17,2855.

[18] S. G. Mohamed, T. F. Hung, M. H. Hsiehe and B. J. Lee, *RSC Adv.*, 2013,3,20143.

[19] N. Du, Y. F. Xu, H. Zhang, J. X. Yu, C. X. Zhai and D. R. Yang, *Inorg. Chem.*, 2011,50,3320.

[20] D. Deng and J. Y. Lee, *Nanotechnology*, 2011,22,355.

[21] B. Liu, B. Y. Liu and G. Z. Shen, *ACS Appl. Mater. Interfaces*, 2013,

5,10011.

[22] Y. C. Qiu, S. H. Yang, H. Deng and W. S. Li, *J. Mater. Chem.*, 2010,20, 4439.

[23] W. Luo, X. L. Hu, Y. M. Sun and Y. H. Huang, *J. Mater. Chem.*, 2012, 22,8916.

[24] K. Karthikeyan, D. Kalpana and N. G. Renganathan, *Ionics*, 2009,15,107.

[25] M. Davis, C. Guemeci and B. Black, *RSC Adv.*, 2012,2,2061.

[26] B. Liu, D. S. Tan, X. F. Wang, D. Chen and G. Z. Shen, *Small*, 2013, 9,1998.

[27] G. Zhou, J. Zhu, Y. J. Chen and T. H. Wang, *Electrochim. Acta*, 2014, 123,450.

[28] G. Pandolfo and A. F. Hollenkamp, *J. Power Sources*, 2006,157,11.

[29] J. Bae, M. K. Song, Y. J. Park, J. M. Kim, M. L. Liu and Z. L. Wang, *Angew. Chem.*, *Int. Ed.*, 2011,50,1683.

[30] Q. F. Wang, X. F. Wang and G. Z. Shen, *Nano Energy*, 2014,8,44.

[31] F. X. Bao, X. F. Wang and X. Y. Liu, *RSC Adv.*, 2014,4,2393.

[32] H. L. Wang, Q. M. Gao and L. Jiang, *Small*, 2011,7,2454.

[33] S. V. Bangale and R. D. Prakshale, *J. Porous Mater.*, 2012,2,20.

[34] B. Liu, J. Zhang, X. F. Wang, G. Chen, D. Chen, C. W. Zhou and G. Z. Shen, *Nano Lett.*, 2012,12,3005.

[35] D. Choi, G. E. Blomgren and P. N. Kumta, *Adv. Mater.*, 2006,18,1178.

[36] M. D. Stoller and R. S. Ruoff, *Energy Environ. Sci.*, 2010,3,1294.

[37] L. Yang, S. Cheng, Y. Ding, X. B. Zhu, Z. L. Wang and M. L. Liu, *Nano Lett.*, 2012,12,321.

[38] X. Y. Lang, A. Hirata, J. T. Fu and M. W. Chen, *Nat. Nano-technol.*, 2011,6,232.

[39] D. W. Wang, F. Li, W. C. Ren, Z. G. Chen, J. Tan, Z. S. Wu, I. Gentle, G. Q. Lu and H. M. Cheng, *ACS Nano*, 2009,3,1745.

[40] H. Sun, X. You, J. Deng and H. S. Peng, *Angew. Chem.*, *Int. Ed.*, 2014, 53,6664.

Graphene oxide-BaGdF$_5$ nanocomposites for multi-modal imaging and photothermal therapy

Hao Zhang[a], Huixia Wu[a,*], Jun Wang[a],
Yan Yang[a], Dongmei Wu[b], Yingjian Zhang[c],
Yang Zhang[a], Zhiguo Zhou[a], Shiping Yang[a]

[a] The Key Laboratory of Resource Chemistry of Ministry of Education, Shanghai Key Laboratory of Rare Earth Functional Materials, Shanghai Municipal Education Committee Key Laboratory of Molecular Imaging Probes and Sensors, Shanghai Normal University
[b] Shanghai Key Laboratory of Magnetic Resonance, Department of Physics, East China Normal University
[c] Department of Nuclear Medicine, Fudan University Shanghai Cancer Center, Department of Oncology, Shanghai Medical College & Center for Biomedical Imaging, Fudan University

1. Introduction

As we all know, chemotherapy, radiotherapy and surgery are important therapeutic approaches for malignant tumors. Unfortunately, these treatment methods would cause strong side effects or toxicity and result in terrible sequelae or relapse after several treatments, so researchers are seeking more effective ways for cancer therapy. Photothermal therapy (PTT), as a novel method for cancer treatment, has been widely investigated recently. In comparison with traditional approaches, PTT is a minimally invasive yet highly efficient treatment modality due to its precise energy delivery to target tissue and the sensitivity of tumor tissue to temperature increase [1,2]. This type of therapy utilizes the large absorption cross section and high photothermal conversion efficiency of nanomaterials in the near infrared (NIR) region. To date, a variety of nanomaterials, such as gold nanostructures [3], palladium nanosheets [4], metal sulfide nanoparticles (NPs) [5 - 7], tungsten oxide nanowires [8], carbon nanomaterials (carbon nanotubes and nano-graphenes) [9,10], and various organic NPs [11 - 13] have been demonstrated to have potential PTT applications.

Graphene, a well known two-dimensional (2D) carbon material with excellent electronic, optical, thermal, and mechanical properties, has been extensively studied in the past decade [14,15]. Recently, great effort has also been devoted to explore potential applications of graphene in biomedical fields, including nanocarriers for drug and gene delivery [16,17], biosensing platforms [18,19], molecular imaging agents [20], and photothermal agents for tumor therapy [10,21,22]. Owing to the strong NIR absorption and good biocompatibility, nano-sized graphene and its derivatives are particularly attractive as photothermal agents for application in cancer PPT [10,21 - 25]. The results of PTT using nano-graphene reveal excellent tumor destruction effects and low toxicity of nano-graphene with biocompatible coatings [10, 21 - 23]. Considering their large surface area, graphene or graphene oxide (GO) nanosheets can be integrated with various types of NPs to form multifunctional nanomaterials for different application purposes [26, 27]. In particular, the combination of functional NPs with graphene or GO will integrate different diagnostic and therapeutic modalities into one single system [28, 29]. Such graphene-based multifunctional nanomaterials will realize simultaneous imaging and therapy administrations and have great potential to improve the therapeutic efficacy of tumors.

Nowadays, magnetic resonance (MR) and X-ray computed tomography (CT) imaging modalities are widely used for various experimental and clinical applications. MR imaging is a noninvasive and nonionizing imaging method that can offer high sensitivity and good discrimination for soft tissues. Gadolinium (Gd^{3+}) metal ion-based complexes (e. g. Gd-DTPA) are currently being used clinically as T_1 relaxation agents due to their unique high spin paramagnetism. Recently, a serial of Gd-based nanomaterials, such as Gd_2O_3 NPs [30], Gd-doped upconversion NPs [31], and $GdVO_4$: Eu ultrathin nanosheets [32] have also been developed for T_1-weighted MR imaging enhancement. However, MR imaging is not suitable for imaging in patients who possess magnetic hardware, and it also shows no signal for high density calculus and calcification. In comparison, CT affords better spatial and density resolution than other imaging modalities, and it could give high-resolution 3D anatomic structure information of tissues based on their differential X-ray absorption ability. The clinically used iodine-based small molecular CT contrast agents are subject to severe limitations including short imaging time, renal toxicity and vascular permeation [33, 34]. To overcome the shortages of iodine agents, several new nanoparticulate CT contrast agents with high atomic number metal elements, such as Au [35], Bi_2S_3 [36], TaO_x [37] and WO_x [34] nanomaterials have been developed. Nevertheless, even if highly efficient CT agents were employed, the low sensitivity and poor resolution for soft tissue still limit the clinical application of CT technology. To satisfy the high requirements of efficiency and accuracy for the clinical diagnosis, combination of multi-modal data is often required. It is believed that the combination of MR imaging with CT modality could achieve more useful information of soft tissues or tumors with much enhanced accuracy [38,39]. Some contrast agents integrated with both MR and CT imaging elements, such as Gd(III)-chelated Au NPs [40], FePt bimetallic NPs [41], and Fe_3O_4/TaO_x core/shell NPs [42] have been designed for dual mode MR/CT imaging applications. As we know, Gd-containing nanomaterials can be used as MR contrast agents, while Ba and Gd have large K-edge values ($Ba_{K\text{-edge}}$: 37.4 keV, $Gd_{K\text{-edg}}$: 50.2 keV) and high X-ray mass absorption coefficients (at 60 keV,

Ba: 8. 51 cm²/g, Gd: 1. 18 cm²/g; at 80 keV, Ba: 3. 96 cm²/g, Gd: 5. 57 cm²/g) [43]. Therefore, BaGdF₅ NPs can play as a promising dual mode MR/CT imaging contrast agent [44].

Herein, BaGdF₅ NPs were directly grown on the surface of GO nanosheets by a solvothermal method in the presence of polyethylene glycol (PEG). The resulting GO/BaGdF₅/PEG nanocomposites combine CT imaging, MR imaging, and PPT functions into one system, which will make it possible to realize simultaneous dual-modality MR/CT imaging and photothermal ablation of tumors. Besides the extensive characterization by a variety of microscopic and spectroscopic techniques, the *in vitro* cytotoxicity and *in vivo* toxic effect of GO/BaGdF₅/PEG were also evaluated. Both MR and CT contrast behaviors of GO/BaGdF₅/PEG *in vitro* and *in vivo* were investigated in detail. Photothermal ablation of HeLa tumors in nude mouse models is finally achieved by intravenous injection of GO/BaGdF₅/PEG and subsequent 808-nm laser irradiation at the tumor sites (Fig. 1).

2. Experimental section

2. 1 *Chemicals and materials*

Graphite powder, Gd(NO₃)₃ · 6H₂O, BaCl₂ · 2H₂O, NH₄F, ethylene glycol (EG), PEG ($M_w = 1500$), and other chemicals were all purchased from Sinopharm Chemical Reagent Co. , Ltd. Deionized water with resistivity higher than 18 MΩ cm was used in all experiments. GO was prepared by a modified Hummers' method using natural graphite powder as a starting material (Supporting information).

2. 2 *Synthesis of GO/BaGdF₅/PEG*

The aqueous suspension of GO (8 mL, 10 mg/mL) was centrifuged to remove the supernatant, and then the collected GO

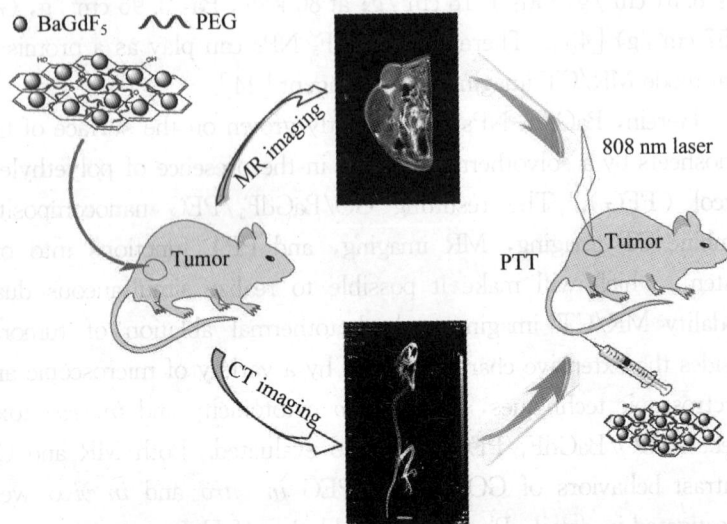

Fig. 1 A schematic diagram of MR/CT imaging and NIR PTT using the GO/BaGdF$_5$/PEG nanocomposites.

(80 mg) was fully dispersed in 20 mL of EG. Gd(NO$_3$)$_3$ · 6H$_2$O (25. 2 mg) and BaCl$_2$ · 2H$_2$O (13. 6 mg) were dissolved in another 30 mL of EG containing 0. 5 g of PEG to form a homogeneous solution, which was then introduced to the above GO suspension under vigorous stirring. After that, 10 mL of EG containing NH$_4$F (11. 2 mg) was added to the above mixture. The mixed solution was agitated for another 30 min and then transferred into a stainless Teflonlined autoclave (100 mL) and kept at 190 °C for 24 h. After the reaction, the system was naturally cooled down to room temperature. The prepared samples were separated by centrifugation, washed several times with ethanol and water to remove other residues.

2. 3 Characterization

Transmission electron microscopy (TEM) images were obtained on a JEOL JEM-2100 high-resolution transmission electron microscope. Morphological analyses were performed with a Veeco Multimode

IIIa atomic force microscope (AFM). Fourier transform infrared (FT-IR) spectra were recorded on a Nicolet Avatar 370 FT-IR spectro-photometer using KBr pellets. X-ray diffraction (XRD) patterns were determined by a Rigaku DMAX 2000 diffractometer using Cu-Kα radiation ($\lambda = 0.15405$ nm). Thermal gravimetric analyses (TGA) were operated with a Shimadzu DTG-60H thermal analyzer in a flowing air atmosphere at a heating rate of 10℃/min. Ultraviolet-visible-NIR (UV-vis-NIR) absorption spectra were obtained with a BeckMan coulter DU 730 spectrophotometer.

2.4 Cell culture

HeLa and L929 cell lines, which were kindly provided by the Institute of Biochemistry and Cell Biology, SIBS, CAS (China), were maintained in Roswell Park Memorial Institute (RPMI) 1640 medium, supplemented with 10% fetal bovine serum (FBS). Cell cultures were incubated in a 5% CO_2 humidified incubator at 37℃. The cells were routinely harvested by treating with a trypsin-ethylene diamine tetraacetic acid (EDTA) solution (0.25%).

2.5 Photothermal experiments in solution

To examine the photothermal behavior of GO/BaGdF₅/PEG, the aqueous solutions (4 mL) of the material with different concentrations (25, 50, 75, 100, 150 and 200 μg/mL) were exposed to an 808-nm NIR laser at a power density of 0.4 W/cm² for 10 min (The distance between the solution and the laser head is 5 cm). The temperature of the solutions was monitored using an infrared thermal imaging system. To assess the NIR photostability of GO/BaGdF₅/PEG, the UV-vis-NIR absorption spectra of the solutions before and after irradiation were measured. Furthermore, five cycles of laser on/off were performed by irradiating the aqueous solution of GO/BaGdF₅/PEG (100 μg/mL) for 10 min using an 808-nm laser (laser on), followed by cooling down to room temperature without the laser irradiation (laser off).

2.6 MTT assays

HeLa and L929 cell lines were used to assess the *in vitro* cytotoxicity of $GO/BaGdF_5/PEG$. Cells were seeded into a 96-well cell culture plate at a density of 5×10^4 cells/well in RPMI-1640 medium at 37℃ and 5% CO_2 for 24 h. Then, the cells were exposed to serial concentrations of $GO/BaGdF_5/PEG$ (0, 50, 100, 150, 200, 300 and 400 $\mu g/mL$) and further incubated for 12 or 24 h. Finally, the cell viability was assessed using the MTT assays. The optical absorption of formazan at 490 nm was measured by an enzyme-linked immunosorbent assay reader (Multiskan MK3, USA).

2.7 MR imaging in vitro

MR imaging of $GO/BaGdF_5/PEG$ in aqueous solution and relaxivity measurements were performed with a 0.5 T Niumag Imaging and Analyzing system NMI20-Analyst. T_1-weighted MR images were acquired with a conventional spin-echo sequence (repetition time (TR) = 200 ms, echo time (TE) = 200 ms). The concentration of Gd^{3+} was determined using a high-resolution sector field inductively coupled plasma atomic emission spectroscopy (ICP-AES) instrument (Varian).

MR imaging of $GO/BaGdF_5/PEG$-treated HeLa cells was performed with a 3.0 T system (3 T Siemens Magnetom Trio). Cells were incubated with different concentrations of $GO/BaGdF_5/PEG$ (0, 25, 50, 100 and 200 $\mu g/mL$) for 4 h at 37℃ in the cell culture medium. The cells were then washed three times using PBS solution, collected, and dispersed in PBS containing 0.5% xanthan gum before MR measurements. The imaging parameters were as follows: TR = 6000 ms, width = 95.62 mm, height = 120.00 mm, depth = 29.70 mm, voxel size = $0.47 \times 0.47 \times 3.30$, flip angle = 120°. The cells were digested in concentrated nitric acid at 90℃ for 6 h followed by dilution to 25 mL with H_2O. The amount of Gd^{3+} uptake into the cells was determined by the same ICP-AES instrument.

2.8 X-ray attenuation measurements

CT scans were performed using a GE Light Speed VCT 64-detector CT (GE Amersham Healthcare System, Milwaukee, WI). Aqueous solutions of $GO/BaGdF_5/PEG$ and the clinically used CT contrast agent Iohexol (for comparison) with different concentrations were prepared in 2.0-mL Eppendorf tubes and placed in a self-designed scanning holder. Imaging parameters were as follows: slice thickness = 0.625 mm, pitch = 0.984:1, voltage = 80 kV, current = 500 μA, field of view (FOV) = 512×512, gantry rotation time = 0.4 s, table speed = 40 mm/rotation, view = 84 × 84. Contrast enhancement was determined in Hounsfield units (HU) for each sample with different concentrations.

2.9 Photothermal ablation of HeLa cells in vitro

HeLa cells were cultured in a 12-well cell culture plate containing RPMI-1640 medium supplemented with 10% FBS for 24 h at 37℃ and 5% CO_2, and then incubated with different concentrations of $GO/BaGdF_5/PEG$ (0, 50, 100, 150, 200 and 250 $\mu g/mL$) for another 4 h. After removing the excess material by PBS washing and adding fresh medium, the cells were exposed to an 808-nm laser (0.4 W/cm^2) for 10 min. After incubated for another 1 h, the cell viabilities were measured by standard MTT assays. Similarly, to investigate the influence of different laser power density on the photothermal ablation of HeLa cells, the $GO/BaGdF_5/PEG$ in RPMI-1640 medium (200 $\mu g/mL$) was incubated with the cells for 4 h at 37℃ and 5% CO_2. Then, the cells were exposed to an 808-nm laser with different laser power density (0, 0.1, 0.2, 0.3, 0.4 and 0.5 W/cm^2) for 10 min and cultured for additional 1 h before MTT assays. The cell viability values were all normalized to control untreated cells. All measurements were done in quadruplicate.

The *in vitro* PTT effects of GO/BaGdF$_5$/PEG with different concentrations (100 and 200 μg/mL) were also evaluated by flow cytometry (FCM). HeLa cells in a 12-well cell culture plate were incubated with GO/BaGdF$_5$/PEG solutions for 4 h. The GO/BaGdF$_5$/PEG-treated cells were exposed to an 808-nm laser for 10 min with the power density of 0.4 W/cm^2. The cells were incubated for another 1 h, harvested by 0.25% trypsin-EDTA solution, and then stained with Annexin V-fluorescein isothiocyanate (FITC) and propidium iodide (PI) for 15 min. The final cells were analyzed with a flow cytometer (Beckman Coulter, Quanta SC, USA). The collected data were analyzed by Flow Jo software 7.6.5.

Confocal microscopic imaging was performed with a Leica TCS SP5 confocal microscope. HeLa cells were cultured in a 12-well cell culture plate in the absence or presence of GO/BaGdF$_5$/PEG (100 and 200 μg/mL) for 4 h, and then exposed to laser irradiation (808 nm, 0.4 W/cm^2) for 10 min. After irradiation, the cells were cultured for another 1 h, and then costained with calcein-AM and PI for confocal microscopic imaging. Calcein-AM and PI were excited by the 488 and 543 nm lasers, respectively.

2.10 MR imaging in vivo

In vivo MR imaging was performed in tumor mice model using a 3.0 T system (3 T Siemens Magnetom Trio). The healthy nude mice (body mass ~20 g) were provided by Shanghai Laboratory Animal Center, Chinese Academy of Science, Shanghai, China (Warrant No. SCXK [Shanghai] 2012 - 0002). All animal operations were conducted in accordance with the guidelines of the Institutional Animal Care and Use Committee. The HeLa tumor models were generated by subcutaneous injection of 1×10^7 HeLa cells in PBS (0.2 mL, pH= 7.4) into the left lateral abdominal wall of each nude mouse, and tumors were grown for 10 - 14 days prior to MR imaging. HeLa tumor-bearing nude mice were anesthetized with chloral hydrate solution (10 wt%), and then PBS solution of GO/BaGdF$_5$/PEG (200 μL, 20 mg/kg body weight) was intravenously injected into the nude mice via the tail vein. We obtained MR images before and 1, 4 and 24 h after injection. The T_1-weighted sequence was as follows: TR = 200 ms, TE = 12 ms, matrix = 320 × 100, FOV = 80 × 60, flip angle = 90°, slice thickness = 1.5 mm.

2.11 CT imaging in vivo

Nude mice bearing HeLa tumors were anesthetized by an inhalational anesthesia system, and then PBS solution of GO/BaGdF$_5$/PEG (100 μL, 20 mg/kg body weight) was intratumorally injected into the HeLa tumor model. CT imaging was performed both before injection and at 0.5 h post-injection. The mice were scanned by a Siemens Biograph micro-CT scanner with following imaging parameters: voltage = 60 kV, current = 500 μA, FOV = 512 × 512, gantry rotation time = 0.5 s.

2.12 Tumor PTT in vivo

HeLa tumor models were used during *in vivo* tumor therapy, which was initiated when the tumors reached an approximate size of 100 – 150 mm^3. The mice were randomly divided to 4 groups (4 mice per group). Two groups of the mice were only intravenously injected with 200 μL of PBS or GO/BaGdF$_5$/PEG solution (2 mg/mL) via the tail vein. The other two groups after intravenous injection with 200 μL of PBS or GO/BaGdF$_5$/PEG solution were irradiated with an 808-nm laser on tumor region for 10 min at a power density of 0.5 W/cm^2. The irradiation was carried out at 24, 48 and 72 h after injection. The tumor volume and body weight were monitored every day for 20 days. The tumor sizes were measured by a caliper and calculated using the equation: volume = (tumor length) × (tumor width)^2/2. Relative tumor volumes were expressed as V/V_0 , where

V_0 is the tumor volume when the treatment was initiated.

After PTT, the mice of each group were sacrificed. The blood was collected for blood biochemistry assays. Major organs (heart, liver, spleen, lung and kidneys) and tumors of the mice were harvested, fixed in 4% formaldehyde, processed routinely into para-ffin, sectioned at 5 mm, stained with hematoxylin & eosin (H&E) for histopathological analysis.

3. Results and discussion

3. 1 Characterization of GO/BaGdF$_5$/PEG

The initial GO for preparing GO/BaGdF$_5$/PEG was made from natural graphite powder by using a modified Hummers' method [45]. TEM (Fig. 2a) and AFM (Fig. 2b) images reveal that the asprepared GO nanosheets are 60 – 300 nm in lateral width (mean size $\sim$ 200 nm) (Fig. 2d) and mostly single layered (topographic height $\sim$ 1. 0 nm) (Fig. 2c). The FT-IR spectrum (Fig. 3a) of GO exhibits the presence of C = O (1737 cm^{-1}), C = C (1626 cm^{-1}) and C-O (1100 $\sim$ 1300 cm^{-1}) functional groups [46]. The average zeta potential of the GO is measured to be-20. 1 mV (Fig. S1). The oxygen-containing surface functional groups and the negative surface potential benefit the adhesion of Ba^{2+} and Gd^{3+} ions on the surface of GO for subsequent growth of BaGdF$_5$ NPs.

The GO/BaGdF$_5$/PEG nanocomposites were synthesized by the solvothermal treatment of a mixture of GO, Gd(NO$_3$)$_3$, BaCl$_2$, NH$_4$F and PEG in hydrophilic solvent EG. The PEG used here is to endow the resulting nanocomposites with good water solubility and biocompatibility. The FT-IR spectrum (Fig. 3a) of the resulting GO/BaGdF$_5$/PEG shows several new characteristic absorbance peaks at 2923 cm^{-1} (asymmetric CH$_2$ stretching), 2852 cm^{-1}(symmetric CH$_2$ stretching), 1462 cm^{-1} (C-C stretching), and 1120 cm^{-1} (C-O stretching) [47], attributed to the presence of PEG in the nanocomposites. Owing to the existence of PEG, GO/BaGdF$_5$/PEG shows good dispersion in water, physiological saline, PBS, RPMI – 1640 medium, and FBS (Fig. S2). The XRD pattern of the resulting GO/BaGdF$_5$/PEG is shown in Fig. 3b. The observed diffraction peaks are in accordance with the standard cubic phase of BaGdF$_5$ (JCPDS 24-0098). The characteristic peak of original GO at 11. 3° disappears, because the attached NPs prevent the restacking of carbon sheets [48].

The TEM image (Fig. 3c) shows the morphological information of GO/BaGdF$_5$/PEG. The GO/BaGdF$_5$/PEG sheets show good separation, and their mean sheet size is smaller than that of the original GO due to the hydrothermal treatment. The BaGdF$_5$ NPs are modified uniformly and firmly onto the surface of GO and the average size of the NPs is 20. 6 ± 2. 1 nm. The selected area electron diffraction (SAED) pattern (Fig. 3d) confirms the good crystallinity of BaGdF$_5$ NPs with cubic phase structure. The high-resolution TEM (HRTEM) image of a single NP (Fig. 3e) shows the clear lattice fringe with a measured d-spacing of 0. 21 nm, which matches well with the (220) lattice plane of cubic phase of BaGdF$_5$. The energy dispersive X-ray spectroscopy (EDS) of GO/BaGdF$_5$/PEG indicates the presence of C, Ba, Gd and F elements (Fig. 3f). Ba, Gd and F are attributed to the BaGdF$_5$ NPs, and C signal originates from the supporting GO and the carbon film on the TEM copper grid. The weight content of BaGdF$_5$ in the GO/BaGdF$_5$/PEG nanocomposites is estimated to be 42% by assuming that GO and PEG have been completely decomposed at 800℃, as indicated by the results of TGA (Fig. S3).

Fig. 3g shows the UV-vis-NIR absorption of GO/BaGdF$_5$/PEG, GO, and BaGdF$_5$/PEG. The BaGdF$_5$/PEG solution is essentially transparent at wavelength more than 700 nm. Compared to as-made GO, GO/BaGdF$_5$/PEG exhibits dramatically enhanced NIR absorption, which is due to the apparent reduction of GO during the

426 学思林

hydrothermal synthesis of GO/BaGdF$_5$/PEG [29]. In addition, the absorption of GO/BaGdF$_5$/PEG at 808 nm linearly increases with the increase of concentration (Fig. S4). Thus, GO/BaGdF$_5$/PEG should be more effective than GO in terms of photothermal heating under the NIR laser irradiation. The absorbance of GO/BaGdF$_5$/PEG nano-composites at wavelengths below~575 nm is lower than GO. This may be due to the attachment of BaGdF$_5$ NPs on the GO sheets. BaGdF$_5$ NPs may hinder the π→π* transitions of partially reduced GO at UV to near UV region. Meanwhile, the BaGdF$_5$ NPs show very weak absorption in this wavelength range.

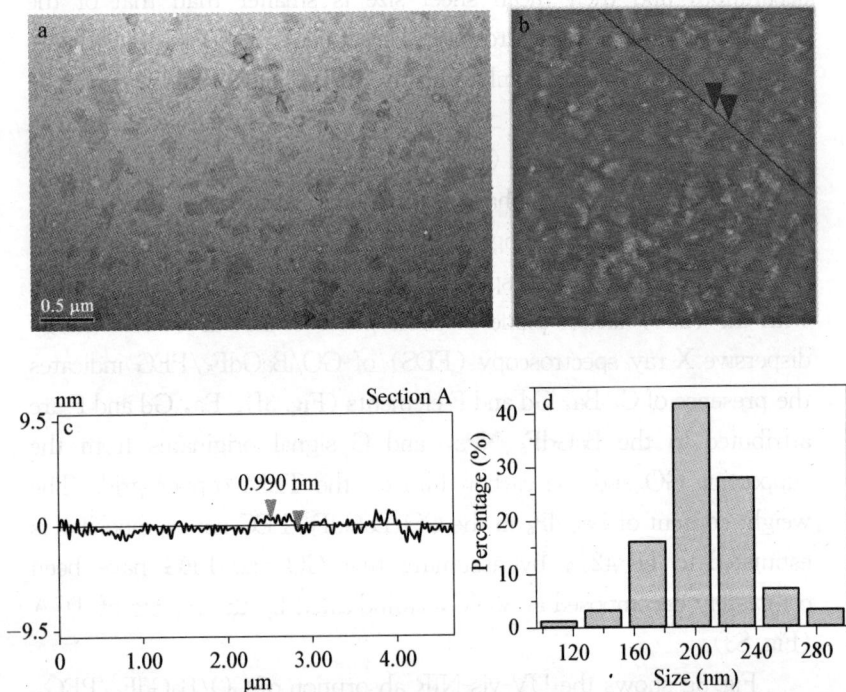

Fig. 2 Characterization of as-prepared GO. TEM image (a), AFM image (b), height histogram (c), and size distribution obtained from TEM images (d) for as-prepared GO.

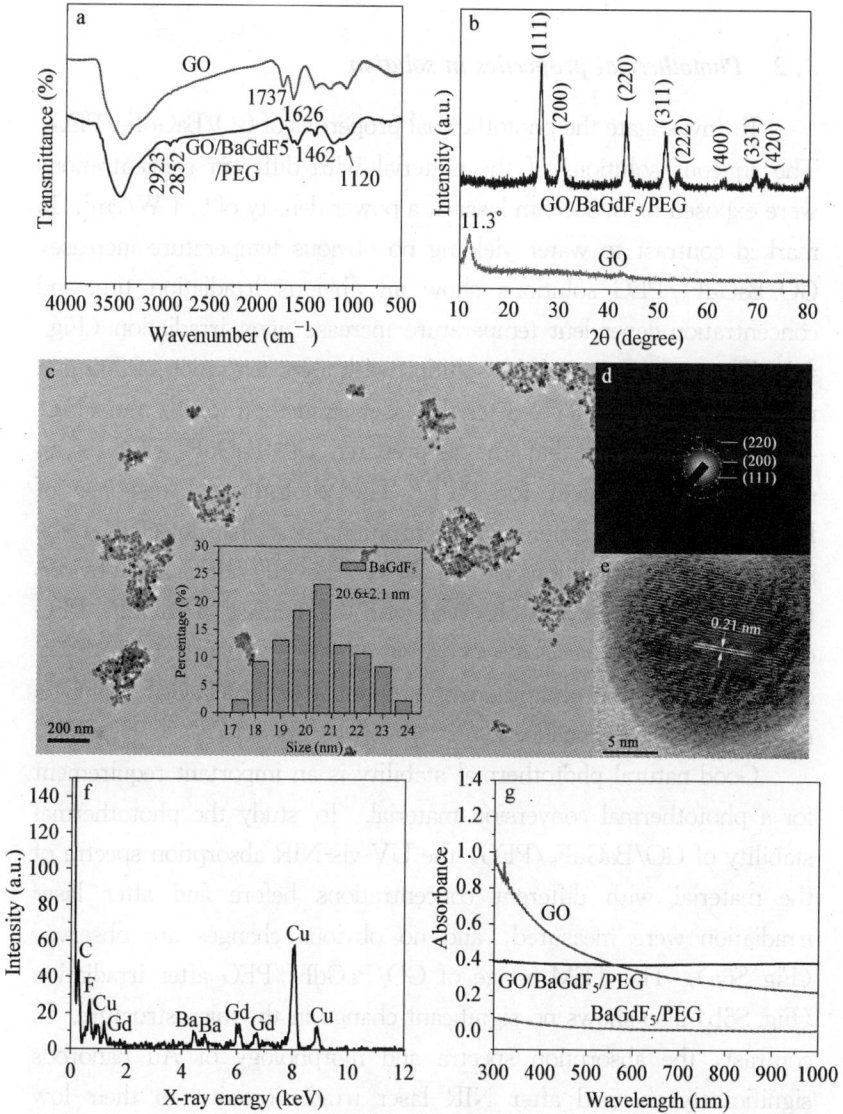

Fig. 3 The characterization of GO/BaGdF₅/PEG. FT-IR spectra (a) and XRD patterns (b) of GO and GO/BaGdF₅/PEG; TEM image (c), SAED pattern (d), HRTEM image (e), and EDS spectrum (f) of GO/BaGdF₅/PEG. Cu signal comes from the copper grid. The inset in (c) is the size distribution of BaGdF₅ on the surface of GO; (g) UV-vis-NIR absorption of GO/BaGdF₅/PEG (100 μg/mL), GO (100 μg/mL), and BaGdF₅/PEG (500 μg/mL).

3. 2 *Photothermal properties in solution*

To investigate the photothermal properties of GO/BaGdF$_5$/PEG, The aqueous solutions of the material with different concentrations were exposed to an 808-nm laser at a power density of 0. 4 W/cm^2. In marked contrast to water yielding no obvious temperature increase, GO/BaGdF$_5$/PEG solutions show an obvious irradiation time-and concentration-dependent temperature increase upon irradiation (Fig. 4a). The temperature of the solution with a concentration of 200 μg/mL was raised by ~33℃ after the laser irradiation for 10 min (Fig. 4b), demonstrating that the as-prepared GO/BaGdF$_5$/PEG is an encouraging nano-agent for PTT. The photothermal response of BaGdF$_5$/PEG with different concentrations was also detected at the same irradiation conditions as that for GO/BaGdF$_5$/PEG. No obvious temperature variation was observed with the increase of BaGdF$_5$/PEG concentration even at a concentration up to 3 mg/mL (Fig. S5), confirming that the photothermal properties of GO/BaGdF$_5$/PEG is rooted in the GO nanosheets.

Good natural photothermal stability is an important requirement for a photothermal conversion material. To study the photothermal stability of GO/BaGdF$_5$/PEG, the UV-vis-NIR absorption spectra of the material with different concentrations before and after laser irradiation were measured, and no obvious changes are observed (Fig. S6a). The TEM image of GO/BaGdF$_5$/PEG after irradiation (Fig. S6b) also shows no significant change in the microstructure. In contrast, the absorption spectra and morphology of Au nanorods significantly changed after NIR laser irradiation due to their low photothermal stability [49]. Furthermore, five cycles of laser on/off experiments (Fig. 4c) reveal that the temperature increase of the GO/BaGdF$_5$/PEG solution (100 μg/mL) remains good stability and reproducibility in each cycle. Therefore, these results demonstrate that GO/BaGdF$_5$/PEG has excellent photothermal stability.

a

b

c

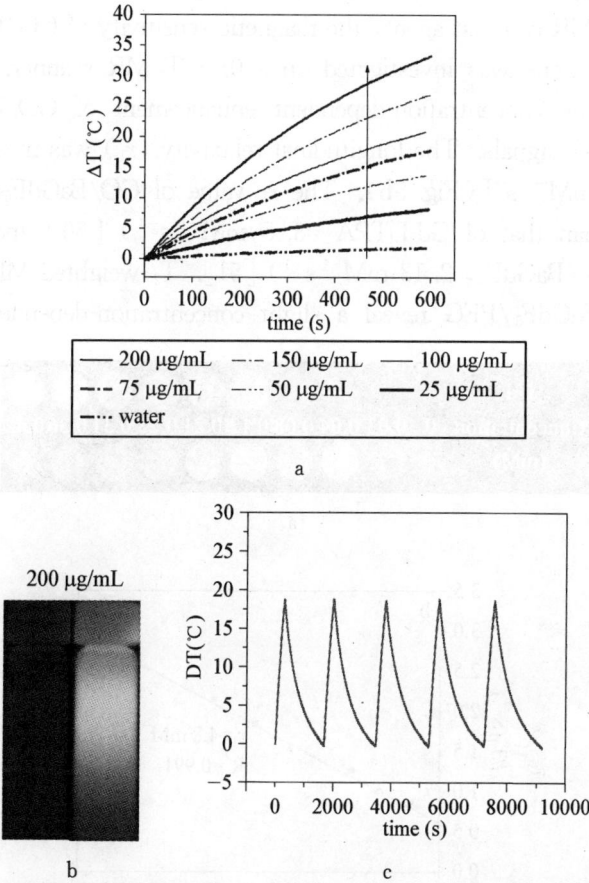

**Fig. 4   Photothermal properties of GO/BaGdF₅/PEG in aqueous solution. (a)
Temperature increase of pure water and GO/BaGdF₅/PEG solutions with different
concentrations under an 808-nm laser irradiation at a power density of 0. 4 W/cm² for
10 min; (b) Infrared thermal images before and after 10 min of laser irradiation for
GO/BaGdF₅/PEG with the concentration of 200 μg/mL; (c) The photothermal cycling
(five cycles of laser on/off) of GO/BaGdF₅/PEG (100 μg/mL) in water.**

3. 3   *MR and CT imaging of GO/BaGdF₅/PEG in solution*

Gd-containing nanomaterials have great potential to be used as
T_1-contrast agents for MR imaging due to their positive MR contrast

effects. To determine whether GO/BaGdF$_5$/PEG could be used as a positive MR contrast agent, the magnetic sensitivity of GO/BaGdF$_5$/PEG solutions was investigated on a 0.5 T MR scanner. Fig. 5a reveals the concentration-dependent enhancement of GO/BaGdF$_5$/PEG in T_1 signals. The longitudinal relaxivity (r_1) was measured to be 4.8 mM^{-1} s^{-1} (Fig. 5b). The r_1 value of GO/BaGdF$_5$/PEG is higher than that of Gd-DTPA (3.5 mM^{-1} s^{-1}) [50] and similar materials (BaGdF$_5$, 2.13 mM^{-1}s^{-1}) [51]. T_2-weighted MR images of GO/BaGdF$_5$/PEG reveal a slight concentration-dependent dark-

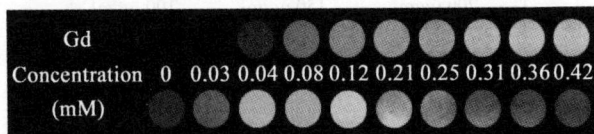

a

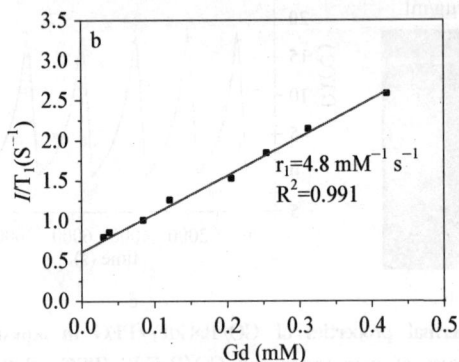

b

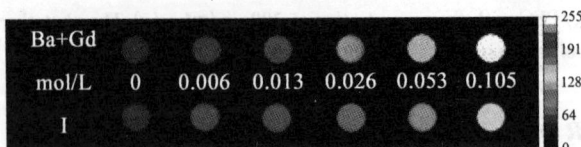

c

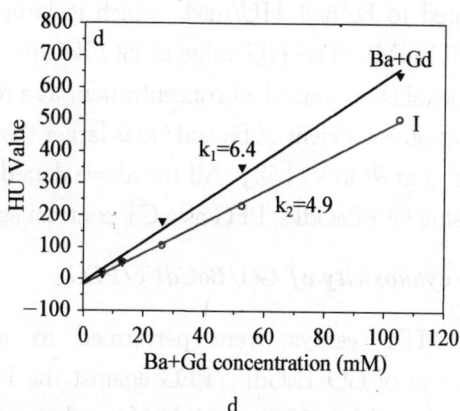

Fig. 5 MR and CT imaging of GO/BaGdF$_5$/PEG in aqueous solution. (a) T$_1$-weighted MR images of GO/BaGdF$_5$/PEG solutions with different Gd concentrations; (b) Plot of 1/T$_1$ versus Gd concentration. Longitudinal relaxivity (r$_1$) was derived from linear fitting of the plot; (c) *In vitro* CT images of GO/BaGdF$_5$/PEG (upper panel) and Iohexol (lower panel) with different concentrations of Ba+Gd or I; (d) CT value (HU) of GO/BaGdF$_5$/PEG and Iohexol as a function of Ba+Gd or I concentrations.

ening effect. The transverse relaxivity (r$_2$) was calculated to be 5. 8 mM^{-1}s^{-1} (Fig. S7). The ratio of r$_2$/r$_1$ is 1. 2, suggesting that GO/BaGdF$_5$/PEG can be used for T$_1$-weighted imaging.

Owing to the high atomic number and X-ray attenuation coefficient of Ba and Gd (at 80 keV, Ba: 3. 96 cm^2/g, Gd: 5. 57 cm^2/g) [43], the GO/BaGdF$_5$/PEG nanocomposites hold great promise for CT contrast agents. To assess CT contrast efficacy of GO/BaGdF$_5$/PEG, the CT phantom images of GO/BaGdF$_5$/PEG were acquired with different concentrations (Fig. 5c). Following the increase of concentration, the CT signal intensity is gradually enhanced, resulting in brighter images. And importantly, GO/BaGdF$_5$/PEG produces higher contrast than Iohexol, a conventional iodine-based CT contrast agent. The CT value, which is measured in Hounsfield units (HU), increases linearly with the concentration for both GO/BaGdF$_5$/PEG and Iohexol (Fig. 5d). Nevertheless, the X-ray absorption coefficient of GO/BaGdF$_5$/

PEG is calculated to be 6. 4 HU/mM, which is larger than that of Iohexol (4. 9 HU/mM). The HU value of GO/BaGdF$_5$/PEG is higher than that of Iohexol at an equivalent concentration, as a result of the fact that the attenuation coefficient of Ba and Gd is larger than that of iodine (I) (I: 3. 51 cm^2/g at 80 keV) [52]. All the above data demonstrate the feasibility of using GO/BaGdF$_5$/PEG as a CT contrast agent.

3. 4   *In vitro cytotoxicity of GO/BaGdF$_5$/PEG*

Standard MTT essays were performed to investigate the cytotoxicity effects of GO/BaGdF$_5$/PEG against the HeLa and L929 cell lines (Fig. 6). After 12 and 24 h of incubation with different concentrations of GO/BaGdF$_5$/PEG, these two cell lines give similar results of cell viabilities. Even incubated for 24 h at a concentration up to 400 μg/mL, the HeLa and L929 cells still kept a high viability above 80%, demonstrating negligible cytotoxicity of the material. The low cytotoxicity of GO/BaGdF$_5$/PEG provides a basic condition for the following cell and animal experiments.

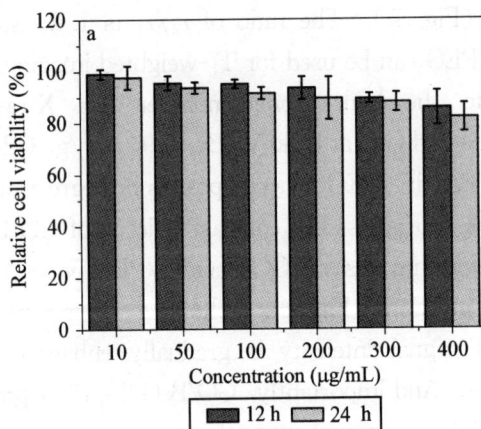

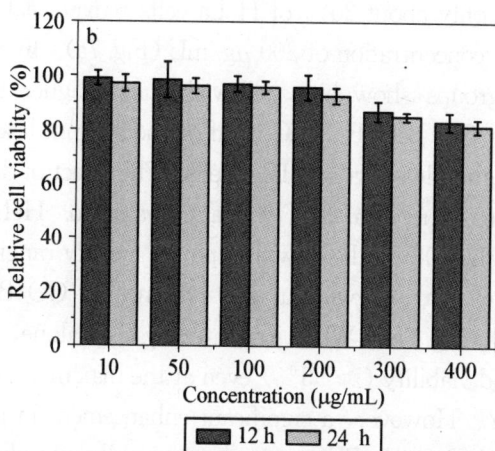

Fig. 6 *In vitro* **cytotoxicity experiments. Cell viability data obtained from the MTT assays of HeLa (a) and L929 (b) cells incubated with GO/BaGdF₅/PEG at different concentrations for 12 and 24 h.**

3. 5 PTT of cancer cells in vitro

The PTT effect of GO/BaGdF₅/PEG on cell viability was first investigated with different concentrations of the material or different energies of laser. HeLa cells were incubated with GO/BaGdF₅/PEG for 4 h, followed by irradiation with an 808-nm laser. The cell viability after irradiation was measured using MTT assays. As controls, HeLa cells were treated similarly with GO/BaGdF₅/PEG without laser irradiation and were laser irradiated in the absence of the material. Herein, we chose an incubation time of 4 h because enough nonocomposites were taken up by the cancer cells after 4 h of incubation (Fig. S8a). Although such an incubation time is not long enough for complete internalization of the uptaken material (Fig. S8b), some nano-composites localized on the cell membrane can result in more effective photothermolysis of cancer cells [53]. As expected, the relative viabilities of the cells decrease with the increase of GO/ BaGdF₅/PEG concentration under the laser irradiation (0. 4 W/cm²,

10 min), and only about 20% of HeLa cells remain viable at a GO/BaGdF$_5$/PEG concentration of 200 μg/mL (Fig. 7a). In contrast, the two control groups show high cell viabilities (higher than 90%), indicating that GO/BaGdF$_5$/PEG itself or the 808 nm laser irradiation alone have negligible effect on HeLa cells. The effect of different laser power densities on *in vitro* PPT was also evaluated. HeLa cells were irradiated by the 808-nm laser with a power density ranging from 0.1 to 0.5 W/cm^2 with or without the presence of GO/BaGdF$_5$/PEG (200 μg/mL) (Fig. 7b). When irradiated by laser alone, the cells still exhibited good viability (> 95%) even at the maximun power density of 0.5 W/cm^2. However, a significant enhancement in photothermal ablation of GO/BaGdF$_5$/PEG-treated cancer cells was observed as we increased the laser power density. About 80% cell lethality was reached when the power density was increased to 0.4 W/cm^2. Apparently, the *in vitro* PTT effect of GO/BaGdF$_5$/PEG depends on both the material concentration and the laser energy. Compared with the results reported elsewhere [54, 55], the power intensities of laser used here are significantly lower to obtain similar *in vitro* PTT results under the same therapeutic dosage of the materials.

The photothermal ablation of cancer cells using GO/BaGdF$_5$/PEG was further evidenced by FCM experiments (Fig. S9a). As indicated in Fig. 7c, the cells treated with GO/BaGdF$_5$/PEG of different concentrations (100 and 200 μg/mL) only or laser irradiation alone show high viabilities (above 97% of live cells), indicating that neither GO/BaGdF$_5$/PEG treatment nor 808-nm laser irradiation alone can cause obvious destructive effects to HeLa cells. However, the cells treated with both material and laser shows substantially higher cell apoptosis and necrosis. At a treating concentration of 100 μg/mL, the apoptosis and necrosis rates after irradiation increased to 19.7% (13.9% for early apoptosis and 5.8% for late apoptosis) and 8.0%, respectively. When HeLa cells treated with 200 μg/mL of GO/BaGdF$_5$/PEG were exposed to an 808 nm laser for 10 min, the cell viability significantly reduced to 20. 6%, and higher apoptosis (24. 1% for early apoptosis and 38. 1% for late apoptosis) and necrosis (17. 2%) rates were detected. Therefore, the photothermal ablation of cancer cells using GO/BaGdF$_5$/PEG in our case is mostly due to apoptosis but partly due to necrosis.

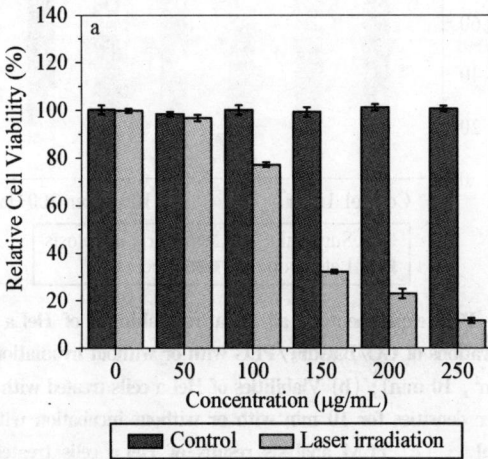

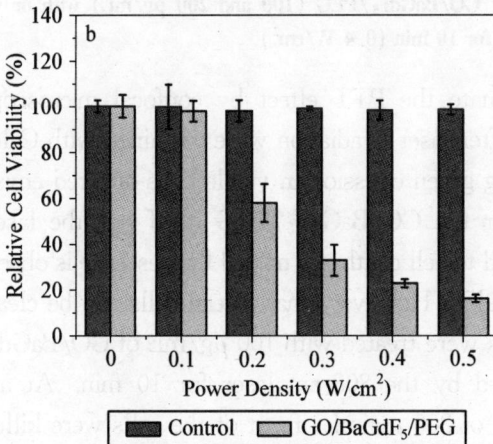

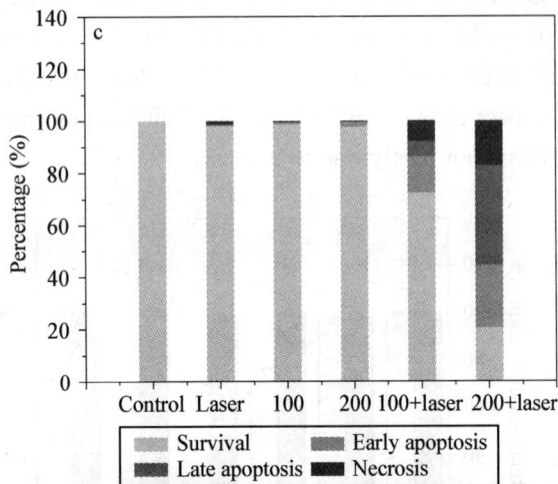

Fig. 7 *In vitro* **PTT experiments.** (a) **Relative viabilities of HeLa cells treated by different concentrations of GO/BaGdF$_5$/PEG with or without irradiation by the 808-nm laser (0. 4 W/cm^2 , 10 min); (b) Viabilities of HeLa cells treated with laser irradiation at different power densities for 10 min with or without incubation with GO/BaGdF$_5$/ PEG (200 μg/mL); (c) FCM analysis results of HeLa cells treated with different concentrations of GO/BaGdF$_5$/PEG (100 and 200 μg/mL) with or without 808-nm laser irradiation for 10 min (0. 4 W/cm^2).**

To evaluate the PTT effect by confocal microscopic imaging, HeLa cells after laser irradiation were costained with Calcine AM and PI, producing green emission in viable cells and red emission in dead cells. Neither the GO/BaGdF$_5$/PEG itself nor the laser irradiation alone can lead to cell death, as no red fluorescence is observed in these cases (Fig. S9b). However, many dead cells can be clearly observed after the cells were treated with 100 μg/mL of GO/BaGdF$_5$/PEG and then irradiated by the 808-nm laser for 10 min. At an incubation concentration of 200 μg/mL, most of the cells were killed after laser irradiation. The confocal microscopic imaging results are consistent with the above FCM data.

3. 6   MR imaging in vitro and in vivo

To testify the diagnostic potential of the GO/BaGdF$_5$/PEG nanocomposites as a T$_1$-weighted MR contrast agent, HeLa cells were incubated with different concentrations of GO/BaGdF$_5$/PEG, and then the MR signal intensity of the treated cells was investigated on a 3. 0T system. Fig. 8a reveals a significant concentration-dependent contrast enhancement on the T$_1$-weighted images of GO/BaGdF$_5$/PEG-treated cells. The increase in signal intensity is attributed to the enhanced cellular uptake of Gd with increasing GO/BaGdF$_5$/PEG concentration, as indicated by the quantitative ICP-AES analysis results (Fig. 8b).

In view of the favorable MR contrast performance *in vitro*, further application of GO/BaGdF$_5$/PEG for MR imaging *in vivo* was investigated with HeLa tumor-bearing nude mice. The PBS solution of GO/BaGdF$_5$/PEG (20 mg/kg body weight) was administrated to the mice via tailvein injection. The acquired T$_1$-weighted MR images are shown in Fig. 8c, which indicates time-dependent brightening in the tumor site. At 24 h post-injection, the MR image of the tumor exhibits obvious brightness enhancement as compared to that without injection. The MR signal intensity in tumor was further quantitatively analyzed (Fig. 8d). The signal intensity in tumor site increases remarkably by 3. 7 times after injection for 24 h. Owning to the enhanced permeation and retention (EPR) effect, GO/BaGdF$_5$/PEG could be passively accumulated into tumors [56]. The obvious increase in MR signal intensity at tumor sites after injection suggests that GO/BaGdF$_5$/PEG can display the tumor sites to guide the NIR PTT of tumors without damaging the surrounding normal tissues.

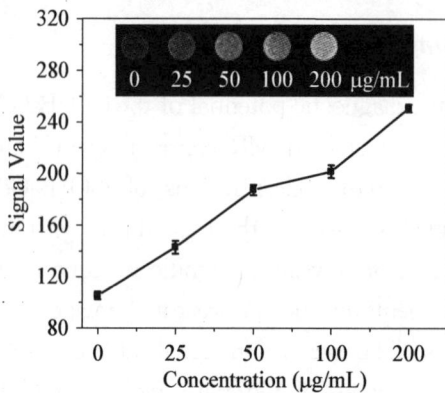

a

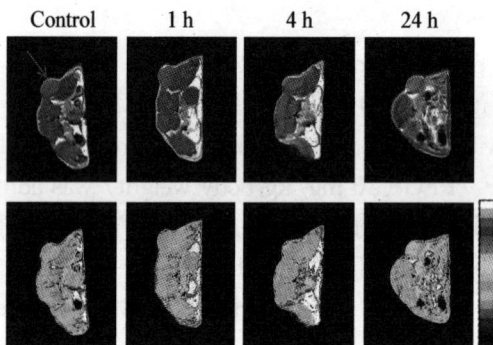

b

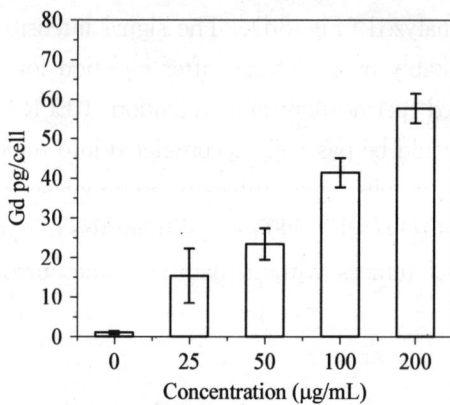

c

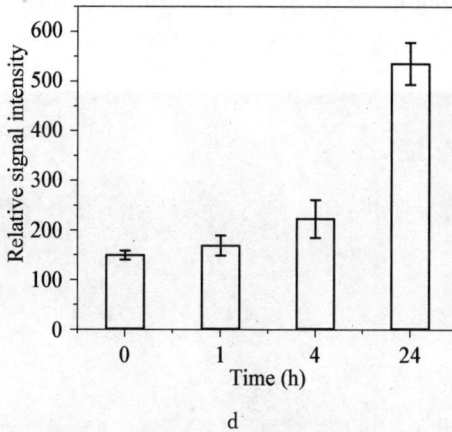

d

Fig. 8 MR imaging *in vitro* and *in vivo*. (a) T$_1$-weighted MR images of HeLa cells incubated with different concentrations of GO/BaGdF$_5$/PEG and the signal intensity of the labeled HeLa cells, as a function of the GO/BaGdF$_5$/PEG concentration; (b) The Gd uptake content in HeLa cells after incubation with different concentrations of GO/BaGdF$_5$/PEG; (c) T$_1$-weighted MR images of the tumor at different time after injection; (d) the relative MR signal intensity (The signal of tumor minus that of muscle) in tumor analyzed by the ImageJ software.

3. 7　CT imaging in vivo

To investigate the feasibility of GO/BaGdF$_5$/PEG as a CT imaging probe, we carried out the CT imaging in HeLa tumor-bearing mice using a small animal micro-CT system. GO/BaGdF$_5$/PEG was intratumorally injected into the tumor model in a nude mouse with a dose of 20 mg/kg of body weight. The mouse was scanned by the micro-CT system before and after injection. The X-ray transverse CT image acquired at 0.5 h after injection reveals that the signal in the tumor site has been obviously enhanced compared to the untreated mouse (Fig. 9a). The signal value (HU) of treated tumor is 426 ± 20, which is significantly higher than the untreated one (156 ± 10). The 3D volume-rendered (VR) CT images shown in Fig. 9b also reveal an enhanced signal in the treated tumor site, demonstrating that GO/

BaGdF$_5$/PEG might serve as a promising contrast agent for CT imaging *in vivo*.

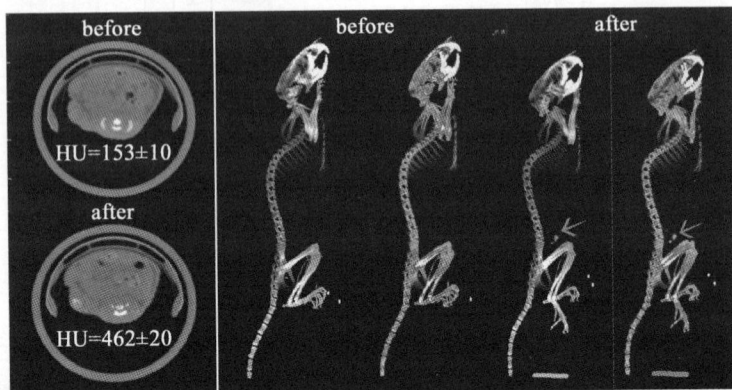

Fig. 9　CT imaging of mice *in vivo*. (a) X-ray transverse CT images of tumor before and after intratumoral injection. The CT values of tumor site are 153 ± 10 HU (before injection) and 462 ± 20 HU (0.5 h after injection); (b) the 3D VR CT images before and after intratumoral injection.

3.8　*In vivo cancer PTT*

Encouraged by the favorable MR/CT imaging results and excellent *in vitro* PTT effect of GO/BaGdF$_5$/PEG, we then carried out the study about using GO/BaGdF$_5$/PEG for photothermally ablating HeLa tumor model *in vivo*. Four nude mice bearing HeLa tumors were intravenously injected with GO/BaGdF$_5$/PEG at a dose of 20 mg/kg. At 24, 48 and 72 h after injection, the HeLa tumors were exposed to an 808-nm laser at the power density of 0.5 W/cm^2 for 10 min. Three other groups (4 mice for each group), including PBS injected mice, PBS injected mice exposed to laser, and GO/BaGdF$_5$/PEG injected mice without laser irradiation, were used as controls. An infrared thermal camera was used to record the local temperature change during laser irradiation. Fig. 10a and b reveals that the surface temperature of the tumors increases by 11℃ after irradiation and the final temperature reaches 48℃, which is high enough for photothermal ablation of tumors *in vivo* [10, 22]. As a control group, the PBS injected mice only shows slight increase to 39℃. Therefore, in addition to MR and CT imaging, the GO/ BaGdF$_5$/PEG nanocomposites can also serve as a good photothermal imaging agent for tumor imaging.

After the beginning of *in vivo* therapy, the tumor growth and body weight were monitored and measured for 20 days. All mice were alive over the entire treatment period. The change of relative tumor volume and body weight for all groups with the time is shown in Fig. 10c and d, respectively. The typical photographs of the four group mice are shown in Fig. S10. As expected, the GO/BaGdF$_5$/PEG nanocomposites resulted in a significant suppression of tumor growth after laser irradiation. The tumor volume was significantly reduced in initial four days after irradiation, and then no obvious growth in tumor volume was observed in the remaining 15 days. In marked contrast, the tumors of the other three groups increased rapidly over the entire experiment period, suggesting that GO/BaGdF$_5$/PEG injection only or laser irradiation alone can not inhibit the tumor growth. The body weight of all groups increased steadily during the treatment (Fig. 10d), illustrating that all the mice lived in a comfortable environment and the PTT did not bring significant side effects.

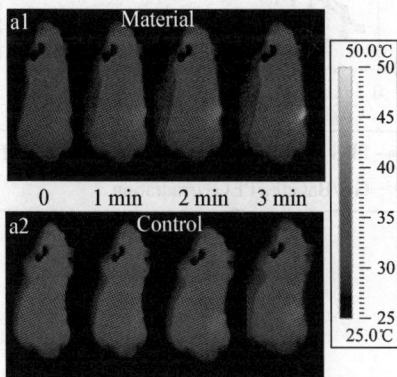

a

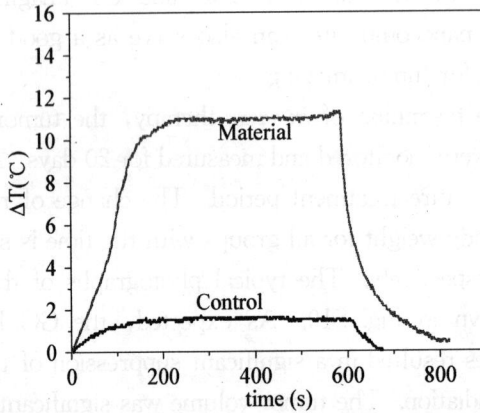

b

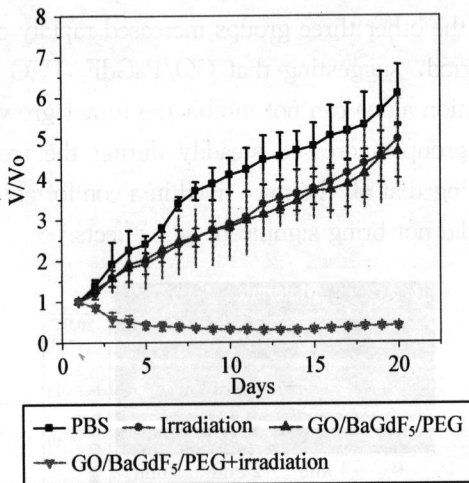

c

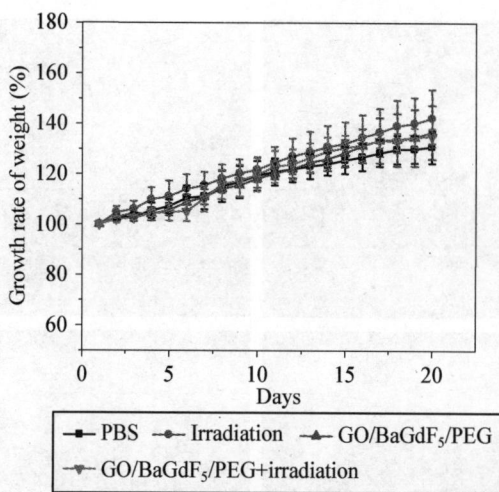

d

Fig. 10 *In vivo* photothermal therapy using GO/BaGdF$_5$/PEG. (a) Infrared thermal images of HeLa tumor-bearing mice with (a1) or without (a2) injection of GO/BaGdF$_5$/PEG exposed to 808-nm laser irradiation (0. 5 W/cm^2) for 10 min (24 h post-injection); (b) The temperature change (ΔT) of tumor after laser irradiation; (c) Growth curves of HeLa tumors in different groups of mice after various treatments. The tumor volumes were normalized to their initial sizes; (d) Body weight of mice in different groups.

After the treatment, tumor tissues of each group were harvested for histological examinations. According to the results of H&E staining (Fig. 11), the tumor tissues treated with both GO/BaGdF$_5$/PEG and laser irradiation (Fig. 11d) show common features of thermonecrosis such as loss of nucleus, cell shrinkages, and coagulation [57,58]. However, no obvious damage is exhibited in the tumor tissues treated with either GO/BaGdF$_5$/PEG or laser irradiation alone. Histological examination results further confirm the successful destruction of tumor cells by the photothermal effect of GO/BaGdF$_5$/PEG.

Finally, the potential *in vivo* toxicity of GO/BaGdF$_5$/PEG after treatment was also investigated. There is no noticeable organ damage

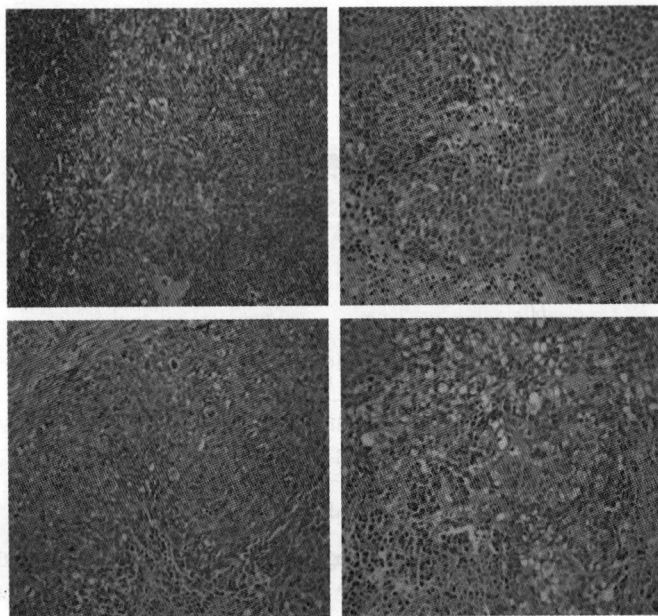

Fig. 11　H&E-stained histology images of tumor issues of different groups after various treatments: (a) PBS only, (b) laser irradiation only, (c) GO/BaGdF$_5$/PEG only, (d) both GO/BaGdF$_5$/PEG and laser irradiation.

or inflammatory lesion in all major organs of mice 20 days after PTT, as indicated by the H&E staining results (Fig. S11). Serum biochemistry assay was also carried out after the treatment, and all the measured important parameters of liver and kidney functions fell within normal ranges (Fig. S12) [59]. These results demonstrate that the GO/BaGdF$_5$/PEG nanocomposites are not obviously toxic to the mice at our experimental dose.

4. Conclusions

A GO-based multifunctional platform has been fabricated through the direct growth of BaGdF$_5$ NPs on GO nanosheets using a solvothermal method. The as-prepared GO/BaGdF$_5$/PEG shows good stability in physiological solutions and low cytotoxicity even at high concentrations. Owing to the inherent magnetic property and high X-ray absorption coefficient, GO/BaGdF$_5$/PEG can be used as a promising T$_1$-weighted MR and X-ray CT duel-mode contrast agent. The strong NIR absorbance and good photothermal effect make GO/BaGdF$_5$/PEG an excellent photothermal agent for *in vivo* photothermal cancer treatment. Moreover, histological examination and serum biochemistry assay reveal no apparent toxicity of GO/BaGdF$_5$/PEG to the mice after treatment. Findings from this work suggest that the GO/BaGdF$_5$/PEG nanocomposites hold great application potential in MR/CT bimodal imaging-guided photothermal therapy of cancer. GO/BaGdF$_5$/PEG may be further conjugated with different targeting ligands to construct multifunctional systems for targeted theranosis of cancers.

Acknowledgments

This work is supported by the Shanghai Natural Science Foundation (13ZR1430300), the Shanghai Municipal Education Commission (14ZZ128), the National Natural Science Foundation of China (Grant No. 21271130), the Opening Project of State Key Laboratory of High Performance Ceramics and Superfine Microstructure (SKL201212SIC), Program for Changjiang Scholars and Innovative Research Team in University (No. IRT1269), Shanghai Science and Technology Development Fund (13520502800), and International Joint Laboratory on Resource Chemistry (IJLRC).

Appendix A. Supplementary data

Supplementary data related to this article can be found at http://dx. doi. org/10. 1016/j. biomaterials. 2014. 11. 055.

References

[1] Zhou F, Wu S, Wu B, Chen WR, Xing D. Mitochondria-targeting single-walled carbon nanotubes for cancer photothermal therapy. Small 2011;7:2727 - 2735.

[2] Yu J, Javier D, Yaseen MA, Nitin N, Richards-Kortum R, Anvari B, et al. Self-assembly synthesis, tumor cell targeting, and photothermal capabilities of antibody-coated indocyanine green nanocapsules. J Am Chem Soc 2010; 132: 1929 - 1938.

[3] Huang X, El-Sayed IH, Qian W, El-Sayed MA. Cancer cell imaging and photothermal therapy in the near-infrared region by using gold nanorods. J Am Chem Soc 2006;128:2115 - 2120.

[4] Huang X, Tang S, Yang J, Tan Y, Zheng N. Etching growth under surface confinement: an effective strategy to prepare mesocrystalline Pd nanocorolla. J Am Chem Soc 2011;133:15946 - 15949.

[5] Cheng L, Liu J, Gu X, Gong H, Shi X, Liu T, et al. PEGylated WS_2 nanosheets as a multifunctional theranostic agent for in vivo dual-modal CT/photoacoustic imaging guided photothermal therapy. Adv Mater 2014;26:1886 - 1893.

[6] Liu T, Wang C, Gu X, Gong H, Cheng L, Shi X, et al. Drug delivery with PEGylated MoS_2 nano-sheets for combined photothermal and chemotherapy of cancer. Adv Mater 2014;26:3433 - 3440.

[7] Zhou M, Zhang R, Huang M, Lu W, Song S, Melancon MP, et al. A chelator-free multifunctional [64Cu]CuS nanoparticle platform for simultaneous micro-PET/CT imaging and photothermal ablation therapy. J Am Chem Soc 2010;132:15351 - 15358.

[8] Chen Z, Wang Q, Wang H, Zhang L, Song G, Song L, et al. Ultrathin PEGylated $W_{18}O_{49}$ nanowires as a new 980 nm-laser-driven photothermal agent for efficient ablation of cancer cells in vivo. Adv Mater 2013;25:2095 - 2100.

[9] Murakami T, Nakatsuji H, Inada M, Matoba Y, Umeyama T, Tsujimoto M, et al. Photodynamic and photothermal effects of semiconducting and metallic-enriched single-walled carbon nanotubes. J Am Chem Soc 2012; 134: 17862 - 17865.

[10] Yang K, Zhang S, Zhang G, Sun X, Lee ST, Liu Z. Graphene in mice: ultrahigh in vivo tumor uptake and efficient photothermal therapy. Nano Lett 2010;10:3318 - 3323.

[11] Song X, Gong H, Yin S, Cheng L, Wang C, Li Z, et al. Ultra-small iron oxide doped polypyrrole nanoparticles for in vivo multimodal imaging guided photothermal therapy. Adv Funct Mater 2014;24:1194 – 1201.

[12] Liu Y, Ai K, Liu J, Deng M, He Y, Lu L. Dopamine-melanin colloidal nanospheres: an efficient near-infrared photothermal therapeutic agent for in vivo cancer therapy. Adv Mater 2013;25:1353 – 1359.

[13] Yang J, Choi J, Bang D, Kim E, Lim E-K, Park H, et al. Convertible organic nanoparticles for near-infrared photothermal ablation of cancer cells. Angew Chem Int Ed 2011;50:441 – 444.

[14] Zhu Y, James DK, Tour JM. New routes to graphene, graphene oxide and their related applications. Adv Mater 2012;24:4924 – 4955.

[15] Huang X, Qi X, Boey F, Zhang H. Graphene-based composites. Chem Soc Rev 2012;41:666 – 686.

[16] Liu Z, Robinson JT, Sun X, Dai H. PEGylated nanographene oxide for delivery of water-insoluble cancer drugs. J Am Chem Soc 2008; 130: 10876 – 10877.

[17] Chen B, Liu M, Zhang L, Huang J, Yao J, Zhang Z. Polyethylenimine-functionalized graphene oxide as an efficient gene delivery vector. J Mater Chem 2011;21:7736 – 7741.

[18] Tang LAL, Wang J, Loh KP. Graphene-based SELDI probe with ultrahigh extraction and sensitivity for DNA oligomer. J Am Chem Soc 2010;132:10976 – 10977.

[19] Zhou M, Zhai Y, Dong S. Electrochemical sensing and biosensing platform based on chemically reduced graphene oxide. Anal Chem 2009;81:5603 – 5613.

[20] Peng C, Hu W, Zhou Y, Fan C, Huang Q. Intracellular imaging with a graphene-based fluorescent probe. Small 2010;6:1686 – 1692.

[21] Robinson JT, Tabakman SM, Liang Y, Wang H, Sanchez Casalongue H, Vinh D, et al. Ultrasmall reduced graphene oxide with high near-infrared absorbance for photothermal therapy. J Am Chem Soc 2011;133:6825 – 6831.

[22] Yang K, Wan J, Zhang S, Tian B, Zhang Y, Liu Z. The influence of surface chemistry and size of nanoscale graphene oxide on photothermal therapy of cancer using ultra-low laser power. Biomaterials 2012;33:2206 – 2214.

[23] Markovic ZM, Harhaji-Trajkovic LM, Todorovic-Markovic BM, Kepic DP, Arsikin KM, Jovanovic SP, et al. In vitro comparison of the photothermal anticancer activity of graphene nanoparticles and carbon nanotubes. Biomaterials 2011;32:1121 – 1129.

[24] Akhavan O, Ghaderi E. Graphene nanomesh promises extremely efficient in

vivo photothermal therapy. Small 2013;9:3593 – 3601.

[25] Li JL, Hou XL, Bao HC, Sun L, Tang B, Wang JF, et al. Graphene oxide nanoparticles for enhanced photothermal cancer cell therapy under the irradiation of a femtosecond laser beam. J Biomed Mater Res Part A 2014; 102: 2181 – 2188.

[26] Artiles MS, Rout CS, Fisher TS. Graphene-based hybrid materials and devices for biosensing. Adv Drug Deliv Rev 2011;63:1352 – 1360.

[27] Liang YY, W HL, Casalongue HS, Chen Z, Dai HJ. TiO_2 nanocrystals grown on graphene as advanced photocatalytic hybrid materials. Nano Res 2010;3: 701 – 705.

[28] Hu SH, Chen YW, Hung WT, Chen IW, Chen SY. Quantum-dot-tagged reduced graphene oxide nanocomposites for bright fluorescence bioimaging and photothermal therapy monitored in situ. Adv Mater 2012;24:1748 – 1754.

[29] Yang K, Hu L, Ma X, Ye S, Cheng L, Shi X, et al. Multimodal imaging guided photothermal therapy using functionalized graphene nanosheets anchored with magnetic nanoparticles. Adv Mater 2012;24:1868 – 1872.

[30] Fang J, Chandrasekharan P, Liu XL, Yang Y, Lv YB, Yang CT, et al. Manipulating the surface coating of ultra-small Gd_2O_3 nanoparticles for improved T_1-weighted MR imaging. Biomaterials 2014;35:1636 – 1642.

[31] Park YI, Kim JH, Lee KT, Jeon KS, Na HB, Yu JH, et al. Nonblinking and non-bleaching upconverting nanoparticles as an optical imaging nanoprobe and T_1 magnetic resonance imaging contrast agent. Adv Mater 2009; 21: 4467 – 4471.

[32] Hu H, Li D, Liu S, Wang M, Moats R, Conti PS, et al. Integrin $\alpha_2\beta_1$ targeted $GdVO_4$: Eu ultrathin nanosheet for multimodal PET/MR imaging. Biomaterials 2014;35:8649 – 8658.

[33] Haller C, Hizoh I. The cytotoxicity of iodinated radiocontrast agents on renal cells in vitro. Invest Radiol 2004;39:149 – 154.

[34] Zhou ZG, Yu C, Shi XY, Wang MW, Liu W, Sun YN, et al. Tungsten oxide nanorods: an efficient nanoplatform for tumor CT imaging and photothermal therapy. Sci Rep 2014;4:3653.

[35] Kim D, Park S, Lee JH, Jeong YY, Jon S. Antibiofouling polymer-coated gold nanoparticles as a contrast agent for in vivo X-ray computed tomography imaging. J Am Chem Soc 2007;129:7661 – 7665.

[36] Rabin O, Manuel Perez J, Grimm J, Wojtkiewicz G, Weissleder R. An X-ray computed tomography imaging agent based on long-circulating bismuth sulphide nanoparticles. Nat Mater 2006;5:118 – 122.

[37] Oh MH, Lee N, Kim H, Park SP, Piao Y, Lee J, et al. Large-scale synthesis of bioinert tantalum oxide nanoparticles for X-ray computed tomography imaging and bimodal image-guided sentinel lymph node mapping. J Am Chem Soc 2011;133:5508 - 5515.

[38] Xing H, Bu W, Zhang S, Zheng X, Li M, Chen F, et al. Multifunctional nanoprobes for upconversion fluorescence, MR and CT trimodal imaging. Biomaterials 2012;33:1079 - 1089.

[39] Chen Q, Li K, Wen S, Liu H, Peng C, Cai H, et al. Targeted CT/MR dual mode imaging of tumors using multifunctional dendrimer-entrapped gold nanoparticles. Biomaterials 2013;34:5200 - 5209.

[40] Alric C, Taleb J, Duc GL, Mandon C, Billotey C, Meur-Herland AL, et al. Gadolinium chelate coated gold nanoparticles as contrast agents for both X-ray computed tomography and magnetic resonance imaging. J Am Chem Soc 2008; 130:5908 - 5915.

[41] Chou SW, Shau YH, Wu PC, Yang YS, Shieh DB, Chen CC. In vitro and in vivo studies of FePt nanoparticles for dual modal CT/MRI molecular imaging. J Am Chem Soc 2010;132:13270 - 13278.

[42] Lee N, Cho HR, Oh MH, Lee SH, Kim K, Kim BH, et al. Multifunctional Fe_3O_4/TaOx core/shell nanoparticles for simultaneous magnetic resonance imaging and X-ray computed tomography. J Am Chem Soc 2012;134:10309 - 10312.

[43] Zeng S, Tsang MK, Chan CF, Wong KL, Hao J. PEG modified BaGdF₅: Yb/Er nanoprobes for multi-modal upconversion fluorescent, in vivo X-ray computed tomography and biomagnetic imaging. Biomaterials 2012;33:9232 - 9238.

[44] Yang D, Dai Y, Liu J, Zhou Y, Chen Y, Li C, et al. Ultra-small BaGdF₅-based upconversion nanoparticles as drug carriers and multimodal imaging probes. Biomaterials 2014;35:2011 - 2023.

[45] Hummers WS, Offeman RE. Preparation of graphitic oxide. J Am Chem Soc 1958;80:1339.

[46] Liu K, Zhang JJ, Cheng FF, Zheng TT, Wang C, Zhu JJ. Green and facile synthesis of highly biocompatible graphene nanosheets and its application for cellular imaging and drug delivery. J Mater Chem 2011;21:12034 - 12040.

[47] Bai J, Liu Y, Jiang X. Multifunctional PEG-GO/CuS nanocomposites for near-infrared chemo-photothermal therapy. Biomaterials 2014;35:5805 - 5813.

[48] Pham TA, Choi BC, Jeong YT. Facile covalent immobilization of cadmium sulfide quantum dots on graphene oxide nanosheets: preparation, characterization, and optical properties. Nanotechnology 2010;21:465603.

[49] Zhou Z, Sun Y, Shen J, Wei J, Yu C, Kong B, et al. Iron/iron oxide core/ shell nanoparticles for magnetic targeting MRI and near-infrared photothermal therapy. Biomaterials 2014;35:7470 – 7478.

[50] Weinmann HJ, Brasch RC, Press WR, Wesbey GE. Characteristics of gadolinium-DTPA complex: a potential NMR contrast agent. Am J Roentgenol 1984;142:619 – 624.

[51] Zhao Q, Lei Z, Huang S, Han X, Shao B, Lü W, et al. Facile fabrication of single-phase multifunctional BaGdF$_5$ nanospheres as drug carriers. ACS Appl Mater Interfaces 2014;6:12761 – 12770.

[52] http://physics.nist.gov/PhysRefData/XrayMassCoef/.

[53] Tong L, Zhao Y, Huff TB, Hansen MN, Wei A, Cheng JX. Gold nanorods mediate tumor cell death by compromising membrane integrity. Adv Mater 2007;19:3136 – 3141.

[54] Liao MY, Lai PS, Yu HP, Lin HP, Huang CC. Innovative ligand-assisted synthesis of NIR-activated iron oxide for cancer theranostics. Chem Commun 2012;48:5319 – 5321.

[55] Dong B, Xu S, Sun J, Bi S, Li D, Bai X, et al. Multifunctional NaYF$_4$: Yb^{3+}, Er^{3+} @ Ag core/shell nanocomposites: integration of upconversion imaging and photothermal therapy. J Mater Chem 2011;21:6193 – 6200.

[56] Rhyner MN, Smith AM, Gao X, Mao H, Yang L, Nie S. Quantum dots and multifunctional nanoparticles: new contrast agents for tumor imaging. Nanomedicine 2006;1:209 – 217.

[57] Xiao Q, Zheng X, Bu W, Ge W, Zhang S, Chen F, et al. A core/satellite multifunctional nanotheranostic for in vivo imaging and tumor eradication by radiation/photothermal synergistic therapy. J Am Chem Soc 2013;135:13041 – 13048.

[58] Hu SH, Fang RH, Chen YW, Liao BJ, Chen IW, Chen SY. Photoresponsive protein-graphene-protein hybrid capsules with dual targeted heat-triggered drug delivery approach for enhanced tumor therapy. Adv Funct Mater 2014;24:4144 – 4155.

[59] Cheng L, Yang K, Chen Q, Liu Z. Organic stealth nanoparticles for highly effective in vivo near-infrared photothermal therapy of cancer. ACS Nano 2012; 6:5605 – 5613.

A highly selective magnetic sensor for Cd^{2+} in living cells with (Zn, Mn)-doped iron oxide nanoparticles

Yang Zhang[a], Jinchao Shen[a], Hong Yang[a],
Yan Yang[a], Zhiguo Zhou[a], Shiping Yang[a, b]

[a] The Key Laboratory of Resource Chemistry of Ministry of Education, Shanghai Key Laboratory of Rare Earth Functional Materials, and Shanghai Municipal Education Committee Key Laboratory of Molecular Imaging Probes and Sensors, Shanghai Normal University
[b] No. 3 People Hospital Affiliated to Shanghai Jiao Tong Unive-rsity, School of Medicine

1. Introduction

Cd^{2+} can cause serious environmental and health problems, and easily pass through the blood into the liver and kidney or be transported into the lungs by smoking [1]. For the requirement of the rapid detection, a number of Cd^{2+}-selective sensors have been designed by utilizing electrochemical [2 - 6], chromogenic [7 - 9], and fluorogenic properties [10 - 12]. Because of the accumulation in organisms and carcinogenesis of Cd^{2+}, the method of detecting Cd^{2+} in living cells or tissues is greatly necessary. Up to date, only the fluorescent method has been widely used to detect it in the biological system [13 - 15]. By comparison, a magnetic sensor, which can be carried out in turbid and light-impermeable media and even in the whole tissue due to no limitation of light scattering and photo-bleaching, has been paid great attention by scientists. Recently, many magnetic sensors have been designed in biological targets such as bacteria [16,17], proteins [18,19], viruses [20], and nucleic acids (DNA and mRNA) [21,22]. However, few magnetic sensors for metal ions, especially in biological system have been reported. Ma and Xu's groups have reported a magnetic probe for Hg^{2+} and Pb^{2+} based on the oligonucleotide conjugated magnetic nanoparticles, respectively [23,24]. Atanasijevic's group described a magnetic sensor for Ca^{2+} based on iron oxide nanoparticles [25]. Our group also reported a magnetic sensor for Hg (II) based on thymidine-functionalized supermagnetic iron oxide nanoparticles [26].

Herein, we designed a novel magnetic sensor based on ethyl 1-(2-(3′, 4′-dihydroxyphenyl)-2-oxoethyl)-1H-1,2,3-triazole-4-carboxylate (ETC) coordinated (Zn, Mn)-doped iron oxide nanoparticles [ETC-(Zn, Mn)Fe₃O₄NPs] for the cellular detection of Cd^{2+} (scheme 1). Two phenolic hydroxyls of ETC can coordinate to the surface of (Zn, Mn) Fe₃O₄ NPs. By use of the selective coordination interaction between 1,2,3,-triazole unit and Cd^{2+}. Cd^{2+} can induce the assembly of ETC-(Zn, Mn)Fe₃O₄ NPs accompanied by the increase of T_2 value of water protons. Furthermore, ETC-(Zn, Mn)Fe₃O₄ NPs were allowed to detect Cd^{2+} in living cells with the change of T_2 value and magnetic resonance (MR) imaging.

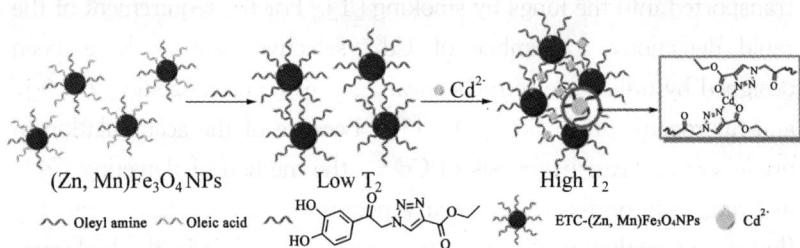

(Zn, Mn)Fe₃O₄ NPs   Low T_2 High T_2

⌇⌇ Oleyl amine ⌇⌇ Oleic acid   ETC-(Zn, Mn)Fe₃O₄NPs   Cd²⁺

Scheme 1 Rational strategy for the detection of Cd^{2+} in living cells by ETC-(Zn, Mn) Fe₃O₄ NPs.

2. Experimental

2.1 Reagents

Benzyl oxide, iron(III) acetylacetonate [$Fe(acac)_3$], manganese (II) acetylacetonate [$Mn(acac)_2$] were purchased from Aladdin. Oleylamine (70%), oleic acid (90%), and 3-hydroxytyramine hydrochloride were obtained from Sigma-Aldrich. Zinc (II) acetylacetonate [$Zn(acac)_2$] and 2-chloro-3′, 4′-dihydroxyacetophenone were purchased from TCI. NaN_3 was purchased from Sinopharm Chemical Reagent Co. Ltd.

2.2 Characterization

The morphology of nanoparticles was observed with a JEOL JEM-2010 transmission electron microscopy. The hydrodynamic diameter was measured by dynamic light scattering (DLS) with a Malvern Zetasizer Nano ZS model ZEN3600. The concentration of Fe was measured by inductively coupled plasma emission spectrometry (ICP-MS) (Vistampxicp Varian, USA). The hysteresis loop was determined by VSM-236 Vibrating Sample Magnetometer (Lake Shore, USA). The ^1H NMR spectra were recorded on a Bruker AVANCE 400 spectrometer. The double-distilled water ($>18MΩ$ cm) was prepared by SUPER SERIES NW Ultra-pure Water System (Heal Force).

2.3 Synthesis of $(Zn, Mn)Fe_3O_4$ NPs

$Zn(acac)_2$ (0.11 g, 0.4 mmol), $Mn(acac)_2$ (0.15 g, 0.6 mmol) and $Fe(acac)_3$ (0.71 g, 2 mmol) were dispersed in benzyl oxide (20 mL) in the presence of oleylamine (1.6 g, 6 mmol) and oleic acid (1.7 g, 6 mmol) in a three-neck round bottom flask. The resulting mixture was heated at 200℃ for 2 h, then 300℃ for 1 h. After the product was cooled down to room temperature, nanoparticles were precipitated by the addition of ethanol, and then separated by centrifugation at 12000 rpm for 8 min. The obtained nanoparticles were as seeds for the next step.

Zn(acac)$_2$ (0. 11 g, 0. 4 mmol), Mn(acac)$_2$ (0. 15 g, 0. 6 mmol), Fe(acac)$_3$ (0. 71 g, 2 mmol) and the above seeds (84 mg) were dispersed in benzyl oxide (20 mL) in the presence of oleylamine (0. 54 g, 2 mmol) and oleic acid (0. 56 g, 2 mmol) in a three-neck round bottom flask. The resulting mixture was heated at 200℃ for 1 h, then 300℃ for 0. 5 h. After the product was cooled down to room temperature, the obtained nanoparticles as new seeds were separated according to the above procedure.

To increase the diameter of (Zn, Mn) Fe$_3$O$_4$ NPs, the similar procedure was repeated excepted the above new seeds (96 mg) was used.

2. 4   Synthesis of ETC

2-chloro-3′, 4′-dihydroxyacetophenone (1. 0 g, 5. 4 mmol) and sodium azide (0. 42 g, 6. 5 mmol) was dissolved in 20 mL of DMSO, and stirred for 12 h at room temperature. 50 mL of water was added to the above solution, and then extracted with diethyl ether (125 mL). The obtained organic layers were concentrated under the vacuum. The 2-azido-3′, 4′-dihydroxyacetophenone was purified by the flash chromatography using CH$_2$Cl$_2$ as a eluent: ^{1}H NMR (400 MHz, DMSO-d_6) δ 7. 18 (dd, $J = 8. 4$, 2. 3 Hz, 1H), 7. 02 (d, $J = 2. 3$ Hz, 1H), 6. 20(d, $J = 8. 4$ Hz, 1H), 5. 50 (s, 2H), 4. 48 (s, 2H).

The mixture of 2-azido-3′, 4′-dihydroxyacetophenone (0. 2 g, 1 mmol), ethyl propiolate (0. 15 g, 1. 5 mmol), CuSO$_4$ • 5H$_2$O (7 mg), and sodium ascorbate (0. 02 g) in 20 mL THF/H$_2$O mixture (v : v=1 : 2) was stirred at room temperature for 12 h. Water was added to the reaction solution. The precipitate was filtered off, and then further purified by recrystallizing with hexane and ethyl acetate mixture solution. ^{1}H NMR (400 MHz, DMSO-d_6) δ 8.68 (s, 1H), 7.50 (d, $J = 8.5$ Hz, 1H), 7.41 (s, 1H), 6.89 (d, $J = 8.4$ Hz, 2H), 6.10 (s, 2H), 5.98 (s, 1H), 4.36-4.28 (m, 4H), 1.31 (t, $J = 7.1$ Hz, 5H).

2.5 Synthesis of ETC-(Zn, Mn)Fe$_3$O$_4$ NPs

A mixture of ETC (66 mg, 0.23 mmol), dopamine hydrochloride (7 mg, 0.046 mmol), and anhydrous sodium carbonate (66 mg, 0.62 mmol) were dispersed in water (10 mL). (Zn, Mn) Fe$_3$O$_4$ NPs (30 mg) in pyridine (10 mL) were added to the above solution. The mixture was stirred at room temperature for 24 h under the nitrogen atmosphere. The nanoparticles were centrifuged at 16000 rpm for 10 min, and purified with water by the redispersion/centrifugation process for three times.

2.6 ETC-(Zn, Mn)Fe$_3$O$_4$ NPs as a magnetic sensor for Cd^{2+}

The T_2 value was measured on a 0.5 T magnet NMI20-Analyst (Shanghai, Niumag Corporation) (TW = 6000 ms, SW = 100 kHz, SF = 18 MHz, RG1 = 25db, DRG1 = 3.). ETC-(Zn, Mn)Fe$_3$O$_4$ NPs were dispersed in water (0.34 μg/mL Fe). Various concentration of Cd^{2+} was added into the solution of ETC-(Zn, Mn) Fe$_3$O$_4$ NPs. The combined solution was mixed for 25 min. The change of T_2 value was calculated as follows.

$$\Delta T_2 = T_{2\,(\text{MNPs, Cd}^{2+})} - T_{2(\text{MNPs})}$$

$T_{2(\text{MNPs})}$ was the average T_2 of the solution of ETC-(Zn, Mn) Fe$_3$O$_4$ NPs. $T_{2(\text{MNPs, Cd}^{2+})}$ was the average T_2 of the solution of ETC-(Zn, Mn)Fe$_3$O$_4$ NPs after the addition of Cd^{2+} with the different concentration.

The limit of detection (LOD) was calculated by the following formula.

$$LOD = \frac{KS_b}{S}$$

S_b was the standard deviation of the blank measures (repeating 20 times), $K = 3$, S is the sensitivity of the method.

2.7 The selectivity of ETC-(Zn, Mn)Fe₃O₄ NPs for Cd²⁺

A variety of metal ions (Na^+, K^+, Mg^{2+}, Al^{3+}, Cr^{3+}, Mn^{2+}, Ca^{2+}, Pb^{2+}, Hg^{2+}, Fe^{3+}, Fe^{2+}, Zn^{2+}, Cu^{2+}) (0.3 μM) were added into the solution of ETC-(Zn, Mn)Fe_3O_4 NPs (0.34 μg/mL Fe), respectively. The combined solution was mixed for 25 min. The competition experiments were performed in the solution of ETC-(Zn, Mn)Fe_3O_4 NPs containing 0.3 μM Cd^{2+} and one of the other metal ions (0.3 μM). The T_2 value was measured using the same parameters shown in section 2.6.

2.8 MTT assay

Hela cells were seeded in 96-well plates for the incubation for 12 h. Then the cells were divided into two groups. In group one, ofter the incubation for 4 h, each well was treated with the different concentration of Cd^{2+} (0, 0.3, 2, and 10 μM, respectivcly) for another 1 h to evaluate the cytotoxicity of Cd^{2+} with the different concentration. In group two, each well was incubated with ETC-(Zn, Mn)Fe_3O_4 NPs (0.34 μg/mL Fe) for 4 h, and then incubated with Cd^{2+} with the different concentration (0, 0.3, 2, and 10 μM, respe-ctively) for another 1 h. to assess the state of HeLa cells during the detection process. Therefore, MTT solution (5 mg/mL in PBS) (20 μL) was added to each well of the two groups. After the incubation for 4 h, then the medium was removed, DMSO (150 μL) was added to each well. The absorption at 490 nm was recorded on a Thermo Scientific Varioskan Flash.

2. 9 *ETC-(Zn, Mn)Fe_3O_4 NPs as a magnetic sensor for Cd^{2+} in living cells*

HeLa cells were seeded in 6-well flat bottomed plates. HeLa cells were incubated with the solution of ETC-(Zn, Mn) Fe_3O_4 NPs (0. 34 μg/mL Fe) under 5% CO_2 for 4 h, then incubated for another 1 h after the addition of different concentration of Cd^{2+} (0. 3, 2, and 10 μM, respectively). HeLa cells were rinsed with phosphate-buffered saline (PBS) for three times, then MR imaging was performed. For control experiments, HeLa cells were incubated with the solution of ETC-(Zn, Mn)Fe_3O_4 NPs (0. 34 μg/mL Fe) for 4 h, or incubated with different concentration of Cd^{2+} (0. 3, 2, and 10 μM, respectively) for 1 h. The parameters were the similar to those shown in section 2. 6 except D_0 was equal to 1500 ms.

3. Results and discussion

3. 1 *Synthesis and characterization of ETC-(Zn, Mn)Fe_3O_4 NPs*

According to a seed-mediated growth method [27], we adopted (Zn, Mn)Fe_3O_4 NPs with a diameter of 6. 5 ± 1. 4 nm (Fig. 1a) as seeds, and synthesized (Zn, Mn) Fe_3O_4 NPs with a diameter of 12. 5 ± 2. 0 nm (Fig. 1b). The X-ray diffraction revealed a typical spinel structure which matched with the standard card of $ZnFe_2O_4$ and $MnFe_2O_4$ (Fig. 1c). The formula of nanoparticles confirmed by ICP-MS was $(Zn_{0.4}Mn_{0.3}Fe_{0.3})Fe_2O_4$. To perform the detection and water solubility ability of (Zn, Mn) Fe_3O_4 NPs, ETC and dopamine hydrochloride were coated on the surface of nanoparticles by the ligand exchange method, which was confirmed by FT-IR spectra (Fig. S1). After the ligand exchange reaction, the stretching vibration peak of—NH_2,—C=O,—C—N—were located at 3413, 1723, and 1337 cm^{-1}, respectively, indicating that ETC and dopamine hydrochloride were successfully coated on the surface of (Zn, Mn)Fe_3O_4 NPs.

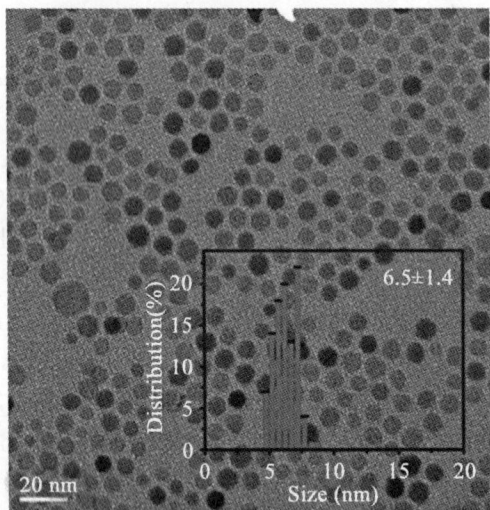

a

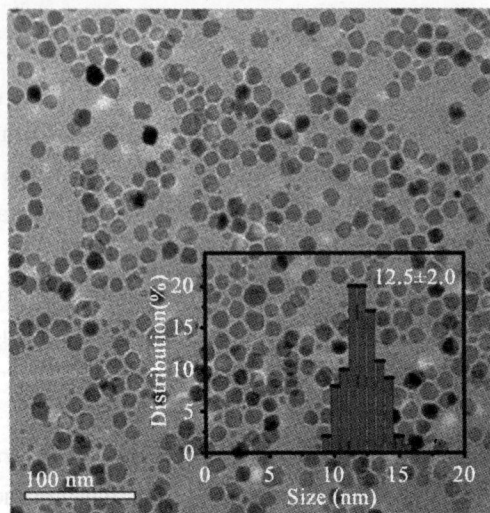

b

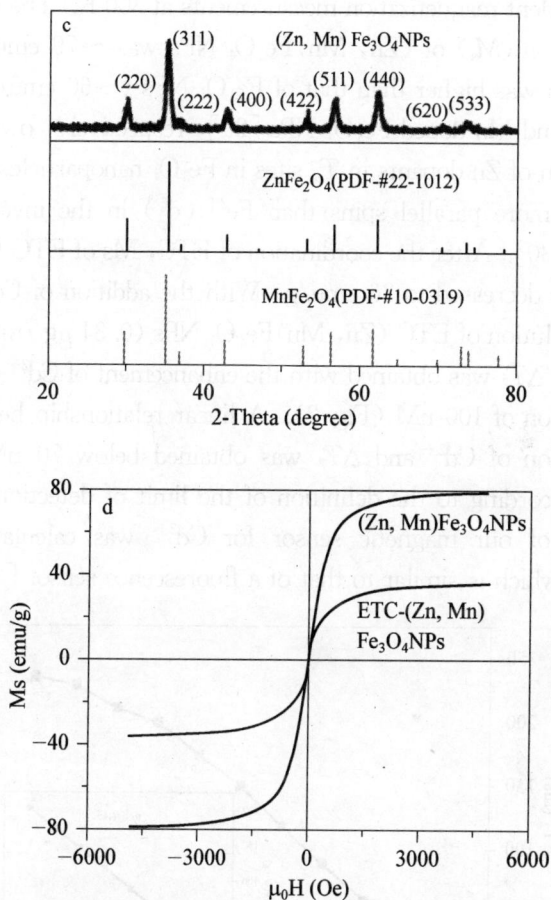

Fig. 1 (a) A typical TEM image of (Zn, Mn) Fe₃O₄ NPs (seeds) and their size distribution (inset). (b) A typical TEM image of (Zn, Mn) Fe₃O₄ NPs and their size distribution (inset). (c) X-ray diffraction pattern of (Zn, Mn) Fe₃O₄ NPs. (d) The room temperature hysteresis loops of (Zn, Mn) Fe₃O₄ NPs (red) and ETC-(Zn, Mn) Fe₃O₄ NPs (black). (For interpretation of the references to color in this figure legend the reader is referred to the web version of this article.)

3.2 ETC-(Zn, Mn)Fe₃O₄ NPs as a magnetic sensor for Cd²⁺

The magnetic property of (Zn, Mn)Fe₃O₄ NPs was evaluated by

field-dependent magnetization measurements at 300 K. The saturation magnetization (M_s) of (Zn, Mn)Fe$_3$O$_4$ NPs was ~79 emu/g (Fig. 1d), which was higher than that of Fe$_3$O$_4$ NPs (~60 emu/g) [28], Zn-doped and Mn-doped Fe$_3$O$_4$ NPs [29], respectively, owing to the contribution of Zn dopants in T_d sites in Fe$_3$O$_4$ nanoparticles [29] and Mn^{2+} has more parallel spins than Fe^{2+} (d^6) in the inverse spinel structure [30]. After the coordination of ETC, Ms of ETC-(Zn, Mn) Fe$_3$O$_4$ NPs decreased to 36 emu/g. With the addition of Cd^{2+} to the aqueous solution of ETC-(Zn, Mn)Fe$_3$O$_4$ NPs (0. 34 μg /mL Fe), an increase in ΔT_2 was obtained with the enhancement of Cd^{2+} within the concentration of 100 nM (Fig. 2). A linear relationship between the concentration of Cd^{2+} and ΔT_2 was obtained below 70 nM (Fig. 2 inset). According to the definition of the limit of detection (LOD), the LOD of our magnetic sensor for Cd^{2+} was calculated to be 3. 5 nM, which is similar to that of a fluorescence sensor [31].

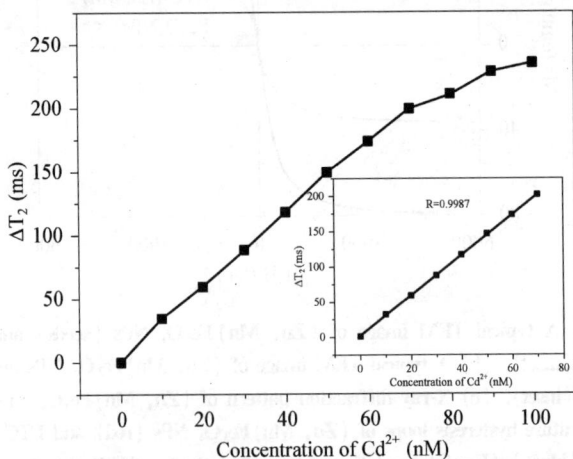

Fig. 2. The changes of ΔT_2 as a function of the concentration of Cd^{2+} (0. 34 μg /mL Fe). Inset: the linear correlation between ΔT_2 and the concentration of Cd^{2+}.

3. 3 The mechanism of Cd²⁺ detection

To investigate the mechanism of Cd^{2+} detection, the aggregation behavior of the magnetic sensor in the presence of Cd^{2+} was measured by atomic force microscopy (AFM). As shown in Fig. 3a and b, many disperse and bright spots were seen on the background in the solution of ETC-(Zn, Mn)Fe_3O_4 NPs (0. 34 μg /mL Fe). On the contrary, in the presence of 0. 3 μM Cd^{2+}, the aggregated spots were obtained. These results suggested that Cd^{2+} should induce the aggregation of ETC-(Zn, Mn)Fe_3O_4 NPs due to the special coordination between the 1,2, 3-triazole unit and Cd^{2+} [7] (Scheme 1). The aggregation behavior of ETC-(Zn, Mn) Fe_3O_4 NPs with Cd^{2+} ion was also confirmed by dynamic light scattering (DLS). The hydrodynamic diameter of ETC-(Zn, Mn)Fe_3O_4 NPs changed from ~246 to ~552 nm with the increase of the concentration of Cd^{2+} from 0 to 100 nM (Fig. 3c). The diameter of ETC-(Zn, Mn)Fe_3O_4 NPs in the aqueous solution was ~ 246 nm exceeded the diffusing distance of water molecules, which should be in the static diphase(SD) regime [32]. The magnetic field induced by ETC-(Zn, Mn) Fe_3O_4 NPs was not averaged by the Brownian movement, and water protons did not undergo the magnetic field in homogeneity. Therefore, they had little magnetic interaction and showed a high T_2 value. After the addition of

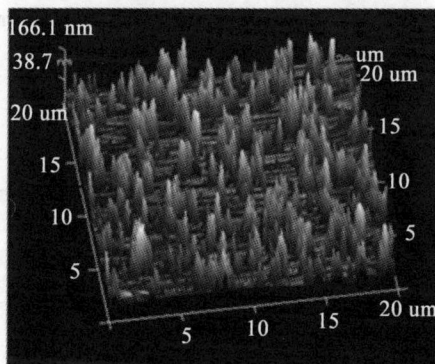

a

b

c

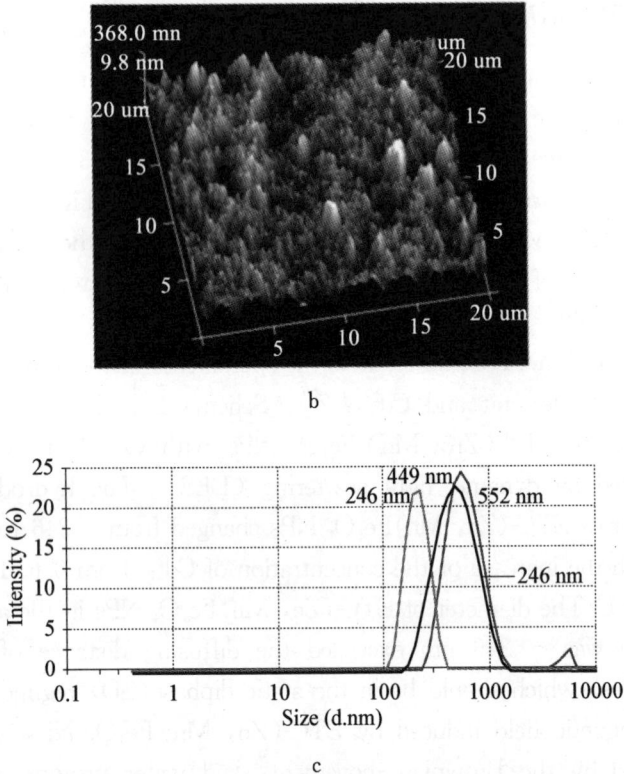

Fig. 3 Atomic force microscopy (AFM) images of ETC-(Zn, Mn)Fe$_3$O$_4$ NPs (a), and with the addition of Cd^{2+} (b). (c) The changes of hydrodynamic diameter of ETC-(Zn, Mn)Fe$_3$O$_4$ NPs (0. 34 μg /mL Fe) (246 nm), ETC-(Zn, Mn) Fe$_3$O$_4$ NPs in the presence of Cd^{2+} (50 nM, 449 nm; 100 nM, 552 nm). (For interpretation of the references to color in this figure legend, the reader is referred to the web version of this article.)

Cd^{2+}, the diameter of ETC-(Zn, Mn) Fe$_3$O$_4$ NPs increased and the system moved into the echo-limited (EL) regime, which resulted in the increment of T_2 value.

3. 4 The selectivity of a magnetic sensor for Cd^{2+}

The specificity of the magnetic sensor (0. 34 μg /mL Fe) was tested by using other metal ions, instead of Cd^{2+}, including Hg^{2+}, Mg^{2+}, Al^{3+}, K$^+$, Na$^+$, Pb^{2+}, Fe^{3+}, Fe^{2+}, Mn^{2+}, Cr^{3+}, Zn^{2+}, Cu^{2+}, and Ca^{2+} with the concentration of 300 nM. Nearly no obvious changes of T_2 value were observed (Fig. 4). To further confirm the effect by other metal ions, the competition experiments was done, in which Cd^{2+} was mixed with one of the other metal ions. No significant variation in the ΔT_2 was observed (Fig. 4). The result was perhaps attributed to the special coordination interaction between ETC and Cd^{2+}[7].

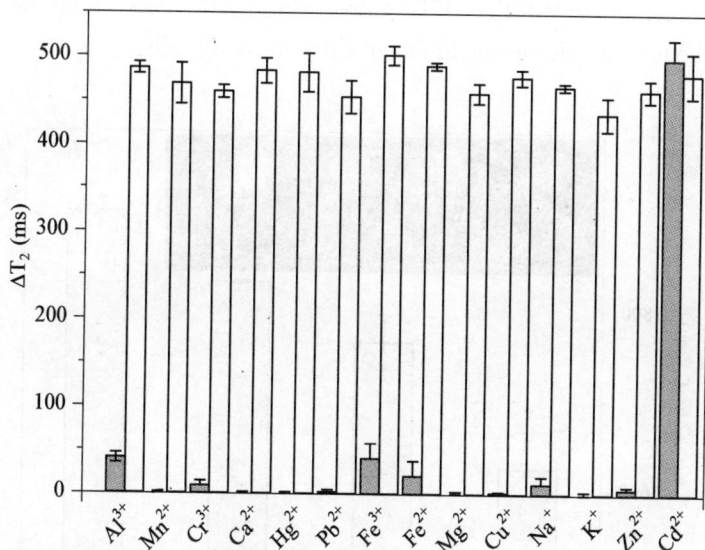

Fig. 4　Black: the ΔT_2 values of ETC-(Zn, Mn)Fe$_3$O$_4$ NPs (0.34 μg/mL Fe) in the presence of different metal ions (0.3 μM) (Al^{3+}, Mn^{2+}, Cr^{3+}, Ca^{2+}, Hg^{2+}, Pb^{2+}, Fe^{3+}, Mg^{2+}, Cu^{2+}, Na$^+$, K$^+$, Zn^{2+}, Cd^{2+}). Blank: the ΔT_2 values of ETC-(Zn, Mn)Fe$_3$O$_4$ NPs (0.34 μg/mL Fe) containing 300 nM Cd^{2+} to the selected metal ions (300 nM).

3.5　*A magnetic sensor for Cd^{2+} in living cells*

To determine the application of ETC-(Zn, Mn)Fe$_3$O$_4$ NPs for Cd^{2+} detection in living cells, T_2 value and MR imaging of HeLa cells were performed. After the incubation of ETC-(Zn, Mn)Fe$_3$O$_4$ NPs (0. 34 μg /mL Fe), T_2 value was $\sim$1600 ms, suggesting that ETC-(Zn, Mn)Fe$_3$O$_4$ NPs were internalized in HeLa cells. As expected, after the incubation of ETC-(Zn, Mn)Fe$_3$O$_4$ NPs (0. 34 μg /mL Fe), then the incubation of Cd^{2+} from 0. 3 to 10 μM, T_2 value increased from $\sim$1760 to $\sim$1900 ms (Fig. 5). The increase of T_2 value in HeLa cells was also confirmed by the brightness in T_2-weighted MR imaging with the increase of Cd^{2+} (Fig. 5 inset). MTT assay confirmed the cells were still alive during the detection for Cd^{2+} (Fig. S2). This result demonstrated that ETC-(Zn, Mn) Fe$_3$O$_4$ NPs could be an excellent magnetic sensor to detect Cd^{2+} in living cells.

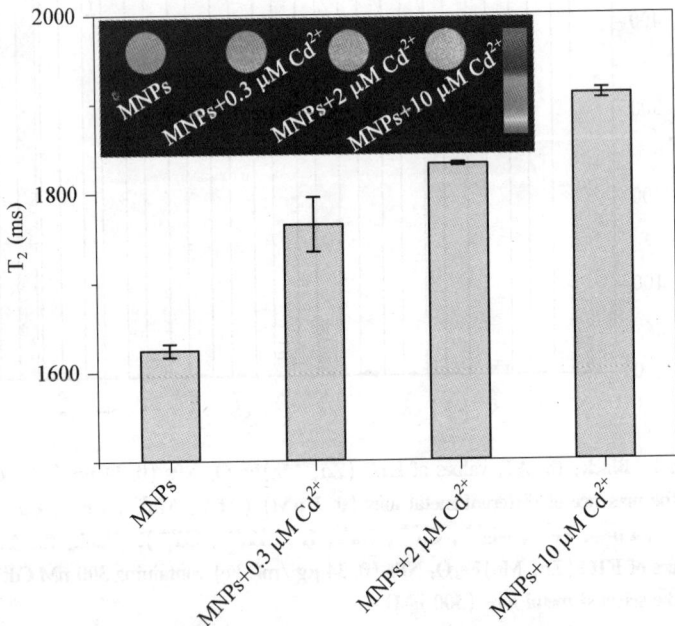

Fig. 5 T_2 **values and MR imaging (inset) in HeLa cells. HeLa cells incubated with ETC-(Zn, Mn)Fe$_3$O$_4$ NPs and then incubated with different concentration of Cd^{2+} (0. 3, 2 and 10 μM, respectively).**

4. Conclusions

In conclusion, a magnetic sensor for detecting Cd^{2+} in living cells has been successfully prepared. ETC-(Zn, Mn) Fe_3O_4 NPs could capture Cd^{2+} effectively *via* special groups of ETC, which showed a selective and sensitive detection of Cd^{2+} in living cells. This method exhibits a simple, rapid and efficient way for detecting Cd^{2+}, which has great potential application in biological system.

Acknowledgements

This work was partially supported by National Natural Science Foundation of China (Nos. 21271130 and 21371122), Program for Changjiang Scholars and Innovative Research Team in University (No. IRT1269), Shanghai Science and Technology Development Fund (Nos. 12ZR1421800 and 13520502800), Shanghai Pujiang Program (13PJ1406600), Shanghai Municipal Education Commission (No. 13ZZ110), Shanghai Normal University (DYL201305) and International Joint Laboratory on Resource Chemistry (IJLRC).

Appendix A. Supplementary data

Supplementary data associated with this article can be found, in the online version, at http://dx. doi. org/10. 1016/j. snb. 2014. 10. 074.

References

[1] L. Jarup, A. Akesson, Current status of cadmium as an environmental health problem, Toxicol. Appl. Pharmacol. 238(2009)201 - 208.

[2] E. L. S. Wong, E. Chow, J. Justin Gooding, The electrochemical detection of cadmium using surface-immobilized DNA, Electrochem. Commun. 9 (2007) 845 - 849.

[3] Y. Wei, R. Yang, X.-Y. Yu, L. Wang, J.-H. Liu, X.-J. Huang, Stripping voltammetry study of ultra-trace toxic metal ions on highly selectively adsorptive porous magnesium oxide nanoflowers, Analyst 137(2012)2183 – 2191.

[4] C. Babyak, R. B. Smart, Electrochemical detection of trace concentrations of cadmium and lead with a boron-doped diamond electrode: effect of KCl and KNO₃ electrolytes, interferences and measurement in river water, Electroanalysis, 16(2004)175 – 182.

[5] R.-X. Xu, X.-Y. Yu, C. Gao, J.-H. Liu, R. G. Compton, X.-J. Huang, Enhancing selectivity in stripping voltammetry by different adsorption behaviors: the use of nanostructured Mg-Al-layered double hydroxides to detect Cd(II), Analyst, 138(2013)1812 – 1818.

[6] Y. Wei, Z.-G. Liu, X.-Y. Yu, L. Wang, J.-H. Liu, X.-J. Huang, O₂-plasma oxidized multi-walled carbon nanotubes for Cd(II) and Pb(II) detection: evidence of adsorption capacity for electrochemical sensing, Electrochem. Commun. 13(2011)1506 – 1509.

[7] H. Li, Y. Yao, C. Han, J. Zhan, Triazole-ester modified silver nanoparticles: click synthesis and Cd²⁺ colorimetric sensing, Chem. Commun. (2009)4812 – 4814.

[8] A. M. López_Marzo, J. Pons, D. A. Blake, A. Merkoçi, High sensitive gold-nanoparticle based lateral flow immunodevice for Cd²⁺ detection in drinking waters, Biosens. Bioelectron. 47(2013)190 – 198.

[9] J. Yin, T. Wu, J. Song, Q. Zhang, S. Liu, R. Xu, et al. , SERS-active nanoparticles for sensitive and selective detection of cadmium ion (Cd²⁺), Chem. Mater. 23(2011)4756 – 4764.

[10] M. Taki, M. Desaki, A. Ojida, S. Iyoshi, T. Hirayama, I. Hamachi, et al. , Fluorescence imaging of intracellular cadmium using a dual-excitation ratiometric chemosensor, J. Am. Chem. Soc. 130(2008)12564 – 12565.

[11] S. Sumiya, Y. Shiraishi, T. Hirai, Mechanism for different fluorescence response of a coumarin-amide-dipicolylamine linkage to Zn(II) and Cd(II) in water, J. Phys. Chem. A 117(2013)1474 – 1482.

[12] X. Liu, N. Zhang, J. Zhou, T. Chang, C. Fang, D. Shangguan, A turn-on fluorescent sensor for zinc and cadmium ions based on perylene tetracarboxylic diimide, Analyst 138(2013)901 – 906.

[13] T. Cheng, Y. Xu, S. Zhang, W. Zhu, X. Qian, L. Duan, A highly sensitive and selective OFF-ON fluorescent sensor for cadmium in aqueous solution and living cell, J. Am. Chem. Soc. 130(2008)16160 – 16161.

[14] X. Peng, J. Du, J. Fan, J. Wang, Y. Wu, J. Zhao, et al. , A selective fluorescent sensor for imaging Cd^{2+} in living cells, J. Am. Chem. Soc. 129 (2007)1500 - 1501.

[15] A. Bencini, F. Caddeo, C. Caltagirone, A. Garau, M. B. Hurstouse, F. Isaia, et al. , An OFF-ON chemosensor for biological and environmental applications: sensing Cd^{2+} in water using catanionic vesicles and in living cells, Org. Biomol. Chem. 11(2013)7751 - 7759.

[16] H. Lee, T. -J. Yoon, R. Weissleder, Ultrasensitive detection of bacteria using core-shell nanoparticles and an NMR-filter system, Angew. Chem. Int. Ed. 48 (2009)5657 - 5660.

[17] C. Kaittanis, S. A. Naser, J. M. Perez, One-step, nanoparticle-mediated bacterial detection with magnetic relaxation, Nano Lett. 7(2006)380 - 383.

[18] A. A. Kulkarni, A. A. Weiss, S. S. Iyer, Detection of carbohydrate binding proteins using magnetic relaxation switches, Anal. Chem. 82 (2010) 7430 - 7435.

[19] M. Zhao, L. Josephson, Y. Tang, R. Weissleder, Magnetic sensors for protease assays, Angew. Chem. Int. Ed. 42(2003)1375 - 1378.

[20] J. M. Perez, F. J. Simeone, Y. Saeki, L. Josephson, R. Weissleder, Viral-induced self-assembly of magnetic nanoparticles allows the detection of viral particles in biological media, J. Am. Chem. Soc. 125(2003)10192 - 10193.

[21] D. Alcantara, Y. Guo, H. Yuan, C. J. Goergen, H. H. Chen, H. Cho, et al. , Fluorochrome-functionalized magnetic nanoparticles for high-sensitivity monitoring of the polymerase chain reaction by magnetic resonance, Angew. Chem. Int. Ed. 51(2012)6904 - 6907.

[22] M. V. Yigit, D. Mazumdar, H. -K. Kim, J. H. Lee, B. Odintsov, Y. Lu, Smart "Turn-on" magnetic resonance contrast agents based on aptamer-functionalized superparamagnetic iron oxide nanoparticles, ChemBioChem 8 (2007)1675 - 1678.

[23] W. Ma, C. Hao, W. Ma, C. Xing, W. Yan, H. Kuang, et al. , Wash-free magnetic oligonucleotide probes-based NMR sensor for detecting the Hg ion, Chem. Commun. 47(2011)12503 - 12505.

[24] L. Xu, H. Yin, W. Ma, L. Wang, H. Kuang, C. Xu, MRI biosensor for lead detection based on the DNAzyme-induced catalytic reaction, J. Phys. Chem. B 117(2013)14367 - 14371.

[25] T. Atanasijevic, M. Shusteff, P. Fam, A. Jasanoff, Calcium-sensitive MRI contrast agents based on superparamagnetic iron oxide nanoparticles and

calmodulin, PNAS 103(2006)14707 - 14712.

[26] H. Yang, Z. Tian, J. Wang, S. Yang, A magnetic resonance imaging nanosensor for Hg (II) based on thymidine-functionalized supermagnetic iron oxide nanoparticles, Sens. Actuators B: Chem. 161(2012)429 - 433.

[27] S. Sun, H. Zeng, D. B. Robinson, S. Raoux, P. M. Rice, S. X. Wang, et al. , Monodisperse MFe_2O_4 (M=Fe, Co, Mn) nanoparticles, J. Am. Chem. Soc. 126(2003)273 - 279.

[28] J. Wang, C. Zeng, Z. Peng, Q. Chen, Synthesis and magnetic properties of $Zn_{1-x}Mn_xFe_2O_4$ nanoparticles, Physica B 349(2004)124 - 128.

[29] J.-T. Jang, H. Nah, J.-H. Lee, S. H. Moon, M. G. Kim, J. Cheon, Critical enhancements of MRI contrast and hyperthermic effects by dopant-controlled magnetic nanoparticles, Angew. Chem. Int. Ed. 121(2009)1260 - 1264.

[30] H. Zhu, S. Zhang, Y.-X. Huang, L. Wu, S.-H. Sun, Monodisperse M_x $Fe_{3-x}O_4$ (M=Fe, Cu, Co, Mn) nanoparticles and their electrocatalysis for oxygen reduction reaction, Nano Lett. 13(2013)2947 - 2951.

[31] S. Sarkar, R. Shunmugam, Unusual red shift of the sensor while detecting the presence of Cd^{2+} in aqueous environment, ACS Appl. Mater. Interfaces 5 (2013)7379 - 7383.

[32] J. Cha, Y.-S. Kwon, T.-J. Yoon, J.-K. Lee, Relaxivity control of magnetic nanoclusters for efficient magnetic relaxation switching assay, Chem. Commun. 49(2013)457 - 459.

(原载于 Sensors & Actuators B Chemical 2015 年第 207 期)

Rapid and label-free Raman detection of azodicarbonamide with asthma risk

Menghua Li, Xiaoyu Guo,
Hui Wang, Ying Wen, Haifeng Yang

The Education Ministry Key Lab of Resource Chemistry, Shanghai Key Laboratory of Rare Earth Functional Materials, Shanghai Municipal Education Committee Key Laboratory of Molecular Imaging Probes and Sensors and Department of Chemistry, Shanghai Normal University

1. Introduction

Each year, a large quantity of people worldwide face a variety of health risks due to food safety [1]. Rapid identification and detection of the presence of the poisonous substances in food is one of the vital tasks in analytical chemistry and sensor development field. Azodicarbonamide (ADA) is a yellow to orange crystalline powder, previously applied in rubber products and food packaging applications [2]. Due to the bleaching and oxidability of ADA, it is approved as a food additive existing in flour products such as steamed bread for serving as a flour bleaching agent ·or an improving agent in some countries. ADA can react with moist flour as an oxidizing agent and form dough. When ADA mixed with the wet flour, it can release active oxygen and make the thiol groups of flour proteins oxidize to disulfide bridges [3]. As a consequence, the protein chain could link with each other and constitute a three-dimensional network structure. To a large degree, this 3D structure can improve the elasticity, toughness and uniformity of the dough significantly, especially the strength and flexibility of the paste. As a food additive, the maximum amount of ADA can be tolerated in flour to 45 mg/kg (ppm) in the United States and China, in accordance with Code of Federal Regulations: Cereal Flours and Related Products. However, it has been deemed as toxic as melamine and Sudan Red in European Union, Australia, Singapore and Japan. The European Union classified ADA as a toxicant whose presence may generate a risk to human health. All of them are illegal food additives and banned in those countries. In Singapore, when someone use ADA can bring about up to 15 years imprisonment and a fine of $450000 [4]. ADA may cause respiratory issues, allergies and asthma, according to World Health Organization Concise International Chemical Assessment Document 16: Azodicarbonamide. What's more, the consumption of ADA may augment the allergic reaction to other ingredients in food. More seriously, semicarbazide (SEM), ADA's decomposition product, shows limited genotoxicity in vitro and carcinogenicity and has been proved to cause tumors [5]. The sensitive and selective methods are required to determine the trace ADA in the complex matrix.

To date, HPLC-MS/MS [6] and LC-MS/MS [4] have been used for detection of ADA. Wang et al. used LC-MS/MS to detect ADA in flour and flour products with a good linearity in the range of 0. 5 - 10 mg/L ($r^2 = 0.9991$) and a quantification limit of 1. 0 mg/ kg [4]. Although these methods have the advantages of accurate detection of ADA at a low concentration, they require complicated pre-processing, cost more and are time-consuming. In this sense, it is urgent for us to develop a simple, robust and rapid method for the quantification determination of trace ADA in real samples.

Surface-enhanced Raman scattering (SERS) is a rapid, noninvasive and powerful spectroscopic technique with huge sensitivity [7, 8]. It carries forward the capability of furnishing molecular fingerprint information of Raman spectroscopy, which possesses distinct molecular selectivity and multiplex ability in systems [9]. The effect of SERS was observed on the roughened silver electrode with pyridine monolayer for the first time [10]. As a powerful method, SERS-based signal measurement and molecular identification will provide an unparalleled occasion for researching in analytical chemistry [11], biomedicine [12, 13], and life science [14, 15]. SERS enhancement factors include two proverbial theoretical mechanisms: long-range electromagnetic (EM) enhancement and short-range chemical enhancement (CE). On account of localized surface plasmon resonance (LSPR), the electromagnetic field on the surface of metal is magnified. The enhancement near fields is primarily preferred at small gaps between nanoparticles which are known as "hot spots" [16 – 18]. The junctions among nanoparticles in the "hot spots" can maximize the localized electric field, thus amplifying the SERS signals of analytes [19]. While CE is realized by transforming the scattering cross section of the molecules absorbed on the metal surface, which depends on the chemical properties of the analytes. Consequently, the enhancement of SERS signals is mainly due to EM enhancement [20, 21]. In recent years, great efforts have been made to synthesize highly active noble metal nanoparticles substrates in colloids or films through tuning shape and size as well as functionality [22 – 25].

Holding the wish for SERS application in food and environmental monitoring [26 – 29] and SERS-based diagnose [30,31], it is of the essence for exploring the appropriate synthesis methods to develop the high performance nanostructures for improving the sensitivity and reproducibility of SERS [32]. In amongst, bimetallic silver-coated gold colloids (Au@Ag NPs) were prepared for identification of toxic food additives. Such colloids can form closely packed of silver and gold nanoparticles but not aggregated on the solid surfaces to elevate SERS signal [33], which takes advantage of the strong SERS signal of silver and the uniform shape and size of gold [34]. As a perspective application, the Au@Ag NPs can be extended for the on-site analysis of trace toxic food additives to guarantee the food safety.

So far, there is no systematic report in literature regarding the SERS-based detection of trace ADA in products. Herein, we proposed a label-free method to detect trace ADA in flour and its relative products by means of the dispersed Au@Ag NPs, depending on the advantage of Raman spectroscopy providing the inherent molecular fingerprint of the analytes [35]. As a model application as well as a good result, SERS determination of ADA in flour and steamed bread exhibited great sensitivity and reproducibility with rapidness, simplicity and low cost, which could be employed for on-field monitoring the quality of food in markets.

2. Experimental

2.1 *Chemicals and materials*

Silver nitrate (AgNO₃), hydrogen tetrachloride (HAuCl₄ · 4H₂O), L-ascorbic acid (L-AA) and tri-sodium citrate (TC) were obtained from Sigma-Aldrich (USA). Azodicarbonamide was purchased from Sinopharm Chemical Reagent (Shanghai, China). Sodium chloride (NaCl) was obtained from Jiangsu Qiangsheng Chemical Co., Ltd. Sugar, milk, yeast, flour and steamed bread were purchased from a local supermarket. All other reagents were of analytical reagent grade and used without further purification. Ultrapure water (18 MΩcm) was produced using a Millipore water purification system and used for all solution preparations.

The surface plasmon resonance spectra of the prepared gold colloids and Au@Ag colloids were measured using 760CRT UV-visible spectrophotometer (Shanghai Precision and Scientific Instrument Co., Ltd.). The morphology of the Au@Ag NPs was measured with a JEOL JEM-2000 FX transmission electron microscopy (TEM) operating at 200 kV and a JEOL JEM-2100 high-resolution transmission electron microscope (HR-TEM) instrument. Those samples were pretreated by dropping the colloids onto a carbon coated Cu grid. Field emission scanning electron microscopy (FESEM) (Hitachi S-4800) was used for imaging the topography. Raman experiment was conducted using a Portable Stabilized R. Laser Analyzer with a narrow line width diode laser at 785 nm with an adjustable power of the maximum at 300 mW.

2. 2 Preparation of gold nanoparticles (Au NPs)

Colloidal gold was prepared via reduction of $HAuCl_4$ by tri-sodium citrate (TC) using Frens method [36]. Briefly, 0. 25 mL of 0. 1 M $HAuCl_4$ was added to 100 mL of ultrapure water and heated to boiling under vigorous stirring. Then, 1. 5 mL of 1% TC was injected into the mixture as quickly as possible. The colloid was kept boiling and stirring for 30 min until it turned wine red.

2. 3 Synthesis of Au@Ag NPs

Au@ Ag core-shell colloids were synthesized using the method reported by Liu and Han [34]. Briefly, 10 mL of the above Au NPs was added to a beaker, followed by 1. 5 mL of 0. 1 M ascorbic acid (AA) as reductive agent was mixed with gold colloids under vigorous stirring at room temperature. Then, 3. 5 mL of 1 mM $AgNO_3$ solution was added to the mixture drop by drop. The $AgNO_3$ solution was reduced by AA and the Ag continuously grew at the surface of the gold. With the increase of $AgNO_3$ solution, the color of the colloids was changing from wine red to orange-yellow. After stirring for another 30 min, the Au@Ag NPs were obtained.

2. 4 SERS determination of ADA

1 mM ADA solution was prepared by dissolving the sample powder into the ultrapure water and heating it at 40℃. Next dilute the solution with water to the various predetermined concentrations (1×10^{-4} M, 1×10^{-5} M, 1×10^{-6} M and 1×10^{-7} M). Then 2 mL of Au@Ag NPs solution was taken out and centrifuged at 9000 rpm/min

for 10 min, followed by decanting the supernatant. Following above step, we mixed 4 μL of the concentrated substrate with 4 μL of as-prepared ADA solution and then dropped them onto the aluminum foil paper. The Raman spectra were collected using a portable Raman spectrometer (Portable Stabilized R. Laser Analyzer). The excitation laser is 785 nm with a power of 300 mW.

For real application, in brief, 2 g of flour and flour product were added to 100 mL of ultrapure water to make stock solutions, respectively. Soon afterwards, 0. 0116 g of ADA was separately added to the above stock solutions. The concentrations of ADA in flour and flour product are both 1 mM. The stock ADA flour and flour product solutions weve diluted with the corresponding flour and flour product stock solutions to a range of concentrations. Then the mixture was ultrasonically treated for 15 min. After ADA dissolving in the real samples, 4 μL of as-prepared mixture was mixed with 4 μL of the concentrated Au@Ag substrate and dropped onto the aluminum foil paper. The SERS spectra were recorded after they dried at room temperature and measured in the same way as described in aforementioned section.

2. 5 *Density functional theory (DFT) calculation of ADA*

Calculation of ADA vibrations was based on Becke-Lee-Yang-Parr nonlocal gradient correction method with a type of basis set 6-311G, shortly named as B3LYP/6-311G. First, ADA molecular structure was optimized using B3LYP/6-311G in Gaussian 03 software and then the vibrational modes were calculated.

3. Results and discussion

3. 1 *Characterizations of Au@Ag NPs*

The surface plasmon resonance (SPR) spectra of Au NPs, Ag NPs and Au@Ag NPs are shown in Fig. 1A. The color of Au@Ag

colloids is quite different from the Au colloids and the Ag colloids,
which can be observed from inset picture of Fig. 1A. The gold and
silver colloids present the strong plasmon bands at 527 and 422 nm,
respectively. However, after the Au@Ag core-shell colloids are
synthesized, two different plasmon absorption peaks of the hybrid
nanostructures are emerged. This is due to the grown of the silver
shell and the plasmon resonance of the gold core is damped and blue-

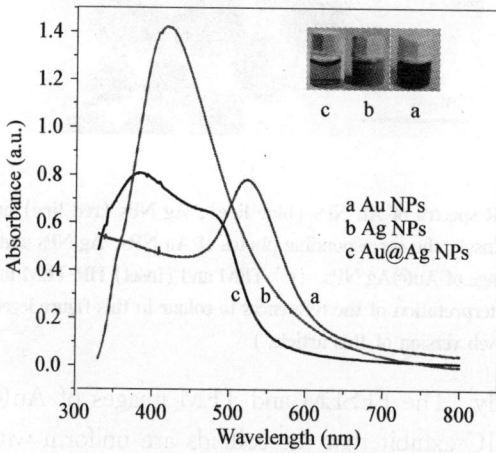

A

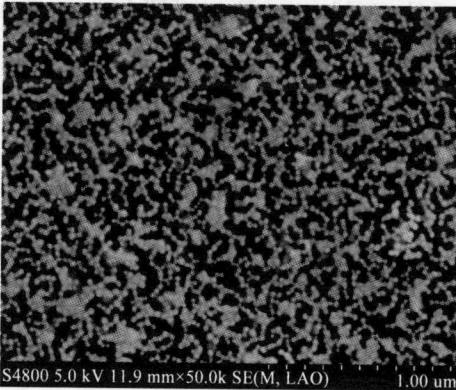

B

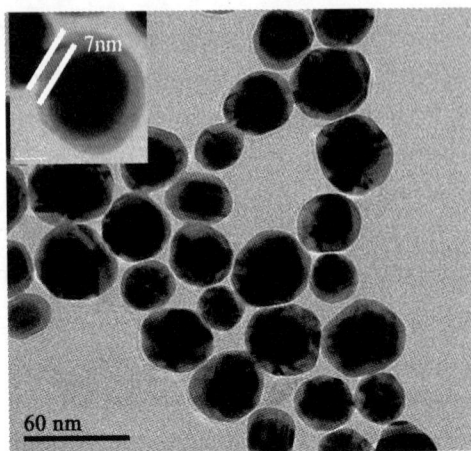

C

Fig. 1 (A) SPR spectra of Au NPs (blue line), Ag NPs (red line) and Au@Ag NPs (black line). (Inset: the corresponding photos of Au NPs, Ag NPs and Au@Ag NPs). (B) FESEM image of Au@Ag NPs. (C) TEM and (inset) HR-TEM images of Au@Ag colloids. (For interpretation of the references to colour in this figure legend, the reader is referred to the web version of this article.)

shifted quickly. The FESEM and TEM images of Au@Ag NPs in Fig. 1B and 1C exhibit that the colloids are uniform with an average diameter of ~40 nm, which demonstrating a highly selective growth of silver shell on the gold core. From TEM image of Au@Ag NPs at the large scale the size distribution is relatively uniform around 40 nm. (see Fig. S1, Supporting Information). The Ag shell thickness is about 7 nm.

3. 2 The SERS performance of different substrates

In order to demonstrate the Raman enhancement effect of the Au @Ag NPs, SERS spectra of ADA mixed with Au@Ag NPs, Au NPs and Ag NPs were recorded in Fig. S2. The colloidal silver was prepared via reduction of $AgNO_3$ by sodium citrate using the method of Lee [37]. The average diameter of pure Ag NPs is ~60 nm. One drawback of Lee's Ag NPs is not uniform. Additionally, the Lee's Ag

NPs are easy to severely aggregate. The Au@Ag NPs possess a broad and strong SPR effect. Consequently, the well-dispersed Au@Ag NPs (40 nm) generate stronger SERS signals.

3.3 Portable Raman detection of ADA in aqueous solution

The procedure for SERS detection of ADA and the models of the corresponding nanoparticles step by step is described in Scheme 1. In detail, 2 mL of Au@Ag NPs solution was taken out and centrifuged at 9000 rpm/min for 10 min, followed by decanting the supernatant. Following above steps, we mixed 4 μL of the concentrated substrate with 4 μL of as-prepared ADA solution, dropped them onto the aluminum foil paper and then remained 3 min until it dried. It should be mentioned that the all Raman spectra were obtained when the laser spot was focused on to the "coffee ring" of dried mixture of ADA and colloids at the surface of aluminum foil paper. The "coffee ring" effect for Raman test could integrate and concentrate the analytes on the closely packed Au@Ag NPs ring, consequently enhancing the SERS

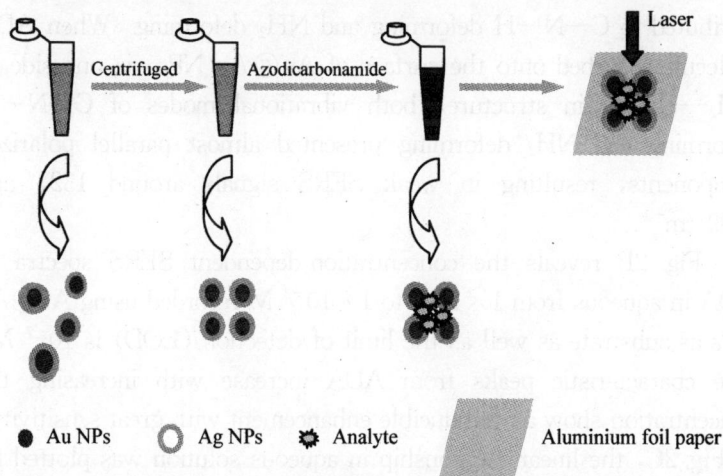

Scheme 1 Schematic diagram of the method proposed for direct detection of ADA measured by the portable Raman spectrometer using Au@Ag as Raman amplifier.

intensity [38].

Fig. 2A shows the SERS spectrum of ADA at the 1×10^{-4} M concentration mixed with Au@Ag NPs and the normal Raman spectrum of ADA solid powder. The differences between normal Raman and SERS spectra could be due to both the electromagnetic (i. e. , localized surface plasmon resonance) and chemical (i. e. , charge transfer) interactions between analytes and substrate surfaces [39]. It is well known, as conducting SERS experiment, some IR-active bands could be seen [40, 41], such as the SERS band at 1028 cm^{-1} in this work. Referring to IR spectrum of ADA, a band about 1120 cm^{-1} could be visible. (See Fig. S3, Supporting Information). Additionally, this band shift might be from the interaction of Ag shell and the NH_2—C=O moiety of ADA. On the other side, according to the surface selection rule for SERS [42, 43], the vibrational modes with vertical polarized components with respect to the surface ought to be enhanced, and the vibrational modes with parallel polarized components with respect to the surface will not be enhanced. The strong lines near 1340 and 1580 cm^{-1} in the solid spectrum could be attributed to C—N—H deforming and NH_2 deforming. When ADA molecule adsorbed onto the surface of Au@Ag NPs via one side of NH_2—C=O in structure, both vibrational modes of C—N—H deforming and NH_2 deforming presented almost parallel polarized components, resulting in weak SERS signals around 1321 and 1599 cm^{-1}.

Fig. 2B reveals the concentration-dependent SERS spectra of ADA in aqueous from 1×10^{-7} to 1×10^{-3} M recorded using Au@Ag NPs as substrate as well as the limit of detection (LOD) is 10^{-7} M. The characteristic peaks from ADA increase with increasing the concentration show a reproducible enhancement with great sensitivity. In Fig. 2C, the linear relationship in aqueous solution was plotted by the SERS intensities of the peak at 1028 cm^{-1}, 1321 cm^{-1} and 1599 cm^{-1} versus the concentrations of ADA. Based on the maximum permitted level of flour is 45 mg/kg (3.9×10^{-4} M) according to

FDA and National standard of China (GB2760 - 2011), we chose the concentrations of ADA from 1×10^{-4} to 1×10^{-3} M to plot the linear relationship. Moreover, when the concentration is less than 1×10^{-4} M, the signals are not at the linear trend shown in Fig. 2C. The linearity given in Fig. 2C exhibits an excellent linear relationship between the SERS intensity and the concentration of ADA. Due to the band at 1028 cm^{-1} displays the highest linearity, therefore, it could be observed for quantitative detection of ADA in real application.

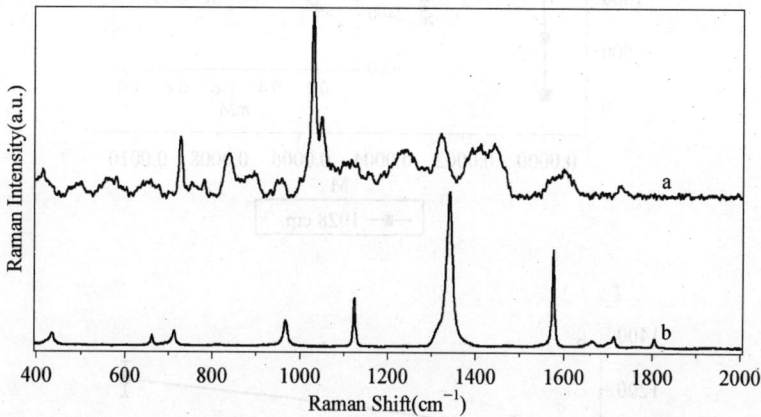

A

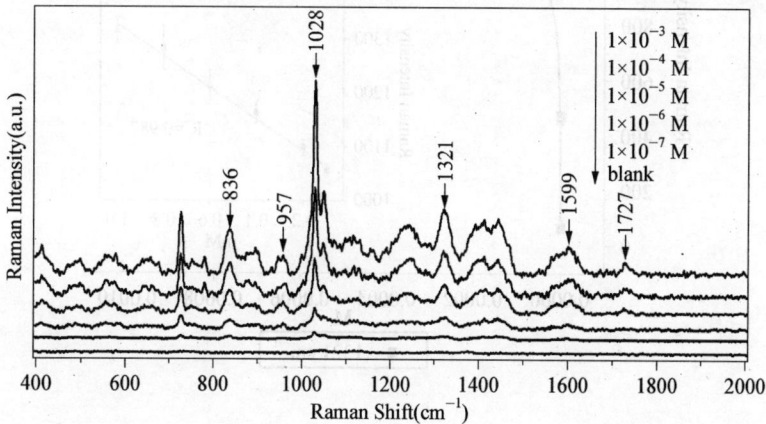

B

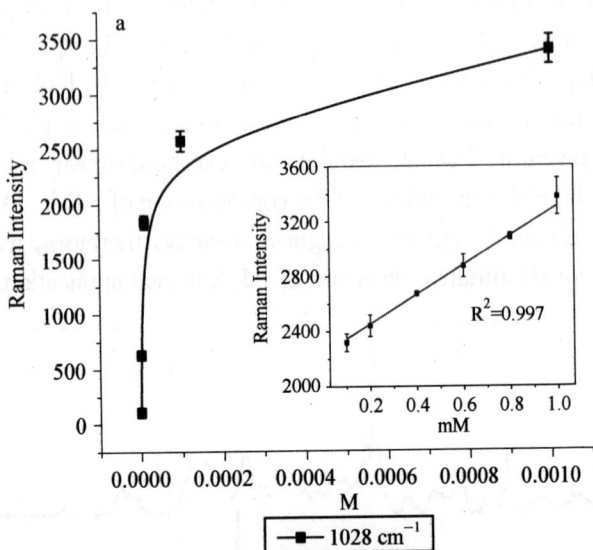

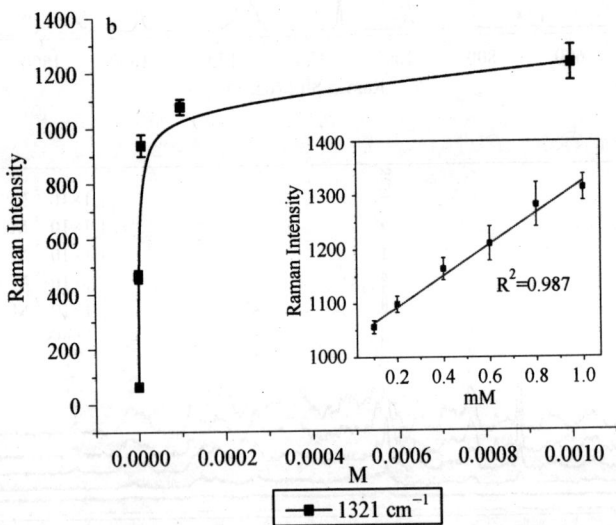

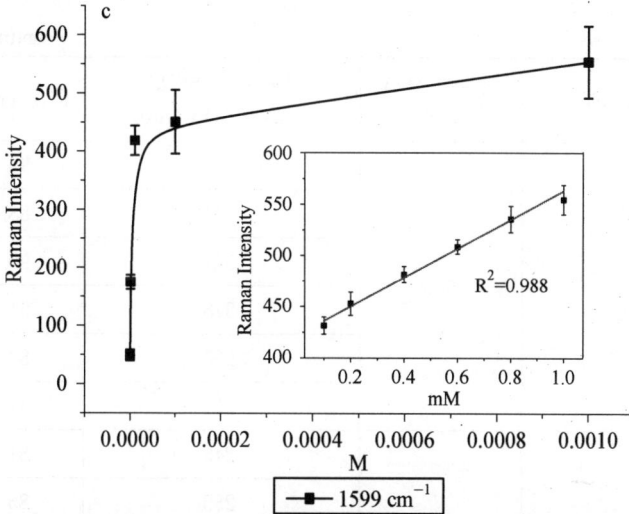

Fig. 2 (A) (a) SERS spectrum of ADA at the 1×10^{-4} M concentration in Au@Ag NPs; (b) Normal Raman spectrum of ADA solid powder. (B) Concentration-dependent SERS detection of ADA from 1×10^{-7} to 1×10^{-3} M in aqueous solution measured with a Portable Stabilized R. Laser Analyzer with a narrow line width diode Laser at 785 nm with a power of 300 mW. (C) (a), (b) and (c) are SERS intensities at 1028 cm^{-1}, 1321 cm^{-1} and 1599 cm^{-1} versus the concentrations of ADA in aqueous solution, respectively. (Inset: the linear correlations of Raman intensity at 1028 cm^{-1}, 1321 cm^{-1} and 1599 cm^{-1} with the concentration changing from 1×10^{-4} M to 1×10^{-3} M in aqueous solution).

Table 1 Recovery values for the analysis of steamed bread spiked with ADA ($n = 5$).

Sample	Spiked ADA (μM)	Proposed SERS method ADA (μM)	Recovery (%)
Flour	300	255	85.00
		269	89.67
		280	93.33
		276	92.00
		265	88.33
		556	92.67

continued

Sample	Spiked ADA (μM)	Proposed SERS method ADA (μM)	Recovery (%)
	600	572	95. 33
		533	88. 83
		541	90. 17
		548	91. 33
		250	83. 33
		261	87. 00
Steamed bread	300	245	81. 67
		255	85. 00
		247	82. 33
	600	504	84. 00
		520	86. 67
		500	83. 33
		512	85. 33
		517	86. 17

The main bands and assignments based on the B3LYP/6-311G level calculation are listed in Table S1. A Raman peak at 836 cm^{-1} is assigned to $\delta(N—H)$ and a band around 957 cm^{-1} could be due to $\delta(C—N = N) + \upsilon(C—N)$. $\delta(H—N—H) + \upsilon(C = O) + \upsilon(C—N)$ contributes to a peak at 1028 cm^{-1}, and a band centered at 1321 cm^{-1} is from $\delta(H—N—H) + \upsilon(C—N) + \delta(N—C = O)$. Raman bands at 1599 and 1727 cm^{-1} belong to $\upsilon(N = N)$ and $\upsilon(C = O) + \upsilon(C—N)$, respectively.

Fig. S4 exhibits the results for the detection of the reproducibility and stability of Au @ Ag-based SERS method. The SERS spectra recorded nine different samples are given in Fig. S4A and the statistical results using Raman intensity at 1028 cm^{-1} in Fig. S4B show a good reproducibility.

3. 4   Detection of ADA in real sample

As a kind of complex matrices, SERS-based protocol of determining ADA will suffer from serious interferences from the compositions in steamed bread including milk, AA, yeast, NaCl, flour and sugar. For the robustness of the proposed SERS assay, SERS spectra of milk, AA, yeast, NaCl, flour and sugar were acquired and shown in Figure S5. After examining those spectra carefully, we found that the characteristic peaks of ADA had no contaminant by the Raman bands from the observed interferences.

With regard to the real samples, the treatment approach may have a great influence on the detection of ADA existed in flour and flour product. As shown in Scheme S1, semicarbazide (SEM) will be formed during moisture environment and high temperature heating process [4]. In addition, starch, the main ingredient of flour, is insoluble in room temperature. When heating it to 53℃ above, the physical properties of the starch turn to change obviously. Therefore, pasting of starch makes the flour denature. Based on those reasons, detection of the real samples was conducted under room temperature to avoid the side effect due to temperature. Considering the possible byproducts shown in scheme S1, such as semicarbazide, Wang et al. found little influence of semicarbazide on their detection of ADA using LC-MS/MS [4]. Regarding biurea, we recorded the normal Raman spectra of powder ADA and 10^{-1} M aqueous ADA given in Fig. S6. It is clearly seen in Fig. S6, that there is no difference between both normal Raman spectra. In consequence, the possible byproducts do not impact on the detection of ADA.

The concentration-dependent SERS signals of ADA spiked into the flour and steamed bread is illustrated in Fig. 3. The characteristic vibrating bands of the analytes appeared and became stronger and stronger with the increase of ADA amount. The limits of detection (LOD) of ADA in flour and steamed bread are 10 μM (1. 16 ppm) and 20μM (2. 32 ppm), which are much lower than the maximum permitted level of flour (45 mg/kg according to FDA and National standard of China (GB2760 - 2011). It can be easily found that the proposed SERS assay with the sufficient LOD could be used to conduct analysis in real samples.

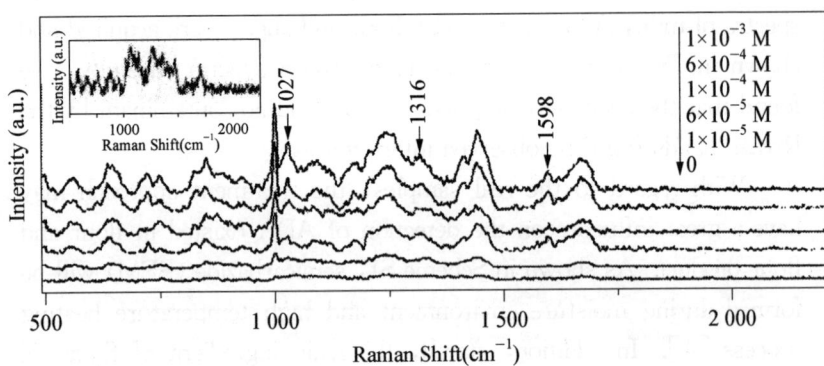

A

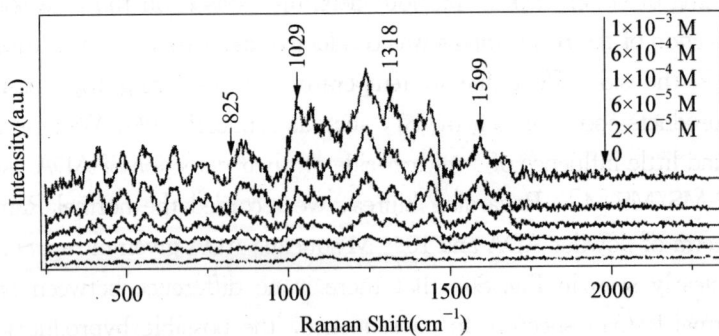

B

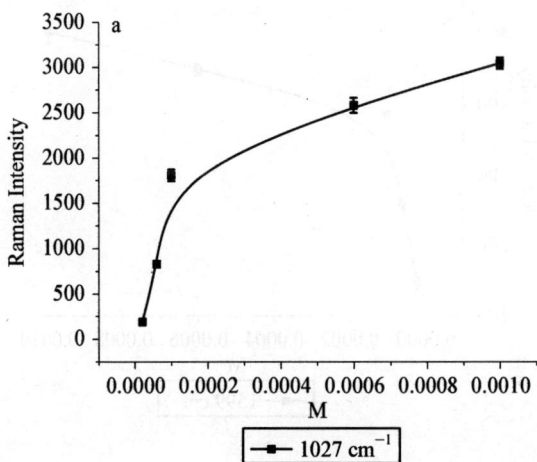

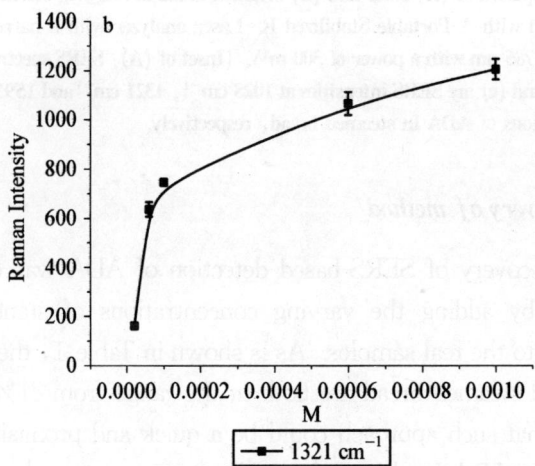

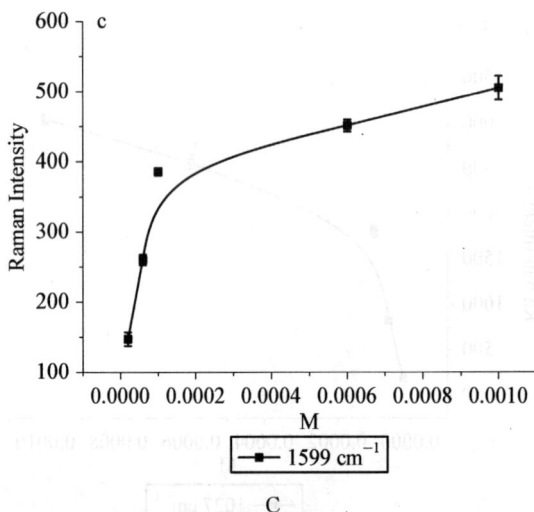

Fig. 3 SERS spectra of (A) flour and (B) steamed bread at Au@Ag colloids spiked with ADA, recorded with A Portable Stabilized R. Laser analyzer with a narrow line width diode Laser at 785 nm with a power of 300 mW. (Inset of (A): SERS spectrum of flour). (C) (a), (b) and (c) are SERS intensities at 1028 cm^{-1}, 1321 cm^{-1} and 1599 cm^{-1} versus the concentrations of ADA in steamed bread, respectively.

3.5 Recovery of method

The recovery of SERS-based detection of ADA was carried out five times by adding the varying concentrations of standard ADA solutions into the real samples. As is shown in Table 1, the recoveries of flour and steamed bread are both in the range from 81% to 95%, justifying that such approach could be a quick and promising method to screen the ADA level in real samples.

4. Conclusion

With the aim of rapid and label-free detection of azodicarbonamide in flour and flour product by SERS method, we made the core-shell

Au@Ag nanoparticles, which have a strong plasmon resonance. The strong surface absorption of NH_2-containing ADA brought it to bind the SERS substrate and a novel SERS protocol with the high sensitivity and spectral selectivity of azodicarbonamide was successfully developed. This approach turns out to be reproducibility and reliability. A linearity range of SERS detection of ADA was from 1×10^{-4} M to 1×10^{-3} M as well as a LOD was 0. 1 μM. The facile assay can be performed in a short time less than 20 min and without a complex sample pretreatment process. As a consequence, this SERS-based method may be suggested as an alternative method to realize rapid, sensitive and online detection of ADA in product by a portable Raman spectrometer for food safety.

Acknowledgements

This work is supported by the National Natural Science Foundation of China (No. 21475088), PCSIRT (IRT1269) and International Joint Laboratory on Resource Chemistry (IJLRC).

Appendix A. Supplementary data

Supplementary data associated with this article can be found, in the online version, at http://dx. doi. org/10. 1016/j. snb. 2015. 04. 103

References

[1] J. S. Lauren. Chemical food safety issues in the United States: Past, present, and future. J. Agric. Food Chem. 57 (2009) 8161 – 8170.

[2] N. O. Gregory, B. H. Timothy, D. W. Gregory. Semicarbazide formation in flour and bread. J. Agric. Food Chem. 56 (2008) 2064 – 2067.

[3] R. Ginn, L. Wilson, S. V. C. De Souza, M. B. Dela Calle, E. M. B. Berendsen; Determination of semicarbazide in baby food by liquid chromatography/tandem mass spectrometry: interlaboratory validation study. J. AOAC Int. 89 (2006) 728 – 734.

[4] J. Ye, X. H. Wang, Y. X. Sang, Q. Liu. Assessment of the determination of azodicarbonamide and its decomposition product semicarbazide: investigation of

variation in flour and flour products, J. Agric. Food Chem. 59 (2011) 9313 - 9318.

[5] A. Becalski, B. P.-Y. Lau, D. Lewis, S. W. Seaman, Semicarbazide formation in azodicarbonamide-treated flour: a model study, J. Agric. Food Chem. 52 (2004) 5730 - 5734.

[6] M. B. De La Calle, E. Anklam. Semicarbazide: occurrence in food products and state-of-the-art in analytical methods used for its determination, Anal. Bioanal. Chem. 382 (2005) 968 - 977.

[7] S. M. Nie, S. R. Emory, Probing single molecules and single nanoparticles by surface-enhanced Raman scattering. Science 275(1997) 1102 - 1106.

[8] E. C. Le Ru, M. Meyer, P. G. Etchegoin, Proof of single-molecule sensitivity in surface enhanced raman scattering (SERS) by means of a two-analyte technique. J. Phys. Chem. B 110 (2006) 1944 - 1948.

[9] K. Faulds, W. E. Smith, D. Graham. Evaluation of surface-enhanced resonance Raman scattering for quantitative DNA analysis. Anal. Chem. 76 (2004) 412 - 417.

[10] M. Fleischm, P. J. Hendra. A. McQuilla, Raman spectra of pyridzne adsorbed at a silver electrode. J. Chem. Phys. Lett. 26 (1974) 163 - 166.

[11] Y. Y. Zhu, C. L. Qu, H. Kuang, L. G. Xu, L. Q. Liu, Y. F. Hua, L. B. Wang, C. L. Xu, Simple, rapid and sensitive detection of antibiotics based on the side-by-side assembly of gold nanorod probes, Biosens. Bioelectron. 26 (2011) 4387 - 4392.

[12] M. D. Hodges, J. G. Kelly, A. J. Bentley, S. Fogarty, I. I. Patel, F. L. Martin, N. J. Fullwood. Combining immunolabeling and surface-enhanced Raman spectroscopy on cell membranes, ACS Nano 5 (2011) 9535 - 9541.

[13] Y. Zeng, J. J. Pei, L. H. Wang, A. G. Shen, J. M. Hu, A sensitive sequential 'on/off' SERS assay for heparin with wider detection window and higher reliability based on the reversed surface charge changes of functionalized Au@Ag nanoparticles, Biosens. Bioelectron. 66 (2015) 55 - 61.

[14] T. Y. Liu, K. T. Tsai, H. H. Wang, Y. Chen, Y. H. Chen, Y. C. Chao, H. H. Chang, C. H. Lin, J. K. Wang, Y. L. Wang, Functionalized arrays of Raman-enhancing nanoparticles for capture and culture-free analysis of bacteria in human blood, Nat. Commun. 2 (2011) 538 - 545.

[15] Y. T. Li, D. W. Li, Y. Cao, Y. T. Long, Label-free in-situ monitoring of protein tyrosine nitration in blood by surface-enhanced Raman spectroscopy, Biosens. Bioelectron. 69 (2015) 1 - 7.

[16] M. Moskovits, Surface-enhanced Raman spectroscopy: a brief retrospective, J. Raman Spectrosc. 36 (2005) 485 – 496.

[17] M. Quinten, Local fields close to the surface of nanoparticles and aggregates of nanoparticles, Appl. Phys. B 73 (2001) 245 – 255.

[18] J. M. McMahon, S. Li, L. K. Ausman, G. C. Schatz, Modeling the effect of small gaps in surface-enhanced Raman spectroscopy, J. Phys. Chem. C 116 (2012) 1627 – 1637.

[19] N. P. W. Pieczonka, R. F. Aroca, Single molecule analysis by surfaced-enhanced Raman scattering, Chem. Soc. Rev. 37 (2008) 946 – 954.

[20] K. Kneipp, H. Kneipp, J. Kneipp, Surface-enhanced Raman scattering in local optical fields of silver and gold nanoaggregates from single-molecule Raman spectroscopy to ultrasensitive probing in live cells. Acc. Chem. Res. 39(2006) 443 – 450.

[21] M. Moskovits. Surface-enhanced spectroscopy. Rev. Mod. Phys. 57 (1985) 783 – 826.

[22] J. P. Camden, J. A. Dieringer, J. Zhao, R. P. Van Duyne, Controlled plasmonic nanostructures for surface-enhanced spectroscopy and sensing, Acc. Chem. Res. 41(2008)1653 – 1661.

[23] W. N. Leng, A. M. Kelley. Surface-enhanced hyper-Raman spectra and enhancement factors for three SERS chromophores. SEHRS spectra on Ag films at pulse energies below 2 pJ, J. Am. Chem. Soc. 128 (2006) 3492 – 3493.

[24] S. J. Lee, A. R. Morrill, M. Moskovits. Hot spots in silver nanowire bundles for surface-enhanced Raman spectroscopy, J. Am. Chem. Soc. 128 (2006) 2200 – 2201.

[25] D. K. Lim, K. S. Jeon, J. M. Nam, Y. D. Suh, Nanogap-engineerable Raman-active nanodumbbells for single-molecule detection, Nat. Mater. 9(2010) 60 – 67.

[26] T. T. Lou, Y. Q. Wang, J. H. Li, H. L. Peng. H. Xiong, L. X. Chen, Rapid detection of melamine with 4-mercaptopyridine-modified gold nanoparticles by surface-enhanced Raman scattering. Anal. Bioanal. Chem. 401 (2011)333 – 338.

[27] R. A. Halvorson. P. J. Vikesland, Surface-enhanced Raman spectroscopy (SERS) for environmental analyses, Environ. Sci. Technol. 44(2010)7749 – 7755.

[28] L. H. Oakley, D. M. Fabian, H. E. Mayhew, S. A. Svoboda, K. L.

Wustholz. Pretreatment strategies for SERS analysis of indigo and Prussian blue in aged painted surfaces, Anal. Chem. 84 (2012) 8006 – 8012.

[29] Y. Q. Wang, B. Yan, L. X. Chen, SERS tags: novel optical nanoprobes for bioanalysis, Chem. Rev. 113 (2013) 1391 – 1428.

[30] N. L. Rosi, C. A. Mirkin. Nanostructures in biodiagnostics, Chem. Rev. 105 (2005)1547 – 1562.

[31] R. A. Álvarez-Puebla, L. M. Liz-Marzán, SERS-based diagnosis and biodetection, Small 6 (2010) 604 – 610.

[32] M. J. Banholzer, J. E. Millstone, L. D. Qin, C. A. Mirkin. Rationally designed nanostructures for surface-enhanced Raman spectroscopy. Chem. Soc. Rev. 37 (2008)885 – 897.

[33] M. Fan, G. F. Andrade, A. G. Brolo. A review on the fabrication of substrates for surface enhanced Raman spectroscopy and their applications in analytical chemistry, Anal. Chim. Acta 693 (2011) 7 – 25.

[34] B. H. Liu, G. M. Han, Z. P. Zhang, R. Y. Liu, C. L. Jiang, S. H. Wang, M. Y. Han. Shell thickness-dependent Raman enhancement for rapid identification and detection of pesticide residues at fruit peels, Anal. Chem. 84 (2011) 255 – 261.

[35] X. X. Han, B. Zhao, Y. Ozaki. Label-free detection in biological applications of surface-enhanced Raman scattering. Trends Anal. Chem. 38 (2012) 67 – 78.

[36] G. Frens, Controlled nucleation for the regulation of the particle size in monodisperse gold suspensions, Nat. Phys. Sci. 241 (1973) 20 – 22.

[37] P. C. Lee, D. Meisel, Adsorption and surface-enhanced raman of dyes on silver and gold sols, J. Phys. Chem. 86 (1982) 3391 – 3395.

[38] R. D. Deegan, O. Bakajin, T. F. Dupont, G. Huber, S. R. Nagel, T. A. Witten. Capillary flowasthe cause of ring stains fromdried liquid drops, Nature 389(1997) 827 – 829.

[39] S. K. Islam, M. Tamargo, R. Moug, J. R. Lombardi, Surface-enhanced Raman scattering on a chemically etched ZnSe surface, J. Phys. Chem. C 117 (2013)23372 – 23377.

[40] M. T. Sun, Y. R. Fang, Z. Y. Zhang, H. X. Xu. Activated vibrational modes and Fermi resonance in tip-enhanced Raman spectroscopy. Phys. Rev. E 87 (2013)020401 – 020405.

[41] D. D. Whitmore, P. Z. El-Khoury, L. Fabris, P. Chu, G. C. Bazan, E. O. Potma, V. A. Apkarian. High sensitivity surface-enhanced Raman scattering in solution using engineered silver nanosphere dimers, J. Phys. Chem. C 115

(2011)15900 – 15907.

[42] M. Moskovits, Surface selection rules, J. Chem. Phys. 77 (1982) 4408 – 4416.

[43] M. Moskovits, J. S. Suh. Surface selection rules for surface-enhanced Raman spectroscopy: Calculations and application to the surface-enhanced Raman spectrum of phthalazine on silver, J. Phys, Chem. 88(1984)5525 – 5530.

（原载于 Sensors & Actuators B Chemical 2015 年第 216 期）

Gd(III) complex conjugated ultra-small iron oxide as an enhanced T_1-weighted MR imaging contrast agent

Li Wang[,a] Hongwei Zhang[,a] Zhiguo Zhou[,a]
Bin Kong[,a] Lu An[,a] Jie Wei[,a] Hong Yang[,a]
Jiangmin Zhao[b] and Shiping Yang[a, b]

[a] The Key Laboratory of Resource Chemistry of Ministry of Education, Shanghai Key Laboratory of Rare Earth Functional Materials, Shanghai Municipal Education Committee Key Laboratory of Molecular Imaging Probes and Sensors, Shanghai Normal University
[b] No. 3 People Hospital Affiliated to Shanghai Jiao Tong University School of Medicine

Introduction

In the past decades, various diagnosis of molecular imaging techniques have been applied including X-ray computed tomography (CT),[1-4] magnetic resonance (MR) imaging,[5-9] optical imaging,[10-14] ultrasound (US),[15-18] positron emission tomography (PET),[19-21] and single-photon-emission computed tomography (SPECT).[22-24] Among them, MR imaging has attracted increasing attention in medical diagnosis because of itsnon-invasive property, high spatial resolution, and minimal damage to humans[25] In order to improve the spatial resolution and definition, an MR imaging contrast agent should be applied. lonven tionally, MR imaging contrast agents can be classified into T_1 and T_2 contrast agents,[26] which lead to brighter and darker images, respectively.

To date, many MR imaging contrast agents have been reported, and have their merits and drawbacks. For example, T_2-weighted contrast agents possess a high feasibility for the detection of a lesion, but they have poor resolution and magnetic susceptibility artifacts.[8] T_1-weighted contrast agents with a brighter MR imaging give an advantage in spatial resolution.[27, 28] However, the conventional ionic complexes used as T_1-weighted contrast agents have a low transverse relaxation rate and short retention time.[29] In order to address these problems, nanoparticulated T_1-weighted contrast agents have been developed to achieve the large longitudinal relaxation rate (r_1) and long retention time, such as MnO,[30] Mn_3O_4,[31, 32] Gd_2O_3,[33] and ultra-small Fe_3O_4 nanoparticles.[34] Even so, the great demand for excellent longitudinal relaxivity (r_1) means improvements are still necessary.

Herein, we synthesizeda Gd(III) complex conjugated ultra-small Fe_3O_4 NPs (Fe_3O_4 @ DOPA (Gd-DTPA) NPs) to combine the advantage of a Gd(III) complex and ultra-small Fe_3O_4 NPs to obtain a nanoparticulated T_1-weighted contrast agent with an enhancement of the longitudinal relaxivity (r_1). We dynamically integrated a Gd(III) complex with ultra-small Fe_3O_4 NPs by ligand exchange with dopamine and a condensation reaction of dopamine (DOPA) and diethylenetriaminepentaacetic acid dianhydride (DTPAda), then coordinated with Gd(III) ions (Scheme 1), in which the Gd complex and ultra-small Fe_3O_4 NPs[35, 36] have a good T_1-weighted contrast. The brighter T_1-weighted contrast effect was observed both in aqueous solution and *in vitro* owing to the strong interaction between them. Importantly, blood vessels in mice were obviously brightened on the T_1-weighted MR images after the injection of Fe_3O_4 @DOPA (Gd-DTPA)NPs.

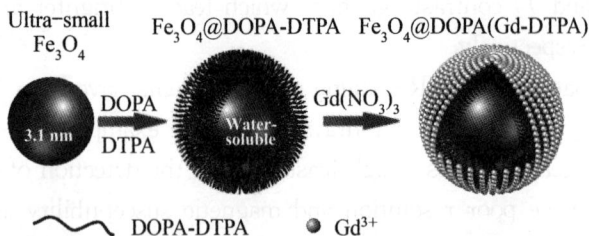

Scheme 1   The schematic illustration of Fe₃O₄ @ DOPA (Gd-DTPA) NPs.

Experimental

Materials

Sodium oleate, $FeCl_3 \cdot 6H_2O$, oleic acid, and tris (hydroxymethyl)-aminomethane-HCl (Tris-HCl) were purchased from Shanghai Sinopharm Chemical reagent Co. , Ltd. Oil alcohol was purchased from TCI Chemical Industry Co. , Ltd. Dopamine hydrochloride (DOPA • HCl) was purchased from Alfa Aesar Chemical Co. , Ltd. Diethylenetriaminepentaacetic acid dianhydride (DTPAda) was purchased from Sigma-Aldrich company. Water used in all the experiments was purified using a Milli-Q Plus 185 water purification system (Millipore, Bedford, MA) with a resistivity greater than 18 $M\Omega cm^{-1}$.

Synthesis of dopamine-modified ultra-small Fe₃O₄ nanoparticles (Fe₃O₄ @DOPA NPs)

Ultra-small Fe_3O_4 NPs were synthesized according to the literature. [34] The obtained Fe_3O_4 NPs (5 mL, 4 mgmL^{-1}) was mixed with DOPA • HCl (100 mg) in 10 mL THF. Then 20 mL ethanol was added and the mixture was stirred under a nitrogen atmosphere at room temperature for 12 h. After centrifugation, the product was washed with ethanol three times. The obtained Fe_3O_4 NPs (denoted as Fe_3O_4 @ DOPA NPs) were dispersed in 20 mL DMF for further use.

Synthesis of Gd (III) complex conjugated ultra-small Fe_3O_4 nanoparticles [Fe_3O_4@DOPA(Gd-DTPA) NPs]

Diethylenetriaminepentaacetic acid dianhydride (DTPAda) (46 mg) and triethylamine (5 mL) were added to the DMF solution of Fe_3O_4@ DOPA NPs (5 mgmL^{-1}, 10 mL), and then stirred at room temperature under a nitrogen atmosphere for 12 h. After the product was centrifuged and washed with 1% triethylamine DMF solution twice, ethanol twice and water once, respectively. The DOPA- and DTPA-modified Fe_3O_4 nanoparticles [denoted as Fe_3O_4@DOPA(DTPA) NPs] were stored in 10 mL 0.05 M Tris-HCl solution. $Gd(NO_3)_3$ · $6H_2O$ (30 mg) and the prepared Fe_3O_4@DOPA(DTPA) NPs were placed in a 25 mL flask, and stirred under a nitrogen atmosphere for 12 h. Afterwards the solution was centrifuged and washed with deionized water three times. The obtained Gd(III) complex conjugated ultra-small Fe_3O_4 nanoparticles [denoted as Fe_3O_4@DOPA(Gd-DTPA) NPs] were dispersed in deionized water.

MR imaging in aqueous solution

Various concentrations of Fe_3O_4@DOPA(DTPA) NPs, Gd-DTPA, Fe_3O_4@DOPA(DTPA) NPs with the Gd-DTPA complex, and Fe_3O_4@DOPA(Gd-DTPA) NPs were prepared for MR imaging study, respectively. The longitudinal relaxation time (T_1) and transverse relaxation time (T_2) were measured (at 298 K) and T_1, T_2-weighted MR images were performed with a 3.0 T system (3T Siemens Magnetom Trio). T_1-weighted MR images were acquired using a conventional spin-echo sequence under the following parameters: TE=12 ms, TR=100 ms, 150 ms, 200 ms, 300 ms, 500 ms, 700 ms, 1000 ms, 1500 ms, 2500 ms, 220 × 320 matrices, 82 × 120 mm field of view, 140 Hz per Px of bandwidth, a slice thickness of 3 mm. T_2-weighted MR images were acquired using a fast spinecho sequence to reduce acquisition time under the following parameters: TR=1000 ms, TE=13.8 ms, 27.6 ms, 41.4 ms, 55.2 ms, 69 ms,

82. 8 ms, 220×320 matrices, 82×120 mm field of view, 220 Hz per
Px of bandwidth, and a slice thickness of 3 mm. Longitudinal
relaxation rate (r_1) and transverse relaxation rate (r_2) were calculated
from the fitting of $1/T_1$, $1/T_2$ and metal ion concentration, respectively.

MR imaging *in vitro*

A human cervical carcinoma cell line (HeLa) was provided by the
Shanghai Institutes of Biological Sciences (SIBS), CAS, China. HeLa
cells were seeded into a 12-well plate with a density of $1×10^5$ cells per
well. The cells were incubated with Fe_3O_4@DOPA(DTPA) NPs,
Gd-DTPA, Fe_3O_4@DOPA(DTPA) NPs plus Gd-DTPA, and Fe_3O_4
@DOPA(Gd-DTPA) NPs with the same concentration of Fe ions (1.
08 mM) or Gd ions (0. 36 mM) for 12 h, respectively. After
incubation, the culture medium was removed and washed with PBS
three times. Then cells were trypsinized, centrifuged, and dispersed
in PBS. The relaxation time and MR imaging measurements of HeLa
cells were performed immediately. We calculated the T_1 relaxation
time decreased the rate by the following equation:

$$\frac{|T_1 - T_{1,0}|}{T_{1,0}} ×100\%$$

MR imaging *in vivo*

The MR imaging *in vivo* was performed on BALB/c mice.
150 μL of Fe_3O_4@DOPA(Gd-DTPA)NPs(Fe: 0. 21 mmol kg^{-1},
Gd: 0. 07 mmol kg^{-1})was injected through a tail vein injection. *In
vivo* MR imaging experiments were recorded using a 3. 0 T system
before and after the injection for 0. 5 h and 1. 5 h, respectively. T_1-
weighted MR images were acquired using a conventional spin-echo
sequence with the following parameters: TR/TE=16/6. 7 ms, 320×
150 matrices, 60×60 mm field of view, 140 Hz per Px of bandwidth,
a slice thickness of 0. 5 mm. The healthy male Kunming (KM) mice
were provided by the Shanghai Laboratory Animal Center, Chinese

Academy of Science, Shanghai, China (Warrant no. SCXK [Shanghai] 2012 – 0002). All animal operations were conducted in accordance with the guidelines of the Institutional Animal Care and Use Committee.

Characterization

TEM was collected on a JEOL JEM-2010 transmission electron microscope operating at an accelerating voltage of 200 kV. X-ray diffraction (XRD) was carried out using a Rigaku DMAX 2000 diffractometer equipped with $Cu/K\alpha$ radiation. FT-IR spectra were recorded on a Nicolet Avatar 370. UV-Vis-NIR absorption spectra were collected on a DU 730 UV-visible spectrophotometer (Nucleic acid, protein analyzer). The hysteresis loop (300 K) was measured using a superconducting quantum interference magnetometer (SQUID, MPMSXL). The concentration of metal ions was determined by induct-ively coupled plasma mass spectrometry (ICP-MS, VISTAMPXICP VARIAN). The MR imaging and relaxation time *in vitro* were performed in a 0. 5 T NMR120-Analyst system (Niumag Corporation, Shanghai, China). The zeta potential and hydration radius were tested by a Malvern Zetasizer Nano ZS model EN3690 (Worcestershire, U. K.) equipped with a standard 633 nm laser.

Results and discussion

Synthesis and characterization

Generally, Fe_3O_4 NPs have been synthesized by the co-precipitation method, hydrolysis, hydrothermal method, micro-emulsion method, sol-gel method, high temperature pyrolysis, and *etc*. Recently, the use of ultra-small Fe_3O_4 NPs as T_1-weighted MR contrast agents has been reported.[34] Based on these reports, we synthesized ultra-small Fe_3O_4 NPs by high temperature pyrolysis according to the literature.[34] As shown in Fig. 1A, the synthesized ultra-small Fe_3O_4 NPs were spherical with an average diameter of

3. 1±0. 7 nm and were well dispersed in hexane. The high resolution TEM images (Fig. 1B) showed that the as-synthesized Fe_3O_4 NPs were highly crystalline with a lattice spacing of 0. 17 and 0. 21 nm, matching the d spacing for the (422) and (400) crystal planes of Fe_3O_4, respectively, which can also be found in the XRD pattern (Fig. 1C). For the Gd complex conjugated on the surface of Fe_3O_4 NPs, DOPA was used to coat the Fe_3O_4 NPs surface by a ligand

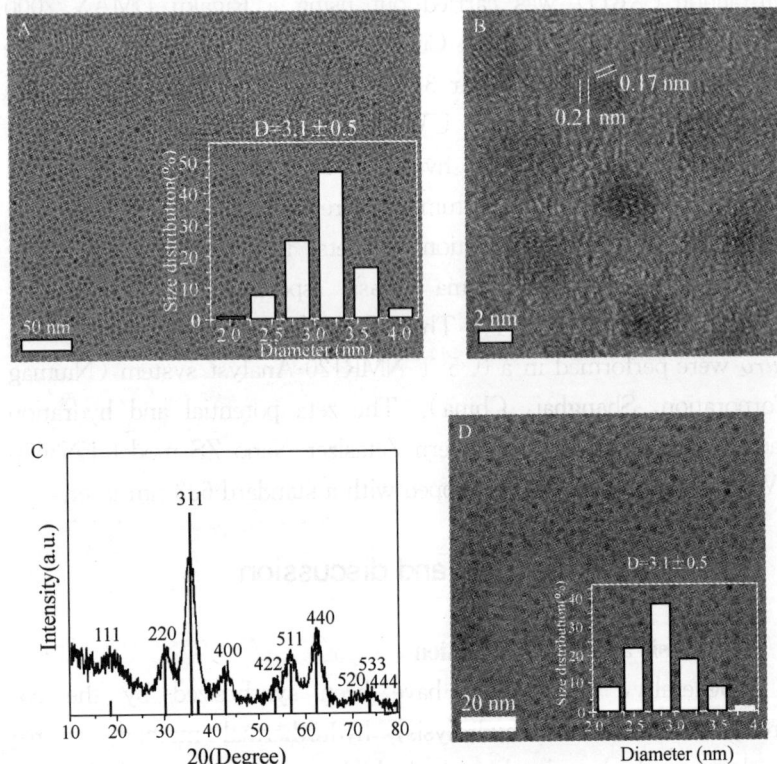

Fig. 1 TEM (A) and HRTEM (B) images of ultra-small Fe_3O_4 NPs. The inset in A is the size distribution of ultra-small Fe_3O_4 NPs. (C) The XRD pattern of ultra-small Fe_3O_4 NPs (the powder diffraction standard card is JCPDS no. 65－3107. (D) TEM image of Fe_3O_4@DOPA(Gd-DTPA) NPs. The inset is the size distribution of Fe_3O_4@DOPA(Gd-DTPA) NPs.

exchange method. In the next step, DTPAda was reacted with the amine group of Fe_3O_4 @ DOPA NPs *via* the construction of amide bonds. Finally, with the strong chelation interaction between Gd(III) ions and the carboxyl group of DTPA, Fe_3O_4 @DOPA(Gd-DTPA) NPs was obtained. As shown in Fig. 1D, the formed Fe_3O_4@DOPA (Gd-DTPA) NPs are stable in water with an average diameter of 3. 4±0. 7 nm, indicating no obvious change of Fe_3O_4 NPs after the multistep modifications.

In order to confirm the successful construction of Fe_3O_4@DOPA (Gd-DTPA) NPs, the FT-IR spectra, hydrodynamic radius, and zeta potential were measured (Fig. 2). As illustrated in Fig. 2A, the distinct absorption peaks at 2915 and 2851 cm^{-1} were attributed to the C—H stretching vibration of the methyl and methylene groups of oleic chains, respectively. After the ligand exchange, the obvious reduction of the absorption peak at 2915 and 2851 cm^{-1} indicated that dopamine was successfully modified on the surface of Fe_3O_4 NPs. After the attachment of DTPA ligands, a strong characteristic peak located at 1682 cm^{-1} that resulted from the C = O stretching vibration was observed in Fe_3O_4 @ DOPA (DTPA) NPs. The blue shift of the carboxyl peak suggested a surface of Fe_3O_4@DOPA(DTPA) NPs. The surface potential of Fe_3O_4@DOPA NPs varied from 23. 5±0. 6 mV to−11. 1±0. 5 mV of Fe_3O_4 @ DOPA(DTPA) NPs, which further indicated that DTPA with a negative charge had been successfully conjugated to the surface of the NPs. Further coordination between Fe_3O_4@DOPA(DTPA) NPs and Gd(III) ions resulted in a decrease of the surface charge to−3. 22±0. 40 mV due to the coordination of Gd(III) ions with the carboxylate group of the DTPA ligand. The formed Fe_3O_4 @ DOPA(Gd-DTPA) NPs were water dispersible and stable with a hydrodynamic radius of about 70 nm with little change after the surface modifications.

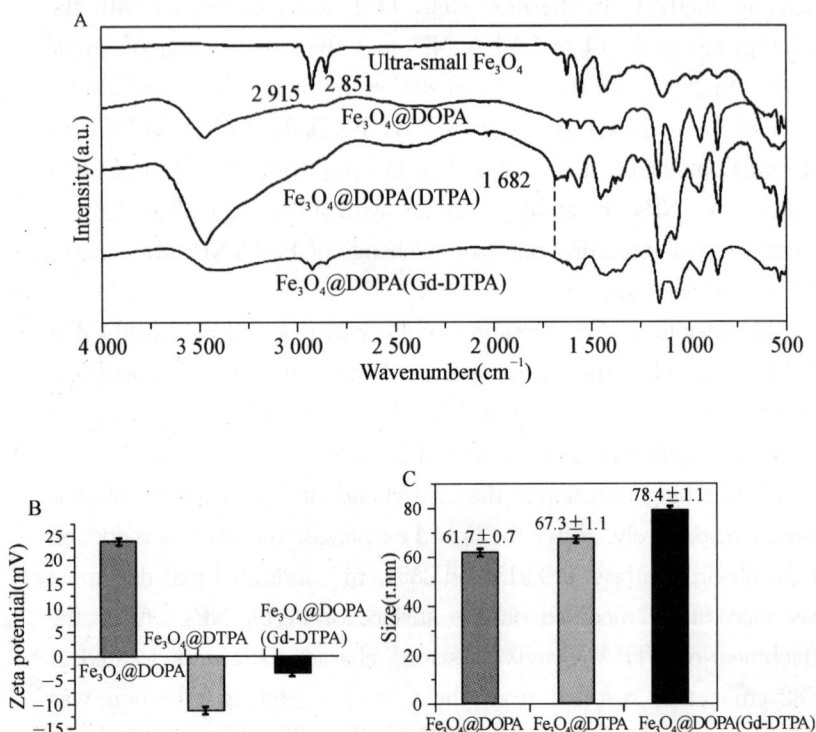

Fig. 2 (A) FT-IR spectra of Fe_3O_4, $Fe_3O_4@DOPA$, $Fe_3O_4@DOPA(DTPA)$, and $Fe_3O_4@DOPA(Gd-DTPA)$ NPs, respectively. Zeta-potential (B) and hydrodynamic radius (C) of $Fe_3O_4@DOPA$, $Fe_3O_4@DOPA(DTPA)$ and $Fe_3O_4@DOPA(Gd-DTPA)$ NPs, respectively.

Magnetic and relativity properties

In order to investigate the magnetic properties, the hysteresis loop of $Fe_3O_4@DOPA(Gd-DTPA)$ NPs was recorde (Fig. S1 †). Their magnetization at room temperature decrease to 30 emu g^{-1}, which was the reason that they could be used as a T_1 MR imaging agent.[34] To validate the contrast ability, the longitudinal relaxation time (T_1) and transverse relaxation time (T_2) of $Fe_3O_4@DOPA$ (DTPA) NPs, Gd-DTPA, the mixture solution of $Fe_3O_4@DOPA$ (DTPA) and Gd-DTPA [$n(Fe) : n(Gd) = 3 : 1$], and $Fe_3O_4@$

DOPA(Gd-DTPA) NPs $[n(Fe) : n(Gd)=3 : 1]$ were examined in a
3.0 T MR system. The r_1 and r_2 are presented in Fig. 3A and B.
Compared to the commercially available MR contrast of Gd-DTPA
($r_1=3.65$ mM^{-1}S^{-1}, $r_2=6.17$ mM^{-1}S^{-1}, $r_2/r_1=1.69$), Fe_3O_4@
DOPA(DTPA)NPs ($r_1=1.89$ mM^{-1}S^{-1}, $r_2=16.62$ mM^{-1}S^{-1}, $r_2/$
$r_1=8.79$) have a smaller value of r_1 and larger r_2 and r_2/r_1, which
indicated its weaker effect as a T_1 contrast agent. The mixed solution
of Fe_3O_4@DOPA(DTPA) and Gd-DTPA $[n(Fe) : n(Gd)=3 : 1]$
showed a similar r_1 value ($r_1=3.53$ mM^{-1}S^{-1}, $r_2=48.04$ mM^{-1}
S^{-1}, $r_2/r_1=13.61$) to that of Gd-DTPA, but r_2 and r_2/r_1 was much
higher than that of Gd-DTPA. Therefore, the T_1-weighted MR
imaging effect of the above mixed solution was inferior to that of Gd-
DTPA. Fe_3O_4@DOPA(Gd-DTPA) NPs possessed the larger r_1 value
($r_1=9.97$ mM^{-1}S^{-1}, $r_2=57.3$ mM^{-1}S^{-1}, $r_2/r_1=5.73$) than those
of Gd-DTPA, Fe_3O_4@DOPA(DTPA), and Fe_3O_4@DOPA(DTPA)
plus Gd-DTPA $[n(Fe) : n(Gd)=3 : 1]$, while the ratio of r_2/r_1 was
smaller. Therefore, we can draw the conclusion that the Fe_3O_4@DOPA
(Gd-DTPA) NPs are an excellent candidate as a T_1– weighted MR
contrast agent. As shown in Fig. 3C, compared to other groups, Fe_3O_4
@DOPA(Gd-DTPA) NPs have the better T_1-weighted imaging effect.

The r_1 of Fe_3O_4@DOPA(Gd-DTPA) NPs is 3 times higher than
that of Gd-DTPA, and 5 times higher than that of Fe_3O_4@DOPA
(DTPA) NPs. To explain the significantly increased value of r_1 after

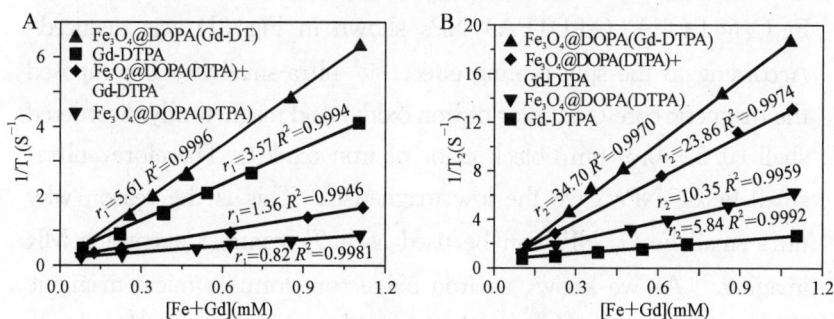

C

Fe₃O₄@DOPA(GD-DTPA)							
[Fe+Gd(mM)]	0.8098	0.6302	0.3496	0.2614	0.2041	0.0852	0.0000
Gd-DTPA							
[Gd](mM)	1.1047	0.7068	0.5456	0.3788	0.2220	0.1024	
Fe₃O₄@DOPA(DTPA) +Gd-DTPA							
+Gd-DTPA(mM)	1.2411	1.0520	0.7874	0.4172	0.3189	0.2700	
Fe₃O₄@DOPA(DTPA)							
[Fe](mM)	0.6724	0.5561	0.4512	0.3896	0.2588	0.1901	

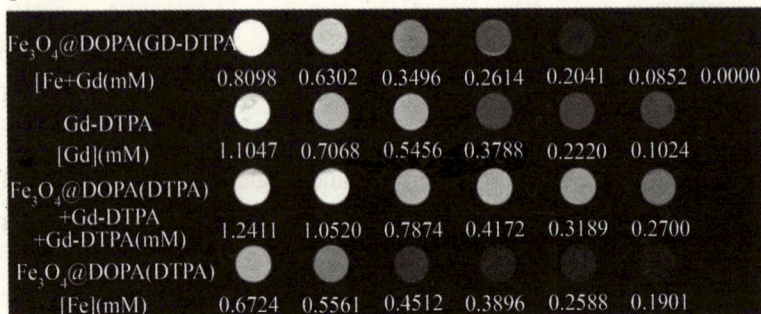

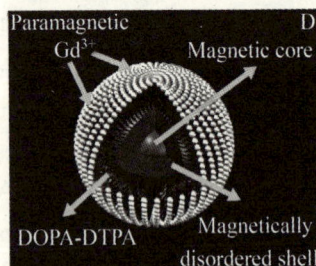

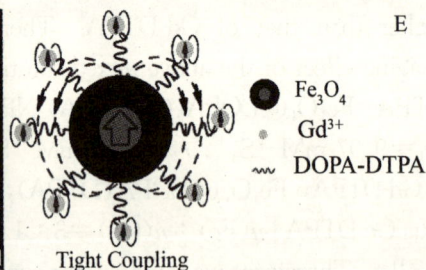

Fig. 3 Plots of (A) $1/T_1$ and $1/T_2$ (B) against concentrations of (Fe+Gd) ions. (C) T_1 MR imaging of Fe₃O₄@DOPA(DTPA) NPs, Gd-DTPA, Fe₃O₄@DOPA (DTPA) NPs plus Gd-DTPA [(n(Fe) : n(Gd)=3 : 1], and Fe₃O₄@DOPA(Gd-DTPA) NPs [(n(Fe) : n(Gd)=3 : 1], respectively. (D) The deduced construction of Fe₃O₄@DOPA(Gd-DTPA) NPs. (E) The interaction of ultra-small Fe₃O₄ and Gd-DTPA.

the Gd was complex conjugated to Fe₃O₄@DOPA NPs, the model of Fe₃O₄@DOPA(Gd-DTPA) NPs shown in Fig. 3D was deduced. According to the spin canting effect,[35-37] ultra-small Fe₃O₄ composed the magnetic core (red color of iron oxide) and magnetically disordered shell (0. 5 - 0. 9 nm, black color of iron oxide). Therefore, ultra-small Fe₃O₄ NPs gave the low magnetism. This is the reason why ultra-small Fe₃O₄ NPs can be used as a T_1 contrast agent for MR imaging.[34] As we know, an iron oxide core forms a micro-magnetic field under an external magnetic field. After Gd ions were abundantly coated to the Fe_3O_4 surface connected by DOPA-DTPA with a distance of ~ 1.88 nm, the micro-magnetic field strongly affected the magnetic field of Gd-DTPA, which resulted in the formation of a new and integral magnetic material. The internal interaction is illustrated in Fig. 3E. The tight coupling of Fe_3O_4 NPs and the Gd complex enabled them have a greater impact on the surrounding water, leading to the reduction of T_1 time.[9] On the contrary, the micro-magnetic field weakened quickly as the distance increased. In the mixed solution of the Gd(III) complex and Fe_3O_4 NPs, the micro-magnetic field of Fe_3O_4 NPs have no influence on Gd-DTPA.

In vitro MRI performance

To evaluate the effect of $Fe_3O_4@DOPA(Gd\text{-}DTPA)$ NPs as a T_1-weighted contrast agent *in vitro*, the cytotoxicity assay was performed used HeLa cells as a model cancer line. HeLa cells were incubated with different concentrations of $Fe_3O_4@DOPA(Gd\text{-}DTPA)$ NPs (0, 25, 50, 75, 100, 150, 200, 250, 500 μgmL^{-1}) for 12 h and 24 h at 37℃, respectively. As presented in Fig. 4A, even with concentrations of $Fe_3O_4@DOPA(Gd\text{-}DTPA)$ NPs up to 500 μgmL^{-1}, cell viability was still up to 83% after incubation for 24 h, indicating a low cytotoxicity of the nanoparticles in HeLa cells. To further investigate the biocompatibility of $Fe_3O_4@DOPA(Gd\text{-}DTPA)$ NPs, hemolysis experiments were also carried out. The hemolytic percentage of red blood cells with different concentrations of NPs are shown in Fig. 4C. With incubated concentrations up to 400 μgmL^{-1}, the hemolytic percentage was only $\sim 0.5\%$. The graph in Fig. 4D intuitively proves a very low hemolytic activity of $Fe_3O_4@DOPA(Gd\text{-}DTPA)$ NPs. Combined with the MTT assay and hemolysis experiments, $Fe_3O_4@DOPA(Gd\text{-}DTPA)$ NPs should be applied further *in vitro*.

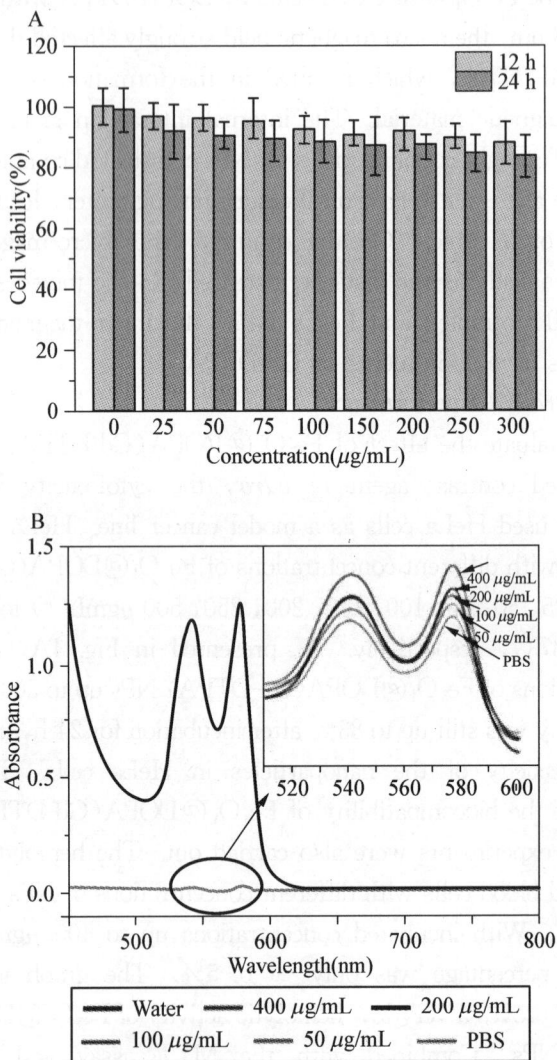

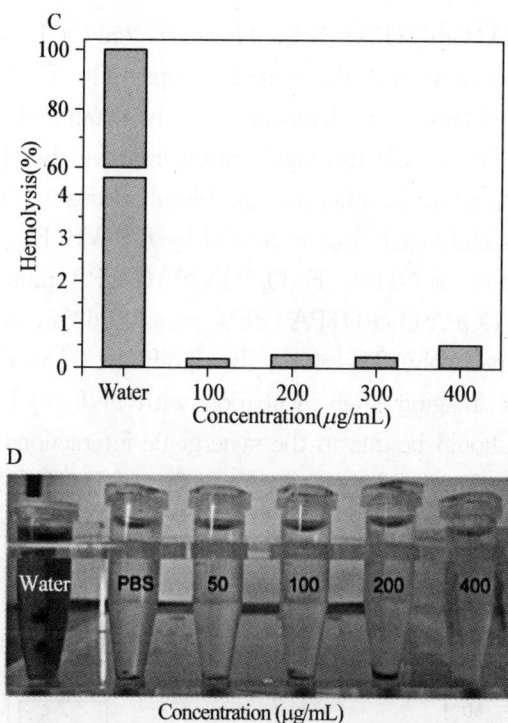

Fig. 4 (A) *In vitro* cell viability of HeLa cells incubated with Fe_3O_4 @DOPA(Gd-DTPA) NPs incubated with different concentrations for 12 and 24 h at 37℃, respectively. (B) The visible absorption of blood treated with water, PBS, Fe_3O_4 @DOPA(Gd-DTPA) NPs (0, 50, 100, 200, 400 μgmL^{-1}), respectively. (C) The hemolysis percentage of water and Fe_3O_4 @DOPA(Gd-DTPA) NPs (0, 50, 100, 200, 400 μgmL^{-1}, respectively). (D) A picture of the hemolysis experiments.

To discuss the effect of Fe_3O_4 @DOPA(Gd-DTPA) NPs for T_1-weighted MR imaging *in vitro*, the changes in the T_1 value in HeLa cells were measured after incubation with Fe_3O_4 @ DOPA(DTPA) NPs, Gd-DTPA, Fe_3O_4 @DOPA(DTPA) plus Gd-DTPA $[n(Fe) : n(Gd) = 3 : 1]$, and Fe_3O_4 @ DOPA (Gd-DTPA) NPs $[n(Fe) : n(Gd) = 3 : 1]$ ($n(Fe) = 1.08$ mM) for 12 h at 37℃, respectively (Fig. 5). The value of T_1 decreased $\sim 61.9\%$ after incubation with

Fe_3O_4@DOPA(Gd-DTPA) NPs. However, only a 1. 6%- 24. 0% reduction was observed in the control groups. The T_1-weighted MR images were obtained simultaneously. It is notable that Fe_3O_4 @ DOPA(Gd-DTPA) NPs can significantly improve the effect of MR imaging compared to the other groups. Simultaneously, the content of Gd uptake by HeLa cells was measured by ICP-MS(Fig. S2 †). The content of Gd in Gd-DTPA, Fe_3O_4@DOPA(DTPA)plus Gd-DTPA, and Fe_3O_4 @ DOPA (Gd-DTPA) NPs was 0. 062%, 0. 24%, and 0.093%, respectively. Therefore, the significant enhancement of T_1-weighted MR imaging after incubation with Fe_3O_4 @ DOPA (Gd-DTPA)NPs should be due to the synergistic interactions of effect of their good uptake and the excellent r_1 value of Fe_3O_4 @DOPA(Gd-DTPA)NPs.

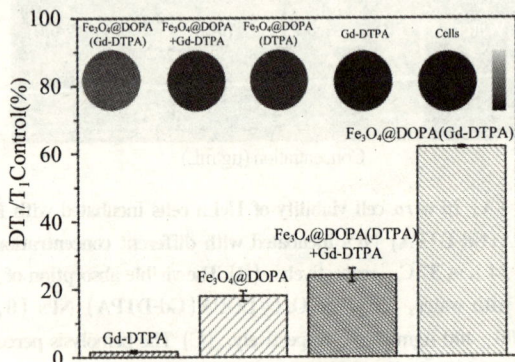

Fig. 5 The changes of the T_1 value in HeLa cells before and after incubation with Fe_3O_4 @ DOPA (DTPA) NPs, Gd-DTPA, Fe_3O_4 @ DOPA (DTPA) plus Gd-DTPA [(n (Fe) : n(Gd) =3 : 1], and Fe_3O_4 @DOPA(Gd-DTPA) NPs [(n(Fe) : n(Gd) =3 : 1]. The insets are the T_1-weighted MR imaging of HeLa cells after incubation.

In vivo MRI performance

The T_1-enhanced MR imaging on a BALB/c mouse was conducted on a 3 T MRI scanner (Fig. 6). After the injection of Fe_3O_4 @ DOPA (Gd-DTPA) NPs (Fe: 0. 21 mmol kg^{-1}, Gd:0. 07 mmol kg^{-1}), blood vessels were obviously brightened on the T_1-weighted MR images, demonstrating that Fe_3O_4 @ DOPA (Gd-DTPA) NPs can enhance T_1 relaxation in the circulating system. The signals increasingly brightened along with the circulating time. The profiles of MR imaging *in vivo* indicated that Fe_3O_4@DOPA(Gd-DTPA)NPs should be excellent candidates as a T_1 MR imaging agent.

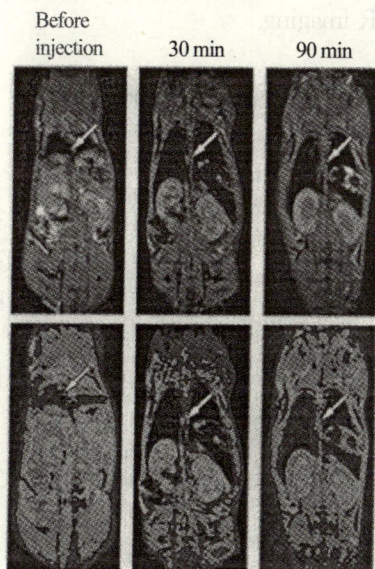

Fig. 6 T_1-weighted MR imaging at different times before and after the injection of Fe_3O_4 @ DOPA (GD-DTPA) NPs (Fe: 0.21 mmol kg^{-1}, Gd: 0.07 mmol kg^{-1}). The white and black arrows correspond to a selection of vessels.

Conclusion

We successfully synthesized ultra-small Fe_3O_4 @ DOPA (Gd-DTPA) NPs by chemically combining ultra-small Fe_3O_4 NPs and medically applied Gd-DTPA. Fe_3O_4 @DOPA(Gd-DTPA) NPs have an excellent T_1-weighted MR contrast effect. Fe_3O_4 @ DOPA (Gd-DTPA) NPs have low cytotoxicity, a small hemolysis ratio, and good biocompatibility. Compared to Gd-DTPA, they have a better T_1-weighted MR contrast effect *in vitro* and *in vivo*. The enhanced T_1-weighted MR contrast effect promises tremendous potential in biomedical and clinical applications of the novel Fe_3O_4 @ DOPA (Gd-DTPA) NPs in MR imaging.

Acknowledgements

This work was partially supported by the National Natural Science Foundation of China (nos 21271130 and 21371122), Program for Changjiang Scholars and Innovative Research Team in University (no. IRT1269), Shanghai Science and Technology Development Fund (nos 13520502800 and 10411953400), Shanghai Pujiang Program (13PJ1406600), Shanghai Municipal Education Commission (nos 13ZZ110 and 14YZ073), Shanghai Normal University (no. SK201339), and International Joint Laboratory on Resource Chemistry (IJLRC).

References

[1] D. Huo, J. Ding, Y. X. Cui, L. Y. Xia, H. Li, J. He, Z. Y. Zhou, H. W. Wang and Y. Hu, *Biomaterials*, 2014,35,7032 – 7041.

[2] N. Lee, H. R. Cho, M. H. Oh, S. H. Lee, K. Kim, B. H. Kim, K. Shin, T.-Y. Ahn, J. W. Choi, Y.-W. Kim, S. H. Choi and T. Hyeon, *J. Am. Chem. Soc.* , 2012,134,10309 – 10312.

[3] V. Amendola, S. Scaramuzza, L. Litti, M. Meneghetti, G. Zuccolotto, A. Rosato, E. Nicolato, P. Marzola, G. Fracasso, C. Anselmi, M. Pinto and M. Colombatti, *Small*, 2014,10,2476 – 2486.

[4] Z. Zhou, B. Kong, C. Yu, X. Shi, M. Wang, W. Liu, Y. Sun, Y. Zhang, H. Yang and S. Yang, *Sci. Rep.* , 2014,4,3653.

[5] H. B. Na, I. C. Song and T. Hyeon, *Adv. Mater.* , 2009,21,2133 – 2148.

[6] H. Yang, C. Qin, C. Yu, Y. Lu, H. Zhang, F. Xue, D. Wu, Z. Zhou and S. Yang, *Adv. Funct. Mater.*, 2013, 24, 1738 – 1747.

[7] Z. Zhou, L. Wang, X. Chi, J. Bao, L. Yang, W. Zhao, Z. Chen, X. Wang, X. Chen and J. Gao, *ACS Nano*, 2013, 7, 3287 – 3296.

[8] Z. Zhao, Z. Zhou, J. Bao, Z. Wang, J. Hu, X. Chi, K. Ni, R. Wang, X. Chen, Z. Chen and J. Gao, *Nat. Commun.*, 2013, 4, 2266.

[9] J.-S. Choi, J.-H. Lee, T.-H. Shin, H.-T. Song, E. Y. Kim and J. Cheon, *J. Am. Chem. Soc.*, 2010, 132, 11015 – 11017.

[10] X. Hu, Q. Wang, Y. Liu, H. Liu, C. Qin, K. Cheng, W. Robinson, B. D. Gray, K. Y. Pak, A. Yu and Z. Cheng, *Biomaterials*, 2014, 35, 7511 – 7521.

[11] L. Zhan-Jun, Z. Hong-Wu, S. Meng, S. Jiang-Shan and F. Hai-Xia, *J. Mater. Chem.*, 2012, 22, 24713 – 24720.

[12] J. Gao, K. Chen, R. Luong, D. M. Bouley, H. Mao, T. Qiao, S. S. Gambhir and Z. Cheng, *Nano Lett.*, 2011, 12, 281 – 286.

[13] H. Wang, F. Ke, A. Mararenko, Z. Wei, P. Banerjee and S. Zhou, *Nanoscale*, 2014, 6, 7443 – 7452.

[14] M. A. Bruckman, K. Jiang, E. J. Simpson, L. N. Randolph, L. G. Luyt, X. Yu and N. F. Steinmetz, *Nano Lett.*, 2014, 14, 1551 – 1558.

[15] L. An, H. Hu, J. Du, J. Wei, L. Wang, H. Yang, D. Wu, H. Shi, F. Li and S. Yang, *Biomaterials*, 2014, 35, 5381 – 5392.

[16] Z. Liu, T. Lammers, J. Ehling, S. Fokong, J. Bornemann, F. Kiessling and J. Gätjens, *Biomaterials*, 2011, 32, 6155 – 6163.

[17] M. G. Shapiro, P. W. Goodwill, A. Neogy, M. Yin, F. S. Foster, D. V. Schaffer and S. M. Conolly, *Nat. Nanotech nol.*, 2014, 9, 311 – 316.

[18] H. Ke, X. Yue, J. Wang, S. Xing, Q. Zhang, Z. Dai, J. Tian, S. Wang and Y. Jin, *Small*, 2014, 10, 1220 – 1227.

[19] S. A. Kwee, J. Lim, A. Watanabe, K. Kromer-Baker and M. N. Coel, *J. Nucl. Med.*, 2014, 55, 905 – 910.

[20] X. Yang, H. Liu, C. K. Sun, A. Natarajan, X. Hu, X. Wang, M. Allegretta, R. D. Guttmann, S. S. Gambhir, M.-S. Chua, Z. Cheng and S. K. So, *Biomaterials*, 2014, 35, 6964 – 6971.

[21] B. M. Paterson, K. Alt, C. M. Jeffery, R. I. Price, S. Jagdale, S. Rigby, C. C. Williams, K. Peter, C. E. Hagemeyer and P. S. Donnelly, *Angew. Chem. Int. Ed.*, 2014, 53, 6115 – 6119.

[22] F.-Y. Su, E.-Y. Chuang, P.-Y. Lin, Y.-C. Chou, C.-T. Chen, F.-L. Mi, S.-P. Wey, T.-C. Yen, K.-J. Lin and H.-W. Sung, *Biomaterials*, 2014,

35,3641 - 3649.

[23] Y. -H. Kim, J. Y. Moon, E. -O. Kim, S. -J. Lee, S. H. Kang, S. K. Kim, K. Heo, Y. Lee, H. Kim, K. -T. Kim, D. Kim, M. S. Song, S. -W. Lee, Y. Lee, S. S. Koh and I. -H. Kim, *Cancer Lett.* , 2014, 344, 223 - 231.

[24] T. J. Wadas, E. H. Wong, G. R. Weisman and C. J. Anderson, *Chem. Rev.* , 2010, 110, 2858 - 2902.

[25] B. -T. Doan, S. Meme and J. -C. Beloeil, in *The Chemistry of Contrast Agents in Medical Magnetic Resonance Imaging*, John Wiley & Sons, Ltd, 2013, pp. 1 - 23.

[26] M. Colombo, S. Carregal-Romero, M. F. Casula, L. Gutierrez, M. P. Morales, I. B. Bohm, J. T. Heverhagen, D. Prosperi and W. J. Parak, *Chem. Soc. Rev.* , 2012, 41, 4306 - 4334.

[27] J. J. Yang, J. Yang, L. Wei, O. Zurkiya, W. Yang, S. Li, J. Zou, Y. Zhou, A. L. W. Maniccia, H. Mao, F. Zhao, R. Malchow, S. Zhao, J. Johnson, X. Hu, E. Krogstad and Z. -R. Liu, *J. Am. Chem. Soc.* , 2008, 130, 9260 - 9267.

[28] P. Caravan, *Chem. Soc. Rev.* , 2006, 35, 512 - 523.

[29] D. T. Puerta, M. Botta, C. J. Jocher, E. J. Werner, S. Avedano, K. N. Raymond and S. M. Cohen, *J. Am. Chem. Soc.* , 2006, 128, 2222 - 2223.

[30] H. B. Na, J. H. Lee, K. An, Y. I. Park, M. Park, I. S. Lee, D. -H. Nam, S. T. Kim, S. -H. Kim, S. -W. Kim, K. -H. Lim, K. -S. Kim, S. -O. Kim and T. Hyeon, *Angew. Chem, Int. Ed.* , 2007, 46, 5397 - 5401.

[31] H. Yang, Y. Zhuang, H. Hu, X. Du, C. Zhang, X. Shi, H. Wu and S. Yang, *Adv. Funct. Mater.* , 2010, 20, 1733 - 1741.

[32] H. Hu, A. Dai, J. Sun, X. Li, F. Gao, L. Wu, Y. Fang, H. Yang, L. An, H. Wu and S. Yang, *Nanoscale*, 2013, 5, 10447 - 10454.

[33] T. Paik, T. R. Gordon, A. M. Prantner, H. Yun and C. B. Murray, *ACS Nano*, 2013, 7, 2850 - 2859.

[34] B. H. Kim, N. Lee, H. Kim, K. An, Y. I. Park, Y. Choi, K. Shin, Y. Lee, S. G. Kwon, H. B. Na, J. -G. Park, T. -Y. Ahn, Y. -W. Kim, W. K. Moon, S. H. Choi and T. Hyeon, *J. Am. Chem. Soc.* , 2011, 133, 12624 - 12631.

[35] T. Ninjbadgar and D. F. Brougham, *Adv. Funct. Mater.* , 2011, 21, 4769 - 4775.

[36] U. I. Tromsdorf, O. T. Bruns, S. C. Salmen, U. Beisiegel and H. Weller, *Nano Lett.* , 2009, 9, 4434 - 4440.

[37] S. Linderoth, P. V. Hendriksen, F. Bødker, S. Wells, K. Davies, S. W.

Charles and S. Mφrup, *J. Appl. Phys.* , 1994,75,6583 - 6585.

[38] J. M. D. Coey, *Phys. Rev. Lett.* , 1971,27,1140 - 1142.

[39] H. Yang, T. Ogawa, D. Hasegawa and M. Takahashi, *J. Appl. Phys.* , 2008,103,07D526.

（原载于 Journal of Materials Chemistry B 2015 年第 7 期）

Pt/Single-stranded DNA/graphene nanocomposite with improved catalytic activity and CO tolerance

Mengzhu Li, Yuxia Pan, Xiaoyu Guo, Yinhua Liang, Yiping Wu, Ying Wen and Haifeng Yang

The Education Ministry Key Lab of Resource Chemistry, Department of Chemistry Shanghai Normal University

Introduction

The rapid increase in the energy demands of people's daily lives and the rapid consumption of fossil fuel reserves are two important environmental concerns facing humanity.[1] Therefore, it is becoming increasingly important to look for green and eff-icient energy sources instead of fossil-based fuels. Nowadays, for instance, proton exchange membrane fuel cells (PEMFCs), direct methanol fuel cells (DMFCs), and direct formic acid fuel cells (DFAFCs) have been extensively investigated for their Potential as candidates of fossil fuel cells.

All the fuel cells are expected to possess the common characteristics of high energy density and low environmental pollution as compared to traditional energy sources. Amongst these, methanol is regarded as one of the most appropriate fuels for direct alcohol fuel cells, thanks to its low molecular weight, simple structure, and very high energy density as well as its low cost,[2] perfectly meeting the actual needs for new energy. In order to develop the practical applications of alcohol-based fuel cells, the key point for technical development is focused on the design of novel and superior anodic catalytic materials as well as optimizing the synthesis pes.

As a matter of fact, platinum (Pt) shows the highest electrocatalytic ability for the methanol oxidation reaction (MOR) on the anode among the metal catalysts. However, there are still unsolved problems, which largely limit the application of Pt in fuel cells. One severe barrier is the poisoning of the Pt electrode by CO during the MOR, due to CO tightly occupying active sites on the surface of the catalyst. [3]

According to previous research work,[4] oxygen-containing surface species ($e. g.$, OH) formed on adjacent bimetallic catalyst sites could improve the ability to remove the adsorbed CO (CO_{ad}) from the catalyst surface. Based on this mechanism, called bifunctional assay, a strategy is extended to synthesis alloy Pt with other oxophilic elements such as Pd^5, Ru^6, Sn^7, Au^8 and Fe^9, which offer abundant active sites for the adsorption of methanol and the formation of OH specie. Papakonstantinou et $al.$, investigating graphene oxide (GO) /Pt-based MOR, found that the presence of many oxygen groups on the surface of graphene could accelerate the oxidation of CO_{ad} at the active Pt sites. [10] Due to the fact that GO is not a conductive support, the GO/Pt-based catalyst exhibited the advantage of not being affected by CO poisoning but the catalytic activity was inhibited to a great extent. Alternatively, reduced graphene oxide (RGO) with the greater surface to volume ratio (theoretically 2600 $m^2 g^{-1}$)[11] and good conductive feature[12] could also be used as a carbon support no which to electrodeposit the Pt catalyst. Moreover, residual oxygen species in RGO provide nucleation centres or sites for loading the catalysts. [13] In addition, lots of edges and defects on the RGO assist in facilitating electron transport and accelerating mass transfer kinetics at the electrode surface, contributeing to the high activity of Pt. [14] Furthermore, during the methanol oxidation process, RGO is simultaneously oxidized and the oxidation of the carbon supports is found to promote the Pt activity.

In the present work, we firstly try to respectively electrodeposit Pt onto the surfaces of GO and RGO dispersed by single-stranded DNA (ssDNA) to explore an optimization method for elevating the catalytic activity of the Pt nanocatalyst. As is well known, ssDNA has a much greater affinity to bind the graphene than double-stranded DNA.[15] The possible reason is that ssDNA interacts more stronglyr with the graphene basal plane through π-π stacking in its open structure.[16] Astonishingly, we found that ssDNA provided abundant oxygen groups, which could enhance the resistance of the catalyst to CO poisoning. In turn, the nucleobase containing multiple nitrogen atoms in exocyclic amino and imino functional groups served as favourably defined sites to facilitate the formation of uniform cotton-flower-like Pt (cf-Pt) nanoparticles (NPs),[17] which eventually produced superior electrochemically active surface areas (ECSAs). Last but not least, when a voltage range from-0.2 - 1.2 V is applied, irreversible oxidative damage of guanine and adenine in ssDNA will be induced,[18] depleting the oxygen produced in CH_3OH electrooxidation and restraining the conversion of Pt to PtO in such a reaction system. As an interesting finding, this proposed novel ssDNA-RGO/cf-Pt anode showed not only high catalytic activity for methanol oxidation but also an excellent CO tolerance.

Experimental

Materials

Hexachloroplatinic (IV) acid hexahydrate ($H_2PtCl_6 \cdot 6H_2O$), trisodium citrate dihydrate ($Na_3C_6H_5O_7$, $\geqslant99\%$), and graphite were purchased from Sinopharm Chemical Reagent (China). Fish sperm DNA sodium salt (fsDNA) was purchased from Aladdin. Pt black was obtained from Sigma-Aldrich. Sodium chloride (NaCl, $\geqslant99.5\%$) was purchased from Shanghai RichJoint Chemical Reagent (China) All the chemicals and reagents were used as received. Ultrapure water (18.2

MΩ cm) was used throughout the experiments

Synthesis of DNA-modified RGO

Graphene oxides (GO) was prepared from graphite powder by the modified Hummer's method.[19] First of all, natural fsDNA (4 mg, 5 mg, 6 mg or 7 mg) was suspended in 10 mL water and heated at 100℃ for 2 h to obtain ssDNA. After the GO dispersion (1 mgmL^{-1}, 5 mL) was mixed with a ssDNA solution, this mixture was reduced by sodium citrate (1 wt%, 2 mL) for 2 h under 100℃. Then, NaCl (0.4675 g, 50 mM) was added to the suspension to remove the excess $Na_3C_6H_5O_7$ by multiple centrifugation steps and double-distilled water rinsing. The resultant DNA-modified RGO solution (containing 0.5 mgml^{-1} RGO) was termed ssDNA-RGO.

Modification of the anode

Before electrodeposition, the glassy carbon electrode (GCE) with a diameter of 3 mm was polished by 0.3 μm and 0.05 μm alumina powders followed by Sequential ultrasonication in doubly distilled water, absolute ethanol and doubly distilled water for 3 min. Then, 10 μL of ssDNA-RGO with different quantities of DNA were dropped onto the surface of the GCE and then dried under an infrared lamp. The 10 μL aqueous solution of GO (0.5 mgmL^{-1}), GO (0.5 mgmL^{-1}) and ssDNA (6 mgmL^{-1}, 10 mL) were also immobilized onto the surface of the GCE for control experiments.

The electrodeposition was conducted at an optimized potential of-0.2 V in 19 mM H_2PtCl_6 and 20 mM KCl solution and the deposition amount of Pt was evaluated through controlling final capacity to be 0.5052 μg. For a comparison, the commercial Pt-black modified GCE was also made by directly casting 10.0 μL of aqueous Pt-black (0.5 mg mL^{-1}) onto a cleaned electrode surface and the amount of Pt was kept the same as for the electrodeposition case.

Electrochemical measurements

The electrochemical experiments were performed using a CHI660D potentiostat (Shanghai Chenhua Instrumental Co., China) under ambient temperature in a cell, consisting of a modified GCE as a working electrode, Ag/AgCl (in 3 M KCl solution) as the reference electrode, and a Pt wire as a counter electrode. Scanning electron microscopy (SEM) and energy dispersive spectrometey (EDS) were carried out using a Hitachi S-4800 scanning electron microsc-ope. UV-vis spectra were recorded using a 760-CRT double beam ultraviolet-visible spectrophotometer (Shanghai Precision and Scient-ific Instrument Co. , Ltd). Raman observations were performed with a confocal microprobe Raman system (LabRam II, Dilor, France) and X-ray photoelectron spectroscopy (XPS; PHI 5000 VersaProbe) was used to identify the chemical composition of the surface of the resultant anode material.

Results and discussion

The procedure for preparing the ssDNA-RGO/cf-Pt hybrid is shown in Scheme. 1. First of all, natural dsDNA was heated to obtain ssDNA at 100℃ for 2 h. Then, keeping the temperature at 100℃, the GO dispersion was mixed with ssDNA and sodium citrate was injected to reduce GO to RGO to prepare the ssDNA-RGO hybrid system.

The preparation process of the ssDNA-RGO hybrid system was monitored using UV-vis spectroscopy. As showed in Fig. 1(A), a strong UV-vis absorption band for GO at 236 nm corresponds to the $\pi \rightarrow \pi *$ transitions of $C=C$ and a weak band around 300 nm is due to the $n \rightarrow \pi *$ transitions of $C=O$.[20] After the reduction reaction, the absorption red-shift peak of the ssDNA-RGO could be seen at 254 nm due to the restored electronic conjugation within the graphene sheets. Digital photos of the GO (pale brown), ssDNA-RGO (black), and RGO (black) in water were also taken. Clearly shown in Fig. 1(B), the ssDNA-RGO hybrid is dispersed in water in a uniform way with long-term stability ($>$ 3 months). Without ssDNA modification,

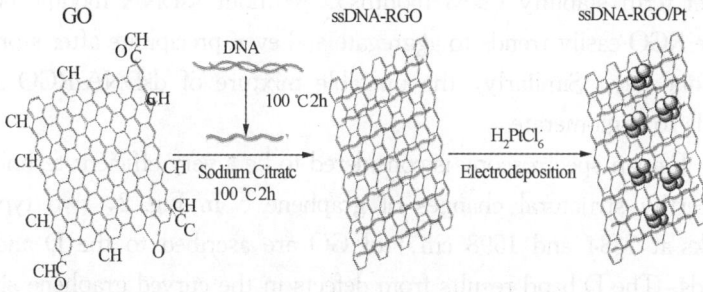

Scheme 1 Schematic illustration of the procedure for preparing ssDNA-RGO/Pt hybrid

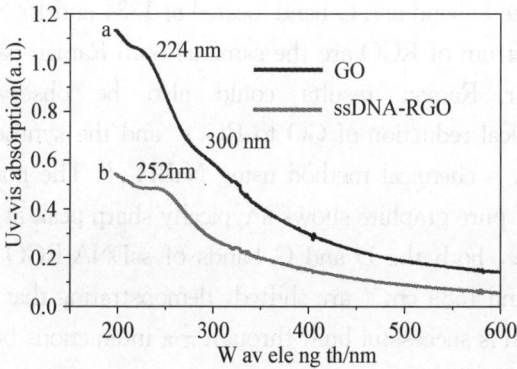

A

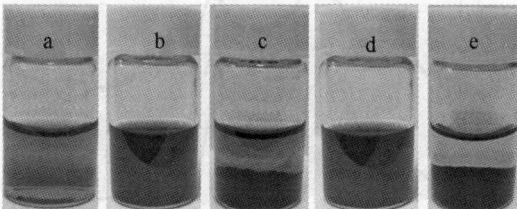

B

Fig. 1 (A) UV-vis absorption results of GO (a), ssDNA-RGO (b). (B) Optical photos of GO (a), ssDNA-RGO (b), RGO (c), ssDNA-RGO after three months (d), dsDNA-RGO (e)

paper term stability （＞3 months）. Without ssDNA modification, pure RGO easily trends to aggregate and even precipitate after storage for one day. Similarly, the unstable mixture of dsDNA-RGO also tends to agglomerate.

Raman spectroscopy is considered to be a very efficient technique to certify structural changes of graphene.[21] In Fig. 2, two typical peaks at 1334 and 1598 cm^{-1} of GO are ascribed to the D and G bands. The D band results from defects in the curved graphene sheet as an indication of disordered structures of GO and the G band is from the vibration of sp^2-bonded structures in a carbon 2D hexagonal lattice.[22] The D band and G band located at 1334 and 1598 cm^{-1}in the Raman spectrum of RGO are the same as both Raman bands of GO. The similar Raman results could also be observed in the electrochemical reduction of GO to RGO[23] and the synthesis of RGO from GO by a chemical method using NaBH$_4$.[24] The normal Raman spectrum of pure graphite shows a typically sharp peak at 1580 cm^{-1}. Interestingly, both the D and G bands of ssDNA-RGO observed at 1327 cm^{-1}and 1589 cm^{-1} are shifted, demonstrating that the ssDNA-RGO system is successful built through π-π interactions between

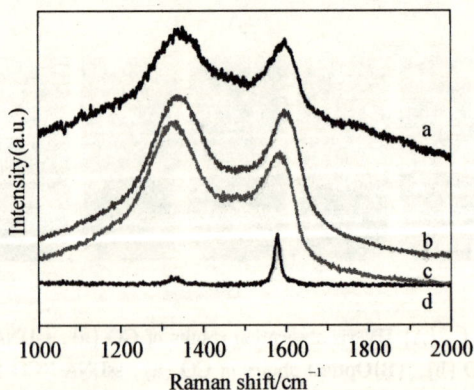

Fig. 2   Raman spectra of GO （a）, RGO （b）, ssDNA-RGO （c）, and graphite （d）.

single-stranded DNA and the graphene basal plane. [25] The calculation of the intensity ratio I_D/I_G can identify the degree of disorder of such carbon materials. The value of I_D/I_G (1. 17) for ssDNA-RGO is larger than for GO (1. 01), RGO (1. 07), which is attributad to the decrease in the average size of the sp^2. [26] Herein, ssDNA acts as an outstanding dispersant to improve the dispersion efficiency of RGO in water *via* π-π interactions.

The electrodeposition of cf-Pt nanoparticles onto a ssDNA-RGO modified GCE was investigated using SEM. The SEM image of ssDNA-RGO in Fig. 3 (A) shows the typical lamellar structure of RGO with intrinsic rumples. Fig. 3(B) proves that the cf-Pt NPs are homogeneously deposited on the surface of RGO. The cf-Pt NPs in Fig. 3(C) could be ascribed to the favourable nucleation and defined electrodeposition sites along the DNA lattice provided by the exocyclic amino and imino groups in nucleobases. The clear image of cf-Pt NPs directly deposited on the crinkle of ssDNA-RGO in Fig. 3(D) exhibits the tight interaction between the ssDNA and cf-Pt NPs. As a comparison experiment, when Pt NPs were electrodeposited on the surface of the pure RGO and GO, the corresponding SEM and TEM images shown in Fig. S1 depict the severe aggregation of the spherical Pt NPs at their surfaces. According to size statistic graphs in Fig. S2, the sizes of ssDNA-RGO/cf-Pt, GO/ Pt and RGO/ Pt are mainly in the ranges of 200 – 800 nm, 100 – 255 nm and 10 – 35 nm, respectively. Clearly, the cf-Pt clusters on the ssDNA-RGO exhibit and open structure, which could be expected to facilitate the mass transfer process and elevate the active area of pt.

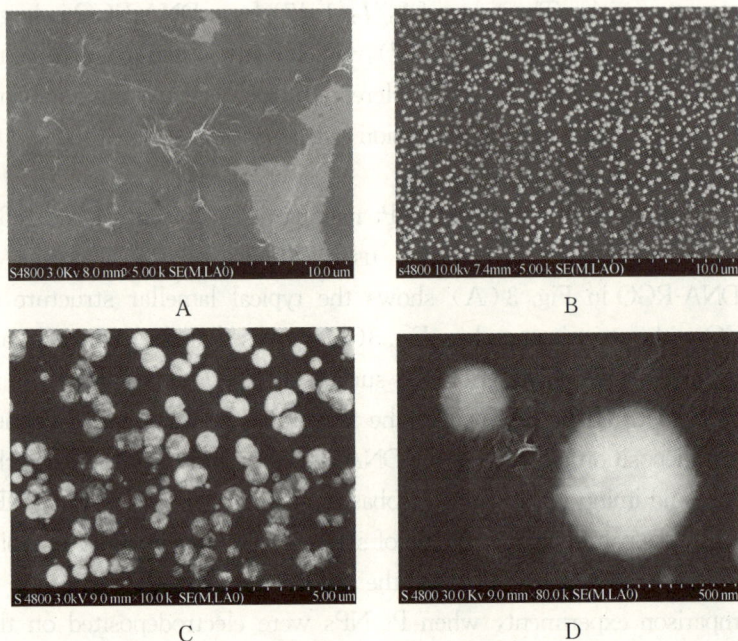

Fig. 3 SEM images of (A) ssDNA-RGO, and (B-D) ssDNA-RGO/ct-Pt shown at different scales

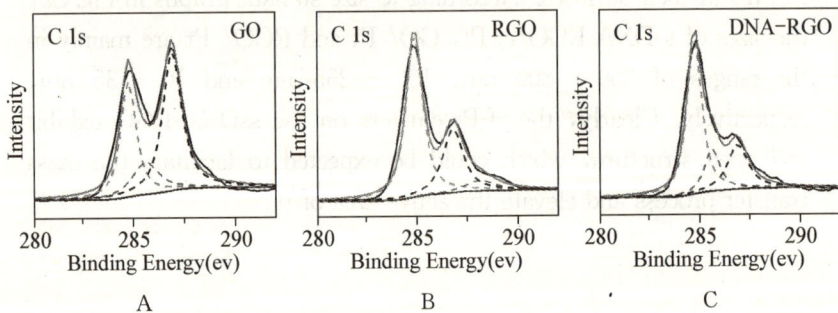

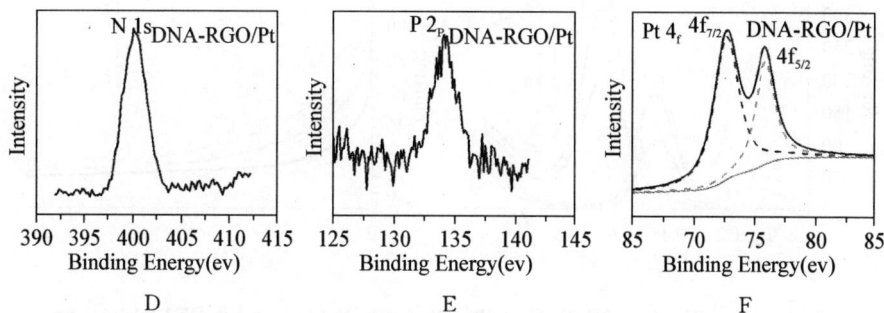

Fig. 4 **XPS spectra of the (A) carbon 1s of GO, (B) carbon 1s of RGO, (C) carbon 1s of ssDNA-RGO/cf-Pt, (D) nitrogen 1s of ssDNA-RGO/cf-Pt, (E) phosphorus 2p of ssDNA-RGO/cf-Pt, and (F) platinum 4f of ssDNA-RGO/cf-Pt.**

In Fig. 4(A), XPS analyze of the surface functionalization of GO, RGO, and ssDNA-RGO, provides the composition information. For the GO sheets, the fitted C_{1s} peaks located at 284. 7, 285. 6 and 286. 8 eV correspond to $C = C/C-C$, C-OH and C-O-C bonds,[27] respectively. when GO was reduced to RGO, with the loss of oxygen moieties it generated new sp^2 C-C bonds. Correspondingly in Fig. 4 (B) showing the XPS spectrum of RGO, a peak from C-OH disappeared and a new peak corresponding to $C=O$ is observed. In turn, the increasing intensity of $C=C/C-C$ can be easily found in the spectral range of 285. 5 – 289. 0 eV. After the formation of ssDNA-RGO, in Fig. 4(C), the novel peak at 286. 2 eV is related to the C-N bond of ssDNA.[28] The XPS data of the nitrogen 1 s (400. 2 eV) and phosphorus 2p (134. 3 eV) in Fig. 4(D) and (E) also confirm the successful modification of ssDNA on the surface of RGO. In addition, the O 1 s XPS peak of GO is located at 532. 6 eV and for RGO, the O 1 s XPS peak red shifts to 532. 8 eV as shown in Fig. S3 while two O 1 s XPS peaks due to ssDNA-RGO are present at 532. 6 and 535. 9 eV. The latter peak located at 535. 9 eV may be due to O-

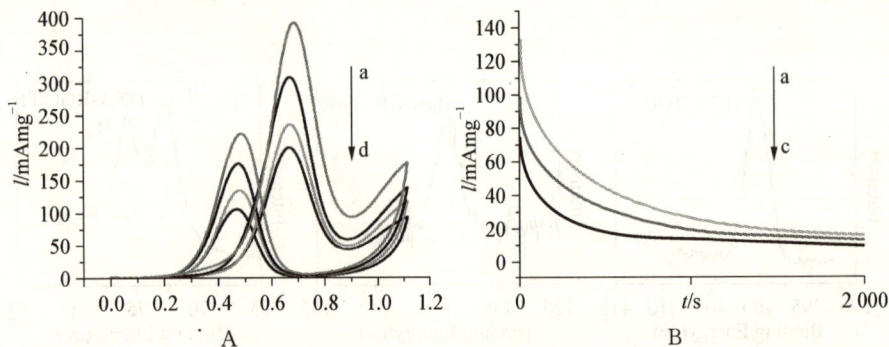

Fig. 5 (A) CVs of ssDNA-RGO/cf-Pt with 6 mg DNA(a), 5 mg DNA (b), 4 mg DNA(c), 7 mg DNA(d) in 0. 5 M H_2SO_4 +1 M CH_3OH at a scan rate of 50 mVs^{-1}, (B) Chronoamperometry curves of ssDNA (6 mg)-RGO/Pt(a), RGO/Pt (b), pure Pt (c) in 0. 5 M H_2SO_4 +1 M CH_3OH at 0. 6 V.

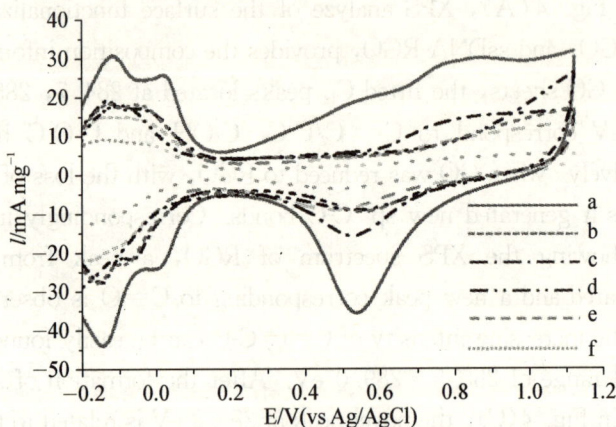

Fig. 6 CVs of ssDNA (6mg)-RGO/cf-Pt (a), RGO/Pt (b), GO/Pt (c), pure Pt (d), ssDNA/Pt (e) and ssDNA (6mg)-GO/Pt (f) in 0. 5 M H_2SO_4 with a scan rate of 50 mV s^{-1}.

Table 1 Elemental atomic Concentration from XPS data

Sample	Atomic concentration%					
	C(%)	O(%)	C/O ratio	N(%)	P(%)	Pt(%)
GO	65.40	34.60	1.89			
RGO	73.31	26.69	2.74			
ssDNA-RGO	64.87	35.13	1.85			
ssDNA-RGO/cf-Pt	62.30	33.74	1.85	3.22	0.74	0.034

containing groups in the ssDNA. As shown in the Pt XPS spectrum of ssDNA-RGO/cf-Pt shown in Fig. 4(F), the positive shifts of both peaks referring to Pt $4f_{7/2}$ and Pt $4f_{5/2}$ can be seen at 72.8 and 76.1 eV, compared to the XPS bands of metallic Pt at 71.4 (Pt $4f_{7/2}$) and 74.6 eV(Pt $4f_{5/2}$).[29] The possible reason is that the shifts of both

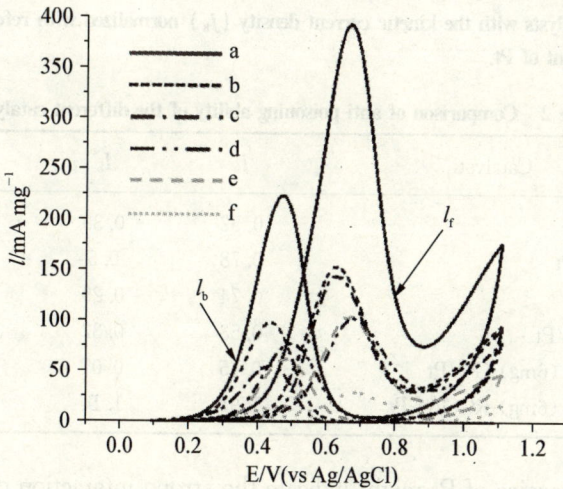

A

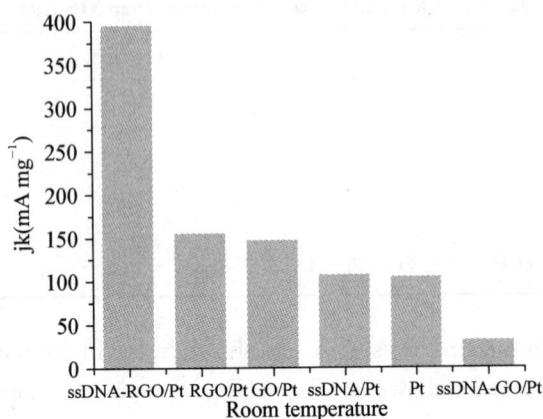

B

Fig. 7　(A)CVs of ssDNA (6 mg)-RGO/cf-Pt (a), RGO/Pt (b), GO/Pt (c), pure Pt (d), ssDNA/Pt (e) and ssDNA (6 mg)-GO/Pt (f) in nitrogen saturated aqueous solution of 0.5 M H_2SO_4, with a scan rate of 100 mVs^{-1}. (B) Mass activity of different catalysts with the kinetic current density (j_k) normalized with referred to the loading amount of Pt.

Table 2　Comparison of anti-poisoning ability of the different catalysts

Catalyst	I_f	I_b	I_f/I_b
Pt	0.52	0.39	1.33
RGO/Pt	0.78	0.5	1.56
GO/Pt	0.74	0.29	2.56
ssDNA/Pt	0.53	0.32	1.67
ssDNA (6mg)-GO/Pt	0.15	0.07	2.14
ssDNA (6mg)-RGO/cf-Pt	1.98	1.14	1.75

binding energies of Pt might indicate the strong interaction of Pt with heteroatoms in the ssDNA-RGO system, especially the nitrogen and phosphate moieties in the ssDNA after carefully comparing with the XPS bands of nitrogen 1s at 400.5 eV and phosphorus 2p at 133.6 eV, given in the literature.[30] The EDS results shown in Fig. S4† also mark the presence of N, Pt, O and C and further verifies the successful formation of ssDNA-RGO/cf-Pt.

As Shown in Fig. 5(A), through the observation of a change in the CVs with the increase in the amount of DNA from 4 mg to 7 mg, the superior catalytic activity of the ssDNA-RGO/cf-Pt composite for methanol electrooxidation than the other could be found when 6 mg DNA is used. The durability and long-term activity of the DNA-RGO/cf-Pt composite within 2000 s shows better performance than commercial Pt NPs and RGO/Pt as shown in Fig. 5(B)

The electrochemical behaviour of the resultant ssDNA-RGO/cf-Pt, RGO and commercial Pt modified GCEs were observed using a cyclic voltammetry (CV) method in nitrogen saturated 0. 5 M H_2SO_4 aqueous solution at a potential scan rate of 100 mV s^{-1} (Fig. 6). The ECSA (active surface area) can be calculated by measuring the columbic charge collected in the hydrogen adsorption and desorption region between-0. 2 and 0. 1 V. According to the following equation,[31] ECSAs=Q_H/mC (where 0. 21 mC cm^{-2} charge is required to oxidize a monolayer of H_2 on the surface of Pt, and m refers to the platinum loading), ECSAs of commercial DNA-GO/Pt, DNA/Pt, Pt NPs, RGO/Pt, GO/Pt and DNA-RGO/cf-Pt were 11. 8 m^2 g^{-1}, 40. 1 m^2 g^{-1},96. 8 m^2 g^{-1}, 95. 3 m^2 g^{-1}, 112. 3 m^2 g^{-1}, and 234 m^2 g^{-1}, respectively. The greater ECSA shows the more catalytically active sites available for electrochemical reaction and simultaneously reflects the conductive pathway available at the surface of the electrode for transfer electrons, which is due to the open strusture of cotton-flower Pt clusters formed with the aid of ssDNA and the very large surface area of the RGO. Therefore, the presence of ssDNA in DNA-RGO/cf-Pt is also a key factor to improve the catalytic activity of Pt.

According to Fig. 7(A), the optimal ssDNA-RGO/cf-Pt modified GCE exhibits the highest current density (1. 98 mA cm^{-2}), which is 2. 5 fold greater than RGO/Pt and 3. 8 fold greater than commercial Pt NPs. In Fig. 7(B), mass activities of DNA-RGO/cf-Pt, commercial Pt NPs, RGO/Pt, GO/Pt, ssDNA/Pt and ssDNA-GO/Pt are 391. 9,

99. 6, 154. 1, 140. 4, 154. 1 and 28. 5 mA mg^{-1}, respectively.

It should be mentioned that the optimal ssDNA-RGO/cf-Pt GCE exhibits the highest electrocatalytic activity and superior CO tolerance capability but the latter is lower than GO/Pt. The difference between GO and RGO lies in the number of oxygen groups. As described above, GO sheets with abundant oxygen groups have better anti-poisoning ability. The forward anodic peak at around 0. 7 V marked as I_f refers to the oxidation of methanol and the backward anodic peak at around 0. 5 V marked as I_b refers to the oxidation of CO$_{ads}$-like species. [32] The ratio I_f/I_b represents the CO tolerance ability of catalysts. In Table 2, the I_f/I_b ratio of GO/Pt (2. 56) is larger than that 1. 56 of RGO/Pt(1. 56). Considering the atomic concentrations in Table 1, the carbon/ oxygen ratio of GO is 1. 89, which is smaller than that of RGO (2. 74). Unfortunately, the GO sheets are not good conductors, hindering the electron transport rate as well as resulting in a decrease in its catalytic ability as shown in Fig. 7 (B). The smallest carbon/oxygen ratio for ssDNA-RGO was evaluated to be 1. 85 on the basis of the XPS results tabulated in Table 1. However, the I_f/I_b of ssDNA-RGO/cf-Pt is just 1. 75, which is lower than ssDNA RGO/Pt and GO/Pt as shown in Table 2. This phenomenon might be due to its excellent catalytic activity generating more CO species during the methanol oxidation process to occupy the active sites of Pt compared with the case of RGO/Pt, Nitrogen functional groups in ssDNA-RGO/cf-Pt from ssDNA play a role in not only producing cotton-flower-like Pt with an enhanced electroactivity but also in adsorbing water, resulting in OH adsorption onto the ssDNA-RGO/ cf-Pt surface, which should greatly contribute to the resistance of CO-poisoning. What's more, OH groups in the phosphate backbone of the ssDNA as a Pt formation site (see Fig. 7(A)) might also contribute towards the improvement in the CO tolerance of DNA-RGO/cf-Pt. As proposed above, the CO tolerance of DNA-GO/Pt should be the best, but the I_f/I_b ratio of DNA-GO/Pt(2. 14) is smaller than that of GO/

Pt. One contribution may be due to the DNA which reduces the oxygen groups of GO in the snythesis of the DNA-GO hybrid.[33] Obviously in Table 2, without RGO, ssDNA/Pt Possesses Poor catalytic ability due to its non-conducting characteristics. The proposed mechanism is described in the following equations:

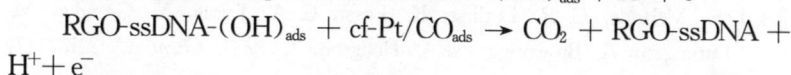

$$RGO\text{-}ssDNA + H_2O \rightarrow RGO\text{-}ssDNA\text{-}(OH)_{ads} + H^+ + e^-$$
$$RGO\text{-}ssDNA\text{-}(OH)_{ads} + cf\text{-}Pt/CO_{ads} \rightarrow CO_2 + RGO\text{-}ssDNA + H^+ + e^-$$

Conclusions

We successfully employed ssDNA to readily disperse graphene oxides in water and then added a reducing agent to synthesize ssDNA-RGO composites. Pt nanoparticles were easily deposited onto the surface of the ssDNA-RGO modified CGE with possessed a very large surface area and good conductivity. Due to the presence of nitrogen sites and phosphates moieties in the ssDNA, the Pt nanoparitcles exhibited a cotton-flower-like structure, exhibiting high catalytic activity for methanol oxidation. Oxygen residual species (*e. g.* , OH) on the surface of the RGO, and OH species formed from water caught by nitrogen functional groups in the ssDNA could accelerate the oxidation of CO_{ad}, which is beneficial for improving CO_{ad} removal. Therefore, the ssDNA-RGO/cf-Pt catalyst showed the advantage of inhibiting CO poisoning to greater extent. We found that the ssDNA played a vital role not only in the good dispersion of RGO as the support for the formation of the open structure of Pt with high activity, but also the enhancement of its CO tolerance.

Acknowledgements

This work is supported by the National Natural Science Foundation of China (no. 21475088), PCSIRT (IRT1269) and International Joint Laboratory on Resource Chemistry (IJLRC), Shanghai Key Laboratory of Rare Earth Functional Materials, and Shanghai Municipal Education Committee Key Laboratory of Molecular Imaging Probes and Sensors.

References

[1] M. Armand, and J. M. Tarascon, *Nature*, 2008,451,652 - 657.

[2] M. M. Liu, R. Z. Zhang, and W. Chen, *Chem. Rev*, 2014,114,5117 - 5160.

[3] J. M. Leger, *J. Appl. Electrochem*, 2001,31,767 - 771.

[4] F. McBride, G. R. Darling, K. Pussi, C. A. Lucas, Y. Grunder, M. Darlington, A. Brownrigg and A. Hodgson, *J. Phys. Chem. C*, 2013,117, 4032 - 4039.

[5] S. J. Guo, S. J. Dong, and E. K. Wang, *ACS Nano*, 2010,4,547 - 555.

[6] S. Y. Bong, Y. R. Kima, I. Kima, S. H. Woo, S. H. Uhmb, J. Y. Lee and H. Kima, *Electrochem. Commun*, 2010,12,129 - 131.

[7] V. R. Stamenkovic, M. Arenz, C. A. Lucas, M. E. Gallagher, P. N. Ross, and N. M. Markovic, *J. Am. Chem. Soc*, 2003,125,2736 - 2745.

[8] Y. J. Hu, H. Zhang, P. Wu, H, Zhang, B. Zhou, and C. X. Cai, *Phys. Chem. Chem. Phys.* , 2011,13,4083 - 4094.

[9] W. Chen, J. M. Kim, S. H. Sun and S. W. Chen, *Langmuir*, 2007,23,11303 - 11310

[10] (*a*) S. Sharma, A. Ganguly, P. Papakonstantinou, X. P. Miao, M. X. Li, J. L. Hutchison, M. Delichatsios, and S. Ukleja, *J. Phys. Chem. C*, 2010, 114,19459 - 19466; (*b*) I. Fampiou and A. Ramasubramaniam, *J. Phys. Chem. C*, 2012,116,6543 - 6555; (*c*) A. Ambrosi and M. Pumera, *Chem. - Eur. J*, 2010,16,10946 - 10949.

[11] Y. X. Liu, X. C. Dong, and P. Chen, *Chem. Soc. Rev.* , 2012,41,2283 - 2307.

[12] N. Zhang, Y. H. Zhang, and Y. J. Xu, *Chem. Soc. Rev*, 2014,43,8240 - 8254.

[13] (*a*) M. Q. Yang, X. Y. Pan, N. Zhang and, Y. J. Xu, *CrystEngComm*, 2013,15,6819 - 6828; (*b*) R. Kou, Y. Y. Shao, D. H. Mei, Z. M. Nie, D. H. Wang, C. M. Wang, V. V. Viswanathan, S. Park, I. A. Aksay, Y. H. Lin, Y. Wang, and J. Liu, *J. Am. Chem. Soc.* 2011,133,2541 - 2547.

[14] N. Zhang, Y. H. Zhang and, Y. J. Xu, *Nanoscale*, 2012,4,5792 - 5813

[15] (*a*) J. N. Tiwari, K. C. Kemp, K. Nath, R. N. Tiwari, H. G. Nam and K. S. Kim, *ACS Nano*, 2013,7,9223 - 9231; (*b*) J. N. Tiwari, K. Nath, S. Kumar, R. N. Tiwari, K. C. Kemp, N. H. Le, D. H. Youn, J. S. Lee and K. S. Kim, *Nat. Commun.* , 2012,486,43 - 51; (*c*) W. Lv, M. Hui, F. M.

Liang, L. Jin, L. Cui, J. Zhi and Q. H. Yang, *J. Mater. Chem*, 2010, 20, 6668 – 6673.

[16] (a) V. Georgakilas, M. Otyepka, A. B. Bourlinos, V. Chandra, N. Kim; K. C. Kemp, P. Hobza, R. Zboril and K. S. Kim, *Chem. Rev.*, 2012, 112, 6156 –6214; (b) A. J. Patil, J. L. Vickery, T. B. Scott and S. Mann, *Adv. Mater.*, 2009, 21, 3159 – 3164.

[17] K. Qu, L. Wu, J. S. Ren and X. G. Qu, *ACS. Appl. Mater. Interfaces*, 2012, 4, 5001 – 5009.

[18] (a) I. V. Yang and H. H. Throp, *Inorg. Chem*, 2000, 39, 4969 – 4976; (b) M. E. Napier, D. O. Hull and H. H. Throp, *J. Am. Chem. Soc*, 2005, 127, 11952 –11953.

[19] (a) G. T. Liu, H. F. Chen, G. M. Lin, P. P. Ye, X. P. Wang, Y. Z. Jiao, X. Y. Guo, Y. Wen and H. F. Yang, *Biosens. Bioelectron*, 2014, 56, 26 – 32; (b) W. S. Hummers and R. E. Offeman, *J. Am. Chem. Soc*, 1958, 80, 1339; (c) M. Q. Yang and Y. J. Xu, *Phys. Chem. Chem. Phys.*, 2013, 15, 19102 – 19118.

[20] M. M. Liu, R. Liu and W. Chen, *Biosens. Bioelectron*, 2013, 45, 206 – 212.

21. J. C. Chacón-Torres, L. Wirtz and T. Pichler, *ACS Nano*, 2013, 7, 9249 – 9259.

[22] M. M. Zhang, J. M. Xie, Q. Sun, Z. Yan, M. Chen and J. J. Jing, *Int. J. Hydrogen Energy*, 2013, 38, 16402 – 16409.

[23] Y. Y Jiang, Y. Z. Lu, F. H. Li, T. S. Wu, L. Niu and W. Chen, *Electrochem. Commun*, 2012, 19, 21 – 24.

[24] M. Y. Yen, C. C. Teng, M. C. Hsiao, P. I. Liu, W. P. Chuang, C. C. M. Ma, C. K. Hsieh, M. C. Tsai and C. H. Tsai, *J. Mater. Chem*, 2011, 21, 12880 –

[25] 12888Stankovich, D. A. Dikin, G. H. B. Dommett, K. M. Kohlhaas, E. J. Zimney, E. A. Stach, R. D. Piner, S. T. Nguyen and R. S. Ruoff, *Nature*, 2006, 442, 282 – 286; C. H. Hsu, H. Y. Liao, Y. F. Wu and P. L. Kuo, *ACS. Appl. Mater. Interfaces*, 2011, 3, 2169 – 2172.

[26] C. H. Hsu, H. Y. Liao, Y. F. Wu and P. L. Kuo, *ACS. Appl. Mater. Interfaces*, 2011, 3, 2169 – 2172.

[27] W. Y. Kim and K. S. Kim, *Nat. Nanotechnol*, 2008, 3, 408 – 412.

[28] J. P. Avinash, L. V. Jemma, B. S. Thomas and M. Stephen, *Adv. Mater.*, 2009, 21, 3159 – 3164.

[29] V. Singha, D. Jounga, L. Zhai, S. Das, S. I. Khondaker and S. Seal, Prog. Mater. Sci., 2011, 56, 1178 – 1271.

[30] D. A. Stevens, M. T. Hicks, G. M. Haugen and J. R. Dahn, *J. Electrochem.*

Soc, 2005,152,2309 – 2315.

[31] B. Lim, M. Jiang, P. H. C. Cama, E. C. Cho, J. Tao, X. Lu, Y. Zhu and Y. Xia, *Science*, 2009,324,1302 – 1305.

[32] L. Gao, W. Yue, S. S. Tao and L. Z. Fan, *Langmuir*, 2013,29,957 – 964.

[33] A. A. Kornyshev, *Phys. Chem. Chem. Phys*, 2010,12,12352 – 12378.

(原载于 Journal of Materials Chemistry A 2015 年第 3 期)

Construction of Dandelion-like Clusters by PtPd Nanoseeds for Elevating Ethanol Eletrocatalytic Oxidation

Yuxia Pan, Xiaoyu Guo, Mengzhu Li, Yinhua Liang, Yiping Wu, Ying Wen, Haifeng Yang

The Education Ministry Key Lab of Resource Chemistry Department of Chemistry Shanghai Normal University

1. Introduction

Among the fuels fed to direct liquid fuel cells, ethanol is a promising energy in the direct ethanol fuel cell (DEFC) reaction for several reasons [1,2]: (1) low toxicity; (2) easy to be stored and transported; (3) higher energy density (ethanol 8030 Wh kg^{-1}, methanol, 6100 Wh kg^{-1}) from the nature of 12 electron transfer upon complete oxidation; (4) low permeability when it across proton exchange membrane. However, without the help of an active anode catalyst, the ethanol oxidation reaction (EOR) at the anode is the sluggish process, which hinders the implementation of the DEFC technology [1]. Thus, developing novel catalysts for EOR is necessary.

Designing the Pt-based bimetallic heteronanostructures is critical to improvement of catalytic activities for highly promising catalysts comparing with monometallic Pt nanostructures [3]. It has been widely reported that a large number of Pt-based bimetallic nanoparticles for the electrocatalytic applications exhibit synergistically enhanced performance, involving PtAu, PtCu, PtPd, PtRu, and PtNi [4-8]. In addition, Pt-based bimetal can also reduce the loading of

Pt in a catalyst and improved Pt utilization efficiency. Among various metals, Pd is a better candidate to form bimetallic nanocrystals with Pt because both of them share the same face-centered cubic crystal structure and have a minor lattice mismatch of 0.77% [9]. As well known, the catalytic and electrocatalytic activity of platinum and palladium nanostructures highly depends on the morphology of the nanoparticles [4]. In the literature, for increasing the activity of PtPd nanostructure catalysts, PtPd tetrahedrons, three-dimensional PtPd nanostructures, Pd@Pt core-shell nanocrystals, and Pt on Pd have been made [10 - 13]. Recent studies have also shown that porous materials with high specific surface area and a high density of low-coordinated atoms, steps, edges, and kinks are of great interest for fuel cell electrocatalysts, especially for electrooxidation of small organic fuels and the oxygen reduction reaction [14,15]. Under these guidances, the shape-controlled synthesis of nanocrystals enclosed by open-structure surfaces is a promising direction for catalyst design [14].

In present paper, we successfully synthesized a PtPd nanostructure with highly branched, using hexadecylpyridinium chloride monohydrate (HDPCl) as a soft template. The as-prepared PtPd nanostructures looked like dandelion. What's more, each branch of dandelion constructed by PtPd nanoseeds can provide more active sites. The single nanoseed in dandelion-like PtPd nanoclusters (DPtPdNC) is about 2 - 5 nm and the mean thickness of branch is only 2.5 nm. The selection of HDPCl, which has Cl_2^- anion group, long alkyl chain, and rigid pyridinium group as the shape-directing agent, plays key role to the formation of dandelion-like nanoclusters in massive way. The nanocrystal composition was confirmed by X-ray diffraction (XRD) and X-ray photoelectron spectroscopy (XPS). We further observed the PtPd nanostructures's catalytic activity toward ethanol electrooxidation in alkaline media. Our results showed that the dandelion-like PtPd nanostructures exhibited higher electrocatalytic activity than the home-made dandelion Pd nanoclusters (DPdNC), the Pd-black and Pt-black catalyst due to the synergistic and electronic effects.

2. Results and Discussion

2. 1 *Synthesis of Dandelion-like PtPd Nanoclusters*

A synthetic procedure is surmised in Scheme 1. At the beginning of experiment, HDPCl formed micelle via sufficient mixing. With the addition of freshly made AA solution, metal ions were rapidly reduced to form tiny nanoseeds. As the reaction progressing, the tiny nanoseeds finally attached each other [16] to develop dandelion-like structure. The formation of bimetallic DPtPdNC can be confirmed by UV-visible absorption spectroscopy. As indicated in Figure S1a, the absorption peak at 310 nm is from $PdCl_4^{2-}$. After the complete reaction, the $PdCl_4^{2-}$ ions are reduced to Pd and the band at 310 nm is vanished in Figure S1b. Moreover, the intensities of absorption more than 420 nm in Figure S1b are higher than Figure S1a, which means the increase of nanoparticles [17].

Transmission electron microscopy (TEM) images of the as-prepared representative products were taken. As shown in Fig. 1a, the product is highly open dandelion-like structure. An average size of 40 nm for nanoclusters consists of tiny nanoseeds with 2 – 5 nm in diameter (a proposed optimal size for electrocatalysts) [18]. Fig. 1b depicts a high resolution TEM (HRTEM) image of the DPtPdNC, in which the lattice fringes show interplanar spacing of 0. 224 nm and the dihedral angle (70°) in the branch regions corresponding to the {111} plane of the PtPd face centered cubic structure [19]. It was further noted that no obvious grain boundaries between nanoparticles, due to highly lattice match of Pt and Pd [20]. Fig. 1c shows TEM image of home-made DPdNC using same synthesis method as the DPtPdNC. Clearly, as mentioned above, HDPCl played the dominated role in shape control, resulting in that the morphologies of bimetallic PtPd nanoclusters and monometallic Pd nanoclusters were same dandelion structure. Selected area electron diffraction (SAED) pattern in Fig. 1d confirms that the crystalline structures of the DPtPdNC involve {111}, {200} and {220} planes. The energy dispersive X-ray spectroscopy (EDX) mapping of Pt and Pd are shown in Fig. 1e, showing that the Pt and Pd in dandelion morphology are uniformly dispersive. Mostly importantly, the branch surface is of several atomic steps (indicated as dotted square in Fig. 1b), which could act as highly catalytic sites [21].

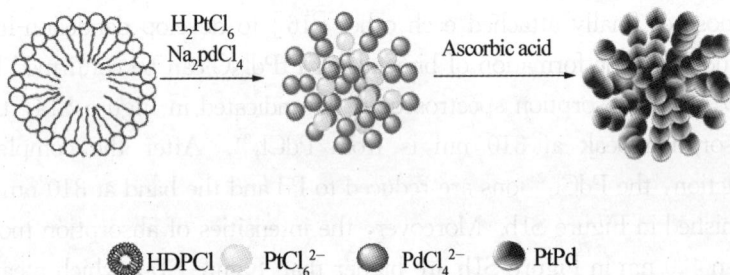

Scheme 1. A synthetic procedure of dandelion PtPd nanoclusters.

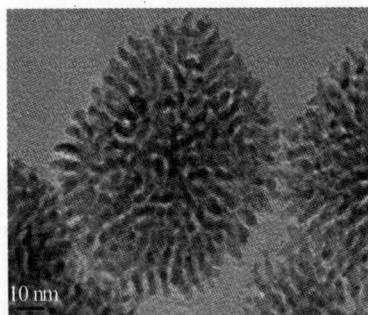

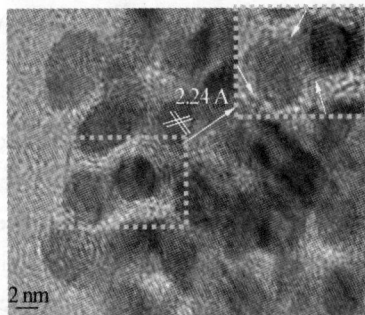

(a)   (b)

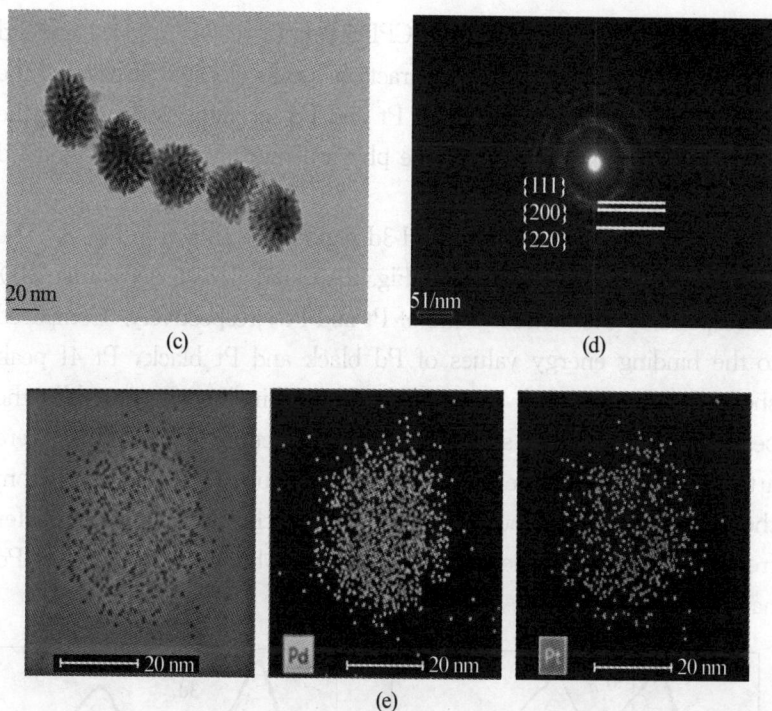

Fig. 1 TEM images of DPtPdNC structures (scare bar: 10nm) (a) and DPdNC structure (c) recorded at different magnifications. (b) HRTEM image taken from the part of a single DPtPdNC structure. (d) SAED pattern of DPtPdNC (e) EDX mapping images. The green and red colours correspond to Pd and Pt elements, respectively. (For interpretation of the references to color in this figure legend, the reader is referred to the web version of this article.)

The yield of the special morphologies for the DPtPdNC is almost 100% as shown in Figure S2A. On counting 185 particles, the size distribution of nanoparticles is found to be very uniform and controllable (Figure S2B). A typical EDX analytical result of DPtPdNC in Figure S2C presents the Pt and Pd peaks, hinting the successful synthesis of bimetallic DPtPdNC. An XRD pattern of DPtPdNC shown in Figure S3 supports the result from SAED pattern. The three apparent diffraction peaks at $2\theta = 39.9°$, $46.5°$, and $67.5°$ can be due to the $\{111\}$, $\{200\}$ and $\{220\}$ planes of DPtPdNC crystal, respectively. By comparing the JCPDS data of Pt (65 - 2868) and Pd (46 - 1043), each three diffraction peaks located between the corresponding peaks positions of Pt and Pd strongly evidence for the formation of alloy rather than the physical mixture of tiny Pt and Pd nanoparticles.

XPS analysis of Pt 4f and Pd 3d regions are shown in Fig. 2. The binding energies of 71. 1 eV (Fig. 2A) and 335. 6 eV (Fig. 2B) correspond to the metallic state of Pt and Pd, respectively. Compared to the binding energy values of Pd black and Pt black, Pt 4f peak shows an obvious shift towards the lower binding energy while the peak of Pd 3d slightly shifts in positive direction. These shifts were attributed to the change of the electronic structure, originating from the special heterogeneous interfaces[22] (electron in part transfer from Pd to Pt) and the defects in domains between the Pt and Pd nanoseeds in DPtPdNC.

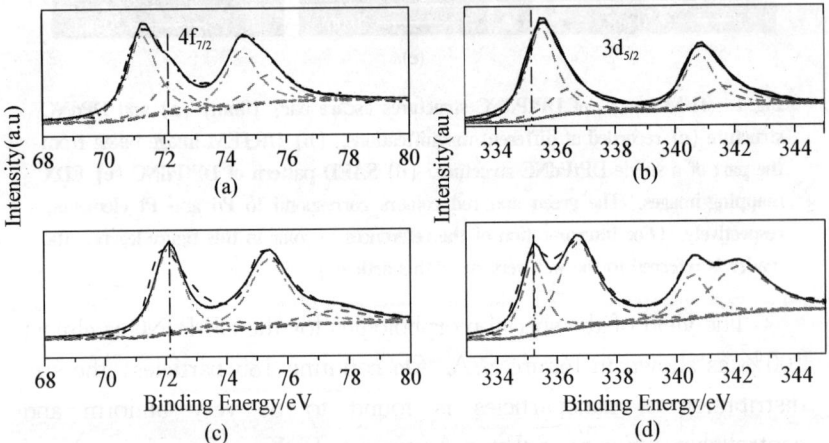

Fig. 2 XPS spectra of DPtPdNC (A) Pt 4f (B) Pd 3d (C) XPS spectrum of Pt 4f from Pt black (D) XPS spectrum of Pd 3d from Pd black.

2. 2 Catalytic Activity of Dandelion-like PtPd Nanoclusters

For examining the electrocatalytic performance of DPtPdNC,

electrochemical measurements were carried out in N_2-purged 0. 1 M KOH solution as shown in Figure S4. As well known, the electrochemically active surface areas (ECSAs) provide important information regarding the available electrochemically active sites, which is essential for evaluating the electrocatalytic activity. ECSAs for four different modified GCEs were obtained from current peak of metal oxide reduction, assuming 0. 405 mC cm^{-2} for the reduction of a monolayer of PdO on the catalyst surface[23] and 0. 210 mC cm^{-2} for the reduction of a monolayer of PtO, after subtracting the double-layer correction. As shown in Table S1, DPtPdNC and DPdNC exhibit large ECSAs, owing to their relatively unique subunits less than 5 nm in branches and highly open nanotunnels, which could be expected to have a significant percentage of atoms on the exposure surface. As an effective way, branching improves the specific surface area of the catalysts [20]. Consequently, the as-synthesized DPtPdNC offer two advantages over previously reported common nanostructures: a) The branches composed of nanoseeds have abundant surface atoms of Pt and Pd; b) As-prepared nanocomposites possessing numerous nanotunnels are beneficial to the molecular kinetic and exposure of inside electrocatalytic sites, further amplifying the synergistic effect from the strong electronic interaction of Pt and Pd. (Fig. 3).

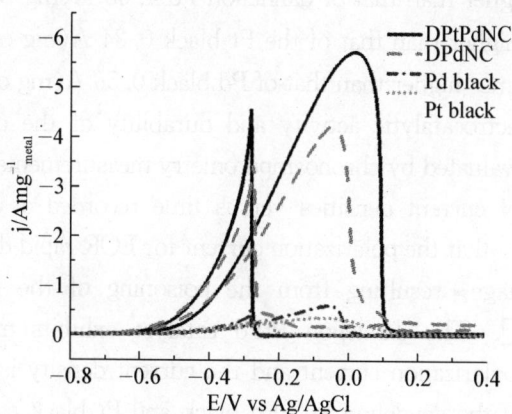

(A)

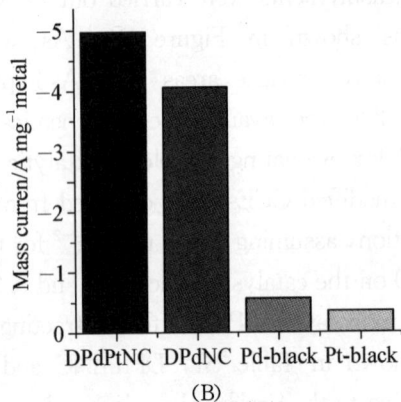

(B)

Fig. 3. (A) CVs of DPtPdNC, home-made DPdNC, Pd black, Pt black catalyst at 50 mV s^{-1} in 0.5 M NaOH containing 1.0 M ethanol. (B) Mass activity specific activity recorded at-0.1V vs Ag/AgCl.

Therefore, it can be estimated that the rich edges and corner atoms derived from the branches formed by unique nanoseeds structures, contribute to the superior merit for enhancing ethanol catalytic activity. Clearly, the mass current density at-0.1V of DPtPdNC in the positive direction sweep 4.95 A(mg of metal)$^{-1}$ is ~ 1.2 times higher than that of dandelion Pd 4.03 A(mg of metal)$^{-1}$, ~14 times higher than that of the Pt black 0.34 A(mg of metal)$^{-1}$, and ~8.8 times higher than that of Pd black 0.56 A(mg of metal)$^{-1}$.

The electrocatalytic activity and durability of the catalysts for EOR were evaluated by chronoamperometry measurements. In Fig. 4, the curves of current densities versus time recorded at-0.15 V for 10000 s show that the polarization current for EOR rapid decline at the beginning stage, resulting from the poisoning of the intermediate species [24]. The dandelion PtPd catalyst exhibits much slower decrease of polarization current and the current density is still higher than those of the dandelion Pd, Pd black and Pt black catalysts over the entire time scale.

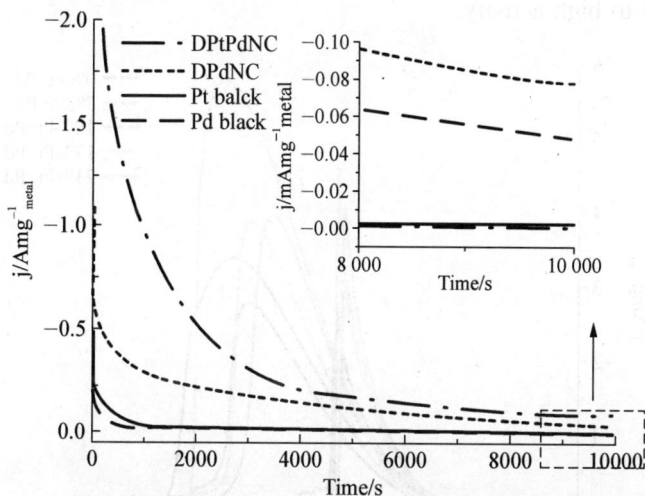

Fig. 4 Current-time curves of ethanol oxidation reactions at-0. 15 V (vs.
Ag/AgCl) in 0. 5 M NaOH containing 1. 0 M ethanol. Insert figure: the
magnified curves between 8000 ~ 10000 s.

2. 3 *Tuning Atomic Composition*

It should be mentioned that the different mole ratios of the Pt and
Pd to form the bimetallic DPtPdNC were also closely investigated.
With the increase of platinum content, the oxidation potential of
ethanol at the corresponding DPtPdNC modified GCE is more negative
as seen in Fig. 5. Interestingly, a suitable loading Pt such as 7%
decorated into 93% Pd branches demonstrates an optimum activity
towards EOR compare to other catalysts. High electrocatalytic
performance with such low loading Pt could be ascribed to the effective
utilization of both the exterior and interior surfaces of the dandelion
structure [25]. The possible mechanism is tentatively described that
the more Pt and Pd heterogeneous interfaces in exposure should be
dependent on the due ratio of Pt and Pd because of easier reduction of

Pd ions (0. 591 V vs. SHE) than Pt ions (0. 775 V vs. SHE), leading to high activity.

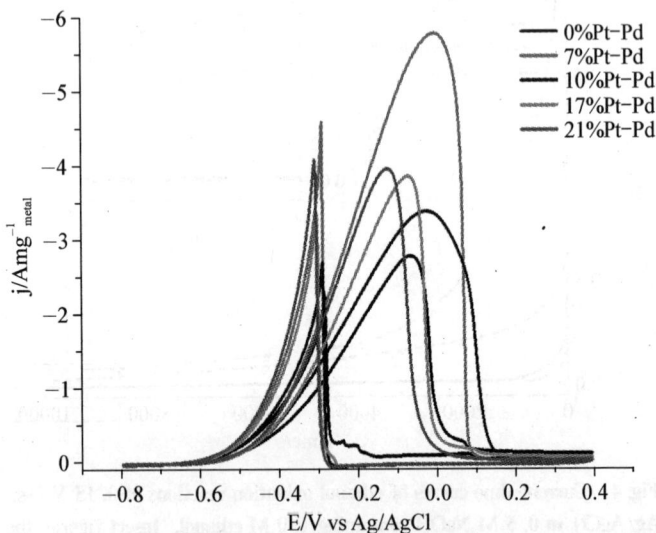

Fig. 5   CVs of DPtPdNC with different percentage of Pt (from ICP) at 50 mV s⁻¹ in 0. 5 M NaOH containing 1. 0 M ethanol.

Based on this study, the formation of dandelion-like PtPd nanostructure with the assistance of HDPCl could be reproducible [26] under certain temperature such as herein 40 ℃. Not only that, but the morphology of the nanostructures could be varying the concentration of the HDPCl aqueous solution [27] as well as the size of the DPtPdNC may be tunable by varying the concentration of ascorbic acid [28]in future work.

3. Experimental Section

3. 1 *Materials*

Hexachloroplatinic (Ⅳ) acid hexahydrate ($H_2PtCl_6 \cdot 6H_2O$) and Hexadecylpyridinium chloride monohydrate (HDPCl, $\geqslant$99. 0%)

were purchased from Sinopharm Chemical Reagent (China). Sodium tetrachloropalladate (Ⅱ) (Na_2PdCl_3, 99. 995%), L-ascorbicacid (AA, >99. 0%), Pd black, and Pt black were obtained from Sigma-Aldrich. All the chemicals and reagents were used as received. Ultrapure water (18. 2 MΩ cm) was used throughout the experiments.

3. 2 *Synthesis of Dandelion PtPd Nanoclusters*

In synthesis of dandelion PtPd nanoclusters (DPtPdNC), 10 mL aqueous solution containing 15 mM Na_2PdCl_4, 15 mM H_2PtCl_6 and 30 mg HDPCl was added in a 25 mL beaker. After homogeneously mixing, 0. 6 mL 0. 1 M AA was quickly injected under stirring. And then the resulting mixture was kept undisturbed at 40 ℃ for 4 h. During the reaction, the color of the solution changed from brownish yellow to black. After reaction finished, the final product was centrifuged at 15,000 rpm for 10 min and washed with ultrapure water several times to remove the residual soft templates.

3. 3 *Characterization*

TEM and HRTEM images were taken by a JEOL JEM-2000 FX operated at 200 kV equipped with energy dispersive spectrometer. UV-vis absorption spectra were collected using a 760-CRT double beam UV-vis spectrophotometer (Shanghai Precision and Scientific Instrument Co., Ltd). X-ray photoelectron spectroscopy (PHI 5000 VersaProbe) was performed to identify the chemical composition of the surface of the observed nanocomposites. The metals amount in nanoparticles were determined with inductively coupled plasma-atomic emission spectroscopy (ICP-AES, Varian VISTA-MPX) and the sample structure was determined by X-ray diffraction (Rigacu D/Max-2000, monochromatic Cu Kα radiation).

3. 4 *Electrochemical Measurement*

The electrochemical experiments were carried out using a

CHI660D potentiostat (Shanghai Chenhua Instrumental Co. , Ltd. , China) at room temperature in a conventional three-electrode cell, consisting of a modified glass carbon electrode (GCE) (3 mm in diameter) as a working electrode, an Ag/AgCl (in 3 M KCl solution) as the reference electrode, and a platinum wire serving as a counter electrode. The GCEs were respectively coated with 10 μL of DPtPdNC, dandelion Pd nanoclusters, Pd black and Pt black at same mole, and dried at 4 ℃. Ethanol oxidation reaction (EOR) measurements were performed in a solution of 0. 5 M NaOH containing 1. 0 M C_2H_5OH at a scan rate of 50 mV s^{-1}. Mass current densities were normalized by the loaded metal amounts which were determined by ICP.

4. Conclusions

In summary, we have developed a controllable soft template-based synthesis of dandelion-like PtPd nanostructures in high yields by reduction of metal precursor with ascorbic acid. Furthermore, the bimetallic dandelion nanoparticles with several branches constructed by relatively unique seeds produce huge ECSAs, providing abundant active sites for catalysis. The DPtPdNC exhibited a much higher catalytic activity for EOR attributed to the Pt and Pd synergistic effect and exposing heterogeneous interfaces. The proposed synthesis method demonstrated a facile and efficient approach for the development of high-performance catalysts for fuel cells.

Acknowledgements

This work is supported by the National Natural Science Foundation of China (No. 21475088), PCSIRT (IRT1269) and International Joint Laboratory on Resource Chemistry (IJLRC), Shanghai Key Laboratory of Rare Earth Functional Materials, and Shanghai Municipal Education Committee Key Laboratory of Molecular Imaging Probes and Sensors.

Appendix A. Supplementary data

Supplementary data associated with this article can be found, in the online version, at http://dx. doi. org/10. 1016/j. apcatb. 2015. 01. 205.

References

[1] W. X. Du, Q. Wang, D. Saxner, N. A. Deskins, D. Su, J. E. Krzanowski, A. I. Frenkel, X. W. Teng, Highly active iridium/iridium-tin/tin oxide heterogeneous nanoparticles as alternative electrocatalysts for the ethanol oxidation reaction, J. Am. Chem. Soc. 133 (2011) 15172 – 15183.

[2] M. Z. F. Kamarudin, S. K. Kamarudin, M. S. Masdar, W. R. W. Daud, Review: Direct ethanol fuel cells, Int. J. Hydrogen Energ 38 (2013) 9438 – 9453.

[3] B. Lim, M. Jiang, P. H. Camargo, E. C. Cho, J. Tao, X. M. Lu, Y. M. Zhu, Y. N. Xia, Pd-Pt bimetallic nanodendrites with high activity for oxygen reduction, Science 324 (2009) 1302 – 1305.

[4] Y. J. Kang, X. C. Ye, J. Chen, Y. Cai, R. E. Diaz, R. R. Adzic, E. A. Stach, C. B. Murray, Design of Pt-Pd binary superlattices exploiting shape effects and synergistic effects for oxygen reduction reactions, J. Am. Chem. Soc 135 (2013) 42 – 45.

[5] H. J. You, F. L. Zhang, Z. Liu, J. X. Fang, Free-Standing Pt-Au Hollow Nanourchins with Enhanced Activity and Stability for Catalytic Methanol Oxidation, ACS Catalysis 4 (2014) 2829 – 2835.

[6] B. Y. Xia, H. B. Wu, X. Wang, X. W. Lou, One-pot synthesis of cubic PtCu₃ nanocages with enhanced electrocatalytic activity for the methanol oxidation reaction, J. Am. Chem. Soc 134 (2012) 13934 – 13937.

[7] S. I. Choi, S. Xie, M. Shao, J. H. Odell, N. Lu, H. C. Peng, L. Protsailo, S. Guerrero, J. Park, X. H. Xia, J. G. Wang, M. J. Kim, Y. N. Xia, Synthesis and characterization of 9 nm Pt-Ni octahedra with a record high activity of 3. 3 A/mg(Pt) for the oxygen reduction reaction, Nano lett. 13 (2013) 3420 – 3425.

[8] Y. Zhang, M. Janyasupab, C. W. Liu, X. X. Li, J. Q. Xu, C. C. Liu, Three Dimensional PtRh Alloy Porous Nanostructures: Tuning the Atomic Composition and Controlling the Morphology for the Application of Direct

Methanol Fuel Cells, Adv. Funct. Mater. 22 (2012) 3570 - 3575.

[9] H. Zhang, M. S. Jin, Y. N. Xia, Enhancing the catalytic and electrocatalytic properties of Pt-based catalysts by forming bimetallic nanocrystals with Pd, Chem. Soc. Rev. 41 (2012) 8035 - 8049.

[10] A. X. Yin, X. Q. Min, Y. W. Zhang, C. H. Yan, Shape-selective synthesis and facet-dependent enhanced electrocatalytic activity and durability of monodisperse sub-10 nm Pt-Pd tetrahedrons and cubes, J. Am. Chem. Soc. 133 (2011) 3816 - 3819.

[11] C. Zhu, S. Guo, S. Dong, Rapid, general synthesis of PdPt bimetallic alloy nanosponges and their enhanced catalytic performance for ethanol/methanol electrooxidation in an alkaline medium, Chemistry-A European Journal, 19 (2013) 1104 - 1111.

[12] H. Zhang, Y. Yin, Y. Hu, C. Li, P. Wu, S. Wei, C. Cai, Pd@Pt Core-Shell Nanostructures with Controllable Composition Synthesized by a Microwave Method and Their Enhanced Electrocatalytic Activity toward Oxygen Reduction and Methanol Oxidation, J. Phys. Chem. C 114 (2010) 11861 - 11867.

[13] Z. M. Peng, H. Yang, Synthesis and Oxygen Reduction Electrocatalytic Property of Pt-on-Pd Bimetallic Heteronanostructures, J. Am. Chem. Soc. 131 (2009) 7542 - 7543.

[14] N. Tian, Z. Y. Zhou, N. F. Yu, L. Y. Wang, S. G. Sun, Direct Electrodeposition of Tetrahexahedral Pd Nanocrystals with High-Index Facets and High Catalytic Activity for Ethanol Electrooxidation, J. Am. Chem. Soc. 132 (2010) 7580 - 7581.

[15] Y. Lu, Y. Jiang, W. Chen, Graphene nanosheet-tailored PtPd concave nanocubes with enhanced electrocatalytic activity and durability for methanol oxidation, Nanoscale, 6 (2014)3309 - 3315.

[16] Y. Wang, S. I. Choi, X. Zhao, S. F. Xie, H. C. Peng, M. Chi, C. Z. Huang, Y. N. Xia, Polyol Synthesis of Ultrathin Pd Nanowires via Attachment-Based Growth and Their Enhanced Activity towards Formic Acid Oxidation, Adv. Funct. Mater. 24 (2014) 131 - 139.

[17] Y. T. Yu, B. Q. Xu, Shape-controlled synthesis of Pt nanocrystals: an evolution of the tetrahedral shape, Appl. Organometal. Chem. 20 (2006) 638 - 647.

[18] W. Liu, P. Rodriguez, L. Borchardt, A. Foelske, J. P. Yuan, A. K. Herrmann, D. Geiger, Z. K. Zheng, S. Kaskel, N. Gaponik, R. Kätz, T. J. Schmidt, A. Eychmüller, Bimetallic aerogels: high-performance electrocatalysts

for the oxygen reduction reaction, Angew. Chem. Int. Ed. 52 (2013) 9849 –
9852.

[19] X. Q. Huang, Y. J. Li, Y. J. Li, H. L. Zhou, X. F. Duan, Y. Huang,
Synthesis of PtPd bimetal nanocrystals with controllable shape, composition,
and their tunable catalytic properties, Nano lett. 12 (2012) 4265 – 4270.

[20] L. Wang, Y. Nemoto, Y. Yamauchi, Direct synthesis of spatially-controlled
Pt-on-Pd bimetallic nanodendrites with superior electrocatalytic activity, J.
Am. Chem. Soc. 133 (2011) 9674 – 9677.

[21] L. Wang, Y. Yamauchi, Metallic Nanocages: Synthesis of Bimetallic Pt-Pd
Hollow Nanoparticles with Dendritic Shells by Selective Chemical Etching, J.
Am. Chem. Soc. 135 (2013) 16762 – 16765.

[22] L. X. Ding, C. L. Liang, H. Xu, A. L. Wang, Y. X. Tong, G. R. Li,
Porous Hollow Nanorod Arrays Composed of Alternating Pt and Pd
Nanocrystals with Superior Electrocatalytic Activity and Durability for Methanol
Oxidation, Adv. Mater. Interfaces 1 (2014) 1400005. .

[23] Z. Zhang, K. L. More, K. Sun, Z. Wu, W. Li, Preparation and
Characterization of PdFe Nanoleaves as Electrocatalysts for Oxygen Reduction
Reaction, Chem. Mater. 23 (2011) 1570 – 1577.

[24] X. Chen, Z. Cai, X. Chen, M. Oyama, Green synthesis of graphene-PtPd
alloy nanoparticles with high electrocatalytic performance for ethanol oxidation,
J. Mate. Chem. A 2 (2014) 315 – 320.

[25] M. M. Liu, Y. Z. Lu, W. Chen, PdAg Nanorings Supported on Graphene
Nanosheets: Highly Methanol-Tolerant Cathode Electrocatalyst for Alkaline
Fuel Cells, Adv. Funct. Mater. 23 (2013) 1289 – 1296.

[26] F. Ksar, G. K. Sharma, F. Audonnet, P. Beaunier, H. Remita, Palladium
urchin-like nanostructures and their H_2 sorption properties, Nanotechnology,
22 (2011) 305609.

[27] S. J. Ye, D. Y. Kim, S. W. Kang, K. W. Choi, S. W. Han, O. O. Park,
Synthesis of chestnut-bur-like palladium nanostructures and their enhanced
electrocatalytic activities for ethanol oxidation, Nanoscale, 6 (2014) 4182 – 4187.

[28] X. Q. Huang, Y. J. Li, Y. Chen, E. Zhou, Y. X. Xu, H. L. Zhou, X. F.
Duan, Y. Huang, Palladium-Based Nanostructures with Highly Porous
Features and Perpendicular Pore Channels as Enhanced Organic Catalysts,
Angew. Chem. Int. Ed 52 (2013) 2520 – 2524.

Highly Sensitive Naphthalimide-Based Fluorescence Polarization Probe for Detecting Cancer Cells

Ti Jia, Congying Fu, Chusen Huang,
Haotian Yang, and Nengqin Jia

The Education Ministry Key Laboratory of Resource Chemistry and Shanghai Key Laboratory of Rare Earth Functional Materials, Department of Chemistry, College of Life and Environmental Sciences, Shanghai Normal University

■ INTRODUCTION

The past decades have witnessed significant advances in fluorescence based sensing technology including development of new fluorescence sensing mechanism and measurement instrumentation. [1, 2] Fluorescence sensing technology has been viewed as a powerful and versatile toolbox in the fleld of physiology and molecular biology, environmental monitoring and clinical diagnosis with the advantage of high selectivity and sensitivity, spatiotemporal resolution, and visibility. [2-5] However, the fluorescence intensity based assay might be interfered with by some environmental factors such pH changes, fluorescence self-quenching, and large background signal. Thus, self-calibration should be required for improving the accuracy and reliability of the fluorescence sensing technology. Recently, two major self-referencing approaches including the fluorescence ratiometric method[6] and lifetime detection[7-10] were developed for overcoming the obstacles of fluorescence intensity based assay, which makes the detection sufficiently reliable. Despite these efforts, rapid, simple, and convenient self-referencing fluorescence detection techniques are still urgently needed especially for cancer diagnosis. [6, 11-13]

Fluorescence polarization (FP) measurement is another self-referencing fluorescence sensing technology. Because the polarization value (P) is deflned as the ratio of fluorescence intensities parallel ($I_{//}$) and perpendicular ($I_{\perp}$) with respect to plane-polarized excitation light (eq 1, detailed information, please see ref 14), the fluorescence polarization-based signal is less dependent on dye concentration and environmental interference, which makes FP measurement an attractive alternative to fluorescence intensity-based detection. [15, 16] Mean-while, FP assay is a "mix and measure" technique without separation of the free and bound ligands, which make FP more convenient for real-time monitoring of the dynamic changes of biomacromolecules including membrane lipid mobility, [17-19] DNA-protein and protein-protein interactions, [20, 21] and folding of G-quadruplex motif, [22] as well as the hyaluronidase activity[23] at the molecular level. [24-26] Apart from detection of biomacromolecules, recent years have also witnessed substantial progress in aptamer based fluorescence polarization measure-ment in determining small molecules such as Ochratoxin A, [27, 28] ATP, [29-31] adenosine, and adenosine monophosphate, [32] as well as L-tyrosinamide. [33, 34]

$$p = \frac{I_{\parallel} - GI_{\perp}}{I_{\parallel} + GI_{\perp}} \qquad G = I_{HV}/I_{HH} \qquad (1)$$

Table 1. Lifetime and Photostability of Naphthalimide-Based BIO Compared to Other Fluorescent Dyes

	fluorescein dyes	rhodamine dyes	cyanine dyes	BODIRY dyes	naphthalimide dyes	BIO
lifetime(ns)	4^a	$2-4^a$	1^a	6^b	$7-8^c$	6.26^d
photostability	low^e	low^e	low^b	relatively high^f	relatively high^e	relatively high

	fluorescein dyes	rhodamine dyes	cyanine dyes	BODIRY dyes	naphthalimide dyes	BIO
used in fluorescence polarization assay	common	common	rare	common	rare	this work

[a] Refs 35, 36. [b] Ref 37. [c] Ref 38. [d] Data was acquired by single-photon counting technique (detailed information in Supporting Information). [e] Ref 49. [f] Ref 52.

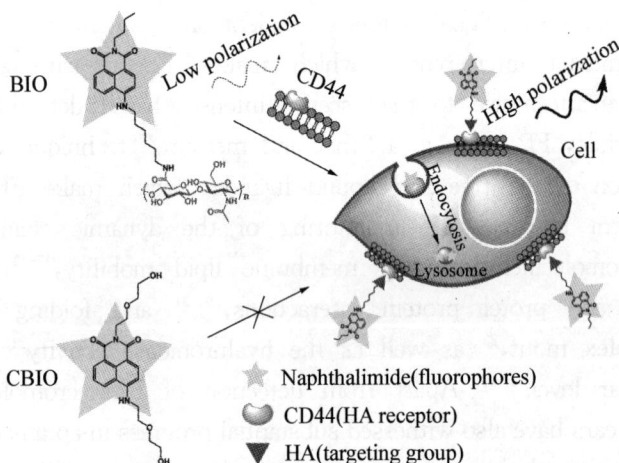

Figure 1 **Illustration of fluorescence polarization probe BIO in the detection of CD44 in situ on cell membranes and intracellular transport CD44 via endocytosis.**

However, most of these fluorescence polarization probes were constructed by introducing fluorescein (or its derivatives such as FAM, a commercially available dye), rhodamine, and cyanine dyes, which have relatively short excited-state lifetimes (less than 4 ns)[35, 36] compared to BODIPY and naphthalimide dyes (lifetimes of naphthalimide and BODIPY dyes were above 6 ns, Table 1).[37, 38] In addition, the longer excited-state lifetimes of BODIPY and naphthalimide dyes could make the signal of fluorescence polarization more sensitive to binding interactions over a larger molecular weight range.[37] Some BODIPY based fluorescence polarization probes have been used for detection of biological samples,[39-42] but the naphthalimide-based fluorescence polarization probes are still rarely investigated in the biological assay (Table 1). Furthermore, most fluorescence polarization probes for cancer diagnosis were mainly based on determination of concentration of biomarker in cancer cells. There are only a few fluorescence polarization probes developed for direct detection of cancer cells.[43-45] Due to the significant role of direct capture of cancer cells, especially in circulating tumor cell (CTC) detection, development of a sensitive and convenient approach for direct detection of cancer cells will contribute to the potential clinical utilization in early cancer diagnosis.[46, 47] Herein, a first naphthalimidebased fluorescence polarization probe was designed and synthesized for sensitive and direct detection of cancer cells.

The working principle of this naphthalimide-based fluo-rescence polarization technology is illustrated in Figure 1. The cancer cell-target fluorescence polarization probe (BIO) was prepared from 4-amino-1,8-naphthalimide dye and chemically modified hyaluronic acid (HA). Considering the longer excited-state lifetimes and greater photostability of naphthalimidecompared with fluorescein and rhodamine dyes,[38, 48, 49] the 4-amino-1,8-naphthalimide was introduced into BIO to emit the fluorescence polarization signal. At the same time, we have chosen HA as a specific ligand for direct targeting of cancer cells because HA serves as a key signaling molecule in regulating cancer metastasis through the interaction with CD44 (a HA receptor), and the overexpressed CD44 is closely related to cancerous angiogenesis and other types of tumor progression. Consequently, the increase in the fluorescence polarization signal of BIO will become remarkable only upon capturing the target cancer cells. Compared to other current technologies for detection of cancer cells, BIO contains the following advantages: (a) the fluorescence polarization signal from BIO is a self-referencing signal which could not be interfered with by environment

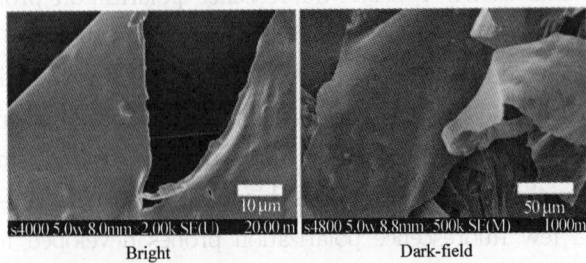

Bright   Dark-field

a

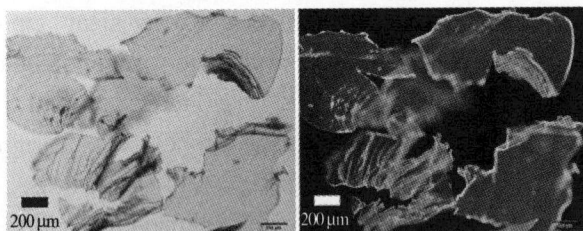

b

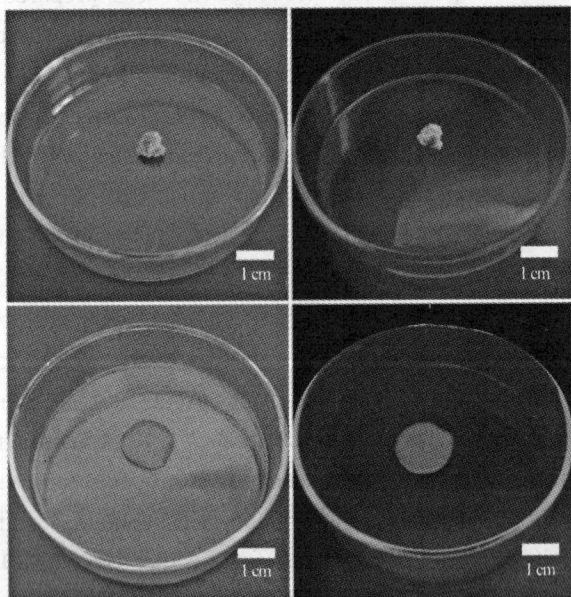

c

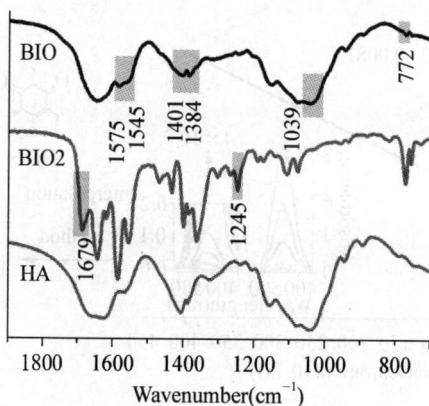

d

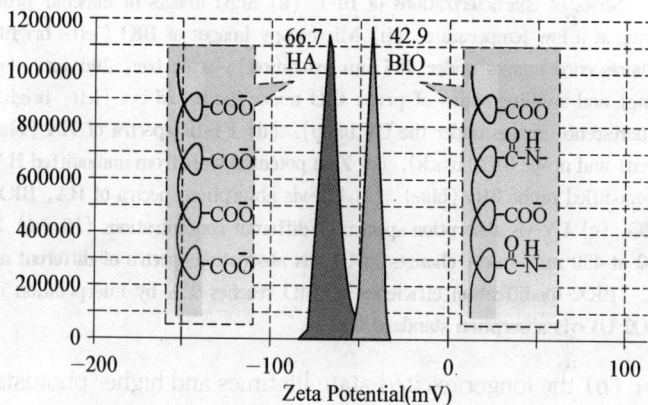

e

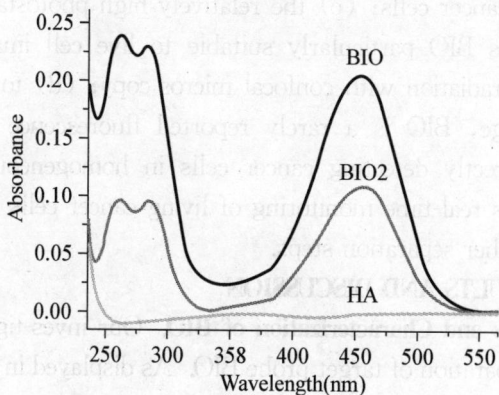

f

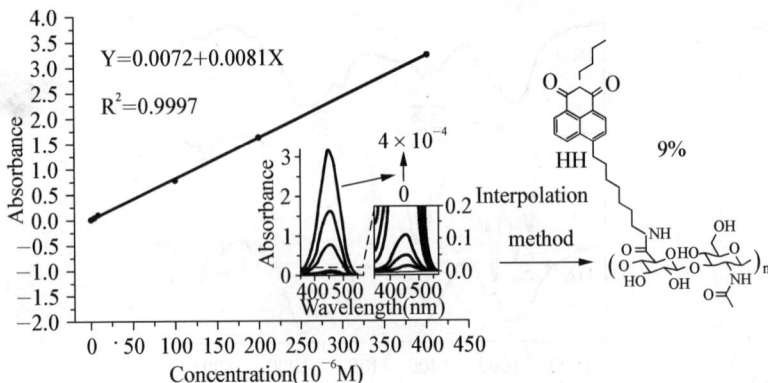

Figure 2　Series of characterizations of BIO. (a) SEM images of lamellar probe BIO after drying at a low temperature. (b) Microscopy images of BIO (left: bright field, right: fluorescence images under 405 nm exictation), scale bar, 200 μm. (c) Dry (shrinking) and swelling status of probe BIO under the naked eye (left: bright field, right: fluorescence images under the UV lamp). (d) FT-IR spectra of HA (blue) and BIO2 (red) and probe BIO (black). (e) Zeta potential shift from unmodiffed IIA (red) to BIO2-modifled probe BIO (blue). (f) UV-vis absorption spectra of HA, BIO2, and probe BIO. (g) UV-vis absorption spectra of different concentrations ($(0-4) \times 10^{-4}$ M) BIO2 at 450 nm. Inset: changes in UV-vis absorption spectra of different amounts of BIO2. (BIO2-modiffcation efficiency of BIO reaches 9% by interpolation analysis upon BIO2 UV-vis absorption standard line.)

factors; (b) the longer excited-state lifetimes and higher photostability of 4-amino-1,8-naphthalimide makes BIO more sensitive and accurate in detecting cancer cells; (c) the relatively high photostable naphthalimide makes BIO particularly suitable to live cell imaging under continuous irradiation with confocal micros-copy; (d) to the best of our knowledge, BIO is a rarely reported fluorescence polarization probe for directly detecting cancer cells in homogeneous solution, which enables real-time monitoring of living cancer cells without cell lysis and further separation steps.

■ **RESULTS AND DISCUSSION**

Synthesis and Characterization of BIO. Our inves-tigation began with the preparation of target probe BIO. As displayed in Scheme S1,

N-butyl-4-(6'-aminohexyl) amino-1, 8-naphthalimide (BIO2) was initially prepared through a facile procedure. [50, 51] Then BIO was prepared by conjugation of BIO2 and HA through the amide bond. The chemical structures of BIO were characterized by IR (Figure 2d), zeta potential, and UV-vis spectra (Figure 2f). The peaks at 1545 and 1384 cm^{-1} can be attributed to the N-H and C-N bands in the amide bond of BIO, and the strength of the peak at 772 cm^{-1} of BIO decreased compared with that of BIO2, which was ascribed to the disappearance of the primary amine of BIO2 through the formation of an amide bond. The peak at 1039 cm^{-1} is from the HA (Figure 2d). Similarly, the zeta potential of BIO was-42. 9 mV which is relatively positive compared to that of HA (-66. 7 mV, Figure 2e), because some of the carboxylic acids in HA were replaced by amine groups of BIO2 through the formation of amide bonds. A maximum absorption at about 450 nm appeared in the UV-vis spectra of BIO also suggesting that BIO2 was successfully conjugated to HA. Furthermore, through the interpolation analysis based on the UV-vis absorption standard line, we observed that the BIO2 modiflcation efficiency of BIO reaches 9%. All these results suggest that BIO was successfully synthesized. Meanwhile, the morphology of BIO was also investigated in both solid state and water solution. Transmission electron microscopy (TEM) images reveal a lamellar structure in the dry form (Figure 2a), which also emitted yellow fluorescence at 405 nm excitation under microscopy (Figure 2b). After BIO was added into water, it swelled and became water-soluble. The water solubility of BIO makes it suitable for further application in biological samples under physiological conditions. Meanwhile, DLS (dynamic light scattering) analysis of BIO in water solution suggested that the hydrodynamic diameter of BIO was centered at 634. 8 nm (Figure S2), and no other peak was observed in DLS analysis, indicating a pure BIO in water solution.

Fluorescence Lifetime of BIO and Cell Viability. Then, by using the single-photon counting technique (Edinburgh FL 900, detailed procedure in Supporting Information), the fluorescence lifetime of BIO was determined to be 6. 26 ns (Table 1). Compared with fluorescein, rhodamine, and cyanine dyes, the naphthalimide-modiffed BIO displayed a relatively longer lifetime, which was beneflcial for sensitive detection of HeLa cells through changes of the fluorescence polarization signal.

The cell cytotoxicity of BIO was also tested by MTT using a standard methyl thiazolyl tetrazolium (MTT) assay. During the concentration between 0 and 150 μg mL^{-1}, BIO exhibited no cell cytotoxicity (Figure S3) when the incubation time was 12 h. Even as the incubation time extends to 24 h, there was no obviously decrease in cell viability (Figure S3). All these results suggested that BIO could be used in the biological samples, especially for the detection of live cells.

Fluorescence Polarization Response of BIO to HeLa Cells. Next, we investigated the fluorescence polarization sensing behavior of BIO toward HeLa cells. Initially, pH titration was conducted in water. As shown in Figure S1, no signiflcant difference in fluorescence of BIO was observed over the pH range of 6. 5 - 10. Thus, a PBS buffer (pH 7. 4, containing 1% DMSO) was chosen as the test medium. Then, we tested the effect of BIO concentration on the fluorescence polarization assay. As indicated in Figure 3a, 14. 56 μg mL^{-1} of BIO was conducive to fluorescence polarization assay. If the concentration of BIO was higher or lower, the sensitivity of the fluorescence polarization signal would be decreased. Thus, 14. 56 μg mL^{-1} of BIO was used in the following assay. To obtain the optimal incubation time of interaction between BIO and HeLa cells, the dynamic changes of the fluorescence polarization signal of BIO were recorded through continuous observation. As displayed in Figure 3b, after 10^5 cells mL^{-1} of HeLa cells were added into PBS buffer containing 14. 56 μg mL^{-1} of BIO, the fluorescence polarization signal changed quickly within 15 min and then reached a plateau after 25 min. This result demonstrated

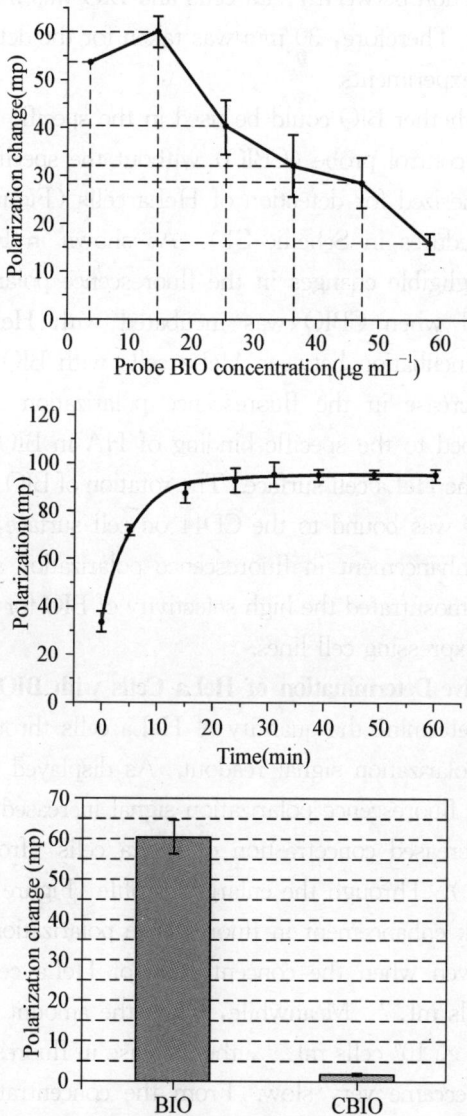

Figure 3 (a) Concentration effect of fluorescence polarization probe BIO on the polarization assay. The amount of detected target HeLa cells is 10^5 cells mL^{-1}. (b) Time correlation dynamics curve of fluorescence polarization probe BIO (14. 56 μg mL^{-1}) for HeLa cells (10^5 cells mL^{-1}). (c) Fluorescence polarization response of BIO and control probe CBIO for HeLa cells (10^5 cells mL^{-1})

that the interaction between HeLa cells and BIO was nearly complete within 25 min. Therefore, 30 min was taken for the detection time in the following experiments.

To test whether BIO could be used in the specific recognition of HeLa cells, a control probe (CBIO) without the specific HA ligand was also synthesized for detection of HeLa cells (Figure 1, detailed synthetic procedures in Scheme S1). As shown in Figure 4c and Figure S4, negligible changes in the fluorescence polarization signal were observed when CBIO was incubated with HeLa cells. By contrast, the incubation between HeLa cells with BIO resulted in a remarkable increase in the fluorescence polarization signal, which could be ascribed to the speciflc binding of HA in BIO to the CD44 expressed on the HeLa cell surface. The rotation of BIO might become slow after BIO was bound to the CD44 on cell surface, which could result in an enhancement in fluorescence polarization signal. These results also demosntrated the high selectivity of BIO for determination of CD44-overexpressing cell lines.

Quantitative Determination of HeLa Cells with BIO. Then, BIO was used to determine the quantity of HeLa cells through the direct fluorescence polarization signal readout. As displayed in Figure 4a, the changes in fluorescence polarization signal increased upon gradual addition of increased concetra-tion of HeLa cells (from 0 to 1×10^6 cells mL^{-1}). Through the enlarged profile (Figure 4a, inset), a clear and quick enhancement in fluorescence polarization signal could be obtained even when the concentration of HeLa cells fell below 2.5×10^2 cells mL^{-1}. Meanwhile, when the amount of HeLa cells increased to 1×10^6 cells mL^{-1}, the increase in fluorescence polariz-ation signal beccame very slow. From the concentration-dependent fluorescence polarization changes, the limit of detection (LOD) of BIO for HeLa cells was about 85 cells mL^{-1} (S/N=3). Additionally, we take the logarithm of fluorescence polarization changes and concentration of HeLa cells, which was deflned as ($\log(\Delta)$ and log

a

b

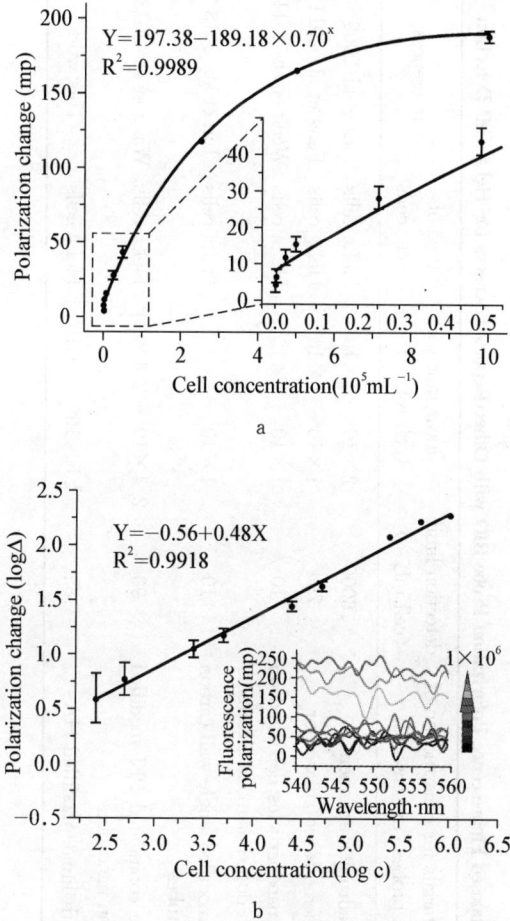

Figure 4　Quantitative analysis of the HeLa cells using fluorescence polarization assay based on BIO (14. 56 μg mL^{-1}). (a) Fluorescence polarization response of BIO to different concentration of HeLa cells (($0-1$) $\times$ 10^6 cells mL^{-1}). Inset: Enlarged profile of fluorescence polarization changes depending on low concentration of HeLa cells (($0-5$) $\times$ 10^4 cells mL^{-1}). (b) Logarithmic behavior of fluorescence polarization changes with different concentration of HeLa cells. Inset: fluorescence polarization response of BIO for different amounts of HeLa cells (($0-1$) $\times$ 10^6 cells mL^{-1}). Error bar represents s. d.

Table 2. Comparisons of the Proposed Fluorescence Polarization Probe BIO with Other Reported Sensors for HeLa Cell Detection

detection technique	materials for construction of probes (or sensors)	detection limit (cell mL^{-1})	linear range (cell mL^{-1})	type of cancer cells	references
chemiluminescence	G-quadruplex aptamers	6000	$2 \times 10^3 - 6 \times 10^5$	HeLa cells	Li et al. 2009[53]
electrochemical (impedance)	graphene based aptasensor	794	$1 \times 10^3 - 1 \times 10^6$	HeLa cells	Feng et al. 2011[54]
electrochemical (AC impedimetric approach)	gold nanoparticles deposited on boron-doped diamond electrode	10	$1 \times 10^1 - 1 \times 10^5$	HeLa cells	Weng et al. 2011[55]
electrochemical (DPV)	PEI modified single-wall carbon nanotubes	10	$1 \times 10^1 - 1 \times 10^6$	HeLa cells	Liu et al. 2013[56]
electrochemical (impedance)	folate conjugated PEI modified carbon nanotubes	90	$2.4 \times 10^2 - 2.4 \times 10^5$	HeLa cells	Wang et al. 2013[57]
fluorescence polarization	naphthalimide modified HA	85	$2.5 \times 10^2 - 1 \times 10^6$	HeLa cells	This work

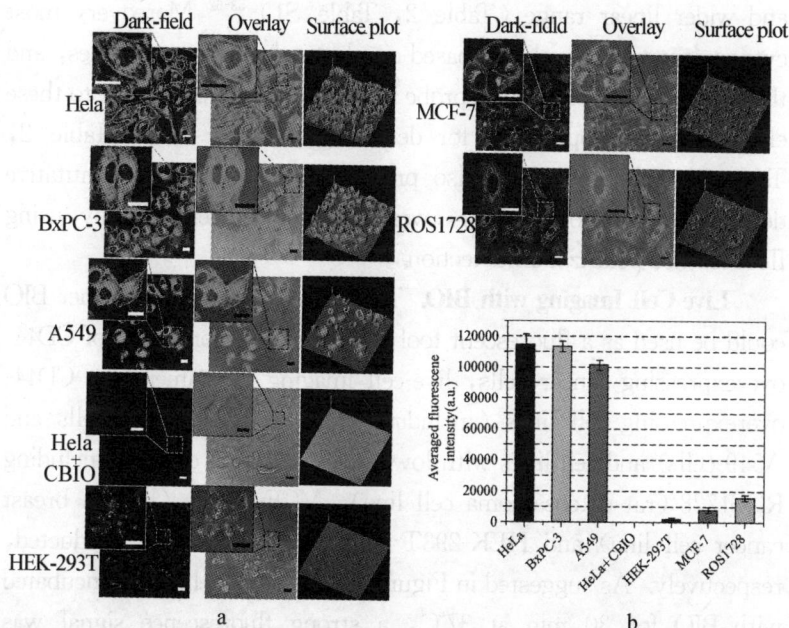

Figure 5 Live cell imaging on six types of cell lines with CD44 expression in different levels with BIO and control probe CBIO. (a) Confocal microscopy images (dark-field and overlay) of CD44-overexpressing cell lines (HeLa cells, BxPC-3 cells, and A549 cells) and cell lines with low expression of CD44 (MCF-7 cells, ROS1728 cells (rat osteosarcoma cell line), and HEK-293T cells) incubated with probe BIO, and HeLa cells incubated with control probe CBIO for 30 min at 37 ℃. (b) Histogram showing the semiquantitative calculation of averaged fluorescence intensity (FI) of each cell in the displayed images. Scale bars are 20 μm.

(c), respectively. With a linear regression by *Origin* 8. 0 software, a linear relationship between (log(Δ) and log(c) was observed (Figure 4b, $R^2 = 0.9918$). Therefore, a linear relationship between changes of fluorescence polarization signal and the concen-trations of HeLa cells (changes from 2.5×10^2 cells mL^{-1} to 1×10^6 cells mL^{-1}, Figure 4b) can be deduced. The obtained linear curve makes quantitative detection of HeLa cells very convenient over this concentration range. Compared to some of the other cytosensors for cancer cells, the probe BIO exhibited a relatively lower detection limit and wider linear range (Table 2, Table S1).[53-62] Moreover, most cytosensors were developed based on electrochemical approaches, and the fluorescence polarization probe BIO could be an alternative to these electrochemical approaches for detection of cancer cells (Table 2, Table S1). Finally, BIO also presents a platform for quantitative determination of other CD44-overexpressing cancer cells by using fluorescence polarization detection.

Live Cell Imaging with BIO. To further investigate whether BIO could be used as a fluorescent tool for visualized monitoring of CD44-overexpressing cancer cells, live-cell imaging exepriments in CD44-overexpressing cell lines (including HeLa cells, BxPC-3 cells and A549 cells) and cell lines with low-level expression of HA (including ROS1728 (rat osteosarcoma cell line), MCF-7 cells (human breast cancer cell line) and HEK-293T cells) with BIO were conducted, respectively. As suggested in Figure 5a, after the cells were incubated with BIO for 30 min at 37℃, a strong fluorescence signal was obtained in HeLa cells, BxPC-3 cells, and A549 cells upon 458 nm excitation with the confocal microscopy, while the BIO-treated ROS1728, MCF-7, and HEK-293T cells produced a relatively weak fluorescence signal. Meanwhile, treatment of HeLa cells with the control probe CBIO only leads to a negligible fluorescence signal. Additionally, through the semiquantitative calculation of averaged emission intensity in cells (Figure 5b), we can see clearly that there

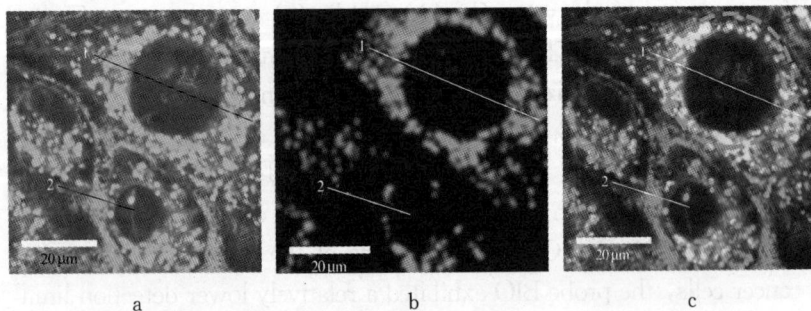

a   b   c

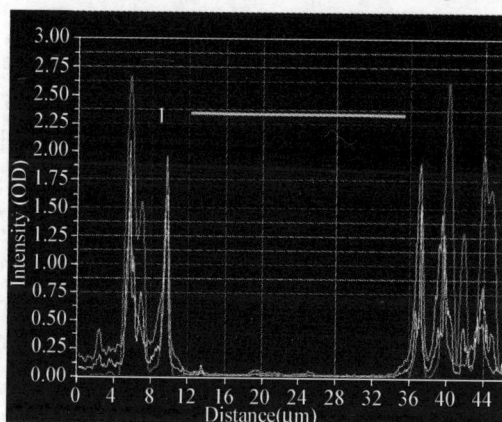

d

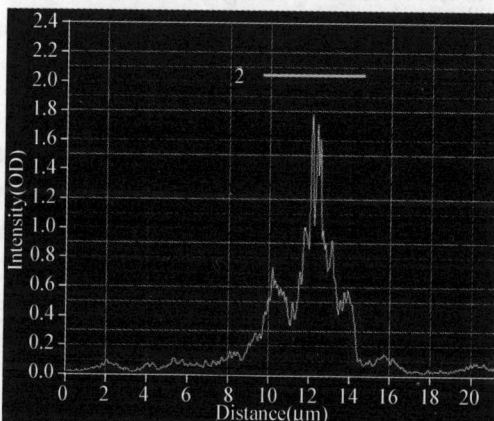

e

Figure 6 Fluorescent image of target HeLa cells co-stained with BIO and commercial lysosome-probe Red DND-99. (a) Confocal microscopy image of HeLa cells incubated with BIO (14. 56 μg mL^{-1}) (λ_{ex}=458 nm, λ_{em}=510 - 590 nm, green). (b) Confocal microscopy image of HeLa cells stained with Red DND-99(50 nM) (λ_{ex}=633 nm, λ_{em}=640 - 795 nm, red). (c) Overlay image of (a) and (b) (Pearson's correlation R_r = 0. 815 and overlap coefficient R_r = 0. 835 of lysosome colocalization in dashed circular area). (d) Intensity profile of regions of interest (ROI) (1, lysosome-location) across HeLa cells. (e) Intensity profile of regions of interest (ROI) (2, cell-membrane-location) across HeLa cells. Scale bars are 20 μm.

was an approximately 6-fold enhancement in fluorescence intensity of BIO-treated HeLa, BxPC-3, and A549 cells compared to BIO-treated ROS1728, MCF-7, and HEK-293T cells. This result demonstrated that HeLa cells, BxPC-3 cells, and A549 cells contain a high level of CD44, and there was low-level expression of ROS1728, MCF-7, and HEK-293T cells, which was partially supported by a previous study that reveals an overexprssion of CD44 on HeLa cells, BxPC-3 cells, and A549 cells and low-level expression of CD44 in ROS1728 cells, MCF-7 cells, and HEK-293T cells. [63-65] It is interesting that this result also indentifled that ROS1728 cells expressed only a little amount of CD44. There is little study revealing the expressed amount of CD44 on ROS1728, which might be potentially useful for understanding bone remodeling. [66] For the CBIO treated HeLa cells, the semiquantitative calculation of averaged emission intensity only emits a background signal, which indicated that speciflc binding of BIO to HeLa cells occurred through the specific interaction between HA of BIO and CD44 on live cells. All these results indicated that BIO was a highly selective probe for determining CD44-overexpressing HeLa cells, and this fluorecence polarization technique with BIO could be potentially used for detecting other CD44-overexpressing cancer cells.

Subcellular Distribution Study of BIO on HeLa Cells. Encouraged by the speciflc interaction of BIO with CD44-overexpressing HeLa cells, the subcellular distribution of BIO on HeLa cells was flnally investigated. As displayed in Figure 5a and Figure S5, a strong fluorescence signal mainly concentrated in the cell membrane and dot-like vesicular in cytoplasm was observed, suggesting a membrane and lysosomal localization. Then, a colo-calization experiment was performed by co-staining HeLa cells with LysoTracker Red DND-99 (a commercially available probe for speciflc staining of lysosomes). Through the fluorescence signal obtained under confocal microscopy, the subcellular localization of BIO could be visualized. As illustrated in Figure 6, a strong green fluorescecne signal was from BIO, and the red fluorescence signal was attributed to the localization of LysoTracker Red DND-99 stained lysosomes. The merged images of BIO and LysoTracker Red DND-99 stained signal showed the strong yellow fluorescence, which mainly localized in lysosomes (Figure 6a, b, c). Through the plot analysis of regions interest (ROI) across the HeLa cells (line 1 in Figure 6a, b, cd), we can observe that some of the BIO stained singal and LysoTracker Red DND-99 stained lysosomes overlapped well. This result depicted that some BIO was localized in lysosomes. Additionally, plot analysis of ROI also suggested a strong green fluorescence signal on cell membrane (line 2 in Figure 6a, b, c, e). Thus, the high selectivity of BIO for HeLa cells was mainly based on the speciflc interaction of HA of BIO with CD44 on HeLa cell membranes. Then, some BIO penetrated into HeLa cells through a CD44-mediated endocytosis and flnally localized in lysosomes. [63, 67, 68]

■ CONCLUSION

In summary, a naphthalimide-based fluorescence polarization probe (BIO) was designed and synthesized for selective and direct detection of CD44-overexpressing HeLa cells. To the best of our knowledge, BIO was the flrst naphthalimide-modiffed HA based fluorescence polarization probe for detection of cancer cells. Compared to previous fluorescein (or rhodamine)-modiffed HA based fluorescence polarization probe, BIO with the naphthalimide fluorophore embodies the relatively high photostability and longer lifetime. Through the direct readout of changes in fluorescence polarization signal of BIO, we have described a new approach for detection of CD44-overexpressing HeLa cells in no more than 25 min. Importantly, this fluorescence polarization technique permits an accurate and quantative determination of HeLa cells through the self-referencing fluorescence polarization signal. This fluorescence polarization based technique for direct detection of cancer cells also presents potential utilization in CTC detection. Finally, the subcellular distribution of BIO on HeLa cells was investigated through the confocal microscopy assay, which could further indentify the high selectivity of BIO for cancer cells with overexpressed CD44. On the basis of BIO, a direct and real-time tool has been developed for detecting cancer cells in homogeneous solution, which enables monitoring of living cancer cells without cell lysis and further separation steps and could offer more accurate information for cancer clinical diagnosis.

■ ASSOCIATED CONTENT

* Supporting Information

Additional materials and methods. The Supporting Information is available free of charge on the ACS Publications website at DOI: 10. 1021/acsami. 5b02429.

■ AUTHOR INFORMATION

Corresponding Authors

* E-mail: huangcs@shnu. edu. cn.

* E-mail: nqjia@shnu. edu. cn.

Notes

The authors declare no competing flnancial interest.

■ ACKNOWLEDGMENTS

We thank National Natural Science Foundation of China (Grants 21302125, 21373138), Doctoral Fund of Ministry of Education of China (Grant No. 20133127120005) Program for Shanghai Sci. &. Tech. Committee (Grants 13ZR1458800, 12JC1407200), Shanghai Science and Technology Innovation Foundation for College Students.

■ ABBREVIATIONS

FP, fluorescence polarization; HA, hyaluronic acid

References

[1] Lakowicz, J. R. In *Topics in Fluorescence Spectroscopy*; Lakowicz, J. R. , Valeur, B. , Czarnik, A. W. , Eds. ; Springer, 1991; Vol. 4 ,pp1 - 68.

[2] de Silva, A. P. ; Gunaratne, H. Q. N. ; Gunnlaugsson, T. ; Huxley, A. J. M. ;

McCoy, C. P. ; Rademacher, J. T. ; Rice, T. E. Signaling Recognition Events with Fluorescent Sensors and Switches. *Chem. Rev.* 1997, *97*, 1515 – 1566.

[3] Chan, J. ; Dodani, S. C. ; Chang, C. J. Reaction-based Small-Molecule Fluorescent Probes for Chemoselective Bioimaging. *Nat. Chem.* 2012, *4*, 973 – 984.

[4] Stennett, E. M. S. ; Ciuba, M. A. ; Levitus, M. Photophysical Processes in Single Molecule Organic Fluorescent Probes. *Chem. Soc. Rev.* 2014, *43*, 1057 – 1075.

[5] Li, H. ; Fan, J. ; Peng, X. Colourimetric and Fluorescent Probes for the Optical Detection of Palladium Ions. *Chem. Soc. Rev.* 2013, *42*, 7943 – 7962.

[6] Fan, J. ; Hu, M. ; Zhan, P. ; Peng, X. Energy Transfer Cassettes Based on Organic Fluorophores: Construction and Applications in Ratiometric Sensing. *Chem. Soc. Rev.* 2013, *42*, 29 – 43.

[7] Levitt, J. A. ; Kuimova, M. K. ; Yahioglu, G. ; Chung, P. -H. ; Suhling, K. ; Phillips, D. Membrane-Bound Molecular Rotors Measure Viscosity in Live Cells via Fluorescence Lifetime Imaging. *J. Phys. Chem.* C 2009, *113*, 11634 –11642.

[8] Nie, S. ; Zare, R. N. Optical Detection of Single Molecules. *Annu. Rev. Biophys. Biomol. Struct.* 1997, *26*, 567 – 596.

[9] Barker, S. L. R. ; Clark, H. A. ; Swallen, S. F. ; Kopelman, R. ; Tsang, A. W. ; Swanson, J. A. Ratiometric and Fluorescence-Lifetime-Based Biosensors Incorporating Cytochrome c and the Detection of Extra-and Intracellular Macrophage Nitric Oxide. *Anal. Chem.* 1999, *71*, 1767 – 1772.

[10] Kuimova, M. K. ; Yahioglu, G. ; Levitt, J. A. ; Suhling, K. Molecular Rotor Measures Viscosity of Live Cells via Fluorescence Lifetime Imaging. *J. Am. Chem. Soc.* 2008, *130*, 6672 – 6673.

[11] Kucherak, O. A. ; Oncul, S. ; Darwich, Z. ; Yushchenko, D. A. ; Arntz, Y. ; Didier, P. ; Mély, Y. ; Klymchenko, A. S. Switchable Nile Red-Based Probe for Cholesterol and Lipid Order at the Outer Leaflet of Biomembranes. *J. Am. Chem. Soc.* 2010, *132*, 4907 – 4916.

[12] Rossignol, R. ; Gilkerson, R. ; Aggeler, R. ; Yamagata, K. ; Remington, S. J. ; Capaldi, R. A. Energy Substrate Modulates Mitochondrial Structure and Oxidative Capacity in Cancer Cells. *Cancer Res.* 2004, *64*, 985 – 993.

[13] Shynkar, V. V. ; Klymchenko, A. S. ; Kunzelmann, C. ; Duportail, G. ; Muller, C. D. ; Demchenko, A. P. ; Freyssinet, J. -M. ; Mely, Y. Fluorescent Biomembrane Probe for Ratiometric Detection of Apoptosis. *J. Am. Chem. Soc.* 2007, *129*, 2187 – 2193.

[14] Johnson, I. ; Spence, M. *The Molecular Probes Handbook: A Guide to Fluorescent Probes and Labeling Technologies*, 11th ed; Life Technologies Corporation, 2010; Chapter 1, pp 44 - 46.

[15] Jameson, D. M. ; Ross, J. A. Fluorescence Polarization/Anisotropy in Diagnostics and Imaging. *Chem. Rev.* 2010, *110*, 2685 - 2708.

[16] Checovich, W. J. ; Bolger, R. E. ; Burke, T. Fluorescence Polarization-A New Tool for Cell and Molecular Biology. *Nature* 1995, *375*, 254 - 256.

[17] Fuchs, P. ; Parola, A. ; Robbins, P. W. ; Blout, E. R. Fluorescence Polarization and Viscosities of Membrane Lipids of 3T3 Cells. *Proc. Natl. Acad. Sci.* 1975, *72*, 3351 - 3354.

[18] Martin, C. E. ; Thompson, G. A. Use of Fluorescence Polarization to Monitor Intracellular Membrane Changes During Temperature Acclimation. Correlation with Lipid Compositional and Ultrastructural Changes. *Biochemistry* 1978, *17*, 3581 - 3586.

[19] Schachter, D. ; Shinitzky, M. Fluorescence Polarization Studies of Rat Intestinal Microvillus Membranes. *J. Clin. Invest.* 1977, *59*, 536 - 548.

[20] Jameson, D. M. ; Seifried, S. E. Quantification of Protein-Protein Interactions Using Fluorescence Polarization. *Methods* 1999, *19*, 222 - 233.

[21] Lundblad, J. R. ; Laurance, M. ; Goodman, R. H. Fluorescence Polarization Analysis of Protein-DNA and Protein-Protein Inter-actions. *Mol. Endocrinol.* 1996, *10*, 607 - 612.

[22] Zhang, D. ; Shen, H. ; Li, G. ; Zhao, B. ; Yu, A. ; Zhao, Q. ; Wang, H. Specific and Sensitive Fluorescence Anisotropy Sensing of Guanine-Quadruplex Structures via a Photoinduced Electron Transfer Mechanism. *Anal. Chem.* 2012, *84*, 8088 - 8094.

[23] Murai, T. ; Kawashima, H. A Simple Assay for Hyaluronidase Activity Using Fluorescence Polarization. *Biochem. Biophys. Res. Commun.* 2008, *376*, 620 - 624.

[24] Borenstain, V. ; Barenholz, Y. Characterization of Liposomes and Other Lipid Assemblies by Multiprobe Fluorescence Polarization. *Chem. Phys. Lipids* 1993, *64*, 117 - 127.

[25] Bachovchin, D. A. ; Brown, S. J. ; Rosen, H. ; Cravatt, B. F. Identif-ication of Selective Inhibitors of Uncharacterized Enzymes by High-Throughput Screening with Fluorescent Activity-Based Probes. *Nat. Biotechnol.* 2009, *27*, 387 - 394.

[26] Heyduk, T. ; Ma, Y. ; Tang, H. ; Ebright, R. H. Fluorescence Anisotropy:

Rapid, Quantitative Assay for Protein-DNA and Protein-Protein Interaction. In *Methods in Enzymology*, Sankar, A., Ed.; Academic Press, 1996; pp. 492 –503.

[27] Cruz-Aguado, J. A.; Penner, G. Fluorescence Polarization Based Displacement Assay for the Determination of Small Molecules with Aptamers. *Anal. Chem.* 2008, *80*, 8853 – 8855.

[28] Zhao, Q.; Lv, Q.; Wang, H. Identification of Allosteric Nucleotide Sites of Tetramethylrhodamine-Labeled Aptamer for Noncompetitive Aptamer-Based Fluorescence Anisotropy Detection of a Small Molecule, Ochratoxin A. *Anal. Chem.* 2013, *86*, 1238 – 1245.

[29] Cui, L.; Zou, Y.; Lin, N.; Zhu, Z.; Jenkins, G.; Yang, C. J. Mass Amplifying Probe for Sensitive Fluorescence Anisotropy Detection of Small Molecules in Complex Biological Samples. *Anal. Chem.* 2012, *84*, 5535 –5541.

[30] Liu, J.; Wang, C.; Jiang, Y.; Hu, Y.; Li, J.; Yang, S.; Li, Y.; Yang, R.; Tan, W.; Huang, C. Graphene Signal Amplification for Sensitive and Real-Time Fluorescence Anisotropy Detection of Small Molecules. *Anal. Chem.* 2013, *85*, 1424 – 1430.

[31] Huang, Y.; Zhao, S.; Chen, Z.; Shi, M.; Liang, H. Amplified Fluorescence Polarization Aptasensors Based on Structure-Switching-Triggered Nanoparticles Enhancement for Bioassays. *Chem. Commun.* 2012, *48*, 7480 –7482.

[32] Perrier, S.; Ravelet, C.; Guieu, V.; Fize, J.; Roy, B.; Perigaud, C.; Peyrin, E. Rationally Designed Aptamer-Based Fluorescence Polar-ization Sensor Dedicated to the Small Target Analysis. *Biosens. Bioelectron.* 2010, *25*, 652 – 1657.

[33] Ruta, J.; Perrier, S.; Ravelet, C.; Fize, J.; Peyrin, E. Noncompetitive Fluorescence Polarization Aptamer-Based Assay for Small Molecule Detection. *Anal. Chem.* 2009, *81*, 7468 – 7473.

[34] Zhu, Z.; Schmidt, T.; Mahrous, M.; Guieu, V.; Perrier, S.; Ravelet, C.; Peyrin, E. Optimization of the Structure-Switching Aptamer-Based Fluorescence Polarization Assay for the Sensitive Tyrosinamide Sensing. *Anal. Chim. Acta* 2011, *707*, 191 – 196.

[35] Nau, W. M.; Mohanty, J. Taming Fluorescent Dyes with Cucurbituril. *Int. J. Photoenergy* 2005, *7*, 133 – 141.

[36] Marquez, C.; Nau, W. M. Polarizabilities Inside Molecular Containers. *Angew. Chem., Int. Ed.* 2001, *40*, 4387 – 4390.

[37] Johnson, I. , Spence, M. T. Z. *Molecular Probes Handbook*: *A Guide to Fluorescent Probes and Labeling Technologies* , 11th ed. ; Invitrogen Life Technologies: Carlsbad, CA, USA, 2010.

[38] Ren, J. ; Zhao, X. ; Wang, Q. ; Ku, C. ; Qu, D. ; Chang, C. ; Tian, H. Synthesis and Fluorescence Properties of Novel Co-facial Folded Naphthalimide Dimers. *Dyes Pigments* 2005, *64* ,179 – 186.

[39] Zhao, G. ; Meier, T. I. ; Kahl, S. D. ; Gee, K. R. ; Blaszczak, L. C. BOCILLIN FL, a Sensitive and Commercially Available Reagent for Detection of Penicillin-Binding Proteins. *Antimicrob. Agents Chemother.* 1999, *43*, 1124 –1128.

[40] Banks, P. ; Harvey, M. Considerations for Using Fluorescence Polarization in the Screening of G Protein-Coupled Receptors. *J. Biomol. Screening* 2002, *7*, 111 – 117.

[41] Banks, P. ; Gosselin, M. ; Prystay, L. Impact of a Red-Shifted Dye Label for High Throughput Fluorescence Polarization Assays of G Protein-Coupled Receptors. *J. Biomol. Screening* 2000, *5* ,329 – 334.

[42] Schade, S. Z. ; Jolley, M. E. ; Sarauer, B. J. ; Simonson, L. G. BODIPY-α-Casein, a pH-Independent Protein Substrate for Protease Assays Using Fluorescence Polarization. *Anal. Biochem.* 1996, *243* ,1 – 7.

[43] Deng, T. ; Li, J. ; Zhang, L. ; Jiang, J. ; Chen, J. ; Shen, G. ; Yu, R. A Sensitive Fluorescence Anisotropy Method for the Direct Detection of Cancer Cells in Whole Blood Based on Aptamer-Conjugated Near-Infrared Fluorescent Nano-particles. *Biosens. Bioelectron.* 2010, *25* ,1587 – 1591.

[44] Tsuda , H. ; Maeda, H. ; Kishimoto, S. Fluorescence Polarization with FDA in Leukaemic Cells: A Clear Difference Between Myelogenous and Lymphocytic Origins. *Br. J. Cancer* 1981, *43* ,793 – 803.

[45] Kornilova, A. Y. ; Algayer, B. ; Breslin, M. ; Addona, G. H. ; Uebele, V. Development of A Fluorescence Polarization Binding Assay for Folate Receptor. *Anal. Biochem.* 2013, *432* ,59 – 62.

[46] Cristofanilli, M. ; Budd, G. T. ; Ellis, M. J. ; Stopeck, A. ; Matera, J. ; Miller, M. C. ; Reuben, J. M. ; Doyle, G. V. ; Allard, W. J. ; Terstappen, L. W. M. M. ; Hayes, D. F. Circulating Tumor Cells, Disease Progression, and Survival in Metastatic Breast Cancer. *New Engl. J. Med.* 2004, *351*, 781 –791.

[47] Paterlini-Brechot, P. ; Benali, N. L. Circulating Tumor Cells (CTC) Detection: Clinical Impact and Future Directions. *Cancer Lett.* 2007, *253*,

180 -204.

[48] Wang, Q. ; Ren, J. ; Qu, D. ; Zhao, X. ; Chen, K. ; Tian, H. ; Erk, P. Synthesis and Luminescent Properties of Some Novel Naphthalimide Dimers. *Dyes Pigments* 2003, *59*, 143 - 152.

[49] Huang, C. ; Yin, Q. ; Zhu, W. ; Yang, Y. ; Wang, X. ; Qian, X. ; Xu, Y. Highly Selective Fluorescent Probe for Vicinal-Dithiol-Containing Proteins and In Situ Imaging in Living Cells. *Angew. Chem. , Int. Ed.* 2011, *50*, 7551 -7556.

[50] Huang, C. ; Li, H. ; Luo, Y. ; Xu, L. A Naphthalimide-Based Bifunctional Fluorescent Probe for the Differential Detection of Hg^{2+} and Cu^{2+} in Aqueous Solution. *Dalton Trans* . 2014, *43*, 8102 - 8108.

[51] Un, H. ; Wu, S. ; Huang, C. ; Xu, Z. ; Xu, L. A Naphthalimide-Based Fluorescent Probe for Highly Selective Detection of Histidine in Aqueous Solution and Its Application in In Vivo Imaging. *Chem. Commun.* 2015, *51*, 3143 - 3146.

[52] Hinkeldey, B. ; Schmitt, A. ; Jung, G. Comparative Photostability Studies of BODIPY and Fluorescein Dyes by Using Fluorescence Correlation Spectroscopy. *ChemPhysChem* 2008, *9*, 2019 - 2027.

[53] Li, T. ; Shi, L. ; Wang, E. ; Dong, S. Multifunctional G-Quadruplex Aptamers and Their Application to Protein Detection. *Chem. -Eur. J.* 2009, *15*, 1036 - 1042.

[54] Feng, L. ; Chen, Y. ; Ren, J. ; Qu, X. A Graphene Functionalized Electrochemical Aptasensor for Selective Label-Free Detection of Cancer Cells. *Biomaterials* 2011, *32*, 2930 - 2937.

[55] Weng, J. ; Zhang, Z. ; Sun, L. ; Wang, J. A. High Sensitive Detection of Cancer Cell with A Folic Acid-Based Boron-Doped Diamond Electrode Using an AC Impedimetric Approach. *Biosens. Bioelectron.* 2011, *26*, 1847 - 1852.

[56] Liu, J. ; Qin, Y. ; Li, D. ; Wang, T. ; Liu, Y. ; Wang, J. ; Wang, E. Highly Sensitive and Selective Detection of Cancer Cell with A Label-Free Electrochemical Cytosensor. *Biosens. Bioelectron.* 2013, *41*, 436 - 441.

[57] Wang, Z. ; Chen, S. ; Hu, C. ; Cui, D. ; Jia, N. An Enhanced Impedance Cytosensor Based on Folate Conjugated-Polyethyleni-mine-Carbon Nanotubes for Tumor Targeting. *Electrochem. Commun.* 2013, *29*, 4 - 7.

[58] Qian, Z. ; Bai, H. ; Wang, G. ; Xu, J. ; Chen, H. A Photo-electrochemical Sensor Based on CdS-Polyamidoamine Nano-Composite Film for Cell Capture and Detection. *Biosens. Bioelectron.* 2010, *25*, 2045 - 2050.

[59] Yang, G. ; Cao, J. ; Li, L. ; Rana, R. K. ; Zhu, J. -J. Carboxymethyl Chitosan-Functionalized Graphene for Label-Free Electrochemical Cytosensing. *Carbon* 2013, *51*, 124 – 133.

[60] Gu, M. ; Zhang, J. ; Li, Y. ; Jiang, L. ; Zhu, J. Fabrication of A Novel Impedance Cell Sensor Based on the Polystyrene/Polyaniline/ Au Nanocomposite. *Talanta* 2009, *80*, 246 – 249.

[61] Li, T. ; Fan, Q. ; Liu, T. ; Zhu, X. ; Zhao, J. ; Li, G. Detection of Breast Cancer Cells Specially and Accurately by An Electrochemical Method. *Biosens. Bioelectron.* 2010, *25*, 2686 – 2689.

[62] Hao, C. ; Yan, F. ; Ding, L. ; Xue, Y. ; Ju, H. A Self-Assembled Monolayer Based Electrochemical Immunosensor for Detection of Leukemia K562A Cells. *Electrochem. Commun.* 2007, *9*, 1359 – 1364.

[63] Tran, T. H. ; Choi, J. Y. ; Ramasamy, T. ; Truong, D. H. ; Nguyen, C. N. ; Choi, H. -G. ; Yong, C. S. ; Kim, J. O. Hyaluronic Acid-Coated Solid Lipid Nanoparticles for Targeted Delivery of Vorinostat to CD44 Overexpressing Cancer Cells. *Carbohyd. Polym.* 2014, *114*, 407 – 415.

[64] Harada, H. ; Nakata, T. ; Hirota-takahata, Y. ; Tanaka, I. ; Nakajima, M. ; Takahashi, M. F-16438s, Novel Binding Inhibitors of CD44 and Hyaluronic Acid. *J. Antibiot.* 2006, *59*, 770 – 776.

[65] Takada, M. ; Yamamoto, M. ; Saitoh, Y. The Significance of CD44 in Human Pancreatic Cancer: I. High Expression of CD44 in Human Pancreatic Adenocarcinoma. *Pancreas* 1994, *9*, 748 – 752.

[66] Yadav, V. K. ; Ryu, J. -H. ; Suda, N. ; Tanaka, K. F. ; Gingrich, J. A. ; Schütz, G. ; Glorieux, F. H. ; Chiang, C. Y. ; Zajac, J. D. ; Insogna, K. L. ; Mann, J. J. ; Hen, R. ; Ducy, P. ; Karsenty, G. Lrp5 Controls Bone Formation by Inhibiting Serotonin Synthesis in the Duodenum. *Cell 135*, 825 –837.

[67] Qhattal, H. S. S. ; Liu, X. Characterization of CD44-Mediated Cancer Cell Uptake and Intracellular Distribution of Hyaluronan-Grafted Liposomes. *Mol. Pharmaceutics* 2011, *8*, 1233 – 1246.

[68] Sun, H. ; Benjaminsen, R. V. ; Almdal, K. ; Andresen, T. L. Hyaluronic Acid Immobilized Polyacrylamide Nanoparticle Sensors for CD44 Receptor Targeting and pH Measurement in Cells. *Bioconjugate Chem.* 2012, *23*, 2247 –2255.

（原载于 Acs Applied Materials & Interfaces 2015 年第 7 期）

Sensitive detection of tumor cells by a new cytosensor with 3D-MWCNTs array based on vicinal-dithiol-containing proteins (VDPs)

Yanan Xu, Hui Wu, Chusen Huang, Caiqin Hao,
Beina Wu, Chongchong Miao, Shen Chen, Nengqin Jia

The Education Ministry Key Laboratory of Resource Chemistry,
Shanghai Key Laboratory of Rare Earth Functional Materials and
Shanghai Municipal
Education Committee Key Laboratory of Molecular Imaging Probes
and Sensors, Department of Chemistry, Shanghai Normal University

1. Introduction

The homeostasis of cellular redox environment is one of the most important foundations of living systems. Among the important factors associated with redox homeostasis and signaling, vicinal dithiol-containing proteins (VDPs) with space-closed thiol groups was especially attractive for its direct involvement of many biological processes through the interconvert between protein vicinal dithiols and disulfides in protein synthesis and post translational modification (Maron et al. , 2013; Poole and Nelson, 2008; Reddie and Carroll, 2008; Ying et al. , 2007). Commonly, mammalian cell surface (exofacial membrane) is rich in disulfide bonding, which can maintain the structure and functionalities of cells in the presence of oxidizing extracellular environment (Ali and Hynes, 1978; Hynes and Destree, 1977). However, recent studies demonstrated that VDPs were also present on mammalian cell membrane. And as the reductive form of protein thiols, these cell-surface vicinal dithiols on VDPs display key roles in maintaining extracellular redox homeostasis and cellular functions, which is found to be responsible for cancer (Lee et al. , 2014; Weiss et al. , 2001; Yang et al. , 2007), platelet function (Sugatani et al. , 1987), and human immunodeficiency virus type 1 (HIV-1) (Mat-thias and Hogg, 2003; Ou and Silver, 2006; Sahaf et al. , 2005). Especially, VDPs are overexpressed in aggressive tumors and the tumor cells become more dependent on these vicinal dithiols of VDPs such as Trx and TrxR system (Dilda et al. , 2008; Lu et al. , 2007; Zhang et al. , 2007). Many efforts have been devoted to studying of the functionality of VDPs including identification of new functional VDPs by arsenite-affinity chromatography (Huang et al. , 2011; Krauth-Siegel et al. , 2005; McStay et al. , 2002; Schuppe-Koistinen et al. , 1994), development of fluorescent probes for specific detection of VDPs, and synthesis of new drug candidates for cancer therapy based on the active vicinal dithiols of VDPs. All these studies were based on the active vicinal dithiols of VDPs. Thus the high levels of vicinal dithiols of VDPs in cancer cells will become a potential biomarker for aggressive tumors. Capturing and detection of cancer cells can provide an easy and effective way for monitoring the progression of cancer and their related biological processes (Galanzha et al. , 2009; Uhr, 2007; Xu et al. , 2009). Therefore, development of rapid, selective and economical approach for detection of cancer cells is highly desirable. Recent years have witnessed a great development in the field of electrochemical biosensors for the rapid, selective, and sensitive detection of cancer cells with low cost. However, to best of our knowledge, there are no electrochemical biosensors reported for capturing and sensitive detection of cancer cells based on the vicinal dithiols of VDPs.

The applications of three dimensional (3D)-nanostructured electrodes are highly desirable for the improvement in the performance of electrochemical biosensors (Mendes et al. , 2007; Zhu et al. , 2014). Especially, three-dimensional (3D) array or vertically aligned structure with functionalized nanohybrids, based on a solid basement, has shown excellent performance in enhancement of surface area and low cytotoxicity (Malhotra et al. , 2010; McCune et al. , 2012). A number of 3D-structure is used as ideal support in bio-sensing and biomedical fields (Han et al. , 2014; Kim et al. , 2011; Sardesai et al. , 2011). For instance, 3D synthetic biodegradable polymer scaffold promotes cell survival without affecting cytochrome oxidase activities, allowing actual liver function more complete simulation (Kim et al. , 1998). Other research uses IrO_2-Hemin-TiO_2 nanowire arrays to detect glutathione and Hela cells extracts by photoelectrochemical detection (Tang et al. , 2013). Due to the electrochemical property of the superior electron transfer and efficient electrical conductivity, carbon nanotubes (CNTs) were typically used as the ideal leader in ultrasensitive, nanostructured electrochemical sensing platform design (Rawson et al. , 2012; Tu et al. , 2009). Some study has demonstrated that well aligned multiwalled carbon nanotubes (MWCNTs) array embedded in a SiO_2 matrix was significant for improving the sensitivity of electrochemical detection method (Li et al. , 2002). Herein, we take MWCNTs as the nanostructured surface for constructing the target electrochemical biosensor. In addition, some studies have suggested that trivalent arsenic based compounds could bind to VDPs efficiently (Donoghue et al. , 2000; Huang et al. , 2013). Our previous work is also found that 2-p-aminophenyl-1,3,2-dithiarsenolane (VTA2) is a highly selective acceptor for vicinal dithiols of VDPs in cells. Due to the overexpressed levels of vicinal dithiols of VDPs in tumor cells, VTA2 was introduced into the MWCNTs as the selective ligand in construction of our target electrochemical biosensor.

Up to now, no electrochemical techniques for the detection of vicinal cancer cells based on that the higher levels of vicinal dithiols of VDPs were present in cancer cells compared to the low levels of vicinal dithiols of VDPs in the normal cells. Here is an attempt to design a cytosensor based on 3D-MWCNTs@VTA2 modified indium tin oxide (ITO) electrode for detecting VDPs overexpressing tumor cells. The ITO electrode was also used as a platform for fabricating VTA2@MWCNTs structure not only due to its conductivity for electrochemical signal collection, but also for that the captured cancer cells could be tracked directly by optical microscope technology. This constructed electrochemical cytosensor may enable for a dual functional detection of cancer cells based on both electrochemical and optical image technology.

2. Experimental

2. 1　Materials and reagents

MWCNTs were purchased from Shenzhen Nanotech Port Co. pphenylenediamine (AP) was purchased from Aladdin. Indium Tin Oxide (ITO, resistivity$=10-15\Omega$) was purchased from Zhuhai kaivo company. Other Reagents were of analytical grade and used without further purification. The 10 mM phosphate buffer solution (PBS, pH 7. 4) containing 14 mM KH_2PO_4, 87 mM Na_2HPO_4, 2. 7 mM KCl and 137 mM NaCl. Ultrahigh purity H_2O (18. 2 MΩ) was used throughout the experiments.

2. 2　Preparation of arylamine film on ITO electrode

Indium tin oxide (ITO) electrodes (resistivity$=10-15$ Ω) were cut into 2 cm $\times$ 0. 3 cm and rinsed by ultrahigh purity water (18. 2 MΩ), ethanol, and then ultrasonic washing in acetone and isopropyl alcohol. The electrochemical working area is controlled via use of epoxy glue with a size of 2 mm $\times$ 3 mm. For the preparation of arylamine film, p-phenylenediamine (7. 25 mL, 10 mM) hydrochloric acid solution was rapidly added to $NaNO_2$ (2. 1 mL, 1 M) solution in an ice bath and allowed for 15 min complete reaction. The arylamine film was electrografted to the ITO surface by cycling once from-0. 6 to

0. 4 V vs SCE ($v = 100$ mV s^{-1}), followed by depositing at-0. 6 V for 2 min. To block the further reduction of the diazonium salt, two final cyclic voltammetric scans were performed.

2. 3　Fabrication of the 3 D-MWCNTs @ VTA 2 cytosensor

Firstly, target ligand VTA2 was synthesized, and the detailed synthetic procedures were demonstrated in the supplementary materials. Then, the cytosensor was fabricated as following process (Fig. 1A). Acid-treated shortened MWCNTs (5 mg, 1 mg mL^{-1}) dispersed in DMSO solution (5 mL) containing amide condensation agent (HATU, 5 mg, 1 mg mL^{-1}) and VTA2 (5 mg, 1 mg mL^{-1}), and then shaked for 30 min at room temperature. Then the VTA2 @ MWCNTs were vertically anchored to arylamine modified ITO electrodes at 65℃ for 24 h. After preparation, the cytosensors, VTA2@ MWCNTs/ITO electrodes, were rinsed with phosphate buffer solution (PBS, 10 mM, pH 7. 4) and dried for subsequent cell detections.

2. 4　Apparatus

All electrochemical experiments containing electrochemical impedance spectroscopy (EIS), cyclic voltammetry (CV) and differential pulse voltammetry (DPV) were performed with a CHI 660B electrochemical workstation (Shanghai Chenhua Co. Ltd., China). A standard three-electrode cell was used during the experiment. The functionalized ITO electrode as a working electrode with a SCE reference electrode and a Pt wire counter electrode. The electrolyte consists of a 10 mM pH 7. 4 PBS solution containing K_3 Fe. $(CN)_6$ (10 mM), K_4 Fe $(CN)_6$ (10 mM) and KCl (0. 1 M). The impedance spectra were recorded within the frequency ranging from 10^{-2} to 10^5 Hz with signal amplitude of 5 mV. The value of R_{et} (the diameters of Nyquist diagrams) was obtained by fitting with ZsimpWin software version 3. 10. The differential pulse voltam-metry (DPV) measurements were performed from-0. 2 to 0. 6 V with a pulse amplitude of 50 mV and width of 0. 02 s.

Atomic force microscopy (AFM) images were obtained on the Bruker AXS GmbH at MultiMode Nanoscope.

3. Results and discussion

3. 1 Fabrication and characterization of the 3D-MWCNTs@VTA2 cytosensor

To fabricate a cytosensor with 3D array of VTA2@MWCNTs, the ITO electrode is initially modified by arylamine layer through electrochemical reduction of the aryl diazonium cation. As schematically illustrated in Fig. 1A, electrochemical reduction was applied to

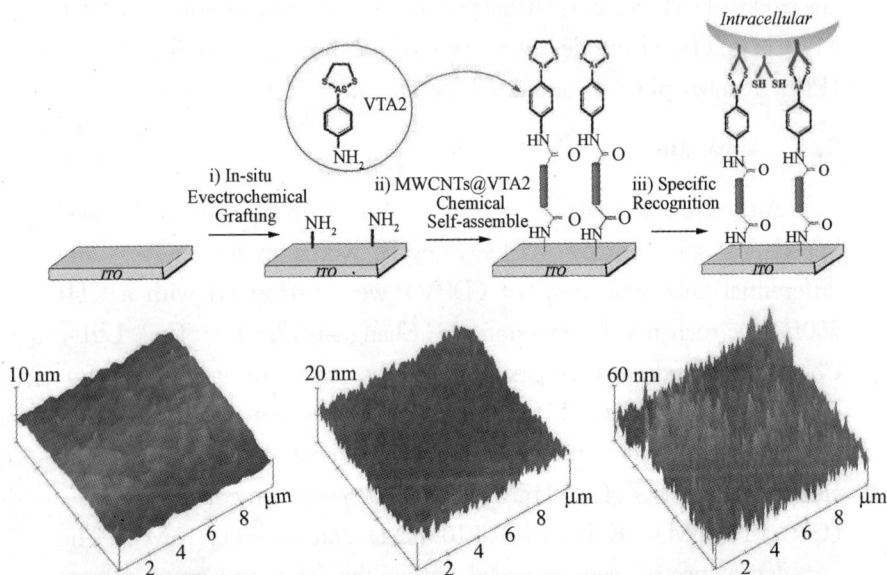

Fig. 1 (A) Schematic illustration of assembling processes of 3D-MWCNTs @ VTA2 cytosensor for detection of VDPs overexpressed tumor cell. (B) The corresponding AFM images of (a) bare ITO electrode, (b) arylamine modified ITO and (c) MWCNTs@ VTA2 modified ITO electrode.

control the functionalization of ITO surface, electrochemical reduction of the aryl-diazonium salt anchored to the ITO substrate by forming an arylamine layer. The mechanism for formatting a multilayer film structures has been proposed previously (Delamar et al. , 1992; Doppelt et al. , 2007). The in situ generating of aryl diazonium cation grafted to ITO surface is shown in Fig. S1A (see the supplementary materials), it can be seen that one reduction peak appeared at-0. 15 V on the first scan of cyclic voltammograms (CVs) from-0. 6 V to 0. 4 V, indicating the reduction of the aryl diazonium salt and its electrografting on the ITO electrode. On the consecutive scan, at the ITO electrode, no subsequent cathodic peak is observed for the reduction of the aryl diazonium cation due to the blocking nature of the formed arylamine film, suggesting that the arylamine film with approximate thickness had electrodeposited on the electrode surface and thus hindered further reduction of aryl diazonium cation (Delamar et al. , 1992; Doppelt et al. , 2007). Furthermore, to confirm this surface modification, electrochemical behavior of the probe [Fe $(CN)_6]^{3-/4-}$ was performed and the resulting CVs are shown in Fig. S1B. At the unmodified ITO electrode, a couple of well-defined redox peaks of the probe $[Fe(CN)_6]^{3-/4-}$ were investigated, whereas this characteristic CV peaks completely vanished at the arylamine film modified electrode, which could further verify that ITO surface was well functionalized by aryl diazonium cation and thereby modified by the arylamine film.

Following that, VTA2@MWCNTs structure was then prepared by covalent interaction between amine group of VTA2 and carboxyl group of MWCNTs. The target cytosensor was finally synthesized by a covalent tether between VTA2 @ MWCNTs and arylamine functionalized ITO via amide bonds. Atomic force microscopy (AFM) was used to characterize the surface topology of layer-by-layer assembling on the ITO electrode (Fig. 1B), displaying vertically aligned carbon nanotubes array with an average length of ～60 nm.

The root-mean-squared surface roughness (rms) values of bare ITO, arylamine modified ITO surface and MWCNTs@VTA2 anchored ITO surface were 0.818 ± 0.09, 2.781 ± 0.37 and 4.818 ± 0.32 nm, respectively. Obviously, the increase in roughness and the results of AFM demonstrate the 3D surface structure of MWCNTs@VTA2 modified ITO electrode is built. Furthermore, the stepwise assembly on the ITO electrode could be efficiently detected by electrochemical impedance spectroscopy (EIS) and CV. EIS is regarded as a powerful tool for probing the interface features of the surface modified electrodes, and its impedance spectra includes a semicircle portion and a linear line portion, which correspond to the electron transfer process and diffusion process, respectively. The diameter of the semicircle represents the elec-tron-transfer resistance (R_{et}) at the electrode surface. Fig. S2A shows Nyquist diagrams changed substantially after step-by-step assembly of arylamine, VTA2@MWCNTs, HL-60 cells on the ITO electrodes using $[Fe(CN)_6]^{3-/4-}$ as a redox probe. At a bare ITO electrode, the redox process of the probe showed a low electrontransfer impedance (R_{et}) value (curve a). After the successive conjugation of arylamine and VTA2@MWCNTs, the R_{et} value obviously increased (curve b, c), suggesting the VTA2@MWCNTs had successfully assembled on the ITO modified electrode and thereby blocked the electron exchange between the redox probe. Especially, after HL-60 cells (4.8×10^3 cells mL^{-1}) were attached to the VTA2@MWCNTs modified electrode, owing to the dielectric behavior of cells for interfacial electron transfer processes (Chen et al., 2013; Zhang et al., 2010), a barrier of the cell membrane would further hamper the redox probe close to the electrode surface and thus the R_{et} value increased greatly (curve d), which could be applied as a rapid and label-free strategy for detection of tumor cells and bio-analysis. In addition, cyclic voltammetric characteristics of the redox probe at these modified electrodes (Fig. S2B) were also consistent with the EIS results.

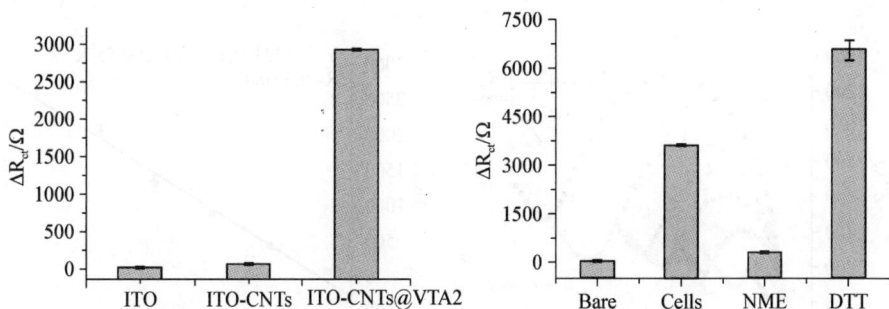

Fig. 2 Histogram of electrochemical impedance spectroscopy for (A) ITO, ITO-CNTs, ITO-CNTs@VTA2 coincubated with HL-60 cells (9.8×10^6 cells mL^{-1}) separately, and (B) for control experiments of Dithiothreitol (DTT) and N-ethylmaleimide (NEM)-treated MWCNTs@VTA2 modified ITO electrode co-incubated with HL-60 cells (9.8×10^6 cells mL^{-1}), respectively.

The corresponding histogram of typical electrochemical impedance spectroscopy for ITO, ITO-CNTs, and ITO-CNTs @ VTA2 incubated with the same concentration of HL-60 cells (9.8×10^6 cells mL^{-1}) is illustrated in Fig. 2A. The increase in corresponding histograms shows different anchor ability for tumor cells, and it can be observed that ITO-CNTs@VTA2 exhibited a highly selective for cancer cells. We can deduce that this higher specificity might be ascribed to the specific interaction between VTA2 anchored to ITO-CNTs@VTA2 and overexpressed vicinal dithiols of VDPs in cancer cells. To further verify the process of VTA2 bound to vicinal dithiols of VDPs, the VTA2@MWCNTs modified ITO electrode co-incubated with Dithiothreitol (DTT) or N-ethylmaleimide (NEM) in HL-60 cells (9.8×10^6 cells mL^{-1}) was studied by using electrochemical impedance spectroscopy (EIS) (Fig. 2B). The DTT treated cells-anchored ITO electrode showed enhanced higher in an electron transfer resistance (R_{et}) response than the cell-coated ITO electrode (without reagent treated), which was explained that DTT reagent was used to reduce disulfide bonds, and enable higher levels of vicinal dithiols of

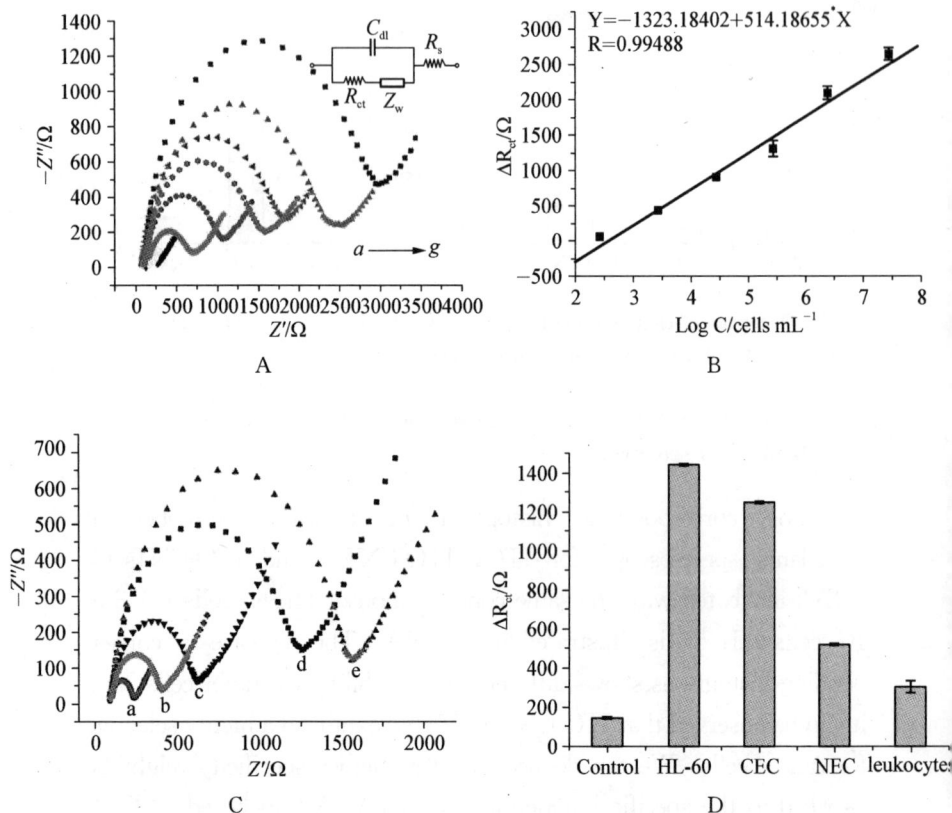

Fig. 3 (A) Typical EIS responses of bare ITO (a) and VTA2@MWCNTs modified ITO electrode after capture of HL-60 cells with different concentrations: (b) 2.7×10^2, (c) 2.7×10^3, (d) 2.7×10^4, (e) 2.7×10^5, (f) 2.7×10^6, (g) 2.7×10^7 cells mL^{-1}. Inset was the corresponding equivalent circuit model. (B) Calibration curve between logarithm values of cells concentration and impedance for detecting HL-60 cells. (C) EIS responses of (a) VTA2@MWCNTs modified ITO electrode and after respective incubation with (b) leukocytes (mouse bone marrow leukocytes), (c) NEC (human pancreatic cancer adjacent tissue cells), (d) CEC (human pancreatic cancer cells) and (e) HL-60 cells. (D) Corresponding histogram of impedance data into R_{ct} values. The concentration of all kinds of cells was same (1.0×10^5 cells mL^{-1}).

VDPs expressed by cells. However, a strongly decreased response was observed on the NEM treated cells-anchored ITO electrode. It is attributed to NEM that it is commonly used thiol-alkylation reagent that can in situ block vicinal dithiols of VDPs in cells, which could reduce the levels of vicinal dithiols of VDPs in cells, and there was little efficient sites for binding by VTA2 in ITO-CNTs @ VTA2. These results suggested that ITO-CNTs@VTA2 was a highly specific cytosensor for cancer cells through the specific interaction between VTAF2 in ITO-CNTs@VTA2 and vicinal dithiols of VDPs in cells.

3. 2   Detection performances and selectivity of the cytosensor

To attain adequate target conjugation and ideal cell capturing capacity of the constructed cytosensor, the suitable concentration of VTA2 and incubating time of ITO-CNTs@VTA2 biosensor for cell detection were firstly optimized (Fig. S3). Then the assay performances of the proposed cytosensor in the detection of HL-60 cells were investigated. The cytosensor was based on the measurement of electron transfer resistance (R_{et}) with $[Fe(CN)_6]^{3-/4-}$ as a redox probe. As electrochemical impedance spectroscopy (EIS) response immediately changed due to the electronic shielding effect from the cell membrane and the electron-transfer impedance (R_{et}) depended on the surface coverage of the cells anchored onto the electrode surface, herein, EIS was applied for quantitative determination of tumor cells. Fig. 3A illustrates its EIS response with increasing concentration of tumor cells ranging from 2.7×10^2 to 2.7×10^7 cells mL^{-1} measured in the presence of $[Fe(CN)_6]^{3-/4-}$ as a redox probe and the equivalent circuit model inset in Fig. 3A, representing the typical electrochemical interface, was used to fit the impedance data into R_{et} values. It can be seen that electron transfer resistance, R_{et}, increased with the increasing cell concentration. The relationship between ΔR_{et} ($\Delta R_{et} = R_{amp}$-R_{blank}) and logarithm concentrations of HL-60 cells in the range from 2.7×10^2 to 2.7×10^7 cells mL^{-1} was fitted linearly with the equation $\Delta R_{ct}(\Omega) = -1323.18402 + 514.18655 \times \lg C_{[HL-60]}$ (cells mL^{-1}) with a correlation coefficient $R = 0.99488$ (Fig. 3B). Additionally, based on its transparent characteristics of the ITO electrode, the process for capturing different concentrations of cells could be visualized by optical microscope technology (Fig. S4). This result from direct observation of HL-60 cells with different concentrations on the VTA2@MWCNTs-ITO modified electrode was consistent with the response in EIS (Fig. 3A). The detection limit of the proposed cytosensor was estimated to be approximately 90 cells mL^{-1}(signal-to-noise, $S/N = 3$) which are much lower than those reported cytosensors (Table S1 in the supplementary materials). The relative standard deviations (RSD) of five ITO electrodes with the same modified procedure independently were 4.1% and 5.7% at the cell concentrations, 2.7×10^3 and 2.7×10^6 cells mL^{-1}, signifying an acceptable precision. All these results provide a good performance of the VTA2 @ MWCNTs/ITO electrode in the quantitative determination of HL-60 cells.

Further, the selectivity of the VTA2@MWCNTs/ITO biosensor was evaluated by measuring its electrochemical impedance spectroscopy (EIS) response toward tumor cells and human normal cells (Fig. 3C). Generally, there is overexpressed VDPs on tumor cells compared to normal cells, which suggested the higher levels of vicinal dithiols of VDPs were present in cancer cells. Here, we chose the same concentration (1.0×10^5 cells mL^{-1}) of cancer cells including HL-60 cells and CEC (human pancreatic cancer cells) as the VDPs overexpression cell lines, normal cells including NEC (human pancreatic cancer adjacent tissue cells) and mouse bone marrow leukocytes as the VDPs normal-expression cell lines. Fig. 3D illustrates that the HL-60 cells gave the highest response in EIS signal. And CEC treated cytosensor also showed the similar EIS signal. By contrast, the mouse bone marrow leukocytes (or NEC) treated cytosensor responded negatively in this experiment, and a quite much lower EIS signal was obtained. In addition, the selectivity of the VTA2 @ MWCNTs/ITO biosensor was also assessed by DPV measurements (Fig. S5, supplementary materials). These data demonstrate that there are overexpressed VDPs on tumor cells and the levels of vicinal dithiols present on tumor cells are higher than normal cells. Thus, the higher levels of vicinal dithiols (or the overexpressed VDPs) could become a new biomarker for cancer cells. It is especially interesting to note that the human pancreatic cancer adjacent tissue cells (NEC) gave little response compared with the response of the Human pancreatic cancer cells (CEC) cell lines, which further confirmed that our proposed cytosensor (ITO-CNTs@VTA2) could selectively determine cancer cells based on the higher levels of vicinal dithiols of VDPs.

4. Conclusions

In summary, we have designed a new cytosensor (ITO-CNTs@VTA2) based on 3D-like VTA2@MWCNTs array for detection of tumor cells via specific recognition of VDPs expression patterns on the cellular surface. Three-dimensional architecture MWCNTs array equipped with excellent conductivity and enhanced surface area performed as an appropriate sensing layer for the attachment of large populations of VTA2 molecules and could be beneficial for the proposed cytosensor to achieve highly selective and sensitive detection of VDPs overexpressed cancer cells. The VTA2@MWCNTs-coated ITO modified electrode presented wide linear range, low detection limit and fast response as well as direct visualized observation in the detection of HL-60 tumor cells. Another novel features of this constructed assay system is that the small-molecule ligand VTA2 conjugated with MWCNTs affords an alternative to antibody-based biosensor. A detection limit for tumor cells on the biosensor was equivalent to or better than other antibody-based measurement systems. Therefore, with a simple and effective 3D nanoscale components assembling on a sensing surface, this electrochemical cytosensing provides a feasible and sensitive method for the detection of cancer cells and may hold great promise in clinical applications for early diagnosis of cancer.

Acknowledgments

This work was supported by the National Natural Science Foundation of China (21373138, 21302125), National 973 Project (2010CB933901), Shanghai Sci. & Tech. Committee (12JC1407200, 13ZR1458800), program for Changjiang Scholars and Innovative Research Team in University (IRT1269), Doctoral Fund of Ministry of Education of China (Grant no. 20133127120005).

Appendix A. Supplementary material

Supplementary data associated with this article can be found in the online version at http://dx. doi. org/10. 1016/j. bios. 2014. 11. 008.

References

[1] Ali, I. U., Hynes, R. O., 1978. Biochim. Biophys. Acta (BBA) — Biomembr. 510,140 – 159.

[2] Chen, Z., Liu, Y., Wang, Y., Zhao, X., Li, J., 2013. Anal. Chem. 85, 4431 – 4438.

[3] Delamar, M., Hitmi, R., Pinson, J., Saveant, J. M., 1992. J. Am. Chem. Soc. 114,5883 – 5884.

[4] Dilda, P. J., Ramsay, E. E., Corti, A., Pompella, A., Hogg, P. J., 2008. J. Biol. Chem. 283,35428 – 35434.

[5] Donoghue, N., Yam, P. T. W., Jiang, X. -M., Hogg, P. J., 2000. Protein Sci. 9,2436 – 2445.

[6] Doppelt, P., Hallais, G., Pinson, J., Podvorica, F., Verneyre, S., 2007. Chem. Mater. 19,4570 – 4575.

[7] Galanzha, E. I., Shashkov, E. V., Kelly, T., Kim, J. -W., Yang, L., Zharov, V. P., 2009. Nat. Nano 4,855 – 860.

[8] Han, D. , Kim, Y. -R. , Kang, C. M. , Chung, T. D. , 2014. Anal. Chem. 86,5991 – 5998.

[9] Huang, C. , Yin, Q. , Meng, J. , Zhu, W. , Yang, Y. , Qian, X. , Xu, Y. , 2013. Chem. -Eur. J. 19,7739 – 7747.

[10] Huang, C. , Yin, Q. , Zhu, W. , Yang, Y. , Wang, X. , Qian, X. , Xu, Y. , 2011. Angew. Chem. Int. Ed. 50,7551 – 7556.

[11] Hynes, R. O. , Destree, A. , 1977. Proc. Natl. Acad. Sci. USA 74, 2855 –2859.

[12] Kim, J. H. , Patra, C. R. , Arkalgud, J. R. , Boghossian, A. A. , Zhang, J. , Han, J. H. , Reuel, N. F. , Ahn, J. H. , Mukhopadhyay, D. , Strano, M. S. , 2011. ACS Nano 5,7848 – 7857.

[13] Kim, S. S. , Utsunomiya, H. , Koski, J. A. , Wu, B. M. , Cima, M. J. , Sohn, J. , Mukai, K. , Griffith, L. G. , Vacanti, J. P. , 1998. Ann. Surg. 228,8 – 13.

[14] Krauth-Siegel, R. L. , Bauer, H. , Schirmer, R. H. , 2005. Angew. Chem. 117,698 – 724.

[15] Lee, M. H. , Jeon, H. M. , Han, J. H. , Park, N. , Kang, C. , Sessler, J. L. , Kim, J. S. , 2014. J. Am. Chem. Soc. 136,8430 – 8437.

[16] Li, J. , Stevens, R. , Delzeit, L. , Ng, H. T. , Cassell, A. , Han, J. , Meyyappan, M. , 2002. Appl. Phys. Lett. 81,910 – 912.

[17] Lu, J. , Chew, E. H. , Holmgren, A. , 2007. Proc. Natl. Acad. Sci. USA 104,12288 – 12293.

[18] Malhotra, R. , Patel, V. , Vaque, J. P. , Gutkind, J. S. , Rusling, J. F. , 2010. Anal. Chem 82,3118 – 3123.

[19] Maron, B. A. , Tang, S. S. , Loscalzo, J. , 2013. Antioxid. Redox Signal. 18, 270 – 287.

[20] Matthias, L. J. , Hogg, P. J. , 2003. Antioxid. Redox Signal. 5,133 – 138.

[21] McCune, M. , Zhang, W. , Deng, Y. , 2012. Nano Lett. 12,3656 – 3662.

[22] McStay, G. P. , Clarke, S. J. , Halestrap, A. P. , 2002. Biochem. J. 367,541 – 548.

[23] Mendes, P. M. , Yeung, C. L. , Preece, J. A. , 2007. Nanoscale Res. Lett. 2, 373 – 384.

[24] Ou, W. , Silver, J. , 2006. Virology 350,406 – 417.

[25] Poole, L. B. , Nelson, K. J. , 2008. Curr. Opin. Chem. Biol. 12,18 – 24.

[26] Rawson, F. J. , Yeung, C. L. , Jackson, S. K. , Mendes, P. M. , 2012. Nano Lett. 13,1 – 8.

[27] Reddie, K. G. , Carroll, K. S. , 2008. Curr. Opin. Chem. Biol. 12,746 – 754.

[28] Sahaf, B. , Heydari, K. , Herzenberg, L. A. , Herzenberg, L. A. , 2005. Arch. Biochem. Biophys. 434,26 – 32.

[29] Sardesai, N. P. , Barron, J. C. , Rusling, J. F. , 2011. Anal. Chem. 83,6698 – 6703.

[30] Schuppe-Koistinen, I. , Moldeus, P. , Bergman, T. , Cotgreave, I. A. , 1994. Eur. J. Biochem. /FEBS 221,1033 – 1037.

[31] Sugatani, J. , Steinhelper, M. E. , Saito, K. , Olson, M. S. , Hanahan, D. J. , 1987. J. Biol. Chem. 262,16995 – 17001.

[32] Tang, J. , Kong, B. , Wang, Y. , Xu, M. , Wang, Y. , Wu, H. , Zheng, G. , 2013. Nano Lett. 13,5350 – 5354.

[33] Tu, W. W. , Lei, J. P. , Ding, L. , Ju, H. X. , 2009. Chem. Commun. , 4227 – Uhr, J42W9. , 2007. Nature 450,1168 – 1169.

[34] Weiss, N. , Zhang, Y. Y. , Heydrick, S. , Bierl, C. , Loscalzo, J. , 2001. Proc. Natl. Acad. Sci. USA 98,12503 – 12508.

[36] Xu, Y. , Phillips, J. A. , Yan, J. , Li, Q. , Fan, Z. H. , Tan, W. , 2009. Anal. Chem. 81,7436 – 7442.

[37] Yang, Y. , Song, Y. , Loscalzo, J. , 2007. Proc. Natl. Acad. Sci. USA 104, 10813 – 10817.

[38] Ying, J. , Clavreul, N. , Sethuraman, M. , Adachi, T. , Cohen, R. A. , 2007. Free Radic. Biol. Med. 43,1099 – 1108.

[39] Zhang, J. J. , Cheng, F. F. , Zheng, T. T. , Zhu, J. J. , 2010. Anal. Chem. 82,3547 – 3555.

[40] Zhang, X. , Yang, F. , Shim, J.-Y. , Kirk, K. L. , Anderson, D. E. , Chen, X. , 2007. Cancer Lett. 255,95 – 106.

[41] Zhu, B. , Niu, Z. , Wang, H. , Leow, W. R. , Li, Y. , Zheng, L. , Wei, J. , Huo, F. , Chen, X. , 2014. Small 10,3625 – 3631.

(原载于 Biosensors & Bioelectronics 2015 年第 66 期)

Functionalized Au nanoparticles for label-free Raman determination of ppb level benzopyrene in edible oil

Shuyue Fu, Xiaoyu Guo, Hui Wang,
Tianxi Yang, Ying Wen, Haifeng Yang

The Education Ministry Key Lab of Resource Chemistry, Shanghai Key Laboratory of Rare Earth Functional Materials, Shanghai Municipal Education Committee Key Laboratory of Molecular Imaging Probes and Sensors and Department of Chemistry, Shanghai Normal University

1. Introduction

Benzo(a)pyrene (BaP), a kind of highly toxic pollutant in ecosystems [1], is often derived from incomplete combustion such as cigarettes [2], gas [3], thermal cooking [4], diesel exhaust and wood smoke particles [5]. BaP as a chronic toxicity could easily adhere to human skin or muscles [6, 7] to cause carcinogenesis [8, 9]. In China, $PM_{2.5}$ loading BaP in the atmosphere will increase cancer risk [10]. Therefore it is quite necessary to develop an ultrasensitive method for quickly detecting the trace BaP.

So far, sensors for detecting BaP have attracted much attention and numerous efforts have been devoted to develop the detection of BaP by high-performance liquid chromatography (HPLC) [11], gas chromatography with flame ionization detector (GC-FID) or mass spectrometer (GC-MS) [12-14], fluorescence [15], electrochemistry [16] and so on. Most above-mentioned methods suffer from complicated pretreatment of samples, which limited their online detection applications.

Ag-and Au-nanoparticles-based Surface-enhanced Raman scattering (SERS) method is a label-free technique with extreme sensitivity at trace level [17-22]. Normally SRES substrate for detecting BaP requires a surface modification process due to weak adsorption of BaP on metallic surface. For example, Ag nanoparticles (NPs) and Au NPs could modified by dithiocarbamate calix[4]arene to produce hydrophobic surface and then they could be used to detect polycyclic aromatic hydrocarbons by SERS technique[23-25]. However, such modification procedure is also complicated.

According to Chinese national standard (GB 2716 – 2005), BaP concentration in qualified edible oil should be less than 10 μgL^{-1} level. We try to directly detect trace BaP in edible oil by SERS technique to meet the requirement of quick screen in market. Obviously, SERS detection for trace BaP in edible oil will suffer from the interference of the bulk oil Raman signals. In this work, Au NPs [26, 27], inositol hexaphosphate (IP_6) stabilized Au NPs dotted magnetic nanocomposites (AMN)[28] and IP_6 stabilized Au NPs (IP_6-Au NPs)[29] were synthesized to optimize the SERS protocol for detecting BaP. Inositol hexaphosphate (IP_6) as an environmentally benign reagent can not only stabilize Au NPs to provide a stable platform for reproducibly enhancing the Raman signal but also offer a certain hydrophobic interface to capture BaP molecules from bulk oil. Lowest

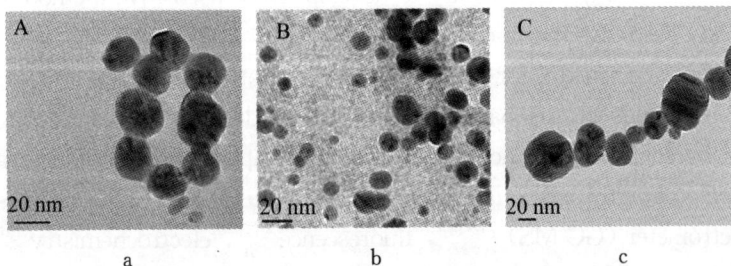

a   b   c

Fig. 1. TEM images of IP_6-Au NPs (A), AMN (B) and Au NPs (C).

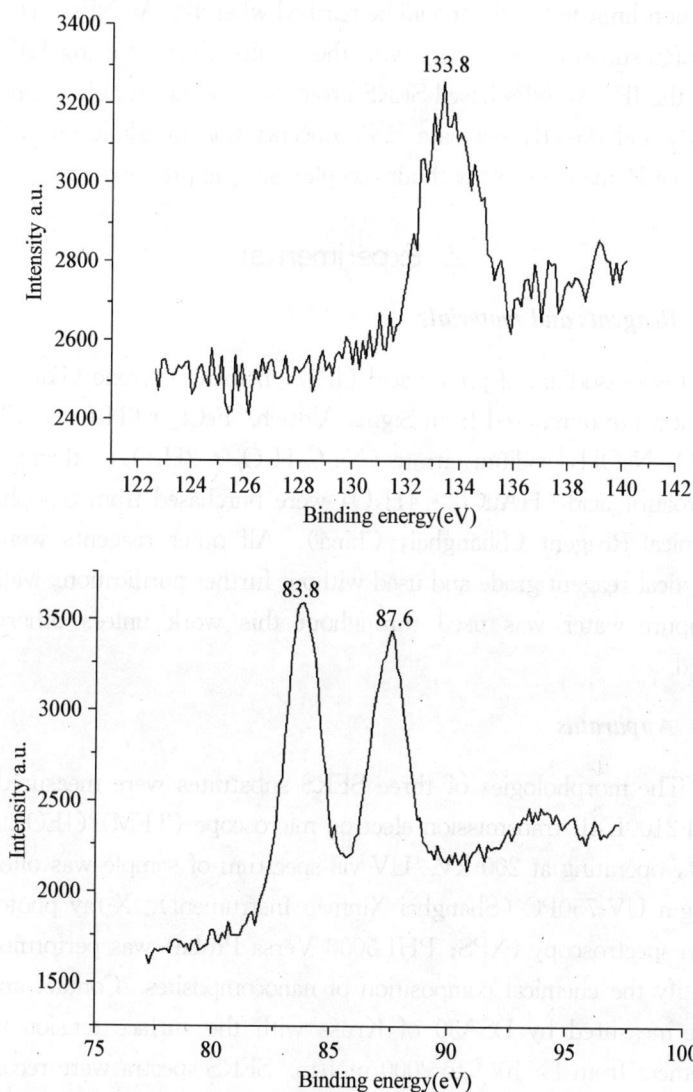

Fig. 2　XPS patterns of the resulting IP$_6$-Au NPs（A）P 2p signal characteristic of phosphates, and（B）Au 4f signal corresponding to the binding energy of metallic Au.

detection limit to 5 μgL^{-1} could be reached when IP_6-Au NPs was used as SERS substrate. Compare with the results obtained using HPLC/MS, the IP_6-Au NPs-based SERS protocol could be reliable to on-site quickly and directly evaluate BaP concentration in edible oil with a portable Raman system without complex sample pretreatment.

2. Experimental

2. 1 *Reagents and materials*

Dodecasodium of phytic acid (IP_6), benzo(a)pyrene (BaP) and pyrene were purchased from Sigma-Aldrich. $FeCl_3 \cdot 6H_2O$, $FeCl_2 \cdot 4H_2O$, NaOH, sodium citrate ($Na_3C_6H_5O_7 \cdot 2H_2O$), ethanol and chloroauric acid ($HAuCl_4 \cdot 4H_2O$) were purchased from Sinopharm Chemical Reagent (Shanghai, China). All other reagents were of analytical reagent grade and used without further purification. Milli-Q ultrapure water was used throughout this work unless otherwise stated.

2. 2 *Apparatus*

The morphologies of three SERS substrates were measured by JEM-2100EXII transmission electron microscope (TEM) (JEOL Co. Ltd), operating at 200 kV. UV-vis spectrum of sample was ollected using a UV-750PC (Shanghai Xinmao Instrument). X-ray photoelectron spectroscopy (XPS; PHI 5000 Versa Probe) was performed to identify the chemical composition of nanocomposites. Contact angles were measured by DSA30 of Kruss with the surface tension measurement from 1×10^{-2} to 2000 mN/m. SERS spectra were recorded using a portable stabilized R. Laser Analyzer (Enwave Co. Ltd). A narrow line width diode laser at 785 nm with an adjustable power of the maximum at 300 mW was also used for online detection purpose.

2. 3 Synthesis of the IP$_6$-Au NPs

IP$_6$-Au NPs were prepared by a method previously reported [29]. 10 mL IP$_6$@Ag colloid solution as precursor [30] was added into 15 mL H$_2$O and stirred under temperature at 50℃. After 10 min, 5 mL HAuCl$_4$ (0. 001 M) was added. After 30 min, 2 mL IP$_6$-Au NPs was taken out and centrifuged at 1000 rpmmin^{-1} for 10 min.

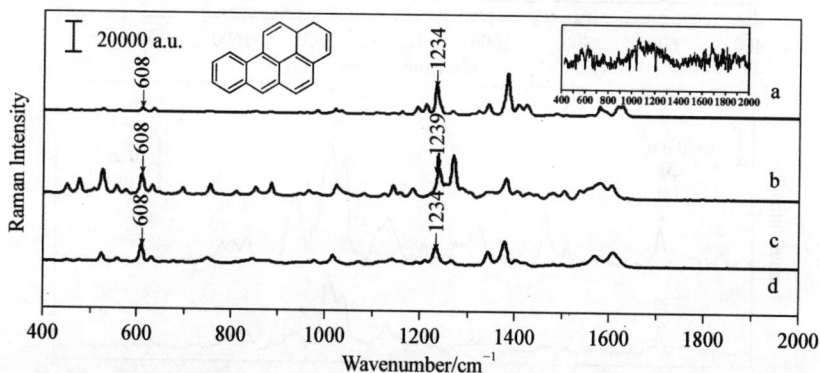

Fig. 3 SERS spectra of BaP (1 g L^{-1}) based on (b) IP$_6$-Au NPs, (c) AMN and (d) Au NPs (inset is the amplification of d) and their respective Raman spectra in the solid state (a). All SERS spectra have been baseline-corrected.

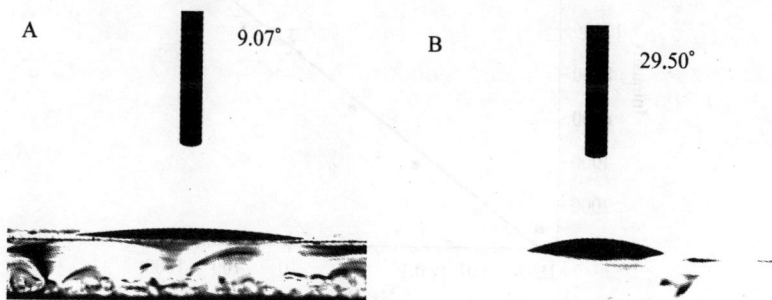

Fig. 4 Pictures and contact angle values of water droplets on sodium citrate-coated (A) and IP$_6$-coated (B) ITO substrates.

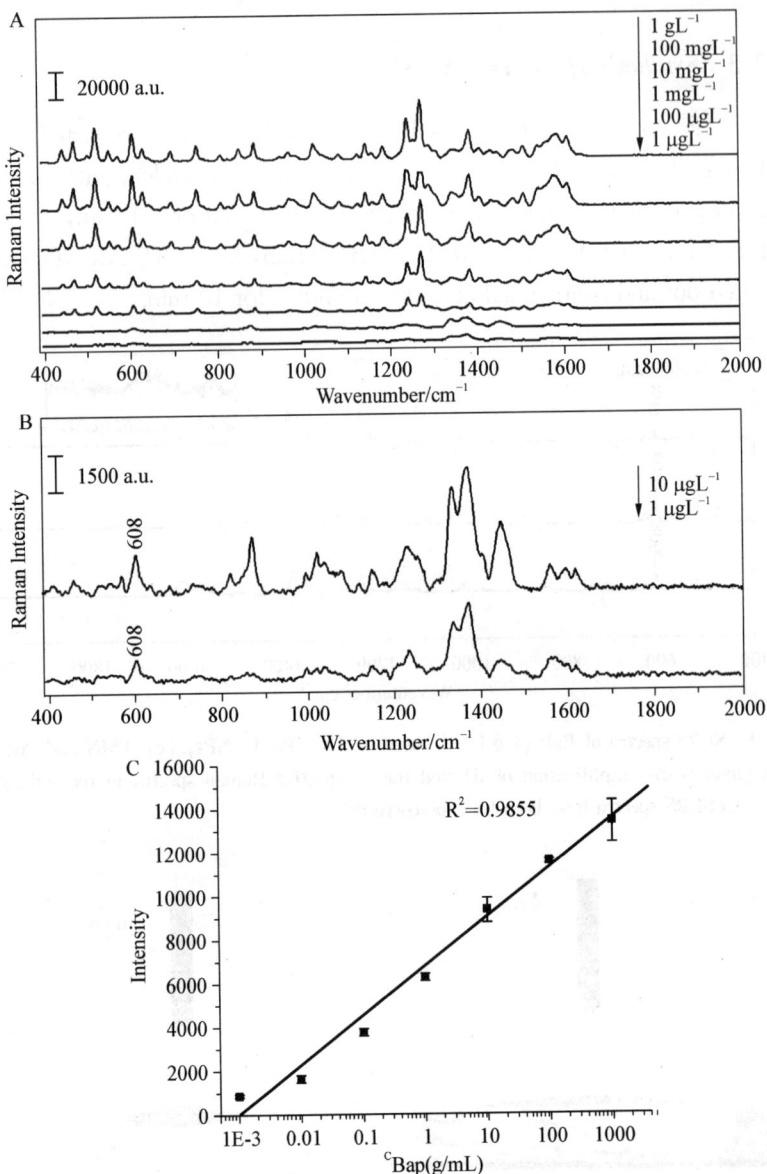

Fig. 5 SERS spectra of BaP in ethanol solution with concentrations from (A) 1 g L⁻¹ 1 μg L⁻¹, (B) 10 μg L⁻¹ and 1μg L⁻¹ and (C) concentration dependence of the SERS intensity for BaP at 608 cm⁻¹ based on IP₆-Au NPs. The data points on this plot are the average for spectra data obtained from three randomly chosen positions on the substrate. Each error bar indicates the standard deviations.

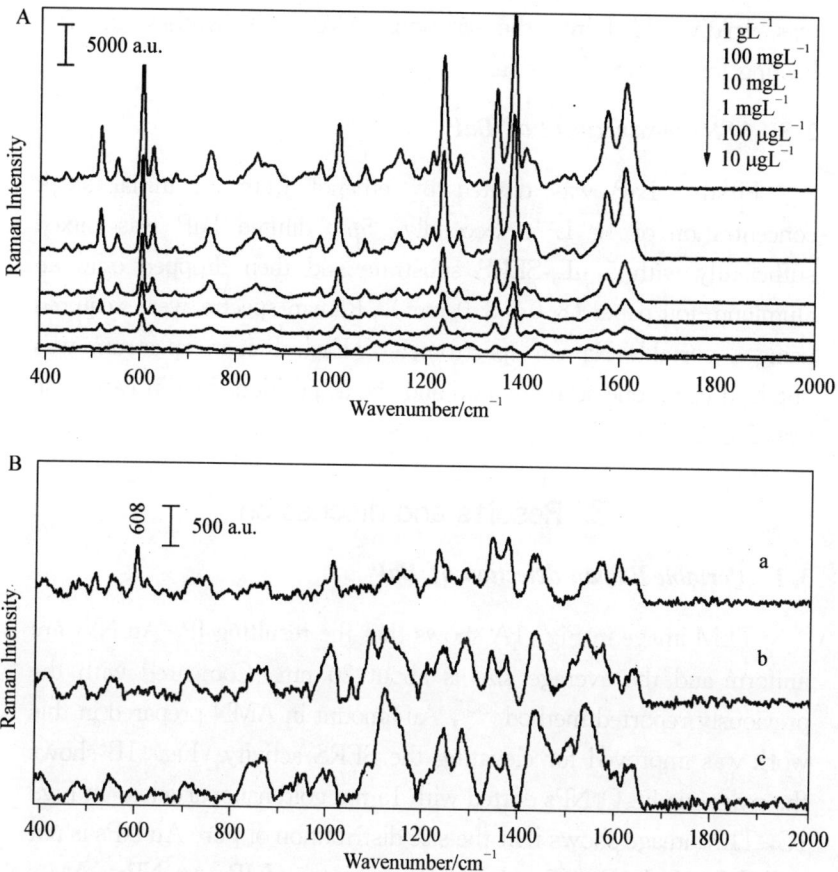

Fig. 6 SERS spectra of BaP in ethanol solution with concentrations from (A) 1 g L^{-1} 10 µg L^{-1}, (B) 10 µg L^{-1} (a) and 1µg L^{-1} (c) after magnetic induction and 10 µg L^{-1} (b) before magnetic induction based on AMN.

2. 4 Synthesis of AMN

AMN was synthesized following the reported method [28]. 2 mL of 1. 9 mg mL^{-1} collected magnetic Fe$_3$O$_4$ NPs were dispersed in 150 mL of ultrapure water and then heated to boiling. After slowly injected 3 mL of 1% chloroauric acid under vigorous stirring, the mixed solution was refluxed for 25 min and 5 mL of 1% sodium citrate was rapidly added into the solution. AMN was synthesized after heating for additional 60 min.

2.5 *SERS measurement of BaP*

Firstly, BaP was diluted by ethanol from an initial stock concentration of 1g L^{-1}. Secondly, 5μL diluted BaP was mixed sufficiently with 5 μL SERS substrate and then dropped onto an aluminum-foil paper (8.0×8.0 cm^2). Raman spectra were acquired using a portable Raman spectrometer. Each Raman spectrum was obtained using one accumulation and the acquisition time in each case was 5 s.

3. Results and discussion

3.1 *Portable Raman detection of BaP*

TEM image in Fig. 1A shows that the resulting IP_6-Au NPs are uniform and the average size is about 20 nm. Compared with the previously reported method [28], Au amount in AMN prepared in this work was improved for elevating the SERS activity. Fig. 1B shows the magnetic Fe_3O_4 NPs dotted with 15 nm gold nanoparticles. In Fig. 1C, TEM image shows that the size distribution of pure Au NPs is not well-defined. In Fig S1, the UV-vis spectra of IP_6-Au NPs, AMN and Au NPs with and without sample in ethanol solution evidence the Stability of such three nanoparticles and show that the average size of pure Au NPs is larger than IP_6-Au NPs and AMN. In Fig. 2, XPS result demonstrates the compositions of Au and P in IP_6-Au NPs, which could be a direct evidence for the presence of IP_6 protection as a stabilized reagent [28, 31].

Raman spectra of 1 g L^{-1} BaP in ethanol solutions were recorded using IP_6-Au NPs, AMN and Au NPs to observe the detection capability. For a comparison, Raman spectrum of solid BaP was also recorded. In Fig. 3a, there are two main peaks at 608 and 1234 cm^{-1}

in normal Raman spectrum, which are corresponded to C-H stretching and C-H in-plane bending [32], respectively. SERS observations of BaP using IP_6-Au NPs and AMN are given in Fig. 3b and Fig. c. However, in the case of Au NPs synthesized without IP_6, no Raman signal from BaP could be seen (Fig. 3d). The possible reason is that the presence of cyclohexane moiety of IP_6 increases the hydrophobicity of nanocomposites to capturing BaP, which is supported by the contact angle test results shown in Fig. 4.

3.2 *Observation of sensitivity*

For meeting the requirement of detection of trace BaP in edible oil, SERS activities of IP_6-Au NPs and AMN are carefully evaluated. The concentration-dependent SERS spectra of BaP in ethanol solution are shown in Fig. 5A. It could be clearly seen on the basis of SERS intensities at 608 cm^{-1} in Fig. 5C, there is the greater linear dynamic range from 1 $\mu g\ L^{-1}$ to 1 g L^{-1} when Raman experiments was recorded with IP_6-Au NPs. SERS spectra of BaP closely examined in the lower concentration from 10 $\mu g\ L^{-1}$ to 1 $\mu g\ L^{-1}$ are given in Fig. 5B. The detection of limit could reach 1 $\mu g\ L^{-1}$. When Raman experiment was conducted to detect a mixture of pyrene and BaP (see Fig. S2). IP_6-Au NPs-based SERS assay for BaP showed a high selectivity due to their different characteristic Raman peaks.

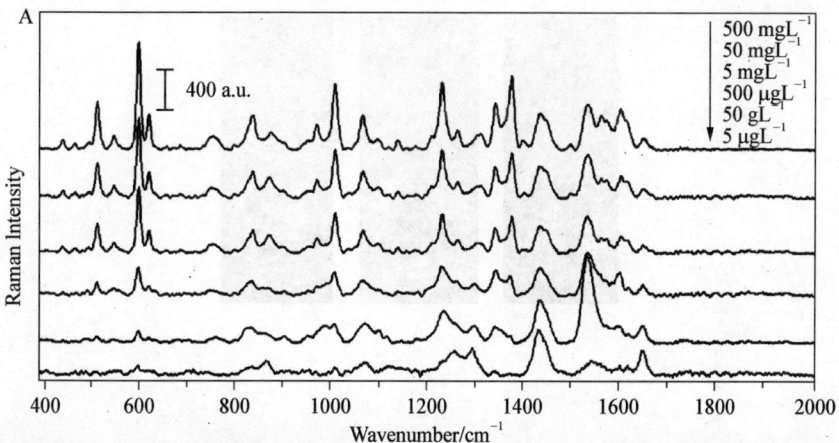

A 500 mgL^{-1} / 50 mgL^{-1} / 5 mgL^{-1} / 500 μgL^{-1} / 50 gL^{-1} / 5 μgL^{-1}

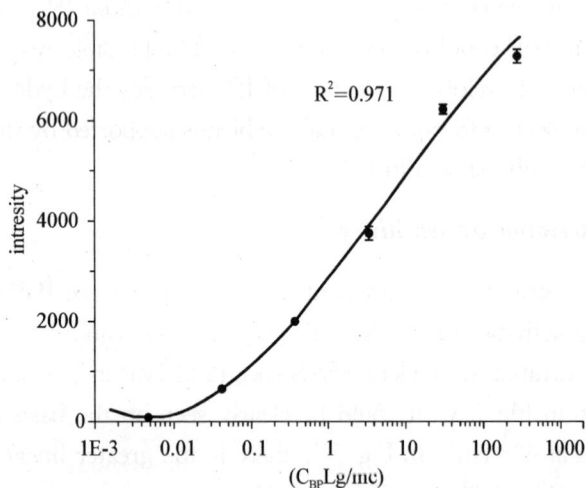

Fig. 7 （A） SERS spectra of BaP in soybean oil with concentrations from 500 mg L^{-1} to 5 μg L^{-1} based on IP$_6$-Au NPs. （B） Concentration dependence of the SERS intensity for BaP at 608 cm^{-1} based on IP$_6$-Au NPs. The data points on this plot are the average for spectra data obtained from three randomly chosen positions on the substrate. Each error bar indicates the standard deviations.

A

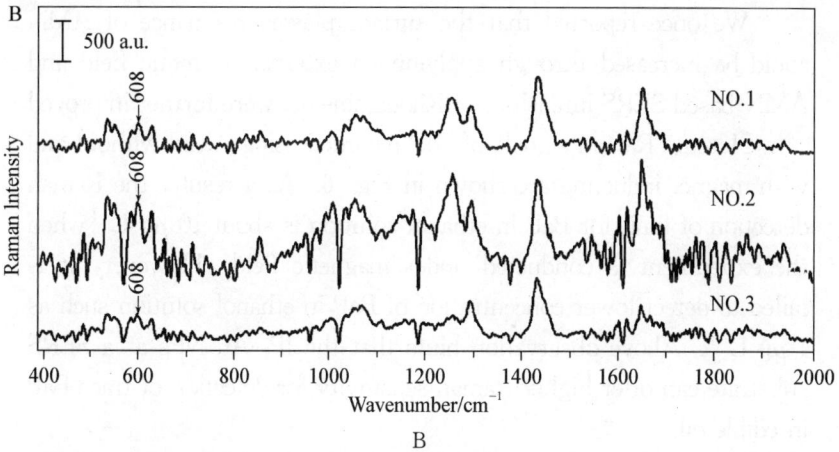

Fig. 8 Photos of BaP in oil samples (A) and IP6-Au NPs-based SERS spectra of BaP in oil samples (B).

Table 1

Sensitivities of various methods for BaP detection.

Analytical method	LOD	References
Electrochemical	2. 8 μgL^{-1}	[16]
HPLC	0. 005μgL^{-1}	[11]
GC-MID	0. 1 μgL^{-1}	[12]
GC-MS	0. 06 μgL^{-1}	[13]
Fluorescence	0. 36 μgL^{-1}	[15]
SERS	20 μgL^{-1}	[30]
SERS	1 μgL^{-1}	This work

Table 2

Comparison of real detection of BaP in edible oil assisted SERS protocol and HPLC-MS.

Sample	This method (μgL^{-1})	HPLC-MS (μgL^{-1})
1	7	3. 5
2	15	17. 5
3	5	2. 2

We once reported that the surface plasma resonance of AMN could be increased through applying an external magnetic field and AMN-based SERS intensities of Rhodamine 6G were further improved [28]. Herein, Raman signals of BaP recorded using AMN without and with magnet inducting are shown in Fig. 6. As a result, the Raman detection of limit for BaP in ethanol solution is about 10 μg L^{-1} when the experiment is conducted under magnetic field. However, it is failed to detect lower concentration of BaP in ethanol solution such as 1 μg L^{-1}. Above observation hints that the IP$_6$-Au NPs as a SERS substrate can offer higher Raman sensitivity for detection of trace BaP in edible oil.

The IP$_6$-Au NPs-based Raman protocol in this work and the previously reported methods for detecting BaP in organic solvents are summarized in Table 1. Apparently, such SERS protocol exhibits the quicker operation (3 min) to determine BaP than the other Raman protocol and electrochemical method. As well known, HPLC, GC and fluorescence spectroscopy also show a high sensitivities for detecting BaP but they need the complicated sampling procedures prior to measurements and Fluorescence inspection of BaP has to be done in the Lab. IP$_6$-Au NPs-based SERS protocol using a portable Raman system seems to be developed as a more convenient method for on-field screening BaP in oil products in markets and factories.

3.3 SERS detection of BaP in edible oils

As mentioned above, BaP in the edible oil is harmful to the health. Without complicated pretreatment, oil is difficult to be directly detected using traditional methods such as HPLC and GC. IP$_6$-Au NPs-based Raman protocol has not only the high selectivity due to its molecular fingerprint information but IP$_6$ modified Au trends to catch trace BaP from bulk oil into SPR vicinity of Au NPs for producing SERS signal. We stimulated the soybean oils spiking different BaP concentrations from 5 μg L^{-1} to 500 mg L^{-1} and their IP$_6$-Au NPs-based SERS spectra were recorded. In Fig. 7A, a peak at 608 cm^{-1} for the indication of BaP could be visible while the concentration is down to 5 μg L^{-1}. The linear correlations ($R^2 = 0.971$) between SERS intensities at 608 cm^{-1} and the concentrations of BaP in the range from 5 μg L^{-1} The linear correlations ($R^2 = 0.971$) between SERS intensities at 608 cm^{-1} and the concentrations of BaP in the range from 5 μgL^{-1} to 500 mg L^{-1} is displayed in Fig. 7B. Consequently, such method could be used to rapidly detect BaP in real oil samples.

BaP concentrations in three oil samples (No. 1, 2 and 3) from China National Food & Safety Supervision and Inspection Center were determined with HPLC-MS and IP$_6$-Au NPs-based Raman protocol. According to SERS results, the concentrations of Bap are estimated at 7 μg L^{-1}, 15 μg L^{-1} and 5 μg L^{-1} for No. 1, 2 and 3 samples, respectively which are tabulated in Table 2 together with the results from HPLC-MS experiments. Obviously, differences between the results obtained by two methods could be seen and undoubtedly, IP$_6$-Au NPs-based SERS protocol exhibited so highly sensitive and selective that it could be applied as a quick method to evaluate BaP concentration in on-market food with a portable Raman system. (Fig. 8).

4. Conclusions

A simple SERS method to detect trace BaP in edible oil without complicatedly tagging and pretreatment was proposed based on the facile synthesis of IP$_6$ stabilized Au NPs. Moreover, IP$_6$ modification for Au NPs increased certainly the hydrophobic capability of the substrate and it was beneficial to catching BaP molecules from bulk oil, bringing ultra SERS sensitivity and selectivity. The LOD for BaP in ethanol solution reached 1 μg L^{-1} while in edible oil LOD is about 5 μg L^{-1}. It is prospective that the IP$_6$-Au NPs-based Raman protocol could be applied as quickly monitoring method to detect BaP on-field for the quality control of commercial oil.

Acknowledgements

This work is supported by the National Natural Science Foundations of China (Grant Nos. 21073121 and 21475088).

Appendix A. Supplementary data

Supplementary data associated with this article can be found, in the online version, at http://dx. doi. org/10. 1016/j. snb. 2015. 01. 134.

References

[1] P. S. Khillare, A. Hasan, S. Sarkar, Accumulation and risks of polycyclic aromatic hydrocarbons and trace metals in tropical urban soils, Environ. Monit. Assess. 186(2014)2907 - 2923.

[2] J. Ono, K. Ogasa, K. Maeda, K. Noguchi, Preferential retention of benzo[a] pyrene in tobacco smoke by β-lactoglobulin in the cigarette filter structure, J. Agric. Food Chem. 29(1981)173 - 177.

[3] M. L. Lee, M. Novotny, K. D. Bartle, Gas chromatography/mass spectrometric and nuclear magnetic resonance spectrometric studies of carcinogenic polynuclear aromatic hydrocarbons in tobacco and marijuana smoke condensates, Anal. Chem. 48(1976)405 - 416.

[4] E. Saito, N. Tanaka, A. Miyazaki, M. Tsuzaki, Concentration and particle size distribution of polycyclic aromatic hydrocarbons formed by thermal cooking, Food Chem. 153(2014)285 - 291.

[5] A. I. Totlandsdal, J. Ovrevik, R. E. Cochran, J. I. Herseth, A. K. Bolling, M. Lag, P. Schwarze, E. Lilleaas, J. A. Holme, A. Kubatova, The occurrence of polycyclic aromatic hydrocarbons and their derivatives and the proinflammatory potential of fractionated extracts of diesel exhaust and wood smoke particles, J. Environ. Sci. Health. , part A. 49(2014)383 - 396.

[6] J. Sowada, A. Schmalenberger, I. Ebner, A. Luch, T. Tralau, Degradation of benzo [a] pyrene by bacterial isolates from human skin, FEMS Microbiol Ecol. 88(2014)129 - 139.

[7] C. Y. Chiu, Y. P. Yen, K. S. Tsai, R. S. Yang, S. H. Liu, Low-dose Benzo (a)pyrene and its epoxide metabolite inhibit myogenic differentiation in human

skeletal muscle-derived progenitor cells, Toxicol. Sci. 138(2014)344 – 353.

[8] J. P. Butler, G. B. Post, P. J. Lioy, J. M. Waldman, A. Greenberg, Assessment of carcinogenic risk from personal exposure to benzo(a)pyrene in the Total Human Environmental Exposure Study (THEES), J. Air Waste Manage. Assoc. 43(1993)970 – 977.

[9] J. Du, Y. L. Li, Z. C. Huang, J. You, Chronic toxicity thresholds for Sediment-associated benzo [a] pyrene in the Midge (*Chironomus dilutus*), Arch Environ. Contam. Toxicol. 66(2014)370 – 378.

[10] B. A. M. Bandowe, H. Meusel, R. J. Huang, K. Ho, J. J. Cao, T. Hoffmann, W. Wilcke, $PM_{2.5}$-bound oxygenated PAHs, nitro-PAHs and parent-PAHs from the atmosphere of a Chinese megacity: Seasonal variation, sources and cancer risk assessment, Sci. Total Environ. 473 – 474(2014)77 – 87.

[11] K. Kato, S. Shoda, M. Takahashi, N. Doi, Y. Yoshimura, H. Nakazawa, Determination of three phthalate metabolites in human urine using on-line solid-phase extraction-liquid chromatography-tandem mass spectrometry, J. Chromatogr. B. 788(2003)407 – 411.

[12] O. S. Olatunji, O. S. Fatoki, B. O. Opeolu, B. J. Ximba, Determination of polycyclic aromatic hydrocarbons [PAHs] in processed meat products using gas chromatography-Flame ionization detector, Food Chem. 156(2014)296 – 300.

[13] W. C. Tseng, P. S. Chen, S. D. Huang, Optimization of two different dispersive liquid-liquid microextraction methods followed by gas chromatography-mass spectrometry determination for polycyclic aromatic hydrocarbons (PAHs) analysis in water, Talanta. 120(2014)425 – 432.

[14] D. Y Shang, M. Kim, M. Haberl, Rapid and sensitive method for the determination of polycyclic aromatic hydrocarbons in soils using pseudo multiple reaction monitoring gas chromatography/tandem mass spectrometry, J. Chromatogr. A. 1334(2014)118 – 125.

[15] M. L. Nahornia, K. S. Booksh, Excitation-emission matrix fluorescence spectroscopy in conjunction with multiway analysis for PAH detection in complex matrices, Analyst. 131(2006)1308 – 1315.

[16] Y. N. Ni, P. P. Wang, H. Y. Song, X. Y. Lin, S. Kokot, Electrochemical detection of benzo(a)pyrene and related DNA damage using DNA/hemin/nafion-graphene biosensor, Anal. Chim. Acta. 821(2014)34 – 40.

[17] X. F. Gu, S. Tian, Q. Zhou, J. Adkins, Z. M. Gu, X. W. Li, J. W. Zheng, SERS detection of polycyclic aromatic hydrocarbons on a bowl-shaped silver

cavity substrate, RSC Adv. 3(2013)25989 - 25996.

[18] X. F. Shi, J. Ma, R. G. Zheng, C. Y. Wang, H. D. Kronfeldt, An improved self-assembly gold colloid film as surface-enhanced Raman substrate for detection of trace-level polycyclic aromatic hydrocarbons in aqueous solution, J. Raman Spectrosc. 43(2012)1354 - 1359.

[19] X. H. Jiang, Y. C. Lai, M. Yang, H. Yang, W. Jiang, J. H. Zhan, Silver nanoparticle aggregates on copper foil for reliable quantitative SERS analysis of polycyclic aromatic hydrocarbons with a portable Raman spectrometer, Analyst. 137(2012)3995 - 4000.

[20] L. Guerrini, J. V. G. Ramos, C. Domingo, S. S. Cortes, Building Highly Selective hot Spots in Ag nanoparticles using bifunctional Viologens; application to the SERS detection of PAHs, J. Phys. Chem. C. 112(2008)7527 - 7530.

[21] D. Li, D. W. Li, J. S. Fossey, Y. T. Long, Portable Surfaced-Enhanced Raman Scattering Sensor for rapid detection of aniline and phenol derivatives by on-site electrostatic preconcentration, Anal. Chem. 82(2010)9299 - 9305.

[22] J. Q. Xue, D. W. Li, L. L Qu, Y. T. Long, Surface-imprinted core-shell Au nanoparticles for selective detection of bisphenol A based on surfaced-enhanced Raman scattering, Anal. Chim. Acta. 777(2013)57 - 62.

[23] L. Guerrini, J. V. G. Ramos, C. Domingo, S. S. Cortes, Functionalization of Ag Nanoparticles with dithiocarbamate Calix arene as an effective supramolecular Host for the Surface-enhanced Raman Scattering detection of Polycyclic aromatic Hydrocarbons, Langmuir. 22(2006)10924 - 10926.

[24] X. F. Shi, Y. H. Kwon, J. Ma, R. G. Zheng, C. Y. Wang, H. D. Kronfeldt, Trace analysis of polycyclic aromatic hydrocarbons using calixarene layered gold colloid film as substrates for surface-enhanced Raman scattering, J. Raman Spectrosc. 44(2013)41 - 46.

[25] L. Guerrini, J. V. G. Ramos, C. Domingo, S. S. Cortes, Sensing Polycyclic aromatic hydrocarbons with dithiocarbamate-functionalized Ag nanoparticles by surface-enhanced Raman Scattering, Anal. Chem. 81(2009)953 - 960.

[26] K. C. Grabar, K. J. Allison, B. E. Baker, R. M. Bright, K. R. Brown, R. G. Freeman, A. P. Fox, C. D. Keating, M. D. Musick, M. J. Natan, Two-Dimensional arrays of colloidal Gold Particles; a flexible Approach to macroscopic metal surfaces, Langmuir. 12(1996)2353 - 2361.

[27] J. B. Jia, B. Q. Wang, A. G. Wu, G. J. Cheng, Z. Li, S. J. Dong, A method to construct a third-generation horseradish Peroxidase Biosensor; self-assembling Gold nanoparticles to three-dimensional sol-gel network, Anal.

Chem. 74(2002)2217 - 2223.

[28] T. X. Yang, X. Y. Guo, H. Wang, S. Y. Fu, J. Yu, Y. Wen, H. F. Yang, Au dotted magnetic network nanostructure and its application for on-site monitoring femtomolar level pesticide, Small. 10(2014)1325 - 1331.

[29] S. Y. Fu, X. Y. Guo, H. Wang, T. X. Yang, Y. Wen, H. F. Yang, Detection of trace mercury ions in water by a novel Raman probe, Sens. Actuators, B. 199(2014)108 - 114.

[30] N. Wang, H. F. Yang, X. Zhu, R. Zhang, Y. Wang, G. F. Huang, Z. R. Zhang, Synthesis of anti-aggregation silver nanoparticles based on inositol hexakisphosphoric micelles for a stable surface enhanced Raman scattering substrate, Nanotechnology. 20(2009)315603 - 3115608.

[31] Y. K. Li, H. M. Yu, C. K. Zhang, L. Fu, G. F. Li, Z. G. Shao, B. L. Yi, Enhancement of photoelectrochemical response by Au modified in TiO_2 nanorods, Int. J. Hydrogen Energy. 38(2013)13023 - 13030.

[32] L. L. Qu, Y. T. Li, D. W. Li, J. Q. Xue, J. S. Fossey, Y. T. Long, Humic acids-based one-step fabrication of SERS substrates for detection of polycyclic aromatic hydrocarbons, Analyst. 138(2013)1523 - 1528.

（原载于 Sensors & Actuators B Chemical 2015 年第 212 期）

A glucose-responsive pH-switchable bioelectrocatalytic sensor based on phenylboronic acid-diol specificity

Peiyi Gao[a], Zhihua Wang[b], Lele Yang[a],
Tengfei Ma[a], Ling Yang[a], Qianqiong Guo[a],
Shasheng Huang[a, b]

[a] Life and Environmental Science College, Shanghai Normal University
[b] Chenzhou No. 1 People's Hospital, Hunan Province

1. Introduction

Stimuli-responsive materials have attracted much attention as their physicochemical properties can undergo dynamic changes in accord with internal alterations and/or external changes in living systems. Switchable and tunable electrochemical interfaces were extensively investigated and applied in electroanalytical and bioelectroanalytical systems [1 – 4], electrooptical systems [5 – 8], magneto-electrochemical systems [9 – 11], fuel cell and energy storage systems [12,13], nano-or microactuators [14], information storage and processing systems [15 – 17], single-electron devices [18], molecular and biomolecular switches [19,20], and controlled wettability systems [21,22].

Recently, stimuli-responsive or "smart" biointerfaces not only focus on single physical signals, such as light [23 – 27], magnetic field [11, 21, 28-36], electrochemical potential [37 – 39], chemical signals like pH changes [40 – 42], or metal cation addition [43 – 45], but also satisfy the needs of double [46] or multiple stimulations [47 – 50] in complex environment. Amid various external stimuli that activate/deactivate biosensor, pH is the most studied one. Many biosensor performances were reversibly affected by the change of pH environment, whose responses were integrated for detection purpose. Besides, many *in vivo* tumor targeting and medicine delivery were designed in combination with pH-responsive polymers [47,51,52] or other biocompatible nanoparticles [53].

Until now, there have been three major kinds of glucose-responsive systems including glucose oxidase (GOD), convanavalin A, and phenylboronic acid [54]. Boronic acid and its derivatives, reported to react with 1,2-, 1,3-or 1,4-diol to create a stable cyclic ester, are a unique class of stimuli-responsive molecules with potential applications as self-healing materials, self-regulated drug-delivery systems, and sensors for the detection of diols like dopamine, sugar and glycoproteins [55]. The complex of the boronic acid is a trigonal boronic acid ester, while the complex of its conjugate base is a tetrahedral boronate ester. They are in equilibrium with each other, with the neutral boronate ester holding a low extent [56]. Boronate groups served as extremely attractive functionalities in probes fluorescently [57 - 59] or electrochemically [60, 61] recognized/detected various species based on boronic acid-diol specificity.

As free carboxylic acid sites of 4-mercaptobenzoic acid (MBA) are sensitive to environmental pH, they are easily protonated/deprotonated in response to the change of pH. Furthermore, since pK_a of 3-aminophenylboronic acid (APBA) in aqueous solution is 8.9 [55], APBA moieties tend to be non-ionic form in lower pH conditions as an electron-deficient Lewis acid with an sp^2-hybridized boron atom, while to be anionic form in higher pH conditions characterized by an electron-rich sp^3 boron atom with tetrahedral geometry. Accordingly, APBA moieties were covalently grafted onto MBA in this paper. Rather than a complex polymerization process to bind to the backbone of poly(acrylic acid) [51] or polymer brushes [46,62], in our developed biosensor, APBA moieties were facilely fabricated onto the MBA-immobilized gold microelectrode. The combination of APBA and MBA using potassium ferricyanide as electroactive probes proved to be sensitive to pH change. GOD is a kind of glycoenzymes that contain lots of sugar residues on their surfaces [63]. Taking advantage of the specific recognition of phenylboronic acid-diol, GOD was accordingly linked here, resulting in a bioelectrocatalytic sensor that was both pH-and glucose-responsive. With the change of pH and/or the presence of glucose, our proposed biosensor acted as a pH switch and produced the corresponding signal. On "ON" state, the biosensor showed a good performance to the detection of glucose both in experimental solution and in disposed serum samples. The general strategy of the method could thus be extended to practical sample detection.

2. Experimental

2. 1 *Chemicals and apparatus*

4-mercaptobenzoic acid (MBA), 3-aminophenylboronic acid monohydrate (APBA), N-hydroxysulfosuccinimide sodium salt (NHS), 1-(3-dimethylaminopropyl)-3-ethylcarbodiimide hydrochloride (EDC), glucose oxidase (GOD, type X-S: from aspergillus niger), glucose, uric acid (UA), ascorbic acid (AA), L-cysteine, lysine, hexaammineruthenium (III) chloride, ferrocenecarboxylic acid, potassium ferricyanide ($K_3[Fe(CN)_6]$), potassium ferrocyanide ($K_4[Fe(CN)_6]$), $MgCl_2$, $CaCl_2$, Na_2SO_4 and $NaNO_3$ were purchased from Sigma-Aldrich Company (Shanghai, China). All chemicals were of analytical grade and were used as received. Milli Q 18. 2 $M\Omega$ water was used throughout the experiments.

The buffer solution was prepared by 0. 1 mol L^{-1} phosphate buffered saline (PBS) containing 10 mmol L^{-1} KCl adjusted to different pH values. In fact, the actual pH range of PBS was from 5. 8 to 8. 0, in order to simulate the biological environment that was faintly acidic or alkaline, two ends were chosen for comparison throughout the experiment. The base solution for detection was 0. 1 mol L^{-1} PBS containing 1 mmol L^{-1} potassium ferricyanide as electroactive probes.

Electrochemical measurements were performed on a CHI 660D electrochemical workstation (CH Instruments, Shanghai, China). A modified gold microelectrode (GME, 100 μm in diameter, CH Instrument) was used as the working electrode, an Hg/HgO electrode and a platinum wire electrode were used as reference and counter electrode, respectively.

2. 2 Assemblies of biosensors

The electrochemical biosensor was prepared as follows. The GME was polished successively with 0. 3 and 0. 05 μm alumina powder to produce a smooth, shiny surface, and then cleaned ultrasonically in acetone and pure water. Later, it was pretreated by cleaning with piranha solution (v/v = 3/1, concentrated $H_2SO_4/30\%$ H_2O_2, caution!) for 15 min. Then it was electrochemically cleaned in 0. 5 mol L^{-1} H_2SO_4 by cycling from 0 to 1. 6 V until a stable gold reductive wave was observed at a scan rate of 100 mV s^{-1}, thoroughly rinsed with water and dried with nitrogen.

The GME treated according to the process described above was soaked into 2 mmol L^{-1} MBA/ethanol solution for 4 hours to fabricate MBA-immobilized gold microelectrode (MBA-GME). After rinsing with ethanol and pure water to remove physically adsorbed molecules, it was further immersed into 2 mmol L^{-1} APBA aqueous solution for 2 hours with the addition of EDC and NHS to get APBA-modified sensor (APBA-MBA-GME), which was rinsed with water thoroughly and stored in pH 7. 0 PBS for further use.

100 mg GOD was dissolved in 500 μL water, and the resulting solution was incubated with the as-prepared APBA-MBA-GME sensor at 4 ℃ for 2 hours to form GOD-immobilized device (GOD-APBA-MBA-GME).

2. 3 *Electrochemical measurements*

The electrochemical measurements were conducted in a 10 mL electrochemical cell with a three-electrode system. Differential pulse voltammetry (DPV) was performed in base solution with an initial potential of-0. 2 V, final potential of 0. 6 V, step potential of 0. 004 V and amplitude of 0. 05 V. Cyclic Voltammetry (CV) was performed in base solution with initial potential of 0. 6 V, high potential of 0. 6 V, low potential of-0. 2 V at different scan rates. Electrochemical impedance spectroscopy (EIS) was performed with initial potential of 0. 188 V, high frequency of 100 000 Hz, low frequency of 0. 1 Hz and amplitude of 5 mV in 0. 1 mol L^{-1} PBS (pH 7. 0) containing 5 mmol L^{-1} $K_3[Fe(CN)_6]$ and 5 mmol L^{-1} $K_4[Fe(CN)_6]$, respectively.

EIS data were modeled by Randle's equivalent circuit and fitted by ZSimpWin software.

2. 4 *Disposal of serum samples*

Drug-free human blood samples were collected from healthy volunteers at Chenzhou No. 1 People's Hospital. 2 mL human serum containing 0. 2 mg GOD (with a specific activity of 100 μmol/min/mg) was incubated for 18 h at 37 ℃ to remove inherent glucose in the serum. Then the pH of the serum was adjusted to 8. 5 using diluted NaOH solution to destroy the activity of GOD, which irreparably lost its catalytic activity under the condition of pH < 3 or pH > 8 [58]. The pretreated serum adjusted to 5. 8 was diluted 10 times by PBS. Different concentration of glucose was added to the diluted serum samples to prepare the spiked samples.

3. Results and discussion

3. 1 *Schematic illustration*

The immobilization of APBA to MBA acted as " command

interfaces", having two surface states: one of them allowed easy access of soluble electroactive probes to the conducting electrode support, while another state had restricted access for the electroactive probes. As shown in Fig. 1, in the absence of glucose, when the GOD-APBA-MBA-GME was immersed in pH 5. 8 base solution, partially unreacted MBA moieties were exposed outside, with free carboxylic acid groups protonized; meanwhile, APBA moieties were in non-ionic forms, both the two kinds of structural changes were conducive to electron transfer (eT) between the anion electroactive probe potassium ferricyanide in solution and electrode surface, resulting in a distinctly amplified current signal performed as eT "ON" (state 1, Fig. 1). Due to the fact that electron-withdrawing substituents reduce the pK_a of APBA [64], the binding of APBA to MBA would accordingly lower its pK_a. Therefore, when it was soaked in pH 8. 0 base solution, the residual-COOH groups of MBA were deprotonized to anions, and APBA moieties were transformed to tetrahedral boronate anions. Both the two factors resulted in the charge repulsion, restricting access of electroactive probes to the conducting electrode support, leading to a poor current signal as eT "OFF" state (state 2, Fig. 1). On the contrary, in the presence of glucose, when the GOD-APBA-MBA-GME was immersed in pH 5. 8 base solution, electron transfer was facilitated with the help of GOD, and a further amplified signal was obtained biocatalytically (state 3, Fig. 1). Yet, even in the presence of glucose, the eT "OFF" biosensor was hindered to transfer electron (state 4, Fig. 1).

This switch originated from the different states of the moieties bound on the electrode surface: in one of them (pH = 5. 8), the combination of APBA and MBA moieties was protonated and allowed the quasi-diffusion translocation providing the electrochemical accessibility for the electroactive redox probes, while in another state (pH = 8. 0), the combination was deprotonated restricting the electrochemical process. Accordingly, when the GOD-APBA-MBA-GME was

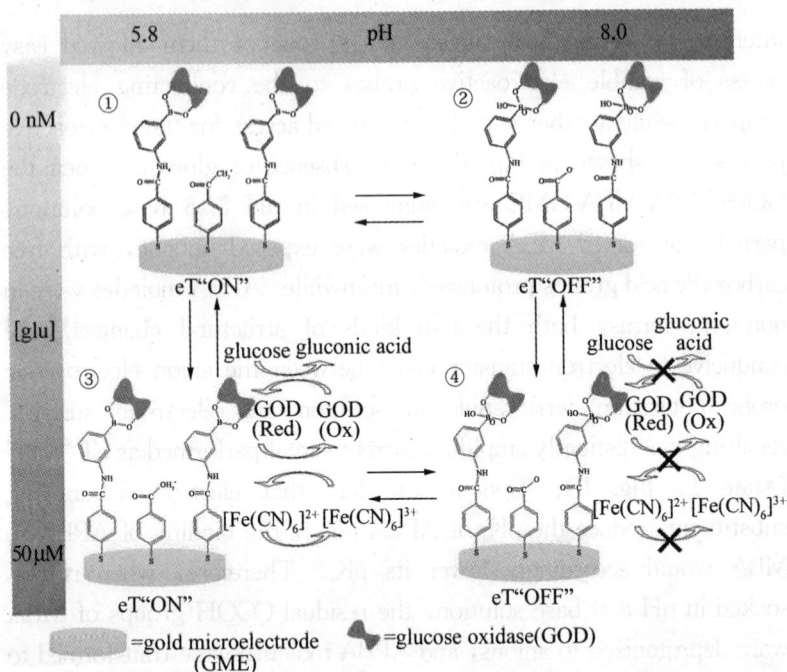

Fig. 1 Schematic illustration for the response of glucose and H⁺. GOD-APBA-MBA-GME performed in ①acidic condition in the absence of glucose as eT "ON"; ②alkaline condition in the absence of glucose as eT "OFF"; ③ eT "ON" in acidic condition in the presence of glucose; and ④ eT "OFF" in alkaline condition in the presence of glucose.

on eT "ON" state, it turned to state 1 or state 3 in response to the existence of glucose. The catalytically amplified anodic current could be employed to the detection of glucose.

3. 2 Formation of the biosensor

To confirm the formation of the bioelectrocatalytic sensor, EIS was compared after each modification step. Fig. S1 showed the Nyquist plots obtained by bare GME (a), MBA-GME (b), APBA-MBA-GME (c) and GOD-APBA-MBA-GME (d) in 0.1 M PBS solution (pH 7.0) containing 5 mmol L^{-1}[Fe(CN)$_6$]$^{3-/4-}$. Inset of Fig. S1 was a modified Randle's equivalent circuit utilized to model the EIS data for the present system. Herein, R$_s$ stood for solution resistance, C was the interface capacitance, W was the Warburg element and R_{et} was the electron transfer resistance directly measured as the semicircle diameter. The plot for the bare GME (a) exhibited small R_{et} value of 8111 Ω. When MBA moieties were modified onto GME, the R_{et} dramatically increased to 37500 Ω (plot b), an evident proof of the successful modification. However, the binding of APBA showed a great decline to about 32770 Ω (plot c), suggesting a better conductivity of the APBA-MBA-combined film. It was probably because APBA moieties were in non-ionic form in pH 7. 0 base solution as a result of its lower pK_a. Compared with the deprotonated MBA moieties, the formation of amide bonds and the existence of non-anionic boronate ions would neutralize the negative charges, which were conducive to electron transfer of the electroactive anion probes. Further immobilization of GOD again soared the R_{et} value to 58920 Ω (plot d), indicating the successful binding of macromolecules.

3. 3   Reversible pH switch

To investigate the properties of our developed biosensor, GOD-APBA-MBA-GME was first studied in the absence of glucose from pH 5. 8 to 8. 0, where an obvious quasi-reversible redox signal was achieved in pH 5. 8 base solution as eT "ON" state (red curve "a" in Fig. 2A) but almost no current signal was achieved in pH 8. 0 base solution as eT "OFF" state (black curve "b" in Fig. 2A). Detailed information was displayed in Fig 2B, when the biosensor was performed in pH 5. 8, the anodic current reached ~171 nA. With the growth of pH value, there was a clear decline in current signal. When it was performed in pH 8. 0 base solution, the anodic current was seriously hindered to ~ 20 nA. To confirm the stability of the biosensor, it was run in pH 5. 8 and pH 8. 0 base solution alternately for five cycles (Fig 2C). Fortunately, there was little attenuation in anodic current at the two different conditions. The sharp and stable contrast in current occurred upon the change of pH like a pH switch.

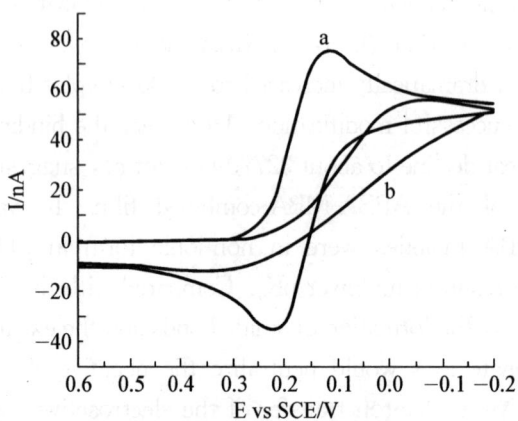

A

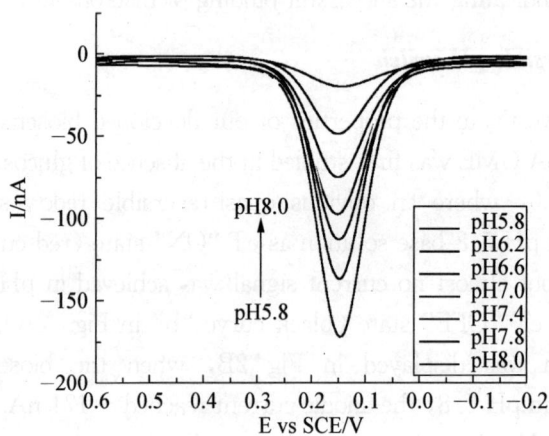

B

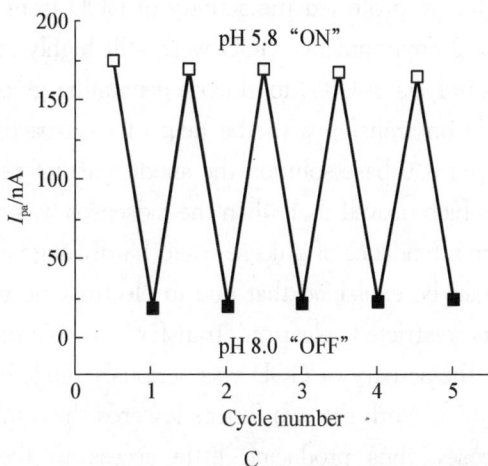

C

Fig. 2 In the absence of glucose, (A) CVs of GOD-APBA-MBA-GME performed in pH 5.8 base solution (red curve "a") as eT "ON" state, and in pH 8.0 base olution (black curve "b") as eT "OFF" state. (B) DPVs of GOD-APBA-MBA-GME at different pH values ranging from 5.8 to 8.0. (C) pH switch of GOD-APBA-MBA-GME run in pH 5.8 ("ON" state) and pH 8.0 ("OFF" state) base solution alternately for five cycles.

In the presence of glucose, an evident transformation of redox curve was observed in pH 5.8 base solution as eT "ON" state (red curve "a" in Fig. 3A), probably due to the catalytic effect of GOD to glucose, but a further suppressed current signal was observed in pH 8.0 base solution as eT "OFF" state (black curve "b" in Fig. 3A). Fig. 3B was the DPVs of GOD-APBA-MBA-GME performed in different pH base solution in the addition of 30 μmol L^{-1} glucose. In pH 5.8 base solution, the anodic current reached $\sim$225 nA, 54 nA higher than that in the absence of glucose. Herein, little potential shift was observed, for the concentration of glucose was too slight to influence the oxidative potential of the larger amount of electroactive probe. It demonstrated that the existence of glucose for the biosensor in acidic condition had little inhibiting effect on the eT "ON" state. On an average, the isoelectric point of GOD was investigated to be around 4-5 due to the residues of the free carboxyl groups [65]. The existence of glucose protected the activity of GOD from inactivation. Thus in pH 5. 8 environment, GOD were still highly-activated, and probably the catalysis of GOD to glucose generating gluconic acid and promoting electron transfer with the help of electroactive mediator. However, in pH 8. 0 base solution the anodic current reduced to less than 20 nA, which proved that when the biosensor was on eT "OFF" state, even the attendance of glucose could hardly augment the anodic current. It could be explained that due to electrostatic repulsion, eT "OFF" state restricted electron transfer to electrode support. Furthermore, the activity of GOD was seriously hindered in pH 8. 0 environment [65]. Both the two factors lowered the catalysis effect of GOD to glucose, thus producing little access to the transfer of electron. To confirm the stability of the biosensor in the presence of glucose, it was run in pH 5. 8 and pH 8. 0 base solution alternately for five cycles as well (Fig 3C), where there was little attenuation in anodic current at the two different conditions. The sharp and stable contrast was not affected by the addition of glucose, and the switch of GOD-APBA-MBA-GME between eT "ON" and eT "OFF" state still existed with the combination of glucose and pH changes.

A

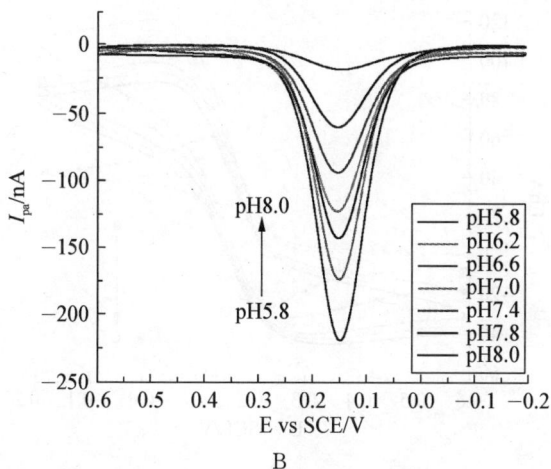

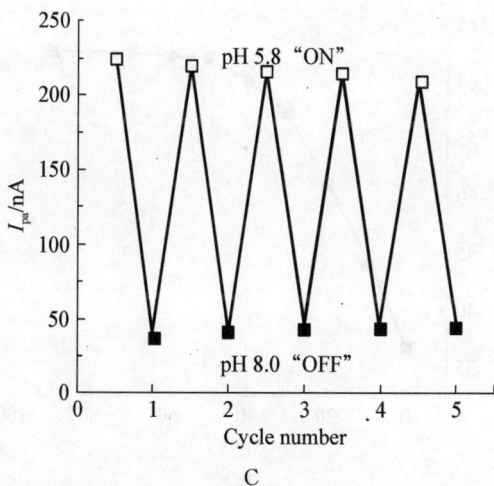

Fig. 3 In the presence of 50 μmol L⁻¹ glucose, (A) CVs of GOD-APBA-MBA-GME performed in pH 5. 8 base solution (red curve "a") as eT "ON" state, and in pH 8. 0 base olution (black curve "b") as eT "OFF" state. (B) DPVs of GOD-APBA-MBA-GME at different pH values ranging from 5. 8 to 8. 0. (C) pH switch of GOD-APBA-MBA-GME run in pH 5. 8 ("ON" state) and pH 8. 0 ("OFF" state) base solution alternately for five cycles.

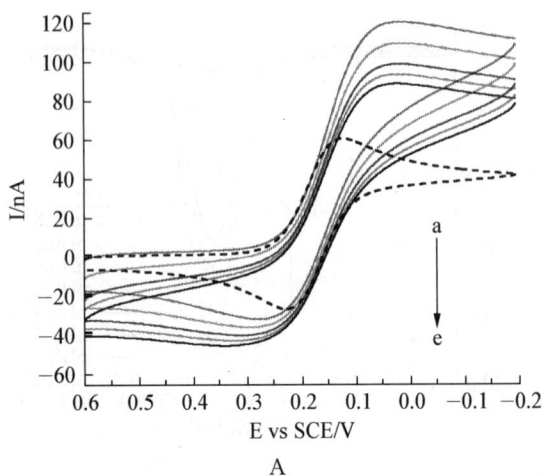

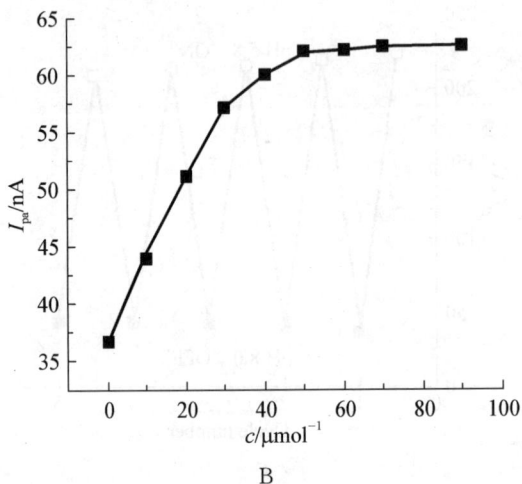

Fig. 4 (A) CV curves of the GOD-APBA-MBA-GME performed on "ON" state in pH 5. 8 base solution containing 0 μmol L^{-1} (black dash curve), 10 μmol L^{-1} (a), 20 μmol L^{-1} (b), 30 μmol L^{-1} (c), 40 μmol L^{-1} (d) and 50 μmol L^{-1} (e) glucose. (B) Correlation of glucose concentration to anodic current, where reaching a current plateau for after the addition of 50 μmol L^{-1} glucose.

The origin for the switching effect may originate from several reasons: (1) electrostatic repulsion of the mediator by depronoted

MBA and tetrahedral anion boronic acid, which evidently generated an eT "OFF" state. (2) effect of pH on the activity of GOD. The activity of GOD in pH 5. 8 promoted the catalysis of glucose, while in pH 8. 0 GOD was inactivated. (3) desorption of GOD from the multilayer as a function of alkaline pH range. In pH 8. 0 environment, GOD was seriously inactivated leading to slight desorption from the electrode multilayer, and the catalysis effect was affected accordingly. The electrostatic changes of multilayer and the catalysis effect of GOD facilitated the switching between eT "ON" and eT "OFF" as a pH switch.

3. 4 Optimum conditions for analyses

Different electroactive probes had different influence on the electrochemical performance. As shown in Fig S2, ferrocenecarboxylic acid, hexaammineruthenium (III) chloride, and potassium ferricyanide were chosen for comparison for the same GOD-APBA-MBA-GME in pH 5. 8, pH 7. 0 and pH 8. 0 as acidic, neutral and alkaline conditions, respectively. It was observed that using ferrocenecarboxylic acid, the anodic current decreased slightly with the increase of pH value (Fig S2A). While the use of hexaammineruthenium (III) chloride led to an opposite result, where a little increase in anodic current was found with the increase of pH value (Fig S2B). However, using potassium ferricyanide as electroactive probe, the anodic current reduced greatly with the increase of pH value (Fig S2C). It might be that ferrocenecarboxylic acid and potassium ferricyanide were anions in aqueous solution, which would promote electron transfer in acidic environment while repel in alkaline environment. What's more, potassium ferricyanide exhibited a better electrochemical behavior for its more negative charges carried. However, as cations in aqueous solution, hexaammineruthenium (III) chloride was inhibited to transfer electron in acidic condition but was promoted in alkaline condition. What achieved above indirectly explained part of the mechanism of the GOD-APBA-MBA-GME; that was to say, the devised biosensor was mainly based on the electrostatic interaction between the probes and the modified multilayer on the electrode surface. As the pH of base solution chan-

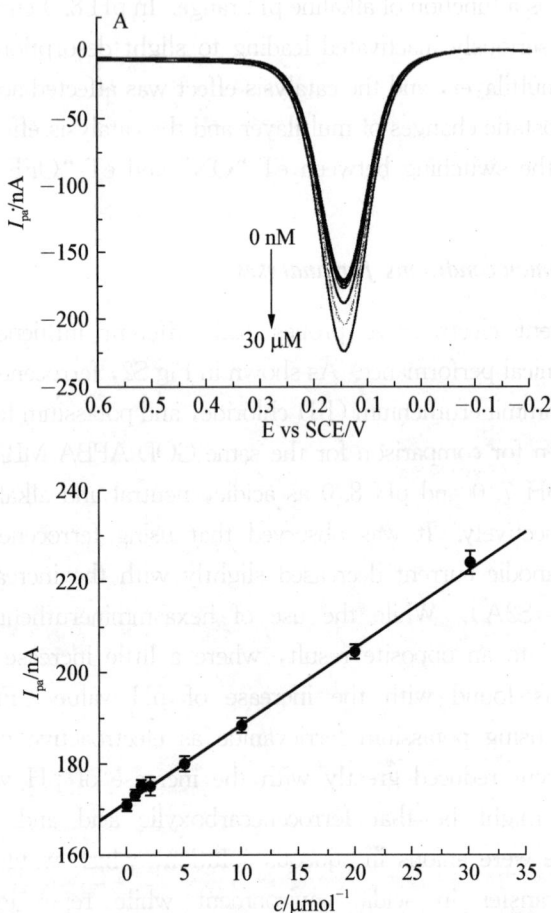

Fig. 5 (A) Quantitative detection of glucose for the GOD-APBA-MBA-GME on "ON" state in pH 5. 8 base solution, the concentration being 0 nmol L^{-1}, 500 nmol L^{-1}, 1 μmol L^{-1}, 2 μmol L^{-1}, 5 μmol L^{-1}, 10 μmol L^{-1}, 20 μmol L^{-1} and 30 μmol L^{-1}, respectively. (B) The plot of anodic current versus the concentration of glucose. Error bars represented standard deviations from three measurements.

ged, the charges of the multilayer varied accordingly, leading to charge attraction/repulsion between the probe and electrode surface, and thus significant anodic current differences were obtained.

3.5 *Effect of fabrication process*

Each fabrication process was probably affected by the change of pH values as well. Fig S3 showed GME, MBA-GME and APBA-MBA-GME performed in different pH base solution ranging from 5.8 to 8.0. As could be seen, the variation of pH had almost no effect on the GME (Fig S3A), but had an observable influence on the MBA-GME (Fig S3B), and a more evident current difference was observed for the APBA-MBA-GME (Fig S3C). It was probably because MBA moieties were sensitive to pH environment, and APBA moieties experienced structural transformation upon the change of pH environment. As a consequence, it was confirmed that the pH switch was attributed to not only the structural change of APBA but also MBA moieties immobilized on the electrode surface. Compared to APBA-MBA-GME, though the linkage of GOD through specific recognition of boronic acid-diol slightly inhibited the anodic current when the biosensor was immersed in pH 5.8 base solution as eT "ON" state (Fig 2B), the presence of glucose amplified the anodic current catalytically (Fig 3B). Therefore, we could conclude that whether in the presence of glucose or not, the GOD-APBA-MBA-GME performed as a pH switch as well.

3.6 *Properties of "ON" state*

It had been demonstrated above that the GOD-APBA-MBA-GME worked efficiently in pH 5.8 base solution as eT "ON" state. In order to know more about our devised bioelectrosensor, follow-up investigations were conducted. Firstly, CVs at different sweep rates were performed in the absence of glucose (Fig S4A). Taking the anodic current as an example, it proved to be proportional to the square root of scan rate by Randles-Sevcik equation for a diffusion-controlled electrochemical process, with a linear equation $I_{pa} = 7.7704 \, v^{1/2} + 23.6089$, R^2 being 0.99997 (Fig S4B). This behavior of the surface-modified electrode originates from the quasi-diffusional translocation of the electroactive units bound to the flexible multilayer tethered to the electrode surface. Due to the structural complexity and incomplete bound of APBA to MBA moieties, we could qualitatively conclude that the electron transport between the conductive support and the electroactive centers proceeded upon the quasi-diffusional translocation.

As the GOD-APBA-MBA-GME had selective response to glucose, base solution containing different concentration of glucose was prepared to investigate its extending range. Fig 4A showed CV curves of the bioelectrocatalytic sensor performed in 0 μmol L^{-1} (black dash curve), 10 μmol L^{-1} (a), 20 μmol L^{-1} (b), 30 μmol L^{-1} (c), 40 μmol L^{-1} (d) and 50 μmol L^{-1} (e) glucose in pH 5.8 base solution, where the biosensor was on "ON" state. Obviously observed, the catalytic oxidation of glucose significantly changed the CV curves, and the anodic current increased with the increase of glucose concentration, reaching a current plateau for 50 μmol L^{-1} (Fig 4B). It could also be seen that there was a linear correlation in the range of 0 to 30 μmol L^{-1} glucose. Therefore, 30 μmol L^{-1} was chosen as the optimum glucose concentration for the investigation of other factors.

Different response time (15s, 30s, 60s, 90s and 120s) was investigated in 30 μmol L^{-1} glucose in pH 5.8 base solution (Fig. S5). It was found that after 30s, there was little increase in anodic current. Accordingly, 30s was chosen as the response time for quick detection of glucose in all the investigations in this paper. The stability in anodic current probably resulted from the stable activity of GOD in pH 5.8 environment [65].

3. 7 *Quantitative detection*

To verify the linearity, a more detailed quantitative experiment was carried out for the GOD-APBA-MBA-GME in pH 5. 8 base solution as an eT "ON" state. As shown in Fig 5A, the increase of glucose concentration led to the growth of anodic current, and a linear correlation from 0 to 30 μmol L^{-1} glucose was achieved (Fig 5B), with a detection limit of 348 nmol L^{-1} (S/B=3) and a dynamic range extending to 50 μmol L^{-1}.

3. 8 *Specificity and stability of the bioelectrocatalytic sensor*

In measurement of real samples some electroactive species in the serum may influence the performance of the bioelectrocatalytic sensor. Some common organic and inorganic substances were examined as possible interferents in the determination of 30 μmol L^{-1} glucose by adding the appropriate amount of interferents to the test solution. The results suggested that for the determination of 30 μmol L^{-1} glucose, organic compounds like UA (100 μmol L^{-1}), AA (100 μmol L^{-1}), L-cysteine (100 μmol L^{-1}) and lysine (100 μmol L^{-1}), and inorganic ions like Ca^{2+} (100 μmol L^{-1}), Mg^{2+} (100 μmol L^{-1}), SO_4^{2-} (100 μmol L^{-1}) and NO_3^{-} (100 μmol L^{-1}) had little influence on the anodic current (Fig. S6), mainly due to the specific catalytic interaction between GOD and glucose, indicating a good specificity of our developed biosensor.

As GOD was vulnerable to the environment, the GOD-APBA-MBA-GME could only be stored in 0. 1 M PBS (pH 7. 0) at 4 ℃ for several days. However, the APBA-MBA-GME was quite stable and was able to be stored in 0. 1 M PBS (pH 7. 0) at 4 ℃ for more than two months, and the response current of the biosensor decreased slightly. As a result, the GOD-APBA-MBA-GME could be freshly fabricated for detection of glucose.

Table 1 Determination of glucose in human serum samples*

Sample	Original found by this method	Added (μmol/L)	Found (μmol/L)	Recovery (%)	RSD (n=3,%)
1#	ND	0	0	—	—
2#	ND	10.0	10.5	105.0	5.7
3#	ND	20.0	19.1	95.5	3.9
4#	ND	30	28.9	96.3	3.5

3.9 *Determination of glucose in human serum samples*

In order to evaluate the feasibility of the proposed device in real sample detection, the GOD-APBA-MBA-GME was applied to the determination of glucose in human serum samples. After pretreatment to remove the original amount of glucose, the diluted samples were spiked with standard gulcose. The average results of three parallel experiments obtained by standard addition method were shown in Table 1, with the RSD lower than 5.7% and the average recoveries in the range of 95.5%-105%, all of which demonstrated the potential application of our developed bioelectrocatalytic sensor for the detection of glucose in human serum samples. Furthermore, after pretreatment of human serum samples, GOD had totally oxidized glucose to gluconic acid. Sample 1# in Table 1 showed that in the absence of glucose and presence of gluconic acid generated, response was not detected. It could indirectly conclude that the presence of gluconic acid as an input factor had little influence on the biosensor.

4. Conclusions

In summary, facilely fabricated, our proposed biosensor showed an amplified anodic current in pH 5.8 base solution as "ON" state, yet a prohibited anodic current in pH 8.0 base solution as "OFF" state. When on "ON" state, the biosensor showed a good linearity for the detection of glucose ranging from 0 to 30 μmol L^{-1}, with a detection limit of 348 nmol L^{-1} (S/B = 3) and a dynamic range extending to 50 μmol L^{-1}. Glucose-responsive, pH-switchable and catalytically-amplified, our biosensor provided a new method for the detection of glucose in the form of pH switch in human serum sample. There was not much literature about pH switch based on boronic acid for the detection of glucose, and the amplified signal to small amount of glucose led to more accurate sensitivity and less deviation. We hoped the "ON" state of the pH switch would be practical to more complicated *in vitro* and *in vivo* environment.

Acknowledgements

This work was supported by the Project of the National Science Foundation of People's Republic of China (21275100), Shanghai Leading Academic Discipline Project (S30406) and Key Laboratory of Resource Chemistry of Ministry of Education.

Appendix A. Supplementary data

Supplementary data associated with this article can be found, in the online version, at http://dx. doi. org/10. 1016/j. elec-tacta. 2014. 11. 054.

References

[1] X. Zuo, S. Song, J. Zhang, D. Pan, L. Wang, C. Fan, A target-responsive electrochemical aptamer Switch (TREAS) for reagentless detection of nanomolar ATP, J. Am. Chem. Soc. 129(2007)1042.

[2] E. Katz, Y. Weizmann, I. Willner, Magnetoswitchable reactions of DNA monolayers on electrodes: gating the processes by hydrophobic magnetic nanoparticles, J. Am. Chem. Soc. 127(2005)9191.

[3] E. Katz, L Sheeny-Haj-Ichia, A. F. Buckmann, I. Willner, Dual biosensing by magneto-controlled bioelectrocatalysis, Angew. Chem., Int. Ed. 41 (2002) 1343.

[4] J. J. Gooding, C. Wasiowych, D. Barnett, D. B. Hibbert, J. N. Barisci, G. G. Wallace, Electrochemical modulation of antigen-antibody binding, Biosens.

Bioelectron. 20(2004)260.

[5] J. Lanzo, M. De Benedittis, B. C. De Simone, D. Imbardelli, P. Formoso, S. Manfredi, G. Chidichimo, Photoelectrochromic switchable nematic emulsion, J. Mater. Chem. 17(2007)1412.

[6] H. Gu, Z. Ng, T. C. Deivaraj, X. Su, K. P. Loh, Surface plasmon resonance spectroscopy and electrochemistry study of 4-Nitro-1, 2-phenylenediamine: a switchable redox polymer with nitro functional groups, Langmuir 22 (2006)3929.

[7] V. Chegel, O. Raitman, E. Katz, R. Gabai, I. Willner, Photonic transduction of electrochemically-triggered redox-functions of polyaniline films using surface plasmon resonance spectroscopy, Chem. Commun. 10(2001)883.

[8] D. R. Rosseinsky, L. Glasser, H. D. B. Jenkins, Thermodynamic clarification of the curious ferric/potassium ion exchange accompanying the electrochromic redox reactions of Prussian blue, iron (III) hexacyanoferrate (II), J. Am. Chem. Soc. 126(2004)10472.

[9] E. Katz, I. Willner, Hydrophobic magnetic nanoparticles induce selective bioelectrocatalysis, Chem. Commun. 32(2005)4089.

[10] E. Katz, I. Willner, Switching of directions of bioelectrocatalytic currents and photocurrents at electrode surfaces by using hydrophobic magnetic nanoparticles, Angew. Chem. , Int. Ed. 44(2005)4791.

[11] E. Katz, R. Baron, I. Willner, Magnetoswitchable electrochemistry gated by alkyl-chain-functionalized magnetic nanoparticles: control of diffusional and surface-confined electrochemical processes, J. Am. Chem. Soc. 127 (2005)4060.

[12] E. Katz, I. Willner, A biofuel cell with electrochemically switchable and tunable power output, J. Am. Chem. Soc. 125(2003)6803.

[13] S. K. Brayshaw, A. Harrison, J. S. Mclndoe, F. Marken, P. R. Raithby, J. E. Warren, A. S. Weller, Sequential reduction of high hydride count octahedral rhodium clusters [Rh$_6$ (PR$_3$)$_6$ H$_{12}$] [BAr$_4^F$]$_2$: redox-switchable hydrogen storage, J. Am. Chem. Soc. 129(2007)1793.

[14] M. Lahav, C. Durkan, R. Gabai, E. Katz, I. Willner, M. E. Welland, Redox activation of a polyaniline-coated cantilever: an electro-driven microdevice, Angew. Chem. , Int. Ed. 40(2001)4095.

[15] J. Areephong, W. R. Browne, N. Katsonis, B. L. Feringa, Photo-and electrochromism of diarylethene modified ITO electrodes-towards molecular based read-write-erase information storage, Chem. Commun. 37(2006)3930.

[16] E. Katz, I. Willner, A quinine-functionalized electrode in conjunction with hydrophobic magnetic nanoparticles acts as a "Write-Read-Erase" information storage system, Chem. Commun. 45(2005)5641.

[17] R. Baron, A. Onopriyenko, E. Katz, O. Lioubashevski, I. Willner, S. Wang, H. Tian, Am electrochemical/photochemical information processing system using a monolayer-functionalized electrode, Chem. Commun. 20 (2006)2147.

[18] E. Katz, O. Lioubashevski, I. Willner, Magneto-switchable single-electron charging of Au-nanoparticles using hydrophobic magnetic nanoparticles, Chem. Commun. 10(2006)1109.

[19] E. Katz, O. Lioubashevsky, I. Willner, Electromechanics of a redox-active rotaxane in a monolayer assembly on an electrode, J. Am. Chem. Soc. 126 (2004)15520.

[20] M. V. Voinova, M. Jonson, Electronic transduction in model enzyme sensors assisted by a photoisomerizable azo-polymer, Biosens. Bioelectron. 20 (2004)1106.

[21] E. Katz, L. Sheeney-Hai-Ichia, B. Basnar, I. Felner, I. Willner, Magnetoswitchable controlled hydrophilicity/hydrophobicity of electrode surfaces using alkyl-chain-functionalized magnetic particles: application for switchable electrochemistry, Langmuir 20(2004)9714.

[22] X. Wang, A. B. Kharitonov, E. Katz, I. Willner, Potential-controlled molecular machinery of bipyridinium monolayer-functionalized surfaces: an electrochemical and contact angle analysis, Chem. Commun. 13(2003)1542.

[23] M. Lion-Dagan, E. Katz, I. Willner, Amperometric transduction of optical signals recorded by organized monolayers of photoisomerizable biomaterials on Au electrodes, J. Am. Chem. Soc. 116(1994)7913.

[24] I. Willner, M. Lion-Dagan, S. Marx-Tibbon, E. Katz, Bioelectrocatalyzed amperometric transduction of recorded optical signals using monolayer-modified Au-electrodes, J. Am. Chem. Soc. 117(1995)6581.

[25] A. Doron, M. Portnoy, M. Lion-Dagan, E. Katz, I. Willner, Amperometric transduction and amplification of optical signals recorded by a phenoxynaphthacenequinone monolayer electrode: photochemical and pH-gated electron transfer, J. Am. Chem. Soc. 118(1996)8937.

[26] N. Liu, D. R. Dunphy, P. Atanassov, S. D. Bunge, Z. Chen, G. P. Lopez, T. J. Boyle, C. J. Brinker, Photoregulation of mass transport through a photoresponsive azobenzene-modified nanoporous membrane, Nano Lett. 4

(2004)551.

[27] S. Bonnet, J. P. Collin, Ruthenium-based light-driven molecular machine prototypes: synthesis and properties, Chem. Soc. Rev. 37(2008)1207.

[28] I. M. Hsing, Y. Xu, W. Zhao, Micro-and nano-magnetic particles for applications in biosensing, Electroanal. 19(2007)755.

[29] I. Willner, E. Katz, Magnetic control of electrocatalytic and bioelectrocatalytic processes, Angew. Chem. Int. Ed. 42(2003)4576.

[30] R. Hirsch, E. Katz, I. Willner, Magneto-switchable bioelectrocatalysis, J. Am. Chem. Soc. 122(2000)12053.

[31] J. Wang, A. N. Kawde, Magnetic-field stimulated DNA oxidation, Electrochem. Commun. 4(2002)349.

[32] R. Laocharoensuk, A. Bulbarello, S. Mannino, J. Wang, Adaptive nanowire-nanotube bioelectronic system for on-demand bioelectrocatalytic transformations, Chem. Commun. 32(2007)3362.

[33] J. Wang, Adaptive nanowires for on-demand control of electrochemical microsystems, Electroanal. 20(2008)611.

[34] O. A. Loaiza, R. Laocharoensuk, J. Burdick, M. C. Rodriguez, J. M. Pingarron, M. Pedrero, J. Wang, Adaptive orientation of multifunctional nanowires for magnetic control of bioelectrocatalytic processes, Angew. Chem. Int. Ed. 46(2007)1508.

[35] J. Wang, M. Scampicchio, R. Laocharoensuk, F. Valentini, O. Gonzalez-Garcia, J. Burdick, Magnetic tuning of the electrochemical reactivity through controlled surface orientation of catalytic nanowires, J. Am. Chem. Soc. 128 (2006)4562.

[36] J. Lee, D. Lee, E. Oh, J. Kim, Y. P. Kim, S. Jin, H. S. Kim, Y. Hwang, J. H. Kwak, J. G. Park, C. H. Shin, J. Kim, T. Hyeon, Preparation of a magnetically switchable bioelectrocatayltic system employing cross-linked enzyme aggregates in magnetic mesocellular carbon foam, Angew. Chem. Int. Ed. 44(2005)7427.

[37] H. Ma, D. J. Rroctor, E. Kierzek, R. Kierzek, P. C. Bevilacqua, M. Gruebele, Exploring the energy landscape of a small RNA hairpin, J. Am. Chem. Soc. 128(2006)1523.

[38] B. V. I. Chegel, O. A. Raitman, O. Liubashevski, Y. Shirshov, E. Katz, I. Willner, Redox-Switching of electrorefractive, electrochromic, and conductivity functions of Cu^{2+}/polyacrylic acid films associated with electrodes, Adv. Mater. 14(2002)1549.

[39] M. Jahn, H. Chen, J. Mullegger, J. Marles, R. A. J. Warren, S. G. Withers, Thioglycosynthases: double mutant glycosidases that serve as scaffolds for thioglycoside synthesis, Chem. Commun. 3(2004)274.

[40] P. R. Ashton, R. Ballardini, V. Balzani, I. Baxter, A. Credi, M. C. T. Fyfe, M. T. Gandolfi, M. Gomez-Lopez, M. V. Martinez-Diaz, A. Piersanti, N. Spencer, J. F. Stoddart, M. Venturi, A. J. P. White, D. J. Williams, Acid-base controllable molecular shuttles, J. Am. Chem. Soc. 120 (1998)11932.

[41] F. Coutrot, C. Romuald, E. Busseron, A new pH-switchable dimannosyl[c2] Daisy chain molecular machine, Org. Lett. 10(2008)3741.

[42] C. J. Richmond, A. D. C. Parenty, Y. F. Song, G. Cooke, L. Cronin, Realization of a "Lockable" molecular switch via pH-and redox-modulated cyclization, J. Am. Chem. Soc. 130(2008)13059.

[43] G. Nishimura, K. Ishizumi, Y. Shiraishi, T. Hirai, A thiethylenetetramine bearing anthracene and benzophenone as a fluorescent molecular logic gate with Either-Or switchable dual logic functions, J. Phys. Chem. B 110(2006)21596.

[44] R. P. Fahlman, M. Hsing, C. S. Sporer-Tuhten, D. Sen, Duplex pinching: a structural switch suitable for contractile DNA nanoconstructions, Nano Lett. 3 (2003)1073.

[45] Y. Shiraishi, Y. Tokitoh, T. Hirai, A fluorescent molecular logic gate with multiply-configurable dual outputs, Chem. Commun. 42 (2005) 5316.

[46] H. Liu, Y. Li, K. Sun, J. Fan, P. Zhang, J. Meng, S. Wang, L. Jiang, Dual-responsive surfaces modified with phenylboronic acid-containing polymer brush to reversibly capture and release cancer cells, J. Am. Chem. Soc. 135 (2013) 7603.

[47] D. Roy, J. N. Cambre, B. S. Sumerlin, Triply-responsive boronic acid block copolymers: solution self-assembly induced by changes in temperature, pH, or sugar concentration, Chem. Commun. 16(2009)2106.

[48] L. A. Tziveleka, P. Bilalis, A. Chatzipavlidis, N. Boukos, G. Kordas, Development of multiple stimuli responsive magnetic polymer nanocontainers as efficient drug delivery systems, Macromol. Biosci. 14(2014)131.

[49] Y. Li, K. Xiao, W. Zhu, W. Deng, K. S. Lam, Stimuli-responsive cross-linked micelles for on-demand drug delivery against cancers, Adv. Drug Deliver. Rev. 66(2014)58.

[50] J. F. Mano, Stimuli-responsive polymeric systems for biomedical applications, Adv. Eng. Mater. 10(2008)515.

[51] N. Schuwer, H. A. Klok, Tuning the pH sensitivity of poly(methacrylic acid) brushes, Langmuir 27(2011)4789.

[52] M. T. Fenske, W. Meyer-Zaika, H. G. Korth, H. Vieker, A. Turchanin, C. Schmuck, Cooperative self-assembly of discoid dimmers: hierarchical formation of nanostructures with a pH switch, J. Am. Chem. Soc. 135(2013)8342.

[53] R. Liu, P. Liao, J. Liu, P. Feng, Responsive polymer-coated mesoporous silica as a pH-sensitive nanocarrier for controlled release, Langmuir 27 (2001)3095.

[54] Q. Wu, L. Wang, H. Yu, J. Wang, Z. Chen, Organization of glucose-responsive systems and their properties, Chem. Rev. 222(2011)7855.

[55] J. N. Cambre, B. S. Sumerlin, Biomedical applications of boronic acid polymers, Polymer 52(2011)4631.

[56] J. Li, Z. Wang, P. Li, N. Zong, F. Li, A sensitive non-enzyme sensing platform for glucose based on boronic acid-diol binding, Sensor. Actuat. B-Chem. 161(2012)832.

[57] Z. Guo, I. Shin, J. Yoon, Recognition and sensing of various species using boronic acid derivatives, Chem. Commun. 48(2012)5956.

[58] S. Liu, F. Shi, X. Zhao, L. Chen, X. Su, 3-aminophenyl boronic acid-functionalized CuInS$_2$ quantum dots as a near-infrared fluorescence probe for the determination of dopamine, Biosens. Bioelectron. 47(2013)379.

[59] J. Peng, Y. Wang, J. Wang, X. Zhou, Z. Liu, A new biosensor for glucose determination in serum based on up-converting fluorescence resonance energy transfer, Biosens. Bioelectron. 28(2011)414.

[60] H. Yao, F. Chang, N. Hu, pH-switchable bioelectrocatalysis based on layer-by-layer films assembled through specific boronic acid-diol recognition, Electrochim. Acta 55(2010)9185.

[61] Q. Wang, I. Kaminska, J. Niedziolka-Jonsson, M. Opallo, M. Li, R. Boukherroub, S. Szunerits, Sensitive sugar detection using 4-aminophenylboronic acid modified grapheme, Biosens. Bioelectron. 50(2013)331.

[62] H. B. Liu, Q. Yan, C. Wang, X. Liu, C. Wang, X. H. Zhou, S. J. Xiao, Saccharide-and temperature-responsive polymer brushes grown on gold nanoshells for controlled release of diols, Colloids and Surfaces A: Physicochem. Eng. Aspects 386(2011)131.

[63] J. Anzai, Y. Kobayashi, Construction of multilayer thin films of enzymes by means of sugar-lectin interactions, Langmuir 16(2000)2851.

[64] C. Zhang, M. D. Losego, P. V. Braun, Hydrogel-based glucose sensors:

effects of phenylboronic acid chemical structure on response, Chem. Mater. 25 (2013)3239.

[65] N. C. Foulds, C. R. Lowe, Enzyme entrapment in electrically conducting polymers immobilization of glucose oxidase in polypyrrole and its application in amperometric glucose sensors, Faraday Trans. 82(1986)1259.

（原载于 Electrochimica Acta 2014 年第 151 期）

DYT1 directly regulates the expression of *TDF1* for tapetum development and pollen wall formation in Arabidopsis

Jing-Nan Gu[a], Jun Zhu, Yu Yu[b], Xiao-Dong Teng[a],
Yue Lou[a], Xiao-Feng Xu[a], Jia-Li Liu[a] and Zhong-Nan Yang[a]

[a] Development Center of Plant Germplasm Resources, College of Life and Environment Sciences, Shanghai Normal University
[b] Shanghai Huangxing School

INTRODUCTION

The anther is the male organ that produces pollen for plant reproduction. The mature anther consists of four somatic cell layers, namely the epidermis, endothecium, middle layer, and tapetum enclosing gametophyte cells. The tapetum originates from the L2 layer as one of three germ layers, L1, L2 and L3, in the stamen primordial (Goldberg *et al.*, 1993). As the innermost of the four somatic cell layers surrounding male gametophytes, the tapetum plays an essential role in pollen development (Mariani *et al.*, 1990; Sanders *et al.*, 1999). Tapetal fate determination depends on the signaling pathway triggered by several leucine-rich repeat receptor-like protein kinases (LRR-RLKs) during the early stage of anther development. Dysfunction of these pathways leads to additional microsporocytes lacking the tapetal cells, resulting in complete male sterility (Canales *et al.*, 2002; Zhao *et al.*, 2002; Yang *et al.*, 2003; Albrecht *et al.*, 2005; Colcombet *et al.*, 2005; Ma, 2005; Jia *et al.*, 2008).

During anther development, the tapetum undergoes dramatic morphological differentiation to form the binuclear secretory cell, which is packed with ribosomes, mitochondria, Golgi bodies, endoplasmic reticulum and vesicles (Stevens and Murray, 1981; Bedinger, 1992). During male gametogenesis, the tapetal cells provide the precursors of sporopollenin for pollen exine formation, the callase complex (also termed β-1,3-glucanase) to release microspores from the tetrad, and numerous elaioplasts and cytoplasmic lipid bodies for pollen coat formation (Mascarenhas 1975; Stieglitz, 1977; Pacini and Juniper, 1979; Hesse and Hess 1993).

In Arabidopsis, several transcription factors regulate the tapetum and its functions. *DYT1* encodes a putative basic helix loop helix (bHLH) transcription factor, and *TDF1* encodes a putative R2R3 MYB transcription factor. Mutations in these two genes cause tapetal hypertrophy extending into the locule and resulting in sporophytic male sterility (Zhang *et al.* , 2006; Zhu *et al.* , 2008). The transcription factor *ABORTED MICROSPORES (AMS)* encodes a bHLH family protein that plays an important role in tapetum development and pollen wall formation (Sorensen *et al.* , 2003; Xu *et al.* , 2010). Another member of the R2R3 MYB family, MS188/ MYB80, apparently regulates sexine formation (Zhang *et al.* , 2007; Zhu *et al.* , 2010). MALE STERILITY1 (MS1), a nuclear protein with PHD-finger motifs, is essential for tapetum development at the post-meiotic phase (Wilson *et al.* , 2001; Ito *et al.* ,2007; Yang *et al.* , 2007). These transcription factors form a genetic pathway (DYT1-TDF1-AMS-MS188/MYB80 - MS1) for tapetal development and function (Zhu *et al.* , 2011).

Cytological evidence indicates that the majority of the precursor materials of the pollen wall originate from the tapetum (Heslop-Harrison, 1962; Dickinson and Heslop-Harrison, 1968). The pollen wall consists of two main layers, the outer exine layer and the inner intine layer. The exine is further divided into the sexine and the nexine (Scott, 1994). Recently, MS188/MYB80 and TEK have been reported to control sexine formation and nexine formation, respectively (Zhang *et al.* , 2007; Lou *et al.* , 2014). Both are directly regulated by AMS (Lou *et al.*, 2014). The sexine layer most likely consists of sporopollenin, which is derived from long-chain fatty acids, oxygenated aromatic rings and phenylpropionic acids (Piffanelli *et al.*, 1998; Ariizumi and Toriyama, 2011). Multiple enzymes in the tapetum, including ACOS5, CYP703A2, CYP704B1, MS2, PKSA and PKSB are involved in the biochemical pathways for sexine formation (Morant *et al.*, 2007; de Azevedo Souza *et al.*, 2009; Dobritsa *et al.*, 2009, 2010; Kim *et al.*, 2010; Chen *et al.*, 2011).

DYT1 functions during the early stage of tapetum development. Transcriptome analysis showed that many genes in the tapetum are downregulated in the *dyt1* mutant (Feng *et al.*, 2012). However, detailed regulation of the tapetum remains unclear. Here, we show that DYT1 directly binds the promoter of TDF1 during tapetum development. Furthermore, a transgenic rescue assay demonstrated that DYT1 regulates the expression of genes for pollen wall formation, primarily via TDF1.

RESULTS

The promoter region (−550 to −463 bp) of *DYT1* is essential for its expression

Previous studies showed that the 631 bp promoter fragment of DYT1 is sufficient to drive its expression for its function in the anther (Song *et al.*, 2009). This promoter region contains specific *cis*-acting elements including MYB, WRKY, ARR1, GATABOX, GTGANTG10, ACGTBOX, W-box, and DOF components according to the PLACE database (http://www. dna. affrc. go. jp/PLACE/) (Higo *et al.*, 1999) (Table S1). We created constructs with GUS driven by different lengths of the *DYT1* promoter fragments (Figure 1a), and transformed the constructs into wild-type. GUS activity could be detected in transgenic lines with promoter fragments of 631 and 550 bp (Figure 1b,c). *In situ* hybridization was used to analyze the expression pattern of GUS driven by the 550 bp fragment. During anther stage 4, the tapetal cells are differentiated when the four-lobed anther pattern is established (Sanders *et al.*, 1999). A weak GUS signal was detected in the anther at this stage (Figure 1i). At stages 5 and 6, when the tapetal layer is clearly present in the anther and the microcytes undergo meiosis, the GUS signal was highest in the tapetum compared to the low level in the meiocytes (Figure 1j,k). At stage 7, when meiosis is complete and the tetrad is formed, the GUS signal was significantly reduced (Figure 1l). The GUS expression pattern driven by the 550 bp fragment was similar to the *DYT1* expression in the wild type (Zhang *et al.*, 2006; Zhu *et al.*, 2011). However, no GUS staining was observed in the transgenic plants with the *DYT1* promoters of 463, 331, 180 and 91 bp, respectively (Figure 1d-g). These results suggest that the promoter region (-550 to -463 bp) contains essential motifs for *DYT1* expression.

DYT1-GFP is specifically localized in tapetal cells

To further understand the function of DYT1 during anther development, we created a DYT1-GFP fusion protein driven by the 631-bp native *DYT1* promoter (Figure 2a). After transformed into heterozygous ($dyt1$-2/+) plants, we identified a transgenic line with a homozygous ($dyt1/dyt1$) background using closely linked markers (Figure 2c and Table S2). This transgenic line exhibited a fully fertile phenotype (Figure 2b), indicating that the DYT1 GFP fusion protein was enable to rescue the sterile phenotype of the $dyt1$ mutation. In the wild type, GFP fluorescence was not observed in the anther. In the transgenic line, GFP fluorescence was not detected at stage 4 (Figure. 2d). At stage 5, the GFP signal was initially present within the tapetal cells (Figure 2e). At stage 6, a stronger GFP signal was detected in the tapetal cells, which formed a circle within the locule. In meiocytes, the DYT1 GFP fluorescence was not observed (Figure 2f,g). At the tetrad stage (stage 7), the GFP signal was weakly detected in the tapetal cells. No GFP signal was observed in tetrads (Figure 2h,i). At stage 8, when the microspores are released from the tetrads, GFP fluorescence was not detected in the anther (Figure 2j,k). These results indicate that the DYT1 is strictly localized in tapetal cells, which is consistent with its role in tapetal development.

ChIP assay demonstrates that DYT1 is associated with the TDF1 promoter

TDF1 is a transcriptional regulator downstream of DYT1 and is involved in tapetum development and function (Zhu *et al.*, 2008). In *dyt1-2*, *TDF1* is barely detected (Zhu *et al.*, 2011). Previous studies showed that DYT1 bind to the G-box (TCACGTGA) of target gene promoters (Feng *et al.*, 2012). However, no G-box is presented in the 1000 bp promoter region of *TDF1*. There are three E-box motifs (CANNTG) in this region, which is a variant of the G-box. We used chromatin immunoprecipitation (ChIP) with a GFP monoclonal antibody to determine whether DYT1-GFP directly binds to the promoter of *TDF1*. Four probes were designed in the promoter region of *TDF1* (Figure 3a). Quantitative ChIP-PCR (qChIP-PCR) showed no significant enrichment of the *TDF1* promoter fragment in the wild type (Figure 3b). By contrast, the *pTDF1-3* fragment of the *TDF1* promoter was increased when GFP monoclonal antibodies were used (+AB) compared with the -AB samples (Figure 3c). No significant increase in the other three *TDF1* promoter fragments was observed

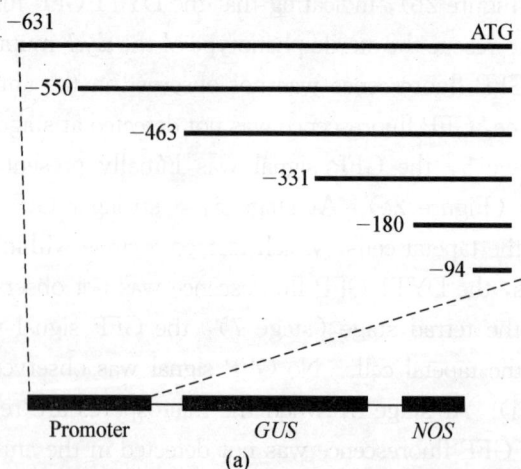

(a)

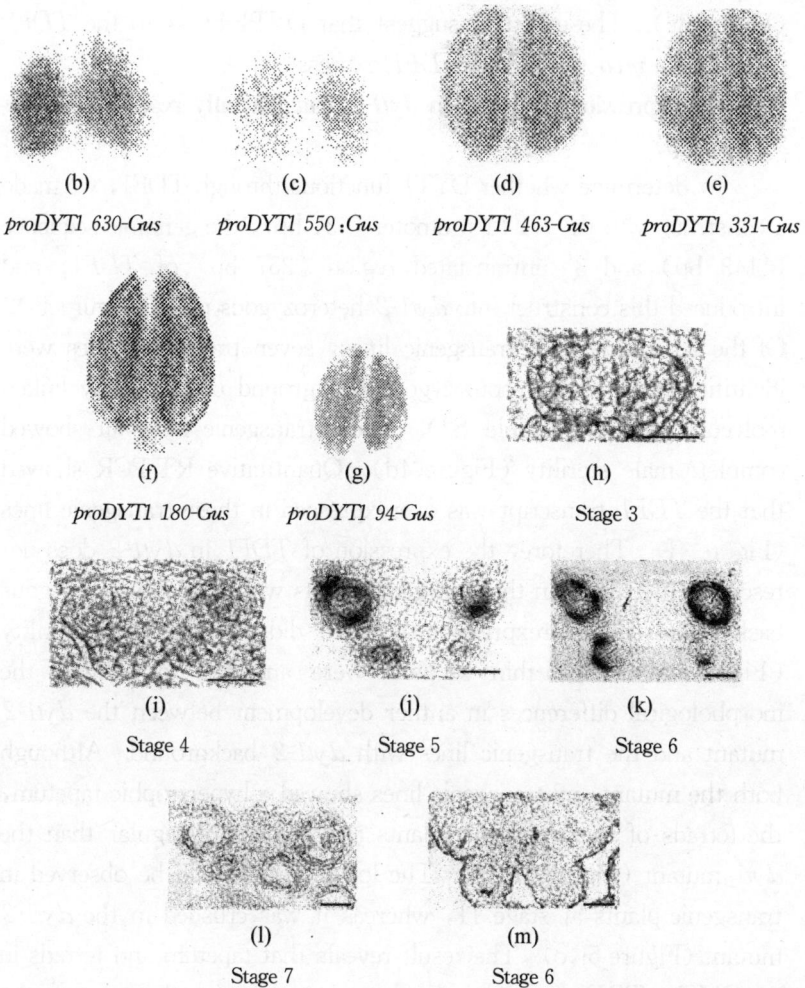

(b)

(c)

(d)

(e)

proDYT1 630-Gus   *proDYT1 550 ; Gus*   *proDYT1 463-Gus*   *proDYT1 331-Gus*

(f)

(g)

(h)

proDYT1 180-Gus   *proDYT1 94-Gus*   Stage 3

(i)

(j)

(k)

Stage 4   Stage 5   Stage 6

(l)

(m)

Stage 7   Stage 6

Figure 1. Promoter analysis of DYT1. (a) Construction of GUS driven by different length fragments of the DYT1 promoter. (b-g) GUS activity of the transgenic lines with different length fragments of the DYT1 promoter. (b) The anther of proDYT1-630 : Gus. (c) The anther of proDYT1-550 : Gus. (d) The anther of proDYT1-463 : Gus. (e) The anther of proDYT1-331 : Gus. (f) The anther of proDYT1-180 : Gus. (g) The anther of proDYT1-94 : Gus. (h)-(l) *In situ* hybridization analysis of transgenic lines with GUS RNA Probe during anther development. ProDYT1-550 : Gus anthers from stages 3 (h), 4 (i), 5 (j), 6 (k), 7 (l). (m) Stage 6 anther hybridized with the sense probe. Bars=40 μm.

(Figure 3c). These results suggest that DYT1 binds to the *TDF1* promoter *in vivo* to regulate *TDF1* expression.

The expression of TDF1 in *dyt1-2* can partially rescue the *dyt1-2* phenotype

To determine whether DYT1 functions through TDF1, we made a construct with the *DYT1* promoter (631 bp), the genomic sequence (1143 bp) and 3′ untranslated region (257 bp) of *TDF*1, and introduced this construct into *dyt1-2* heterozygous plant (Figure 4a). Of the 23 independent transgenic lines, seven transgenic lines were identified to be *dyt1-2* homozygous background using closely linked molecular markers (Table S2). These transgenic lines all showed complete male sterility (Figure 4d). Quantitative RT-PCR showed that the *TDF1* transcript was overexpressed in these transgenic lines (Figure 4f). Therefore, the expression of *TDF1* in *dyt1-2* does not rescue the fertility. In the transgenic plants with *dyt1-2* heterozygous background, the overexpression of *TDF1* did not affect their fertility (Figure 4e). Semi-thin sections were analyzed to identify the morphological differences in anther development between the *dyt1-2* mutant and the transgenic lines with *dyt1-2* background. Although both the mutant and transgenic lines showed a hypertrophic tapetum, the tetrads of the transgenic plants appeared more regular than the *dyt1* mutant (Figure 5h, m). The locule space could be observed in transgenic plants at stage 11, whereas it was crushed in the *dyt1-2* mutant (Figure 5j,o). The result reveals that tapetum and tetrads in *proDYT1∷TDF*1 transgenic lines are less defective than that in the *dyt1-2* plants.

We used the *proDYT1∷TDF*1 transgenic line to identify the genes regulated by DYT1 via TDF1. The *SPL*, *EMS*1, *SERK1*, *SERK2* and *TPD*1 have been reported to be important for early anther development and tapetal fate determination, Genetic studies showed that these genes function upstream of *DYT1* (Yang *et al.*, 1999; Ma, 2005; Zhang *et al.*, 2006). The qRT-PCR showed that the expressions of these genes were either increased or nearly normal in *pro-DYT1 :: TDF1* transgenic plants. This result is consistent with previous studies that these genes act upstream of *DYT1*. Additionally, the GAMYB-like genes, *AtMYB33* and *At-MYB65* play a redundantly role for tapetum development (Millar and Gubler, 2005). The double mutant of them showed the similar tapetal defect compared with that in *dyt 1*. These genes likely act at approximately the same stage as *DYT1* (Zhang *et al.*, 2006). The expression of

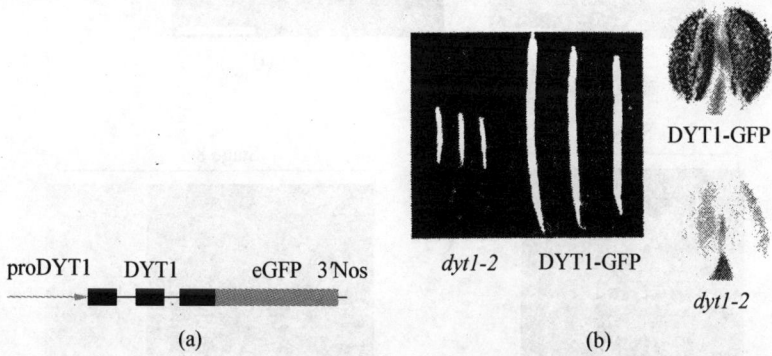

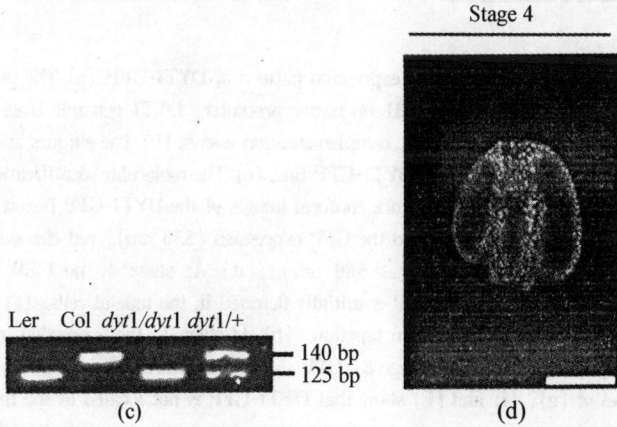

proDYT1   DYT1   eGFP 3'Nos
(a)

dyt1-2   DYT1-GFP

DYT1-GFP

dyt1-2

(b)

Stage 4

Ler Col *dyt*1/*dyt*1 *dyt*1/+
— 140 bp
— 125 bp
(c)

(d)

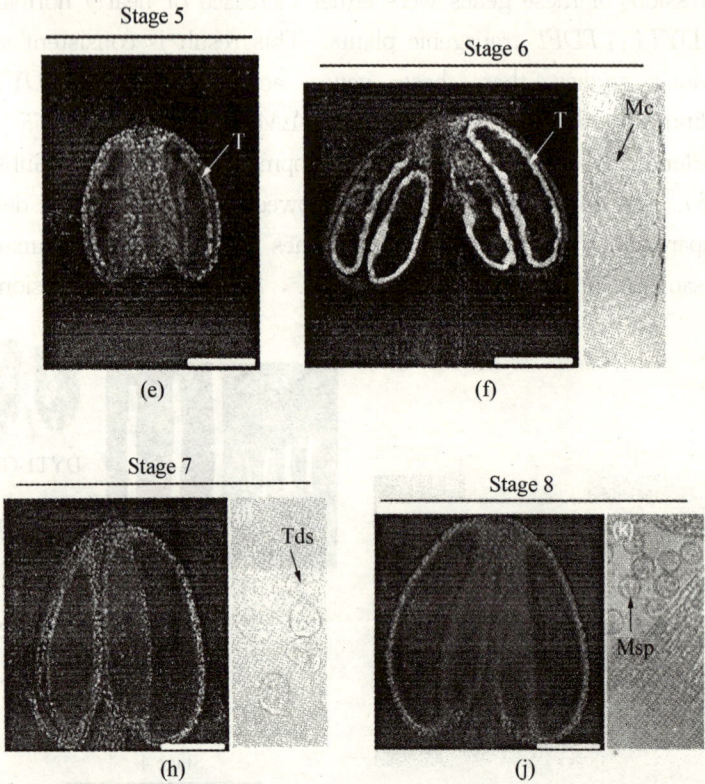

Figure 2. Genetic complement and expression pattern of DYT1-GFP. (a) The proDYT1:
DYT1-GFP constructs including 631 bp native promoter, DYT1 genomic fragment and
GFP coding region used for genetic complementation assays. (b) The siliques and stained
anthers of *dyt1-2* and proDYT1:DYT1-GFP line. (c) The molecular identification of the
dyt1 mutated site. (d-k) Fluorescence confocal images of the DYT1-GFP fusion protein.
The green channel in (d-k) showed the GFP expression (530 nm), red channel showed
the chlorophyll autofluorescence (> 560 nm). (d) At stage 4, no GFP signal is
observed. (e) At stage 5, the GFP is initially detected in the tapetal cells. (f) At stage
6, the GFP is strongly expressed in tapetum. (h) At stage 7, the expression of GFP is
dramatically decreased. (j) At stage 8, GFP signal disappeared in anther. The bright-
field images of (g), (i) and (k) show that DYT1-GFP is not located in the meiocytes,
tetrads and microspores, respectively. T, tapetum; Mc, meiocytes; Td, tetrads; Msp,
microspores, Bars=40 μm.

these genes was up-regulated in *proDYT1* :: *TDF1* transgenic plants (Figure 4h). The transcription factors *AMS*, *MS188/MYB80*, *MS1*, and *TEK* are essential for tapetum development and pollen wall formation. They act downstream of DYT1 and TDF1 (Zhu *et al.*, 2008, Lou *et al.*, 2014). The expression of these genes was nearly restored to the level in the wild type (Figure 4g). These results suggest that DYT1 regulates the expression of these transcription factors via *TDF1* for tapetum development and pollen wall formation.

Genes for pollen wall synthesis act downstream of *TDF1*

During anther development, tapetal cells are active in the biosynthesis of phenylpropanoids, steryl esters, long-chain alkanes, and flavonoids for exine formation (Hernould *et al.*, 1998; Scott *et al.*, 2004). Although pollen grains are ruptured in the locule of transgenic lines during the late stage (Figure 5o), the expression of the regulators for exine formation, *AMS*, *MS188/MYB80* and *TEK*, are recovered in the transgenic line. We determined whether the exine precursors of the pollen wall were synthesized in the tapetal cells of the transgenic plants. The diethyloxadi-carbocyanine iodide ($DIOC_2$) and Tinopal were utilized to stain the fatty acid content of exine and cellulose materials in the transgenic line and mutant plant (Regan and Moffatt, 1990; Lou *et al.*, 2014). In the wild type, the red fluorescence of $DIOC_2$ staining was observed in the tapetum and microspores and the blue fluorescence of Tinopal staining showed cell outline in the anther (Figure 6a). In the transgenic plants, the red fluorescence was also detected in the defective tapetum and ruptured pollen, indicating that some exine materials were synthesized in these cells (Figure 6c). However, no red fluorescence was observed in the anther of *dyt1-2* mutant (Figure 6b). This result indicated that the materials for the pollen wall could be synthesized when the *TDF1* expressed.

In *Arabidopsis*, *ACOS5*, *CYP703A2*, *CYP704B1*, *MS2*, *PKSA*, *PKSB* and ABCG26 are involved in sporopollenin synthesis and transport (Morant *et al.*, 2007; de Azevedo Souza *et al.*, 2009;

Dobritsa et al. , 2009; Kim et al. , 2010; Quilichini et al. , 2010; Chen et al. , 2011). The expression of these genes was significantly down regulated in the *dyt1-2* mutant. However, the expression levels of these genes in the transgenic plants were restored to the level of the wild type (Figure 6d). These results indicate that the expression of the exine-related genes is restored and that the materials for the pollen wall are synthesized in the transgenic lines. Therefore, the normal expression of *TDF1* is *dyt1* is sufficient to drive the expression of the exine-related genes directly or indirectly for the synthesis of the pollen wall materials.

DISCUSSION

DYT1 is required for early tapetum development and function

During anther development, SPL/NZZ is a key regulator that controls the early differentiation of primary sporogenous cells into

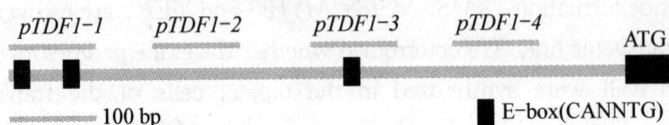

(a)

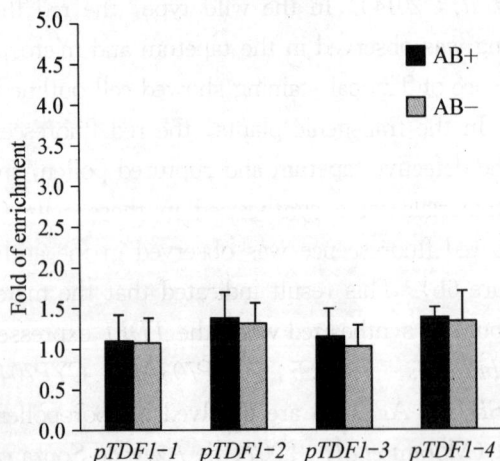

(b)

DYT1-GFP

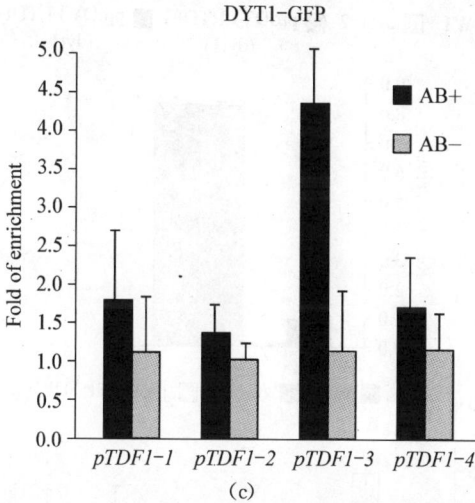

(c)

Figure. 3   TDF1 is a direct target of DYT1. (a) The black box indicates the potential DYT1-binding sites in the TDF1 promoter region (1 kb). The grey short lines show the fragments amplified in the ChIP-PCR assays. (b, c) The enrichments of TDF1 promoter were confirmed by ChIP-quantitative PCR (qPCR) with the primer sets (pTDF1-1, pTDF1-2, pTDF1-3, pTDF1-4), using the wild-type (b) and DYT1-GFP (c) samples. Fold of enrichment is calcu lated from three independent replicates. Error bars represent the standard deviation (n = 3). AB+, presence of antibody; AB-, absence of antibody.

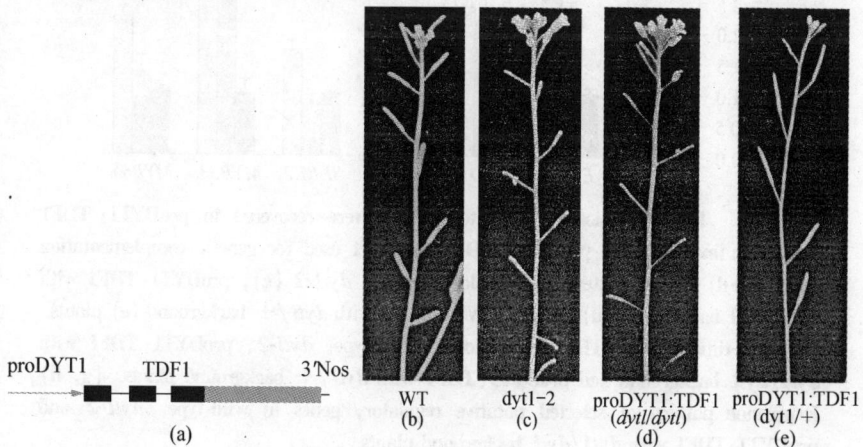

proDYT1   TDF1   3′Nos

(a)

WT
(b)

dyt1-2
(c)

proDYT1:TDF1
(*dyt1/dyt1*)
(d)

proDYT1:TDF1
(dyt1/+)
(e)

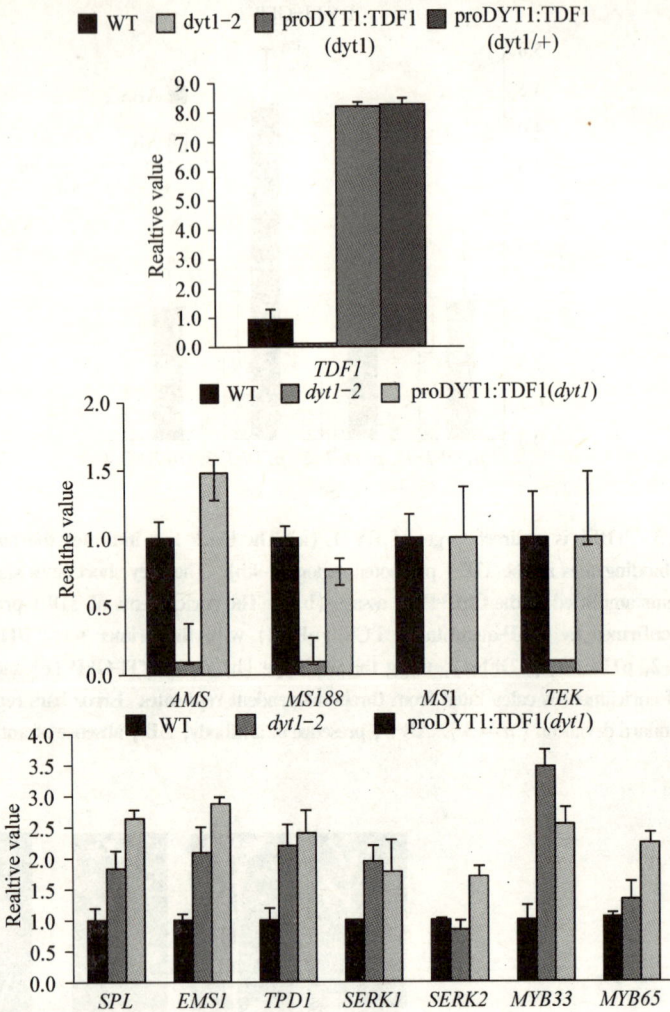

Figure 4   The expression of regulatory genes were recovered in proDYT1:TDF1 transgenic line. (a) The proDYT1:TDF1 construct used for genetic complementation assay. (b-d) The main stem of the wild-type (b), *dyt1-2* (c), proDYT1:TDF1 with *dyt1/dyt1* background (d), and proDYT1:TDF1 with *dyt1/+* background (e) plants. (f) Real-time PCR of TDF1 expression in wild-type, *dyt1-2*, proDYT1:TDF1 with *dyt1/dyt1* background and proDYT1:TDF1 with *dyt1/+* background plants. (g, h) Expression pattern of selected putative regulatory genes in wild-type, *dyt1-2* and proDYT1:TDF1 with *dyt1/dyt1* background plants.

microsporocytes (Schiefthaler *et al.*, 1999; Yang *et al.*, 1999). Tapetum fate determination requires a signaling pathway between reproductive and non-reproductive cells, such as the EMS1/TPD1-dependent pathway(s) (Zhao *et al.*, 2002; Yang *et al.*, 2003). *DYT1* is a critical transcription factor for early tapetum development acting downstream of *SPL*, *EMS1* and *TPD1* (Zhang *et al.*, 2006; Chang *et al.*, 2011). Using promoter-GUS analysis, we determined that the promoter region (−550 to −463 bp) of *DYT1* contains important *cis*-elements essential for *DYT1* expression (Figure 1). These elements are putative binding sites for MYB, WRKY, and bZIP family proteins. Of the upstream regulators, *SPL* encodes a putative MADs-Box transcription factor. However, no MADs-Box binding site was found in the essential region (Table S1). It is likely that there are some other factors that can bind to the essential *cis*-elements of the *DYT1* promoter to regulate its expression. The identification of these factors will contribute to understanding the early events of tapetum development.

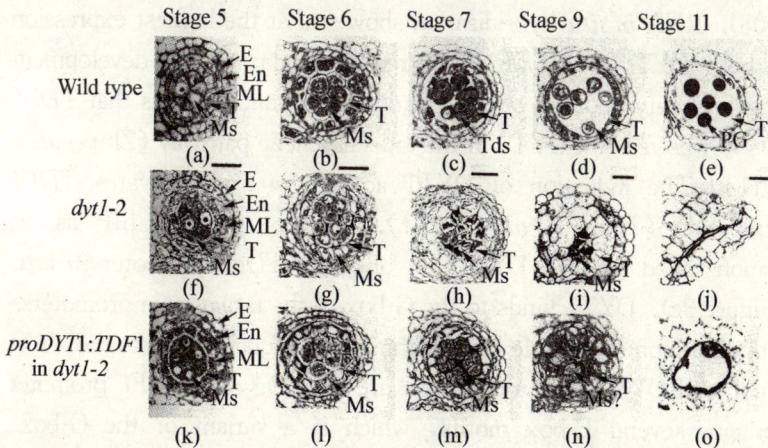

Figure 5   TDF1 partially rescues *dyt1-2* phenotype. Anther cross-section from wild-type (a-e), *dyt-2* mutant (f-j) and proDYT1:TDF1 transgenic lines (k-o). E, epidermis; En, endothecium; ML, middle layer; Ms; microsporocyte; Msp, microspore; T, tapetum; Tds, tetrads. Bar=20 μm.

During anther development, the primary sporogenous cells (PSCs) and primary parietal cells (PPCs) are derived from the archesporial cells in the L2 layer of the primordium. PSCs continue dividing, giving rise to a central sporogenous mass, and the PPCs develop to form three concentric parietal layers, including the tapetum (Goldberg et al., 1993). The DYT1 transcript was initially detected both in PPCs and PSCs based on in situ hybridization (Figure 1j; Zhang et al., 2006). The DYT1 transcript levels were highest in the tapetum and low in the meiocytes at stages 5 and 6 (Figure 1j, k). However, DYT1-GFP was only detected in the tapetal cells from stage 5 to stage 7 (Figure 2e-h), indicating that the DYT1 only accumulates in the tapetal cells. The tapetum localization of the DYT1 is consistent with its function in normal tapetal development. There may exist an unknown mechanism that regulates the translation of DYT1 during early anther development.

DYT1 directly regulates TDF1 expression in the tapetum

The tdf1 mutant exhibits increased vacuolation and dysfunction of the tapetum, which is similar to the dyt1 mutant (Zhu et al., 2008). RNA in situ hybridization showed that the highest expression of both DYT1 and TDF1 occurred at similar tapetal development stages. Analysis of the dyt1 tdf1 double mutant suggests that TDF1 acts downstream of DYT1 in the tapetal genetic pathway (Zhu et al., 2011). The induction of DYT1 activity in vivo activates TDF1 expression (Feng et al., 2012). In this study, ChIP assays demonstrated that the DYT1 can bind the TDF1 promoter in vivo (Figure 3c). DYT1 binds to the G-box of the target gene promoters. Any mutation in a single base of the G-box sequence affects the direct binding of DYT1 in vitro (Feng et al., 2012). The TDF1 promoter contains several E-box motifs, which is a variant of the G-box. However, the EMSA assay utilizing the DYT1 recombinant protein showed that DYT1 does not bind to the E-box motif on the promoter of TDF1 in vitro. However, the DYT1 could bind to the G-box motif

(Figure S1). Recently, CIB1, a bHLH protein, has been reported to form heterodimers with other CIB proteins to bind E-boxes *in vitro* (Liu *et al.*, 2014). In addition, DYT1 interacts with other bHLH proteins (Feng *et al.*, 2012). It is likely that DYT1 and several other bHLH proteins form a heterodimer to bind to the E-box motif of the *TDF*1 promoter to regulate its expression.

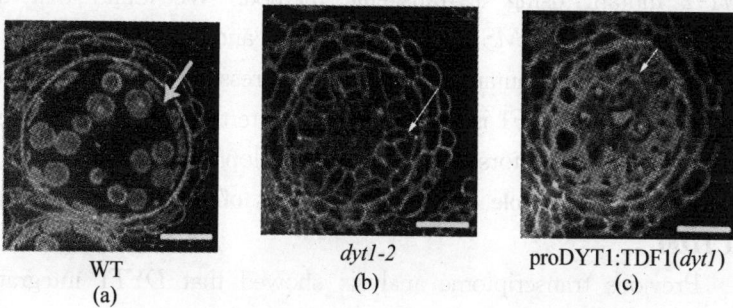

WT
(a)

dyt1-2
(b)

proDYT1:TDF1(*dyt1*)
(c)

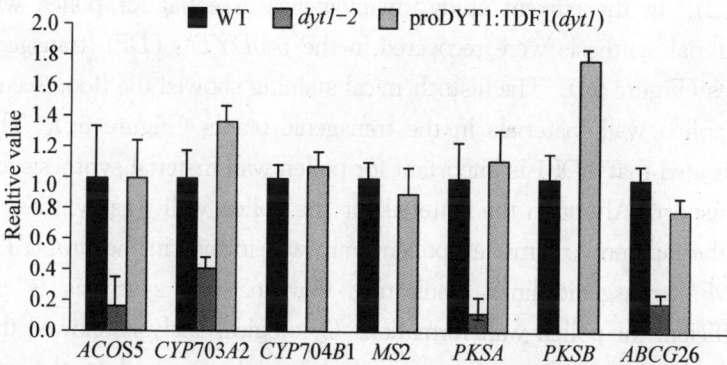

Figure 6. Pollen wall material synthesis in proDYT1 : TDF1. (a-c), Cytochemical staining of semi-thin sections of wild-type, *dyt1-2*, proDTY1 : TDF1 plants at stage 10. The red fluorescence indicates DiOC₂ could stain the sporopollenin precursors. The blue fluorescence indicates the Tinopal which binds to the cellulose. (a) Wild-type tapetal cells exhibit red fluorescence. (b) No red fluorescence are detected in the *dyt1-2* tapetum. (c) Red fluorescence is observed in pro-DYT1 : TDF1 tapetal cells. The arrows point to tapetal cells. (d) The expression pattern of selected pollen wall material synthesis-related genes in wild type, *dyt1-2* and proDYT1 : TDF1 plants. Bar=40 μm.

The transcription factors TDF1, AMS, MS188/MYB80, TEK and MS1 are essential for tapetal development and functions (Zhu *et al.*, 2011, Lou *et al.*, 2014). In the *dyt*1 mutant, the expression of these proteins is very low. Feng *et al.* (2012) proposed that DYT1 might regulate distinct temporal patterns of gene expression through feed-forward loops. In the present study, we expressed TDF1 in the *dyt*1-2 mutant using a transgenic method. We found that the expression of *AMS*, *MS*188/*MYB*80, *TEK* and *MS*1 was restored in the *dyt*1 knockout mutant with normal expression of *TDF*1 (Figure 4g). Therefore, TDF1 is sufficient to activate the expression of these transcriptional regulators during anther development.

DYT1 plays a role during the synthesis of pollen wall materials via *TDF1*

Previous transcriptome analysis showed that *DYT*1 integrates multiple biological processes for pollen development (Feng *et al.*, 2012). In the current study, many genes essential for pollen wall material synthesis were recovered in the *proDYT1 : TDF1* transgenic lines (Figure 6d). The histochemical staining showed the fluorescence of pollen wall materials in the transgenic plants (Figure 6c). This indicated that TDF1 is important for pollen wall material synthesis and transport. Although the material for the pollen wall was synthesized in the tapetum, no mature pollen grain was formed in the *proDYT1 : TDF1* transgenic lines, indicating that material synthesis is not sufficient for pollen wall formation. Cytological analysis showed that the tapetum development remained abnormal compared to the wild type. Therefore, the normal tapetal development is important for pollen formation and *DYT1* likely regulates several other genes essential for tapetum development and pollen formation.

EXPERIMENTAL PROCEDURES

Plant materials

Both the wild-type and mutant plants are the Landsberg *erecta* (L*er*) ecotype of Arabidopsis. Plants were grown under 16-h light/8-

h dark conditions at approximately 22℃. The *dyt1-2* mutant was isolated from EMS mutation lines as described by Song *et al*. (2009).

Analyses of the DYT1 promoter

The promoter fragments of *DYT1* were amplified by PCR with specific primers and ligated into the multiple cloning sites of a modified binary vector pBI121 to construct the DYT1∶∶GUS vectors, which were then introduced into the wild-type plants. The seeds of transformed plants were screened for kanamycin-resistant seedlings, which were transferred to the soil. GUS staining was performed according to the method of Jefferson *et al*. (1987).

In situ **hybridization**

Non-radioactive RNA *in situ* hybridization was performed as described in the Digoxigenin (DIG) RNA Labeling Kit (Roche, http∶//lifescience. roche. com/) and the PCR DIG Probe Synthesis Kit (Roche). The PCR product was cloned into the pSK vector and sequenced. The plasmid DNA was completely digested and prepared for transcription templates With T3 or T7 RNA polymerase (Roche) respectively. The Olympus BX-51 digital camera took the photos.

ChIP

Young flower buds were collected for ChIP assay as described by Haring *et al*. (2007). The experimental procedure and reagents preparation were as described (Yang *et al*. , 2013). The DNA from immunocomplexes Was dissolved with water and used for qChiP-PCR analysis. The C_t difference (ΔC_t) between the AB+ and AB− samples were obtained. The fold enrichment was calculated as $2^{(-\Delta C_t)}$. In this experiment, wild type was used as a control.

Microscopy

Nikon D7000 camera was used to photograph, and Olympus DP70 camera to take flower images (Nikon, http∶//www. nikon. com/). Alexander's solution was used as described (Alexander, 1969). DYT1 GFP in the anther was observed using a Carl Zeiss confocal laser scanning microscope (LSM 5 PASCAL; Zeiss, http∶//

www. zeiss. com). The procedure of semi-thin section and $DiOC_2$ staining were performed as described previously (Zhang *et al.*, 2007; Lou *et al.*, 2014). The sections were photographed by BX51 camera (Olympus, http://www. olympus-global. com/en/).

Quantitative PCR

Quantitative PCR analysis was performed as described by Lou *et al.* (2014). The β-tubulin gene was analysis as a positive control, and each sample had three replicates. The relative expression levels were calculated according to cycle number. The relevant primer sequences we designed are provided in Table S2.

Sequence data from this article can be found in the GenBank/ EMBL data libraries under accession numbers *DYT1* (AT4G21330), *TDF1* (AT3G28470), *AMS* (AT2G16910), *MS188/MYB80* (AT5G56110), *TEK* (AT2G42940), *MS1* (AT5G22260), *SPL* (AT4G27330), *EMS1* (AT5G07280), *TPD1* (AT4G24972), *SERK1* (AT1G71830), *SERK2* (AT1G34210), *MYB33* (AT5G06100), *MYB65* (AT3G11440), *ACOS5* (AT1G62940), *CYP703A2* (AT1G01280), *CYP704B1* (AT1G69500), *MS2* (AT3G11980), *PKSA* (AT1G02050), *PKSB* (AT4G34850), *ABCG26* (AT3G13220) and TUB (AT5G23860).

ACKNOWLEDGEMENTS

This work was supported by grants from the National Science Foundation of China (31100227) and the Innovation Program of Shanghai Municipal Education Commission (12YZ087).

SUPPORTING INFORMATION

Additional Supporting Information may be found in the online version of this article.

Figure S1. DYT1 recombinant protein binds to G-box rather than E-box motif.

Figure S1. Cis-acting elements are shown in DYT1 promoter region.

Table S2. List of primers used in this study.

References

[1] Albrecht, C. , Russinova, E. , Hecht, V. , Baaijens, E. and de Vries, S. (2005) The Arabidopsis thaliana SOMATIC EMBRYOGENESIS RECEPTOR-LIKE KINASES1 and 2 control male sporogenesis. *Plant Cell*, 17,3337 – 3349.

[2] Alexander, M. P. (1969) Differential staining of aborted and nonaborted pollen. *Stain Technol*. 44,117 – 122.

[3] Ariizumi, T. and Toriyama, K. (2011) Genetic regulation of sporopollenin synthesis and pollen exine development. *Annu. Rev. Plant Biol*. 62, 437 –460.

[4] de Azevedo Souza, C. , Kim, S. S. , Koch, S. , Kienow, L. , Schneider, K. , McKim. S. M. , Haughn, G. W. , Kombrink, E. and Douglas, C. J. (2009) A novel fatty Acyl-CoA Synthetase is required for pollen development and sporopollenin biosynthesis in Arabidopsis. *Plant Cell*, 21,507 – 525.

[5] Bedinger, P. (1992) The remarkable biology of pollen. *Plant Cell* 4, 879 –887.

[6] Canales, C. , Bhatt, A. M. , Scott, R. and Dickinson, H. (2002) EXS, a putative LRR receptor kinase, regulates male germline cell number and tapetal identity and promotes seed development in Arabidopsis. *Curr. Biol.* 12,1718 – 1727.

[7] Chang, F. , Wang, Y. , Wang, S. and Ma, H. (2011) Molecular control of microsporogenesis in Arabidopsis. *Curr. Opin. Plant Biol*. 14,66 – 73.

[8] Chen, W. , Yu, X. H. , Zhang, K. , Shi, J. , De Oliveira, S. , Schreiber, L. , Shanklin, J. and Zhang, D. B. (2011) Male Sterile 2 encodes a plastid-localized fatty acyl-aCP reductase required for pollen exine development in *Arabidopsis thaliana*. *Plant Physiol*. 157,842 – 853.

[9] Colcombet, J. , Boisson-Dernier, A. , Ros-Palau, R. , Vera, C. E. and Schroeder, J. I. (2005) Arabidopsis SOMATIC EMBRYOGENESIS RECEPTOR KINAS-ES1 and 2 are essential for tapetum development and microspore matu ration. *Plant Cell*, 17,3350 – 3361.

[10] Dickinson, H. G. and Heslop-Harrison, J. (1968) Common mode of deposition for the sporopollenin of sexine and nexine. *Nature*, 220,926 – 927.

[11] Dobritsa, A. A. , Shrestha, J. , Morant, M. , Pinot, F. , Matsuno, M. , Swanson, R. , Møller, B. L. and Preuss, D. (2009) CYP704B1 is a long-

chain fatty acid omega-hydroxylase essential for sporopollenin synthesis in pollen of Arabidopsis. *Plant Physiol*. 151,574 – 589.

[12] Dobritsa, A. A. , Lei, Z. , Nishikawa, S. , Urbanczyk-Wochniak, E. , Huhman, D. V. , Preuss, D. and Sumner, L. W. (2010) LAP5 and LAP6 encode anther-specific proteins with similarity to chalcone synthase essential for pollen exine development in Arabidopsis. *Plant Physiol*. 153,937 – 955.

[13] Feng, B. , Lu, D. , Ma, X. , Peng, Y. , Sun, Y. , Ning, G. and Ma, H. (2012) Regulation of the Arabidopsis anther transcriptome by DYT1 for pollen development. *Plant J*. 72,612 – 624.

[14] Goldberg, R. B. , Beals, T. P. and Sanders, P. M. (1993) Anther development: basic principles and practical applications. *Plant Cell*, 5, 1217 –1229.

[15] Haring, M. , Offermann, S. , Danker, T. , Horst, I. , Peterhaensel, C. and Stam, M. (2007) Chromatin immunoprecipitation: optimization, quantitative analysis and data normalization. *Plant Methods*, 3,11.

[16] Hernould, M. , Suharsono. S. , Zabaleta, E. , Carde, J. P. , Litvak, S. , Araya, A. and Mouras, A. (1998) Impairment of tapetum and mitochondria in engineered male-sterile tobacco plants. *Plant Mol. Biol*. 36,499 – 508.

[17] Heslop-Harrison, J. (1962) Origin of exine. *Nature* 195,1069 – 1071.

[18] Hesse, M. and Hess, M. W. (1993) Recent trends in tapetum research. A cyto-logical and methodological review. *Plant Syst. Evol*. 7,127 – 145.

[19] Higo, K. , Ugawa, Y. , Iwamoto, M. and Korenaga, T. (1999) Plant cis-acting regulatory DNA elements (PLACE) database: 1999. *Proc. Natl Acad. Sci. USA*, 27,297 – 300.

[20] Ito, T. , Nagata, N. , Yoshiba, Y. , Ohme-Takagi, M. , Ma, H. and Shinozaki, K. (2007) Arabidopsis MALE STERILITY1 encodes a PHD-type transcription factor and regulates pollen and tapetum development. *Plant Cell*, 19,3549 –3562

[21] Jefferson, R. A. , Kavanagh, T. A. and Bevan, M. W. (1987) GUS fusions:β-glucuronidase as a sensitive and versatile gene fusion marker in higher plants. *EMBO J*. 6,3901 – 3907.

[22] Jia, G. , Liu, X. , Owen, H. A. and Zhao, D. (2008) Signaling of cell fate determination by the TPD1 small protein and EMS1 receptor kinase. *Proc. Natl. Acad. Sci. USA*, 105,2220 – 2225.

[23] Kim, S. S. , Grienenberger, E. , Lallemand, B. *et al*. (2010) LAP6/ POLYKETIDE SYNTHASE A and LAP5/POLYKETIDE SYNTHASE B

encode hydroxyalkyl alpha-pyrone synthases required for pollen development and sporopollenin biosynthesis in *Arabidopsis thaliana*. *Plant Cell*, 22,4045 – 4066.

[24] Liu, Y. , Li, X. , Li, K. , Liu, H. and Lin, C. (2014) Multiple bHLH proteins form heterodimers to mediate CRY2-dependent regulation of flowering-time in Arabidopsis, *PLoS Genet*, 9, e1003861.

[25] Lou, Y. , Xu, X. F. , Zhu, J. , Gu, J. N. , Blackmore, S. and Yang, Z. N. (2014) The tapetal AHL family protein TEK determines nexine formation in the pollen wall. *Nat. Commun.* 5,3855.

[26] Ma, H. (2005) Molecular genetic analyses of microsporogenesis and microgametogenesis in flowering plants. *Annu. Rev. Plant Biol.* 56, 393 –434.

[27] Mariani, C. , Beuckeleer, M. D. , Truettner, J. , Leemans, J. and Goldberg, R. B. (1990) Induction of male sterility in plants by a chimaeric ribonuclease gene. *Nature*, 347,737 – 741.

[28] Mascarenhas, J. P. (1975) The biochemistry of angiosperm pollen development. Bot. *Rev.* 41,259 – 314.

[29] Millar, A. A. and Gubler, F. (2005) The Arabidopsis GAMYB-like genes, MYB33 and MYB65, are microRNA-regulated genes that redundantly facilitate anther development. *Plant Cell*, 17,705 – 721.

[30] Morant, M. , Jørgensen, K. , Schaller, H. , Pinot, F. , Møller, B. L. , Werck-Reichhart, D. and Bak, S. (2007) CYP703 is an ancient cytochrome P450 in land plants catalyzing in-chain hydroxylation of lauric acid to provide building blocks for sporopollenin synthesis in pollen. *Plant Cell*, 19, 1473 –1487.

[31] Pacini, E. and Juniper, B. E. (1979) The ultrastructure of pollen grain development in the olive (*Olea europaea*). II. Secretion by the tapetal cells. *New Phytol.* 83,165 – 174.

[32] Piffanelli, P. , Ross, J. H. E. and Murphy, D. J. (1998) Biogenesis and function of the lipidic structures of pollen grains. *Sex. Plant Reprod.* 11,65 – 80

[33] Quilichini, T. D. , Friedmann, M. C. , Samuels, A. L. and Douglas, C. J. (2010) ATP-binding cassette transporter G26 is required for male fertility and pollen exine formation in Arabidopsis. *Plant Physiol.* 154,678 – 690.

[34] Regan, S. M. and Moffatt, B. A. (1990) Cytochemical analysis of pollen development in wild-type arabidopsis and a male-sterile mutant. *Plant Cell*, 2,

877 - 889.

[35] Sanders, P. M. , Bui, A. Q. and Goldberg, R. B. (1999) Anther developmental defects in *Arabidopsis thaliana* male-sterile mutants. *Sex. Plant Reprod.* 11,297 - 322.

[36] Schiefthaler, U. , Balasubramanian, S. , Sieber, P. , Chevalier, D. , Wisman, E. and Schneitz, K. (1999) Molecular analysis of NOZZLE, a gene involved in pattern formation and early sporogenesis during sex organ development in *Arabidopsis thaliana*. *Proc. Natl Acad. Sci. USA*. 96. 11664 - 11669.

[37] Scott, R. J. (1994) Pollen exine: the sporopollenin enigma and the physics of pattern. In *Molecular and Cellular Aspects of Plant Reproduction* (Scott, R. J. and Stead, M. A. , eds). Cambridge, UK: University Press, pp. 49 - 81.

[38] Scott, R. J. , Spielman, M. and Dickinson, H. G. (2004) Stamen structure and function. *Plant Cell*, 16, (Suppl), S46 - S60.

[39] Song, Y. , Li, H. , Shi, Q. L. , Jiang, H. , Chen, H. , Zhong, X. L. , Gao, J. F. , Cui, Y. L. and Yang, Z. N. (2009) The Arabidopsis bHLH transcription factor DYT1 is essential for anther development by regulating callose dissolution. *J. Shanghai Norm. Univ.* 38,174 - 182.

[40] Sorensen, A. M. , Kröber, S. , Unte, U. S. , Huijser, P. , Dekker, K. and Saedler, H. (2003) The Arabidopsis ABORTED MICROSPORES (AMS) gene encodes a MYC class transcription factor. *Plant J*. 33,413 - 423.

[41] Stevens, V. A. and Murray, B. G. (1981) Studies on heteromorphic self-incompatibility systems: the cytochemistry and ultrastructure of the tapetum of *Primula obconica*. *J. Cell Sci.* 50,419 - 431.

[42] Stieglitz, H. (1977) Role of beta-1, 3-glucanase in postmeiotic microspore release. *Dev. Biol.* 57,87 - 97.

[43] Wilson, Z. A. , Morroll, S. M. , Dawson, J. , Swarup, R. and Tighe, P. J. (2001) The Arabidopsis MALE STERILITY1 (MS1) gene is a transcriptional regulator of male gametogenesis, with homology to the PHD-finger family of transcription factors. *Plant J*. 28,27 - 39.

[44] Xu, J. , Yang, C. , Yuan, Z. , Zhang, D. , Gondwe, M. Y. , Ding, Z. , Liang, W. , Zhang, D. and Wilson, Z. A. (2010) The ABORTED MICROSPORES regulatory network is required for postmeiotic male reproductive development in *Arabidopsis thaliana*. *Plant Cell*, 22,91 - 107.

[45] Yang, W. C. , Ye, D. , Xu, J. and Sundaresan, V. (1999) The SPOROCYTELESS gene of Arabidopsis is required for initiation of sporogenesis and encodes a novel nuclear protein, *Genes Dev.* 13,2108 - 2117.

[46] Yang, S. L. , Xie, L. F. , Mao, H. Z. , Puah, C. S. , Yang, W. C. , Jiang, L. , Sundaresan, V. and Ye, D. (2003) Tapetum determinant1 is required for cell specialization in the Arabidopsis anther. *Plant Cell* , 15,2792 – 2804.

[47] Yang, C. , Vizcay-Barrena, G. , Conner, K. and Wilson, Z. A. (2007) MALE STERILITY1 is required for tapetal development and pollen wall biosynthesis. *Plant Cell* , 19,3530 – 3548.

[48] Yang, J. , Tian, L. , Sun, M. X. , Huang, X. Y. , Zhu, J. , Guan, Y. F. , Jia, Q. S. and Yang, Z. N. (2013) AUXIN RESPONSE FACTOR17 is essential for pollen wall pattern formation in Arabidopsis. *Plant Physiol*. 162, 720 – 731.

[49] Zhang, W. , Sun, Y. , Timofejeva, L. , Chen, C. , Grossniklaus, U. and Ma, H. (2006) Regulation of Arabidopsis tapetum development and function by DYSFUNCTIONAL TAPETUM1 (DYT1) encoding a putative bHLH transcription factor. *Development*, 133,3085 – 3095.

[50] Zhang, Z. B. , Zhu, J. , Gao, J. F. , *et al.* (2007) Transcription factor AtMYB103 is required for anther development by regulating tapetum development, callose dissolution and exine formation in Arabidopsis. *Plant J*. 52,528 – 538.

[51] Zhao, D. Z. , Wang, G. F. , Speal, B. and Ma, H. (2002) The excess microsporocytes1 gene encodes a putative leucine-rich repeat receptor protein kinase that controls somatic and reproductive cell fates in the Arabidopsis anther. *Genes Dev*. 16,2021 – 2031.

[52] Zhu, J. , Chen, H. , Li, H. , Gao, J. F. , Jiang, H. , Wang, C. , Guan, Y. F. and Yang, Z. N. (2008) Defective in Tapetal development and function 1 is essential for anther development and tapetal function for microspore maturation in Arabidopsis. *Plant J*. 55,266 – 277.

[53] Zhu, J. , Zhang, G. Q. , Chang, Y. H. , Li, X. C. , Yang, J. , Huang, X. Y. , Yu, Q. B. , Chen, H. , Wu, T. L. and Yang, Z. N. (2010) AtMYB103 is a crucial regulator of several pathways affecting Arabidopsis anther development. *Sci. China Life Sci*. 53,1112 – 1122.

[54] Zhu, J. , Lou, Y. , Xu, X. F. and Yang, Z. N. (2011) A genetic pathway for tapetum development and function in Arabidopsis. *J. Integr. Plant Biol*, 53, 892 – 900.

Withholding Response to
Self-Face Is Faster Than to Other-Face

Min Zhu, Yinying Hu, Xiaochen Tang,
Junlong Luo, Xiangping Gao

Education College, Shanghai Normal University

Adults' response to self-face is faster than that to other-face (Devue & Brédart, 2011; Keenan et al. , 1999; Sui & Humphreys, 2013), which refers to self-face advantage (Ma & Han, 2010). Numerous studies have indicated that self-face captures attention quickly and can be prioritized processing (Pannese & Hirsch, 2010; Platek, Thomson, & Gallup, 2004). For example, Sui and Han (2007) used an implicit face-recognition task in which participants were instructed to discriminate the head orientation of their own and familiar faces. They found that response to self-face was faster than that to familiar faces. As a meaningful and salient stimulus, self-face conveys not only visual face features, but also something about self-reference (Brédart, Delchamber, & Laureys, 2006), implying self-consciousness (Gallup, 1977), self-awareness (Devue & Brédart, 2011; Gallup, 1998) and theory of mind (Gallup, 1982; Keenan, Gallup, & Falk, 2003).

Up to now, all studies have limited at the influence of self-face on the production of approaching responses. We initiatively explored whether self-face would interact with a process, which needs to withdraw responses, namely response inhibition. As a hallmark of executive control, response inhibition refers to the suppression of no longer required or inappropriate actions (Logan & Cowan, 1984; Verbruggen & Logan, 2008). The paradigms of studying response inhibition are various and debated. Three main paradigms are antisaccade, go/no-go, and stop-signal tasks (SST; Dillon & Pizzagalli, 2007). Moreover, SST is the most suitable paradigm to study response inhibition (Logan & Cowan, 1984; Verbruggen & De Houwer, 2007; Ver-bruggen & Logan, 2008), because it is purer than the rests (details in Dillon & Pizzagalli, 2007). A standard SST consists of a go task and a stop task. Participants are asked to make a choice reaction time task of the visual stimuli in the go task, while withholding their motor response when they hear an auditory tone (i. e. , stop signal) right after the visual stimuli (the stop task). The delay between the go stimulus and the stop signal (SSD) can be set dynamically to manipulate the probability of inhibition (Bissett & Logan, 2011). The method is called tracking procedure — SSD is adjusted after every trial. If the current stop is successful, the next stop trial's SSD will increase to make the inhibition harder; if the current stop is unsuccessful, the next stop trial's SSD will decrease to make the inhibition easier. Logan and Cowan (1984) proposed a horse race model to explain the findings from SST. They suggest that there is a race between the go process and the stop process. When the stop process finishes before the go process, participants will inhibit successfully and suppress their response (a signal inhibit trial); when the go process finishes before the stop process, participants will execute response and inhibit unsuccessfully (a signal response trial). The latency of the stop process, namely the stop-signal reaction time (SSRT) can be regarded as an index of inhibitory control. SSRT cannot be measured directly; however, the horse race model makes it possible to estimate it. When the tracking procedure produced p (respond — signal) equal to 0. 50, SSRT is calculated by using mean go RTs to subtract mean SSD, which is called the mean method (details in Verbruggen & Logan, 2009). The findings of human's inhibition, for instance who with attention deficit hyperactivity disorder (Alderson, Rapport, & Kofler, 2007) or chronic metham-phetamine abuse (Monterosso, Aron, Cordova, Xu, & London, 2005) showed that the SSRTs in the experiment group was longer than that in the control group. Shorter SSRTs are associated with more efficient inhibition (Dillon & Pizzagalli, 2007).

Limited but increasing studies indicated the attribute of stimuli had an effect on response inhibition. Researchers explored whether emotional stimuli interfered with response inhibition. By using a modified stop-signal task, they found emotional pictures prolonged both response and stopping latencies regardless of the valence of the emotional stimuli (Kalanthroff, Cohen, & Henik, 2013; Verbruggen & De Houwer, 2007), but relevant to the arousal of the emotional stimuli (Pessoa, Padmala, Kenzer, & Bauer, 2012). Though behavior data showed that SSRT was not influenced by the emotion, functional magnetic resonance imaging data revealed the brain activation engaged in emotion inhibition was special, as activity in primary motor cortex was lower in stop-signal response trials accompanied by a fearful face relative to neutral (Sagaspe, Schwartz, & Vuilleumier, 2011). It was also found that erotic images and painful video clips impaired the inhibitory control in men (Yu, Hung, Tseng, Tzeng, Muggleton, & Juan, 2012). When stimuli were associated with reward, the performance of response inhibition was facilitated (Boehler, Hopf, Stoppel, & Krebs, 2012). Consequently, it is convinced that a stimuli's attribute such as emotional content can influence executive control processes (Pessoa, 2009). In the present study we addressed the issue whether the self-face would interact with response inhibition.

As self-face is a kind of high salient stimuli (Pannese & Hirsch, 2011) and easier to capture attention, the approaching response to self-face is faster than to other-face. In another words, response to self-face is more impulsive. In the go task, frequent go stimuli set up a prepotent response tendency, as 25% of the trials were stop trials, which was a low-probability condition (Chen, Muggleton, Juan, Tzeng, & Hung, 2008; Li, Huang, Constable, & Sinha, 2006). We proposed that the prepotent response tendency to self-face would be stronger than that to other-face in the go task. While in the stop task, how self-face advantage influencing SSRT is unpredictable. Since the response to self-face is shortened, the go process of self-face is faster compared with other-face, and then it will always finish before the stop process. Therefore response inhibition after self-face should be harder in stop trials. However, Logan and Cowan (1984) suggested that the go process and the stop process were independent. The performance of withholding response to self-face may not be impaired by the fast response to self-face. Self-face processing demands less attention resources (Tong & Nakayama, 1999), then there are more attention resources being used in the stop process. As successful inhibition depends on attention resource (Logan & Cowan, 1984; Pessoa et al. , 2012), it assumes that more inhibition control will be recruited to self-face, which facilitates response inhibition. Accordingly, SSRT is expected to be shorter when the stimulus is self-face. Mean-while in the stop response trials (unsuccessful inhibition) in which processes are ballistic, participants cannot inhibit and response impulsively. Self-face may have a response advantage in such impulsive condition. Then the stronger response tendency to self-face is also reflected by faster RTs in the stop response trials. Thus, SRRT of self-face is faster than that of other face.

Method

Participants
Twenty-four undergraduate and graduate students (13 women) took part in this study. The age was ranged from 19 to 26 years old ($M = 22.91$ years; $SD = 1.61$ years). All participants were right-

handed and had normal or corrected-to-normal vision, and they all signed informed consent prior to the experiment. This study was approved by the local ethics committee of Shanghai Normal University.

Stimuli

Pictures selected from the standard Chinese Facial Affective Picture System were employed as "other-face" for participants.

Each participant in the experiment was photographed in a frontal position before the experiment. Self-face pictures for him or her were taken in same condition: in front of a black background, expressing neutrally, or pronouncing different speech sounds. Different poses were used to maintain participants' interest during testing and to minimize potential reliance on local cues, such as the shape of the mouth, for recognition (Keyes & Brady, 2010). Using Adobe Photoshop, the parts up the eyebrow and below the jaw of the photographs were removed and cropped to 260×300 pixels. All pictures were converted to grayscale (see Figure 1).

Procedure

We employed a modified version of SST (see Figure 2) according to the work of Bissett and Logan (2011). Stimuli were facial pictures with half self-faces and half other-faces. The experiment was programmed using E-Prime 2.0 (Psychology Software Tools, Inc., Pittsburgh, PA, USA). Each trial started with a fixation presented for 500 ms, then followed by a face picture remained on the screen for 500 ms. Participants were instructed to discriminate the identity of the face by pressing different keys as quickly and accurately as possible. The responding keys were keyboard number 1 and number 0, one for self-face and the other for other-face, which counterbalanced across participants, using the right and left index finger, respectively. The next was a blank screen for 1000 ms. Occasionally, a stop signal (70 dB, 100 ms, 500 Hz) occurred briefly following the face picture, to indicate participants to withhold their response whosever the face was. The initial SSD was set at 250 ms and dynamically adjusted according to separate tracking procedures for each type of pictures. The SSD increased by 50 ms if the participant succeeded in inhibiting and decreased by 50 ms if the participant failed to inhibit, which ensured the probability of successful inhibition by 0.50 (Verbruggen & Logan, 2009).

The experiment was consisted of a practice session and a main task session. There were two parts in the practice session. The first practice part was a go task with 12 trials. In this part, participants were instructed to respond to the pictures as quickly and accurately as possible and to make sure 100% accuracy. In the second practice part, stop signals occasionally occurred in the go task (stop-signal practice). The instruction indicated to participants to withhold their response when they heard the stop signal and emphasized not to wait for the potential stop signal. In this part, participants were given feedback on speed and accuracy after 24 trials. To enter the main task, participants should respond with accuracy above 83% and RT below 800 ms. The occurrence percentage of the stop signal was 25%, namely there were 84 stop trials. There were three blocks of 336 trials in the main task. After each block, participants would get a feedback on RT and accuracy, as well as the percentage of trials on which they responded while the picture remained on the screen (also see Bissett & Logan, 2011). Then participants were compelled to take a rest for at least 4 s.

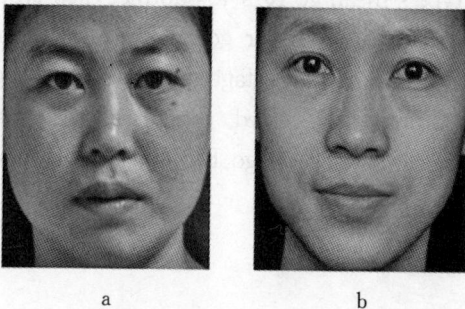

a   b

FIGURE 1. Samples of face stimuli, a self-face picture (a) and an other-face picture (b).

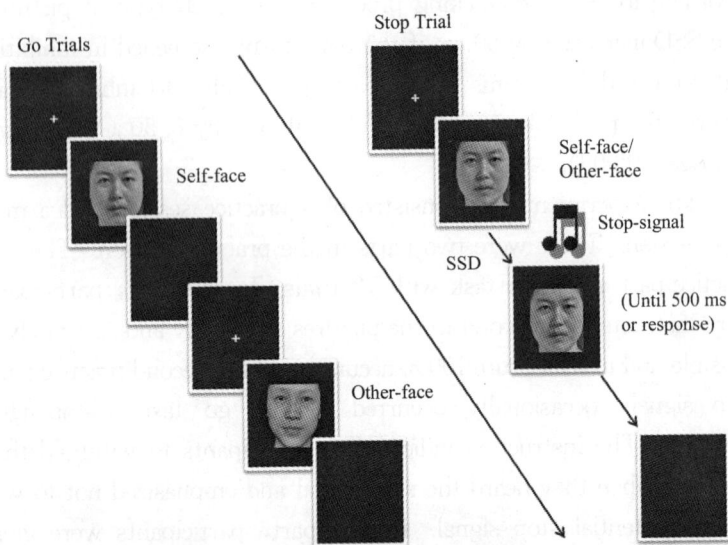

FIGURE 2. Task trials, illustrating two go trials and a stop trial.

Data Analysis

The go trial RTs of each type of pictures were calculated by excluding incorrect trials and trials with RTs more than three standard deviations away from mean go RTs for each face type, which referred to previous studies (Kalanthroff et al., 2013; Pessoa, et al., 2012). SSD was calculated by averaging the stop signal delays of stop trials for each type. According to the mean method, SSRT was calculated by using each type's mean go RTs to subtract each type's mean SSD. Paired T-test was carried out for go trial accuracy, correct go RT, SRRT, SSD, SSRT, and percentage of successful stopping under the two facial conditions. Repeated measures analyses of variance (ANOVA) were conducted on go RT and SRRT to investigate the influence of the signal on RTs.

Results

The rejection rates of trials with go RTs for self-face and other-face more than three standard deviations from the mean were 1. 36% and 1. 75%, respectively. Table 1 shows the behavioral performance of the participants. The mean accuracy in the go task was all above 95%, Paired t test of accuracy of different face types showed no significant difference, $t(23) = 0.90$, $p = 0.375$.

According to assumption of the tracking procedure, the stopping-success rates would be 50%. Based on this assumption, one-sample t test of the stopping-success rates taken for each stimulus type showed that both successful inhibition percentages did not differ significantly from 50%: self-face, $t(23) = 0$, $p = 1$; other-face: $t(23) = -0.92$, $p = 0.366$, which indicated that the experiment procedure was successful. As SSD was dynamically adjusted according to participants' performance of inhibition, mean SSD was calculated, $t(23) = 2.71$, $p = 0.013$, $\eta^2 = 0.24$, revealing that SSD following self-face was significantly longer than that following other-face.

Analysis of mean RTs for correct response in each stimulus type in the go task revealed no significant difference, $t(23) = 0.02$, $p = 0.986$, RTs for self-face were not significantly shorter than those for other-face.

The paired t test showed a significantly shorter SSRT when inhibiting response following self-face, $t(23) = -3.12$, $p = 0.005$, $\eta^2 = 0.30$. Consistent with the race-model assumption of independence of go and stop processed (Logan, 1984), there was no significant correlation between go RT and SSRT, for neither other-face ($r = 0.228$) nor self-face ($r = 0.094$).

TABLE 1. Behavioral Data

	Self		Other	
	M	SD	M	SD
Go trial accuracy(%)	95.92	1.95	96.38	2.32
Go trial RT (ms)	482.44	54.45	482.34	49.08
SRRT (ms)	455.78	48.44	474.12	41.47
Mean SSD	270.54	75.04	243.25	77.89
SSRT (ms)	211.91	57.02	239.09	72.72
Percentage stop success (%)	50.00	2.47	49.38	3.32

Note. RT=reaction time; SSD=stop signal delay; SRRT=stop response reaction time.

Notably, the RT difference between the go trials and the stop response trials (i. e. , SRRT) was larger for self-face than for other-face (26. 66 ms vs. 8. 22 ms, respectively; see Figure 3). This difference was further verified by a repeated measures ANOVA on RTs from both the no signal response (go) and signal response (stop response) conditions, which showed no main effect of face types, $F(1, 23) = 2.41$, $p = 0.135$, $\eta^2 = 0.095$. The response conditions' main effect was significant, $F(1,23) = 12.01$, $p = 0.002$, $\eta^2 = 0.343$. As motor execution was too fast to be suppressed by inhibition, RTs were generally shorter in the stop response trials (Sagaspe et al. , 2011). A significant interaction between face types and response conditions was found, $F(1,23) = 8.94$, $p = 0.007$, $\eta^2 = 0.28$. Further simple effect analysis indicated, RTs of self-face in the stop response trials was significantly shorter than that in the go trials, $F(1,23) = 19.02$, $p < 0.001$. No significant difference of other-face was found between the two kinds of trials, $F(1,23) = 2.09$, $p = 0.162$.

Discussion

The present study used a modified stop-signal task to examine how self-face advantage interacted with response inhibition, in which self-faces and other-faces were presented as stimuli. The findings showed that RTs of self-face were faster than that of other-face not in the go task but in the stop response trials. Self-face recognition studies have manifested that adult's response to his or her own face is faster than other-face (Devue & Brédart, 2011; Keenan et al. , 1999; Sui & Han, 2007; Sui & Humphreys, 2013). Whereas, it is also tested that self-face advantage is affected by the experimentally manipulated context. The boss effect showed that participants responded more slowly to self-face than to the advisor's face as the fear of negative evaluations from influential superiors modulated self-face recognition (Ma & Han, 2009). When an individual's self concept was threatened by priming with negative traits, the response to self-face was not shorter than that of other-face (Ma & Han, 2010). Further study found comparison with important others collaborating with self-concept threat weakened the self-face advantage (Guan, Zhang, Qi, Hou, & Yang, 2012). Therefore, it is reasonable to infer that self-face advantage is mediated by the task context.

Although there was no significant difference between self go RTs and other go RTs, there was a significant difference for SRRTs. In the stop response trial, RTs of self-face were faster than that of other-face. In such situation, participants can't inhibit their motor response as go process finishes before stop process (Verbruggen & Logan, 2009), so it is impulsive to response to stop signal. Our results showed that self-face processing was faster than other-face processing in the impulsive condition, which indicated that self-face advantage did exist in the motor execution process. The further analysis of face types and response conditions (go trials vs. stop response trials) was consistent with previous study that RTs in the stop response trials were shorter compared with those in the go trials (Sagaspe et al. , 2011). This RTs improvement effect was significant for self-face rather than for other-face, which demonstrated self-face process was quite different from other-face process when interacting with inhibition

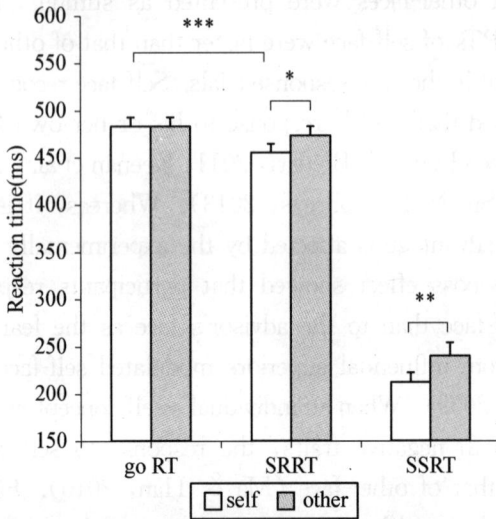

FIGURE 3 Reaction times (RTs) in three conditions, mean go reaction times (go RT), stop response reaction times (SRRT) and stop-signal reaction times (SSRT). * $p<.05.$ ** $p<.01.$ *** $p<.001.$

process, especially in which participants failed to withhold their motor action. Combined with the performance in the go trials and stop response trials, it suggests that participants may have slowed their response speed to stimuli in the go task, which had an especially obvious effect on self-face advantage.

The novelty of current study is that it explores whether self-face is different from other-face in interacting with response inhibition. Our results showed that SSRT of self-face was shorter relative to that of other-face, which indicated that response inhibition to self-face was stronger. Researchers suggested that successful performance in response inhibition involved inhibitory mechanisms as well as other processes, including perceptual processing and attention (Pessoa, 2009; Pessoa et al., 2012). In previous studies, emotional faces as salient stimuli enhanced sensory representations of the stop stimulus, leading to stop-signal processing being facilitated and consequently improved inhibitory performance (Pessoa et al. , 2012). When emotional stimuli serving as primes present prior to response stimuli, the SSRT for emotional condition is longer than for neutral condition (Kalanthroff et al. , 2013; Verbruggen & De Houwer, 2007), as emotional stimuli in the go task consuming too much attentional resource interrupt the inhibition processing. Salient stimuli capture attention, which affecting both go process and stop process. As a response stimulus in present study, though self-face did not influence the go process significantly, it interacted with the stop process. The attention resource consumed by self-face in the go task is less than that by other-face in the go task (Tong & Nakayama, 1999), from which the inhibition control benefits. In other words, more cognitive resource is used to help inhibit successfully. Thus the SSRT of self-face is shorter.

Studies about impulsive violent offenders (Chen et al. , 2008), drug abuse (Franken & Muris, 2006; Kimbrel, Nelson-Gray, & Mitchell, 2007) and alcohol abuse (Franken & Muris, 2006) showed that high impulsive actions were associated with inhibition deficit. Consequently, healthy adults should have strong inhibition control ability to respond to strong response tendency. Gray (1987) proposed a personality model to explain the cause of inhibition of prepotent behavior, which consists of a behavioral activation system (BAS) and a behavioral inhibition system (BIS). RT in the go task is an indicator of prepotent response tendency related to BAS and faster go RTs index a stronger BAS (Chen et al. , 2008; Logan, Schachar, & Tannock, 1997). SSRT is regarded as an indicator of BIS and shorter SSRT is associated with stronger BIS (Avila & Parcet, 2001; Chen et al. , 2008; Logan, et al. , 1997). In the present study, though the BAS triggered by self-face was not stronger than that triggered by other-face in the go task, it was reflected in the stop response trials that response tendency to self-face was stronger than to other-face. Otherwise, self-face's SSRT is shorter. Therefore, it is reasonable to speculate that self-face has stronger BIS to overcome stronger BAS.

In summary, self-face advantage was not in the go task but in the stop response trials. Meanwhile, response inhibition to self-face was more efficient. Therefore, the processing mechanism of self-face might be characterized by a strong response tendency and a corresponding strong inhibition control.

ACKNOWLEDGMENTS

We thank Gordon D. Logan and Patrick Bissett for providing their e-prime procedure to us for reference and the anonymous reviewer for his/her comments reported about this article.

FUNDING

This research was supported by the Innovation Program of Shanghai Municipal Education Commission (12ZS117).

References

[1] Alderson, R. M. , Rapport, M. D. , & Kofler, M. J. (2007). Attention-deficit/hyperactivity disorder and behavioral inhibition: A meta-analytic review of the stop-signal paradigm. *Journal of Abnormal Child Psychology*, 35, 745 –758.

[2] Avila, C. , & Parcet, M. A. (2001). Personality and inhibitory deficits in the stop-signal task: The mediating role of Gray's anxiety and impulsivity. *Personality and Individual Differences*, 31,975 – 986.

[3] Bissett, P. G. , & Logan, G. D. (2011). Post-stop-signal slowing: Strategies dominate reflexes and implicit learning. *Journal of Experimental Psychology: Human Perception and Performance*, 38,746 – 757.

[4] Boehler, C. N. , Hopf, J. M. , Stoppel, C. M. , & Krebs, R. M. (2012). Motivating inhibition-reward prospect speeds up response cancellation. *Cognition*, 125,498 – 503.

[5] Brédart, S. , Delchambre, M. , &. Laureys, S. (2006). One's own face is hard to ignore. *The Quarterly Journal of Experimental Psychology*, *59*,46 – 52.

[6] Chen, C. Y. , Muggleton, N. G. , Juan, C. H. , Tzeng, O. J. , &. Hung, D. L. (2008). Time pressure leads to inhibitory control deficits in impulsive violent offenders. *Behavioural Brain Research*, *187*,483 – 488.

[7] Devue, C. , &. Brédart, S. (2011). The neural correlates of visual self-recognition. *Consciousness and Cognition*, *20*,40 – 51.

[8] Dillon, D. G. , &. Pizzagalli, D. A. (2007). Inhibition of action, thought, and emotion: A selective neurobiological review. *Applied and Preventive Psychology*, *12*,99 – 114.

[9] Franken, I. H. , Muris, P. , &. Georgieva, I. (2006). Gray's model of personality and addiction. *Addictive Behaviors*, *31*,399 – 403.

[10] Gallup, G. G. J. (1982). Self-awareness and the emergence of mind in primates. *American Journal of Primatology*, *2*,237 – 248.

[11] Gallup, G. G. J. (1998). Self-awareness and the evolution of social intelligence. *Behavioral Processes*, *42*,239 – 247.

[12] Gallup, G. G. J. (1977). Self-recognition in primates: A comparative approach to the bidirectional properties of consciousness. *American Psychology*, *32*,329 – 338.

[13] Gray, J. A. (1987). *The psychology of fear and stress*. New York, NY: Cambridge University Press.

[14] Guan, L. L. , Zhang, Q. L. , Qi, M. M. , Hou, Y. , &. Yang, J. (2012). Self-concept threat and comparison with important others weaken self-face advantage altogether. *Acta Psychologica Sinica*, *6*,010.

[15] Kalanthroff, E. , Cohen, N. , &. Henik, A. (2013). Stop feeling: Inhibition of emotional interference following stop-signal trials. *Frontiers in Human Neurosc-ience*, *7*,78.

[16] Keenan, J. P. , Gallup, G. G. , &. Falk, D. (2003). *The face in the mirror: The search for the origins of consciousness*. New York, NY: Harper Collins.

[17] Keenan, J. P. , McCutcheon, B. , Sanders, G. , Freund, S. , Gallup, G. G. , &. Pascual-Leone, A. (1999). Left hand advantage in a self-face recognition task. *Neuropsychologia*, *37*,1421 – 1425.

[18] Keyes, H. &. Brady, N. (2010). Self-face recognition is characterized by "bilateral gain" and by faster, more accurate performance which persists when faces are inverted. *The Quarterly Journal of Experimental Psychology*, *63*, 840 – 847.

[19] Kimbrel, N. A. , Nelson-Gray, R. O. , & Mitchell, J. T. (2007). Reinforcement sensitivity and maternal style as predictors of psychopathology. *Personality and Individual Differences*, *42*,1139 - 1149.

[20] Li, C. S. R. , Huang, C. , Constable, R. T. , & Sinha, R. (2006). Gender differences in the neural correlates of response inhibition during a stop signal task. *Neuroimage*, *32*,1918 - 1929.

[21] Logan, G. D. , & Cowan, W. B. (1984). On the ability to inhibit thought and action: A theory of an act of control. *Psychological Review*, *91*,295 - 327.

[22] Logan, G. D. , Schachar, R. J. , & Tannock, R. (1997). Impulsivity and inhibitory control. *Psychological Science*, *8*,60 - 64.

[23] Ma, Y. N. , & Han, S. H. (2009). Self-face advantage is modulated by social threat: Boss effect on self-face recognition. *Journal of Experimental Social Psychology*, *45*,1048 - 1051.

[24] Ma, Y. N. , & Han, S. H. (2010). Why we respond faster to the self than to others? An implicit positive association theory of self-advantage during implicit face recognition. *Journal of Experimental Psychology: Human Perception and Performance*, *36*,619 - 633.

[25] Monterosso, J. , Aron, A. R. , Cordova, X. , Xu, J. , & London, E. D. (2005). Deficits in response inhibition associated with chronic methamphetamine abuse. *Drug and Alcohol Dependence*, *79*,273 - 277.

[26] Pannese, A. , & Hirsch, J. (2010). Self-specific priming effect. *Consciousness Cognition*, *19*, 962 - 968.

[27] Pannese, A. , & Hirsch, J. (2011). Self-face enhances processing of immediately preceding invisible faces. *Neuropsychologia*, *49*,564 - 573.

[28] Pessoa, L. (2009). How do emotion and motivation direct executive function? *Trends in Cognitive Sciences*, *13*,160 - 166.

[29] Pessoa, L. , Padmala, S. , Kenzer, A. , & Bauer, A. (2012). Interactions between cognition and emotion during response inhibition. *Emotion*, *12*, 192 -197.

[30] Platek, S. M. , Thomson, J. W. , & Gallup, G. G. Jr. (2004). Crossmodal self-recognition: The role of visual, auditory, and olfactory primes. *Consciousness and Cognition*, *13*,197 - 210.

[31] Sagaspe, P. , Schwartz, S. , Vuilleumier, P. (2011). Fear and stop: A role for the amygdala in motor inhibition by emotional signals. *Neuroimage*, *55*, 1825 - 1835.

[32] Sui, J. , & Han, S. (2007). Self-construal priming modulates neural

substrates of self-awareness. *Psychological Science*, *18*, 861 – 866.

[33] Sui, J. , & Humphreys, G. W. (2013). The boundaries of self face perception: Response time distributions, perceptual categories, and decision weighting. *Visual Cognition*, *21*, 415 – 445.

[34] Tacikowski, P. , & Nowicka, A. (2010). Allocation of attention to self-name and self-face: An ERP study. *Biological Psychology*, *84*, 318 – 324.

[35] Tong, F. , & Nakayama, K. (1999). Robust representations for faces: Evidence from visual search. *Journal of Experimental Psychology: Human Perception and Performance*, *25*, 1016 – 1035.

[36] Verbruggen, F. , & De Houwer, J. (2007). Do emotional stimuli interfere with response inhibition? Evidence from the stop signal paradigm. *Cognition and Emotion*, *21*, 391 – 403.

[37] Verbruggen, F. , & Logan, G. D. (2008). Response inhibition in the stop-signal paradigm. *Trends in Cognitive Sciences*, *12*, 418 – 424.

[38] Verbruggen, F. , & Logan, G. D. (2009). Models of response inhibition in the stop-signal and stop-change paradigms. *Neuroscience & Biobehavioral Reviews*, *33*, 647 – 661.

[39] Yu, J. , Hung, D. L. , Tseng, P. , Tzeng, O. J. L. , Muggleton, N. G. , & Juan, C. H. (2012). Sex differences in how erotic and painful stimuli impair inhibitory control. *Cognition*, *124*, 251 – 255.

(原载于 Journal of Motor Behavior 2014 年第 2 期)

Influence of Entrepreneurial Experience, Alertness, and Prior Knowledge on Opportunity Recognition

Yu Li, Pei Wang, and Ya-jun Liang

Department of Psychology, Shanghai Normal University

To reduce employment pressure, the Chinese government and universities recently united their efforts to support university students' entrepreneurship (Hao, Sun, & Yuen, 2015; Mok, 2015). Therefore, we integrated theory and practice to examine Chinese university students' entrepreneurship in this study. Our purpose was to analyze the factors that influence opportunity recognition, which is the central issue of entrepreneurship (Shane, 2000; Shane & Venkataraman, 2000; Short, Ketchen, Shook, & Ireland, 2010), from the psychology perspective.

Entrepreneurship is very important for the creation of jobs, economic and societal development of nations, and overall innovation (Frese & Gielnik, 2014; van Praag & Versloot, 2007), and is defined as the identification and exploitation of business opportunities within the individual-opportunity nexus (Shane & Venkataraman, 2000). For an entrepreneur, one of the most important challenges is identifying and seizing opportunities (Short et al. , 2010). Thus, researchers have paid special attention to investigating how entrepreneurs recognize these opportunities and use them to create new products and services (Zhu, 2005).

Opportunity recognition refers to the process by which entrepreneurs seek "something out there" that has potential value (Ardichvili, Cardozo, & Ray, 2003). Cognitive psychologists have discussed the opportunity recognition process mainly from two different perspectives. One is based on the feature analysis model, the focus of which is the features of opportunity. In this model, emphasis is placed on the importance of entrepreneurial experience and knowledge to identify opportunities. (Larsen & Bundesen, 1996). Many previous researchers have used the novice-experienced entrepreneurs contrast as a general paradigm to explore differences in opportunity recognition between entrepreneurs with low versus high levels of experience. These researchers primarily compared individuals with different amounts of entrepreneurial experience, including entrepreneurs, managers, and graduate students with Master of Business Administration degrees. Results showed that experienced entrepreneurs' opportunity recognition is better than that of novices (Baron, 2009; Baron & Ensley, 2006; Grégoire, Barr, & Shepherd, 2010). Further, they also have higher levels of *prior knowledge*, which refers to entrepreneurs' familiarity with, or having information about, the market, industry, technology, and customer demand (Baron, 2006; Hisrich, Langan-Fox, & Grant, 2007; Tang, Kacmar, & Busenitz, 2012). According to the feature analysis model, entrepreneurial experience and prior knowledge have a direct influence on opportunity recognition.

The second perspective is based on the models of pattern recognition, in which prototype, exemplar, and schema models are integrated into a single cognitive framework (Ács & Audretsch, 2010; Alvarez & Barney, 2007). Individuals' opportunity recognition depends on prototypes or schema at the beginning. As they gain more expertise and knowledge, key features of entrepreneurial opportunity may be linked together, thereby allowing these individuals to automatically identify complex patterns (Baron, 2006). As a basic schema, *entrepreneurial alertness* refers to the capacity to recognize existing opportunities, such as those emerging from changes in technology, markets, government policies, and competition (Dew, Read, Sarasvathy, & Wiltbank, 2009; Tang et al., 2012). On the basis of the cognitive framework perspective, entrepreneurial alertness has a direct influence on opportunity recognition, whereas entrepreneurial experience and prior knowledge do not. Although in both models opportunity recognition is considered as a complex cognitive process that involves feature analysis, the mechanisms and key effects differ.

Although many scholars have focused on how entrepreneurial experience, entrepreneurial alertness, and prior knowledge influence opportunity recognition (Baron, 2006; Hisrich et al., 2007; Tang et al., 2012), few have paid attention to university students' opportunity recognition. Thus, we are the first to have explored the influence of entrepreneurial experience, entrepreneurial alertness, and prior knowledge with a sample of Chinese university students, using the novice — experienced entrepreneurs contrast paradigm. Therefore, we proposed the following hypotheses:

Hypothesis 1: In a Chinese context, entrepreneurial university students' opportunity recognition will be significantly better than that of nonentrepreneurial university students.

Hypothesis 2a: Entrepreneurial alertness will have a direct positive influence on opportunity recognition.

Hypothesis 2b: Prior knowledge will have an indirect positive influence on opportunity recognition.

Hypothesis 3a: Entrepreneurial alertness will positively influence opportunity recognition of nonentrepreneurial university students.

Hypothesis 3b: Prior knowledge will positively influence opportunity recognition of entrepreneurial university students.

Method

Participants

The entrepreneurial university student group comprised 144 graduate and undergraduate students with an entrepreneurial tenure of between 3 months and 2 years. They had founded their own company or innovatively developed new fields in the job market. A further 150 students without any entrepreneurial experience comprised the nonentrepreneurial university student sample.

Participants whose responses to the scale items had a large amount of missing data were excluded from further analysis. Thus, the final sample comprised 94 entrepreneurial university students (66 men, 28 women) and 114 nonentrepreneurial university students (63 men, 51 women). All of the participants were compensated with US $1. 60 for taking part in the study, were aged between 18 and 28 years old, and were recruited from universities in Shanghai.

Measures

Opportunity recognition. Opportunity recognition was measured with Keh, Foo, and Lim's (2002) scale, which we revised for the purposes of this study to include background information outlining an opportunity recognition situation and six opportunity feature descriptions. The background information was as follows:

> Mr. Liang has worked for 3 years in a multinational corporation after graduating from university and has been promoted to the position of department manager. Now, he has a large income and a large development space. However, he has always been full of entrepreneurial enthusiasm and wishes to create his own industry. Once, he accidentally discovered an entrepreneurial project.

All six opportunity feature descriptions included the same two test items that Keh et al. (2002) used, to which the participants respond using a 7-point scale (ranging from 1 = *totally disagree* to 7 =*totally agree*). In this study, the Cronbach's coefficient of internal consistency for these two items was . 81.

Entrepreneurial alertness. Entrepreneurial alertness was measured using Miao's (2008) Entrepreneurial Alertness Questionnaire, which includes three dimensions: prospecting, sensitive foresight, and reframing. In this study the Cronbach's coefficient of internal consistency was between . 82 and . 86. Participants respond to the items on a 5-point scale ranging from 1 (*never true*) to 5 (*always true*).

Prior knowledge. Prior knowledge was measured using Shane's (2000) Prior Knowledge Questionnaire, which includes two dimensions: special interest and domain knowledge. In this study the Cronbach's coefficient of internal consistency was between . 84 and . 88. Participants respond to the items on a 5-point scale ranging from 1 (*never true*) to 5 (*always true*).

Procedure

The first step was to revise the opportunity recognition measure that had been developed by Keh et al. (2002), which involved the following steps: First, we interviewed eight entrepreneurial university students, each of whom had a business in a different domain that had been established for between 1 and 4 years, about their entrepreneurial project and opportunity recognition. Second, through transcribing the recordings of the content of these interviews and conducting a semantic analysis, we obtained the six characteristics of university students' entrepreneurial opportunity recognition, comprising project novelty, consumer demand, market prospect, profit margins, industry change, and capital need. Next, we combined the six opportunity feature dimensions with corresponding descriptive statements that we located in opportunity recognition questionnaires developed by Timmons

(1999) and Miao (2005). The resulting revised scale included background information and six opportunity feature descriptions. All six opportunity features included two test items, that is, "I will consider investigating the entrepreneurial plan" and "This is a real entrepreneurial opportunity that I will not miss."

Participants completed the three scales via email or using paper and pencil.

Results

Analysis using t tests revealed that although entrepreneurial university students were better able to recognize various opportunity features than nonentrepreneurial students were, the difference between the two groups was not significant, $M = 9.33$, $t(206) = 1.68$, $p = .95$.

We used entrepreneurial alertness and prior knowledge as predictors to conduct a stepwise regression. As is shown in Table 1, entrepreneurial alertness significantly predicted opportunity recognition, $t(206) = 3.16$, $p = .002$, whereas prior knowledge affected opportunity recognition through its impact on entrepreneurial alertness (see Figure 1).

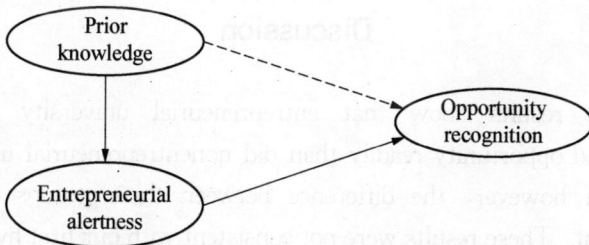

Figure 1   *Path diagram showing the influence of university students' entrepreneurial alertness and prior knowledge on opportunity recognition.*

Note. Solid arrows denote a direct influence. The dotted arrow denotes an indirect influence.

Table 1. *Regression Results of University Students' Entrepreneurial Alertness on Opportunity Recognition*

Step	Opportunity recognition				Entrepreneurial alertness			
	R^2	β	F	p	R^2	β	F	p
Alertness	. 21	. 22	9. 99	. 002				
Prior knowledge			~~. 51~~	~~. 50~~	114. 90	~~. 001~~		

On the basis of a cluster analysis, we conducted a 3 (entrepreneurial alertness: high, medium, and low) × 3 (prior knowledge: high, medium, and low) analysis of variance (ANOVA) to test the effect of entrepreneurial university students' alertness and prior knowledge. We found a significant main effect of prior knowledge, $F(2,208) = 3.12$, $p = .04$, but not of alertness or interaction.

Further, we conducted a 3 (entrepreneurial alertness: high, medium, and low) × 3 (prior knowledge: high, medium, and low) ANOVA to test the effect of nonentrepreneurial university students' alertness and prior knowledge. We found a significant main effect of entrepreneurial alertness, $F(2,208) = 3.41$, $p = .03$, but not of prior knowledge or interaction.

Discussion

The results show that entrepreneurial university students recognized opportunity readily than did nonentrepreneurial university students; however, the difference between these groups was not significant. These results were not consistent with our first hypothesis or with some previous research findings (Baron, 2009; Dew et al., 2009). Some scholars have stated that entrepreneurial experience is not overly important for successful recognition of entrepreneurial opportunity (Frese & Gielnik, 2014). In fact, there may be disadvantages in having greater experience, such as liabilities, a cognitive fixedness, and "mental ruts" (Gielnik, Krämer, Kappel, & Frese, 2014; Shepherd & DeTienne, 2005; Ucbasaran, Westhead, & Wright, 2009).

Past researchers have taken two different views regarding, opportunity recognition. Those taking the first view argue that individuals who possess, and are widely exposed to prior and new information are able to more easily recognize opportunities, which is the basis of the feature analysis model (Shane, 2000). The different view is that individuals with superior cognitive capabilities, that is, what Kirzner (1997) calls alertness, are able to more easily recognize opportunities, which is the basis of the cognitive framework theory (Ács & Audretsch, 2010; Alvarez & Barney, 2007). In this study, we found that entrepreneurial alertness had a direct significant influence on opportunity recognition, whereas prior knowledge affected opportunity recognition indirectly, through its influence on alertness. These results support Hypotheses 2a and 2b and the cognitive framework theory, according to which entrepreneurial alertness is mainly a schema that relates to perception and thinking, that is, the basic cognitive capacities required to recognize entrepreneurial opportunities (Baron & Ensley, 2006; Gaglio & Katz, 2001). More recent researchers have described alertness as a schema based on a number of cognitive capacities and processes, such as prior knowledge and experience, pattern recognition, information processing skills and social interactions (Tang et al. , 2012). This kind of schema allows entrepreneurs to successfully integrate information and create new causal links to facilitate recognizing opportunities (Shane, 2012), and has received strong and consistent theoretical support (Lim & Xavier, 2015). Prior knowledge relates to the information that an individual accumulates about business markets, technology, and competition. As regards the cognitive framework theory, this knowledge provides entrepreneurs with cognitive and mental structures that are integrated into a professional cognitive framework of comprehending and interpreting new information to further enrich schemata (e. g. , alertness) or prototypes (Shane, 2000; Shepherd & DeTienne, 2005). Our results in this study empirically support this theory; that is, entrepreneurial alertness directly influences opportunity recognition and prior knowledge indirectly influences opportunity recognition through its impact on entrepreneurial alertness (Lim & Xavier, 2015; Shane, 2012).

Our results also show that, for nonentrepreneurial university students, entrepreneurial alertness influenced opportunity recognition, whereas for entrepreneurial university students, prior knowledge influenced opportunity recognition. These results are consisted with Hypotheses 3a and 3b and also support the cognitive frameworks theory. Further, they explain the influence of entrepreneurial alertness and prior knowledge on opportunity recognition. Although these two factors do not directly influence the process of opportunity recognition, they may exist in different processing stages, as follows: First, nonentrepreneurial university students lack knowledge of entrepreneurship, so they depend on schema such as alertness to recognize opportunities (Shane, 2003) and see relationships and patterns in information (Gaglio & Katz, 2001; Gielnik et al. , 2014). Second, entrepreneurial, versus nonentrepreneurial, university students had accumulated much more prior knowledge, which provides significant insights into the process of recognition of opportunity (Venkataraman, Sarasvathy, Dew, & Forster, 2012). Thus, entrepreneurial university students will naturally form particular cognitive frameworks based on their prior knowledge, which are different from those of nonentrepreneurial students. In line with this, when faced with situations of uncertainty, entrepreneurs can automatically recognize and judge opportunities.

In summary, our research findings empirically support and expand the cognitive frameworks perspective of entrepreneurial opportunity recognition, which suggests that our research has theoretical value. Further, our findings also have practical significance in relation to the background of Chinese university students' entrepreneurship and may help to guide Chinese university students' entrepreneurial opportunity recognition at different entrepreneurial stages.

However, there are limitations in this study. First, our sample of entrepreneurial university students included both current and graduated university students, and these two types of participants might have certain differences in opportunity recognition. Future researchers should use a more homogeneous sample of entrepreneurial university students. Second, survey data based on self-reports may be subject to social desirability bias. Future researchers should use more objective measures to examine the opportunity recognition process and the roles that different important factors have in this process. Additionally, as previous scholars have stated, opportunity recognition is a complex process that is influenced by cognitive properties and information corridors, rather than a sudden flash of insight (Alvarez & Barney, 2013; Shane, 2012). Thus, future researchers should develop a more integrated psychological theory beyond the cognitive framework model and use more objective measures to examine the opportunity recognition process and the roles that different important factors have in this process. This will allow for further more thorough exploration of the dynamic process of entrepreneurial university students' opportunity recognition (Frese & Gielnik, 2014).

References

[1] Ács, Z. J. , & Audretsch, D. B. (Eds.). (2010). *Handbook of entrepreneurship research: An interdisciplinary survey and introduction* (2nd ed.). New York: Springer.

[2] Alvarez, S. A. , & Barney, J. B. (2007). Discovery and creation: Alternative

theories of entrepreneurial action. *Strategic Entrepreneurship Journal*, *1*, 11 -26. http://doi. org/bx82qc.

[3] Alvarez, S. A. , & Barney, J. B. (2013). Epistemology, opportunities, and entrepreneurship: Comments on Venkataraman et al. (2012) and Shane (2012). *Academy of Management Review*, *38*, 154 – 157. http://doi. org/5cx.

[4] Ardichvili, A. , Cardozo, R. , & Ray, S. (2003). A theory of entrepreneurial opportunity identification and development. *Journal of Business Venturing*, *18*,105 – 123. http://doi. org/hbm.

[5] Baron, R. A. (2006). Opportunity recognition as pattern recognition: How entrepreneurs "connect the dots" to identify new business opportunities. *Academy of Management Perspectives*, *20*, 104 – 119. http://doi. org/b968q5.

[6] Baron, R. A. (2009). Effectual versus predictive logics in entrepreneurial decision making: Differences between experts and novices: Does experience in starting new ventures change the way entrepreneurs think? Perhaps, but for now, "caution" is essential. *Journal of Business Venturing*, *24*,310 – 315. http://doi. org/dsx85w.

[7] Baron, R. A. , & Ensley, M. D. (2006). Opportunity recognition as the detection of meaningful patterns: Evidence from comparisons of novice and experienced entrepreneurs. *Management Science*, *52*,1331 – 1344. http:// doi. org/b73t9w.

[8] Dew, N. , Read, S. , Sarasvathy, S. , & Wiltbank, R. (2009). Effectual versus predictive logics in entrepreneurial decision-making: Differences between experts and novices. *Journal of Business Venturing*, 24,287 – 309. http://doi. org/bjc246.

[9] Frese, M. , & Gielnik, M. M. (2014). The psychology of entrepreneurship. *Annual Review of Organizational Psychology and Organizational Behavior*, *1*,413 – 438. http://doi. org/5cz.

[10] Gaglio, C. M. , & Katz, J. (2001). The psychological basis of opportunity identification: Entrepreneurial alertness. *Small Business Economics*, *16*,95 – 111. http://doi. org/dz2p4z.

[11] Gielnik, M. M. , Krämer, A. -C. , Kappel, B. , & Frese, M. (2014). Antecedents of business opportunity identification and innovation: Investigating the interplay of information processing and information acquisition. *Applied Psychology*, *63*,344 – 381. http://doi. org/5c2.

[12] Grégoire, D. , Barr, P. , &. Shepherd, D. (2010). Cognitive processes of opportunity recognition: The role of structural alignment. *Organization Science*, *21*,413 – 431. http://doi. org/cjz5rf.

[13] Hao, D. , Sun, V. J. , &. Yuen, M. (2015). Towards a model of career guidance and counseling for university students in China. *International Journal for the Advancement of Counselling*, *37*,155 – 167. http://doi. org/5c3.

[14] Hisrich, R. D. , Langan-Fox, J. , &. Grant, S. (2007). Entrepreneurship research and practice: A call to action for psychology. *American Psychologist*, *62*,575 – 589. http://doi. org/cjk6gw.

[15] Keh, H. T. , Foo, M. D. , &. Lim, B. C. (2002). Opportunity evaluation under risky conditions: The cognitive processes of entrepreneurs. *Entrepreneurship: Theory and Practice*, *27*, 125 – 148. http://doi. org/crq6gq.

[16] Kirzner, I. M. (1997). Entrepreneurial discovery and the competitive market process: An Austrian approach. *Journal of Economic Literature*, *35*, 60 –85.

[17] Larsen, A. , &. Bundesen, C. (1996). A template-matching pandemonium recognizes unconstrained handwritten characters with high accuracy. *Memory &. Cognition*, *24*,136 – 143. http://doi. org/ ck4629.

[18] Lim, W. L. , &. Xavier, S. R. (2015). Opportunity recognition framework: Exploring the technology entrepreneurs. *American Journal of Economics*, *5*, 105 – 111.

[19] Miao, Q. (2005). Cognition-based perspective on entrepreneurial process research [In Chinese]. *Psychological Science-Shanghai*, *28*, 1274 – 1276. http://doi. org/5c4.

[20] Miao, Q. (2008). Entrepreneurs' alertness: The psychological schema of opportunity recognition [In Chinese]. *Chinese Journal of Ergonomics*, *14*, 6 –9. http://doi. org/5c5.

[21] Mok, K. H. (2015). Higher education transformations for global competitiveness: Policy responses, social consequences and impact on the academic profession in Asia. *Higher Education Policy*, *28*,1 – 15. http:// doi. org/5c6.

[22] Shane, S. (2000). Prior knowledge and the discovery of entrepreneurial opportunities. *Organization Science*, *11*,448 – 469. http://doi. org/ffg4m6.

[23] Shane, S. (2003). When are universities the locus of invention? In C. Steyaert

& D. Hjorth (Eds.), *New movements of entrepreneurship* (pp. 145 – 159). Aldershot, UK: Edward Elgar.

[24] Shane, S. (2012). Reflections on the 2010 AMR Decade Award: Delivering on the promise of entrepreneurship as a field of research. *Academy of Management Review*, 37, 10 – 20. http://doi. org/ fhkw8r.

[25] Shane, S. , & Venkataraman, S. (2000). The promise of entrepreneurship as a field of research. *Academy of Management Review*, 25, 217 – 226. http:// doi. org/d9f3kn.

[26] Shepherd, D. A. , & DeTienne, D. R. (2005). Prior knowledge, potential financial reward, and opportunity identification. *Entrepreneurship: Theory and Practice*, 29, 91 – 112. http://doi. org/ df7npf.

[27] Short, J. C. , Ketchen, D. J. , Jr. , Shook, C. L. , & Ireland, R. D. (2010). The concept of " opportunity " in entrepreneurship research: Past accomplishments and future challenges. *Journal of Management*, 36, 40 – 65. http://doi. org/dzqswc.

[28] Tang, J. , Kacmar, K. M. , & Busenitz, L. (2012). Entrepreneurial alertness in the pursuit of new opportunities. *Journal of Business Venturing*, 27, 77 – 94. http://doi. org/chnc37.

[29] Timmons, J. A. (1999). *New venture creation: Entrepreneurship for the 21st century* (5th ed.). New York: McGraw-Hill.

[30] Ucbasaran, D. , Westhead, P. , & Wright, M. (2009). The extent and nature of opportunity identification by experienced entrepreneurs. *Journal of Business Venturing*, 24, 99 – 115. http://doi. org/dmz2tv.

[31] van Praag, C. M. , & Versloot, P. H. (2007). What is the value of entrepreneurship? A review of recent research. *Small Business Economics*, 29, 351 – 382. http://doi. org/bqdwd3.

[32] Venkataraman, S. , Sarasvathy, S. D. , Dew, N. , & Forster, W. R. (2012). Reflections on the 2010 AMR Decade Award: Whither the promise? Moving forward with entrepreneurship as a science of the artificial. *Academy of Management Review*, 37, 21 – 33. http://doi. org/fm687t.

[33] Zhu, R. -H. (2005). Entrepreneurship research: Theoretical schools and development trends [In Chinese]. *Studies in Science of Science*, 23, 688 – 696. http://doi. org/5c7.

（原载于 Social Behavior & Personality An International Journal 2015 年第 9 期）

Online Emotion Regulation Questionnalre for Adolescents: Development and Preliminary Validation[*]

Dengfeng Xie, Jiamei Lu, Zhangming Xie

Dengfeng Xie, Education Science College, Shanghai Normal University, and Department of Ideological and Political Education, West Anhui University; Jiamei Lu, Education Science College, Shanghai Normal University; Zhangming Xie, Educational and Counseling Center of Students' Mental Health, West Anhui University.

Internet usage has become an important part of adolescents' lifestyle (Mishna, McLuckie, & Saini, 2009), and there has been growing interest in adolescents' emotion regulation in an online social networking context (Hormes, Kearns, & Timko, 2014; Kuss & Griffiths, 2011). *Emotion regulation* refers to shaping the emotions the individual has, when the individual has them, and how the individual experiences or expresses these emotions (Gross, 2014). *Online emotion regulation* is a specific example of emotion regulation that involves managing emotion arousal in a network community, and

* This study was supported by the Key Projects of Philosophy and Social Sciences Research, Ministry of Education Research on the Status Quo of China's Contemporary Youth's Affective Quality (No. 13JZD046), Ministry of Education, Humanities, and Social Science Research Funds (No. 13YJC190010), and Social Development Research Funds of Anhui Province (No. AHSK11 – 12D348).

that is concerned with the development of Internet social functioning. Developing healthy emotion regulation produces positive outcomes in young people's socialization, which is the basic condition for harmonious interpersonal relationships (Min'er & Dejun, 2000; Xie, 2013). Online emotion regulation requires strengthening, maintaining, or reducing emotion intensity during online person-to-person interactions, which represents a core motivation for promoting character and building a harmonious online environment. *Promoting character* consists of self-management, prosocial competencies, social moral cognition, communicative competency, and emotion competency. Contemporary researchers in the area of personality theory regard emotion regulation as a core component of personality functioning and an important predictor of psychological adjustment and social competence (Thompson & Meyer, 2007).

Emotion regulation is an experience that is common to all human societies; however, the varying moral and social rules associated with different situations affect the individual emotion regulation process (Tsai, 2007). At present, disorderly online interactions (e. g. , cyberbullying, network fraud) and a loss of self-disciplined communication via the Internet often occur. Online deviant behaviors do not cause negative social emotions, like guilt, shame, and fear; on the contrary, they give rise to enjoyable emotions (e. g. , contentment, amusement; Caspi & Gorsky, 2006). Furthermore, in previous research it has been found that when individuals are exposed to the happiness of others in an online context, this results in a feeling of depression (Turkle, 2012). According to Walther's (2001) social information processing theory, one of the main reasons that individuals experience these emotion problems online is that they do not immediately receive feedback information from the other person, especially nonverbal cues (e. g. , posture, interpersonal distance, facial expressions, mimicry; see also Constantin, Kalyanaraman, Stavrositu, & Wagoner, 2002; Walther & D'Addario, 2001). This lack of nonverbal expression means that the mechanism of interpersonal emotion on the Internet is different from face-to-face social interactions (Wang, 2007).

According to Gross (2014), emotion regulation has three core features, comprising the activation of a regulatory goal, the engagement of regulatory processes, and the modulation of the emotion trajectory. However, most existing emotion regulation strategy questionnaires are not based on this general model of emotion regulation, and cover only a portion of the effective emotion regulation modes (Phillips & Power, 2007; Zhang, Pan, Wang, Shen, & Qiu, 2012). In this study, our aim was to explore the basic structure and characteristics of youth network emotion regulation and to develop and validate a questionnaire of online emotion regulation for adolescents.

Method

Participants

Participants aged 18 years or older signed their own consent forms, and the guardians of those aged under 18 signed the informed consent form before the data collection commenced. This consent procedure and the study itself were approved by the Research Ethics Committee of Shanghai Normal University.

The initial group of participants for the exploratory factor analysis comprised 320 adolescents from one junior high school and two senior high schools in China. However, eight participants failed to complete the whole set of questionnaires, so their responses were excluded from the analyses, meaning that 97.5% of the adolescents provided valid responses. The gender was evenly distributed between boys ($n = 130$) and girls ($n = 182$). The majority of the participants had logged many hours online every day in the last 3 months, comprising either 3 hours daily ($n = 138$), between 3 and 6 hours ($n = 128$), or more than 6 hours ($n = 46$). The second group of participants comprised 223 (79 boys and 144 girls) students from one junior high school and two senior high schools in China, aged between 13 years and 22 years. The participants in the two groups combined consisted of 535 (209 boys and 326 girls) people. The mean age of the participants was 16. 8 years ($SD = 1.4$).

Validation

For assessing validity, internal consistency was used to indicate construct homogeneity. In addition, the measure was correlated with several objective self-report questions to assess criterion validity. According to the theory of emotion adjustment functioning, healthy emotion regulation is an adaptive result that mediates the relationship between the individual and the environment and determines the mood of the individual in terms of aspects such as physical arousal, thereby increasing the flexibility and effectiveness of the subjective experience and expressive behavior. Thus, in this study, we used Internet-related emotion experience as a correlation criterion of the questionnaire. Participants answered the following self-report question: "What positive emotions do I feel when I am online?"

Measure Construction

We developed the Online Emotion Regulation Questionnaire for Adolescents (Chinese version) using previous online psychology and behavioral research and qualitative work with teenagers, with reference to interview outlines designed by the Taiwanese scholar Jiang (1987). Before developing the items for the questionnaire, we conducted interviews and focus group discussions with junior and senior high school students to gather information regarding the characteristics of online emotion regulation, which is important to ensure that the written items will be appropriate to the adolescents' lives. We conducted focus group discussions separately with 10 junior high school (five boys and five girls) and 14 senior high school (seven boys and seven girls) students, who were part of the selected sample groups. All of these individuals had experience with emotion regulation in an online community and regularly took an active role in a network community.

In the focus groups, we started by defining online emotion regulation and outlining the basic elements of the online emotion regulation process, which were as follows: situation selection, situation modification, attentional deployment, cognitive change, and response modulation (Gross, 1998). We then conducted a general discussion about emotion regulation in the network communities to which the participants belonged. Next, we asked the participants to write down the physical representation and inner experiences that occurred when they were successfully regulating emotion arousal. In addition, we conducted 50 semistructured interviews of 15 to 25 minutes each with individual participants (22 men and 28 women, mean age$=20\pm1.3$ years). During these interviews, the participants were asked more generally about their strategies for self-regulation of online emotions and about the self-efficacy of their emotion self-regulation under the induced forms of affect. An example online emotion scenario is as follows: "I am labeled a dummy when online without a reason being given."

These processes resulted in our reaching the conclusion that online emotion regulation can be divided into the following five dimensions (Xie, Huang, & Xie 2014): emotion perception (description and recognition of one's own or another's emotion state and cognitive ability), emotion expression (emotion behavior and control of the present situation), emotion reflection (individual adjustment, process of reflection, and evaluation of the mood), emotion regulation strategies (method for coping with emotion problems), and self-efficacy of emotion regulation (feeling of competence when the individual regulates his or her emotion).

Each item in the questionnaire measures the frequency of the individual experiencing that problem in the last 3 months. The response format is a 5-point Likert-type scale, where 1 = *strongly* disagree and 5 = *strongly agree* .

Data Analysis

Exploratory factor analysis, confirmatory factor analysis, calculation of reliability coefficients, and Pearson's correlation analysis were performed using SPSS version 13. 0 and AMOS version 7. 0 software.

Results

Item Analysis

Data from the initial group of participants were used to for the exploratory factor analysis to decrease the number of items. According to the online emotion regulation score, the top 27% were allocated to the high score group and the bottom 27% were the low score group. The scores for items were compared between the high group and the low group by using t tests to check the items' degree of identification. According to the results, there were highly significant differences between the high and low groups. Correlation analysis was used to evaluate the correlation between items and the total score; the results showed the correlation index to be between . 36 and . 65 ($p<.001$), indicating that the design of the items was of a good quality. Thus, the final Online Emotion Regulation Questionnaire for Adolescents consisted of 20 items.

Explanation of Factors

Using the preliminary data, we performed an exploratory factor analysis with varimax rotation to maximize the variance of the squared loadings of each factor in a matrix, which allowed us to identify the underlying structure of the original variables. A factor weight of . 30 was the minimum cutoff point for an item, so this process produced different (albeit associated) factors (Floyd & Widaman, 1995), each reflecting a dimension of online emotion regulation. The detailed results are shown in Table 1.

Online Emotion Regulation... 689

Before performing principal components factor analyses, we assessed the suitability of the data for factor analysis. The approximate chi square of Bartlett's test of sphericity = 1585. 259, $df = 190$, and Kaiser—Meyer—Olkin (KMO) measure of sampling adequacy=. 744. The significance ($p < 0.5$) of the Bartlett's test of sphericity and values above . 60 for the KMO index were considered to be acceptable (Cudeck, 2000). According to the gravel diagram and the percentage of variance explained, we found the rubble figure to stabilize the main starting point from the third factor. We then extracted four factors, covering the 20 items, which explained 48. 449% of the total variance. To understand the potential meaning of the items in the respective factors, we established a specific definition for each factor. Thus, the Online Emotion Regulation Questionnaire for Adolescents included the following four dimensions: positive emotion seeking, negative emotion experience, interpersonal emotion support, and mood awareness. *Positive emotion seeking* was defined as a tendency to maintain satisfaction, peace, and pleasure by using humor, leisure activities (e. g. , listening to music, watching television), and self-acceptance. *Negative emotion experience* constitutes such experiences as evaluation of an unpleasant atmosphere, anxiety during maintenance of individual self-esteem, online emotion experience deficit, and feelings of neglect. *Interpersonal emotion support* is a phenomenon that includes interpersonal trust, emotion support, and sharing in an online context. *Mood awareness* is an individual's perception of his or her emotion state in the network environment.

Table 1. *Rotated Loading Matrix from the Factor Analysis*

Items	Component			
	1	2	3	4
1. I show a sense of humor to give myself a pleasurable experience when online.	. 672			

690 学思林

续 表

Items	Component			
	1	2	3	4
2. I use some online leisure activities to cope with pressure.	.608			
3. I experience emotional distress when facing cyber conflict.	.626			
4. I pay attention to my inner feelings when online.	.702			
5. I accept that I experience positive emotions when online.	.695			
6. I can maintain a happy mood on the Internet.	.721			
7. I often feel unhappy in an online social networking context.		.449		
8. Most netizens disagree with my opinions.		.590		
9. I am not aware of others' emotions when online.		.417		
10. I cannot regulate my emotions when I experience conflict with other netizens.		.736		
11. Most netizens express their anger on the Internet.		.630		
12. I cannot remain calm when I am anxious and on the Internet.		.697		
13. Most netizens' rudeness offends me.		.503		
14. My friends provide me with online social support.			.481	
15. My online friends are willing to help me solve my problems.			.754	
16. Trustworthy online peers are uncommon.			.686	
17. My online friends are willing to listen to me when I feel physically or mentally ill.			.752	
18. I often review inappropriate emotions that I have expressed online.				.478
19. I know why I am angry when I am online.				.827
20. I know why I am anxious when I am online.				.799

Note. $N = 312$.

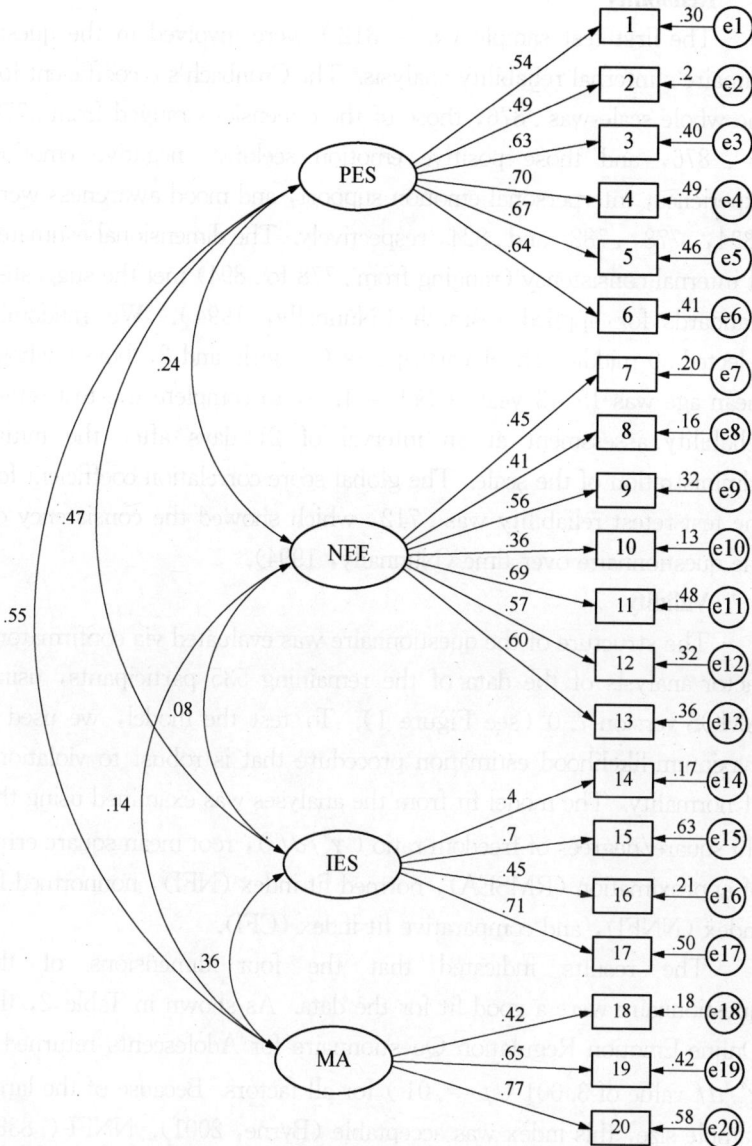

Figure 1 *The structure of the questionnaire.*

Note. PES=positive emotion seeking, NEE=negative emotion experience, IES=interpersonal emotion support, MA=mood awareness.

Reliability

The first test sample ($n = 312$) were involved in the quest-ionnaire's internal reliability analysis. The Cronbach's α coefficient for the whole scale was . 876, those of the dimensions ranged from . 778 to . 876, and those positive emotion seeking, negative emotion experience, interpersonal emotion support, and mood awareness were . 894, . 778, . 782, and . 824, respectively. The dimensional estimates of internal consistency (ranging from . 778 to . 894) met the suggested standards for applied research (Nunnally, 1994). We randomly selected 50 middle school participants (23 girls and 27 boys) whose mean age was 15. 43 years ($SD = 1.2$) to complete the test-retest reliability assessment at an interval of 21 days after the initial administration of the scale. The global score correlation coefficient for the test-retest reliability was . 712, which showed the consistency of the questionnaire over time (Nunnally, 1994).

Validity

The structure of the questionnaire was evaluated via confirmatory factor analysis of the data of the remaining 535 participants, using AMOS version 7. 0 (see Figure 1). To test the model, we used a maximum likelihood estimation procedure that is robust to violations of normality. The model fit from the analyses was examined using the chi square/degrees of freedom ratio (χ^2/df), root mean square error of approximation (RMSEA), normed fit index (NFI), nonnormed fit index (NNFI), and comparative fit index (CFI).

The results indicated that the four dimensions of the questionnaire were a good fit for the data. As shown in Table 2, the Online Emotion Regulation Questionnaire for Adolescents returned a χ^2/df value of 3. 001 ($p =. 01$) for all factors. Because of the large sample size, this index was acceptable (Byrne, 2001). NNFI (. 838) and CFI (. 860) were greater than the benchmark of . 80 and the RMSEA (. 061) met the criterion of acceptability of being under . 08 (Thompson, 2000).

Table 2. *Validity Indicators of the Questionnaire*

	Online emotion regulation	Positive emotion seeking	Negative emotion experience	Interpersonal emotion support	Mood awareness
Validity indicators	.389**	.358**	.149**	.295**	.235**

Note. * $p < .05$, ** $p < .01$, *** $p < .001$.

We used Pearson's correlation analysis to assess the criterion validity for the interval data (i. e., the degree of positive online emotion experience). In Table 2, the results show that there are significant correlations among all of the dimensions of the Online Emotion Regulation Questionnaire for Adolescents and the degree of positive online emotion experience. Thus, the criterion-related validity result supports the generalizability of the validity coefficients.

Discussion

We have empirically confirmed that the pattern of online emotion regulation has a multidimensional structure. The confirmatory factor analysis revealed that the four-factor, 20-item model fit the data well. All of the dimensions of adolescents' online emotion regulation and the level of their positive emotion experiences were significantly correlated, which indicates that the questionnaire has good criterion validity. Analysis of the internal consistency reliability and the test-retest reliability showed that the alpha indices of all items and dimensions achieved an acceptable standard. All of the dimensions of the questionnaire were subjected to a test of reliability and reached a significant level, which indicated that the questionnaire has good reliability.

In this study, we developed the Online Emotion Regulation Questionnaire for Adolescents, which consists of 20 items and the following four dimensions: positive emotion seeking, negative emotion experience, interpersonal emotion support, and mood awareness. This self-report measure can be used to assess functional and dysfunctional online emotion regulation, consisting of internal and external factors. Although the ability to use internal resources is increasing, assessing both internal and external strategies is very important in young people (Phillips & Power, 2007). More flexible usage of all resources tends to be associated with enhanced adaptation to the environment and, therefore, better mental health (Kuppens, Allen, & Sheeber, 2010). Some online emotion regulation strategies are effective at modifying affect, whereas the other strategies put a person at increased risk for psychopathology (Gross & Jazaieri, 2014), which is correlated with deviant behavior, such as Internet addiction and network violence in adolescents (Li, 2013).

Additional research is needed for fine analysis of the dimensions. Despite our findings that the Online Emotion Regulation Questionnaire for Adolescents has high internal consistency, good test-retest reliability, and adequate construct validity, the present study has several limitations that should be addressed in future research. The first limitation is that the results were collected using several select self-report measures of online emotion regulation. In general, self-reported data are affected by the self-perceived competence of the individual providing the data. According to the theory of conditioning, Internet craving is an unconscious psychological reaction (Koob, 2011). Therefore, the data in this study should be further measured along with external and objective approaches, such as neuroscience, behaviorism, and neuropharmacology. Accurate reporting of all aspects of online emotion regulation is challenging because many strategies may be unconscious (Gross, 1998). A second limitation is that our participants might not be completely representative of the entire population of adolescents because they comprised only Chinese young people. Cultural models of self affect whether or not individuals are motivated to use emotion regulation. People in a collectivistic society are more likely to use expressive suppression than are those in an individualistic society (Ford &- Mauss, 2015); therefore, further studies should be conducted to determine whether or not there is a relationship between culture and online emotion regulation. A third limitation is that a large number of the emotion events discussed in the interview in our study concerned netizens (i. e. , individuals who interact online but have few to no opportunities to meet in person), regardless of interaction with peers, family members, teachers, and other people. Future researchers could analyze interpersonal relationships among online and offline situations, and explore adolescents' emotion regulation across different relationship contexts.

Conclusion

Our development of a tool that can be used in assessing individual differences in online emotion regulation will help adolescents to develop skillful and flexible self-regulation, making the world of the Internet a better place (Gross, 2014). According to our findings, the questionnaire we developed is psychometrically valid and reliable. However, extensive work is warranted before it can be used as a fully developed instrument.

References

[1] Byrne, B. M. (2001). *Structural equation modeling with AMOS: Basic concepts, applications, and programming.* Mahwah, NJ: Erlbaum.

[2] Caspi, A. , &- Gorsky, P. (2006). Online deception: Prevalence, motivation, and emotion. *CyberPsychology &- Behavior, 9,* 54 - 59. http://doi. org/b24fmk.

[3] Constantin, C. , Kalyanaraman, S. , Stavrositu, C. , &- Wagoner, N. (2002). *Impression formation effects in moderated chatrooms: An experimental study of gender differences.* Paper presented at the 88th Annual Meeting of the National Communication Association, New Orleans, LA, USA, November 21 -24.

[4] Cudeck, R. (2000). Exploratory factor analysis. In H. E. A. Tinsley &- S. D. Brown (Eds.), *Handbook of applied multivariate statistics and*

mathematical modeling (pp. 265 – 296). San Diego, CA: Academic Press.

[5] Floyd, F. J. , & Widaman, K. F. (1995). Factor analysis in the development and refinement of clinical assessment instruments. *Psychological Assessment*, *7*, 286 – 299. http://doi. org/fq5wrx.

[6] Ford, B. Q. , & Mauss, I. B. (2015). Culture and emotion regulation. *Current Opinion in Psychology*, *3*, 1 – 5. http://doi. org/35z.

[7] Gross, J. J. (1998). The emerging field of emotion regulation: An integrative review. *Review of General Psychology*, *2*, 271 – 299. http://doi. org/bg3k9k.

[8] Gross, J. J. (2014). Emotion regulation: Conceptual and empirical foundations. In J. J. Gross (Ed.), *Handbook of emotion regulation* (2nd ed. , pp. 3 – 20). New York: Guilford Press.

[9] Gross, J. J. , & Jazaieri, H. (2014). Emotion, emotion regulation, and psychopathology: An affective science perspective. *Clinical Psychological Science*, *2*, 387 – 401. http://doi. org/352.

[10] Hormes, J. M. , Kearns, B. , & Timko, C. A. (2014). Craving Facebook? Behavioral addiction to online social networking and its association with emotion regulation deficits. *Addiction*, *9*, 2079 – 2088. http://doi. org/3d9.

[11] Jiang, W. (1987). *Research on emotional adjustment trajectory and model construction*. Unpublished doctoral dissertation, Institute of Education Psychology and Counseling, National Taiwan Normal University, Taiwan, ROC.

[12] Koob, G. F. (2011). Neurobiology of addiction: Toward the development of new therapies. *Annals of the New York Academy of Sciences*, *909*, 170 – 185. http://doi. org/c3zgbs.

[13] Kuppens, P. , Allen, N. B. , & Sheeber, L. B. (2010). Emotional inertia and psychological maladjustment. *Psychological Science*, *21*, 984 – 991. http:// doi. org/bwc6qn.

[14] Kuss, D. J. , & Griffiths, M. D. (2011). Online social networking and addiction—A review of the psychological literature. *International Journal of Environmental Research and Public Health*, *8*, 3528 – 3552. http://doi. org/ cqrtjv.

[15] Li, L. (2013). Prevention of adolescents' Internet addiction: Based on the evidence from research [In Chinese]. *Advances in Psychological Science*, *20*, 791 – 797.

[16] Min'er, H. , & Dejun, G. (2000). The essence of emotion regulation [In Chinese]. *Psychology Science*, *23*, 109 – 110.

[17] Mishna, F. , McLuckie, A. , & Saini, M. (2009). Real-world dangers in an online reality: A qualitative study examining online relationships and cyber abuse. *Social Work Research*, *33*,107 - 118. http:// doi. org/fzsvfq.

[18] Nunnally, J. C. (1994). *Psychometric theory* (3rd ed.). New York: McGraw-Hill.

[19] Phillips, K. F. V. , & Power, M. J. (2007). A new self-report measure of emotion regulation in adolescents: The Regulation of Emotions Questionnaire. *Clinical Psychology & Psychotherapy*, *14*,145 - 156. http://doi. org/btqdp6.

[20] Thompson, B. (2000). Ten commandments of structural equation modeling. In L. G. Grimm & P. R. Yarnold (Eds.), *Reading and understanding MORE multivariate statistics* (pp. 261 - 283). Washington, DC: American Psychological Association.

[21] Thompson, R. A. , & Meyer, S. (2007). Socialization of emotion regulation in the family. In J. J. Gross (Ed.), *Handbook of emotion regulation* (pp. 249 - 268). New York: Guilford Press.

[22] Tsai, J. L. (2007). Ideal affect: Cultural causes and behavioral consequences. *Perspectives on Psychological Science*, *2*,242 - 259. http://doi. org/ftqkm3.

[23] Turkle, S. (2012). *Alone together: Why we expect more from technology and less from each other*. New York: Basic Books.

[24] Walther, J. B. , & D'Addario, K. P. (2001). The impacts of emotions on message interpretation in computer-mediated communication. *Social Science Computer Review*, *19*,324 - 347. http://doi. org/fjsm9q.

[25] Wang, S. (2007). Network-rization and socialization: A study on the factors involved in juveniles growing up [In Chinese]. *Contemporary Youth Research*, *25*,40 - 45.

[26] Xie, D. F. (2013). The differences in children's emotion regulation in a network situation [In Chinese]. *Mental Health Education of Primary and Secondary Schools*, *23*,11 - 13.

[27] Xie, D. F. , Huang, S. L. , & Xie, Z. M. (2014). The characteristics of adolescents' emotion regulation in interpersonal conflict situations [In Chinese]. *Journal of West Anhui University*, *30*,135 - 138.

[28] Zhang, Q. , Pan, F. D. , Wang, L. S. , Shen, Y. J. , & Qiu, L. (2012). Constructing the Questionnaire of Affective Competence for secondary school students [In Chinese]. *Psychological Exploration*, *32*,263 - 266.

（原载于 Social Behavior & Personality An International Journal 2015 年第 6 期）

图书在版编目(CIP)数据

学思林：上海师范大学研究生优秀成果选集/俞钢主编. —上海：上海三联书店,2016.8
ISBN 978-7-5426-5532-5

Ⅰ.①学… Ⅱ.①俞… Ⅲ.①社会科学-文集②自然科学-文集 Ⅳ.①Z427

中国版本图书馆 CIP 数据核字(2016)第 053472 号

学思林——上海师范大学研究生优秀成果选集

主 编 / 俞 钢
责任编辑 / 殷亚平
装帧设计 / 周剑峰
监 制 / 李 敏
责任校对 / 张大伟

出版发行 / 上海三联书店
(201199)中国上海市都市路 4855 号 2 座 10 楼
网 址 / www. sjpc1932.com
邮购电话 / 021 - 22895557
印 刷 / 上海叶大印务发展有限公司

版 次 / 2016 年 8 月第 1 版
印 次 / 2016 年 8 月第 1 次印刷
开 本 / 889×1194 1/32
字 数 / 480 千字
彩 插 / 6
印 张 / 22.25
书 号 / ISBN 978-7-5426-5532-5/Z·116
定 价 / 58.00 元

敬启读者,如发现本书有印装质量问题,请与印刷厂联系 021-66019858